Report from a
Chinese Village

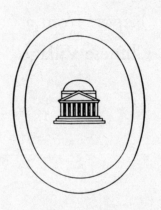

Report from a Chinese Village

▸ BY JAN MYRDAL ◂

Illustrated and with photographs by Gun Kessle

Translated from the Swedish by Maurice Michael

Pantheon Books · A Division of Random House · New York

© 1965, by William Heinemann Ltd.

All rights reserved under International and Pan-American Copyright Conventions. Published in New York by Pantheon Books, a division of Random House, Inc. Manufactured in the United States of America.

Library of Congress catalog card number: 64-18346
Originally published in Swedish as
Rapport från kinesisk © 1963 by Jan Myrdal
H/H

Second Printing

Contents

List of Illustrations

Explanation of Terms Used

1 yuan	Roughly 3 shillings or 42 U.S. cents. Contraction: Y.
Silver dollar	In principle corresponds to the silver value of the Mexican dollar.
Tael of silver	20 or 24 dwt. of silver.
String of cash	These coins, tsien, are small round copper coins with rectangular holes. They are intended to be threaded on a string. A string of 1,000 tsien used to correspond to roughly 20 dwt. of silver.
1 li	550 yds.
1 chi	13¼ in.
1 jin	1 lb. 1½ oz.
1 liang	About 1 oz.
1 mu	0·9 rood.
Ganbu	Originally a professional revolutionary—hence the expression 'join the revolution' when one took a job in government service—now a civil servant or functionary in state industry, the party or some mass organization.
Hsiang	Smaller administrative unit, now done away with. Its area corresponded roughly to that of the present people's communes.
Hsien	Larger administrative unit, often translated as 'county'.
Kang	The domestic clay bed that is heated from underneath.
K.M.T.	Kuomintang, formed in 1912 by Sun Yat-sen as a middle-class democratic national party. Later joined the Comintern, when China's Communist Party became a part of the Kuomintang. Sun Yat-sen died in March 1925. Finally, when the Kuomintang seemed to be victorious all over the country, Chiang Kai-shek carried out his long-planned attack on the communists and leftish elements in the so-called big 'April Massacres' of 1927. The ultimate result of this action was Chiang Kai-shek's flight to Formosa in 1949 together with the remnants of the Kuomintang.

Loess	Layers of wind-blown yellow soil. Fertile. Forms huge deposits in which the rain cuts deep ravines.
Ming tuan	'People's force', defence corps, 'white bandits'. Armed free corps mainly organized as a defence against peasant revolt during the Kuomintang period.
Yamen	A mandarin's official residence, his offices.

Introduction

THIS is a book about people. A description of the villagers of Liu Ling in northern Shensi. I have attempted to reproduce as accurately as possible how these villagers, these individual men and women, portray their own reality; the experiences they remember and the role they believe they have played during one of the great social and political upheavals of modern times, the Chinese revolution. Thus it is not a study of the Chinese village in general and in the abstract, neither is it an account of the different agricultural policies during different periods of that revolution. And this I want to make very clear: the book is meant to be exactly what the title says: 'Report from a Chinese village'.

That also means that the individual interviews in this book can be read as independent stories; *contes;* human documents from a crucial period. I have not sought to write a smooth and easily read book on China where the reader is presented with all the material in a premasticated state and only needs to swallow in order to get his conclusions. I wanted to provide the material that I had found I lacked during my travels in Asia. I want the reader to doubt, to think, to utilize my work in order to understand and interpret what is happening in China, to make it one of the instruments he will use when he tries to arrive at conclusions.

Therefore I have tried to provide all the information on this village that is obtainable, without leaving anything out. I have not compared individual statements with official pronouncements made at government or party level. (That material has been published many times and is easy to find. To have included it in this volume would only have added to its bulk, not to its information.) Nor have I tried to reconcile the statements of the various witnesses, though different individuals gave mutually contradictory and incompatible accounts of the same event. I did this because my conception of the role of a writer is that he should be an interpreter of reality, not a corrector or censor; his duty is to report, not to distort.

I will later return to the question of sources of error, but here one important thing remains to be said: the usefulness of this book to the reader in his search for realities and the validity of my whole argument rests, of course, on my honesty. That goes for any book or study, though many writers try to hide the fact behind an objectivization that is misleading. No writer is as mechanically accurate as an electronic computer; but even a computer is programmed and one always has to ask how was the programming done? What was the bias of the programmer?

Very few writers are subjectively dishonest. The real question is thus not honesty or dishonesty, but what is the code of honesty of this specific writer, i.e. his bias? No human being can be an unbiased observer of other humans. The reader thus has to take my honesty, i.e. that I'm not wilfully changing the facts that I report, on trust. But he has at the same time to remember that I'm biased.

My bias is primarily that of an intellectual and humanistic tradition. My premise is that human beings are, in the last analysis, rational, that they respond in a rational manner to an existing social and material reality. Historical and cultural differences are a part of this reality, but even so the differences between villagers in Sweden, Latin America, China, Great Britain and the United States are not ones of quality. Not only in fiction, but also in fact, are we all brothers under the skin. Thus it is possible to form a judgement and hold opinions and act on these opinions on the basis of facts. The pride of this tradition is that you change your opinions as the facts outgrow them, as the snake changes his skin. You are constant not in your opinion, but in your receptivity to factual information.

I have also a strong social bias. To a large extent it has been formed by the historical tradition of my country, Sweden, a small country where free peasants during the centuries have managed to keep their own power and held off the gentry and the officials that plagued most of Europe, both the British Isles and the Continent: a tradition that even now, in industrialized modern Sweden, makes for an intense distrust of officials. I cannot express this tradition better than did the Peasant Estate of the Swedish Parliament on 9 April 1720 during a grave national crisis in a grim war:

xiv

Give us no more officers to the utter and unavoidable disaster of the country, we will not receive them or give ourselves under their orders or leadership, but we promise and honestly ensure that we, following the honourable example of our forefathers, if the enemy enters the country and highest necessity demands it of us, will go every man from his house and spare neither blood nor life for the defence of the country and the fatherland.

This bias does not make me change what people told me; but it probably makes me a more sympathetic listener to plebeian, peasant, democratic and puritan remembrances than it would a man whose ideals had belonged to the aristocratic tradition in Europe. This peasant bias was also one of the motivations behind the decision to try to write a book of this kind. The revolution in China was a peasant revolution, and the most striking aspect of the whole underdeveloped world is peasant unrest and hunger for land.

But there was also an identification on a deeper level. Not until the book was written and published and I held the volume in my hands did I become conscious of what had been the strongest emotional impulse behind it: a personal, emotional and sub-conscious drive towards identification, which has to be taken into account by a reader whose identifications and responses are different. On my father's side, the family comes from the village of Solvarbo in Dalecarlia, a province that, throughout Swedish history, has been the home of peasant freedom and peasant insurrection ('Oaks and noblemen never pass the Dala river'), and is also, in one way, the most conservative and traditional in the country. (When mentioning me in the provincial press in Dalecarlia they never fail to write: 'Jan Myrdal of Solvarbo lineage'.) Like several other villages in Dalecarlia Solvarbo refused to follow the land reform (unification of holdings) that broke up the Swedish villages during the eighteenth and nineteenth centuries. The reform had to be implemented if one peasant in a village demanded it. But until this day no peasant in Solvarbo has demanded it and during nearly two centuries of convincing arguments from the officials of the Swedish government—they still try—the Solvarbo peasants have refused to be convinced.

As my parents were abroad, I spent my early childhood with my paternal grandparents. Later on I spent nearly every summer with my paternal grandmother. During the war, when my parents were in the United States, she lived with us children. I also spent quite a long time in Solvarbo and met the old people there. During all these years my grandmother talked about our village. And, when I was young, I never quite knew whether the Slott Anders Andersson she talked about was the one that lived in the seventeenth century or the one that lived during her childhood. There was a genealogical consciousness pervading everything she said. Though she had moved from the village, she still existed inside the village framework. When, at the age of ten, I said that I was going to be a writer, she took this to be a writer about Solvarbo, describing village and family. I never became that writer; I never will. That village is dead and gone. Though the peasants refused to conform, Swedish society has changed so fast that the village has lost its meaning, even though it has not physically disappeared. Even our names have disappeared, the Myres, Knuts, Perers have all lost their names through an act of Parliament, so that I'm not Myres Jan Gunnarsson, I'm Jan Myrdal. The law of the land demands it. I knew the old ones and they are dead, I never go to the village. I never even go to the province.

But now I understand that the reason that I identified myself so strongly with these Chinese peasants and this village, Liu Ling, was because they were so close to my own family and tradition. My grandmother telling me of Myr Erik Eriksson as she remembered him, a poor and stubborn petty peasant walking barefoot through the village holding his Sunday shoes, which he never used except inside church; his two oxen, one white and one brown. The ox-driving song from Solvarbo village:

'The earnings are small and the days are long,
Go slow, dear oxen, go slow.
You don't amount to much and neither do I,
But we'll keep on a-struggling with all our might.
Go slow, dear oxen, go slow.'

With this book on China I unburdened myself of my debt to my ancestors. Only afterwards did I become fully conscious of this emotional drive behind my work. So, in a way, I did write the book about our village, even though I wrote of a village in China. During the time I sat in Peking and wrote the book it seems that I—according to what the then Swedish chargé d'affaires in Peking, Stig Brattström, has told me—spoke more about Solvarbo village than about the Sino-Soviet conflict.

I do not believe that this emotional motivation behind my work invalidates my findings; quite the contrary, I hold that no intellectual work can be of any value unless there is a very deep personal and emotional involvement in the issues. In my case, this involvement makes it impossible for me to see the peasants of Liu Ling as mere pawns in a game. And so I cannot see the world as a gigantic chess-board where White plays Red, the 'Free World' plays the 'Socialist Bloc' for checkmate and final supremacy. Of course I see my bias not as prejudice, but as rationality and sanity; the reader might see it differ-ently, but in any case, knowing my bias will make my work more useful to him.

The method I have used to transmit an Asian reality to a 'Western' public is the outcome of my own experiences while travelling in Afghanistan and India in 1958–60, and in Burma and India in 1961–2. During those years I came to experience a frightening gap between the reality that surrounded me and the description of that reality as I read about it. The published material I had to use when trying to draw my own conclusions eventually proved to be unreliable, much too much was speculative, mere 'impressions'. The clarification and formulation of my ideas about social reality and the description of that reality, the problem of what source material could be available and the way to handle it was a long process. It took place in New Delhi during the winter of 1961–2 in discussions that lasted day in and day out for several months. The individuals who in these discussions influenced me deeply were Mr Bertil Mathsson, who at that time headed the regional I.C.A. (International Co-operative Alliance) Study Centre for Asia in New Delhi, and Mrs Kusum Nair, whose book *Blossoms in the Dust* about the Indian villagers made a deep impression on me. My parents Alva and Gunnar Myrdal also influenced my outlook—it would have been strange if they had not, considering that we share several fields of interest and have had an intermittent debate going on for two decades. That these discussions drove me to become conscious of what principles are tenable for an approach to the problem does not, of course, in any way mean that anybody else is responsible for the way I have worked or necessarily agrees that this method of presenting a peasant revolution in an Asian country is the most appropriate.

When, during the four months in China that preceded my stay in the village, I struggled to obtain a clear picture of the tremendous change that has taken place, I found that I lacked certain material that would make it possible for me to have a concrete picture of what happened and how it happened. Not that I lacked literature: the literature on China is enormous. If somebody had the misfortune to request—in a fairy-tale moment when all wishes are granted—that he be given everything published about China, then that poor student would immediately be crushed to death by an avalanche of books. If not a mountain, at least a hillock of excellent and scholarly tomes would mark his resting place. Even so I lacked the one book I had most wanted to read. And as the Chinese development is of such a character that it demands of each of us not to take a stand, but, much more important, to understand clearly why and how, the problem was not just a personal problem. So I decided to try to write such a book that I would have liked to read. A book that was to be concrete and factual, and about one specific village, thus making the question of the 'village in general' understandable. The formal concept behind this book—to try to be the mouthpiece of Asian villagers—is thus the outcome both of my deepest personal needs and my experiences during several years of travel and study in Asia.

When I decided to write on Chinese villagers, I knew that my formal qualifications were nil. That never disturbed me. I left school when I was seventeen, because I found that it hindered my studies. I have never cared for degrees and formalities, they are ladder steps in a career; they can be stepped upon, if you are interested in that kind of career, otherwise you don't need them. My main aim during the short life that is given any of us is to work; study, travel and write. But what really disturbed me was, of course, that my specific qualifications were not large enough. I would have wanted to be a scholar of Chinese as Dr Karlgren, to know the history of science and implements in China like Dr Needham. I don't. This lack of knowledge is a limitation. For some time, therefore, I doubted whether it really was up to me to try to do this work. But when I spoke to young sinologists, I found that they usually were both uninterested in and unfeeling for peasant problems. Their knowledge of Chinese could not help them, as they had no common language with peasants. The best works on Chinese village life, like Martin C. Yang's *A Chinese Village*, were about another period than that of the peasant revolution. Books on the peasant upheaval like *New Earth* by Jack Chen to me read too much like a Red Sunday-school tale: 'Hsinteng county will be more beautiful than ever—a land with-

xviii

out want, without ignorance, a land of science, abundance, democracy and peace.' I did not and do not doubt that in the very long run this will prove correct both in Hsinteng county and every other county in the world. But it is not a picture of the hungry, sweating reality of today or in the next generation. My real qualification I found to be that no one else seemed to want to do what I wanted. I might qualify this statement by adding that I have later met some people who would have liked to do something similar—but they were either not allowed by their own government to go to China or not allowed by the Chinese government to enter China. In this, as in many other situations, I'm happy to be a Swede. Sweden is such an insignificant country that it does not have any mission in the world and thus its government can retain a 'nineteenth-century liberal' attitude towards their intellectuals, and no foreign government needs to see us as 'representatives'. Which brings me to the question of visas and permissions.

When I visited Sweden in the winter of 1960–1, I had preliminary discussions with the embassy of the Chinese People's Republic in Stockholm on the possibility of obtaining a visa for a protracted stay in China. At that time I had been writing about Afghanistan and I was planning a journey to the north-eastern provinces of Burma. I wanted to link this up with China, and thus I asked for permission to go to Sinkiang, which was immediately refused, Inner Mongolia (nomadic culture), western Yunnan (the tribes on the border to Burma) and a village in China proper. Already at that time I was, of course, conscious of the village problem, though I did not see it as clearly as I did a year later after the discussions in New Delhi.

In the spring of 1962, I and my wife, the artist Gun Kessle, received our visas for China and left from New Delhi for Peking. We had been granted visas for one year. Three factors probably played a part in our receiving this permission, apart from the general easiness with which we as Swedes travel around the world: the rather good diplomatic and trade relations between Sweden and the People's Republic; the fact that I was to write for the most influential weekly magazine in Sweden; the general opening-up of China for 'Western' writers and tourists as a strange result of the Sino–Soviet conflict. (While I'm writing this introduction to the English translation, news has come that agreements have just been signed that will send 300 Swedish tourists to China in the spring and summer of 1964.)

Financially the trip was made possible through two large grants from the Swedish State Writers' Fund, advances from my Swedish publishers, Norstedt & Söner, and the weekly magazine *VI*, the organ of the Swedish Consumers' Co-operative and Wholesale Society, plus diverse other magazine and book publishers. And we borrowed. Thus, we financed our journey to China and our travels in China with our own resources. We probably could have become 'invitees'; the Chinese suggested this to us on several occasions, when we spoke of reducing our expenses, and that we did not do so was less because we thought that we would be corrupted—I have never believed myself to be easily corruptible and I don't think that I change my opinions because of small economic gains—but I intensely dislike the international junkets, the pleasure trips at public expense. The big powers, the Soviet Union, the United States, China, France, Great Britain, are all subjecting the writers of small countries like Sweden (and of each other) to well-intentioned economic pressure through different forms of free travel 'with all expenses paid'. Even if I don't think I would be corrupted, I'm against the whole tendency. It has a perverting influence on the intellectual morals of the writer, it runs counter to the free expression of ideas. I can't stop this tendency, but I can at least say no for myself. I distrust free-loaders whether they are capitalists, communists, liberals, conservatives, anarchists or just plain sellers of words. I have never liked being grateful to anybody. And I can't understand how the public—that after all pays for it—can put up with this spectacle of politicians, writers and sundry 'public figures' banqueting their way around the world on a spree of phrases.

But as my funds were by no means unlimited and as there were, and are, few facilities in China today for the tourist with a slim pocketbook, this led to certain conflicts. Our status was that of 'short-time guests' who were supposed to stay a long time and pay their own expenses. We had brought along our bicycles and as that was not quite up to the status of a 'guest' (who ought to ride in a car, which we could not afford) it took some time and discussion before we were granted permission to go on bicycles. We tried to save on living expenses in order to be able to spend the money on travel. (For instance when we wanted to go up the Burma Road from Kunming to the border, we had to hire a car. This cost a thousand dollars. The price was quite normal in that part of the world and, if we had not paid it, we could not have gone the six hundred miles to the border. When travelling, there is always the choice between sleeping up your money or using it in a rational manner.) In Peking we first lived in a good hotel, the Hsin Chiao; it was not too expensive, but it still was too expensive for us to live there for months. Then we succeeded in getting permission to live in a small and inexpensive Chinese hotel, the Beifang, but as the food situation in China was becoming better, this hotel was converted to a restaurant and we were forced out. That was at the time when we left for Liu Ling. When we came back to Peking, we were given the choice of living in a good hotel—at a price we could not afford to pay—or becoming the honoured guests of the Chinese People's Association for Cultural Relations with Foreign Countries. There simply was no third way. Inexpensive lodgings for foreigners did not exist. Still, I succeeded in finding a third way. A Swedish journalist, Sture Kallberg, who lived in the Wai Djau Da lou, the 'Diplomatic Building', had a room I thought he could spare. We moved into it and shared the household expenses and I started to work. Unfortunately, the 'Diplomatic Building' came under the 'Diplomatic Service Bureau' and it seemed that I had contravened all regulations concerning foreigners' residence and this led to strained relations with the Chinese authorities for some time. We had no ration cards and there were interminable discussions with different officials that went on day after day. I can understand the Chinese officials who were responsible for us; I undoubtedly created great difficulties for them, broke all their regulations and tangled up the different bureaucratic organs, but at the same time, I pointed out that I was only interested in having peace and quiet and being allowed to work. In the end we reached a compromise, and even the 'Diplomatic Service Bureau' agreed to let me stay on. It was to be clearly understood that my behaviour in regard to lodging, as in regard to bicycles, was in no way to be construed as a precedent. I'm not criticizing the Chinese; in every country in which I have lived I have had to take up a discussion with the bureaucracy in order to be left in peace to do my work. The Chinese officials were reasonable and it took rather less time to convince them than it has taken in many other countries; also there was no question of corruption. They followed their regulations and I wanted to have these regulations changed. To conclude this section on my economic situation and the way it influenced my work: the final ironical twist to the story was given by the Swedish 'establishment' after this book was published in Sweden, when I was selected to be one of those writers who were to be 'freed from material cares' by being given monthly 'salaries' through the Swedish State Writers' Fund.

Our journeys to Inner Mongolia, at the beginning of our stay in China, and western Yunnan, our last trip during the stay, were interesting. Partly because it is always interesting to travel in an area like eastern Inner Mongolia, which has been closed to strangers for a long time. Just getting somewhere can be a pleasure, if that somewhere is difficult to reach. I have experienced that pleasure several times; when we arrived at Khiva, when we managed to get to the Wakhan corridor, when we went up the Bashgul valley in northern Nuristan. It might be a tainted pleasure, because it is so purely personal (though the pleasure often makes the writing pleasurable to read). But the journeys also were a part of that larger work I had tried to get a grip on for several years: what is happening to the minorities (we visited the same tribes on both sides of the Sino–Burmese border); what is happening to the nomadic cultures; what the conflicts are between the nomads and the agriculturists.

I got much material during these journeys, some of it I have used for articles, some I am planning to use in a larger context. But during our discussions in New Delhi the emphasis shifted to the village. Nomadic cultures still fascinate me, but I have come to see the Asian village and the Asian peasant revolution as the most important aspect of the journey to China. Thus, except for the journeys, I concentrated on getting permission to go to a village and live there for some time. That seemed to me the most important.

One of the prerequisite conditions for travelling in China today is that you accept interpreters and guides. We were given ours by the Chinese People's Association for Cultural Relations with Foreign Countries. I will come back to the question of interpreters, but I just want to point out that you either accept this condition or you don't travel outside Peking, Canton, Shanghai—and more often than not, not even there. I don't like this. But it is a tendency that is spreading from country to country. Even in Sweden we are starting to take in 'invitees', give them guides and see to it that they keep looking at what we want to show them. I'm disturbed by this tendency. It gives strength to my fears that we, all over the world, are moving towards a more 'supervised' form of existence. But in this case I could not just say no, find a third way out or shift the emphasis. Either I have my travel supervised—or I stay at home, quite probably supervised in one way or another even there. However much I dislike it, I have to accept this condition.

We were to be given a free choice of a village to stay in, though there were limitations to this free choice. All military areas were barred, so were the 'closed areas'. No areas in China were in general open for foreigners at that time. But some were much less open than others. We also had certain wishes of our own. I wanted a village that had been part of 'the old liberated areas', a village where the first agrarian revolution had been carried through on a local basis (i.e. not one where the change came as a result of civil war, but one where the change had been a factor leading up to the civil war). Added to this was the purely personal wish of both my wife and myself that, after five summers spent in deserts and on the hot plains of India, we should go somewhere with a slightly better climate. Accordingly, on these grounds I chose the area immediately south of Yenan. Permission for this area was granted. When I reached Yenan the local authorities had a number of villages to suggest, and of those I chose Liu Ling for a number of reasons. In the first place it was a typical village of northern Shensi, not in the sense that it was average—that I doubted—but because it presented certain features of the modern Chinese peasant revolution in their purest form; the leading communists in the village were old peasant revolutionaries, who had carried through their revolution before Mao Tsetung came to Shensi. Then the village had been the scene of some of the earliest experiments in collective and co-operative farming. Also Edgar Snow had visited it a couple of years previously, and this meant that by choosing a village already visited that probably would be described, the reader would have certain leads both to the different perspectives on the village and to the old question of how a description of people and life in a country like China changes with the degree of intensification, i.e. the validity of extensive and impressionistic reporting. Anyone interested in this would do well to read Edgar Snow's *The Other Side of the River*, pp. 475–89 (New York, London, 1962).

I have repeatedly stated that this book is not the *final* truth about China. It is an instrument. No book is more. It is necessary to read other material in order to get a clear picture. For instance, just as I have been writing this introduction I have been reading O. Edmund Clubb (last U.S. Consul General in Peking), *Twentieth Century China* (New York, 1964). It contains among other things a very good section, 'Communist leadership turns to the peasantry', pp. 186–94, that has a direct bearing on what the old peasants of Liu Ling tell about the beginnings of the agrarian revolution. This advice to read further ought to be self-evident. Unfortunately it is not. Too many people—especially students—take the words of *Ecclesiastes* much too literally: 'Of making books there is no end; and much study is a weariness of the flesh.'

We had been given permission to spend one month in a village, and we spent one whole autumn month, from the middle of August to the middle of September, in Liu Ling. The authorities in Yenan were very eager that we should not sleep in the village. They promised to arrange for us to be ferried there and back every day. We wanted, of course, to live in the village, we even demanded to be allowed to do so. The 'Old Secretary' of the village strongly supported us. To him it was a point of honour. After some discussion the Yenan authorities were (with some reluctance) convinced of our point of view. (The reluctance can be interpreted in many ways, one of them is that the Yenan authorities wanted us to be as comfortable as possible. They probably wanted to be kind. It is not their fault that their kindness would have made this book impossible.) We then lived in a stone cave (normally the party secretary's office) and I worked in another (the brigade's conference-room). Since we lived in a cave in a village of caves and ate the village food and the whole time associated with the villagers, it would be easy to say that we lived as one of the people. But that would be a romantic and thus mendacious description of reality. We were the first foreigners to have lived in the village, and the village honour required that our cave should be whitewashed and that we should eat well. We lived considerably better than the villagers. This way of treating strangers and guests is no specific Chinese trait; you meet it in every village in all peasant societies. In the evenings, when we had finished the day's work, the peasants came with gifts from their private plots, melons, corn-cobs, fruit, nuts. It was kind of them; they gave out of their poverty. But it was also pride. I have stayed with peasants in villages in Afghanistan and India and Europe and it has always been the same, the pride of the household, the pride of the village demands that the guest is given the best there is. As a guest in a village you eat well, you also eat with a certain reverence, because you know that you are eating the fruits of the toil and sweat of the people around you. But you never say so to your hosts. There is pride in toil. There is nothing 'objective' about food in a poor peasant village. It does not come out of a tin, neither is it something you carry with you from the city. But I was not one of the villagers. And I was not living like a Chinese peasant.

I spent the first few days visiting all the fifty families in the village, thus obtaining a certain picture of the village and its inhabitants. These first days in the village were rather difficult. Suddenly, after two years, I really was there in the village I had asked for. I had made a thorough nuisance of myself, pulled every string I could, demanded, written, asked, suggested, organized finance, promised to write, and now I was there and it was up to me; if I didn't do what I had set out to do, there was no one but myself to blame. During these first visits I felt depressed; it was difficult to get a grip on the work.

This feeling of uncertainty was increased by the fact that the Chinese authorities seemed to have quite another picture of my function in the village than I had. They thought that I was to work with the peasants in order to get a close understanding of their life. This I had also thought—even written in my visa application—but only if I could stay for many months. When I had only one month I could not do it, no time would have been left for the interviews; the resulting book would have been one of sentiment and description of personal experiences and I did not want to write that kind of book. (It was suggested to me later on in Peking that the permission for me to live in a village probably had been based on the assumption that I was to take part in agricultural labour.) This slight conflict was solved in a practical fashion by the 'Old Secretary'. He pointed out that he himself was doubtful about the value of middle-aged intellectuals for manual labour.

The first fifty interviews had been short. Only on the evening of the second day, when I looked over my notes, was I able to visualize the scope of the work. I found some threads that I could start winding. The material from these first interviews is not published in this volume. They were rather pointless and only gave me a background. The information they contained was later either duplicated in the statistical tables or deepened in the long interviews. On the third day, I selected the first of those people I wanted to interview. After that we worked all the time in the same fashion. My wife, Gun Kessle, walked alone in the village and the surrounding area, sketching and taking photographs, while I interviewed from eight a.m. to noon and from two p.m. to six p.m. In the midday interval and in the evenings I collected material for the 'People say . . .' sections, in general conversations, mostly with the women of the village. In the evenings I arranged my notes, prepared the following day's interviews and discussed the day's work with Gun. (Before falling asleep in the evenings we read. The day before we left Peking I had been to the Dung An bazaar and bought some books in the second-hand bookshop. While in the village I read Goethe's *Italian Tour*; *Water Margin*, the Jackson translation of the Chinese classical novel about the robbers of Liang Shan Po; and Thomas Wolfe's *Of Time and the River*.)

I did not select the people to be interviewed according to a pre-arranged plan. Some people (the economic and political personages of the village) were planned from the beginning, the others I chose one by one. Either because their names cropped up in other interviews, or because I found them interesting in one way or another. Thus even a figure such as Li Hsiu-tang, 'the counter-revolutionary', became clear to me only after ten days. This limits my previous statement that I collected *all* the material I could collect: I collected all the material that I could collect in a month of intense work. I deliberately left the final selection of people to be interviewed open as long as possible. I don't trust rigid plans; they lead to abstractions. But I did *speak* with everybody.

The decision to have an upper limit to the interviews, i.e. not to continue far up in the bureaucratic structure above the village, was contained in the idea of the book itself. But first I had thought of including at least some representative from Yenan, who could give the slightly larger picture of the village in its setting. I even tried to make that interview and spent one morning in Yenan interviewing the local party secretary, a young man. Unfortunately he was too dogmatic, too official to be of any value. (And this is a typical problem all over Asia: the middle echelon of bureaucracy is mostly young and dogmatic and narrow-mindedly inexperienced. The old experienced peasants are illiterate, the bright young administrators are already high up and the old intellectual generation of revolutionaries or 'national figures' are slowly fading away.) I don't blame the young bureaucrat from Yenan. He ran true to type, but when he flatly stated: 'We have here in our part never had any difficulty, never committed a mistake, never made a fault and we have no problems today', I broke off the interview with a few nice, pleasant phrases, and decided that he was not to be included in the book and that I had better go back to the village and talk with the peasants.

During our stay in China I met several higher functionaries, but

only once was this of any value as far as Liu Ling goes. That was when I talked with Mao Tse-tung. During the National Day celebrations in Peking (drinking tea, eating sweets and looking at fireworks) my interpreter for the evening suddenly came to fetch me. I was to be presented to Mao Tse-tung. We were a long line of foreigners and each one in the line had his hand shaken by Mao. As I had the chance I did not move on according to protocol after the handshake, but tried to converse. It ran like this:

I: I have just come back from a trip to the Yenan area.

Mao: That is a very poor, backward, underdeveloped and mountainous part of the country.

I: I lived in a village, Liu Ling. I wanted to study the change in the countryside of China. [I meant historical change; Mao seemed to understand it as just economic.]

Mao: Then I think it was a very bad idea that you went to Yenan. You should have gone to the big agricultural plains. Yenan is only poor and backward. It was not a good idea that you went to a village there.

I: But it has a great tradition—the revolution and the war— I mean, after all, Yenan is the beginning——

Mao [interrupting me]: Traditions—[laughing]. Traditions— [laughing].

Then I was pushed onwards and the conversation ended. It was just that kind of surrealistic and inconsequential conversation of which diplomatic reports are made. The only concrete result was that I had my photograph taken with a laughing Mao Tse-tung.

I also set myself another limit from the beginning. I left out the folklore aspect. Not because I'm not interested—I'm deeply interested in folklore and a large part of my library is devoted to it—but having so little time I had to make a choice and that choice was easy; the folklore has been recorded, the story of the peasants in upheaval has not.

When I say that my wife and I settled down in a village and started interviewing the people, sketching them and taking photographs of them, I know that this immediately makes the reader suspicious. In our societies, the highly industrialized countries of north-western Europe and North America, we are fed up with questionnaires and scientific interviews. When your doorbell rings, you often feel a strong resentment at knowing that outside that door stands a young man with rimless spectacles and a leather briefcase (initials in gold, leather black) who will present some kind of credential and then start asking you how often you wash your feet, what you know of your neighbour's sex life and how you would feel about Malcolm X as President of the U.S.A. And we are all tired of filling up forms (name, date of birth, nationality at birth, maiden name of mother, particulars of education, where first employed, etc. etc.), filing photographs (full face and profile, twelve of each, with signed statement as to when taken and if beard has been grown since then). It might be sampling and scientific social study, but we don't like it, and we don't trust it.

I have never worked that way. I have always worked as I was taught to do, when I started as a cub reporter twenty years ago and was given my first assignment, to interview a hundred-year-old lady: 'Just get her to talk about her life, what she experienced, what she remembered. When? How? And then? That's all there is to it.' (It was not quite all there was to it; the old lady declared that she had lived to a hundred because she had taken a glass of spirits, akvavit, every morning ever since she was ten years old. This, of course, was immediately struck out by the editor. 'Boy! You can't offend the readers; in a newspaper you must know what not to write.' That's why I prefer writing books.)

To interview in this fashion is not a less scientific way of working, but it is a more human way. You don't interview 'subjects' or 'samples'; you get people to talk about their lives and you treat them with the respect that is their due as people. This is also what I meant by saying that I have tried to reproduce these peasants' 'self-portraits', I have not tried to dehumanize a human story, a story that I experienced as epic in the true sense of the word. I also believe—without wanting to start a discussion on the fundamental ideas of sociology at this point—that you give a truer 'profile' of a peasant revolution in this way, than by subjecting the peasant samples to a questionnaire and then converting the answers to algebraic notions and ending up with a symbolic line-drawing of 'the structure of peasant unrest'.

We had two interpreters with us. Apart from these there were no outsiders in the village. The fact that there was no 'politically responsible ganbu' in the village checking on our activity, I then, and now, guess to be because of the personality of the 'Old Secretary', who very much was *the* responsible man in the village.

Our chief interpreter was Pei Kwang-li. She had come with us from

Peking. She was the most flexible, the best linguist and the most hard-working of the interpreters I had come across in China. I had tried several interpreters before getting hold of her, and we had been working together for about two weeks when we arrived at the village. She was supposed to go back to Peking from Yenan and it was only after some quite hard discussion that I managed to take her with me to Liu Ling. She was of great help to me in the village. She was friendly and cheerful and interested in the work. I gathered that she was afterwards criticized for her work with me. When we came back to Peking, she went away on vacation and after that she was not so friendly, natural and relaxed as she had been during the month in Liu Ling. She later on—when the book was finished—interpreted for us during our trip to Yunnan and during that trip she was cold, formal, dogmatic and even (which in China says much) quarrelled violently with us on the grounds that we showed 'anti-Chinese' opinions. As our 'anti-Chineseness' was our opinions about toil and sweat and peasant hunger that she had understood so well in Liu Ling, I cannot explain this change in her behaviour otherwise than that she had through 'criticism and self-criticism' come to evaluate us and our work in a different way and change her opinions about our way of working. Because of this I got rather less information in Yunnan than I had hoped for. But in Liu Ling she was a good companion, hard-working and cheerful.

My other interpreter was Ching Chi, who had been in Liu Ling before. I brought her from Sian. She was talkative, but wanted to improve her English; I managed to put in about a half-hour's lesson each day with her. (I took her story as typical of lao dung, pp. 321-8.) Her duties were mainly those of a secretary—she collected statistical material and made arrangements with those I had selected for interviews, and she also acted as auxiliary interpreter when Pei Kwang-li was asleep. Both girls did a good job. As our time in the village was limited we didn't take any free days, neither could the girls have their accustomed midday rest. We were a small enough group to be able to work without friction, and once I had drawn up the schedule and we had discussed our problems and agreed that time was too short for us to afford to lose even a single hour, they both did their utmost. I am grateful to them that they never asked for time off, even when they quite plainly were ill, or protested at what they were asked to do, however onerous. In principle, I cannot help feeling that in work like this the result achieved is in exact inverse proportion to the number of those taking part.

It is of course clear that the very fact of the arrival of four strangers in the village changed the atmosphere there. That is unavoidable; measuring changes what is measured. Or, as Pei Kwang-li put it, she had been on lao dung and lived in villages, but she had not heard peasants say that much about their lives; she supposed it was because I was a foreigner and put questions in a foreign manner. One of the aspects of Chinese civilization that I like most is the respect it gives to work. Intellectual work is also work and highly respected. This trait is also to be found in other cultures. To be a poet in Iceland, a professor in Germany, an academician in Russia, an intellectual in China means holding an honoured position in society. (This needs to be pointed out because one of the strange features of Anglo-American culture is of course that an expression such as 'to live by one's wits' is condemnatory, while in most other languages the literal translation would be laudatory.) I was a writer and an intellectual, the girls were students, thus the relation between us and the villagers was one of mutual respect. But the girls were women, young women, and in China old men are still the most respected. Judging from the way the girls and the old men behaved to each other it seems to me utterly unlikely that the old men would in any way change what they were saying out of respect (or fear, or what have you) for the girls. But I do think that the fact that they were students made some of the younger and 'literate' peasants want to prove that they too were becoming 'learned'. I don't think it changed their stories, but I believe it strengthened the emphasis on being 'new and learned peasants'. This strengthening is no distortion of the process now taking place in China.

The fact that I worked through interpreters was in itself a source of possible error. I would have preferred having an absolute command of Chinese and living all alone in the village for a year. But because of political and social conditions in China today (in most of Asia, by the way) a 'Westerner' would not be allowed to live absolutely alone and on his own whether he knew Chinese or not. Thus, to hope to collect the story of the Chinese peasants without somebody sitting beside you is unrealistic.

One pre-requisite of this method of working is that the interpreter used must be able to interpret; that is to say, have an absolute command over the language into which he, or she, is translating. All too often one comes across interpreters who have only a limited knowledge of one's own working language and then it is impossible to work with them. My chief interpreter, Pei Kwang-li, had an almost perfect knowledge of the language and—what is even more unusual—was sufficiently acute to follow my way of thinking. She was to me a good interpreter and that was why I guarded her so jealously. To work with an interpreter is like being married; you have to have an absolute mutual rapport. (Not to cause misunderstanding: I don't mean marriage as a form of sex life, but as a form of intense intellectual communication. It does not matter if the interpreter is male or female.)

It is sometimes said that a clever interpreter can systematically suppress or distort information. If she is a bad interpreter, i.e. has but a poor command of the language, she can. But over the years I have worked quite a lot both as an interpreter and with interpreters, and I am convinced that in work such as this, where the interpreting has to be kept up without pause hour after hour, day after day, any such systematic distortion is impossible. It would require a superhuman intellectual effort, as any experienced cross-examining lawyer can tell you. And I certainly never had the shadow of a suspicion that it was being attempted.

The major source of possible error in interpreted material lies in the fact that all the information has to pass linguistic frontiers (*traduttore, traditore* is not just a question of bad translations, but of the impossibility of translation); thus, despite all my precautions, I must have lost certain nuances, maybe also misunderstood information. Obviously I should have preferred it if I had known Chinese like my own language.

But against this one has to set the definite advantages of working through an interpreter. This provides a calm rhythm throughout the interview and makes it possible to concentrate on the main questions. Both the interviewed and the interviewer have time to think. The use of an interpreter also creates an almost 'clinical' atmosphere. If I had been using my own language and working within my own cultural area, I should have found it difficult—or impossible—to ask certain of the questions, both political and personal, that I put to those I interviewed.

In general, I prefer to work with an adept interpreter, even when the language used is one of which I have a reasonably good command. Doing this makes the work matter-of-fact, and emotionally charged questions are cooled down and 'estranged' without becoming impersonal. If I had been Chinese, I should not have been able to ask certain questions; partly because I should not have been able to phrase them, as I should have been so impregnated with Chinese culture that I should see that culture from inside its own value-judgements, and partly because the person I was interviewing would have objected.

There is another possible source of error which the use of interpreters enabled me to reduce. It is inevitable that one feels emotional sympathy for some people and antipathy for others. In ordinary human intercourse this does not matter; in my general literary work, it is one of my—or any writer's—great driving forces, but if I had been submerged in these personal relations to different people in Liu Ling, it could have caused complete shifts in perspective unbeknownst to the reader. As I have already stated, I had a general emotional drive behind my work, but by keeping the interviews 'clinical', as I did (white-washed room, an interpreter and the calm rhythm of interpreted conversation), I believe I am correct in saying that there was never any emotional contact in this sense between myself and those I interviewed. At all events I tried to suppress any such reaction.

When I received answers that seemed doubtful or palpably incorrect, I rephrased the question so as to make sure that I had not misheard or misunderstood. I also made lists of questions to be asked in various connexions, as a result of which most questions were checked by the different people I interviewed. This, of course, led to disparity between answers. (I did not say: 'You say this, but X said that. . . .' I did not want to push the answers in any direction, I wanted to bring out as many aspects of the story as I could; the different ways in which the happenings were seen.)

But, though I certainly must on occasion have misheard or misunderstood, or been misunderstood, or got something wrong because of the interpreting, I believe that I am entitled to claim that, within the limits of my ability, I have succeeded in reproducing what these people really said, and that the interrogations were conducted in such a way that their answers are of real value.

It is another question to what extent those who told me their stories gave correct accounts of the events they had experienced or in which they had taken part. Obviously they are not 'true' accounts, if you define this truth as a 'scientifically objective account', as of an experiment. Such objectivity does not exist when living people are talking about their lives. What is given here is the evidence of the actual participants in the events. It is notorious that no two witnesses give exactly the same account of what happened in even the simplest traffic accident (unless they are perjuring themselves). The evidence in this book is not concerned with a traffic accident, but with a great revolution of profound significance for the lives of each one of the participants.

It is also obvious that the older and illiterate peasants are story-tellers, tellers of tales. They have a life to talk about and what they say often deviates considerably from the 'official line'. The younger and more literate tend to verbalize their experiences in words they have read. Incidentally, this is nothing peculiar to Chinese villagers. Also the general tendency for these accounts is to approximate to the social conception of the events, in this case, the official Chinese interpretation of the history of the revolution. I'm not saying that this history is necessarily wrong, only that the official interpretation influences the individual memories in different degrees. This state of affairs is in no way specifically Chinese. A similar investigation made in Sweden—on the break-up of the village and the origin and development of the farmers' co-operative movement—would give the same result. In assessing these statements, therefore, the same reservations must be made as in assessing any other evidence. But, though every lawyer knows that witnesses' statements are always subjective, none has yet concluded from that that such evidence should be dispensed with and the courts fall back on speculation instead. I want to emphasize that what is self-evident to the lawyer does not always seem so to the social scientist. There has been a tendency both in the 'East' and in the 'West', largely owing to the cold war, to abandon oneself to speculation about 'the other'.

If this book were read as a novel, it might be called a parade of 'positive heroes'; but it is no novel. Here people plead their own cause. They are trying to be honest, but they also want to present themselves as they think they ought to be seen, which naturally means in a positive light. The same thing goes for the village gossip, which I have used, for example, in the 'People say . . .' sections. In this village people do not speak really ill of each other, at least not to younger people or outsiders.

That the peasants in this book do not speak about the famine and the agricultural catastrophe after the 'Great Leap Forward', does not mean that that famine did not exist. Even when I and my wife arrived in China the food situation was precarious. But for several reasons, both climatic and political, these years were not so catastrophic in northern Shensi. One must always keep in mind that China—like India—is a vast country. Conditions can be extremely different in different parts of the country at the same time.

There are many people and many institutions in different countries that made it possible for me to write this book. The organization that was 'responsible' for us, the Chinese People's Association for Cultural Relations with Foreign Countries, had a lot of trouble with us. I am glad though that during the nine months we were in China, although they did not always share my view of the way the work should be done or of what 'reality' was (a long discussion was kept up on this question, 'objectivism' being harmful, etc.) and though we had different views of how the world was developing and argued sharply over practical questions, they never once went back on what they promised to do when we first arrived.

But there is one man I must thank personally, I didn't do it verbally as it would have interfered with the work, and that is the 'Old Secretary', Li Yiu-hua. I respect him as a person and without his understanding of what my work required, this book could never have been written.

J. M.

Fagervik
1964

Part I
Liu Ling Village

36° 34′ North, 109° 28′ East

Liu Ling is a small village lying buried among the loessial hills west of the River Nan, immediately south of Yenan in northern Shensi.

The easiest way of getting there is from Sian. You first go to Tung-kwan, either by branch line train or by bus via Hsienyang. In either event, you continue northwards from Tungkwan by bus up the old Hsienyang–Yulin highway, spending the night at the inn at Hwang-ling. A couple of hundred yards north of this inn is where the 'Yellow Emperor', Hwang-ti, the mythical founder of the Han people and culture, is reputed to have been buried 4,000 years ago. At all events you can visit his tomb and the temple, recently restored, that was put up in his honour. In 1959 the government had a new stone plaque put up there, inscribed: 'Father of the Han people . . .'

This is the heart of China. The first day of your journey takes you through the river country, where China's classical agricultural civilization took shape and the people of Han developed their individuality. It was here that the early forms of the Chinese state came into being, and it was from here that China was united. The second day takes you northward across the loessial plateau with its deeply etched ravines, muddy rivers, treeless bush and cultivated fields. This is a poor part of China, a borderland through which, during long dynasties, the imperial levies marched on their way north to the frontier fortifications at Yulin. Sian was the big capital city of this huge agricultural province, Yulin its border with the realm of the nomads in the north. Yenan is 600 li north of Sian and the same distance south of Yulin. Northern Shensi is bare and barren, its climate hard. The crops fail there every other year, and its people are famed for their toughness, industry and rebellious nature. All through China's long history, northern Shensi has been one of the hotbeds of the unrest that has repeatedly flared up among the peasantry, and a hinterland for the peasant armies of many a

3

civil war. In 1628 the peasants of northern Shensi rose, and the rising spread over the Empire. In 1636 their forces combined under the command of Li Tse-cheng and four years later it was announced that 'all land shall be divided equally between the poor and the rich', while at the same time all taxes were declared abolished for five years. In 1644 Li Tse-cheng rode into Peking at the head of the victorious peasant levies and, as they entered the city, Se-tsung, last emperor of the Ming dynasty, hanged himself to atone for his sins. This victory was soon turned into defeat, however, for the generals of the Ming dynasty preferred to let in foreigners and be conquered by the Manchurians than allow their own peasants to seize power.

In the early 1930s the peasants of northern Shensi rose and drove out the landowners and tax collectors, set up their own soviet republic and formed their own Red Army, which was led by the now legendary Liu Chi-tan. It was to northern Shensi that Mao Tse-tung and the Central Committee of China's Communist Party led China's Red Army of workers and peasants in the Long March, its great 25,000-li retreat. It was 19 October 1935 when the survivors reached Wuchichen in Kuyuan hsien. Then the 'Shensi–Kansu–Ningsia Border Region' was set up with Yenan as its administrative capital, and from there their struggle against the Japanese was directed, and it was from there that the Chinese People's Liberation Army eventually conquered all China.

You leave the bus after Ten-mile Village—before it reaches Yenan—and turn off to the left down a side road leading to the river. You are now heading west. You cross the River Nan by the ford and, as you climb the opposite slope, the white caves of Liu Ling's basic school will be on your right and, above them, the caves of the village itself, dug into Naopanshan. Paths wind up the hillside and the caves lie in rows, one above the other.

The village lies 2,500 feet above sea level, on the loessial plateau with its great hills of loess with their vast eroded slopes. Where the ground is not cultivated, the hills are covered with scrubby bush. The landscape is predominantly ochre in colour. Loess cannot easily absorb large quantities of rain. It can suck up a gentle rain, but here the rain is seldom gentle and so, when it comes, torrents of yellow muddy water gush down across the fields, digging deep furrows in the layers of loess.

Loess is rich and, if it gets water at the right time, can give big yields; but the climate here is a continental one and the rain refuses to come at the right time. The average annual rainfall in Liu Ling is about 20·72

4

in., 54 per cent of which falls in July–August–September. The snowfall is not great, only 3·85 in. of the above total falling in the form of snow. The ground is frost-bound to a depth of 4·2 in. for three months of the year. The winters are cold, dry and dusty, and, the ground being bare, the frost often damages the winter wheat. Spring is also a difficult season with its drought and high winds. Then they have to burn brushwood on the headlands between the fields at night to protect the young corn from the frost, and the smoke hangs heavily over the yellow earth. April and May are months of sunshine and great heat and in them no rain falls. Out of three years they reckon on one good, one middling and one bad harvest. To them there is nothing unusual about crop failure; drought, frost and hail are a constant menace.

The variation in temperature during the twenty-four hours is considerable: up to 20° C. or more. The maximum recorded temperature is 39·7° C., recorded on 29 July 1952, and the minimum —25° C., recorded on 23 January 1956. The year's average is 9·3° C.

Mean temperatures are:

January	7·2°C.	July	23.0°C.
February	2·4°	August	26·6°
March	4·5°	September	15·9°
April	11·4°	October	9·2°
May	16·8°	November	2·6°
June	21·1°	December	4·8°

Sitting on Tashiai, the Old Secretary, Li Yiu-hua, talks about the countryside, farming and women as workers

WHEN I came here twenty-five years ago, only the valley was cultivated. All the fields you see up there on the hillside have been cleared
since then. It is good soil down there in the valley. It yields ten times
as much as that on the slopes. Down there we are able to use a tractor.
We hire one from the tractor station at Yenan. We have only a couple
of hundred mu which can be tilled by tractor, but the Liu Ling People's
Commune has plans to buy one and a couple of lorries; but that cannot
be till the commune has made a bit more out of its factory for agricultural implements. It's only on the actual floor of the valley that there is
any tractor land.

Every member of the labour brigade is given a private plot down there. We reckon 0·4 mu per head, and everyone is included, even infants. The plots are allocated every other year, and people can grow what they like in them. The private plots run from the threshing floor to the melon field, where the temple, shiwa, used to be. You can tell that the plots are private from the way they are all such bits and pieces. It is good land, but not really right for tractors. We try to keep the private plots separate from land that we are going to use the tractor on.

Here, in northern Shensi, we are badly off for temples. We have been liberated a long time here and many of the temples have disappeared. This was a Buddhist temple. They say that the K.M.T. blew it up, before they withdrew in 1935. At all events, more and more of it collapsed after that and we used the stones for other things. You'll find stones from the temple in every cave in Liu Ling. In 1958 there were only a few caves left and we used them as store- and work-rooms, while we were building the Jenhuei canal, which we did that year. Last year we turned everything over to melons. That pays better. But we're going to take the stones with carving on and put them in the school, so that the children have something to look at. The tent on the melon field down there is for the nightwatchman. The fields have to be guarded at night now that the melons are beginning to ripen. There are different kinds of foxes, you see. If you hear music among the melons at night, it will be the nightwatchman. He plays to make the time pass and keep the foxes away.

Up here on the hillside is where we cleared the new ground, and are still clearing. You can see that the fields are of different shapes. The big ones are the collective ones. They are worked by the labour groups. Big fields are more economic than small. You have to have big fields if collective working is to pay better than individual. But there are smaller fields too. There is a lot of ground that is not really suitable for big fields and which, because of that, it would not pay to clear for the collective, so we let ganbus from the town come out and work it on Sundays. We tell them where they may till and in those places they grow what they like. Of course, we don't grant any title to the land. We couldn't do that; but they are allowed to grow what they like and take it home. You can see there are quite a lot of those plots.

In their free time our members are allowed to clear where they like on the hills. That is to say, they may not clear where we could make a big field, but otherwise where they like and as much as they can. Usually, there is never any cause for argument. They are all farmers,

7

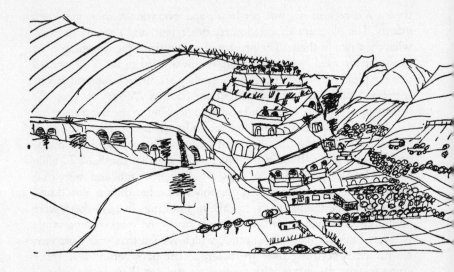

you see, and themselves know where they can break new ground. The only occasions on which we have had to interfere were when someone tried to till the actual track. Wang Chen-chia did that this year. He is not from this village. He began digging down there by the track. Then he began planting vegetables till there was only a narrow foot-path left in the middle, and so Li Hai-kuei had a word with him: 'That's the way we take our animals. Our goats go that way. If you think we are going to try and stop them eating your vegetables, you're very much mistaken. You had better move your vegetables and put them somewhere else, unless you want to feed our goats with them. You must just stir your stumps and climb up the hillside and clear some ground there.' Li Hai-kuei considered that what Wang Chen-chia was doing was inadmissible, because it did not leave room for our oxen any longer. Well, you don't need a meeting to solve that sort of problem. It solves itself. Wang Chen-chia had to go up the hillside and dig up there.

Of course, lots of people have had their eye on the ground down there by the track along the stream, for it's good soil. Ma Hai-hsiu also dug a plot there right beside the track; but he chose cleverly and was able both to get water from the stream and yet leave room for the oxen on the track. You get ten times the yield there that you do up on the hillside. Then the herdsman told him that his plot was too

near the path. Ma Hai-hsiu replied that he had remembered the oxen and left room for them; but the herdsman said that it wasn't enough and that the oxen would walk on to his plot and eat what was growing there, so Ma Hai-hsiu ought to go elsewhere. But Ma Hai-hsiu did not want to do that. He thought it a pity to give up the good soil he had, so instead he built a high wall round his plot. It's so tall no one can get over it. And that's all right.

Ever since we began co-operative farming in this district, we have had this system of five kinds of plot: collective plots in the valley, private plots in the valley, collective plots on the hillside, privately cleared plots on the hillside and ganbu plots on the hillside. We have never given up the principle of having private plots. Here, in this hilly country, work is hard and people need to eat a lot. It is mostly millet we eat. That's filling. Wheat is more of a luxury. There's no strength in it. We eat potatoes sometimes, but they won't keep longer than April. No, millet of various kinds, buckwheat and maize, though we use the maize mostly as fodder. You can eat oats too, but that's really a fodder crop. This has been a dry year, as you can see. The harvest up on the hillside will be a bad one. Down in the valley the weather does not make such a difference as it does up here.

Over there on Loushan we are ploughing for winter wheat just now. We grow wheat two years running, then we take a crop of buckwheat and after that one of millet, and then it's wheat again for another two years. The leader of the labour group selects the best ploughers; they work in teams: three ploughers and a clod-crusher and four ploughers and a clod-crusher, and, in addition, there are five men with mattocks who turn the soil in the places the oxen cannot get at. A man with a wooden plough ploughs one mu a day on the average. He has either one strong ox or two smaller ones.

We go in a lot for goats here. People prefer goat's meat to mutton. Mutton has a rank taste. We usually castrate the billies; that makes their meat tender. We don't use milk. We aren't accustomed to it. Milk is harmful to others than infants. Our women make wine of maize and millet. But we only do that in the winter; in the summer it won't ferment properly, so, if we want anything, we buy spirits in the shop. No, we don't distil ourselves. Of course, we would be allowed to do so, if we wanted. Who could forbid us? But it is simpler and just as cheap to buy our spirits in the shop.

You can see that we have started weeding the fields down there. The women work well. In the old days they weren't worth anything. Women were oppressed then, and people used to say: 'An incompetent man can get about in nine countries, but a competent woman can only get round her cooking stove.' When we began making our revolution, thirty years ago, the emancipation of women was one of the main points in our programme. We sang songs about it. I can still remember them. We had a slogan: 'Free their feet!' Now their feet are free and women can work in the fields, so now, both men and women share in cultivating the land. Thirty years ago we were saying: 'Let both men and women take part in our revolution', and now that has come about. Marriage is free now, too. It's only those directly concerned who have any say in it. That's a good thing. Women are hard workers. Do you see that the women down there have baskets beside them as they weed, but the men don't? That's because the women aren't only weeding, they are also collecting grass for the family's pig.

Since 1960 we have had a loudspeaker in every cave that has electricity. Families pay five yuan a year for them. Everyone wants a radio and this is the cheapest way. We usually have a big loudspeaker outside the cave you are living in, but we took it down so that you should be able to work. Lo Han-hong thought you would find it difficult to write, if the loudspeaker was there. He ought to know. He lives in the cave next to yours and he sometimes writes to the newspapers himself.

The ox-driver there is employed by the labour brigade. He has to cart out manure, when he has time. Otherwise he carts our timber. He fetches it from a place four days' journey away, some 200 li from here. He sleeps in inns on the way. They are all right, not too wonderful and not too awful. Every place of any size has an inn and the ox-drivers foregather there in the evenings. Ai Kou-ming has been an ox-driver since he was quite young. He likes it. We have several big horse carts too.

The graves over there on Loushan are quite new. They belong to the family of Wang Fung-li's father-in-law, Li Yü-teh. Naturally, we don't till that land. One has a right to choose one's own grave, after all. Why should the collective interfere? One doesn't select good arable land for that, if one can help it.

Cave-Building, *Mau Ke-yeh*

PEOPLE in our part of the country prefer living in caves. This is largely because our loessial soil makes cave-building easy and the result is a nicer and better insulated dwelling than an ordinary house. I must have built a good forty caves in my day. My father taught me how to build them, but I'm no specialist. Anybody can build a cave.

There are two kinds of cave: earth ones and stone ones. The earth caves are dug into the hillside. The first thing to do is to find a place with the right kind of soil, hard yellow loessial soil. You cannot build a cave where the soil is sandy. There are lots of places in this valley suitable for building caves. But you can make a mistake. Li Hsiu-tang made one this year when he began building a big cave down at the bottom of the eastern side of Naopanshan behind Chang Chung-wen's pigsty. The earth was damp there and all he achieved was a big hole. The higher up the hillside you dig your cave the better the earth usually is; but it means you have a longer way to the well.

You don't need so many people to build an earthen cave. An ordinary cave of normal size, 18–19 chi long, 9–10 chi high and 8–9 chi wide, including making the kang and cooking stove and chimney, takes about forty work-days. A house of the same size takes the same or a little less, but it isn't so practical and costs more to heat.

Having selected a place where the earth seems to be of the right kind, you smooth the hillside so that you have a vertical face. In doing this you will see what the soil is like to work with. Next, you make a first hole of two by seven chi and dig in for roughly three chi before you start enlarging. As you dig, the kind of soil will show you how large you can make the cave. The harder and closer the soil is, the larger you can make your cave, and vice versa. Having dug out your cave, you polish the earth walls to make them smooth, then you plaster them with mud made of loessial earth. All this time, you leave the outer wall untouched, using just the little opening that you made at the beginning, but once the cave is finished you open up this wall so that you have a door and a window. The window is a lattice frame with paper stretched over it. This makes a good window that lets in the light, but keeps out the wind. Nowadays we also use glass a bit; but glass is expensive and it is seldom one sees a piece more than two by three chi. Besides, glass is not always practical, and it calls for a considerably more complicated structure for the lattice.

At first, caves are slightly damp, but they dry out after three or five months. If the soil is of good quality and hard and firm, you can then build additional caves and store-rooms leading off from the first cave. But if you do that, you make the passages between them rather narrow, roughly two by seven chi.

You cannot build this sort of a cave by yourself. It needs several of you. We usually exchange work and help each other. Up here in northern Shensi people prefer, as I said, to live in caves, because they are warmer in winter and cooler in summer; but down in central Shensi people prefer to live in houses.

But earth caves don't last well, and they can also be dangerous. Even if the soil is of good quality, an earth cave seldom lasts more than two or three generations. Often only thirty years. If the soil is poor and you have help enough to be able to build a whole stone-cave, you can build one that is half and half: half stone cave and half earth cave dug into the hillside. But that is not a good solution. You can tell when an earth cave is nearing the end of its days, because then small pieces begin falling from the roof. You have to be careful when that happens; but you can still use the cave, if you strengthen it.

There are two ways of strengthening. The best method, though one that can only be used for smaller caves, is to take six-inch planks that you soften and bend in steam and fix these up under the curve of the roof one chi apart. These make a good support and the cave can be used for a long time yet. The other method—you saw it used in Yen Chi-yung's cave, he's a carpenter and knows how to do it—is to build a framework with support pillars and stretchers and cross-beams to hold up the roof. But this isn't very practical and it doesn't last either.

Stone caves are better. I have built a number of them. Twenty years ago I planned all the stone caves of Liu Ling's basic school and was in charge of building them. I also was in charge when the three caves we are sitting in now were built. A stone cave calls for more careful planning and considerably more work. You can take it that each stone cave takes roughly 400 work-days. The three caves in this row took the work of seventy men for a whole month. They are thus considerably more expensive to build than both earth caves and ordinary houses; but, while an ordinary house won't go more than thirty years without major repairs, a stone cave will stand for four or five hundred years and not need a thing doing to it. In theory stone caves are indestructible. The only thing requiring maintenance is the paper and woodwork of the windows, for wood will rot in time. But in an ordinary house there is a lot that can rot and fall and need replacing.

In principle, it is best for a cave to face south, because then it will be warmed by the winter sun, which hangs low, and the summer sun, which stands high in the sky, won't reach in; but you cannot pay much attention to that, where earth or stone caves are concerned, for they have to be sited according to the condition of the ground. I have built caves facing all quarters of the compass, but, wherever I could, I have avoided making them face east or west.

Caves, of course, are built with cooking stoves and chimneys, but with both earth and stone caves we usually make an additional outside kitchen for use in summer. That helps to keep the cave cool in summer and the women consider it an advantage to be able to work outdoors. When we do this, we site the outside kitchen in a shady place.

In many places you have to be careful about drainage when building stone caves, but here with us the subsoil water is fairly far down and we have good stone. We have not needed any special drainage either at the school or for this row. We begin by digging the foundations. We excavate ten chi down. The hole corresponds to the outside measurements of the cave-to-be. Then we make a foundation of tamped loess. If this is done carefully, it becomes almost as hard as concrete. On this foundation we build two stone walls, which are the inner long walls of the cave. We make a stone floor. When these inner walls reach a height of six chi above the stone floors we build the inner short walls. Then we reckon out the vault. This has to be a semi-circle and rest on the two inner long walls. We don't calculate with paper and brush. We are farmers and we cannot write or calculate on paper; but we know how it has to be. The inner short wall is a measure for the vault. We put up a frame in the cave and build the vault with stones. This calls for a lot of work, for each stone has to be cut so that it fits exactly. But you soon learn to tell from looking at a stone how it has to be done.

Once the vaulting is finished the cave will stand for hundreds of years. After that we build the outside walls. The smallest distance between the inside of the outer wall and the outside of the inner wall is five chi. The same goes for the distance between the outsides of the inner walls, if one is building several caves one beside the other as in this row. This intervening space is filled with tamped loess. The outside walls of the cave are built up six chi, plus the height of the vault, plus five chi, because the vault has also to be covered with trodden loess. Here too, five chi is the smallest permissible distance between the highest point of the vault and the top of the layer of beaten loess.

Built in this way, the roof needs no maintenance; and, although grass grows on it and we let our goats graze there, no damp can get into the cave. For the sake of drainage we make the roof slope inwards and make a gutter of baked clay there to take the water away. Neither rain nor frost nor weeds can crack the roof. Up in the north, however, where they build similar caves, but of sun-dried bricks, which aren't strong enough to bear the load, the clay roof has to be trodden every year.

We have good stone here. We took some from the old temple when it collapsed; and the rest we quarried over there where the latrines now are. You can see from the look of the hillside that we have used it as a quarry. You build several stone caves at a time, if you can; because it is cheaper to build them in a line, since that saves outer walls.

The last thing to be done to a stone cave is to plaster the walls with fine wet loess mixed with chopped straw and then whitewash them. After that, with the trellis for the window in place and the paper over it, and the door made, it is a good dwelling and one that is easy to keep warm in winter, while it is always cool in summer. And you never need to think about maintenance.

We are planning to rebuild the whole village with stone caves down here; but that is a long-term plan. We haven't yet decided exactly where we are going to build. That also depends on whether we are to get a better water supply. The well here is not as good as it might be. But we have decided in principle to start building the first range in 1963 and 1964. In a few years the whole village will consist of stone caves and they will stand for 500 years without needing repair. That is what makes stone caves the most economical.

The Rhythm of Life

Long talks with Ching Chi and the Old Secretary, Li Yiu-
hua, and shorter ones with practically all the women
of Liu Ling

THE mothers of Liu Ling suckle their babies until they are two or three.
Many go on even longer, especially if it is the last child, or if the
mother wants to avoid having any more children for a time. If a
mother does not herself have milk, she does not get another woman to
suckle her baby. Here, in northern Shensi, a woman does not suckle
another's child. In these cases the baby is given goat's milk. Some
children drink milk up to the age of seven, but never after that. 'Milk
is bad for your health.'

A baby starts being given other food than breast milk when it is
seven months old. It then starts being given a thin gruel of millet and

rice and water; then a thin porridge of millet and water. At one year old, the child starts getting thicker porridge, then noodles and steam-baked bread soaked in gruel, but no vegetables at that age: 'Vegetables are too difficult for children's stomachs to digest.'

At three, when a mother normally stops suckling her child, it starts being given steam bread with bean stuffing, eggs and vegetables. While I was talking with Tuan Fu-yin's wife, she had her youngest daughter on her knee, and there the child sat, clutching its mother's right breast in one hand and a tomato in the other, and taking alternate sucks and bites, while we talked. This was unusual, though.

After three, a child starts to eat with the family. It is given soft, easily masticated food without strong spices. All members of the family help to feed it. Then it begins trying to eat with chopsticks, after which its diet becomes progressively that of the others in the family.

Up to the age of six all children wear trousers open behind. There is no flap or fall arrangement, but the actual fork of the trousers is hemmed on both sides, where in adult garments there is a seam, so that when the child squats or sits, this gapes, forming a large opening through which the child can relieve itself. People reckon that a child ought to be 'house-trained' by the time it is eighteen months and able to walk properly; by three, it should be able to keep itself dry, and by six it is considered to have sufficient control of its bladder to wear trousers with the seam sewn up.

On the whole, boys and girls are treated alike at this age. If a child is an only one and consequently has a lot of people helping look after it, it will be strictly brought up, but otherwise it will be able to play all day and its parents won't bother about it or what it does. In wintertime children stay indoors during the morning and afternoon, playing on the warm kang with their brothers and sisters or, perhaps, the neighbours' children. The kang is the children's place, too, when it rains.

Boys and girls start being treated differently at the age of seven, when boys will be sent by their mothers to collect wild grass for the pig. Girls are not made to help much in such ways, but they are expected to help with the housework. At ten, a girl ought to be able to help her mother unpick quilted jackets and trousers and wash them, and she should also be able to wash vegetables and cook a meal. At this age boys start fetching the water from the well, not by themselves with a carrying pole over their shoulder, but in pairs with a bucket slung on a pole carried between them. The girls mend clothes and help their mothers do the washing in the river. Normally they use nothing but the water. Soap is seldom used, but they do occasionally use soda.

It is not easy to keep the children clean. They are washed in water, and, if very dirty, given a scrub with river sand. Their parents wash when they get back from work. The children are washed in the morning and, if dirty, at night as well. Children go to bed at about half past eight in summertime and at eight in the winter. In the morning they are allowed to lie longer than their parents, not usually waking till seven, and half an hour later in winter, by which time their father is already at work in the fields and their mother busy with the housework. After that they lie on the kang playing and chattering till it is time to go to school.

Between seven and twelve, little girls play hopscotch, and in the afternoons you can see them skipping, either holding their own rope or skipping over one held by two others. They sing counting songs: 'One two two one, one two three three two one, one two three four four three two one, one two three four five', etc., and there is great rivalry to see who can go on longest. They also dance round-dances and sing. Nowadays they are said to sing mostly songs that are 'in tune with the times', like 'Chairman Mao has come to our village to visit us'. Girls 'grind salt' and 'make covers'. Girls and boys do not play together after the age of seven except in school, where the teachers make them play and dance and sing together, but the moment the teacher's eye is off them, they split up into separate groups of boys and girls. Boys of this age play with balls, hoops, diabolo and hopscotch. In wintertime they go sliding. They will sing, but they won't dance unless they are made to.

Most of the children go to school, but not all. The younger parents do send their children to school: 'I want my child to be a ganbu.' Nowadays most people consider that children ought to be taught to read, write and do arithmetic. Even the older women want their children to go to school. It's the grandparents who spoil them. It is always they who are closest to the children. They have the most time for them and talk with them most. If a child goes to its granny and says: 'It's horrid at school', 'I'm so tired', 'It's so cold in school', or 'It's so hot in school', granny will get into a state and say to the child's parents: 'It's too much for the poor child to go to school.' Whenever a child wants to do something its parents won't allow, it has only to go to its grandparents and weep; then the grandparents go to the child's parents and read them a lesson.

Last year a girl called Hu Yen-ching grew tired of school. Her father, Hu Shen-chu, didn't let that disturb him and just told her that she had to go, so then she went to her granny, Ching Chung-ying's wife, and said: 'I don't like school. I don't get good marks. The teachers criticize me. I won't go there any more.' Her grandmother was very upset and said: 'Poor little girl, working so hard! There's no need for you to go to school. Just you stay at home.'

After that, Hu Shen-chu's wife told the school-teachers: 'There's nothing I can do. My mother has made up her mind and I cannot make her change it.' Then Hu Yen-ching moved to her grandmother's, because she thought her parents nagged her about school. She refused to do what her parents said and stuck to her grandmother. It took a year for the party, the school and the collective to convince nine-year-old Hu Yen-ching that she ought to go back to her parents and start going to school again.

At twelve or thirteen girls stop skipping and playing hopscotch and such games, and play cat's-cradle instead. And there is far less talking and joking with boys. After their first menstruation, which may be any time between twelve and sixteen, they become more and more shy and bashful. They talk less, play the fool less often and sing less. They are shy when talking to strangers, especially if they are men. They stay mostly at home and devote themselves to domestic work instead of playing. When they reach eighteen, girls begin getting their trousseau ready, whether they are engaged or not. They make shoes and clothes and bedcovers. At that age they will also have begun helping with the farm work.

There is no corresponding change in boys at this age. They begin playing ball games and ping-pong; then they start working in the fields; but boys are considered to stay childish into their late teens. They are shy if they meet a girl of their own age; but otherwise they are not bashful, not even with married women. People say that a boy always gives the impression of being younger and less mature than a girl of the same age.

There is no special ceremony to mark entry into youth or manhood. The only outward sign of sexual maturity is bashfulness and the end of giggling and chattering. Girls marry at a younger age than boys. There is a shortage of girls in Liu Ling, in fact in all northern Shensi, and so girls often are able to choose between several suitors. The Old Secretary, Li Yiu-hua, said this of the shortage of girls: 'I don't know why it is, but it is a fact. Just look at my family. I have nine grandchildren: six are boys and three are girls. In Liu Ling there are thirty-six boys and twenty-two girls. There have always been far more boys born here than girls; and with us a girl child has never been an unwanted burden, as in other parts of the country. In the old days in Szechwan, in the old society, they used to kill girl babies, because they were just a burden on the family; but with us here in northern Shensi girls have always been precious. We have never looked down on girls so much as people have in other parts of the country. In the old days, parents here in northern Shensi used to get a lot for their daughters when they married them off; thus a girl did not deprive her family, but added to its possessions. That's an important thing to remember. So there was never such a great difference between the way girls and boys were treated here in the old days. We have always been short of manpower and at the same time always had more men than women. That is one of the reasons why widows always marry again here. But I have never been able to fathom why it is that so few girls are born here.'

There are three principal ways of arranging marriages:

(1) The boy and the girl live in the same village. They work together in the fields and they talk together. He likes her and she admires him. They fall in love and, as they know each other, they tell each other and they marry, if their parents agree. They marry of their own free will.

(2) They live in the same village and see each other occasionally. The boy likes the girl and the girl likes the boy, but they dare not tell each other; so each asks some older person to act as go-between and tell the other: 'So-and-so is in love with you.' That's what Lo Han-hong and Li Chin-wa did. He had a job and she was studying. They could not talk to each other and so could only gaze at each other. She noticed that he came out of his cave-office every time she walked past on her way home from Liu Ling school, and he noticed that she walked by, whenever he was looking for her. Then Lo Han-hong asked Li Kuei-ying to talk to Li Chin-wa, and afterwards Li Chin-wa asked Li Yang-ching to talk to Lo Han-hong, and in that way they learned that they loved each other. Then they met and went into Lo Han-hong's cave and talked alone together, and after that they became betrothed. It's mostly boys who get an older person to speak for them.

(3) A person with a son over twenty and not yet married grows anxious lest his son become an old bachelor. He happens to have a relative in another village, who has a neighbour with a daughter who is not yet engaged, so the man takes his son and they go together to visit this relative. The boy and the girl cannot meet otherwise. Things are arranged so that the two can see each other, and afterwards they are asked: 'Did you like him?' 'Did you fall in love with her?' After that, the two young people meet again and perhaps they do fall in love, become engaged and get married. When Chang Chung-liang's younger brother, Chang Chung-wen, was twenty-two and still unmarried, he went to Chitan hsien, where he had an uncle, and his uncle introduced him to a very young girl. They got married and she now has a child of four, though she herself is only twenty-one.

When a girl considers the boys with an eye to choosing one to marry, she looks for one who is strong and healthy and able to work well. Girls attach great importance to behaviour: the boy they choose must be even- not quick-tempered. Appearance is less important. As the girls say: 'We have a long life to live together. He may look handsome now, but his looks will soon go. But if he is faithful and kind and hard-working, we can have a good life together.' Boys who are known to be lazy seldom get married.

When a boy considers a girl, the first thing he asks himself is: 'Can she look after a home?' Next in importance is that she should be even-tempered. Appearance plays a certain part, but not a great one. In Liu Ling no one will say that a girl is ugly or plain, just that she 'looks well enough in her way'.

'In the towns the girls will tell you the same as those in the villages, but they will only do that because it is the thing to say. In reality, town girls want smart, dashing-looking boys.'

The person with the most say in the matter of a girl's marriage is her grandmother, then her grandfather, then her mother; what her father thinks is of least importance. What they all want for the girl they are marrying off—and what the boy's parents are also looking for—is a 'good marriage' to someone who is 'rich', strong and able to work well.

Once they are engaged, the boy and girl meet often. Li Chin-wa and Lo Han-hong spent hours sitting together in his cave. They were always alone then and no one would disturb them. 'We aren't so feudal in Liu Ling that we won't leave them alone together.' But when Lo an-hong goes to see Li Chin-wa, he has to sit with the whole family. Sometimes the two would go to the cinema in the town together.

There is no intercourse prior to marriage. That is held to be immoral. 'No girl in Liu Ling has ever had a baby before she was married. That happens very seldom up here with us in northern Shensi.' The age at which girls normally marry is such that there is no large group of sexually mature but unmarried women.

Later on, when they are to marry, the two young people go to the authorities and register. They have to say how old they are and they are asked: 'Do you love each other? Do you want to marry? Are you doing this of your own free will?' Only after that are they given a marriage licence. Having got that, they are legally married, but it has never yet happened that a couple have begun living together as man and wife after just this legal marriage. There has to be a ceremony as well, and for various reasons there can be an interval of anything up to six months between the legal marriage and the wedding.

A bride's trousseau usually consists of three or four changes of clothes, two new coverlets, one mirror, one or two chests, one cup, one soft cushion, one pillow, and one wash-hand basin, and the bridegroom should have furnished the bridal chamber with one mattress and one thick coverlet. The thicker this coverlet is, the richer and happier the bride's life will be, or so they say.

The wedding is in the bridegroom's home and it will be well attended. There can be more than a hundred guests. All relations, neighbours and friends are invited. There will be wheaten bread, buckwheat noodles and cakes of 'sticky millet' to eat. Altogether there ought to be eight courses; four is the minimum. There should be meat and wine and spirits, and everyone will eat and drink and sing and joke. At the start of the ceremony the guests are seated, gathered round the couple, who stand in front of the table, the bride on the right, the bridegroom on the left. There should be wine and a dish of sweetmeats and melon seeds and cigarettes and a looking-glass on the table; and there should be a picture of Chairman Mao hanging on the wall in front of the couple. The bride takes some flour and puts it in a porcelain bowl. Bride and bridegroom bow low to the portrait of Chairman Mao; then they turn to their parents and bow to them, then they bow to the elders and lastly to their guests.

Then the guests ask them to tell how they fell in love with each other, to tell 'the story of their love', and they both become very embarrassed and look at each other and urge each other to do the telling. And the people call out: 'Quickly! Quickly!' Then the bridegroom will mumble something in a low voice. Some just say a word or two like: 'We met and so we married.' Then all the guests ask lots of questions. They pretend that they have seen the two together and say things like: 'We saw you! You were walking very close together down by the river.' Everyone jokes and tries to make them blush as much as possible. Both bride and bridegroom wear big red paper flowers, which they exchange, and after that they drink wine. Then the guests ask the bride to sing. The couple eat a few sweetmeats from the dish, then they sit down and everyone starts eating and drinking.

Now, the bride and bridegroom are congratulated and everyone drinks. After that, good friends conduct the couple to the bridal chamber. There the bride has to wait on the bridegroom and all their friends. She must light their cigarettes and fill up their cups with wine. Bride and bridegroom sing and everyone drinks wine. About midnight the couple are left alone in the bridal chamber and the guests depart.

On the third day, the couple go to the bride's family with gifts. They take cakes and sweetmeats, dried noodles, handkerchiefs and stockings. Then the bride's mother invites some of her good friends and relations to a dinner with meat and wine and all sorts of good things. After that the couple go back to the bridegroom's family. 'This is our new way of celebrating a wedding. Everyone's wedding has been like that for many years now. But the old people say that it was done differently in the old days.'

The old women say that in the old days you were not allowed to choose whom you married. A young couple were not allowed to meet before the wedding. When a girl was sixteen or seventeen, the marriage-broker would come and say: 'I have seen a young man in such-and-such a place and he does this or that and he is healthy and strong and of good family, and he is rich and even-tempered.' If the girl's mother was interested in the offer, a day would be fixed for the young man to be presented. On the day appointed, the marriage-broker and the suitor would arrive with presents of wine and meat and other good things, as well as cloth for the girl. The girl's mother would take the meat and cook it and warm the wine, and then they would eat and drink. Meanwhile the girl would be kept hidden. She was not meant to meet her suitor. If the mother was satisfied with the suitor after she had seen him, she would say: 'It is well', and then they would settle the financial arrangements.

That done, a propitious day for the wedding would be decided on with the assistance of a wise man. This had to be at least one month away in order to allow the girl time to get her trousseau ready. She had to have four baskets of embroidered shoes, quilted trousers, pieces of cloth, socks, needle and thread, and foot-bindings for her girl-children. All her relations would have to help her get the things ready in time. After this the suitor and marriage-broker would bring the girl's mother all the things the suitor had agreed to give for the girl: money and cloth and meat and wine. The mother would cook the meat and warm the wine and accept the suitor's bride-ransom.

A girl had to weep properly on her wedding day. To begin with, she was decked out with lots of red flowers and ornaments, and then her pigtails were unplaited. Next, she was placed in a palanquin carried by two or four men and taken to the bridegroom's home, her brother going with her. When they reached the bridegroom's home, the bride's brother gave her away. Bride and bridegroom then knelt in the big room in front of a table. The room had to be decorated with flowers and ribbons, and there had to be two red candles on the table and also fruit and sweetmeats. The couple then bowed first to heaven and earth, then to the bridegroom's parents and then to the bride's brother and the marriage-broker and all the relations. After that everyone ate and drank.

In the old days, the main dish used to be wheat-flour noodles, and throughout the ceremony some men sat by the door to see that no widows, cats or dogs got into the room, because in those days these always brought bad luck, especially at a wedding. After everyone had eaten, the curtain before the bridal chamber was pulled aside. At that moment the bride had to look desperate, otherwise people said: 'Look how avid she is!'

The first three days after the bridal night, the bride had to spend sitting on the kang all the time. She was given no more to eat and drink than was necessary for survival, and if she wanted to relieve nature she could do so only at night, creeping out when everyone else was asleep, because if anyone discovered her going out she would be jeered at. During the day she had to hold it in however much it hurt. On the third day the couple went to the bride's mother with gifts. The bride's mother would have invited some close relatives and they would eat meat and drink wine, and afterwards the young couple would return to the bridegroom's home. For the first three years of her marriage a bride was not supposed to go beyond the gate. Some of the old women said that they were allowed to go a little way beyond, but they must not go far and only when it was necessary. 'Well, that was the old way of marrying. It is not practised any longer. It hasn't been employed for many years and it's a long time since anyone bowed to heaven and earth.'

Nowadays, when people marry, they are usually very loving for the first year. Not that they show it in front of others, we don't do that, but you can see it by the way their clothes are better and their shoes whole, and they look happy. But otherwise brides behave in the same way as before. People don't consider a bride properly married until she has had a baby. Until then she is still a girl, even though she is married. She won't dare talk and joke with the others; but everyone will joke with her and her husband. People will stop her on the road and ask: 'Well, are you in love with your husband?' And if the bridegroom is coming back from the town, he will be stopped and asked: 'What have you bought your bride?' They will blush, but they won't joke back till the bride has had her first child. Of course, she will be less bashful than she was before her marriage, but she isn't yet one of the married women. If they don't have any children, people usually adopt a son. That is what Tien Kuei-hua did. Her husband is a ganbu at the coal mines in Yenan. He was deputy party secretary of Liu Ling's People's Commune up to 1961, then he was moved. When they did not have any children, they adopted one. People would rather adopt the child of some close relative with lots of sons, than let their family die out. The adopted son has to be treated well, because he is the family's future. Such adoptions are quite common.

Nowadays divorce is very rare. There having been no free choice of partner under the old system, there was a sudden rush of divorces when the new order began. But that is a thing of the past. If there are children, people think it immoral and wicked to leave them. Even if the marriage is childless, people still consider divorce immoral, because now that people can choose whom they will marry, they will have chosen each other and should put up with the consequences. One can always adopt a child. If, in spite of all this, they still want a divorce, the various organizations, the party, the League of Youth, the women's group, try to instruct them and explain what is the decent thing to do and the one consistent with socialist morality. If they persist, the matter is taken up by the mediation committee of the people's commune, which goes into it thoroughly with them and explains to them why they ought not to divorce, but should live together and agree. If, after all this, they refuse to give in and still want a divorce, they are, of course, entitled to go to the court in Yenan and start proceedings for a divorce; but that has not yet happened in Liu Ling, nor have any divorces been heard of in the neighbouring villages for many years, for it is a long time now since women have been granted equality and marriages have been entered into voluntarily.

Brawling and fighting were said to be unknown in Liu Ling, nor had anyone heard of anyone suffering from jealousy. Infidelity was unheard of in the village, and they had not had any great dramas of passion, let alone *crimes passionnels*. 'It is all due to the fact that we in northern Shensi are different to people from Hopeh and Canton and Shantung and Kiangsu and Fukien. We aren't like they are. Down there, those sorts of thing do happen; but not with us.'

Eye diseases were not common, but stomach disorders were. Most children suffered from tummy-ache and diarrhoea right from infancy till they started going to school, after which the teachers saw to it that they did not sit right on the ground and that they stopped drinking water from the river, with the result that they became healthier. Children's trousers being open meant that they, especially the little girls, were susceptible to inflammation of the bladder. All that the mothers had to say about this was: 'What can we do? The children just run about as they like.' Among the older generation, the women especially suffered from rheumatic pains in their hands and feet, but aches and pains were typical of all old people.

Adults did not drink water that had not been boiled, and they did not eat raw vegetables. 'Raw food and cold food have a nasty taste.' Melons and tomatoes were the exception: they were eaten raw. Tea was a luxury. On the rare occasions when they drank it, it was the cheapest black tea they had.

Meat was party fare and when an animal was slaughtered, they ate everything, even the blood and stomach; but they never ate horse-flesh or mule-flesh: 'It tastes of vinegar'; though they would at a pinch eat donkey, even though they didn't really like the taste. They did not eat sucking-pig or chickens: 'Immature meat is harmful.' Goats, sheep, cattle and pigs were butchered and eaten. If a pig showed signs of being ill, it was butchered and eaten. If it died before it could be butchered, it was buried. If a donkey died of old age it was eaten; if it died of disease or foundered on the road, it was buried. If it fell down the hillside and broke a leg, it was slaughtered and eaten. But horse and mule were never eaten, though some people are said to have eaten even horse-flesh in the great famine.

Almost every household had its cat. Cats were the rat-catchers, but also the children's playmates. There were only five dogs in Liu Ling: two owned collectively and three privately. The collectively owned dogs were the herdsman's dogs. They were fed on millet porridge, vegetables, pumpkins and maize-flour bread. At the slaughtering seasons they got some bones, but otherwise they were vegetarian dogs. They were not used for hunting and did not hunt on their own. The three dogs in private possession were owned by Wang Fung-li, Fu Hai-tsao and Chi Pei-fa. They were not so well fed and got fewer bones. They were watchdogs and pets, mostly pets. But they also acted as guards against foxes and wolves. Foxes took a lot of the villagers' hens.

Only one person in Liu Ling had been in his country's capital; this was the Old Secretary, Li Yiu-hua. One or two had been in Sian, capital of Shensi province. On two or three occasions in the last ten years, they had had foreigners in the village, come out by car from Yenan: 'But you are the first foreigner to have spent the night here or stayed here.' A couple of years before, some young people from Sian had been in Liu Ling doing voluntary agricultural work, lao dung. (Ching Chi was one of them.)

When a couple have their first child, whether boy or girl, their relatives send them presents of dried noodles, wheaten flour, bean flour and eggs. When the baby is a month old, its mother invites their immediate relatives and best friends and all who have sent them presents to a celebration. The celebration consists of two meals, the first of which is eaten at ten in the morning and consists of buckwheat noodles and four other dishes, salted and pickled vegetables. After a noonday rest there is a second meal, which starts at four and consists of steamed wheaten bread, 'sticky millet' cakes and four courses, including mutton and fish. With all this they drink hot spirits out of small cups. The guests bring all sorts of presents: little shoes, baby clothes, etc. But this is only done for the first baby in the family. There is no celebration for the others that may come, and birthdays are not kept.

When a man reaches the age of fifty, he starts getting his coffin

28

ready. He may even have bought the wood for this years before, and has to be good thick wood; but having reached the age of fifty he ca ask a carpenter to make up the coffin, and when it is finished and ready, it is stored either in the labour brigade's store, or in the store-room in the person's own cave. Once they are fifty, men let their beards grow and they also start smoking and drinking spirits. Some younger men smoke and drink spirits, but that is unusual. In wintertime the older men usually have a couple of small cups of hot sixty per cent spirits every day; but they do not need this in summertime.

The great day of a man's life is his sixtieth birthday, for then he has completed his span. If he dies before sixty, it is an unhappy death, but after sixty he can die happy. The next birthday celebrated is his seventieth, then his eightieth and so on, and each is a happy and honourable occasion.

One invites all one's friends and relations to one's sixtieth birthday; so that in the case of a respected man, the entire village will be there. He will regale them with noodles, eggs, meat, wine and spirits. There is a first meal at ten o'clock in the morning and this should consist of buckwheat noodles with meat gravy and four dishes of pickles and vegetables. The second meal is about four o'clock, after a midday siesta, and should consist of thirteen dishes, 'thirteen flowers', eight dishes of pork and mutton and vegetables and that sort of thing, and five dishes of pickles and suchlike. Everyone drinks and makes speeches, saying lucky and luck-bringing things to their host; in fact you eat and drink as much as possible, and talk a lot.

There is no definite age at which a son takes over responsibility for the family from his father. As long as a father can work in the fields, he remains head of the family, but once he is no longer able to do a full day's work, it is usual for the eldest son to take over from him. Big family decisions are not taken by the head of the family alone. On such questions as whether or not to build a new cave, buy a bicycle or cart, and questions of the children's schooling, all the older members of the family confer and reach a joint decision.

In principle, work done in the labour groups is calculated per person and it can also be paid for to the individual; for example, when Li Yang-ching bought her husband a bicycle as a big surprise present, she signed the receipt for her pay herself; but usually all money earned is given to the head of the family. Whichever way is used, it will go into the joint family purse.

When there are several grown-up children in a family, it is normal these days for the children to set up their own households when they marry, thus splitting up the family. Yet, even though split in this way, the family will stick closely together. For example, Ai Ke-liang, who is forty-nine and lives alone, being a widower, has his own cave and is counted as having his own household, yet he lives and eats with his sister, Ai Lan-ying, and her husband, Li Hai-kuei, and he shares all the corn and cash he gets with his sister, Ai Lan-ying, and his younger brother, Ai Ke-kao: 'My wife is dead. I have no children. Whom else have I to give it to now?'

Chen Chung-yuan's wife had had three sons by a previous marriage. (She was first married to Tsao Chen-kuei's uncle.) The eldest, Tsao Chen-yung, married and set up his own household; thereupon the middle son, Tsao Chen-hua, moved across to his newly married brother's cave. The third son, Tsao Chen-yi, had already been accepted for the Chinese People's Liberation Army, being able to get in only because the family at that time had three unmarried sons all over the age of eighteen. Chen Chung-yuan's was the only family in the village that had ever fulfilled that condition and thus Tsao Chen-yi was Liu Ling's only soldier. He had already been three years in the army and had spent all the time in Tibet. He was just a private, but he had been to school and could write. He often wrote to his mother and whenever she got a letter from him, she would take it to someone who was able to read and have it read out to her, weeping all the time as she listened, because she yearned for him so much and was so anxious about her youngest son, who had become a soldier and gone so far away. He had a lot to do in the army, he told her, and was getting on well; also he was hoping to be transferred soon to some other place, from where he might be able to come and see her, for he had been in Tibet ever since the autumn of 1959.

When an old person dies, his or her sons put on white mourning clothes and go and inform all the relations. Then they all discuss when and where the dead person is to be buried. A 'knowledgeable' person is invited to come and say which day will be most propitious and which burial place the best. There used to be one of these 'knowledgeable' men in Liu Ling itself, but he died in 1961. He was called Tung Shi-hai and his widow later moved to Yulin, while his granddaughter has gone to Sian, so that his family is not in Liu Ling any more. He was the last one able to pronounce on such matters and who used the old traditional methods in the search for what would be propitious and bring luck. Now, if there are many members of the older generation in a family, they will insist that a 'knowledgeable' person be fetched from another village, though these are getting more and more difficult to find. The young people do not bother so much about this, but the older generation still think it matters a lot how they are buried.

When a good place for the grave has been found and a propitious day for the funeral decided upon, invitations are sent out to all the relations, who then send gifts of food and money to the sorrowing family, anything from three to five yuan per household. Then they come, even from long distances, to take part in the mournful ceremony. On the first day of the funeral there are three meals: one of buckwheat noodles with meat gravy and pickles at eight o'clock in the morning; then, at midday, they have steamed wheaten bread and eight dishes of vegetables, pork and mutton. After this they all weep until the evening, when, at six o'clock, they have more buckwheat noodles—these being considered lucky—with meat gravy and pickles. After that they weep and talk about the dead man. Then they all go to bed.

Early the next morning the corpse is taken to the grave, the coffin being carried by four good friends. The eldest son heads the procession, holding the dead man's name plaque in front of him; then comes the coffin and then the members of the family in order of generations. They have with them wine and steam bread for the dead person. Everyone weeps as the dead man is being buried.

Our graves are built more or less like potato cellars. First, a perpendicular shaft is dug into the ground and from the bottom of this a horizontal grave chamber is excavated. If a wife dies first, she is buried outside the family's burial place in a temporary grave and moved to join her husband when he dies. In these cases, the wife's bones are collected and put in another coffin, smaller than the ordinary ones, which is then placed beside the dead man's coffin. If the husband dies first, the grave is made large enough for two coffins.

After the coffin has been placed in the grave, the entrance to the grave chamber from the shaft is closed up with stones and the shaft is then filled in, a mound built over it and tombstones placed on this. Then one burns paper money and other things and sets out offerings of wine, steam bread and meat for the dead person. After that everyone returns to the village, and when they get back to the cave, they have

31

another meal of 'sticky millet' cakes, after which the relations disperse to their homes.

On the third day after the funeral, the younger members of the family go to the grave and make offerings of paper money, meat, wine and steamed wheaten bread, weep a lot and then go home. One hundred days after the funeral, they again go to the grave and make offerings. After that, offerings are made once a year. Everyone in Liu Ling, both communists and those not in the party, go to the graves of their ancestors and make offerings. Each family has its burial ground.

As a general rule, widows re-marry unless they are old, that is to say getting on for sixty or more. Tung Yang-chen's mother, for example, Tsao Fong-ying, married Chang Shi-ming and that was considered right. A woman ought not to live alone. But a widow must not marry again until at least a hundred days after her husband's death. If she gives birth to a posthumous child, it is called having a 'moon child'. This happens. Women in mourning must not wear patterned materials, but must dress in white, black, grey or light blue. They must not wear ornaments. If the person who died was under sixty, people will prefer not to talk about him: 'He died an unlucky death.' But if he died after attaining the age of sixty, people will gladly talk about him: 'He died a lucky and happy death.'

Children under twelve may not be buried in their family's burial ground. The older people say: 'Children under twelve have not got fully developed souls. It would bring bad luck to bury them in the family grave.' So they are buried without ceremony up on the hillside. Children under seven are buried without coffins. They are thrust into some natural crevice or hole in the rocks near the village and covered with earth and stones to keep wild animals from getting at them. The older people say that any other way of burying those who die so young is unthinkable. 'It would bring great misfortune upon the entire family.'

The most serious thing one can say about anyone is: 'He has been so bad and behaved so immorally that he has no young generation.' To die without anyone to continue the family is the most dreadful thing that can happen to anyone. That almost happened to Li Yü-teh. He has his family grave on Loushan, for he belongs to the old land-owning family. He never had a son of his own, only two daughters and they, of course, would leave the family as soon as they married. His elder daughter is Li Kuei-fung and she is married. She married Wang Fung-li. Only, instead of her leaving home, Wang Fung-li moved to her home. That was arranged when the marriage was being settled. Li Yü-teh wanted Wang Fung-li to come and live with him and give him a young generation. You can do that if there is no son in the family, in which case sons-in-law can act as sons. Li Kuei-fung's first two babies were girls, so they were called Wang; but her third was a boy and so it was named Li. In this way Li Yü-teh has a grandson who bears his name and will continue the Li family. Thus Li Yü-teh's family will not die out; but if Wang Fung-li's son had been given the name of Wang, the Li Yü-teh family would have died out.

Fu Hai-tsao has saved his stepfather's, Tsao Shen-hung's, family in the same way, partly by bearing both his father's name of Fu and his stepfather's name of Tsao, and partly by giving his child the name of Tsao.

Tables

Prices of consumer goods in the shop in Seven-mile Village

In China the basic unit of currency is the yuan, the rate of exchange for which is, at present, about three shillings or forty-two U.S. cents, but all calculations based on this are quite valueless in assessing the economic situation of these families. Thus, as in all other cases where one has to try to compare countries which have different social and historical assumptions, the prices must not be viewed in relation to those in the United Kingdom or United States, but to China's own reality. Material for doing this is provided in different places in this book. There is no coin for a thousandth of a yuan, but, as in other countries, prices in China are often expressed in thousandths of the currency unit.

Cotton wadding	jin	1·005 Y
Cotton material, simple	chi	0·295
Knitting wool	jin	8·05
Sewing thread	skein	0·15
Handkerchief	each	0·435
Galoshes (rubber shoes)	pair	4·59
Salt	jin	0·16
Sugar	jin	0·80
Sweets	jin	1·32
Vinegar	jin	0·09
Cooking oil	jin	0·72
Biscuits	jin	0·70
Spirits, 60 per cent	jin	1·34
Washing soap	2 cakes	0·435
Electric light bulb, 15-watt	each	0·63
Earthenware jar holding 80 jin of grain	each	9·91
Water cauldron, iron, holding 20 litres	each	7·82
Enamel basin	each	2·10
Enamel mug	each	0·74
Alarm clock	each	16·30
Hand-cart with bicycle wheel	each	125·50
Bicycle	each	178·00
Thermos, 2½ litre	each	2·62

The planned supply of goods

These particulars refer to the position in Yenan hsien in September 1962 and were provided by Lo Han-hong and Liu Hsin-min.

Quite a lot of consumer goods are rationed. This, however, is not called rationing, but 'planned supply of goods', since the main object is 'not to restrict the individual household's consumption to a certain maximum, but to guarantee a certain supply of the goods'.

The country people buy very little of their food. Each family receives its quota of grain from the labour group to which it belongs and, in principle, they produce on their own private plots all else that they require. In theory, a family that considers it requires more grain can buy extra from its labour group after the matter has been put to a meeting of the labour group. This, however, has never yet been done. Families can always grow their own vegetables, tobacco and the like; and they are free to buy in the market vegetables, pork, sweetmeats, everything you eat and drink, except salt and sugar. Many industrial goods are also unrationed: books, paper, earthenware, bicycles, handcarts, electric light bulbs, man-made materials, washing powders (not soap).

Each household has a ration book in which the number of persons in the family is entered. This permits the purchase of one jin of salt per person per month, one jin of paraffin per paraffin lamp per month, one cake of washing soap per person per month, and one skein of sewing thread per household per month.

The department for trade and economy in the people's commune also hands out cotton coupons. The quota for adults for six months was one jin of cotton wadding and 3·7 chi of cotton material, and for children one jin of cotton wadding and 5·2 chi of cotton material. Extra can be obtained after special application has been made to the department for trade and economy.

In addition, there are four other forms of planned supply:

(1) Extra distribution consequent on the planned production of grain having been exceeded. In 1961, after the harvest had been brought in and the grain sold, Liu Ling Labour Brigade received extra permits for 417 chi of cotton material, 120 packets of cigarettes and 24 pairs of galoshes.

These extra amounts were divided up among the labour groups in accordance with their totals of days' work. The distribution was decided on by the authorities of Yenan hsien after all the corn deliveries from the district had been made.

(2) Extra distribution for deliveries of goats. Every goat delivered entitles one to coupons for six chi of cotton material or one sheepskin or goatskin. In this way, in 1961, Liu Ling Labour Brigade received coupons for 192 chi of cotton material and 70 sheepskins or goatskins.

(3) When private goats, pigs or eggs are sold to the state, the household concerned receives, as well as a cash payment, permits to buy, for one goat, six chi of cotton material or one goatskin or sheepskin; for one pig, one set of cotton underclothes *and* one pair of galoshes *and* one or two handtowels; and for one jin of eggs, half a jin of sugar.

(4) Through Liu Ling People's Commune, Liu Ling Labour Brigade receives from Yenan hsien extra permits to buy industrial goods in addition to those already mentioned. This extra distribution depends on the size of the distribution of industrial goods made to

Yenan hsien, and between 1 January 1962 and 1 September 1962 there were eight of them. They comprised blankets, thermos flasks, enamel basins, thick woollen sweaters, wool yarn, galoshes and brocade bed-covers. The total value amounted to 1,443·56 Y.

Prices paid by the state for animal products sold privately

(If sold in the market, animals fetch the market price for that day, but the seller does not receive a permit to buy consumer goods as given above.)

Pigs per jin live weight	0·43	Y
Goats per jin live weight	0·43	
Eggs per jin	0·795	

Prices paid (per jin) by the grain office in Yenan hsien

Wheat	0·10	Y
Millet	0·06	
Millet, 'sticky millet' (*glutinosa Bretsch* or *effusum Alet*)	0·065	
Maize	0·065	
Black beans (*Vicia faba*)	0·08	
Soya	0·08	
Long beans (*Phaseolus vulgaris*)	0·075	
Green beans (*Phaseolus mungo*)	0·10	
Buckwheat	0·065	
Kaoliang	0·065	
Jute seeds	0·15	

Births and Deaths in Liu Ling village, 1 January 1961–1 September 1962

1961
BIRTHS: five sons (to Chang Chung-wen, died at three days; to Li Hai-fu; to Kao Yü-kuei; to Wang Fung-li; and to Tsao Chen-kuei); and two daughters (to Yang Kuei-ying and to Li Hai-ching).
DEATHS: Chang Chung-wen's son (see above); Tung Shi-hai, 71, old age; Fan Yu-lien, 27, heart disease.

1962
BIRTHS: two sons (to Chiang Hao-lu (the day we left Liu Ling); and to Li Hai-kuei; and two daughters to Tung Yang-chen and to Li Hai-fa).
DEATHS: Li Hai-kuei's father, 73, old age; and Mau Ke-yeh's wife, 54, abdominal cancer.

Households in the village of Liu Ling

50 households, 212 persons.

Listed and numbered according to the register as at 15 August 1962. The name of the head of the family is in heavy type. Age is reckoned in the Chinese way: one year at birth and then one year for every calendar year, counting from the new year of the lunar calendar. The households are numbered according to the position of the caves. The first cave is in the bottom row, farthest to the left on the south side. Then follow the caves in the second row, then those in the third, all taken from left to right.

Households in the main village on Naopanshan:

(1)	♂	**Li Hai-yuan**	48
	♀	Chia Fu-lan	50
	♂	Li Te-chua	15
(2)	♀	**Kao Chin-Lan**	26
	♂	Li Ai-ping	8
	♂	Li Chao-ping	2

(The husband, Li Hai-chang, works at the mill in Yenan.)

(3) ♂ **Li Hai-Kuei** 38
   ♀ Ai Lan-ying 34
   ♂ Li Yun-shen 12
   ♂ Li Shan-hsin 5
   ♂ Li Chao-hsiu 1

(4) ♂ **Li Hai-fu** 50
   ♀ Tu Juei-chen 35
   ♂ Li Shi-wa 21
   ♀ Ma Ping 21
   ♀ Li Ai-ai 7
   ♂ Li Lao-hu 2

(5) ♂ **Tu Yi-chen** 43

(6) ♂ **Ching Chung-wan** 48
   ♀ Tu Fang-lan 56

(7) ♂ **Ai Ke-Liang** 49

(8) ♂ **Ai Ke-kao** 37
   ♀ 33
   ♂ Ai 14
   ♂ Ai 11
   ♂ Ai 8
   ♀ Ai 3

(9) ♂ **He Huang-ho** 25
   ♀ Chia Ying-lan 53

(10) ♀ **Li Kuei-ying** 32
   ♂ Li Ho-ping 10
   ♂ Li Shi-ping 6
   ♀ Li Ai-ping 5
   (The husband, Li Teh-chiang, is a
   ganbu and visits her once a month.)

(11) ♀ Chia Ping-fong 76
   ♂ **Li Hai-Ching** 32
   ♀ Yuan Fon-ching 26
   ♀ Li Shan-ling 7
   ♀ Li Chao-ling 1

(12) ♂ **Chang Chung-liang** 33
   ♀ Chi Mei-ying 29
   ♂ Chang 8
   ♂ Chang 5
   ♂ Chang 1

(13) ♂ **Kao Pin-ying** 37
   ♀ Liu Kuei-ying 38
   ♀ Kao 3

(14)	♂	Tsao Yiu-fa	53
	♀	Tung Kuei-ying	48
	♂	**Tsao Chen-kuei**	28
	♀	Chiao Kuei-lan	27
	♀	Tsao Shi-lien	17
	♀	Tsao Ai-ping	7
	♂	Tsao Ma-chuan	4
	♂	Tsao Chu	1
(15)	♂	**Tsao Chen-yung**	28
	♀	....	22
	♂	Tsao Chen-hua	21
(16)	♂	**Chen Chung-yuan**	44
	♀	....	48
	♀	Chen Nü	11
	♀	Chen	7
	♂	Chen	4
(17)	♀	Li Fong-lan	76
	♂	Kao	58
	♂	**Tung Yang-chen**	35
	♀	Kao Kuei-fang	32
	♀	Tung Yuan	12
	♀	Tung Er-wa	10
	♂	Tung Hong-hong	8
	♀	Tung Chiao-wua	1
(18)	♂	**Mau Ke-yeh**	59
(19)	♀	**Fung Yü-lan**	27
	♂	Mau Ying-shin	8
	♂	Mau	6

(The husband, Mau Pei-chin, works in Seven-mile Village as deputy director of Liu Ling People's Commune's Agricultural Implement Factory.)

(20)	♂	**Li Yü-hsin**	46
	♀	Li Shang-wa	16
	♂	Li Shung-chen	11
	♂	Li	7
(21)	♂	**Li Sha-chang**	50
	♀	....	56
	♂	Li	14
(22)	♂	**Chang Chung-wen**	27
	♀	....	21
	♀	Chang	4

40

(23) ♂ **Li Hung-fu** 33
    ♀ 24
    ♂ Li 10
    ♂ Li Shi-ming 7
    ♀ Li 4
(24) ♀ **Tung Chi-lian** 49
    ♂ Chang Shun 9
    (The husband works as carpenter in Kanshuan hsien and visits his family once a month.)
(25) ♀ Wang Yü-lan 62
    ♂ **Liang He-yiu** 33
    ♀ 32
    ♀ Liang Yen-ling 9
    ♀ Liang 3
(26) ♂ **Li Hsiu-tang** 38
    ♀ Li 39
    ♀ Li Chin-wa 18
    ♀ Li Ai-liang 17
    ♂ Li Ta-min 15
    ♂ Li 14
    ♂ Li Shuei-ming 12
    ♂ Li 8
    ♀ Li 6
(27) ♂ Tsao Shen-yung 69
    ♀ 64
    ♂ **Fu Hai-tsao** 39
    ♀ Li Tsuai-ying 35
    ♀ 18
    ♂ Tsao Ming-wa 15
    ♀ Tsao Shan-nü 9
    ♂ 7
(28) ♂ **Chang Shi-ming** 58
    ♀ Tsao Fong-ying 51
    (Mother of Tung Yang-chen by a previous marriage.)
    ♂ Chang Niu-Ming 14
(29) ♂ Ma Chen-hai 65
    ♂ **Ma Juei-ching** 34
    ♀ ... 24
    ♂ Ma 8
    ♀ Ma 5

(30)	♂	**Ching Chung-ying**	54
	♀	. . . .	51
	♂	Liu Ching-tsei	31
	♀	. . . .	26
	♂	Liu	6
	♂	Liu	2
(31)	♀	**Jen Huai-ying**	22

(Her husband works in the coal mines in Tingshuan. He visits her two or four times a year.)

(32)	♀	**Tien Kuei-hua**	38
	♂	Liu Yuan	8

(Her husband is party secretary at the coal mines in Yenan and comes home every week.)

(33)	♂	**Jen Teh-wan**	59
	♀	. . . .	59
	♀	Tuan Fong-ying	29

(Tuan Fong-ying's husband, Jen Teh-wan's son Jen Huai-wan, is party secretary at the pottery in Yenan. He comes home every week.)

	♀	Jen Chiu-yen	8
	♂	Jen	5
	♂	Jen	2
(34)	♂	Li Yü-teh	50
	♀	. . . .	50
	♂	**Wang Fung-li**	31
	♀	Li Kuei-fung	26
	♀	Li Shung	12
	♀	Wang	8
	♀	Wang	4
	♂	Li	2
(35)	♂	**Hu Shen-chu**	33
	♀	Liu	28
	♀	Hu Yen-ching	9
	♀	Hu	3
(36)	♂	**Liu Chen-yung**	30
	♀	Li Yang-ching	29
	♀	Liu Lan-shuan	10
	♀	Liu	5
	♂	Liu	3

(37)	♂	**Yen Chi-yung**	46
	♀	....	34
	♂	Yen An	17
	♂	Yen	14
	♀	Yen	10
	♀	Yen	8
	♀	Yen	3

Households on the Shiwan side of Liu Ling village:

(38)	♀	**Chang Chu-liang**	20

(Her husband, Tuan, works at the mill in Lochuan. He had visited her twice during 1962.)

(39)	♂	**Tuan Fu-yin**	54
	♀	....	48
	♂	Tuan Shao-tang	11
	♀	Tuan	8
	♀	Tuan	3
(40)	♂	**Ma Hung-tsai**	29
	♀	....	25
	♂	Ma	7
	♀	Ma	3
(41)	♂	**Chi Pei-fa**	36
	♀	Tung Chi-fu	29
	♀	Chi	7
	♂	Chi	3
(42)	♂	**Ma Hai-hsiu**	51
	♂	Ma Tsuei-chang	22
	♀	....	18

Household connected to the cattle-sheds:

(43)	♂	**Wang Hsin-wang**	63

Households on the Shiaoyuanchihou side of Liu Ling village, not yet given electricity:

(44)	♀	**Kao Yü-kuei**	29
	♀	Li Ho-ping	10
	♂	Li Shin-ming	4
	♂	Li Choa-ming	2

(The husband, Li Hai-chun, is in charge of Liu Ming's People's Commune's loan department.)

(45)	♂	**Li Yiu-hua**	57
	♀	....	51

43

	♂	Li Hai-fa	30
	♀	She Shiu-ying	26
	♂	Li Hai-tsai	28
	♀	Chang Yü-ying	25
	♂	Li Shuan-tsai	12
	♂	Li Yen-shin	8
	♂	Li Ming-shen	7
	♂	Li Shi-shin	5
	♂	Li Chiao-ming	3
	♀	Li Mei-li	2
	♀	Li Chiao-mei	1
(46)	♂	Li Ying-teh	60
	♀	....	54
	♂	**Li Hsin-chen**	39
	♂	Li Chi-shen	17
(47)	♂	**Shi yü-chich**	58
	♀	....	52
(48)	♀	**Yang Kuei-ying**	30
	♀	Yang	8
	♀	Yang	7
	♀	Tuan	2

(Her husband, Tuan, works in Yenan. Her former husband, Yang Yung-chien, died in 1959.)

(49)	♀	**Yang Fu-Lien**	37
	♂	Li Ai-shen	9
	♀	Li Kou	6

(Her husband, Li Hai-chen, works in Seven-mile Village. He is director of Liu Ling People's Commune Agricultural Implement Factory. He bicycles home every week.)

(50)	♂	**Chiang Hao-lu**	43
	♀	....	39
	♀	Chiang	9
	♂	Chiang	6

Part II
The Road to Power

Pai Yu-teh, veteran ganbu, aged 60

now director of Yenan's Water Regulation Board

THE way the revolution took—well, that's many years ago now and I may have forgotten a lot, but I'll try and tell you what I can remember. I was never able to go to school as a child. What I've learned, I've taught myself in my spare time or at the party school. Now, I can read newspapers and letters, but no more. I am a farmer's son, so perhaps it won't all be as clear as if I had been able to study more.

I came from a peasant home. My father had 100 mu, but it was not good land. It was rocky. I began working when I was seven. I herded cows and goats until 1918, when I began working in the fields. In 1921 I took a job as hand with a farmer called Liang Hung-en in Yenchang, but went back home the next year. I had then been married for several years and we already had three children. I began working on the family's land. The thing was that Father had been adopted by a farmer called Tien, who wanted to prevent his family dying out, and Father had taken his name and so inherited 100 mu in a village called Tien Family's Corner. But, as I said, it wasn't good land, and with us there in Yenan 100 mu was not much. In other parts of China it was only landowners who had so much, but in Yenan there was lots of land and too few people.

In 1927 a peasants' organization was set up here and that was when I first heard of communism. 'Destroy the landowners and do away with taxes,' was the cry, but I wasn't 'aware' at that time, of course. That year we refused to pay taxes. We heard that in the towns the students were fighting against imperialism. The leader of our peasants' organization was Chu Cheng-chiang, a big, strong man known for his integrity and honesty. I don't know if he was a communist. The party was illegal then, of course, and I wasn't a member, so I wouldn't have known about that. Then the K.M.T. came and suppressed us and all our activities stopped. Chu Cheng-chiang had to fly. He died later in Yenan, in 1949.

In 1931, 1932 and 1933 I kept hearing about Liu Chih-tan and how there were revolutionaries in Suiteh and Tsechang who had destroyed the landowners and done away with taxes. That made a deep impression on me. I especially liked the idea of the landowners being destroyed, because landowners lived in luxury, while the people suffered. As I said, the fact that I owned 100 mu myself did not mean that I was a landowner, because it all depends on what sort of land you own. There's land down in the valley and there's land up on the hillside. There are peasants who have 200 mu and are poor. Down in the valley, yields are ten times as great for less work, so you can work it out yourself.

In 1935 Liu Chih-tan was operating in Nanliang and in Wuchi. There was a lot of talk then about the Red Army. In April that year Liu Chih-tan sent a guerrilla group to Thirty-mile Village to wipe out an armed landowner group. The Red Army's slogan was: 'Down with the local landowners! Down with the local despots! Down with imperialism! Divide the land equally! Free the women! Abolish taxes!' Thirty-mile Village was not far away, of course, and I talked about what had happened with my best friend, Han Pei-hsin. He and I worked together and we had already been profoundly impressed by what we had heard of the happenings in Suiteh and Tsechang. Now, we told each other that we ought to go across the hills and see what they

48

were doing in Thirty-mile Village. After all, we wanted everyone to be equal and all bureaucrats and landowners to be destroyed. So, one night, Han Pei-hsin and I set off across the mountain to see if we could find the Red Army. It was chilly and we had only one quilted coat between us, and that was seven years old. Han Pei-hsin later became party secretary in a liberated hsien and died in 1942 of tuberculosis and undernourishment.

When we got to Thirty-mile Village we talked with a propagandist, who wore civilian clothes and was called Wang Shen-hai. He was about thirty, a dumpy chap with a round face. We told him about ourselves and he gave us the job of organizing the poor peasants in the neighbouring village for the cause of the revolution. Later on, I used to meet Wang Shen-hai now and again. He died of high blood pressure in Sian in 1960.

It was now my job to organize the people of the neighbouring villages. I had to find leaders who could help the Red Army and see that it was given food and information and was kept up-to-date with the landowners' plans. In the district there were two detachments of the landowners' armed forces, Ming Tuan, and also a dozen or so police, so I had to work in secret. They used to cut off the head of any of us they happened to get hold of. When I went to a village, it was in disguise. Once there, I visited the poorest villagers, the farmhands and daily labourers, and talked with them. I spoke about the revolution with those I thought I could trust and gave them the job of giving the Red Army all the support it needed.

In the end, the landowners no longer dared stay in the villages at night, but made fortified places for themselves up on the hillside and withdrew to those. After I had organized twenty villages, one of the Ming Tuan detachments fled, but the other remained. Wang Shen-hai then started a guerrilla action. We went to Chaochia, where there was a moneylender and landowner called Chen Chin-ho. We allowed him to escape with his life, but we confiscated all his possessions and all his land. The peasants said to us: 'Don't leave us, because if you do, perhaps he will come back with the Ming Tuan.' We agreed that we would send a 'feather-letter' round the villages. This is a letter with a feather. As soon as it reaches one village, it is sent on to the next, and so everyone knows what is going to be done. By the next morning, six hundred farmers had arrived, and we arranged a mass meeting and elected a revolutionary committee.

49

That, then, was our new government. There were various departments in the committee: a defence department and a land department and a grain department and a department for women's affairs and a department for young communists. We elected Wu Pao-tang our chairman and I was chosen brigade leader for the Red Guard. That was in May 1935.

We had now seized control in both valleys on this side of Yenan and the second Ming Tuan detachment also took refuge in the town. There were five brigades of us and I was leader of one of them. But we had no arms. Not all the landowners had been able to escape with their arms, but it wasn't much they had left behind. So the village blacksmiths took the surplus agricultural implements and made spears out of them; but as there were not even enough of these to go round and we weren't all armed, we made dummy ones. Each of us had three wooden hand grenades. Our uniform was a red armlet. At a distance it looked as if we were heavily armed. We got hold of some silver paper in a shop and used it to cover our wooden bayonets. They glinted in the sun. We frightened the landowners.

The women and children went and kept guard along the roads and outside the villages, and we did not let anyone pass who did not have a permit from our revolutionary committee. Each Brigade had a big red flag, and we carried these in front of us when we marched against Yenan. By June 1935 we had taken the far bank of the river and Yenan was surrounded. There were shortages of food and fuel in the town then. Here, in the Nan valley, we got into contact with Mau Ke-yeh. He and I met in Matan that June, and we discussed what was to be done. He said: 'Ought we not to establish contact with each other?' And we in our brigade thought that we ought and after that we kept in touch.

After this the Red Guard in the hills was increased. We got proper guerrilla detachments. The Land Department and the Trade Unions and Poor Peasants' Association decided to investigate the state of the classes in the villages. We were to find out who were exploiters and who weren't. We were to take away the exploiters' possessions and give the exploited their land. We were very strict and energetic, and we destroyed the landowners as a class. When we turned our attention to a certain Chang Pei-yi, six hundred of the people on his estates came to the meeting and told us how he had oppressed them. It was a long meeting. We found that he had 300,000 jin of grain, 400 goats, 6 donkeys and 21 oxen. He told us that he only owned 10,000 mu, but he really owned more. He had more than 20 villages under him and received 60,000 jin a year in rents. Well, we parcelled up his land and distributed his corn and his animals and his tools and implements. We kept back part as public property to cover the expenses of the Red Army, but the rest we divided up. Chang Pei-yi himself had fled to Yenan, for he knew what his tenants would do with him if they got hold of him. But when we liberated Yenan in 1936, there was the united front against Japan, so he was able to go on living there, and later his daughter joined the revolution and now she's a leading ganbu in Szechwan. Chang Pei-yi lives with her there now.

After each such fight against a landowner, we valued all his possessions. Everything had to have the people's support. We had to divide the man's land up and take his possessions, but we also had to take off part as public property. Everything had to be done publicly and openly. Had we worked in any other way, the people would not have supported us. In each village we would set aside ten mu or so for common needs, the amount depending on the size of the village and quality of the land.

It was at this same time that we heard that Mau Ke-yeh, using cunning and red flags, had succeeded in disarming the whole of one of the landowner's forces and made the landowner fly. You see, there were many ways of defeating the landowners.

After we had surrounded Yenan, the grain, vegetable and fuel situation in the town got worse and worse. As no supplies were being sent in, the enemy had to send out soldiers to plunder the villages, and this of course strengthened the peasants in their hatred of the enemy, making the blockade more and more effective. The peasants joined the guerrillas and fought too.

I became a member of the party in July 1935, the same month that Liu Chih-tan led the Twenty-sixth Army in an attack on Kaochia village, sixty li away. The enemy there sent to Yenan for reinforcements from the 'Peace-conserving Brigade', a special landowners' force, the main task of which was to root out communists. But before the reinforcements could get there from Yenan, the Twenty-sixth Army had taken Kaochia. We knew that reinforcements were on the way, so we laid a trap for them. Leaving only a few Red Army men in the village, the main force withdrew into the broken country round about. When the Peace-conserving Brigade arrived, it was enticed into the village by the thought of an easy victory. After that, we surrounded them and destroyed them. Lo Ting-chen, commander of the Peace-conserving Brigade, was killed and we took twenty prisoners. For three days we reformed the prisoners. 'Our fight is with the landowners,' we told them. 'You are poor people like us. We don't wish you any harm.' Then we gave them a silver dollar each and told them to go home. They went back to Yenan and spoke well of the Red Army. They told how we had control of all the villages, how we were well armed with modern rifles, how we had many flags and many soldiers, though actually we had neither many soldiers nor many rifles. They said this just as an explanation of why they had been defeated. At all events, in this way the fame of the Red Army spread in Yenan and the enemy's morale deteriorated.

On the death of Lo Ting-chen, Li Han-hua took over as commander of the Peace-conserving Brigade. He shrank from nothing and was our most serious opponent.

The Twenty-sixth Army now freed Yenchang, Anting, Chinchien, and thus a large area round Yenan was liberated. The people were in control in Kanchuan and Fuhsian, and then in August of that year, the North-eastern Army arrived under Chang Hsueh-liang, the Young Marshal, and their slogan was 'Root out the communist bands in a month'. That made the landowners happy. They sent messages to their villages: 'Every goat stolen shall be paid for with a head. If anyone has been eating my corn, his whole family shall pay with their lives', and people were terrified. Then the North-eastern Army marched in with its modern weapons. People were afraid and asked us: 'How can we be expected to fight them? How can we save ourselves?' The North-eastern Army had sent to the villages, telling them to send corn to Yenan; so we sent round our propagandists who told them: 'Don't be afraid. When the troops come, we shall hide in the hills and they won't venture there.' We organized peasants on whom we could rely to take grain to Yenan. Every day we sent some people with corn and fodder from the villages, just enough to keep them quiet, but not enough to meet their needs. These men's job was not so much to take the corn, as to reconnoitre and get us information about the morale of the troops in the North-eastern Army and its plans. In this way we knew everything about the enemy, because they thought the villagers who brought them grain were well disposed towards them and they trusted them. These men also took leaflets with them into the town and distributed them.

In September that year I had been chosen to be the one responsible for military work in our hsien, the commander for our military district. But after the arrival of the North-eastern Army at Yenan, we had to retreat some distance from the immediate neighbourhood of the town. Mau Ke-yeh was at Seven-mile Village, where he had an illegal party headquarters. It was a sort of depot for guerrillas and party workers.

Then the Twenty-fifth army came here to the Yenan area, as did our Twenty-sixth Army that had been in Hongshan. The two joined up in Yungping and from there we marched on Laoshan and attacked Kanshoan. But this was just a cunning stratagem. We wanted to lure the enemy out from Yenan; and they did as we expected and tried to relieve Kanshoan, and we lay in ambush for them. It was a bloody fight. We wiped out one enemy division. After that we went on to Yulinchi and Taotsenpo, where we destroyed the enemy's regiment. After that we were able to surround Yenan again and restore the blockade. We now set up a government in Fusze hsien, the thirty li round Yenan. I was elected president of Fusze hsien in November 1935.

We had four garrison detachments, one in each valley round Yenan, and now began really harassing the enemy. We let nothing through to them, and at night we went up on to the hillside and shot at the town. We did not do that to harm them, but to keep them awake and make them waste their ammunition. It was usually enough to light a few fires on the hills and throw firework bangers into the town. Sometimes we shot someone too. The enemy was nervous and had to be in a continual state of readiness and used to shoot blindly into the dark. The morale of the North-eastern Army grew worse and worse. In the end they had neither food nor ammunition, having fired it all off unnecessarily. Then the enemy tried to supply his troops by air, but the planes flew too high. The pilots were Americans hired by Chiang Kai-shek and they didn't want to die, they were just flying for the money. So they dropped pancakes over Kanchuan where the enemy was starving, but the wind caught them and they drifted over to us and we ate them. They were still warm and we laughed loudly at the idea of our starving enemies watching us eat their pancakes. The enemy also dropped ammunition by parachute over Yenan, but it landed on the ice and exploded. In the end the enemy stopped trying to help his troops by air. It was proving too expensive, especially as we got most of it; but even so we were badly off for arms. We were always short of arms.

In September, for example, Ma Ming-fan, chairman of northern Shensi's soviet government, came to us. I told him that we had no arms and he wrote out a piece of paper authorizing me to collect 100 new rifles; but I didn't know much about administration then, so I never asked for ammunition as well. Thus, the paper just said: '100 rifles for Comrade Pai Yu-teh, military commander Fusze hsien.' Then we got five donkeys and went to Taotsenpo where our troops had just destroyed a regiment of the enemy and taken a lot of booty. Well, I got my 100 rifles, unloaded, but the comrades there refused to let me have any ammunition. 'There's nothing about ammunition on your requisition, Comrade!' they said. 'We have no right to hand out ammunition to anyone who just comes and asks for it.' And I had to be content with that, and we set off home with our five pack-donkeys laden with empty rifles. As we were passing Chang-hsin-chuan, we were stopped by the people there. They were having a great meeting. They said to me: 'You usually come here with only one rifle. Now you have many. The enemy's coming today to plunder the village. They are going to take our corn from us, because we have just got the harvest in. They want us to starve to death. So now you must stay and defend us. We won't let you go until you have defeated the enemy and protected us.'

What were we to do? After all, we had no ammunition. I could not let the enemy get hold of our rifles. But on the other hand I couldn't abandon the villagers. In the end I sent off two men with the five laden donkeys and kept eight men with unloaded rifles. Then I got hold of the chairman of the Poor Peasants' Association in the village. He was called Chuen Tien-ying and was a clever chap. We went off into a corner and I said to him: 'I have something I must tell you; but it is a secret and you mustn't let it out to anyone. We have no ammunition. None at all. I'll gladly let you have one rifle if you like, but we have no ammunition.' Then Chuen Tien-ying replied: 'I have some cartridges, left over from when we captured a K.M.T. plunderer.' After that we sent the women and children up on to the hill. The village Red Guard was placed at the foot of the hill, and I and my other soldiers took up position in front of the temple. Then the enemy came. There was a detachment of soldiers and a group of grain requisitioners. It was a whole regiment. At that time the K.M.T. would not venture out of the town unless there was at least a regiment of them. The soldiers surrounded the village and the grain requisitioners came towards the temple. Then I gave my order: 'Don't shoot into the brown. Choose one definite one. Shoot one at a time. See that each bullet hits an enemy!' Then the corn requisitioners arrived. First we shot and killed one. The women and children on the hill shouted our slogan: 'The triumphant Red Army has come!' Then we shot and killed another. And then another. Everyone was now shouting. When five of the enemy had fallen, the enemy fled. We still had five cartridges left. When the enemy fled, we held a great feast. People had more confidence in us than ever. They said: 'This is the real Red Army. Eight men defeat so many of the enemy.' When we got back home after this battle, our garrison certainly had one hundred rifles, but we still had no bullets.

To solve this problem, we sold some of the expropriated landowners' possessions and sent some men to Lochuan, which was occupied by the enemy, and there they bribed the commander and bought some ammunition from him. But he had been cunning and when we tried to shoot with the cartridges, they exploded and made the rifles burst in the faces of those trying them out. There was not much we could do about it. We could not accuse our comrades in Lochuan, but the enemy had outwitted us and taken our silver and given us ammunition that was no good. So then we took the cartridges and emptied out the powder. We moulded our own bullets and made powder from the heads of matches. That worked, and so gradually we acquired both rifles and ammunition for the garrison.

In October 1935 the First Route Army came here at the end of the 'Long March'. It was led by the Central Committee of the Party and Chairman Mao. Thus three armies joined forces: the First Route Army, the Twenty-fifth Army and the Twenty-sixth Army. Mao now led our forces against Fusze and wiped out two enemy regiments in Chilo. The Central Soviet Government was set up in Wayapo. The Central Committee came to us with this message: 'Go north to fight the Japanese! Resist Japan! Form a united front! Chinese do not fight Chinese! Let all unite against the Japanese invaders!' In November our soviet power was set up officially at all levels. It was then that I was elected soviet chairman for Fusze hsien. Till then we had had only a provisional revolutionary government committee. After that, order was restored everywhere.

55

Chairman Mao came to us and spoke of the necessity for forming a united front. The Central Committee now stopped our activities against the landowners. They insisted that we had been guilty of departing from the correct revolutionary way, so we re-investigated the true class circumstances of every family. We had been far too strict, we were told. We were now to fight shoulder-to-shoulder even with landlords.

In January 1936 the three armies were reorganized into the Fifteenth Unity Army and Chairman Mao led this army to the east to fight the Japanese. That left only the Twenty-eighth Recruit Army in Wayapo; but in Shansi there was Yen Hsi-shan. He was the war-lord in Shansi. We sent a message to him saying that we did not want to fight his troops, but wanted to fight with him against Japan to save our country. But then Chiang Kai-shek sent ten divisions to fight us and stop us from fighting against Japan. Liu Chih-tan had been given orders to lead his forces across the Yellow River. He was killed in the fighting at Linshien in March 1936. He was a great hero, our greatest hero of northern Shensi. We had to retreat from Shansi without having made contact with the Japanese. But even so this expedition proved of decisive importance. It opened everyone's eyes. They saw that we wanted to end the civil war and fight Japan.

During this time my job was to see that the blockade of Yenan was maintained effectively. We stayed in occupation of the hills and when the enemy came out to get corn we fell upon him from our ambush. During the daytime we used to assemble up in the hills round Yenan and curse the enemy. We continued organizing the masses and strengthening the power of the soviet.

In February 1936 I was transferred to the United Front that had just been formed. In March I was made responsible for it, and when our troops began marching east, we local party workers were given the job of taking the North-eastern Army in hand and forming a united front against the Japanese; the thing being that the North-eastern Army came from the areas captured by the Japanese and they did not like the idea of having to fight us, while the Japanese occupied their home territories, and they didn't like Chiang Kai-shek not letting them help fight the Japanese in order to recover their homes. So now we began secretly working on them. Their fighting morale was poor, of course; they had no food, they were hungry and cold, and lost all the engagements they were in with us, for they were fighting far from their homes in a war they did not understand.

56

The first conferences between us and the North-eastern Army took place in Tungchwankou, about twenty li from Yenan. Wu Liang-ping, who was then in charge of the propaganda department, represented the Central Committee of the party; the soviet government of northern Shensi was represented by Li Chi-lin, and I and Liu Ping-win represented Fusze hsien. An officer called Chao came from the North-eastern Army. I don't remember his rank, but he was a regimental officer. Then we began our discussion. We sat in a stone cave and had a friendly discussion. That was the first step in our collaboration that finally led to Chiang Kai-shek being taken prisoner in Sian and compelled to go to war with Japan. In that very first meeting we arrived at complete agreement as to the basic principles of our collaboration. These were:

(1) A non-intervention agreement.

(2) We marked out the areas that were occupied by armed forces and those that were to be neutralized. To enter these neutralized areas you had to have permission both from us and them. United Front Offices were to be set up to deal with matters of our collaboration. They were to be set up by us in their territory and by them in ours.

(3) Two markets were to be set up: one by us in the Date Garden. This was to be manned by our people and theirs in conjunction, and there we would sell corn, vegetables and fuel to them, and they would sell arms and ammunition and other war material to us. Only unarmed personnel was to enter these markets.

Our agreement also laid it down that the arrangement was in agreement with the Central Committee's statement that Chinese did not fight Chinese, but stood together to drive out the Japanese aggressors. These were the fundamental principles for our working together and we were in entire agreement about them. We also arranged—and that was made part of our agreement—that we were to stop all hostile acts against each other.

This agreement was, of course, strictly secret. Chiang Kai-shek suspected that something was brewing in the north-west, but he could not prove anything. The difficulty was that we could not include the Ming Tuan, the landowners' 'Peace-conserving Brigade', in the discussions. They were not reliable. We, of course, tried to make propaganda among them, and, of course, they had all been driven out of the countryside and into the town, but they were there and a continual source of disturbance. Militarily, they were under the command of the North-eastern Army, but as they thought this altogether too ineffectual in fighting the communists, they acted on their own. The only way of keeping them in check was for the North-eastern Army to delay issuing them ammunition.

The United Front was hard work. We sold corn to the army at the markets; but the class hatred of the landowners' troops was unquenchable. One night in May 1936 the Peace-conserving Brigade came to our United Front Bureau in the Date Garden. They were under the command of Li Han-hua and in breach of the agreement they were armed. I wasn't in the office at the time, but they took four others prisoner: Li San-chi, Ma Chan-piao, Liu Chung-piao and a comrade called Han, but I have forgotten the rest of his name. These four were responsible for the work of the United Front in the Date Garden open market. But they were irresponsibly credulous and not sufficiently prepared for the class hatred of the landowners, so they were all captured together and had their heads cut off that same night.

The difficult thing here was that the pact between the North-eastern Army and us was secret. We discussed the matter with the North-eastern Army and it was all hushed up. Of course we would have liked to avenge our comrades, but for political reasons we had to pretend that nothing had happened. The important thing was to preserve the United Front. That sort of thing happened quite frequently. I cannot remember that event ever being taken up afterwards, and no plaque was ever put up in their memory. It's like that in all revolutions. Many have to be sacrificed.

It wasn't easy work. The North-eastern Army came by day, but the Peace-conserving Brigade came at night, plundering and murdering. We did not want to shoot and kill them, but persisted in our work for the United Front. But the Peace-conserving Brigade went out into the villages and plundered the farmers' stores of grain and beheaded our ganbus. We refused to let ourselves be provoked and our iron party discipline prevented our own people from hitting back.

We also opened youth clubs in the open markets. We had a variety of printed matter in them, brochures and leaflets with wording like: 'Drive back the invaders and recapture our country.' We held a big market every fifth day and soldiers from the North-eastern Army came to those youth clubs to hear news from home and read our leaflets. I myself was engaged at this time in working on the officers. Later, when the Young Marshal, Chang Hsueh-liang, flew up to Yenan, Chou En-lai went and conferred with him. That was how we distributed our work.

Chou En-lai and Chang Hsueh-liang now reached a general agreement. Our relations with the North-eastern Army were so good that one could say they were friendly. But Chiang Kai-shek had become more and more suspicious. He did not send winter uniforms for the North-eastern Army and he would not pay them either. Not only that, but he had ordered the North-western Army under Yang Hu-chen to go to Sian in order to prevent Chang Hsueh-liang going over to us. Chiang Kai-shek also repeated his orders that the communist bandits, which was what he always called us, were to be wiped out.

Chou En-lai and Chang Hsueh-liang had long discussions about this situation. Something had to be done. We cooked up a plan between us that would solve all our problems; this was that the North-eastern Army should attack us, win a great victory and take lots of booty and make great propaganda out of it. When everything had been worked out, the North-eastern Army attacked Wayapo, where we had our government, as we had arranged. The government and the Central Committee and everyone else had withdrawn to Chitan hsien in good time, and, as we had arranged to fire only into the air, no one was even wounded. We had arranged with the North-eastern Army that we would leave all our unserviceable arms behind in Wayapo together with others the North-eastern Army had lent us for the purpose of being captured. After that Chang Hsueh-liang was able to telegraph to Chiang Kai-shek that he had dealt the communists a shattering blow, that Chairman Mao had fled or been killed in the fighting, his headquarters taken and much booty captured. This report was printed in the newspapers all over the world. Chiang Kai-shek was very happy and at once let the troops have all their back pay. After this, Chiang Kai-shek's confidence in the North-eastern Army was restored and he gave them all the material they needed. We asked the North-eastern Army to organize artillery for us, because we had none, and Chang Hsueh-liang telegraphed to Chiang Kai-shek for guns, saying that he needed modern ones for the final destruction of the power of the soviet. He got the guns and handed them over to us, so that we could together fight the Japanese.

Our relations with the North-eastern Army were now so friendly that we could even deal with the Peace-conserving Brigade; so, when they went out raiding the villages, we shot at them to kill. The Peace-conserving Brigade complained to the North-eastern Army and asked for protection, and, since our agreement was secret, this could not be refused. The North-eastern Army got in touch with us and told us where they were going to attack the following day, promising to withdraw after a brief exchange of shots and tell the Peace-conserving Brigade that our numerical superiority had been too great, but they insisted that we must shoot too. I thought this difficult, because we did not have enough ammunition to be able to waste any shooting into the air. In the end, it was arranged that the day before they attacked anywhere, they would provide us with ammunition so that we had some to use. That is what was done, and thus the Peace-conserving Brigade got no help from the North-eastern Army. When we encountered each other, we and the North-eastern Army both fired, shooting up into the air, and then the North-eastern Army withdrew, and the Peace-conserving Brigade had to retreat as well, because we were shooting at them to kill. As it was difficult for the Peace-conserving Brigade to buy anything in our markets and they were kept from plundering the villages, their men became thinner and thinner. They were always hungry and so gradually they became unsettled and dissatisfied.

In July 1936, the North-western Army arrived and that altered the situation. They had the same slogan as the North-eastern Army: 'Exterminate all communist bands in northern Shensi.' We were not looking for a fight, so we let them occupy all our towns except Chitan, where the Central Committee and the soviet government were, and Wuchin, where we had a big concentration of troops; but the countryside was still ours. We tried to make contact with the men of the North-western Army and made intensive propaganda; but it was far more difficult with them because, coming from a part of the country that was not threatened by the Japanese, they were not so aware of the Japanese menace. Thus we had no success with the rank and file or the N.C.O.s. Our relations with the North-western Army only improved after Chang Hsueh-liang had got in contact with Yang Hu-chen and they had agreed together that, for the sake of their country, they would work with us against the Japanese.

While this was going on, the class struggle in the villages and countryside had had to take second place and we had stopped our attacks on the landowners. Certain of the landowners now took advantage of the situation to return to their villages and settle accounts with their tenants; but on these occasions our guerrillas hit back. We

60

were not going to attack ourselves, but we certainly did not intend to let them attack our people. Shi Chung-je was one who returned thus to his village, Huchua. He was a pig-headed fellow. I went to see him and had a talk with him about forming a United Front with us to fight the Japanese together, but he would not co-operate. He had his own army. It was not big, but even a score of armed men can be dangerous, especially when they have a fortified camp. They treated the villagers very harshly. We decided to break them. We knew where they had their spies and we sent some men to walk along that road saying aloud how worried and anxious they were because they were so few and how they hoped Shi Chung-je's men would not be lying in ambush for them. The spies heard this and hurried to tell Shi Chung-je, who ordered his men to attack the few Red Army men. They made an ambush for our men; but we knew this and were prepared; so that, when they attacked, we took them in the rear. We killed one and took nineteen prisoners. That frightened Shi Chung-je and he wrote to me: 'I was wrong to be less than willing to co-operate. I had not thought the Red Army was so powerful. If you will just order my nineteen men to be let free, I promise to do as the Red Army wants and fight against Japan.' We re-educated our nineteen prisoners. That took us a fortnight. Then we released them. That landowner never dared do anything more. At the time of the happenings in Sian, when all the troops of the North-eastern and North-western Armies withdrew on 13 December 1936, he fled with them and went to Ichian. Later, in 1937, when the Communist Party and K.M.T. were working together, he returned to his house. We looked after him well, and when he died it was of disease.

The Sian happenings were the final result of our long negotiations with the North-eastern Army. On 12 December 1936, when Chang Hsueh-liang and Yang Hu-chen took Chiang Kai-shek prisoner, a plane was sent to Yenan to fetch Chou En-lai for discussions in Sian. These discussions later led to the collaboration between K.M.T. and us in the war against Japan. This was a great defeat for all un-national forces. Both Chang Hsueh-liang and Yang Hu-chen were patriots and Chiang Kai-shek never forgave them. Yang Hu-chen afterwards was murdered in one of the K.M.T.'s concentration camps and Chang Hsueh-liang, as far as I know, is still Chiang Kai-shek's private prisoner in Formosa.

While this was going on in Sian, Li Han-hua, commander of the

Peace-conserving Brigade, had become anxious and afraid of what might happen, and when he saw the plane coming in from the south to land in Yenan, he rushed to the airfield. He thought the plane was coming to help him. But the officers in the plane asked him: 'Who are you?' Li Han-hua answered: 'I am from the big government here in our hsien.' Then the officers said: 'Go away. We don't want to have anything more to do with you.' At that moment Chou En-lai rode on to the airfield. Seeing Li Han-hua and the Peace-conserving Brigade, he said to them: 'Don't worry. The soviet government and the K.M.T. are going to work together now in the struggle against Japan. We are going to set up a great national united front. I shall come back soon, and then I promise to see personally that all your problems are solved.' He said this in a friendly tone and he meant it to be friendly, because he saw that Li Han-hua was dismayed. But Li Han-hua and the Peace-conserving Brigade had no confidence in our promise and fled instead from Yenan that same night and went to Michi. Two detachments of the brigade did stay in Yenan and came over to us. The others ought to have trusted us and mended their ways in time. That's how it was with Li Han-hua.

Li Han-hua was a rich man, a moneylender and landowner, hard and vengeful and bloodthirsty. He had become leader of the Peace-conserving Brigade and he shrank from nothing. He murdered many villagers in the district that year. We spoke to him and gave him a chance to reform and join the United Front against Japan, but he chose to continue to fight the people. Eventually he took himself off to Yulin, where he remarried under a false name. When Yulin was liberated in 1948, he withdrew to a village, but we were on his track and in 1950 we caught him and brought him to Yenan, where he had been the cause of so many people's deaths. Many came to accuse and bear witness to his crimes, and after a proper trial he was condemned to death and we executed him.

His first wife died in 1960, and his second remarried. His sister and her children live in Liu Ling. There are a number of his relatives round here.

After this, I was sent to Hongchuan as party secretary. Then, in 1937, I was sent to the party central school in Yenan, took my exam in 1938 and was sent to the Southern District outside Yenan as party secretary. In February 1941 I became political commissar in the consumers' co-operative in our hsien. In December 1943 I was chosen to be in charge of the production department in Yenan hsien. In April 1949 I resumed my function as political commissar in the consumers' co-operative, which had to be built up again after Hu Tsuang-nan's occupation. In 1951 I was sent to Licha as regional party secretary and, in 1954, I was sent to the regional party school. In March I took my exam and was put in charge of dam construction in Yenan Water Regulation Board. In 1958 I became director of the board. That is all.

Mau Ke-yeh, cave-builder, farmer-
revolutionary, aged 59

OF course, I can always tell you what I remember. But I've never been
to school and can neither read nor write, so perhaps I'll get a date or
something wrong now and again. One forgets, doesn't one? In the old
society things were hard; life was harsh then. Taxation was heavy and
we were not paid much for our corn. In 1926 and 1927 all we got was
two silver dollars for 300 jin, and we had to pay two silver dollars a
month in family tax. We had an ox then and two or three able-bodied
people in the family. We got 5,000 jin in, but more than half went in
taxes. We had no mats on the kang and our bedcover was twenty
inches wide. We never ate our fill and we never had any cash. It was
difficult to manage and things just got worse and worse every year.

My father was a mason. It was he who taught me to build stone
caves. We lived in Yulin, but in 1917 we moved to Yenan district.
People said it was better there. It was usual for people to move round
in those days. One went from one village to the other, from one landowner to the other, trying to find a place with a lower rent. If you were
in debt you could not move. You had to pay your debt first. We were
five in our family and we had a small roll of bedding and a mirror.
When we came down here, we rented sixty mu from a landowner
called Chang. That was eighty li from here. The rental was 900 jin.
We ploughed with the landowner's oxen and he took 1,800 jin for
that. That autumn we harvested 9,000 jin of corn. Father did it all.
I was only half-manpower then. I had a younger sister and a younger
brother. Our landowner was not too hard, but he smoked opium and
by 1924 he had ruined himself and became poor, so that year we moved
to the village of Niuchang twenty li from here.

There, things were a bit better. We had an ox of our own and I was able to do a full day's work. We paid 600 jin rental for sixty mu. We used to get in 5,000–6,000 jin of corn and, when we had paid our taxes and the rent, there was just enough left to enable us to survive. Then came the great famine year of 1928. We starved in 1929 too. We plucked leaves and ate them; and we mixed chaff and elm-bark and made bread of it. The fact that we went so hungry in 1929 was not so much because of the harvest. Taxes and rental had taken their due, of course. But our harvest wasn't so bad. What happened was that I got married that year. That wasn't cheap. I had to pay 120 silver dollars for my wife. The following year I had a wife, I know, but the whole family had to go hungry, of course. We went on living with my parents. I had got a loan from a landowner and government official called Chia to help me pay the price for my wife. Chia lived in Yenan, where he was departmental chief in the K.M.T. administration. The interest on the loan was only two per cent a month, but even so I was never able to pay back the capital. I could not manage more than the interest. In 1935, when we made our revolution, the loan was written off. But Chia was already dead then. He smoked so much opium that he died of it. But I went on paying his widow till we had made our revolution.

In 1930 I moved to Matan Village. Up there in the hills, I could be my own master. It was, of course, common land there and we who broke new ground had to pay only one jin per mu a year. We had to pay taxes too, of course: two silver dollars a month. And we had to pay cash. It was hard work.

In 1935 an army calling itself the Red Army arrived. It was in the countryside. The K.M.T. was in the towns. This Red Army made propaganda and told us: 'The Red Army is good and we are going to divide up all the land and you won't have to pay taxes or rent to anyone any longer.' It was in the month of February 1935 that I met communists for the first time. These were Li Wen-yuan and Wang Hsiao-kang. They were both in their thirties. I met them again in later years, but whether they are alive or dead now, I don't know. They came to us one night and told us: 'We are propaganda-makers for the Red Army and now you are to make a revolution.' We replied: 'All right, we will.' But we didn't think they had any real power; they did not look as though they had and what could we poor farmers do? So we did nothing.

But in March that same year, they came back again. They called us all together for a meeting outdoors and told us to form a poor farmers' association and elect a leader. Then the others pointed to me and said: 'He's a calm and sensible chap and never does things hastily.' So I became leader. And Li Wen-yuan and Wang Hsiao-kang made us speeches and said: 'Why do you pay taxes to the K.M.T.?' Then we replied that we were afraid and that the K.M.T. had plenty of soldiers. But they said: 'Just stop paying taxes and don't be afraid, because the Red Army has its own methods of dealing with the K.M.T.'

They had their government in Lochuan then and the Red Army was commanded by Liu Chih-tan. To begin with, people were afraid of them and said that communists were murderers, but when they came here they were ordinary people and they always said: 'Divide up the land and fight against landowners and despots.' They talked a lot and held lots of meetings, and at the meetings we used to stand up and shout 'Yes, yes!', but we did not really believe in them or that they had any real power.

But in April 1935 the Red Army defeated an armed counter-revolutionary landowners' corps ten li from here. They killed the leader of the Southern District, Mu Hsin-tsai, and took lots of booty. After that they came more often. They also killed other counter-revolutionaries. Then the people saw that the Red Army did have power, and so we stopped driving into the town with our taxes and goods. Instead, we organized ourselves into guerrilla bands. Eight to ten men to each.

We no longer went to the town and we no longer sold grain to the town and we paid no taxes, and those who were K.M.T. no longer dared live out in the country, but began to run away. The town was isolated. It became a dead town. When tax collectors came, we took them prisoner, and, if any were decent, we let them go; the others we killed. So the town became quite isolated. Sometimes we fought Ming Tuan forces that came out from the town. We had spears and home-made rifles. But as all the people in the villages were organized and as the villages helped each other, when a landowner force came out from the town, they could not do anything to us.

In June 1935 we divided up the land. Everything was divided according to the size of each family and the quality of the land. Every-body got a paper with a stamp on it saying he now owned his land. But to begin with there were many who were doubtful and said: 'This is somebody else's land. It will bring us misfortune.' We also divided up the landowners' animals, and those who had none got goats and pigs. Thus, in the year 1935 we put an end to rent and taxes and we wrote off all our debts. We all lived better. Soldiers came out from the town, but when they did that, we villagers went up into the hills. When the soldiers went away, we came back again. K.M.T. wanted to steal our grain, but we hid it and fled up into the hills and K.M.T. had to go back empty-handed, and everyone had lots to eat.

My father had died by this time and in June 1935—no, not June—in May 1935 I was elected platoon leader of our Self-defence Corps. After that, I was quite convinced that the revolution would succeed, though I had doubted sometimes. I had changed my mind like the autumn weather. I was now responsible for a hundred families. We had spears with red tassels; we had knives and twenty homemade rifles. When necessary, all the men in the village assembled and off we marched with our spears, and as we marched along we were joined by the units from all the other villages round about.

The first big action I took part in was in May 1935. We had a message that we were to assemble to do in a landowner who would not surrender voluntarily. We came walking along all the paths with red flags on our spears. The landowner's name was Ma Sho-yen and he was all-powerful in Tsen-sanyan village. He had now barricaded himself in his house and had twenty armed men round him to defend his property. These were his own tenants, and it was their duty to defend him.

We had only twenty Red Army men, but the Self-defence Corps from all the villages had come too. The landowner's house was now surrounded by hundreds of men. We set up red flags on all the hills round about, and there were lots of them, so the horizon was quite red all round Ma Sho-yen. Then we all called to the landowner and held up our spears and said: 'If you don't give us your land and if you don't give us your rifles, you won't survive. You will die tonight.' After a while he came out. He was a big man in his fifties with a moustache, and he said: 'As long as I can keep my life, the land and rifles don't matter.' When we had got the rifles, we let him go off and he ran away to Kanchuan, where he had relatives. No one was even wounded in that action. And as soon as the landowner had fled, the villagers emerged; you see, they had been forced to stay with the landowner because they were afraid he would report them as 'bandits' or 'Red Army-men' and he had told them that if he did that, the

K.M.T. would cut off their heads. They were glad now and we held a big meeting and divided the land up and all the landowner's possessions.

I joined the party in 1935. I had become quite convinced by then and gave myself up body and soul to the revolution. In August 1935 I was elected leader of the district committee. At that time, we had our own revolutionary government in our hsien, and the district—which has now long since had its boundaries changed—consisted of these valleys here. I was responsible for agrarian reform, dividing up the land, fighting the landowners and for the employment of the labour forces. It was hard work, but there were ten of us together in the government then.

Here, in the village of Liu Ling, the landowner was Li Yu-tse. He owned several thousand mu of land. His family was one of the four that ruled Yenan and the area round Yenan. He owned half the valley here. Up as far as Ten-mile Village. But he had fled into the town and we never got hold of him. Then he fell ill and died. Li Hsiu-tang, who lives here in the village, is his son. He was so young at the time that he was given as much land as the rest. His children go to the school like all the others.

This Li Yu-tse had a relation who was a moneylender and a landowner. His name was Li Fa-fu and he lived in Fusichuan, thirty li from here. Li Han-hua, leader of the landowners' armed forces, was his son. He used to come with his men to the villages by night in order to strangle communists. Later, when the K.M.T. troops left Yenan, he fled to Sian. He never ventured here again, but took himself off to Yulin, where he worked for a war-lord called Kao Shua-chen. When Kao Shua-chen died, some time in the 1940s, Li Han-hua hid in a village beyond Yulin and disguised himself as a farmer. But then someone from here happened to go there and recognized him, and in the early '50s we caught Li Han-hua and brought him to Yenan, and there he was brought before the court and condemned and executed.

From April 1935 Yenan was blockaded by us farmers. We did not sell any corn to the town, nor any vegetables, nor fuel. This went on for seventeen months, then Yenan was liberated, the K.M.T. fled and the Red Army marched in. That was the time when the Central Committee and Chairman Mao came up to us in northern Shensi. They stayed here for ten years. The K.M.T. were only 200 li away. But those ten years were a good time. The farmers in the twenty or thirty hsien we controlled had cattle and food and new clothes. Our army was not in the towns; it lay up in the hills. There, the army broke new ground and grew corn. They grew more than they needed for themselves. It was an army that did not live by exploiting the farmer; instead, it helped the farmer. Those years, there was corn in profusion.

In 1938 I went to another type of work. I began in the consumers' co-operative. I became manager of Liu Ling's co-operative shop. Then I handed my land in Matan over to my young brother, took my family and moved here to Liu Ling. There were twelve or thirteen households in the village then. As manager of the shop, I had to buy what the farmers produced and re-sell it. I also had to get hold of consumer goods and sell them to the village. This was quite a new field of activity for me. This was trading, of course, and I had never traded before. But it went all right.

We began collecting capital to make a start. In order to be a member, one did not need to contribute more than thirty or forty cents. Irrespective of the size of one's contribution, one had only one vote. Members could take out their share whenever they wanted. Though we made propaganda for them to stay in. They could take out the yearly dividend or they could leave it standing. After a time, everyone thought that co-operation was a good thing, because it made goods cheaper than they had been, and besides it was the members themselves who gained on all trading.

To begin with, many of the farmers in the district were doubtful of it. They said: 'This is just a trick to lure money out of us.' But then others said to them: 'Even if they cheat us, we shan't lose so much and one can always have a try.' We also made a lot of propaganda for co-operation. The most important argument was that the contribution was so low.

After a couple of years everyone could see that co-operation was a proper way. Because, when they noticed that our goods were always cheaper, and when they saw that they got a big dividend on their shares and also were at liberty to take out their shares when they wanted, everyone was agreed and gradually they began putting in more money. If anyone had no money, he could invest a donkey. If that was done, we valued the donkey and the amount was regarded as share capital. We ended up with 600 donkeys. We increased the dividend too. Before Hu Tsung-nan's attack on us in 1947 the dividend was up at 100 per cent per annum, and we had 300 employees. We had seven shops and were a big undertaking. I was still manager of the shop in Liu Ling.

In those ten years things got better and better in Liu Ling. Our prosperity just increased. New caves, new land brought into cultivation. More and more families moved here. Newcomers were able to borrow money and buy tools from our loans department. But we did not charge interest. We weren't usurers. In this way we increased production the whole time. After harvest the new ground clearers paid back what they had borrowed, then they joined the co-operative society and invested more money with us, so that we could lend more to other newcomers. So we went on building up for ten years.

Those were good years, you see, our Eighth Route Army had put such a lot of land under cultivation for itself, and when it went off to the war, it handed all this land over to the farmers. It gave it to them for nothing. We saw them march off against the Japanese. They had almost no uniforms and very few weapons, and we wondered if such an army would be able to defeat Japan. But then came reports of victories. There were only a few soldiers left in Yenan. Those years we all had big pigs, cattle and corn. Everybody had enough to eat and there was food over. But then came General Hu Tsung-nan.

It was at the turn of 1946-7 that we learned that Hu Tsung-nan and his troops were coming. We had lots of goods then and a big capital. It took a whole month for us to remove our store of goods. Then we buried what was left and fled into the hills. At that time, the co-operative association in the Southern District owned more than eighty room-units, where the school now stands. But that was all destroyed. There was nothing left of the shops and either Hu Tsung-nan's troops found what we had buried, or else people dug it up themselves, when they began getting hungry. Hu Tsung-nan's troops ate up everything there was in the district. The rest they destroyed. People said: 'What are we to do? We have nothing to live for any longer.' So, when I came down from the hills during the occupation and saw that everything had been destroyed and that there were Hu Tsung-nan's troops everywhere, there was no working in the co-operative association any longer for me, for there was no such thing. Instead, I began working politically. I became a guerrilla.

We organized ourselves in Liu Ling. The Nan valley is an important thoroughfare, after all. The big highway to Yulin runs through it.

There were five of us and we had two rifles. One night in April of the year 1947, we made our way across the river and up into the eastern hills. After a month there were forty-eight of us and we had twenty-eight rifles. I was elected leader. The enemy had occupied the valleys and the roads and the towns, and we kept to the hills. We slept by day and operated in the villages by night. We took our arms from the K.M.T. What we did was that, if we saw a small K.M.T. force, we surrounded them and told them to surrender. They soon learned to be afraid of us and surrender. In the first month we took thirty rifles from them. The villagers gave us food and kept us informed of what the K.M.T. was doing. Every time a big K.M.T. formation came, we fled; and every time they split into little groups of eight or ten, we destroyed them. In this way the K.M.T. could not employ small groups, but always had to go about in force and that made things difficult for them.

Actually, the K.M.T. soldiers didn't want to fight at all. If they came to any village by themselves, we took them prisoner and gave them food and spirits and talked with them. If they wanted to go home and get out of the war, we gave them journey money and helped them to get away. In this area round Yenan, we got about twenty K.M.T. men a day to desert. We treated the privates well. When we captured them, they usually said: 'We are farmers too. We too have parents and children and we don't like war, but want to go home to our villages.'

Here, round Yenan, there were three K.M.T. regiments and 2,000 Red guerrillas. K.M.T. tried to organize the population, but they did not succeed. After all, there were only children and old people left in the villages. K.M.T. arranged meetings and appointed section leaders, but these mostly maintained contact with us and told us everything, partly because they didn't like the K.M.T. and partly because they thought it safest to do that.

In our village there is no one who was with the K.M.T. the whole time of the occupation, right to the end. That happened in other villages, but here they withdrew after a time. It was the landowner element and those like Li Hsiu-tang who brought Hu Tsung-nan's troops to Yenan and then bore arms for the K.M.T. and worked for the K.M.T. People were pressed into the K.M.T. army. Tung Yang-chen was one; he was made to be a K.M.T. soldier for several months, before he succeeded in deserting. Tuan Fu-yin stayed here in the village and worked for the K.M.T. There were many among those who had fled into the hills who became anxious about their farms and so went down to the village again. Many of them were captured by the K.M.T. and forced to carry sacks of grain on carrying-poles in Hu Tsung-nan's baggage-train. Ma Hai-hsiu and others had to do this, but they deserted the moment they were left unguarded.

The K.M.T. frightened people. They forced old men to carry two heavy sacks apiece, and, when they could go no farther, the K.M.T. soldiers beat them. Our own army never asked anyone to carry anything and our soldiers were trained always to be courteous and always to say 'thank you', so people said: 'How well behaved and pleasant our own army is! It really is a people's army.' But the K.M.T. used to catch villagers and when they did, two soldiers would hold them and a third question them: 'Have you got the old Eighth here?' They always said that, when they were asking about the Eighth Route Army. Then the one they had caught would say: 'That's difficult to say. They come and they go.' But the soldiers asked: 'Where are they now?' If the villager would not answer that or couldn't, he was beaten. After a time everyone hated the K.M.T. But we in the guerrillas never beat people and never spoke harshly to them, and we operated by night and were far away again by the morning. By day, the K.M.T. organized its sections, but at night the section-leaders fled to us, and so the following day the K.M.T. had to begin all over again.

We in the guerrillas had good sources of information. Every time the K.M.T. asked for guides, they got in touch with us and then we made an ambush and the K.M.T. had a bad time of it. In the end, the K.M.T. thought that we were everywhere and that there were too many of us to count. But that was not so. There were never more than 2,000 of us. But we knew more than they did. If a lot of K.M.T. soldiers came, we hid; but if we knew that there was not many of them, we fought them. The more we fought, the more we won. The villagers also collected arms and ammunition for us, while the K.M.T. were asleep.

There were many fights that year. And the K.M.T. never knew whether they were fighting our army or guerrillas. We demoralized the K.M.T. in every way. We used to fire at their cantonments at night, so that they had to stand by. In that way we prevented them sleeping. We needed only to detail one man to keep a whole K.M.T. cantonment awake night after night. In the end, the K.M.T. began to become tired and irritable. They never got to grips with us.

After that, we saw to it that the privates were not frightened of us. When they came to us, we were friendly to them and talked sense with them and gave them journey money, so that they could get away out of the war. But we, of course, knew what would happen to us if we were captured. They did catch a communist in one of the neighbouring villages, and he was sent to Sian for interrogation, and there they drowned him in the river. So we preferred to die fighting to being taken prisoner. We could always move about in little groups of two or three, but there always had to be a lot of the K.M.T., so that they could guard each other. The officers there beat their own men, too. And the K.M.T. also tortured its prisoners. People did not like that. So the K.M.T. was never able to get the people on its side, despite its occupying the area for thirteen months. They themselves only became more and more demoralized the whole time. The K.M.T. captured several communists hereabouts. But the party managed to rescue most of them.

Well, after that the K.M.T. was forced to flee and we came back. I left political work and went back to the co-operative. We handed in our rifles and were going to start building the shop again. Everything had been destroyed. The K.M.T. had even cut down the trees and there was nothing left of our buildings and our stores. The villagers did not have anything either. Everything had been destroyed. We had certain resources even so. We had outstanding debts of about 1,000 yuan, so we were able to open one shop again. But it could never be as big as it had been. And most of our 300 employees went to other provinces to get trading started there. We were being victorious all over the country then and everybody was needed.

The K.M.T.'s section-leader in Seven-mile Village was called Sze; he fled, but the deputy section-leader was called Yü and he stayed. So, eventually, he was brought before a court. People accused him of having knocked them about and of stealing cows. He was given three years' imprisonment. He came back here afterwards. He died of some illness about a year ago. Li Hsiu-tang was condemned to three or three and a half years' imprisonment and loss of civic rights. He had been responsible for the K.M.T. agents here. He was employed in their espionage department. But his family lived here in Seven-mile Village and he had not escaped with the K.M.T. He hadn't murdered anyone either. If he had, his punishment would have been more severe. He came back some time at the beginning of the 'fifties. He looked after his fifty mu of land single-handed and in the end he was let into the

74

East Shines Red Higher Agricultural Co-operative as one of the last. That was in 1955. He has no right to vote and no civic rights, but his economic rights are the same as everyone else's. He is still under surveillance. You see, he is the only real counter-revolutionary we have here in the village. If he should ever show that he works hard and has become a new person, then he will get his civic rights back. But he hasn't shown any signs of that yet. Of course, his father owned many thousand mu here.

I myself worked with the co-operative shop until the year 1953. Then I was pensioned and returned to the labour group for mutual help as an agricultural worker. In 1954 I joined Liu Ling Farmers' Co-operative. There I was elected chairman of the supervisory committee. That doesn't carry a salary, of course. And I've stayed that all the time. Both when the East Shines Red Improved Agricultural Co-operative was formed, and when we set up Liu Ling People's Commune. Then, I'm on the board of the party organization in Liu Ling too. I'm still quite fit, but I am beginning to get old and I only count as semi-able-bodied. Now, in the people's commune, I work mostly in the vegetable plot. I'm in the labour group for vegetable cultivation. I have a lot of work for the supervisory committee of Liu Ling Labour Brigade. Our job is to see that the different functionaries really do their jobs and that money is not wasted. We haven't had any embezzlement, but there has been occasional negligence, and now and again one or other of the labour leaders has behaved improperly.

Looking back on my life, I can only say that everyone ought to take part in the revolution. It won't be a proper revolution if everyone does not accept his share of responsibility and look after it. Revolution is not a thing you can let others do for you. Even when you are as old as I, you must go on working in the revolution, for there is no pausing in revolution, even if it has different stages.

Chang Shi-ming, aged 58

It's raining again today, so we haven't gone out to the fields, so it doesn't matter, my sitting here chatting. It's good it's raining. If the rain had come a few days later it would have been bad. Though it would have been best if it had come ten days ago in the middle of August. But it's good that the rain comes at all.

We come from Hengshan hsien. We have always been farmers. But we did not have our own land. We rented it. For three generations we rented the same land. There were 120 mu. The landlord's name was Wang Ting-tung. When I was a child, I worked at home. When I was fourteen, I went out to work as herd-boy for Wang Ting-tung. There were ninety sheep in the flock, and it was herded by one shepherd and a boy. I was not given any wages, but I got my food. Three meals a day, millet gruel and 'sticky millet' bread. The shepherd had a lame leg. The landlord lived in the town, he had several houses and stone caves. We had an ordinary earth cave.

Landlords did not eat as we others did. They never used their bodies, and they ate meat and vegetables every day. There were seven or eight persons in Wang Ting-tung's family. He was an incredibly mean person. He made you give back the tiniest coin due to him. He was hard. If people could not pay, he punished them. He did not hit you, but he threatened and swore and took your land and possessions away.

When I was eighteen, I began working with Father in our fields. People hated the landlords, but there was no way of getting round them. 'As long as we have our daily food, we must be satisfied,' people said. 'We must do what our masters say. They own the land and the oxen.' Wang was called 'Wang the Bloodsucker'. In our dialect the two names sounded almost the same: Wang Peng-ton and Wang Ting-tung. Everybody owed him money. And as long as you owed him money, you could not get permission to leave the village in order to look for another landlord, who perhaps gave better terms.

Every year he put up our rental. In 1928—which with us was a normal year without any great crop failure—the rent was 15 jin per mu. In 1929 it was 15 jin per mu. In 1930 18 jin per mu. In 1931 21 jin per mu and that year we could not pay it all. We owed him 600 jin. It was a normal year without crop failure, but there were so many mouths to feed in our family and the rent was so high, that we could not manage to pay it. Then Wang Ting-tung said: 'You must pay your debt before you can have permission to move.'

If one reckoned up all that Grandfather, Father and I paid the landlord for these 120 mu that we rented during three generations, it would make an incalculable number of jin. The landlords ate up people's work. They ate and we worked. I myself have always worked for as far back as I can remember. When I was small, I helped Mother pluck grass for our animals. I have toiled ever since my earliest childhood. We had to give up our land, but we weren't able to move from there, because we owed 600 jin.

After the harvest in 1931, when we did not know what to do, my brother's father-in-law came on a visit. It was winter, and he had come up from Yenan to see his daughter. He was called Tsao San-tung. He told us things were better in Yenan district. There was more land there. He advised us to come down to Yenan and offered to relieve us from our debt to Wang Ting-tung. After a family discussion we decided to move to Yenan. In January 1932 we set off for Yenan. There were nine of us in the family then, Mother and four of us brothers and three wives and a younger sister.

Tsao San-tung lived about thirty li from here. At first we stayed with him, but the water was not so good there and we tried to find out where it was better. Tsao San-tung helped us. I also knew Tsao You-fan. He spoke with the landlord about me and I was given a promise that I could rent land in Liu Ling, here. The landlord's name was Li Yu-tse. He was Li Hsiu-tang's father. Being the eldest of us brothers, I then had to go to Yenan to see him. He lived in a big house in the town. I was shown into his office. He sat and I stood. He wore a Chinese woollen coat and a Western hat. He said: 'You may cultivate my land, but you must pay 600 jin for two ox-lands.' Then he waved me away. In his eyes I was just a beast. That was in the late winter of 1932.

An ox-land was about eighty mu. I had one piece of valley land roughly where the big latrine is now, another piece on the other side of the river, and the rest was hill land. Then I had to hire oxen. I did that from another landlord. He, too, lived in Yenan, and his name was Li Han-hua. He was Li Fa-fu's son and a brother of Li Hsiu-tang's wife. I hired two oxen. I had to pay 300 jin of corn a year for each. In January 1933 I had to borrow 300 jin of corn from Li Yu-tse. When I paid back the loan after the harvest, I paid 420 jin. I had to pay a household tax of two silver dollars every month. That meant that I had to sell 300 jin of corn each time to get the cash. We were poor and there were only two in the family able to work. There was tax on everything, even on killing your pig. We got in 9,000 jin and half went as rent and taxes.

The landlords, of course, Li Fa-fu, Li Han-hua and Li Yu-tse, had thousands of goats, donkeys and oxen, and they just gathered in their rent. They bought and sold grain and they always made money on everything. In the autumn, when we had to sell grain to get the cash to pay our taxes, the price of corn was low; and in the spring, when we had to borrow or buy corn, the price of corn was high. We starved and toiled, but they lived in luxury and profusion and never worked. They ate pork every day; they had steamed wheaten bread and noodles.

In February 1934 people began whispering about the Red Army and how it was saying: 'The poor will not have to pay taxes. The poor will not have to pay rent. Poor people's children shall go to school, and landlords will disappear.' Then the landlords said: 'Don't listen to rumours. The communists are bandits. They want to kill you and take your wives.' The only time I had heard about communists before was some years earlier, before we moved to Yenan. Some communist books had been found in the school at Yulin and people were saying: 'There are communists in Yulin. Track them down and kill them.' It was almost only landowners' children who went to school; and we in the villages only heard of communism when they brought their children home away from school, so that they should not be infected with communism. At that time I had heard someone say something about Sun Yat-sen's ideas, but I did not know what they were. We ordinary farmers did not know anything about politics. That was no concern of ours. Various armies were fighting each other, bringing misfortune over the land. The landlords and K.M.T. plundered and hit and swore and took people for forced labour, and one army was worse than the next; that was all we farmers knew. But now people were whispering about a new and quite different army, which was going to put an end to all injustice.

Then, in March 1934, the first propagandist came to the village of Liu Ling. This was Wang Shen-hai. He was about 30 then and, the last I heard of him, he was in Sian. He is working there now. He came to the village disguised as a donkey driver. He stayed in the village and sought out the poorest and most oppressed. But he also made inquiries as to whether they were respected. Then he took us to some hidden-away place and said: 'In northern Shensi Li Chih-tan and Hsei Tse-chiang are fighting now. They are the commanders of the Red Army. We are making revolution now and getting rid of all landlords and all taxes and oppression. You must make propaganda in all the villages here. But it must be done in secret. Rely only on yourself. Only on the poorest. Do not reveal who I am. In other people's eyes I am just an ordinary donkey driver.' Wang Shen-hai said this to those he trusted. He had a good eye for people, and he was never betrayed to the land-lords, though he lived right in their villages. He tried to select those who were honest and upright and strong and respected, and to win them for the cause of the revolution.

To begin with, we did not have much faith in him. There was, too, an intense propaganda battle in the villages. The landlords sent out agents, who went round the villages saying: 'At first the communists talk very friendlily, but if they come they will plunder you.' Gradually, we became more convinced. We organized the Poor Farmers' Associa-tion. Ma Hai-hsiu was elected president of it. Then we set up a Self-defence Corps and I was elected its platoon leader. Obviously, all this sort of thing was unpaid. That was in April, and then all the landlords began running away to Yenan.

In the daytime, the landlords sent out their armed corps, Ming Tuan, to plunder our corn. But there was the Self-defence Corps then and that co-operated with the guerrillas. We gave the guerrillas infor-mation about the enemy and they helped us protect our corn and hide it.

In October 1934 we organized a committee to divide up the land in the village of Liu Ling. There were seven members on the committee. Tung Chi-hwei was chairman. He was Tung Yang-chen's father and the landlords cut his head off. That happened in 1936, as far as I remem-ber. Li Yu-tse was the one who wanted to have him killed and Li Han-hua was the commander of the brigade that captured him and executed him. He was taken to Yenan and kept there imprisoned for a while, before his head was cut off. The other members of the land distribution committee were Ma Hai-hsiu, Li Fung-hua, who died last year and was Li Hai-kuei's father, Tsao Yiu-fa, who is a herdsman now and Tsao Chen-kuei's father, Ai Ke-liang, who is a herdsman too now, and Ho Chan-yu. This last died of some disease in 1953 or 1954. He had no relatives in the village here and his widow remarried to another village. Besides them, I, too, was a member of the committee.

There were about ten families in the village here, and everyone got land. We also allotted land to the landowner's family. The land was divided up according to the size of the families and the landowner's family got exactly the amount due to it according to the number of persons in it. None of them was living here, but in 1936 Li Hsiu-tang moved out here. He hired day labourers to work his land. His father, Li Yu-tse, was still alive then. He did not die till 1937 or 1938, in the time of the United Front.

Most families were happy to have been given land, but some of them were worried. They did not believe that we could keep power.

'When the landlords come back, we shan't be able to carry away the land we have been allotted,' they said. But, then, gradually they became calmer, as they saw that the power of the landlords was beginning to be broken.

There were nine of us in our family, and we got 100 mu. Those years, life was better than it had been before. Now, after this land reform, I was more politically minded than I had been, and, in August 1935, I joined the party. Then came the period of the United Front during the war with Japan, and up to 1947 there was no hard class struggle out in the countryside, but we helped each other. I was leader of the Self-defence Corps in Liu Ling village all this time. In 1947, when Hu Tsung-nan was approaching Yenan, I was commander of the People's militia in Liu Ling. Our task was, in the event of war, to send food, information and drinking water to the guerrillas. We were the guerrillas' base. In peacetime we were to maintain order in the village, and be responsible for security and on our watch against spies and saboteurs.

One month before Hu Tsung-nan came, a big conference was held in Yenan. All the different local commanders of the people's militia attended. General Chu Teh talked to us, describing the country's military and political situation. He told us that Mao Tse-tung had said: 'Keep Yenan, lose Yenan. Give up Yenan, win Yenan.' To begin with, we did not understand that. How could we keep Yenan by surrendering Yenan? There was a long discussion, and we got up and said that we thought this was wrong. The right thing would be to defend Yenan. But, in the course of the discussion, Chu Teh told us not to be anxious. It was not a question of giving up Yenan for good, but only of making a temporary withdrawal in order to entice Hu Tsung-nan into a trap. 'We are coming back. I promise that,' he said. We had a long discussion and gradually we agreed. 'Hu Tsung-nan is going to be our transport company,' Chu Teh said. 'He is bringing up modern weapons for us.' Then we made a detailed survey of the situation and decided on proper operational plans for our coming work under the occupation. After that, meetings were held with the military representatives in the hsien administration. There we received our orders. This meeting was held ten days before Hu Tsung-nan moved into Yenan. Different ones of us were given different duties. Each one of us was made responsible for his part of the fight.

We had to explain all this to the people, when we got back to Liu Ling. It was not easy. Most people were apprehensive, but we explained the position and quoted what Chu Teh had told us that Mao Tse-tung had said. We tried to explain to them the necessity of surrendering Yenan. It took a long time and some were never entirely convinced. But, in the end, when they saw our troops retreating through the village, they dug pits and buried their corn.

When the K.M.T. marched into the village, the villagers had all fled up into the hills. I myself returned to Liu Ling on 1 May. All the caves were destroyed; that is to say, the doors and window walls had been removed, the timber taken as firewood, so that the caves were little better than dens. As more and more of us came back, we crowded together in the actual village of Liu Ling on Naopanshan. No one dared live on his own, but we lived three or five families to a cave. The K.M.T. soldiers plundered and raped. Here, Chang Chen-pong's wife was raped. She died. He moved to Seven-mile Village. Jen Teh-wan's wife had a girl, her cousin's wife, living with her and she too was raped. It was safest to live together. Before Hu Tsung-nan came, when we were still working to explain to people what the soldiers were really like, many of the villagers had thought they must be quite ordinary people and that it would be all right to live under K.M.T. rule as well. But when the troops did come, they were just as brutal as we had said, and they were guilty of just the violent deeds we had said they would do, and everybody united and spontaneously sought contact with the guerrillas. People were beginning to hate the K.M.T., as they had not done before they had seen them.

When I saw the K.M.T. troops, I thought that there were so incredibly many of them, and sometimes I wondered if we really were going to be able to crush them. People compared them with our own army. No soldier in our Red Army had ever hit people, and none of our soldiers had ever sworn at people. One compared the two armies, and we heard about the first victories.

Li Hsiu-tang stayed on in Liu Ling when we were told Hu Tsung-nan was coming. He went to welcome the K.M.T. troops with boiling water. Then he went to the town. He worked in Yenan for their intelligence service, as a secret agent. He was in the police troops. Well, he was Li Yu-tse's son.

Tuan Fu-yin also stayed on in the village. When he saw Hu Tsung-nan's troops, he thought that the Red Army was finished and that the K.M.T. was victorious and would stay for ever. Tuan Fu-yin worked for the K.M.T. He was appointed K.M.T. leader for Liu Ling village. He gave information to Hu Tsung-nan's police about who were communists and who were not. He informed against the political commissar in our hsiang, Kao She-chi, who lived in Hsiao-chiayuantsa, ten li from here. The K.M.T. arrested him on Tuan Fu-yin's information and tied him to a tree and began flogging him. Then people said: 'He is not from the Eighth Route Army. He isn't a communist. Why are you flogging him? He is just an ordinary farmer.' Everybody said they would go guarantee for him. At first, the K.M.T. wanted to hang him and kill him straight away, but people swore that Kao She-chi had not been a Red; so then they decided to investigate further and took him to a cave, where he was to be kept till their superior officers came. But in the twilight he managed to get loose and went off into the hills. The K.M.T. security police were sitting in another cave. They had thought he was securely tied. He got up into the hills, but having been flogged had made him sickly and he died in August 1947. I used to know him well. We were good friends. He was a farmer from the district here and was the political manager for our hsiang.

Well, after a time, even the K.M.T. had had enough of Tuan Fu-yin. He had always been a liar and now he had lied to ingratiate himself with the K.M.T. In the end, they chucked him out, and he had to go back to being a vegetable hawker. He has always been a weak,

82

lying wretch. When the K.M.T. withdrew, he fled with them, but we found him in Lochuan, when we liberated the town, and condemned him to three years. That was in April 1948. His wife went on living in Liu Ling. When he was released in 1950, he stayed on in Lochuan. His wife used to go down there to see him. He came back here in the end, in 1960, and since then the social care has had to look after him. He can't really work any more, you see. Well, his family had fled to the hills when the K.M.T. came and his cave was as well plundered as all the others; but he thought that the K.M.T. had won, that was all. He has always been stupid and short-sighted and tried to lie his way out of difficulties. When he was young, he was a street-seller in Yenan. That's what he has always been happiest at. Both his sons are working. One is a blacksmith and the other works with textiles.

During the occupation we in the people's militia fought the K.M.T. We called it 'the sparrow-war'. We worked in small groups, and whenever we came across an enemy soldier on his own, we killed him or took him prisoner. Here, we captured ten K.M.T. soldiers. Most were security agents. We knew them. When one of them came to the village, we smiled friendlily and invited him into a cave. They were always ready to eat and drink. We then gave him lots to eat and lots of spirits to drink. We kept pouring out more for him and laughed at everything he said, because then he enjoyed himself and joked a lot. Then, all at once, we held a spear to his back, tied him up and sent him up to the guerrillas. They did the interrogation and then sent the prisoner on to our safe area, where prisoners were kept for three or five months to be re-educated. Some of them then joined us and some were sent back to their villages. Every time we were asked about one of these security police who had disappeared, we replied that we had not seen him in our village; that he must have got somewhere else. They couldn't do anything.

(Chang Shi-ming was tired and breathless. He seemed feverish. Because of the state of his health, I did not want to press him and the rest of the interview was got through in a couple of minutes. J.M.)

In 1955 I joined Liu Ling Farmers' Co-operative. In 1956 we formed the East Shines Red Higher Agricultural Co-operative. In 1958 we formed Liu Ling People's Commune. In 1959 I began working in the grain office in Yenan hsien. I was to help with grain purchases. Had my work in one office. I was pensioned from that one year ago. There was no special reason for that. Now I'm working in the labour group for vegetable cultivation.

People say of Chang Shi-ming: He is greatly respected. He works hard. His health is bad and the chairman of the labour group for vegetable cultivation, Ching Chung-ying, has told him to take it easy and to stop working. But Chang Shi-ming just says: 'Work does no harm.'

His wife says that he has tuberculosis. 'He wasn't allowed to go on working in the grain bureau because of his tuberculosis. They wanted him to stay at home, lying down resting. But he won't.'

Part III
Liu Ling Village Labour Group

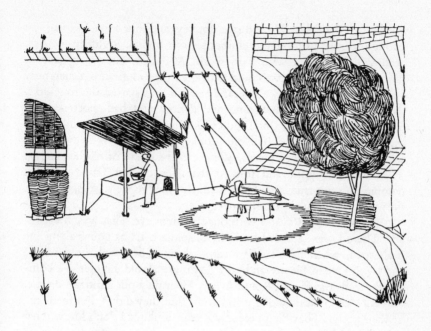

Tung Yang-chen, the martyr's son, K.M.T. deserter, aged 35

I WAS born in the village of Liu Ling. I don't remember much about my childhood. I was told that my father was taken by the white bandits and beheaded, and I used to think that when I was big I would exact vengeance. But I don't know if anyone really ever got hold of those who killed Father. That's all so long ago now. I don't know much about him. Most of those who knew him are dead.

I grew up during the time of the Shensi-Kansu-Ningsia Frontier Region. The land had all been divided up and we had twenty mu down in the valley. It was good land. We had land up on the hillside as well. Our family consisted of my grandmother, stepfather, mother and I. As a child, I herded the cattle. When I was fifteen, I began

87

working in the fields. We had two donkeys and four oxen. We had just enough to give us food and clothes for our bodies. Right up to 1947, each year was filled with hard work. As I said, our work gave us exactly enough so that we could manage. I used to go into Yenan now and again to shop and see opera. They had just started the song-and-dance troupes then. They sang and danced and had short sketches about different things. But I didn't like them, I don't remember any sketch I saw that I liked. The old people say the same. We never go to see the song-and-dance pieces. We go to the opera or to the cinema. Then someone came and told us that General Hu Tsung-nan was coming. 'It's not true,' Stepfather said. But they replied: 'Yes, it is true. Now, Hu Tsung-nan's troops are coming.'

I was sent to Wayapo with our two donkeys. That was in February. There I was captured by K.M.T. soldiers. I was going along the high road, when four soldiers came along. They took hold of me and two of them hit me and said: 'You are an old Eighter'—a communist from the Eighth Route Army. Then they put a muzzle on me. Someone said that they ought to kill me, but they didn't, but made me be their porter. They disappeared with the donkeys. I don't know what they did with them. That was how I became a porter for Hu Tsung-nan's troops. I had to carry seventy-five jin of wheaten flour and an overcoat. At times I had to go from seventy to eighty li a day. Many of us farmers and villagers were caught and became porters. Guards with rifles walked behind us. There were seven guards. I was hungry the whole time, didn't get food and wanted to run away. But I saw what happened to those who tried to run away.

I had a friend from Wayapo, who was called Liu Ying-kwei and was twenty-two years old. He was taken the same day as I, and we worked together. When we got to Lochuan he thought he had had enough of being a porter and he did a bunk. He was caught the next day, and then we porters were assembled. There were twelve of us. The officer said: 'Liu Ying-kwei ran away from us. Now we are going to shoot him.' Then they shot him. Afterwards, the officer said: 'Does anybody else want to run away?' We were all very afraid and answered: 'No, no!' After that I stopped thinking of running away.

In April, all eleven of us were made soldiers. That was in Pinglian and we were in cantonments there for two months. We were given uniforms and rifles. We ought to have been paid for being porters, but we never saw the money. The officers took all the money. Our platoon commander was called Liu. He was a bad-tempered man; he hit people when he was angry. I was often beaten. Sometimes he hit me with a stick, and sometimes he took my rifle and hit me with that. I was hit the most of us eleven new ones. Then we began to march. We marched and marched and everywhere we ate up all the villagers' pigs and poultry. After all, we were hungry too. Then we heard that the Eighth Route Army had taken Yulin. We fought against the Eighth Route Army in Sachiatien. We lost many men. Now we had to recruit new soldiers, and we became veterans. Now we were no longer watched so much; it was we who guarded the new ones. Then we marched on Yenan and we ate up all the goats on the way. We reached Yenan on 13 August. We spent the night in a village just north of Yenan. The one where the pottery is. We thought we were going to be allowed to rest there. But in the night between 14 and 15 August we got orders to break up and march on.

As we marched off, I said that I had to shit and walked out into the kaoliang field with my rifle and squatted. That was in the middle of the night and it was dark. When I had finished and stood up again, they had all marched off and I was alone. So I deserted and went up into the hills. I knew all the paths round here from my childhood. I got back to Liu Ling village that night. When Mother caught sight of me, she laughed and then she cried and then she laughed again. She got my old clothes out, and I changed. After that I made a bundle of my rifle and uniform and went up into the hills. I had told my mother: 'Don't say anything to anyone in the village about my coming back.'

I buried my rifle and uniform, because I didn't want Mother to have them in her cave. Someone could have come and seen them and then the K.M.T. would have shot her. After that I stayed hidden up in the hills the whole time. They used to come up with food for me from the family now and again. Then Hu Tsung-nan withdrew and I came back to Liu Ling and began working in the fields again.

That was a difficult spring and a lot had been destroyed during the occupation. But the work went on as usual. We did at least have seed to sow. Hu Tsung-nan had not found all our grain. The harvest that year was not all that good. But we managed. Then I too joined the labour exchange group. We exchanged one person's work for another's. That was done on a private basis. I hadn't an elected function there. Then we discussed the formation of a labour group for mutual help. I joined. We were all of us agreed. It wasn't a farmers' co-operative, but each one kept his land. We got bigger harvests than before. The problem, of course, was whose land should be tilled first. We decided to take turns. But that did not always work.

Then we began discussing a farmers' co-operative. Most agreed to turn the labour group for mutual help into a farmers' co-operative; but I thought that as I had both animals and land, I ought to be able to manage on my own, and that if I was in want of labour, I could perfectly well hire people. So I said that I had no use for any sort of farmers' co-operative. I kept my independence and worked for myself on my own land.

Then, little by little, people came to me and talked to me. They said: 'Your father had his head cut off by the K.M.T. and you were taken by the K.M.T. and you were made to carry sacks of flour for Hu Tsung-nan's army and were put into their army. When you were a child, you said that you wanted to take vengeance because of your father, but now you want to employ people and become an exploiter yourself. What's the meaning of this?' Then they talked about the advantages of the farmers' co-operative. It was mostly the Old Secretary, Li Yiu-hua, and Ma Juei-ching who talked with me. For a long time I thought about what they had said, and in the end I did see that it was probably best for me to join the farmers' co-operative.

My income increased too, once I did join, because, when I farmed on my own, I had had to hire people and that was difficult and expensive, and when at the end of the year I reckoned it all up, I found that my income was greater now as a member of the farmers' co-operative than in the days when I worked on my own.

Then they began discussing the formation of a higher agricultural co-operative. To begin with I was not at all convinced. I was thinking of the land. We had had good land. In the co-operative we had still had a certain return from our land; but in these discussions it was being said that each should be paid in accordance with the work he did. Not for anything else. Again it was the Old Secretary, Li Yiu-hua, and Ma Juei-ching, Ching Chung-ying and Tsao Chen-kuei who did most of the agitation for this reorganization. I listened to them and thought about it a lot. Then I heard that the party wanted us to form a higher agricultural co-operative and in the end I did apply for membership. But I wasn't elected to anything there either. My income in the

East Shines Red Higher Agricultural Co-operative that first year was 200 jin of corn more than it had been in the first farmers' co-operative. That was a big income.

In 1958 there was a new thing. People were talking then about a people's commune. I decided then, at the very beginning, that I would first hear what the party said and follow it and not argue. Because the party had always been right before. So I just voted yes for the people's commune and left it at that. In the autumn of 1961 I was elected deputy labour leader for Liu Ling Village Labour Group. I was very moved that people had confidence in me. I wanted to work better and show more enthusiasm, and if I planned my work properly and worked hard myself, it would mean that everyone achieved prosperity and happiness.

My task now is being responsible for agricultural production within the labour group. It isn't an easy job. As labour leader one has to have patience. Some of the members are pleasant, others aren't. Some are apathetic and have to be persuaded to work. The work, of course, has to be uniform. As labour leader I have much more to do than when I was an ordinary worker member. I have to organize all the work, get the people out to the fields every day, see that the ploughing and weeding is done properly. In the afternoons I plan the next day's work. I do that while I am working. I think as I go along. Before the others go home for the day, I tell them what has to be done the next day. In that way, they all know what they are to do. Sometimes they have different ideas and suggest that the work be done in a different way; sometimes they think I'm wrong. If so, they point this out to me, but they don't protest against my instructions. After all, I was elected labour leader and it is I who bear the responsibility. Being labour leader is an honorary position of trust.

Most of the members are decent people. Not all, but most. They say: 'Of course, we'll manage to get that field ploughed.' That helps me. Any big questions are always discussed at our meetings. The difficult thing, where I am concerned, is that I can neither read nor write. I have taken part in literacy courses and I did learn a few characters, but I forget them again at once. It's not easy to learn anything once you're grown-up.

The days pass in work. If you look at how the last few days have been for me, you'll know what almost all our weeks are like. The only things that alter are the seasons and the jobs we do.

04.30 Alarm bell rings. My wife and I get up. I smoke a pipe of home-grown tobacco. We don't have anything to eat. I don't even have a glass of warm water in the morning. Then I go out and see that people get off to their work. Ten of them are to plough the wheatfields up on Loushan. Fifteen are to weed. I myself go with the ploughers.

08.00 The food-fetcher brings our breakfasts. This is our first meal of the day. One man in the team is detailed to collect all our breakfast dishes. He goes from household to household. We take it in turn to do this. The one who is doing it, of course, begins work later. He gets his work points for fetching our food. It isn't so easy carrying breakfast dishes with food for ten people.

12.00 We stop our morning's work. We drive the oxen down. They are tired now and need rest. Then we ourselves go home to eat and rest. My wife has food ready. After eating, I sleep for half an hour.

14.00 In the afternoon the ploughers get up potatoes. The others go on weeding.

19.30 When work is over for the day, we go home. I fetch four buckets of water from the well. Then I eat. Then we all go to bed.

Monday, 27 August 1962

04.30 Get up, smoke, ten for ploughing, fifteen for weeding.

08.00 Breakfast.

12.00 Bring oxen down, have dinner, half an hour's sleep.

14.00 All getting up potatoes.

19.20 Potatoes all up. Leader of the labour group, Li Hung-fu, returns from a meeting of the committee of Liu Ling's labour brigade. We hold a labour group meeting in the fields.

Li Hung-fu reports on the committee meeting. We had had our labour group's committee meeting a couple of days earlier, on the 23rd I think. After a short discussion, we agree to the suggestions of the brigade committee. Then we divide up the potato harvest. It is a clear starry night and we don't have to fetch paraffin lamps. After this, everyone goes home taking his potatoes, has supper and goes straight to bed.

Tuesday, 28 August 1962

04.30 Get up, smoke, ten on ploughing, fifteen on weeding.

08.00 Breakfast.

12.00 Dinner. Rest.

14.00 All twenty-five on weeding.
19.00 Home, fetch water, have supper, sleep.

Wednesday, 29 August 1962
04.30 Get up, smoke, ten on ploughing, fifteen on weeding.
08.00 Breakfast.
12.00 Dinner, rest.
14.00 Everybody on weeding.
16.30 Rain, can't work, sit in lee of a mound and wait for it to clear. Rain does not stop, just gets harder.
17.00 Go home, work stops, raining too much. Stay in cave. Sit on kang, resting.
19.30 Supper. Sleep.

Thursday, 30 August 1962
04.30 Get up, smoke, ten on ploughing, fifteen on weeding.
08.00 Breakfast.
12.00 Dinner, rest.
14.00 Everybody on weeding.
19.00 Home, fetch water, have supper, sleep.

Friday, 31 August 1962
This is my free day this week. I can do what I like.
04.30 Get up, smoke, fetch four buckets of water, sweep the yard in front of the cave, go down and see to my private plot of land.
08.00 Home to the cave for breakfast.
09.00 Down to my private plot. Weeding, till it becomes too dark to work.
19.00 Home, have supper, sleep.

There are no mornings when we sleep in. We don't do that in this part of the country. In the busiest time, harvest-time, we don't take our days off. We save them up till later in the year. No, I don't normally go and visit our neighbours in the village. After all, I see them out in the fields every day, so I don't need to visit them in the evenings as well.

It's in the winter that we rest. We collect fuel then. Either sticks and dry wood that we find, or we hack up a little coal. Actually the children are supposed to sweep in front of the cave, but they do it badly and skimp if they can, and when I see that, I do it myself. We bought a bicycle in 1960, and we bought a two-wheeled cart with rubber tyres in 1961. I had been thinking of buying a bicycle for a long time. It is easier to get into the town if you have a bicycle. I ride the bicycle. My wife could not bicycle when we bought it. I have tried to teach her, but she still can't get on without help. I keep the bicycle up in the cave. I get it out when we want to go in to Yenan, then I take her, if she's coming too.

I bicycle into Yenan twice a month. Then I go to the opera. If there's a good opera in Yenan, we stop work at half past five. Perhaps we decide that the whole team will go to the opera. We ride in on seven or eight bicycles, each of us taking a passenger. I usually ride in with the other chaps, but now and again I take my wife and the children. Mostly she does not want to come. She wants to stay with our youngest. She won't take it to the opera. It's such a business. The older children like films best. None of us like song-and-dance. But when there's a film in the village, even Granny goes to it.

The years pass; they are all like one another. We begin with the spring ploughing and continue with it for a month. Then we sow millet, then kaoliang and maize. We plough for the two different kinds of 'sticky millet', that takes ten days, then we sow. We turn the soil for buckwheat and sow buckwheat. Then we begin weeding the fields, and we keep on with that the whole time till we harvest, one field after the other, and then we begin again with the first field. We harvest the wheat and bring it down off the hillside. We begin threshing the wheat and ploughing up the wheatfields. We sow wheat and harvest buckwheat and then the two kinds of 'sticky millet', millet, maize and beans. We bring our harvest down off the hillside. We use carrying-poles to carry it. We thresh, and finish threshing towards the end of the year. Then in January we have winter and then we rest and gather fuel and that sort of thing, unless there's some water-regulating work or something else on the go, and after that we begin the year with ploughing again.

In October we begin preparing the production plan for the next year. That's about all. Now and again we help on water regulation. Harder some years, not so hard others. During the winter twenty men are on repairing and maintaining the terraces we built before. We aren't making anything new this year; and we didn't make anything new last year either. We are just trying to keep it all in good order.

Life goes on. I have four children now. One girl goes to school; she's ten. I have a boy who's eight and a girl who is a hundred days. I also have a daughter of twelve; she went to school for one year, but the teachers sent her home. They said she was too stupid to go to school. That's all.

People say of Tung Yang-chen: Theirs is the biggest and finest cave in Liu Ling. It belonged to Li Hsiu-tang's father, Li Yu-tse. Tung Yang-chen's family was given it, because Tung Chi-hwei, Tung Chang-chen's father, was a hero and a martyr. Everybody loved Tung Chi-hwei. He did so much. He was one of the poor people's leaders and because he was beheaded, when the Red Army came back and was victorious, the biggest cave in the village was allotted to his family. His widow then married Chang Shi-ming.

The Tung Yang-chens aren't so well liked. They had the best land in the valley after it was divided up. They had the biggest caves, three big caves. Well, people don't dislike Tung Yang-chen, but his grandmother, Li Fong-lan, who is The Old Secretary, Li Yiu-hua's, older sister, is very obstinate. She has had the say in that family. She didn't like handing over their land to a collective.

Tung Yang-chen works hard. He always has. He is a good worker. His wife, Kao Kuei-fang, also works very hard. She can carry 100 jin on a carrying-pole. She isn't liked either. Her tongue is so sharp. The women won't talk with her. What she says is so hard and her voice so shrill. Tung Yang-chen's second daughter, Tung Er-wa, doesn't go to school, but is at home looking after the house, because her grandmother is too old now.

Chang Chung-liang, book-keeper, aged 33

WE come from Yulin. I went to school during one winter. That was when I was nine. Mother says that my father was a day-labourer. I myself don't remember him. When I was twelve, Mother got married again to a coalminer. Mother has told me that Father had once borrowed money. He could not pay the interest in time, so just before New Year the moneylender came and took our iron cooking-pot. Mother wept and we were unable to cook anything. Mother told me that herself. I don't remember anything from that time.

My stepfather was a coalminer. He had to sweat hard, and his wage was small. We lived on millet porridge. My uncle told me about the war against Japan. He was a pedlar. I myself saw Japanese bombers fly over our house, when they were on their way to Yenan to bomb it. They flew in a line, like birds. People looked at them and said: 'The Chinese people cannot be subdued by the Japanese.' It was said that the Japanese killed people as one slaughters animals. I wondered why the Japanese hated us Chinese so much. The way they behaved wasn't human. We had never done them any harm.

People said: 'The Eighth Route Army is strong. It will stand up to the Japanese.' I wondered if the Japanese were going to come and occupy us. I wondered, too, whether I shouldn't try to go to Yenan and become a soldier. I was young. When I was nineteen, and the war against Japan was over and the new war against the K.M.T. was going on and Hu Tsung-nan had had to get out of Yenan, we moved here. We had nothing left up in Yulin then. Hu Tsung-nan's troops had marched past that way and had taken our donkey and 300 jin of corn. They had slaughtered and eaten our pig and our goat. My uncle was living in Yenan, and as we had nothing left in Yulin any more, and Yenan had been freed, we walked to Yenan to search for my uncle.

He was living in Shachiakou. We got there after walking for ten days. I went into the cave first. Grandmother saw me and said: 'Has your mother come?' 'Yes,' I said. Then they all laughed and were glad, and Grandmother wept. They fetched Mother into the cave and seated her on the kang. She was very tired after walking from Yulin. Her feet were sore and her legs ached, she said.

That autumn of 1945, we stayed two months with my uncle. After that he found us an abandoned cave which we put in order, and, in January 1949, we began gathering firewood for him. He helped us a lot. In the summer of 1949, we were given land and an ox, and that gave us a lot of grain to eat. The family then consisted of Mother, Stepfather, me and my wife and my small brother and my little sister. We had got our land from Uncle. Another uncle had died the year before, and now we were given twenty-five mu to cultivate. Uncle gave us this without payment, of course. There was no mention of buying the land from him. We had a good harvest and things began to look brighter.

In 1949 a labour exchange group was formed. I had an older cousin living in Liu Ling. He's dead now. He came over to us to ask about Yulin and hear what things were like up there. Then he said to me: 'There's a lot of land to be brought into cultivation at Liu Ling. You can break as much new land there as you like.' My stepfather, my mother and my little sister stayed on in Shachiakou, while I and my wife and my young brother went to Liu Ling.

Here, I began breaking new ground up on the hillside. I joined the labour exchange group. People thought it better to work together, that that made the work easier, and that evening came quicker, if several of you were working together, than if you were working quite alone. To begin with, the group was not organized on a permanent basis, but was a direct agreement between the members to exchange their labour. In 1951 we decided to reorganize the group and put it on a permanent basis as a labour group for mutual help. Ma Juei-ching was its leader. The work went well, but there were lots of quarrels about whose land should be taken first. It was difficult to solve all these problems. Some said: 'Why should his field be taken first? I've got a heavier crop. It ought to be my turn now.' Whatever we did, this went on; so then we began talking about forming a farmers' co-operative. There was Li Yiu-hua's Farmers' Co-operative on the other side of the valley. They were doing better and better. We discussed this. First, we decided to form our own farmers' co-operative, then we joined Li

Yiu-hua's Farmers' Co-operative, which then changed its name to Liu Ling Farmers' Co-operative.

In 1955 Hutoma Village and Wangchiakou Village were also incorporated. We then formed the East Shines Red Higher Agricultural Co-operative. Our incomes had been rising the whole time, so the others had confidence in us. But, of course, there were also some who were against this development. For example, Chen Hung-liang in Hutoma Village. He had a lot of animals, three oxen, two donkeys, and there were two working in the family and only four mouths to feed. He had good fertile land down in the valley. He did not want to join at all; but then people worked out for him in detail how much bigger his income would be in the higher agricultural co-operative, so that in the end he too applied for membership.

In 1954 we formed Liu Ling People's Commune. A people's commune is a coalition of economic organizations. It makes it possible to employ greater labour resources, where these are needed. By this, one can make greater efforts and employ all one's force on one given point, which is much more efficient. We were now able to carry out more jobs that required capital. Our consciousness also increased. The labour groups worked better and we were able to decide to take care of those families which were in need of help.

In December 1958 I was elected book-keeper for Liu Ling Village Labour Group. I had kept the work daybook and the record of people's labour points in the labour group for mutual help. I am now responsible for keeping both the cash book and the grain book. I have to render statements every month to the labour group. But I am only responsible for the books, not for the actual money or grain. The treasurer is in charge of the stores and the cash, and he keeps his own books of what he has in cash and in store. Our two sets of books have to agree. We often check them.

If payments have to be made, Li Hai-ching, who is the one responsible for our finances, signs the bill; I enter the amount in my books and the treasurer pays the amount from his cash and enters the amount in his own books. When in-payments are made, we have to inform Li Hai-ching as well.

This work of mine as book-keeper is, of course, an honorary job, but at the same time it is a lot of work. I am credited with one and a half days' work for it, that is fifteen work points, for the months when there is a lot of work, and ten work points for the months when there is less work. As far as I have been able to see, this is fair. It corresponds more or less to the time I put into keeping the books. I use the evenings and night-time for this work.

I never went to school for more than that one winter, when I was nine; but since then I have attended several reading courses. In addition, I have learned by doing the work. I was compelled to learn quite a bit, while I was keeping the work journal and the record of labour points for the labour group for mutual help. I have also had to learn a lot as book-keeper. I can now read the newspaper and write letters. I can also read simpler books of fiction. I stick most to serial stories in parts with lots of pictures and a few simple characters on each page. The pictures make it possible to understand the characters I don't know.

I am very fond of films. Opera and that sort of thing doesn't appeal to me so much. Opera is a bit old-fashioned. Films have much more variety, more themes, more reality and much more that is funny and makes you laugh. I usually go to the cinema or opera once every ten days. We often have films in Liu Ling; but mostly I take myself into the town. Sometimes I go in with my wife and my eight-year-old son, my other children are far too small to appreciate going to the cinema. But, sometimes, when we have finished work for the day, someone will say: 'Come on, let's ride into town and go to the cinema.' Then we jump on to our bicycles and ride off.

The management committee of the labour group consists of five people. They are elected at the annual meeting of the labour group's members. Usually, it is people who are known to be good workers and to be knowledgeable about farming, and who have the reputation of being fair and honest, who are elected. After the past year's work has been discussed, the committee for the coming year is elected. The labour group has a members' meeting once a month or so. At these, anything can be discussed. The annual meeting is really a number of meetings held together at the end of the year.

First, we have a meeting to elect our delegate to the Liu Ling Labour Brigade's representatives. At this meeting we discuss the opinions the labour group wants ventilated at the meeting of the representatives. A couple of days after the meeting of the representatives, the labour group summons its members for a further meeting. At this the delegate to the representatives reports what was discussed and what was decided at the meeting of the representatives. After this, the chairman of the management committee of the labour group reports on the year's production and on what has been accomplished during the year. Then I inform them of the year's balance and report in detail on the economic situation. Then the member from our labour group who sits on Liu Ling Labour Brigade's supervisory committee reports on how the auditors found our books and our cash and stores. He reports if the auditors have had occasion to criticize anything or if they have had to take action over anything. After that we have a long discussion. This is the longest meeting of the year. At it, everything has to be talked over. Last year, it went on for three days running. My mother was ill, so I had got permission to visit her, but the meeting was held just the same, and when I got back to Liu Ling the discussions were still going on and I attended the last bit of the meeting. There wasn't anything special; there usually isn't. There doesn't need to be any special question for discussion, but everything that has happened has to be gone through and all that has been done during the year.

At the end of the discussion, when the members have approved the committee's work—or made their criticisms—a new committee is elected. The way this is done is that, first, the chairman is elected, the one who will be labour leader, then the deputy leader is chosen and he also becomes deputy labour leader; then we elect the one who is to be financially responsible and supervise the economy and countersign everything, and, finally, the treasurer is elected. The committee is elected. The committee is never elected in a body. Each one is discussed thoroughly before he is elected. When the new committee is elected, the annual meeting is at an end. The committee then meets and discusses the production plan and the labour group's budget for the coming year. When this has been worked out, a new members' meeting is called, and the committee presents its proposals for the coming year's budget and work. The members' meeting discusses these proposals, perhaps changes something in them and thereafter the proposals are handed over to the committee of the labour brigade for approval.

If the committee of the labour brigade has no objections to make, the committee of the labour group again puts forward the year's budget and work plan at a further members' meeting and has them finally approved. If the labour brigade committee should not have approved the budget and work plan, they are referred back to a further members' meeting for discussion and then again laid before the committee of the labour brigade, and so on, until everyone is agreed. The members' meeting of the labour group does thus have the final word.

But this complication does not occur. We keep the labour brigade's committee informed; after all we have representatives on it and we are in continual contact with each other. This is just the way things would have to go in theory, if there should ever be a dispute between the labour group and the committee of the labour brigade. A lot of meetings are held at the turn of the year. There is not much work to do on the land, of course, and the members have time to discuss all questions thoroughly. Everyone wants to say what he thinks.

My wife is a member of the League of Youth, but I myself am neither in the party nor the League of Youth. I have never asked to join.

My cave is next to the office of Wang Kwang-yung, the treasurer of Liu Ling Labour Brigade. On the night of 13 July I heard him and the labour brigade's book-keeper, Lo Han-hong, starting to go through their books. They were discussing why the two books, the book-keeper's and the treasurer's, did not agree. I did not like that. It did not sound nice at all. They were talking so loudly that I could hear it in my cave, so I went straight up to Li Hai-tsai, who is the representative of our labour group on the supervisory committee. I spoke to neither Lo Han-hong nor Wang Kwang-yung nor anyone else, before I spoke with him. Li Hai-tsai then went to Mau Ke-yeh, president of the supervisory committee of Liu Ling Labour Brigade, and they decided that Li Hai-tsai, who can read, should go through the books. They both went down to Wang Kwang-yung's office and took the books. I had gone to bed. Then they checked every account and finally found the mistake. It wasn't embezzlement. It was negligence. On 16 July they came to me and reported what they had done and what they had found. After that it was brought up at a members' meeting.

People say of Chang Chung-liang : He's nothing special. On the whole he's an honest fellow. He isn't very strong. He does not like talking with people. He is by nature uncommunicative and something of a recluse. But he is decent and honest. He has always had the reputation of being prudent and considerate. His wife, Chi Mei-ying, is a member of the League of Youth. She jokes a lot and chatters all day long. Some years ago she attended a course and learned the new scientific methods of delivering babies. Latterly, she has been midwife and attended most of the births in the village. Because of her, most children now survive. She is very liked. Theirs is a happy marriage.

Kao Pin-ying, the one who was strung up, aged 37

IF it doesn't rain worse than it is now, the animals can come down from the hills. Otherwise, they will have to stay up there on the stubble they are ploughing. This soil becomes smooth and slippery if it rains too much, and then they can easily break their legs. But if they can just be kept fat, there is no great risk of their catching a chill. One has to look after them. Anyway, the rain's good. We need rain now.

I'm from Yulin hsien. There were four of us in the family: my parents, myself and a young uncle of mine. We worked as day-labourers and farmhands and life wasn't easy. We heard that the communists here in Yenan were letting people have all the new ground they could break, and that they could keep their crops without deduction. In 1942, my parents died. Then Li San-soi had a talk with me. He had gone down to Yenan in 1941. He had come to Yulin to fetch his family. He said that things were better in Yenan. The Eighth Route Army was a good army. There was a government in Yenan that did not just oppress the farmers. Breakers of new ground didn't need to pay any taxes for the first three years. They could even get help from the government. Then I talked with my uncle; he stayed in Yulin and I went to Yenan with all I possessed in a bundle on my back. I wanted to be my own master and not have anyone over me any more.

I came to the village of Loutzekou, sixty li from here. My grandfather lived there. Grandfather took me to the authorities and I was shown where I could clear land. I became a breaker of new land. I worked on my land and, in 1943, I got an interest-free loan from the co-operative society to enable me to buy an ox. I paid the loan back in 1944. I was enthusiastic and happy and put in a lot of work. I had my own land, I had cleared twenty to thirty mu of hill land myself, and I harvested 3,000 jin and lived in an abandoned cave in the village of Loutzekou. It was hard work and I liked it.

In February 1947, Hu Tsung-nan came. I had hidden all my corn and all my possessions, had buried them and then made off into the hills. When I came down again, the K.M.T. was in the village, they had discovered my corn and stolen all that I had. They ordered me to carry it myself to their H.Q. Then they said that I was from the Eighth Route Army. They tied my hands behind my back and tied a rope round my wrists and strung me up in a tree. My arms were twisted. It hurt. I hung free above the ground and couldn't touch it even with the tips of my toes. Then they said that I was a communist. They whipped me for two hours. I wanted to die.

When you are strung up in this way, your head falls forward and hangs down. They put mud on the nape of my neck, big clods of it. I was young and strong and I didn't faint. But it hurt and I begged them to shoot me and have done with it. But they wouldn't. Instead, they whipped me again, and then they went back to the village and investigated. They discovered that I was just an ordinary breaker of new land and not someone from the Eighth Route Army, so they let me down and told me to get off home.

When the K.M.T. let me go, I went home to my village. I went to my cave and lay down. I was quite alone and I rested on my kang for twenty days. It took a long time before I was fit again. You can see that I still have scars from my flogging all over my body. There was nothing to eat. My neighbours gave me a little food. I just lay quiet. I thought a lot then. I had not been afraid of Hu Tsung-nan's troops before. I had gone off into the hills, just because I did not want to be in the war. But there had been nothing to eat in the hills, and so I had gone back down to the village. I had thought that perhaps Hu Tsung-nan's troops might hit me in the face or swear at me, but one can stand that. I was just an ordinary breaker of new land. I had never taken part in politics, nor been interested in them either. I didn't think they could do anything to me. Yes, I had, of course, been a stretcher-bearer and I had laid mines.

I lay there in my cave thinking about this, and it took me twenty days before I was well enough to get up again. Then one day some guerrillas came to Loutzekou. They were from Shansi and they were led by Liu Shi-hsiu. I went up to him and said: 'I want to join the guerrillas.' That was in April 1947. I was accepted. After two days we left the village. We operated in the surrounding hsiang. One day the villagers let us know that the enemy was going to send out a patrol to plunder. It was to steal corn from the villages. We lay in ambush and captured four rifles and took five prisoners. One of the prisoners was a cook. The others ran away and escaped. We schooled them and then let them go, so that they should be able to tell about the Eighth Route Army's policy towards prisoners-of-war.

One day, when we were in Laoshan, that was in July or August, we heard that the enemy was supposed to be coming along the highway. We laid an ambush and I was on guard. Then I saw a man whom I suspected of reconnoitring for the enemy. I captured him and he was armed. The unit that had strung me up in the tree was the same as the one that was coming. He was from it. I looked at my prisoner and wondered if I should kill him. He had helped to string me up. But I didn't kill him. We were not supposed to do that in spite of everything. I took him prisoner and led him to our headquarters.

There, we questioned him about the enemy. The enemy seemed to be far too strong for our ambush to be successful. We withdrew and sent a message for the regular army. The regulars came in the afternoon. They were commanded by Wang Chang. After that, we wiped out the enemy. We had a meeting after the fight. The regulars praised the guerrillas for their good work and gave us a machine-gun with ammunition, a mortar and several boxes of ammunition, twelve rifles with ammunition and the dead enemies' overcoats. We hadn't had any uniforms before that.

In that fight the enemy lost about 400 men. Of those thirty were killed. The prisoners were re-trained. Some joined us; the others went home to their villages to tell what it was we wanted and how we had treated them. We ourselves hadn't had any losses. The regular army lost a couple, though.

After that the Eighth Route Army marched on Lochuan and we went to my village. We rested there for five days. We were so happy. We had taken a lot of booty. We had a big feast the first evening. We sang in the northern Shensi way. We made up our own words to the song. It's called, 'Walk with the Wind' and you have to make up your own words for it. We had lots of arms now and we all had a big feast, guerrillas and villagers together. Our leader made a speech about the fight and praised various people for what they had done. Then he started the song. He sang: 'The cocks are crowing and the dogs are barking. Our brothers the guerrillas have come back.' Each of us sang a verse. I myself sang: 'There by the ditch the oxen are drinking water and red flags are flying over the hills. I take my guerrilla comrades to my home, the millet gruel is cooking and the steamed bread is hot.'

After these five days we left the village. We had many fights. They were almost all the same. We took part in a fight almost every day. Our task was to protect the population of a certain area, to support the regular army in its struggle, to demoralize the enemy and obtain information about the enemy. I was only wounded once and it wasn't anything serious. I and a comrade were to reconnoitre one of the enemy's forts. We were discovered. That was at Maping Hill, twenty li from here, at the beginning of September. I had a shot wound in the foot. My comrades carried me away and then I was transported on an ox and I lay hidden in Maping for a fortnight. It was often difficult for the wounded. We couldn't take them with us, you see. But I was with a neighbour who had known me since before the war. Four men were killed in our group. We knew each other as one does in a group. Their names were Ho, Chang, Chi and Liu. At the beginning we were fifty, but towards the end we were eighty.

Later I was given a medal: 'Liberation of the Great North-west'. We who were in the guerrillas often meet. Only yesterday I met our leader, Liu Shi-hsiu, in the town. He is head of a labour brigade in another people's commune. But I never have met my tormentors again since the war. But one day in 1960, when I was working in the fields down here, somebody called me. I went up to the road, where two men were standing. They said that they were from the public prosecutor's office and had some photographs they wanted me to look at. They wondered if I recognized any of them. I recognized one of the men in those photographs. It was the one who had given the orders for my hands to be tied behind my back and that I was to be strung up and flogged. I had had time to see my fill of him in 1947, and I shall never forget his face. I told them what I knew about him. They said that now they had caught him and that he had confessed how many people he had had strung up and flogged and executed, and that they were now busy checking his confession. He had caused many people's deaths. They took down my evidence and said that they would get in touch with me, if I was needed, but evidently I wasn't needed to get him condemned, because I never heard from them again. But I was so glad when they showed me his photograph, because I knew then that he had been captured. Now I shall be avenged, I thought. I remembered what had happened and felt hatred in my heart, because it's awful to be strung up as I was.

We did not take part in any fights after March 1948, when Hu Tsung-nan withdrew. We were stationed in the village of Linchen. There we had discussions and meetings, we analysed the fights and studied. Some of us were taken into the regular army; the others were demobilized and allowed to go home. I wanted to join the regular army. I wanted to stay on in the army. I liked the life and at this time we were going ahead all over the country and many people were needed for the army. But they didn't accept me. I was an only son. They accepted only those who had brothers, and they told me that they could not take me, because I was the last of my family and, if I was killed, my family would have died out. I tried to talk them round, but I couldn't. I was demobilized as well.

When I got back to Loutzekou, I found that my neighbours had begun tilling my land. That wasn't a thing I wanted to discuss with them. We don't take land back. You see, I had handed it over to them in order to go to the war, and there was more land to clear. In the guerrillas I had heard that Liu Ling was a good place and I had also met a girl from Liu Ling, so I moved there in October 1948 and married in April 1949.

I began breaking new ground up on the hillside. I had to borrow a cave. It wasn't till 1955 that I had time to build one of my own. I joined the labour exchange group and the 1949 harvest was medium good. There were only two of us in my family, my wife and I, and I was the only one tilling the ground. That was hard. So I joined the labour group for mutual help. I did that in February 1950. Views were divided about the question in our labour exchange group. Four other families and I wanted to form a labour group for mutual help. None of us had land down in the valley and it was difficult for us to till the land alone and the labour exchange arrangements weren't enough. The other four were Jen Teh-wan, Ai Ke-kao and Chi Pei-fa, who all joined another labour group for mutual help, and Yang Yung-chien, who was Yang Kuei-ying's first husband and died a couple of years ago. He and I joined the same labour group for mutual help.

The others weren't so enthusiastic. Some were strongly against the whole thing. There's no need to mention names. Those are matters that don't need to be raked up now. It's all long ago and who they were is of no significance. They had better land and were afraid they would lose their land and preferred to be on their own. There were long discussions. People produced their reasons. I myself said: 'I cannot weed all the weeds in my fields by myself. It takes too long. Co-operation is better. Co-operation will make us strong.' Well, at all events we decided to form a labour group for mutual help in February 1950. There were fifteen families of us and we divided ourselves into two groups. I was leader of one group with seven families. They were Li Hung-fu, Li Hai-ching, Ma Hung-tsai, Li Hai-kuei, Yang Yung-chien and Li Hai-fu. Li Hai-fu and I ran the group. We discussed whose fields should be taken first. We took them in turn. The other group was led by Ma Juei-ching and Fu Hai-tsao. That year the harvest was good. We had no direct difficulties. I liked the work.

I joined Liu Ling's Farmers' Co-operative in 1954. There were long discussions about this for many days. At first I did not understand the point of a farmers' co-operative, but later I did see that it was right. I thought of how it had been when I was a day labourer, and I decided that now I ought not to think of working just for my own good, but that proper united action was needed now. Those most in favour of forming a farmers' co-operative were Li Hai-kuei, Li Hai-ching and Yang Yung-chien, all three of whom had fields on the hillside, and Ma Hung-tsai who had good land down in the valley.

Well, certain people did not want to be in on this, others were so enthusiastic that they raised both hands when we voted. Those in favour of the farmers' co-operative said that, in the old days, the owner of the land became rich and everyone else was poor, but now there was a new age, and now no one would be poor and no one would live on another's labour, but all would work and live well. Most of us, after all, had been farmhands, day labourers or poor tenant farmers, so we understood all that. But there were certain ones—the names are neither here nor there—who said: 'The more there are together, the worse it will just make things. Things have been all right as they are.' But, in the end, everyone was agreed and understood that with a farmers' co-operative there was no question of one gaining at the expense of another, but that all should achieve prosperity together.

At the first meeting, Ma Hai-hsiu was elected treasurer, but the next year, 1955, I was elected treasurer. My job was to be responsible for all cash, all grain and all stores. It is hard work, because you yourself are responsible for everything. One has to be very careful, especially careful as you are dealing with money and corn and tools and instruments, which are not even your own. I thought then that, as people were trusting me, I must be even more careful of their property than I had been of my own. For my work as treasurer I was credited with one day's work a month. All treasurers get the same. Labour leaders, however, get nothing extra.

In 1955 we talked of forming a higher agricultural co-operative. Most were for this. It was only a small minority that was against it. Li Hai-kuei talked with them; he explained to them why they ought to vote for the higher agricultural co-operative. Those who were against it did not like it that the higher agricultural co-operative would do away with the dividend on land. I don't remember how much it was. At any rate it was of no significance to me. Ten jin per mu per year or something like that, I believe it was. But, in the end, Li Hai-kuei persuaded them. I myself was for the higher agricultural co-operative from the very beginning. When I was a farmhand, I got only fifteen old dollars for a whole year's work, so I considered that the principle 'To each according to his work' was the only right one. Of course, it was one's own work that decided everything. Afterwards, we founded the East Shines Red Higher Agricultural Co-operative.

There was no mistrust of the people's commune among us. We considered it the only possibility. We had to develop our joint effort.

And that confirmed the principle 'To each according to his work'. That principle has never been changed with us. Before, the masters had cave after cave of corn, while the people went hungry. The people's commune was better, because it gave possibilities for better water-regulation works and terracing of the hillsides, more order in planting out trees, more cultivation of vegetables and more odd jobs. We in Liu Ling Labour Brigade have managed to carry out big water-regulation works and terracing thanks to the people's commune. My work as treasurer was not at all affected by the people's commune reform. It has been exactly the same all these eight years.

You see, I was never able to go to school as a child. So, one winter when there was not so much agricultural work, I decided to go to a literacy course. Now I can read the newspaper. I read *The Yenan Daily*. But I don't read it every day. I haven't time for that. The labour group subscribes to one copy of *The Yenan Daily*. We read certain articles aloud for the members who can't read, and then the paper goes the round of those who can read.

People say of Kao Pin-ying: He is good-looking, he is a cautious man and has a calm temperament. He was elected treasurer because he works hard and is very scrupulous. He often works cleaning out the shop and stores. He takes his job as treasurer very seriously and looks after the members' possessions in the best possible way. He dries the grain in the sun and actually puts considerably more work into his job than the day's work a month which he is credited with. He spends every free moment on it.

The women often joke with him because he is so cautious. He never hurries: 'Not even if the heavens fell would Kao Pin-ying lengthen his stride.' He is never nervous or anxious. He always thinks a long time and carefully.

His wife Liu Kuei-ying is tall and has bound feet, although she isn't more than thirty-eight. She is from the district. Before, she used to live with her mother, but her mother moved away. In 1959 she kept the labour diary for the women. She did that because the women's leader could not write at that time. She was very mistrustful. She had to write down the women's hours of effective work every day, and they came to her in the evenings to have their hours of work entered. But as the women often go to work in the morning a couple of hours late, she used to ask at what time they had really begun that morning. Then some replied: 'I began at sunrise.' But others said: 'No, she didn't. You see, Liu Kuei-ying was so mistrustful and scrupulous that the women liked making fun of her and getting her to write down, then have to cross it out and re-do it, and then cross that out and write it all over again. In the end, it reached such a pitch that Liu Kuei-ying no longer believed anyone. 'I went an hour later,' one woman might say. 'Have you any proper witnesses for that?' Liu Kuei-ying would ask. She is honest and she is strict and she is careful. There's nothing actually wrong with her. It's just that she doesn't like talking; she is taciturn and doesn't understand a joke.

Kao Pin-ying is henpecked. He is sat on by his wife. He is a kind man, but she is hard. He just smiles kindly at her, but she is like a storm. She was barren for a long time. They had no children. When she finally did have one some years ago, it was a daughter and then she had no milk. The child got goat's milk. But as Liu Kuei-ying didn't suckle it, she ought to have had another child long ago. She hopes to be able to give birth to a son, but it doesn't look as if anything is coming of it.

Actually, the women don't like her so much. She doesn't talk and she never jokes. 'She is one of those who does everything alone.' She isn't such a good worker either. She does her best, but that isn't so much. Besides she's far too finical.

Li Hai-yuan, the one who left the co-operative, aged 48

I AM from Hengshan. We were poor when I was growing up. Father worked on the land, and I helped at home till I was twelve. I never went to school. They didn't want people like us to learn to read and write. I can read a little now, but I learned that after my fortieth birthday. Before, I didn't know even one character. But at my age it isn't so easy to learn. I mean, it is easy to learn to recognize the characters, but it is difficult to remember how to write them and then one forgets easily. I'm always forgetting them.

At all events, I began earning as a farmhand, when I was twelve. I had my board and three silver dollars a year. It was a medium-sized landowner I worked for. I've forgotten his name, but it doesn't matter, landowners are all alike. I wasn't fully grown then, of course, so I wasn't good for a full day's work.

When I was eighteen, I began working for a landowner called Ma Tsu-chuan. I worked as a day labourer for him and at the same time I rented twenty mu from him. The rental was twenty-four jin a mu. I lived with my father then. I then took over my father's debt to Ma Tsu-chuan. It was fifty taels of silver. I don't know how much my father had borrowed to begin with, but my first memory of the debt as a child was that it was ten taels of silver. The interest was fifty per cent a year and with interest on interest and bad harvests we could never pay it back. Although we were paying and paying all the time, the debt grew bigger and bigger. We had too little land for it to pay to have an ox. It was bad land up there in Hengshan.

The taxes were heavy. We had to pay in cash twelve silver dollars a year. In 1931 we weren't able to pay. We just couldn't. Then soldiers came and took me. They put me in prison. Father had to go round to friends and relations and neighbours and beg money. In the end he got twelve silver dollars together. Then I was let out of prison. I early became responsible for the family. I had, of course, taken over Father's debt. But he did not die till 1954.

Then my brothers and my parents moved. The family split up. I took over the debt and the cave and 600 jin of grain, and the others were free of debt. After that they all moved to Yenan. I had Father's debt, so I was compelled to stay behind in Hengshan. I married and we had children—we worked hard. We had eleven children. Ten of them died. [He weeps.] Our eldest daughter died when she was eight. The others when they were seven, four, five and three. They all died. We were poor and we couldn't afford to have the doctor. Doctors weren't for people like us. The only one to survive the illness was my son, Li Te-chua. But it made him deaf and dull-witted. He went to school for four years. Now he's fifteen. He mostly gathers firewood. He's the only one of my family left now. Things were difficult for poor people. Hard work and big debts and nothing but hunger and illness all the time.

In 1945, I had a letter from my aunt, Li Fong-lan; she is Tung Yang-chen's grandmother. In that letter my aunt wrote: 'If life is hard for you, you should know that things are better here. If you come here, the communists will help you. There's land here. I'll help you and the communists won't let anyone who is willing to work starve.' But, of course, I had these fifty taels of silver to pay back, so I couldn't do anything. Ma Tsu-chuan had died, but his family was still there. Debts did not vanish so easily.

In the end, my aunt sent me an ox from Yenan. Oxen fetched high prices then. In that way she paid my debt and I became free. In the month of March according to the moon calendar of the year 1948 I went down to Yenan. When I got there I had a talk with my aunt. She said: 'I'll see you have a cave and food.' I was given some abandoned land and a pig. That was a very difficult year. Ma Hai-hsiu was leader of Liu Ling village then, and it was he who arranged that I got twenty mu of hill land. I didn't have to pay anything. I myself owned the land. In July that year my wife and son came here. They walked. All that we possessed then and had brought with us from Hengshan was an old quilt. We had had to sell the rest because of the debt.

Later, in the year 1949, everything was settled about my land in Liu Ling. I was given a stamped certificate and everything. But it had

been clear from the start that it was to be my own land. It was just that the formalities took time. Originally, Li Hsiu-tang's father had owned the land we took over. It was the first land we had owned. No one had cultivated it before. We were very happy. Before that we had never even dreamed of having our own land. Why should we? We didn't dream of anything. And if we didn't have quilts enough to keep out the winter's cold, we couldn't long for land of our own. That's how it was. But now that we had got land of our own, Father came to me and said: 'You should be grateful to the communists. Without them you would never have got this land. Before, things were just as hard winter and summer, and we worked and worked, but could never pay the land-owner. The debt just grew. Ten of your eleven children died. So be grateful to the communists.'

In 1948, I had begun with the spring work as soon as I came to Liu Ling, but I didn't have time to plough it all and that year my harvest was only 600 jin. But Aunt lent us corn, so that we were able to manage. In 1949, I got 1,200 jin and I didn't have to pay any taxes or other deductions, because breakers of new ground did not have to pay corn tax the first few years.

Then Li Yiu-hua spoke with me about joining his labour group for mutual help. 'You haven't enough corn,' he said. 'You cannot manage alone. It is only when there are several that one can do anything.' When, as I now did, I joined the labour group for mutual help, there were three members in my family. My parents were living with my elder brother, Li Hai-fu. My parents, my elder brother and my younger brother, Li Hai-ching, had all moved here in 1938 leaving me with the debt up there in Hengshan. To be honest, it was difficult for me to keep my family alive in Liu Ling too. We still had only one quilt. The land was not enough. I had been thinking of going out to work as a day labourer again, when Li Yiu-hua spoke with me and said: 'Now, you are to join my labour group for mutual help instead.' Well, I thought, that sounds all right.

My father, of course, was Li Yiu-hua's older brother. Now, Li Yiu-hua told us how we were going to work and how we were to share the income. I had less land and worse land than the other men, but Li Yiu-hua said that after the grain tax had been paid we were all to share the harvest alike. In that way, no one would lose anything, but all would gain. I thought that sounded all right.

That year was very slightly better. I had clothes to put on and enough corn to be able to eat the whole year. The following year we bought a new quilt. The third year, Li Yiu-hua's labour group for mutual help had four cattle and two donkeys. I was labour leader. We worked quite well together. I was the poorest of the four families in the labour group. Things went really well for us.

We worked harder than the others who had land down in the valley. We got up earlier and we rested less and went to bed later. Li Yiu-hua could work very hard and we were all prepared to work. We carried manure up to the fields on the hill. All of us, men and women, worked. We planted trees and we went to a lot of trouble. What was hard was that I had to be awake at night thinking how the work ought to be planned. A lot depended on everything being planned correctly. Hard work and sweat aren't enough by themselves; you also have to think what you are doing.

The fourth year, I had 2,400 jin of corn in store. And then our labour group was to be expanded. Then I thought that I could manage on my own. And if I left the labour group, I had the right to take my share of the common property, which would be two oxen, but if I stayed in the new farmers' co-operative, I should perhaps have more responsibility and have to rack my brains all night.

Li Hai-chun kept the accounts and I talked with him. After that I talked with Li Yiu-hua and the others and I said: 'If the whole village is going to come in, then I'm going out. The more people there are, the more of a burden it will be. More work for me. I shall wear myself out being labour leader. Besides it's not practical taking in all these villagers. Most of them can't work properly. So, if you decide to take the others in, I'm going to leave and take two oxen, and then I shall be able to manage without your help.'

My wife wanted this too. She had said to me: 'We have worked for so many years for landowners and got nothing; you've been a day labourer and possessed nothing. But we have land and two quilts and we have two oxen and it will be better if we manage on our own.' But Father and my brothers did not like me going out. Father talked to me and said: 'You ought not to go out, now that you've benefited from the communists. You came here a pauper and they helped you and you have worked together and you have been well off. It's not right that just you should leave.' But I said: 'I want to manage on my own, whatever you others say.'

Naturally, there was a lot of talk in Li Yiu-hua's Agricultural

Co-operative, as it was called before it changed its name to Liu Ling Agricultural Co-operative, when I left. Li Hai-chen said: 'If you don't like being labour leader, someone else can take on the responsibility, the main thing is that you don't let us down.' But I did not care what they said; the main thing for me was to get those two oxen and be on my own. In the end, the others had to agree to it, of course. The collective's voluntary, after all.

Well, after that I was on my own. My wife looked after the animals and I worked in the fields. I toiled away, scarcely ever sleeping. I worked even harder than before. After a time I began to regret what I had done, but I didn't say so. I wasn't going to give them that pleasure.

For two years I stayed on my own. It was difficult. You couldn't hire farmhands or day labourers any longer. I had to see to everything myself. I sweated my guts out. None of my brothers would help me. Not that I asked them, for that matter. I saw that Liu Ling Agricultural Co-operative was flourishing and I began to think that I was stupid to have left it. But then I thought of how the others would say: 'There! What did we say?' And when I thought of that, I worked harder still because, whatever happened, I did not intend to take the first step. Then in the third year I did not manage to finish my ploughing. I had two mu left. I wasn't going to manage it in time. Then the farmers' co-operative people came along: they stopped and watched me and then, without a word, they began ploughing those two mu for me. There were seventeen of them, and they did the work in less than an hour. I myself would have needed two days. Then I thought: 'It's good to be many.' But we didn't say anything to each other. I said nothing and they said nothing.

Later, when I was weeding a field of maize that I was behind with, they came once again to help me. I didn't really like that. I told them that I would pay them for their work. I didn't like people working without payment. But they replied: 'You are in difficulties and you can't manage this. We are strong and we are many, and we can help you as a brother.' After that they sent Tsao Chen-kuei to help me. But I hadn't asked for any help. I hadn't spoken to anyone. They had just seen for themselves how things were with me and come of their own accord. That was just before I joined the agricultural co-operative.

Liu Ling Farmers' Co-operative had then been re-organized into the East Shines Red Improved Agricultural Co-operative. They had bigger fields than before. The millet fields were very big and I looked at them and they were so beautiful. Just after that they came to me from the East Shines Red Improved Agricultural Co-operative and talked with me. They were polite and asked me to do them the service of joining. They said: 'Do you see how rich we've become? We've pooled all our land now. It's hard farming on your own. Come to us.' I thought they were right and, as they had come to me themselves and been courteous, and I hadn't had to ask them for anything, I said that I would agree to become a member of the East Shines Red Improved Agricultural Co-operative. That was 1955—I was the last in the whole district to join the farmers' collectives.

Then it was suggested that I should be labour leader for a labour group. I accepted this. I was that for two years. I thought it onerous. There was all too much headwork and all too much responsibility. But, however it was, I was better off than when I had been on my own. In 1955, my last harvest on my own, I had got 1,800 jin. In 1956 in the East Shines Red Agricultural Co-operative, I got 2,000 jin and also 60 Y in cash. And, despite having the extra responsibility as labour leader, I had not needed to work so hard.

After being labour leader for two years, I got up at the annual meeting and said: 'I don't want to be labour leader any longer. I don't want to have responsibility for others. I don't like being the one who has the responsibility.' But they just said: 'You work so hard. You organize the work of production so well. We can't do without you, because you are so clever at the work.' After that they elected me again, even though I protested. I didn't like that. That next year I didn't work all that well. It was the first time in my life that I had stopped working hard. After that harvest, the others agreed without discussion to elect a new labour leader.

I thought it so nice being an ordinary farm worker again and not having to be labour leader. You see, if you are labour leader, you have to plan everything, and then you have to urge people on and keep at them, and they get grumpy if you keep at them. They think you are persecuting them, because most people are so lazy and don't really know what work means. I thought it would be so nice only to have to do my work and not have to worry about what others were doing or not doing. It was lovely only having to do farm work and not having to plan. It's not that you have to work less in the fields if you're a labour leader; on the contrary, you can't get a labour group to do anything, if you don't go in front yourself and show them how the work should be done.

Now, as an ordinary worker, my income's increasing all the time. I don't remember properly how much corn I got the second year, but it was a lot. And also I got more than 300 Y in cash. I'm working now on the autumn ploughing. I plough in the mornings and in the afternoons I weed. I plough one mu every morning. I have a one-yoke plough and use the same ox every day. That's the best way. It is a good ox and I am responsible for it and the plough, and I know it well and can get the most out of it.

I really intend to be an ordinary farm worker all my life now. I don't intend ever to let myself be elected to anything, either to be labour leader or anything else that means having responsibility for others. But I have learned enough characters to be able to keep books, if I want. I let the book-keepers and ganbus teach me: the different characters for a work-day and wheat and millet and that sort of thing.

People say of Li Hai-yuan : He is an industrious, tenacious, hard-working man. He is known as a responsible person. No one mentions his leaving the collective. He himself doesn't talk about it either. 'He is a good man and a hard worker. But one must talk about propitious things and good events. One shouldn't mention unpleasantnesses unnecessarily because, whatever else he is, he is a good fellow.'

His wife, Chia Fu-lan, is from a very poor family. Her feet are badly misshapen, because they used to be bound. She is Chia Ying-lan's sister and they say she came to Li Hai-yuan as a child-bride. Their great grief in life is that their son, the only surviving one of their children, became deaf and dull-witted after an illness. Actually Li Te-chua is backward. His parents have built him a cave. They hope that he will marry. But he has no girl. The women think it will be difficult to get him a bride. Chia Fu-lan usually says to the women : 'I have to work harder than other mothers. I have had to see that he got a silk quilt and a fine big cave for himself and lots of things so that he can get married. The girl's parents must be able to see that it is a rich home she is going to, otherwise her mother won't allow the marriage, although they ought to have been transformed in the new society and not think of such things.' But even so the women don't think his parents are going to be able to find a bride for Li Te-chua. But they don't say that to his mother. They are sorry for her.

They have no other children alive. Chia Fu-lan hoped for a long time to be able to have another child, but now the last year she has said: 'Perhaps I look pregnant, but I'm not. I'd like to be and we've tried and tried, but now I'm too old to bear fruit.'

Li Hai-yuan does not talk about this. He does not mention it, but he grieves. He has gone to the party people and spoken to the ganbus who come from the town and said to them: 'Can't you find some specialist in Sian who can make my son well?' The ganbus have tried to help him, but the doctors say there is nothing to be done. After hearing that, he hasn't spoken with anyone about it again. His wife, Chia Fu-lan, however, still hopes that her son will get all right and often speaks with the women about it.

Tables

Management Committee

Li Hung-fu   Chairman, labour leader
Tung Yang-chen   Deputy labour leader
Chang Chung-liang   Book-keeper
Kao Pin-ying   Treasurer
Li Hai-ching   Responsible for economy

Grain Production

	Area 1961 mu	Crop 1961 jin	Area 1962 mu
Wheat	182	20,042	182
Millet	217	37,760	235
'Sticky millet'	156	25,485	145
Maize	133	28,987	120
Beans	86·7	12,552	83
Buckwheat	17	2,300	24
Kaoliang	17	2,677	21
	808·7	129,803	810

Sales of Animal Products

			1961		1962 (1 Jan.–1 Sept.)
Goats		9	63 Y	7	42 Y
Wool	jin	62	49·60	36	28·80
Sheepskins		18	36	8	16
Leather, goat	jin	51	96·90	48	91·20
			245·50		198

Family Incomes, 1961

Head of Household	Days' work	Grain, jin	Cash, Y
Kao Pin-ying	439	2,722	746·36
Chang Chung-liang	321	1,990	545·70
Li Hai-ching	353	2,189	600·10
Tu Yi-chen	173	1,073	294·10
Ai Ke-kao	349	2,164	593·30
He Huang-ho	269	1,668	457·30
Wang Fung-li	572	3,546	972·40
Li Hai-yuan	465	2,883	790·50
Hu Shen-chu	297	1,841	504·90
Jen Teh-wan	173	1,073	294·10
Liu Chen-yung	367	2,275	623·80
Chang Chung-wen	272	1,686	462·40
Liang He-yiu	410	2,542	697·00
Tung Chi-lian	90	558	153·00
Li Hung-fu	348	2,158	585·60
Li Yü-hsin	267	1,655	453·90
Fung Yü-lan	115	713	195·50
Tung Yang-chen	449	2,784	763·30
Ai Ke-liang	203	1,259	345·10
Li Hai-kuei	345	2,139	586·50
Kao Chin-lan	50	310	85·00
Chang Chu-liang	29	179	49·30
Ma Hung-tsai	335	2,077	569·50
Chi Pei-fa	395	2,449	671·50
Li Yiu-hua	1,059	6,516	1,800·30
Li Kuei-ying	73	453	124·10
Jen Huai-ying	59	366	100·30
Li Hai-fu	322	1,996	547·40
Chen Chung-yuan	338	2,096	574·60

Family Incomes, 1961 (continued)

Head of Household	Days' Work	Grain, jin	Cash, Y
Li Hsin-chen	186	1,153	316·20
Li Sha-chang	479	2,970	814·30
Wang (not in Liu Ling Village)	255	1,581	433·50

Social Subsidy from the Labour Group's Assistance Fund, 1961
Only grain

Name	Jin	Reason
Tuan Fong-ying	560	Husband works in Yenan. Parents-in-law old. Shortage of labour.
Tung Chi-lian	220	Alone at home. Son at school. Bound feet.
Li Yü-hsin	300	Widow with three children. Only one person working in the family.
Fung Yü-lan	200	Husband works in Seven-mile Village. Two children, no parents. Works at home.
He Huang-ho	50	Only person working in the family.
Kao Chin-lan	200	Husband works in Yenan. New member. A lot to do at home.
Chang Chu-liang	200	Husband works in Lochuan. On her own.
Li Kuei-ying	300	Husband away working. On her own.

Rewards to Merit Workers, 1961

Tung Yang-chen	Mattock
Kao Pin-ying	Mattock
Li Hung-fu	Mattock
Chang Chung-liang	Mattock
Li Tsuai-ying	Mattock
Li Kuei-ying	Mattock
Kao Kuei-fang	One handkerchief, one pair of stockings
Ai Lan-ying	One handkerchief, one pair of stockings
Li Hai-yuan	Felt mat

Part IV

The Labour Group for Vegetable Cultivation

Ching Chung-ying, leader of the vegetable group, aged 54

I AM from Hengshan. My family has always lived there, but for several generations we have not had the land to make a living from. We had ten mu and Father worked as a day labourer for various landowners. Ours was not good land; it lay high up the hillside. We were five brothers. Life was hard for us and when I was twelve I had to go out and earn.

It was in January 1920 that I began working for a landowner called Wang Kou-ho. I was to get 'two strings of cash' for the year; that is to say from January to October according to the moon calendar. The landowner woke me when the cock crowed. I had to carry the water and shit. I had to do everything. One summer day, when the melons had ripened, I dropped one on the ground and it split open. It was a sheer accident, but Wang Kou-ho was furious and took his mattock and hit me on the head. You can still see the scar. I was unconscious, and it was late afternoon when I came round; I was soaked in blood and he had just left me lying where I fell. [Weeps.] No one knows how the poor people suffered. I was twelve and had no trousers, and the landowner struck me without cause. He often struck me. Everything was my fault. I often got five or six beatings a day. He was a big landowner. He had 600 mu. It was both valley land and hill land.

One day Wang Kou-ho took me with him when he went out to the sheep. That was in the summer and it was hot. We went eight li from the village. At dinner-time I was sent back to fetch his food. First he took off my cloth shoes and pissed in them, then he said: 'You must be back with my food before my piss has dried.' It was a hot summer and I had to run barefoot across sand and I could not stop and rest on the way. I ran as fast as I could, but when I got back the landowner's piss had already dried, because the sun was strong, and Wang Kou-ho beat me after he had eaten. [Weeps.] I was only twelve.

Next year, when I was thirteen, I worked for a landowner called Chou Kuan-yü. I was his herd-boy. It was better there. I had only four beatings the whole year. Though I did get my ears boxed now and again. The following year, I moved to a landowner called Li Teh-chen. He was a decent man and I herded sheep for him and worked one day in the fields. I was getting bigger now. But his son was different. The son was about twenty-five and, when his father wasn't looking, he used to hit me. He thought it fun. He got hold of me and beat me up six times that year. But I tried to keep clear of him and stay within sight of Li Teh-chen. Because as long as he was looking, I wasn't thrashed. That was the last year I had a thrashing.

When I was fifteen years old, I went as farmhand to work in the fields of a landowner called Mau Ko-jen. The following year I moved over to Shou Huei-chen. Now I was reckoned as fully able-bodied. I worked hard. One does.

When I was twenty, the great famine came. That was 1928. One of my brothers died. After that, Father and I and my three other brothers went to Shansi. It was better there. We sold my two youngest brothers. We were forced to do that in order to survive. We got twenty-eight silver dollars for one and twenty silver dollars for the other. I don't know where they went. I have never heard of them since. After that it was only Father and I and my younger brother, Ching Chung-wan. He lives in Liu Ling too now. I fell ill. But I survived and two years later we came back to Hengshan again.

There, I worked as a day labourer. Then gradually we heard about the Red Army. It was supposed to be rather good. They took their land, cattle and corn from the rich and distributed it to the poor people. But I never met a communist till long afterwards. But I remember that Father and I talked about them one night, when I was twenty-six. That was in 1934 and there was revolution in northern Shensi. 'Why should one be a farmhand for others all one's life?' we said. But the Red Army didn't come.

It was only in 1938 that I met a communist. He was called Wu Shen-tsai. He was middle-aged, thirty or thereabouts. He had come up from Yenan to make propaganda. He talked with me in Hengshan. He said: 'You toil all year round for a landowner, but your life is wretched. You gather riches for others, while you go hungry yourself.' Then he talked to me about Yenan. That was in February 1938. After that I talked with Father, and we decided that I should go down to Yenan and see if it were true, as was said, that there people were given land, and that the government there was good. One night I set off for Yenan. When I reached the town, I didn't know where to go, so I asked a woman ganbu. She was polite to me. That surprised me. Then I saw that this was a good place. It was true what people said.

In March, I went back up to Hengshan. Father was ill. I was to fetch Father and the family. When I got there Father was dead. I got there about noon and he had died that morning. After the funeral, we went down to Yenan. That was Mother and I and my younger brother, Ching Chung-wan. The only thing we possessed was an iron pot. We took that with us.

I was given land in Liu Ling, and, since I came here, I have never worked as farmhand for others. I worked hard, but I did not have to

127

toil as I had done when I was a farmhand. And every year life became better. At the beginning of 1947, we had six cattle, three big pigs, two donkeys and 21,000 jin of corn. After that Hu Tsung-nan came. His troops plundered. They stole everything we had. They destroyed everything. They took the seed in the fields to feed their horses. Everything was destroyed. In 1947 we had another famine. After thirteen months' occupation Hu Tsung-nan left us in March 1948. We then had nothing to eat and no seed. There was seed-corn in Lochuan. We got that from the government. That spring I went between Lochuan and Liu Ling with seed. I walked hundreds of li and carried two sacks on a carrying-pole on each trip. At night, I slept on the sacks by the roadside. Then we began building Liu Ling up again.

First we organized a labour exchange group. On the other side of the valley the Old Secretary, Li Yiu-hua, and some others were building up their farmers' co-operative. We watched them. Their working together there seemed to bring them luck. More people meant more strength and more manpower. They did the ploughing better than we and they manured more thoroughly. They had nice harvests. We discussed whether we shouldn't form our own labour group for mutual help. That was in February 1952.

Some of us were for this. I thought it would be good. Mau Ke-yeh and Ma Juei-ching also worked for the proposal. Others were against the idea. Fu Hai-tsao, for example. Their family had more manpower. Both he and his father worked. Also they had good land in the valley. They said: 'We two can manage our fields ourselves. We don't really like the idea of others looking after our land.' Then I went over and talked to them: 'If the others on the other side of the valley can do their job properly, why shouldn't we be able to do so?' I said. Three weeks later, Fu Hai-tsao came to me and said that he had thought it over and that he would join. I was chosen labour leader for Liu Ling Labour Group for Mutual Help and Ma Juei-ching became deputy leader.

The discussions took four evening meetings. Two were held in my cave and two in Mau Ke-yeh's. Then we began working. We got up early in the morning and worked hard. By the autumn of 1953, the Old Secretary's farmers' co-operative, Li Yiu-hua's Farmers' Co-operative, had become very prosperous. They had increased the number of their oxen to seven and they had 120 goats. Although we too had worked hard and had increased the number of our cattle and donkeys, things had gone better for them. We talked about joining his co-operative.

But many were against it. Those who were most against it were Fu Hai-tsao, Li Chiao, Tung Yang-chen and Li Yang-pei (he is dead now). They said: 'Over there they have no valley land, but we have. If they can manage with their poor land, we can do even better without them.' We held many meetings. We kept on at it evening after evening. There was great discussion. 'We have good land,' they said. 'We shall lose on the deal.' That was their only reason and their only argument.

At the first meeting, it had been four for and four against. But in January 1954, when we had the last meeting, I said: 'There are quite a lot of us. We shall have the right to vote. It isn't certain that we shall lose by going over. We shall be in the majority in this farmers' co-operative, so you don't need to be afraid. It will be all right, if we stick together.' Then Fu Hai-tsao said: 'All right. In that case we can join. If it is as you say, then I vote for joining. But we must stick together afterwards.' That gave us a majority for joining Li Yiu-hua's Farmers' Co-operative. When the three others realized this, they gave in. They said: 'All right. Then we'll join too, so that we can stick together.' After that we joined. In this way the whole of Liu Ling's Labour Group for Mutual Help joined Li Yiu-Hua's Agricultural Co-operative.

There were eight of us joined: Fu Hai-tsao, Li Yang-pei, Li Chiao, Li Hung-fu, Mau Ke-yeh, Tung Yang-chen, Ma Juei-ching and I. Later other households joined individually: Li Hai-kuei, Tsao Chen-kuei, Li Yü-hsin and Li Hai-ching. There were four members in Li Yiu-hua's Farmers' Co-operative: Li Yiu-hua, Li Hai-chen, Li Hai-chun and Li Hai-yuan. In the discussions that now began, Li Hai-yuan left the farmers' co-operative and farmed on his own.

In January 1954 we had a long meeting to lay down the rules for the farmers' co-operative. There were eight meetings in a row. We changed the name from Li Yiu-hua's Agricultural Co-operative to Liu Ling Agricultural Co-operative; we chose a leader and various labour leaders. We changed the name to Liu Ling Agricultural Co-operative because people got up at the meetings and said: 'We don't belong to Li Yiu-hua. If we belong to anyone, it's the village of Liu Ling.' Li Yiu-hua was elected leader; Ma Hai-hsiu became deputy leader; Li Hai-chun, Kao Yü-kuei's husband who now works in the offices of the people's commune, became book-keeper, and I became treasurer. Ma Juei-ching became labour leader and Li Hai-kuei deputy labour leader. One year later, in 1955, we comprised thirty-two households.

We held a meeting every time we were to buy anything. We decided what we were going to buy and who should buy it. They said that I was the best one to buy a horse and a mule. We were to have those for the carts. We had already bought a two-wheeled horse-cart with motor-car wheels. It had been a year of good progress. I went to the town and bought a mule that cost 115 Y and a horse that cost 45 Y. People were pleased with my purchases. Especially pleased that I had managed to get the horse so cheap.

Now the others could see that things were going well for us. They saw all the things we bought. They said: 'Things are going well for you. We are just as we were.' Then we told them that they could join; but most of them replied that they didn't want to do that. They had good land down in the valley, of course; they had good donkeys and they had no desire to go in with us. For them it was the good land they had which was the main thing.

For us, the work went better. Of course, at first, people saw to their own fields most and thought the others did things badly, but there was no great antagonism and little by little it was overcome. I myself had not really properly believed in it all, although I had been for the idea and had worked for it. But I saw that it was doing all right. On the other hand, I now thought seriously that I was far too old to be treasurer. At every meeting I got up and said: 'Let the young people look after the cash. I am old and I cannot read and I can't keep books and, if there's a mistake and there's money missing, it would be difficult for me to find out what has happened. Let me get out of doing this.' But the meeting just answered: 'You do the work well and you are honest and there has never been any money missing, and you are painstaking and thorough and you got that horse so cheap. You're the right person to be treasurer.' We had that discussion in March 1955. And when the other sixteen families joined, it just meant more work for me.

I had talked to them and told them to join. I said to Li Yü-teh, Wang Fung-li's father-in-law: 'Although you have a good ox and good land, you have no security as long as you are an individualist and farm by yourself. Do you remember what happened with Kau Yü-hua down in Seven-mile Village? His ox died and the whole family wept for several days, because then he had lost everything. If he had been a member of an agricultural co-operative, he would have been saved.

Then Li Yü-teh said: 'That is true. You are right there. At times it can be a good thing if there are several of you. It can be more secure.' I replied: 'Think about it. If, when you have thought about it, you reach the conclusion that you ought to join, you can speak to our book-keeper, Li Hai-chun.' A week later, Li Yü-teh came and said: 'I have thought now. I shall apply.' He was the last. Then, thirty-two house-holds had joined Liu Ling Agricultural Co-operative. After that, we elected Wang Fung-li, Li Yü-teh's son-in-law, to be labour leader. He was young and energetic, and was known to be a good farmer.

But there were still some who were reluctant. Tung Yang-chen worried for a long time about his land in the valley. He could not let it go; he thought about it the whole time and in the end the others talked to him about it and said: 'Don't be so anxious.' Then he calmed down. In the co-operative, we had one labour team and that was divided into two groups. Each group cultivated an area, but the two groups helped each other.

In February 1956 we formed the East Shines Red Higher Agricul-tural Co-operative. Then we incorporated Wangchiakou and Hutoma villages. We had spent a fortnight making propaganda. In this we had to drive home the socialist principle, 'To each according to his work', all the way. People were agreed about that. That was the right prin-ciple. Wangchiakou was with us about that, but Hutoma Village was not so easy. People there said that Hutoma would lose by it all. They thought that it would be an amalgamation at their expense. Liu Ling had more people and greater power and Hutoma would just be el-bowed aside. It was Mu Ju-tsai, who is now leader of Hutoma Village Labour Group, who was most against this amalgamation. He was not against the socialist principle, he told us; he thought that Hutoma Village could accept that. But he said at several meetings that Hutoma did not want to join up with Liu Ling.

Tung Yang-chen, for his part, did not like losing his land. Because now we were all pooling our land properly and were going to stop paying dividends on land; from then on we were just going to give dividends on actual work. Tung Yang-chen said: 'I have such good land in the valley. Why should I have to lose it? If I too had been one of those who only have poor hill land, then I would have been entirely for this principle, but I happen to have my land in the valley.' Anyway, gradually they were all talked over and we formed the East Shines Red Higher Agricultural Co-operative.

I continued as treasurer for it until April 1956. Then I had a very serious talk with the Old Secretary, Li Yiu-hua, and told him that it really could not go on any longer. Everything had now become so much bigger; it was all too complicated for me. It had not been onerous when it was just a question of looking after the money and stores for a small union of a few households, where everyone knew each other. It had become hard when it was a whole farmers' co-operative with over thirty households, but now that it was an improved agricultural co-operative comprising many villages, I simply could not manage the work any longer. So, a new treasurer for the improved agricultural co-operative was elected at the meeting in April and I moved to the labour group for vegetable cultivation. There I was elected leader in April 1956.

The income from the labour group for vegetable cultivation was large. In 1956 it was roughly 8,000 Y; after that it rose every year by about 1,000 Y. I was responsible for the labour group, but now I had the possibility of having my own treasurer, and I chose Chang Cheng-pong and got him elected. He has moved to Seven-mile Village, but he really is from Liu Ling and has worked as treasurer for the labour group for vegetable cultivation since he was elected in 1956.

In 1958 we became a people's commune, but there was no discussion to speak of and I don't remember anything special happening or anything being changed. The labour group for vegetable cultivation has worked in the same way right from 1956. We decide at our members' meetings how much we are going to cultivate and what we shall grow, we consult with the committee of the labour brigade about our plans and then we take our decisions at the members' meetings. It has been the same every year. There has never been any change at any time in any way after the introduction of the people's commune. All binding decisions have to be taken at our members' meetings. 1956 as 1958 and 1958 as 1962. Sometimes we hold a members' meeting every week, depending on the season and the work. Just now, during the harvest, there has been a short pause of a few weeks, but we shall be holding one in a few days' time immediately after the brigade committee meeting.

Now the green-vegetable season is almost over, and we are on onions now. Every day two of our members drive into Yenan to sell the vegetables. That is an easy and a pleasant job, so we take it in turns. We sell to the vegetable company and what's left we sell in the market. This has been so since 1951. The vegetable company pays twenty per cent less than the market price. But we are bound to go to them first, before we are allowed to sell in the market. We get the best prices in the morning; towards afternoon the market price drops all the time. There are no fixed prices. It's been market price for vegetables all the time since 1956. The vegetable company pays cash when it buys. If we have a lot to do, we can fetch the money later, if we like.

In 1961, the labour group for vegetable cultivation earned roughly 14,000 Y. But this money is not divided directly among the members of the group. We, of course, are part of Liu Ling Labour Brigade and we are the group that brings in the most cash. So, the money is handed over to Liu Ling Labour Brigade in the same way as the other labour groups hand their income over. Then the whole income from the entire labour brigade is divided among the members according to their amount of work. Incidentally, the labour group for vegetable cultivation also grows corn. The deputy labour leader, Fu Hai-tsao, is responsible for corn cultivation.

Three times a day we fetch a load of human excrement from the town. It's thanks to this manure that we can produce so many vegetables. We tip the shit into the big dung-pit on the other side of the road, from which we get the manure for growing our vegetables. Every load we fetch from the town is about 1,000 jin. That makes 3,000 jin a day. We have made an arrangement with the sanitary department of Yenan town administration, allowing us to empty twenty-one latrines a day. We take seven latrines at a time. The sanitary department has allocated all the latrines in Yenan town in this way, and the various labour groups empty them.

The excrement of the people in Liu Ling and the dung from their private pigs goes to their private plots. But if any family has any over, the labour group for vegetable cultivation will pay 0·40 Y cash for two buckets amounting to 100 jin together.

Last year we got electricity here. It reached this side, but not over to Shiaoyuanchihou. We have 220-volt A.C. and it costs 0·25–0·26 Y a kilowatt. Our costs of installation were roughly 10,000 Y. We borrowed part of this. Then the question of a pump cropped up. We are, of course, forced to water our vegetables a lot. We dug the well at the vegetable fields in 1957; that's the best water in the whole district, considerably better than the water here in the village. Vegetables need a lot of water, especially during the dry season. But we had to employ two donkeys and one man every day pumping up the water: one donkey in the morning and one in the evening. Altogether that cost ten yuan a day. Seeing that it was so expensive, we discussed buying an electric pump. In February 1961, the labour brigade decided that we should have an electric pump. That pump pays for itself. The cost of electricity for the pump from 1 January 1962 to 30 July 1962 was thirty-four yuan. We haven't had a bill for the autumn yet.

Things are going very well for us. There are two of us working in the family: my stepson, Liu Ching-tsei, and myself. We work. I am not a party member. I have never been interested in politics. Before, we were oppressed. The poor had no rights. We owned nothing. When I came here I had just an iron pot. Now I should need several ox-carts to move all my things. I have a bicycle and a hand-cart with rubber-tyred wheels. Now, if one works hard, one can live really well.

Fu Hai-tsao, the one who wanted to be a singer, aged 39

WE came to Yenan from Hengshan when I was five. That was during the great famine of 1928. We had been thrown out. My father brought the family with him here. Father starved to death the next year. We went about begging in 1929. We had nothing to eat. Father went to Chaochuan to gather firewood and beg food, but he didn't get any. He was carrying elm leaves and firewood when he fell by the roadside. We waited for him all night. In the morning, when he hadn't come, Mother said: 'Now let's go and see what's happened to him.' Then Mother and Uncle and I walked along the road towards Chaochuan. I was the one who saw him first. He was lying on his face and was dead. The elm leaves and firewood were still there beside him. No one had touched a thing. The elm leaves were for us to eat. He wasn't ill; he had just starved to death. Mother says that he used to be big and strong and had been a good worker, thoughtful and kind to the family and open-handed if anyone was ill. That is my earliest memory: of always being hungry, and of Father lying there dead in the road.

After that, we went into Yenan and lived by begging. Mother begged for us. She did not eat much. Six months later she married Tsao Shen-yung. That's why I am called Fu after my father and Tsao after Stepfather. He was poor. He also had debts of 300 silver dollars. He had an ox and brought in firewood for the town. But it was not easy for him to feed so many people and at the same time pay his debts. He had had to borrow the money from a merchant who had the shop, Yushenkwei, in Yenan town. He charged big interest on his money. Stepfather had bought the ox to enable him to till his land properly. We were living then in Suchianan, fifteen li from here. But he wasn't able to manage his debt, so we had to leave the land and in 1932 we came to Liu Ling. Here Stepfather rented ten mu from Li Hsiu-tang's father. But we worked most fetching firewood from the common lands and transporting it to the town.

I began working with Stepfather when I was eight. We cut firewood up on the hillside. We had to protect the ox from the authorities as well as we could, because the yamen in Yenan, that is the authorities there, used to requisition animals for their transports. Because of that, we had built a special cave for our ox up on the hillside. We drove into the town with the firewood early in the morning, then back to Liu Ling and up on to the hill to cut more wood. The most important thing was that the authorities should not get their eye on us and take our ox from us. In those days, the rentals were thirty jin per mu for hill land and forty-five jin per mu for valley land. We had to pay taxes besides. But we cut the firewood on the common lands. We were poor and I was always hungry. What I remember best of my childhood is that I was never able to eat my fill, but was always hungry. We were oppressed. One day, when I was eleven, Stepfather said to me: 'Child, the sufferings of the poor are going to end now. People are saying that there is a Red Army, which is setting up soviets everywhere and dividing everything up equally among the people. They are even dividing up heaven and earth and giving them to the poor, and if a poor person hasn't any food, they give him something to eat and they give land to those who haven't any and animals to those without.' Stepfather told me about this when we were working up on the common lands. That was before the Red Army came here.

In 1935, the whole of this region became red. The merchant stopped coming to demand his interest. There were eight households in Liu Ling then, and we made a distribution of the land. Many people were worried and anxious. They wondered if the communists would be able to stay in power. 'If we take the land and later the Red Army is beaten, we shall have to bear the blame,' they said. They didn't think the Red Army looked strong enough. One old man called Ai Shen-you said: 'I won't touch anyone's land. I have always been a day labourer and farmhand and I intend to go on being one. That's the safest.' An old woman called Hsiu said: 'I don't want to take any land. I have only one grandson left. He is the last of my family. If I take any of the land, the landowner will kill him when he comes back. And if they cut my grandson's head off, my family will be dead.' Stepfather and Mother discussed the question a great deal. Stepfather thought that we ought not

to take part in dividing up the land; that that would be dangerous and that it was unnecessary to run such a risk. The landowners were strong and they always used to win in the long run. But Mother said: 'There are only three of us in our family. If we don't take any land, we shall die just the same, because we shall starve to death. If the landowner comes back, he can't do more than kill us. So that we might just as well take the land from the beginning and hope for the best.' The communists had people making propaganda here, and they talked with people and in the end persuaded them. They said: 'We are strong enough to deal with the landowners. If we hadn't been strong enough, we should not have begun the revolution. You are all poor and how are you going to be able to live if you don't have any land?' So everyone joined forces and went and divided up Li Yü-tse's land.

I now worked with Stepfather in the fields, and every year he and I discussed what we should grow on our land. We lived very happy lives then. Ganbus often came and held meetings about the three mountains the Chinese people was in the process of casting off itself. I joined the Young Pioneers. There we had classes about which districts were red and liberated and which were held by the Whites or the Japanese. The twelve-year-olds joined the Red Guard. That was usual. After all, we had to learn to defend our land.

The leader of the people in our village was Tung Chi-hwei. He was Tung Yang-chen's father. He was the one who forced the distribution of land through. All the landowners hated him. He was a big strong man with a round face and laughed a lot. Whenever the enemy was on the way from the town making for the village, he sent a message to the soviet area, for we were on the very fringe of it. He organized the Red Guard in the village and scared off the enemy. He put up posters on the telegraph poles and talked with everyone about how we must root out the landowners and their gang.

Tung Chi-hwei had a brother and two children, a son, Tung Yang-chen, and a daughter. His brother took to the hills and became a guerrilla. Nobody knows what happened to him after that. He was probably killed somewhere. Everyone had confidence in Tung Chi-hwei and people asked his advice about everything. Once, when I was listening, he said: 'Things are difficult now, but a time's coming when our difficulties will be overcome and all our enemies crushed, and then everyone will be able to eat their fill and everyone will have clothes and plenty.' He comforted people, when the difficulties came. Everyone had faith in him. But one day the enemy came and caught him. It was Li Hsiu-tang's father who wanted to have him killed, and it was Li Han-hua who took him prisoner. Li Han-hua was Li Hsiu-tang's brother-in-law.

But the people loved Tung Chi-hwei, and they had a letter written and sent to the town saying that they would stand guarantee for him, but that did not help. Li Han-hua had his head cut off. And they did not even hand over the body, and his widow kept weeping loudly for a long time afterwards. But Li Yü-teh had a relative who lived in the town, and he was able to get hold of the body and smuggle it out of the town and hide it under some stones to stop the street-dogs from eating it. He had said: 'After all, it's one of our villagers they have beheaded!' He hid himself at the place of execution and, when the executioners had gone, he took the body and brought it to safety. Later, the body was brought to Liu Ling and buried here. But Tung Chi-hwei really came from Hengshan, so his uncle had him moved up there. But I've heard that the family is now planning to bring him back home to Liu Ling.

In the Young Pioneers, I was trained in bayonet fighting and learned how to use a spear. There, too, we had political talks about the war with Japan. More and more families moved here. There were more and more cattle and donkeys. We had got a lot of land in the land distribution. We had twenty-five mu of fertile land down in the valley and 105 mu up on the hillside. Stepfather and I worked in the fields; we had cattle and lived well.

They had begun teaching me to read and write in the Young Pioneers. I didn't like that. I preferred being outdoors working with Stepfather. But in the end they managed to persuade me to start going to school. I went for three days, then I ran away. Perhaps it was short-sighted, but I had starved when I was young and I never wanted to starve in my life again. We had land now and, if I worked hard in the fields, we would have more to eat. Now, of course, I see that that was a childish way to reason, because if I had really learned to read and write, I would have been of much more use to the village and the people and our country. Now I can hardly read at all.

Then Yenan was bombed by the Japs and everything was de-stroyed and the people there were evacuated. Then the Red Guard was re-organized and made a people's militia and I joined it. That was about 1945, I think. We were to look after the public safety. We were organized like the army, in platoons and so on. At night we kept guard against saboteurs and enemy agents.

The countryside was the most important, because the land and the harvest is the basis of everything, and so Chairman Mao asked us to till twice as much. In that way we should have enough and more than enough. We worked hard. When Hu Tsang-nan came, almost everyone left Liu Ling. We went up into the hills. I was in the people's militia then. We had buried all our possessions and all our corn. Hu Tsung-nan destroyed everything, and his troops ate and ate. They discovered our grain stores, and they stole our cattle. The guerrillas fought against Hu Tsung-nan's troops. They knew their hills, and we in the militia helped them.

At that time I was in Hsuchiachien. There were no K.M.T. soldiers in that village. If any came, we fled. When they left, we came back. We did not work. It was only a few who went out to the fields. We slept by day and at night we fought the K.M.T. We were in a different place every day. We went back to Liu Ling as soon as Hu Tsung-nan fled. At home, everything had been destroyed. They had even broken the mill-stones. It was like building a new farm. We dug up the corn the K.M.T. had not found. It was not much, but more than most people had. We managed. That year we sowed only the valley fields. Our own authorities came back and the people too.

We formed a labour exchange group, so as to be able to get the work done. We worked for each other in turn. Later, in 1952, we re-organized this into a labour group for mutual help. Strictly speaking, it was just the same thing, only better organized. We had now decided to work according to a plan every day and not just as things came along. Ma Juei-ching was made labour leader for the group, and I was elected deputy labour leader. There were eight households in the group. We drew up a timetable, and one day we worked for one household and the next day for another. The one we worked for had to provide food for the whole group. But it was not easy to make a timetable like that. There were many squabbles. Li Chung-ying was the worst; he always wanted to be first. Because it was often important to be the one who got ploughed first or his seed in first. In the end, we agreed to take it in turn. But he was never properly satisfied and then he married a girl from the town and, when his father-in-law died, he left the village and went to live in the house he had inherited.

Being leader of the labour group for mutual help was a thankless task. Every day there was someone who said: 'You are unfair.' Sometimes, for example, a person would say: 'Turn about, turn about! Can't you see that I have many more weeds in my field than he has? Weeds don't bother to grow in turn. If you don't weed my field today, I shall suffer for it.' In the end we chose a small group that had to deal with all such questions. If any was altogether too difficult to resolve, we had to have a democratic discussion. But, as I said, it wasn't easy and I think that these difficulties made certain persons more inclined to form a farmers' co-operative than they otherwise would have been. In 1953, we formed a farmers' co-operative, in which the land was to be employed alike. But then I didn't want to be a member any longer. We had a lot of land and good land, of course; we had cattle and were a small family with four grown-ups and two children and several able to work. I didn't think it looked as though there would be any such freedom in the farmers' co-operative. We knew how to run our own fields, we didn't need anyone to tell us now what we should do. So Stepfather and I agreed not to bother about it, but to manage on our own. Besides, I felt it had been onerous being labour leader. There was nothing but surliness and squabbling. People were never satisfied, and one was always being accused of being unfair and showing favouritism. In the mornings, when I had to fetch people for work, I was often told: 'What are you standing there nagging for?' Well, we discussed all that in the family and decided to farm on our own.

But things went well for the farmers' co-operative, better than for us. People from the village came and talked with us, wanting us to join. Stepfather let himself be persuaded. He talked with me and said: 'We eight neighbour families have worked together so long, we are neighbours and good friends and the others are in the farmers' co-operative and they have bigger incomes.' But I didn't want to. It took time, but in the end Stepfather talked so much about it that I applied to be a member. But I wasn't going to be labour leader.

I was one of the last families to join the co-operative. At the meeting people said: 'You work so hard. You should be elected group leader.' But then I got up and said: 'The group leader has to do as much work in the fields as anyone. But he has to get up earlier in the morning and he has to go to bed later in the evening and all the time he has to be thinking everything out and planning the work. He can only have time for that at night. But he isn't paid anything extra for this, but is just accused of being unfair. I remember what it was like when I was labour leader in the labour group for mutual help. But that was still possible. Because the labour group for mutual help was such that, there, each one owned his own land; but now in this farmers' co-operative, it is socialism, and that means that each is to work according to his ability and be paid according to his work, and that is a principle that I don't yet know; and, as I haven't any experience of it and anyway don't want to, I don't want to be made group leader.' But they elected me even so. And afterwards they came up to me and said: 'We are going to obey you and follow your instructions; we did that before and we shall do so now and we shan't grumble.' But I was still mistrustful and had no wish to do it, so ganbus from the party came to me and said: 'You are a hard worker. There's a lot you can do. One has to serve. And because you work well and can do a lot, you must also serve the people. Having to get up a little earlier in the morning surely isn't anything to complain about. You must serve the cause of the people.' So then I thought over what they had all said and changed my mind and agreed to let myself be elected group leader, and I have worked as that all these years since. In 1955 Liu Ling Farmers' Co-operative was re-organized as the East Shines Red Higher Agricultural Co-operative. I was beginning to have experience of the work and things were going easier. Everyone was to be paid according to the work he performed. The work had to be planned in the best possible way. One had to avoid any form of waste. If the labour group committee meetings are conducted in the right way and the labour leaders are reliable, the work should go smoothly and no unpleasantness arise.

Now we have more households than ever and that means even greater responsibility. There aren't the same households in the group as before. You see, in 1955, we re-organized the labour group. That year we set up the labour group for vegetable cultivation. After that we took the old people into our group. After he's fifty, no one is able to do a full day's work, but he can at least work with vegetables. We increased our production of vegetables. Since 1955, life has improved steadily. There haven't been any sensational changes, but it has become slowly better year by year. Two things have happened since the formation of the people's commune in 1958: we have got an electric water pump, that was decided at the brigade meeting, and last year we increased the vegetable area from twenty-four to fifty-two mu. We decide for ourselves how we are to work and what we shall grow. We have collective management, because everybody discusses everything until we are agreed.

One of the difficulties of working a farmers' collective is the necessity for keeping books. It is difficult to find people who can do this work. As long as we were just a labour group for mutual help, we managed without keeping proper books. Then we just had a simple work daybook. That was kept by Jen Huai-wan, who has now left the village and become party secretary in the pottery at Yenan.

I joined the party in 1955. Before that I was in the armed militia; now that I am older, I am an ordinary militia man. No, we have not introduced any extra remuneration for the labour leader. We aren't thinking of doing so either. It would not be good for production morale. One should be paid for physical work, not for the other. The other must be voluntary and unpaid.

The people who really persuaded me to join the co-operative and made me join the party were the Old Secretary, Li Yiu-hua, and my best friend, Li Hai-chen. I am a couple of years older than he, but he talked seriously with me: 'Now that I have joined, you must join,' he said.

I have always liked singing. No, my mother never sang; she had suffered too much to be bothered with that sort of thing. But under the occupation 1947-8 and the following year, I was a lot together with an old man, who was called Chou. He liked playing and singing. He taught me all I know. He used to say that he was the one who knew most songs in northern Shensi. He got many of us to sing. We used to sing when we went out to work in the mornings, and the older people said: 'Listen to the idiots.' Then old Chou died. But I went on singing. I sing mostly love songs, old songs, you know what I mean. I sing while we are working. It seems to go easier that way. When people are tired and the work is slow, they usually ask me to sing. We sing a lot in the village here now. We make up our own words and create quite new songs. We sing about the things we are thinking of. We sing mostly about love.

One day a man from Peking came. He was called Ching and he worked for some organization. I don't remember what it was called, but it had something to do with music. He travelled about writing down what people sang. When he came to Yenan, he went to Yenan's Art Ensemble and there he was told that I sang a lot and had taught them lots of songs. I had had three singers from that troupe out here for some days and taught them singing. They were called Li and Niu and Chou. They came out to me and sang with me here. Now they told Ching to come and see me. He came to Liu Ling and visited me and asked me to sing. As I sang, he sat beside me and wrote it all down in a little book, just as you are doing. Then he said to me: 'Come with me to Peking! You must study and become a singer. In Peking they will teach you everything. You will do your country great service as a singer. You will travel all over the world.' But Mother said: 'You are my only son. I gave you birth and I have worked and starved for you. Your father and stepfather and all their fathers before them worked on the land. If you go away from us, there is no one else to look after us. There will be no one to bury me.' Then she began to weep. Then I wept too. My wife did not weep. She said nothing at all. She just walked out. Then Ching said that I could at least promise to come to the big festival of folk music in Sian. He promised that I should be able to come home again, if I wanted. 'If you don't want to go to Peking, no one can force you,' he said. 'But you can at all events come to Sian. You must see a big city once in your life. You must know what it is you are missing if you don't come with me to Peking. If you come to Peking, the government will look after you. You and your family will never need to go hungry, even though you aren't working on the land. Your parents won't suffer any hardship.' When he said that, I could not refuse any longer, but decided to go with him to Sian and see what it was like.

But Mother wept and said: 'I shall die and you will never see me again. This is all the thanks I get for starving for you. You just leave us.' You see, of course, I was the only Fu and also the only Tsao left. My wife didn't say anything to me. My stepfather came with me into Yenan, whence I was to take the bus for Sian. We walked in together. He hadn't said anything about my trip, but just before the bus started, he said: 'It would be good, of course, if you did come back.'

I stayed twenty days in Sian. It was a big and beautiful city. We had a music festival the whole time, and when I was free and not singing myself, I went to the opera and recitals and shadow-plays. In the end, I was thinking: 'It is fun singing. I would like to sing all my life. I would like to go to Peking all right.' But Mother had said that she would die if I left the village, and the more I remembered that and the more I thought of Mother, the more I realized that it was impossible for me to go to Peking. After twenty days I said to Ching: 'I must go home now.' He just replied: 'That is a pity.' He gave me a ticket for the bus to Yenan, and I have never seen him since, nor heard of him. And so I returned to Liu Ling. When I came to the cave, Mother said: 'I thought you had gone for ever.'

People say of Fu Hai-tsao: He is a very nice chap. He and Lin Hu-fu are the best-looking men in the village. The women talk a lot about how good-looking he is. He sings very well. His wife is tall and slim. She has a savage temper. She talks aloud and is far from being the gentle wife. He is really rather henpecked at home. There's a standing joke about her: 'If she had married a man with the same temper as she has, their marriage would not have lasted a single day. But she has been lucky.' But she is the best worker among the women in the village. She is as strong as a big man. She can carry a hundred jin and think nothing of it, when other women can scarcely manage fifty. So one can also say that Fu Hai-tsao is a fortunate man to have got such a hard-working and industrious wife. She contributes a lot to the family's economy.

Actually, it is a pity that he did not go to Peking to study. He sings so well. But his mother has a very strong will, and he is her only son. So she wouldn't let go of him. He is very respectful to his stepfather. The older people in the village consider him an example to all the others, because he is the most faithful son in the village. He scolds his wife occasionally despite her temper and his being so nice, but only because she does not show enough respect to his parents.

He is well known for getting up early and going to bed late. He is considered one of the hardest workers in the village. He was elected labour leader, because he is good at organizing the work and does so much himself. Every evening he tells what has to be done the next day.

He speaks rather softly, but he likes a joke. He loves fun. The women like talking with him. He does not always reply, but he has such a good smile. They aren't irritated by his not replying, because he gives them such beautiful smiles. He is always calm and friendly. He is never agitated. He never swears. He never rushes about and he never flies out at you. His is a placid temperament. Perhaps he's a bit slow and it does take him some time to make up his mind; but whatever happens, he is always the same. He never lets himself be upset or ruffled.

He really wanted to go to Peking. In his heart of hearts he badly wanted to be able to sing. But he gave way to his family. The older people praise him for that. They say it shows that he is a good son. The young people, on the other hand, think he did wrong, that he ought to have gone.

Ma Chen-hai, aged 65

I GREW up in the village of Fengchiatsah in Suiteh hsien. It was a small village. My family had always been farmers. We owned fifteen mu and we rented thirty mu from Ma, the landlord. We had to pay thirty-four jin per mu in rent. The landlord, Ma, had a moneylending concern called Tsunteh. We did not borrow money from him, but we were not able to pay our rent. He took interest on it and interest on the interest. It was a high rent. The years were not bad ones and the crops were middling good, but we were six mouths to feed in the family, and in the end our debt had increased to 1,200 jin of grain, so then he took our fifteen mu of land from us. I was twelve or thirteen years old then. There was no way we could get out of it. We could not get out of his clutches. The next year we rented the fields that before had been our own, and had to pay thirty jin per mu rental for them. Father said: 'What can we do? The landowner is hard. He takes our land from us. But they have the money and the power, and there's no way out for us. We must bow to it.' Father had no hope any longer. He did not dare talk with the others in the village. If he had, he would have been suspected of stirring up mischief. Mother just wept. Having four children, it was hard for her to have lost those fifteen mu. She kept saying: 'Life is much worse now.'

I gathered fuel and plucked grass. I looked after our goat and the landowner's donkey. We were to feed it and, if it foaled, the landlord and we were to share equally. During the winter the landlord took the donkey back and rode round gathering his rents. My older brother went to Chitan hsien and started work there as a day labourer. My second brother worked in our fields and I was now fourteen, so I went out as herd-boy. I got five strings of cash a year and three meals a day. I worked for a relation, an uncle. The landlord, Ma, lived forty li away, so we did not see him often. But his agent, the manager of Tsunteh, his moneylending business, had a round, bearded face. He was called Ma Shou-chen. He collected rents and ran the moneylending. He was not a nice person. He was always stiff and dignified. He never smiled. He never showed either anger or pleasure. He was just suave and as hard as stone. We never saw a government official and I have no idea when the dynasty went. At all events, we never noticed anything in our village of those revolutions. Everything stayed the same, and the farmers suffered just as much all the time.

When I was twenty, I began work as a day labourer. I worked now here, now there, and at the same time in Father's fields. I used to earn ten cents and my food for a day's work. I did that for ten years. During those ten years Mother died and I got married. Father had become crippled with rheumatism and unable to work in the fields any longer and so had become doorkeeper for the moneylending business, Tsunteh, and all we brothers had set up households of our own. All our land was now out of the family's hands, and we all rented land from the landowner and did odd work as day labourers as well. We brothers took fifteen mu each of the forty-five mu that father used to rent. The total rental remained the same. It was not a good life. It was even a bit worse than when I was a child.

When I was thirty, I had three children. That made five mouths to feed. The heaviest harvest I ever had was 2,100 jin; 450 jin went to the landlord, leaving 1,650 for seed and the family's food. And that was our best year. On the average we got about 900 jin, and of this the landlord took 450 and we got 450. That wasn't enough and we could not live on it, so I went on going out as a day labourer. We ate wild herbs and made bread out of chaff. We mixed pumpkin and potato with our food. We did not pay taxes. No one in our village did.

I worked by the day for the landlord as well as other people. If one worked hard, they were pleased, and if one didn't work well, they said 'We don't want to see you again.' I was known as a good worker. They often came to me to ask for my help. There was no valley land in my village. All our fields were on the slopes. I cultivated the fifteen mu I rented.

In 1928, there was a famine. There was a bad drought. The whole crop from all the fifteen mu I rented was only 100 jin that year. We could not pay our rent. After the harvest, we were eating grass. Then we walked the fifty li down to the Yellow River. There, we got ourselves, the children and I, across to Shansi. In Shansi I worked as a porter. I carried rice. Then, with the money I earned, I bought and sold corn. In that way, I was able to get enough corn to survive. But we were starving the whole time. I sold all our possessions. That is all long ago now. I was young and strong then, and could bear a lot.

The following year, 1929, was even worse. There was no rain in the first half of the year and the drought was awful. We were starving. We bought chaff from the landowner. It was expensive. We had to pay three silver dollars for a measure, each measure containing thirteen or fourteen jin. I was working as a day labourer. It was not difficult for me to get work then. Many people had moved away from the village, some had died, and there was a shortage of decent labour. I got thirty cents a day. But I could no longer get a jin of corn with a day's work. Though my wage was so much higher, I only got a jin of chaff for a day's work. Rain fell in the second half of the year and there was a harvest of sorts. We got in 400 jin and the landlord took 200 of it.

But 1930 was better. We got 900 jin then. But the landowner claimed 700 jin, saying: 'You paid nothing in 1928 and you owe 250 jin from 1929. But I shall be generous, because times were bad, and not charge interest or interest on interest.' Later, we repaid the debt with between thirty and sixty jin a year.

No, we never heard the K.M.T. mentioned and no one ever said anything about Sun Yat-sen. Or, if anyone did, or about the revolution, I must have forgotten it. We are just uneducated farmers and we forget so easily. Life went on as before. Everything was as usual. But in 1932-3 I heard people talking of the Red Army. 'Now there's a Red Army. When it comes, it will kill all the landowners and landlords,' they said. At this time, officials and officers from the K.M.T. went to other villages, but we never saw any in ours. But the landowner was said to have had dinner with them. So, it was all sudden my discovering that the K.M.T. and the Red Army existed and hearing about the revolution.

Ma Shou-chen, who managed the moneylending business, Tsunteh, and was the landowner's agent, spoke to us about the K.M.T. and the communists. He said: 'The K.M.T. wants what is best for you. The K.M.T. is good. The communists, on the other hand, want to steal your possessions and take your wives from you. The communists will share your wives with each other. The K.M.T. will protect you from that.' No, in our village no one was ever beaten or put in prison by the landowner. That wasn't necessary. Because, if you could not pay the rent, the landowner took the land you owned, and if you did not own land, you had to work to pay off the rent in the future.

I remember the day the Red Guard reached the village. That was in November 1934. People were saying: 'There are Red Guard men in the village.' We were very afraid. I scarcely dared go out. If I did go out and met one of my neighbours, we spoke softly together. One of the neighbours I met on the road said to me in a whisper: 'They're saying we shan't be oppressed any more.' It was only propagandists from the Red Guard that had come to the village, not the armed men of the army, and there was a K.M.T. band in the neighbourhood, so we were cautious. The propagandist who came then was called Kao Wen-shen. He was a man with a swarthy, sunburned face. He was a poor farmer from a neighbouring village, and I knew him. No, I don't know how he got into the Red Army or how he became a propagandist. But now I heard that he was in our village and was talking about the revolution. He stayed one night with us, and then went on somewhere else. Some days later, we heard that he had been executed by the K.M.T. He had come to another village and one of the poor farmers with whom he talked had informed his landlord about him, and the landlord had sent for the K.M.T. and they had come in the night and shot him on the spot. We told each other in whispers what he had said about the revolution and what had happened to him.

The first propagandist with whom I ever talked properly was Ma Chien-hsiang. I knew him well. He was a poor farmer who lived three li from here. He was chosen propagandist after the Red Guard took his village. Afterwards, he became a guerrilla commander. I believe he's still alive. He came to my home one evening and said: 'We ought not to listen to the K.M.T.'s rumours. We are not going to be oppressed by them any longer. We communists are going to destroy all the land-owners and all the war lords and generals and officials and share out the land as equals and then never pay any more taxes or rent to anyone.' I thought that sounded very nice, but I wondered whether poor people really would be able to overthrow the powerful. I could scarcely believe it. It was the winter of 1934–5 that we had these discussions.

But all the same, it was only propagandists who came to us, and the K.M.T. was still there. Everything had to be secret. Kao had been shot. Then, suddenly, all these propagandists vanished. The Red Guard never came and the K.M.T. was still there and everything was the same as before.

Some time later, people again began talking about the communists. They talked about Yenan and what things were like there. It was my younger brother, Ma Cheng-pong, who talked most to me about this. He had a donkey which he used for transport work and was in Yenan several times a year. He said: 'In Yenan there's a Chairman Mao, who has a government there. Life is not bad in Yenan now. The land has been divided up and the poor get enough to eat and can have clothes and fuel and are not oppressed by landowners.' Lots of people talked about this, but it's my brother I remember best. He was my brother, of course, and I had faith in what he told me. There were many people in my district who had started making for Yenan.

In March 1938, I had a talk with my wife about what we should do. I had given the land I had been renting back to its owner and was released from the rental, and we discussed what we ought to do now. 'Seeing it is hard for us here,' she said, 'couldn't you take the boy with you and go down to Yenan? If things really are so good there as people say, you can have a letter written to us or yourself come up and fetch us.' So then I sold all that I owned except my mattock. Then I gave all the money and all our corn to my wife and my two daughters and told them to wait for me. So then, I took my mattock, and I and the boy walked to Yenan. No one bothered to stop us. We were just poor refugees and nobody bothered his head about us. The K.M.T. knew where we were off to all right, but that made no difference, because we were poor.

We got to Yenan in May 1938. We searched out a relation, who had a little tea stall outside the town and there we lived. My relation said: 'There's a boy needed in Liu Ling to herd the beasts.' My boy was twelve years old then, and he went to Liu Ling. I myself began working in the mill at Peichuan. Yenan really was as good as people had said it was. Poor people were building themselves big caves. Everywhere were people moving in. After one year's work one could have corn, money, jute and much, much besides.

I worked at the mill for a month. Then I went over to Liu Ling to see how the boy was getting on. That was in the busiest month and they were weeding the fields. I helped them that day and then I went to Tsao Yu-fao and said: 'I would like to settle here.' 'That will be all right,' he said. So then I searched and found an abandoned cave, and I was told that I could start clearing new ground. I cultivated land up on the hillside, and I was able to borrow seed and tools from the communists. These loans were interest-free. In August 1938, I wrote to my wife, and, later, my brother, Ma Cheng-pong, sent her and my two daughters down to me in Liu Ling. After that, life became better and better every year. Then Hu Tsung-nan came. He stole 240 jin of millet from me. He slaughtered and ate my two pigs and he smashed everything of mine that could be smashed.

We had fled into the hills when Hu Tsung-nan was coming. We had tried to hide our corn first and we took our two pigs with us. We kept them hidden in a ravine. But one day, when I went down into the ravine to feed the pigs, the K.M.T. was there. They boxed my ears, hit me in the face and butchered the pigs on the spot. They swore at me and cursed me. The only payment I received for my pigs was a box on the ears. I did not dare protest or say anything. After that, they took me and my son with them to the town. When we got there, they let me go, but kept my son. When I got back to the village, there were only a few people there. Ten days later my son came back. He had been made to carry sacks of flour for them, but had managed to escape from them one night.

We wanted to be rid of Hu Tsung-nan. Whenever K.M.T. soldiers came to the village, we ran up into the hills. When they left the village, we came down again. The fields up on the hillsides could not be cultivated then. Nothing was grown then. When the corn began to grow up in the valley, Hu Tsung-nan put his horses to graze in the fields. They destroyed it all. Then they were driven out, and we began to work once more. Again life became slowly better and better.

We set up a labour group for mutual help. That is better than working on your own. The young people work together and chatter and sing, and that makes the work easier and go quicker than when they are all working on their own. If one falls ill, then the others look after one's fields in the meantime, and later on one can repay their day's work with one's own work. But there was a lot of squabbling in our labour group for mutual help and quarrelling about who was to be ploughed first. Earlier ploughing often means better crops.

People began talking about a farmers' co-operative. With one we would be able to get over those difficulties, they said, plough up the march lands, pool our oxen and get better crops. I agreed with the idea from the beginning. The harvest was good in the farmers' co-operative. But certain persons who had had more land or better land in the valley, or who had had more beasts, had not worked half as hard as I, because they were wretched workers, yet they got more corn and more money than I. That I thought was unfair and so, when the discussion about the improved agricultural co-operative began, I was from the very beginning all for us introducing the socialist principle. But now I am getting very old, and my son has had to take on responsibility for the family's affairs. But I talk a lot with him.

Life is good now. I do the household work, and at times I go down to our private plot and do a little work there. Mine is a peaceful old age. My two daughters are married and have children. My son is married and has children. I believe I have thirteen grandchildren now, and my eldest granddaughter is twenty and married and has children of her own. I have a calm and peaceful time of it. I spend the daytime with my grandchildren. But I don't see well. My eyes are almost finished and my teeth ache all the time. It is difficult for me to chew. I have toothache the whole time, especially in my left lower jaw.

Some years ago I went to my old village on a visit, but all my relatives were aged or dead, and the young did not know me. I shall have myself buried here in Liu Ling. I've decided that. I have my coffin all ready. It's made of proper thick wood. It's a very fine coffin.

People say of Ma Chen-hai: He is respected. He's an old man and respected.

His son, Ma Juei-ching, works very hard and is a capable person. He is responsible for one of the draught animals. His wife, Fan Yu-lien, died of heart disease last year. Ma Juei-ching married again in July 1962. He has a new wife.

Tables

Management Committee

Ching Chung-ying   Chairman, labour leader
Fu Hai-tsao   Deputy labour leader
Li Hai-fa   Book-keeper
Chang Chen-pong   Treasurer

Family Incomes, 1961

Head of household	Days' Work	Grain, jin	Cash, Y
From Seven-mile Village			
Chang Chen-an	307	1,535	644·70
Chang Chen-pong	279	1,395	585·90
Chang Hu-chen	285	1,425	598·50
Chao Huai-teh	187	935	392·90
From Hutoma Village			
Shueh Shen-huei	163	815	342·30

From Liu Ling Village

Ching Chung-ying	546	2,730	1,148·60
Tien Kuei-hua	119	595	249·90
Ma Juei-ching	266	1,330	558·60
Chang Shi-ming	164	820	344·40
Fu Hai-tsao	578	2,890	1,213·80
Mau Ke-yeh	159	795	333·90
Tsao Chen-yung	447	2,235	938·70
Tsao Chen-kuei	583	2,915	1,224·30
Ching Chung-wan	346	1,730	726·60
Tuan Fu-yin	163	815	343·30
Ma Hai-hsiu	97	485	203·70
Yang Kuei-ying	73	365	153·30
Yang Fu-lien	45	225	94·50
Kao Yü-kuei	36	180	75·60
Shi Yü-chieh	60	300	126·00

Social Subsidies from the Labour Groups' Assistance Fund, 1961:

Name	Jin	Reason
Tuan Fu-yin	200	Only one of five family members working.
Kao Yü-kuei	200	Husband working in Yenan.
Shi Yü-chieh	85	No able-bodied person in family. Recipient occupied mostly on his private plot.
Yang Kuei-ying	160	Husband working in Yenan.
Yang Fu-lien	120	Husband working in Yenan.

Resident in Seven-mile Village

Shu Hsiu-chu	60	Husband studying in Peking.
Chang Chen-pong	300	Only one of the eight members of the family is working.

Resident in Hutoma Village

Shueh Shen-huei	320	Only one person of the seven in family working.

Rewards to Merit Workers, 1961

Resident in Liu Ling Village

Fu Hai-tsao	Mattock
Ma Juei-ching	Mattock

Resident in Seven-mile Village

Chang Chen-an	Mattock
Chang Chen-ping	Scarf

Vegetable Production

	Area 1961 mu	Crop 1961 (round figs)	Area 1962 mu	Crop to 1 Sept. 1962
Chinese cabbage	8	48,000 jin	8	
Potatoes	9	27,000 jin	12	
Yellow carrots	2	6,000 jin	2	
Carrots	1	2,500 jin	1	
Lettuce	2	10,000	2	10,100
Turnips	3	10,500 jin	3	
Cucumber	2	2,000 jin	3	
Egg-fruit	4	12,000 jin	4	13,280 jin
Chilis	3	1,950 jin	3·5	
Leeks	1·5	1,350 jin	1·5	1,350 jin
Onion	2	13,000 bundles of 50	2	
Garlic	2	600 jin	2	618 jin
Tomatoes	3	7,840 jin	4	
Cabbage	5	15,000 jin	7	

Area 1961: 47·5 mu
Value of sales, 1961: 14,998 Y

Area 1962: 54 mu
Value of sales to 1 Sept. 1962: 8,885 Y

Grain Production
No figures for 1961
No figures for 1962

Part V
Liu Ling Labour Brigade

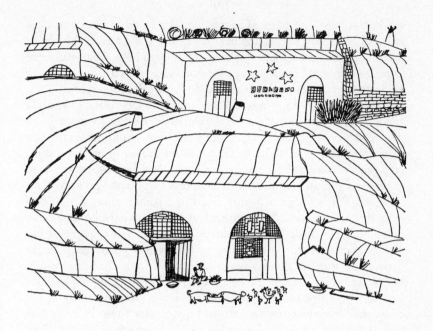

Feng Chang-yeh, leader of the brigade, aged 38

My grandfather and my father and all my ancestors have been farmers. I myself began at the age of seven, herding for others, and at twelve I began working in Father's fields. We had seventy-eight mu in Heng-shan hsien. In the month of January 1948, my wife and my son and I moved to Ten-mile Village. That was during the occupation. My son died later, and since then we have had a daughter. The first year I broke new ground up on the hillside. I was a breaker of new ground. I worked on my own like that for two years. In 1950 I was able to buy an ox, and things were easier then. The following year, 1951, I bought a donkey. In the first six months of 1952 we organized a labour exchange group, and I was elected its leader. There we helped each other with our work. But one never knew if people would turn up or not; it was just as it might be. So, during the next six months, we turned the labour exchange group into a labour group for mutual help. That was more organized. In that labour group, we decided at the start that we were going to turn up at definite times and do the work properly.

In 1953, we had got most of the farmers in the village to join the group. There were proper discussions and divided opinions about doing this. You see, in the labour exchange group, you could choose the best workers to exchange labour with; but in the labour group for mutual help each worker had a certain point rating. His day's work was rated at between one and ten points. At first, those who were good workers wouldn't hear of a permanently organized labour group for mutual help. 'If we exchange labour with a bad worker, we shall only lose by doing so,' they said. Then we discussed matters with them and explained that everyone's work was to be given a point rating in the democratic way, so that no one would suffer by exchanging labour, nor would anyone gain by being lazy or having a poor physique. 'Those who work properly shall have many points, those who work badly shall have few,' we told them. I myself saw from the beginning that this transformation was necessary. If people help one another, everyone can be better off, I thought. But it had to be done properly and properly thought out.

Between December 1953 and January 1954, we discussed turning our labour group into an agricultural co-operative. In general, one can say that those whose land was not good were for the idea; and that those who had good land down in the valley and a lot of manpower were against it. My neighbour, Chao Teh-pa, for example, got up during the discussion and said: 'I don't want to go up the hill and toil on the hill fields. I have good, fertile land down here in the valley, and this agricultural co-operative won't pay me. I can manage by myself.' Well, we reckoned out properly how many days' work he would get in an agricultural co-operative and how much his fields in the valley gave him as it was. We proved to him that large-scale farming and joint effort was much more rational, and that, in actual fact, he would gain by joining the agricultural co-operative. 'I'll hire people,' he replied. We told him that would become rather difficult. There would be no day labourers or farmhands to be had, once we had formed our collective. They would prefer to work for themselves in an agricultural co-operative than for anyone farming on his own. In the end we proved to him that he would get much more corn and more cash for his work if he joined the agricultural co-operative.

'That isn't of any significance,' he replied. 'It may well be that I should earn more. But if I am to choose between earning more and having to climb up the hill and toil there, or earn less and only have to cultivate my own fields down in the valley, then I prefer to earn less and not have to clamber about up on the hill.' After that, we had a serious talk with him. 'You want to hire people to work for you. That's exploitation. Why do you want to become rich on other people's work? Why should only you become rich? You are not going to get anyone to exploit. Choose how you want things to be. Do you want to be rich alone, or do you want us all to be well-off together? Do you want to be a decent person or not? Think about it.' He thought about it and joined.

I was elected leader of Wanchiakou Agricultural Co-operative. After the harvest of 1954, I reckoned that what we had said really was true. We had all got more corn than we had had before. There were two reasons for this. First, we had been able to plan to use our labour more rationally; and, secondly, we had manured better. We had been able to manure better, because we had bought a flock of goats, and because now, as a co-operative, we had detailed two men, who every day drove in to Yenan town and fetched a load of human excrement. This was new and we would not have been able to get it without being organized. We had made an arrangement with the town that we got the shit in return for emptying the latrines. That was a fair exchange. The townspeople were rid of it and we got manure.

There still were people who farmed on their own here and there. We had ten of them. That year we helped them as well. In that way they too had better harvests. We helped them weed, if we had finished weeding our fields and theirs were still unweeded; we also helped them with their harvest. We did not take payment for this. We just let them feed us on the days we worked for them. They wanted to pay all right, but we would not accept anything. We did it to help them, to increase the output for the district and to give them practical proof of the power of collaboration.

The next winter, 1955–6, all the households in our area had joined Wangchiakou Agricultural Co-operative, and then we discussed transforming ourselves into a higher agricultural co-operative. At that time there was our agricultural co-operative, Wangchiakou Agricultural

Co-operative and also Liu Ling Agricultural Co-operative, and, in Hutoma, there was a labour group for mutual help. Well, to begin with, there were a lot who did not want to agree to the change. Again, it was a question of those who had the better land and those with many animals being afraid of losing by it. They did not want their animals to become collective property. 'We don't want to lose our animals,' they said. We proved to them that they would not lose anything economically. The animals would be bought from them by the co-operative, and they would be paid for them in instalments over several years. Now we were going to be more efficient and look after our resources in quite a different way. We were doing all that so that everybody would be able to live better. The discussions went on till late at night. Kou Chen-you, who has a stiff leg and a knee that hurts, said: 'The economic side's all very well, but I am a cripple and I have a horse and I need that for getting into the town and doing my business and I need it when I go to see my relations. So I shall keep my horse and not go in with you again.' So then we all sat down with him and made proper calculations with him. We demonstrated for him that many of his errands to the town would no longer be necessary, when there was a higher agricultural co-operative, because all visits to the town could be organized in a more rational way. As far as visiting relations went, that would be easy to arrange. Everybody knew that he had a bad leg and needed a horse to get about. There would be no difficulty about his borrowing a horse whenever he wanted to visit his relatives. Before, he had not travelled about visiting people in the busiest time of the year, when a horse could not be spared; so there would be no inconvenience or difficulty for him, quite the reverse. Gradually, he became convinced that we were right.

Now, I was elected leader of the East Shines Red Higher Agricultural Co-operative. We comprised four villages: Wangchiakou, Hutoma, Liu Ling and Erchuankou. We had more manpower and were able to do more. Our incomes increased. I have had the job for eight years now. It is a heavy responsibility. The responsibility gets heavier every year. At the same time, the work becomes easier every day, because people's consciousness increases every day.

The whole time, the work has meant having the personal responsibility for everything that happens, all that is done in tilling, looking after the animals, forestry, subsidiary occupations and so on. The leaders of the labour groups are responsible for the day-to-day work, but my task is to co-ordinate all the work and see that all goes smoothly and that we stick to our plans and that we don't distort production. When we went into Liu Ling People's Commune in 1958, I became leader of Liu Ling Labour Brigade. My job and my responsibility remained the same: planning, supervising, training, solving problems, finding out the members' views and listening to them.

The discussion about forming a people's commune was short. Some people thought it an unnecessary measure. Lo Wen-ming and Li Shen-yung in Wangchiakou said: 'Why should we change everything again now? Things are going well as they are. It's just unnecessary trouble and complication and doesn't serve any purpose.' But we discussed and made propaganda. The central committee of the party, of course, had said that we ought to form people's communes. People's communes were supposed to be a more effective employment of man-power, to give greater possibilities for capital investment; with one we should be maintaining the principle of everyone being paid according to the work he did and be able to give more help to those who got into difficulties. We said other things too. After this propaganda work, we joined Liu Ling People's Commune and, instead of the East Shines Red Higher Agricultural Co-operative, we became Liu Ling Labour Brigade.

We had heard about that business of free food. But we didn't think it would be suitable here with us. We simply did not believe in it. We were afraid that it would undermine our members' trust in the principle of the day's work as the unit. It would make consumption independent of the work contributed, and we did not think that would work well. So we discussed this among ourselves quite briefly. After that we decided not to allow any discussion of it outside, among the members. If any such discussion was to start, we would check it. But no one took the idea up.

But the organization of a people's commune also involved changes in our social care. From the beginning we had had no direct social care. Of course, from the very first days of the people's government a state public assistance fund had been set up, and that still exists. Grants are made from it every quarter. These go to certain individual cases: it can be a case of an accident or there can be other specific grounds for giving assistance. We of the labour brigade's committee deal with this and send our suggestions into the people's commune, which passes them on to the administration of the hsien. People can apply for grants from the fund. As a member of the committee, I am responsible for drawing up the proposals. But, of course, this is not social care in the proper sense. But, even when we first formed the East Shines Red Higher Agricultural Co-operative, we started giving social help to the families that needed it. But then we could only help those who were directly incapable of working, cripples and invalids who had been left on their own. The labour group decided what share of the harvest was to go to social help, and the committee of the higher agricultural co-operative saw to the distribution of the labour brigade's grants.

After the introduction of the people's commune, we were able to increase these grants considerably. After that, we were able to give grants not only to those who were actually ill, but also to families which had got into difficulties for one reason or another. It could be a family with many members in it, but few of them able-bodied; or it could be a dwelling-grant for new arrivals or for young people setting up their own home. But the principle remained the same as before. The labour groups decide what portion of the harvest is to go towards this, and then the committee of the labour brigade takes the proposals for grants made by the labour groups and decides what actual amounts each family is to receive. There is thus no difference in the sources, from which we get our resources, to those of social care. But that, of course, is obvious. There is no other source. Work is the only basis. You can't get social care out of the sky. Those who work must themselves agree what proportion of their work they are prepared to hand over to their neighbours, for whom things are difficult. That is a question of social responsibility and solidarity. You can't solve that question by taking the possibility of deciding this from the workers. That would reduce their social consciousness and be the end of solidarity. In the same way, there is no difference in who is entitled to decide; the decision still rests with the members of the labour groups and is taken in general meeting. This, too, is essential in a democratic society. The workers must themselves assume the responsibility. The difference consists in the fact that with the introduction of the people's commune and the big propaganda campaigns we had during that time, the members' consciousness increased and their sense of responsibility was strengthened so greatly that it became possible to introduce rational social care. This is also one of the main points in our propaganda: the mutual responsibility of members.

At the same time, we have to see that the social grants don't become so big that social help is greater than the workers' incomes. One must not undermine the value of work. But one has to see that everyone, even those who for various reasons have got into difficulties, have the possibility to live decent lives. You will understand that better if you will take a look at the figures.

The year before the formation of Liu Ling People's Commune, 1957, we in the East Shines Red Higher Agricultural Co-operative handed over as social help 3,360 jin of corn and 6,000 jin of fuel. During 1958, when Liu Ling People's Commune was formed, these figures rose to 13,900 and 14,000 respectively, and, in 1959, the first whole year with the commune, when we had stabilized the position, 13,300 and 16,000; and last year, 1961, we had got up to 16,300 and 18,000.

There you have the development. I consider this one of the most important changes of recent years. Illness, death and accident are no longer catastrophes. Citizens now have security.

Even if the whole labour brigade should be hit by some natural catastrophe, it would still be possible to apply for help from the hsien administration through the people's commune. The people's commune is the citizen's guarantee of security. It is this requirement of security that has largely been responsible for getting the people's commune accepted. Even the higher agricultural co-operatives were too small to be able to provide a real guarantee.

The labour brigade can also borrow money. If we need to make an investment for which we do not have the means available, we make an application, which is then considered by the management of Liu Ling People's Commune and, if it recommends it—which it always does, because we never make an application unless we have had preparatory discussions with the various persons responsible—it is sent up to the hsien administration for final approval, and the loan is then made by the Yenan branch of the Chinese People's State Bank. The rate of interest can vary, for long-term loans it is usually about $2\frac{1}{2}$ per cent per annum. At the present we have a loan of 4,000 Y for installing electricity.

Then, the people's commune has a loan department, which makes various private loans. Members have to apply to us on the committee of the labour brigade, and we recommend the loan department of the people's commune to make the loan.

Between September 1958 and February 1959, we experimented producing iron by our local method. We have, of course, both coal and iron-ore up in the hills. We built a blast furnace and I was responsible for organizing the work. There were seventy of us working on this. We were given work points for all other work. But this was a non-recurrent phenomenon. I can't remember the exact figures now, but, as far as I can remember, it didn't pay. You had best ask at the people's commune's office; it's some years ago now, but they have the books there. But it wasn't just a question of profitability. We learned the technique, and it's a good thing to be able to do it, if the need should ever arise.

Then, in February 1959, I joined the party. I had been thinking about it for a long time. When I came here in 1948, I had joined the people's militia, as you know. That was when the K.M.T. controlled the area and we were fighting them. Then, gradually, I became more and more conscious; I was given responsible posts and I thought a long time about joining the party. I did so finally in February 1957. When I was a child, I attended school for three winters. Those were the winters when I was eight, nine and sixteen. But I have forgotten most of what I learned there. When I came here, I began trying to learn to read and write. Mostly teaching myself. I learned to read, and the first things I set about reading were the newspaper articles about the collectivization of farming. That was what I was most interested to read about.

I am head of Liu Ling Labour Brigade, of course. I was elected that, and I shall try to explain its structure for you. First, you have the labour groups. They forgather and hold meetings, quite often. All members take part in the meetings. They elect delegates to the Liu Ling Labour Brigade's representation. Each labour group has a certain number of delegates in the representation. The number is calculated according to the number of members in the population. There is one delegate for every thirteen to seventeen individuals in the schedule of population. Infants and old people count as individuals here. But it is only the working members of the labour groups over sixteen who are entitled to vote and who can be elected. The delegates to the representation are elected at the meetings of the labour group.

The representation of the labour brigade holds four ordinary meetings a year: in winter, spring, summer and autumn. The representation is the highest enacting organ in the labour brigade. At the annual meeting, the committee and the supervisory committee report to the representation, their reports are then discussed and accepted, after which a new management committee and supervisory committee are elected, and also the delegates to the Liu Ling People's Commune's representation. These delegates represent about 170 individuals a piece. We have four delegates in the representation of the people's commune. This meets three or four times a year. Our delegates report to the management committee of the labour brigade what decisions have been taken at the meetings of the representation of the people's commune.

A chairman and deputy chairman are elected for the committee of the labour brigade. Then the members of the committee are elected. Then, we of the committee allot the various duties among ourselves. There has to be a representative of every labour group in the brigade on the brigade management committee. If a labour group is large, it ought to have both a male and a female representative. It is not stated anywhere that the leaders of the labour groups should be members of the committee of the labour brigade. But that is customary.

After the representation of the labour brigade has held its annual meeting, the labour groups hold theirs. At these they elect their leaders and committees. All are elected for one year, and have to be re-elected in the proper way every year. You cannot just stay on. The members have the right to dismiss anyone who behaves improperly or who does not represent the members' interests in the right way. This has never happened in our brigade. But last year it did with one of the delegates to the representation of Liu Ling People's Commune. The man's name was Yang, and he was from Yuanchuan Labour Brigade. He had a hot temper. He behaved improperly, swearing at people and being thoroughly unpleasant; but it's not much to talk about. Having been given a post it had gone to his head. At all events the members got together and demanded that he should be dismissed and chose another in his place.

The internal functions of the committee are divided in a number of ways. Partly, there is common responsibility, but then, too, I, as chairman, am directly responsible for, and supervise, all production, except agricultural production. Tsao Chen-kuei, who is deputy chairman, is directly responsible for agricultural production. Then there is also a committee member responsible for each labour group: I am responsible for Wangchiakou village labour group, Lo Han-hong is responsible for Hutoma Village Labour Group. The Old Secretary, Li Yua-hua, is responsible for Liu Ling Village Labour Group, and Ching Chung-ying is responsible for the labour group for vegetable cultivation. Besides, each of us is responsible for certain specific tasks. The division of work within the committee can be seen from the list we drew up this morning. Perhaps you ought to add to that, that this division of duties is made by the committee itself. For example, it is usual that the committee member responsible for public safety is also battalion commander of the people's militia, as he is with us. But it isn't stated anywhere that this has to be so.

The committee of the labour brigade meets every ten days or fortnight. This depends on how urgent the work is and what matters have to be settled. But, of course, we are in continual contact with each other. we have no sub-committees. The supervisory committee is quite separate. No one can be on the supervisory committee and at the same time be one whose work has to be scrutinized. That would be impossible. And it is also laid down in the regulations.

The labour groups have to keep up the small country roads within their areas. They maintain them and are responsible for them. On the other hand, the labour brigade is responsible for the upkeep of that section of the highway which crosses its area, from Seven-mile Village past Ten-mile Village and as far as our boundary with Chaochuan Labour Brigade. In our committee, it is Jen Yü-chen from Hutoma who has the job of seeing to this. He maintains contact with the Department for Highways Construction in Yenan hsien. This calls meetings of the various representatives of the labour brigades concerned and at their meetings they discuss the question of roads and what ought to be done during the year. These meetings then take the requisite decisions about roadworks. The decisions are subsequently implemented by the labour brigades. In principle, every able-bodied member of a labour brigade gives two days' work per annum to the upkeep of the highway. This applies to minor repairs and ordinary maintenance. When it is a case of really big roadworks, such as are of provincial importance, that will be discussed higher up. But we are in this way responsible for the road being kept open.

The postmen are no concern of ours. The post finances itself out of postage receipts. But we are to a certain extent responsible for the school. There are two types of school. Some are schools established by the labour brigades, and with these the labour brigades pay fifty per cent of the school expenses and the state fifty per cent. Some are schools wholly financed by the state, that is to say, the hsien administration. The school we have here, Liu Ling Basic School, is of the latter type and wholly financed by Yenan hsien.

We have a parents' representation for the school and a school committee. This committee, however, has no responsibility for the school's budget: if the school had been of the other type, then this school committee would also have been responsible for the budget, for the salaries and for engaging the teachers. As it is, our responsibility is limited. We discuss the work in the school and correct faults; we discuss the results obtained by the teachers and the behaviour of the pupils. If necessary, we report to those responsible for schools in the hsien administration and ask them to take steps. This school has pupils from three labour brigades and also from Seven-mile Village. Usually, the labour brigades appoint the member on their committee who is responsible for culture and educational matters to serve on the school committee. In our labour group it is Jen Yü-chen who is responsible for culture, but even so I have been appointed as our representative on the school committee. There are seven members of the committee: the head of the school, two teachers elected by the teachers themselves, one representative from Seven-mile Village and one from each of the labour brigades.

Here, in this district, there are a lot of meetings and conferences every year about various matters. They may be concerned with care of cattle, propaganda, forestry, work among women, grain production, the use of artificial manures and so on. Meetings are often held about different matters. In most cases, the committee member responsible for the thing in question is sent to the meeting. In certain cases another member, who is specially interested in the matter, may be sent. If a meeting or conference is called by the administration of the hsien and is held by day, delegates are given an allowance by the hsien of 1·20 Y a day, if they are not given food as well; or of 0·70 Y, if they are provided with food. If the meeting is of such a character that we consider it to deal with a production matter of direct interest to the labour brigade, the representative attending from the labour brigade is credited with one day's work. In this case, he does not receive the hsien administration's allowance. Last year the number of days' work credited in this way by the labour brigade exceeded 250. Ask the book-keeper for the exact figure. If a meeting is held in the evening or in the night, those taking part are not credited with a day's work. It will then take place in their spare time and is an honorary task.

People say of Feng Chang-yeh: He has a brain like an abacus. At first he appears cold and haughty, but he is easy to get into contact with. It is only on the surface that he appears to be distrait. Actually he is listening to everything, though it may not look like it. Then, gradually, you notice that he remembers it all and is thinking of it all. He is always smiling, but he often seems to be looking right through one at something far away. He can calculate anything and work anything out, and when he takes up a problem, it's as though he had an abacus in his head. That is why he was elected chairman. You get accustomed to him, and then gradually you come to like him. He is greatly liked and respected now.

Tsao Chen-kuei, 'The Little Author', aged 28

FATHER moved here from Hengshan in 1927. I myself was born in 1934. I was born here, of course, and have no knowledge from my own experience of what it was like up there, but Father says that his landlord was hard, and that they were not able to manage. When Father heard that there was more land in the area round Yenan, the family moved here. It consisted of Grandfather and Grandmother, Father and Father's younger brother. At that time, there were still landowners in Liu Ling. But in the distribution of land in 1935 we got forty mu of valley land and sixty mu of poor hill land. This had all belonged to Li Hsiu-tang's family. The valley land lay down there and the hill fields were up there on the far side of the valley.

In 1946 I started at the basic school here in Liu Ling. The school was run by the government of the Shensi-Kansu-Ningsia Frontier Region. That was our Red government up here. By that year, 1946, life had become quite good. We had a horse, but no ox. We exchanged days' work with others when we needed to borrow an ox. One ox-day was equivalent to 2½ days' work. With three years' work, we harvested enough for four years' consumption. That means that life was quite good, and that everything was going ahead nicely. We were worse off where clothes were concerned. We were, of course, blockaded by the K.M.T. and had to wear homespun that wasn't always of such wonderful quality. In 1947, Hu Tsung-nan came. The school stopped, and I fled with my parents to the village of Louta up in the hills.

Before this, Father had been up at the front helping our army dig trenches. We ourselves had buried all our corn in response to the government's appeal. We had 2,400 jin in store then. I hadn't been digging, for I was young, of course, and only able to carry light things. During the night of 10 and 11 March 1957, Father came back from the front and said that now the enemy was coming at any moment and that we were to fly, because our army was in full retreat. That night we did all our packing and the next morning we fled into the hills. On the 13th Hu Tsung-nan's troops marched in, but we were then no longer here.

K.M.T. troops also came to the village of Louta. But we did not stay in the village during the day; we just slept there at night. We kept up on the hill. One day, the soldiers came and succeeded in getting our horse and the things we had in our cave. They even took our sieve. Then the soldiers began coming up on to the slopes. We saw them coming up through the bushes. Before that, I had seen only the Eighth Route Army soldiers; but these, who were coming then, had proper uniforms and steel helmets. They shouted and fired into the air, and we were so frightened that we could not even bring ourselves to run away. I know now that we would have been able to run away, but when we saw those soldiers in their uniforms and steel helmets and with rifles, we were quite paralysed. They took us back to the village. They took Father away with them. We were not allowed to go with him.

Everything in our cave in Liu Ling had been destroyed. It had all been smashed or stolen. Only a few people had come back to the village. There was Tung Yang-chen and his grandmother, Li Hai-kuei's and Fu Hai-tsao's mother, and ourselves. They were the only ones on this side. Li Hsiu-tang and his family were on the other side, of course. We had no contact with him and his family. People said that Li Hsiu-tang had joined the K.M.T. then, others say that he fled to the hills and came down after a while and was captured by the K.M.T., and others again say that he had secretly been waiting and longing for the K.M.T. for years and years and had always worked for them. I don't know. People talk such a lot. At all events we had no contact with his family.

All of us who had come back now lived together in the same cave. It was Tu Yi-chen's cave, it had been standing empty and was a double cave with several exits. We all lived in it together. In that way we could help each other.

Father came home little more than a week after we had been taken back to the village. They had flogged him, he told us. He had been kept a prisoner in the village of Koumen. They had accused him of being a communist and of doing transport work for the Eighth Route Army. He couldn't tell them anything about the Eighth Army's transports, not having taken part in them; he had just dug trenches for them and given them food. Father said to the K.M.T. soldiers: 'I am a farmer from the district here. I can prove that.' They kept him locked up, and he talked to the guards and said: 'If any of the older people come back down to the village from the hill, they can confirm that I am just an old farmer from Liu Ling.' Father was kept shut up in a potato cellar. But then Ma Chien-kai, Fen Tse-wen and Liu Tsung-yuan came. All three were old farmers in the village of Koumen. They guaranteed to the K.M.T. that Father really was what he made himself out to be, an ordinary local farmer. After that they let him go. Father still talks about them today and says that they were his true benefactors.

We fetched corn from our buried stores; but someone had discovered them and most of it had been stolen. We don't know whether it was the K.M.T. or someone from the village. Then, in June, we again lost a lot of corn. One night I had dug up thirty jin of the millet we had in one of our hiding places up on the hillside, which had not been plundered. But the very next day a K.M.T. patrol came. We had hidden the millet by spreading it on our kang and putting a blanket over it and then sitting on the blanket. But the K.M.T. soldiers just went straight to the kang, shoved us off on to the floor, lifted the blanket and took all our millet. So then we had nothing to eat. After that Mother and I gathered different herbs during the day, and, at night, I crept up cautiously to one of our hiding places and dug up a little corn. But I only took enough to last for the following day. In that way, if the K.M.T. soldiers came, they were not able to take so much from us. And they did come.

Once again they took our millet. Mother began to weep and

173

pleaded with them: 'Let us keep our millet! We are starving!' But the
soldiers kicked her over and threatened her with their rifles. They said
that she had insulted the K.M.T., and that they would stick their
bayonets through her in various ways. I was so afraid that I didn't know
what to do. The entire family fell on their knees and begged for mercy
for Mother. Tung Yang-chen's grandmother, who is my grandmother
too, also begged for mercy for Mother. Then the soldiers said: 'We
pardon you. But you have forfeited your millet.' So then they took the
millet and went.

One night, we heard the sound of many men and horses in the
village. There were thunderous crashes. We were so afraid that we
stayed right at the back of the cave. Not till the morning did we see
what had happened. The Southern District Co-operative Society had
had seventy or eighty rooms in the village here, where the school now
stands. They had had two-storied houses and a big warehouse and
everything. That night the K.M.T. had pulled it all down, and the
troops had gone off with all the timber. There were only ruins left.
Before, there used to be quantities of big willows here, down by the
river. A whole wood it had been. The K.M.T. cut almost the whole lot
down.

A couple of days before Hu Tsung-nan's troops withdrew, they
had big manœuvres up in the hills. They shot and called and talked
loudly and marched about everywhere. No one knew what they were
doing, or why they were doing it. People did not dare come out of
their caves. The soldiers were shooting all over the place, though there
were neither guerrillas nor Eighth Route Army anywhere near. I was
living then with Hu Chan-yü; he's dead now. A couple of nights later
the enemy nearly took Father again. There were great explosions and
crashes everywhere. There were sounds of troops up on the hillside.
Nobody dared sleep. We were all sitting on the kang and had not lit
any lights. Nobody dared look out through the door to see what was
happening. Suddenly some K.M.T. soldiers walked into the cave.
They shone pocket torches on us and then they took Ai Shen-tang
away with them; he was from Hengshan, but was hiding in Liu Ling.
He was to act as guide for them. Then a solitary K.M.T. soldier came
back. He fetched Father. Father was to be their guide too. But when
they got outside into the dark, Father managed to tear himself free and
get away. He ran up on to the hill and remained hidden there till the
K.M.T. had marched away.

Then we had to start building it all up from the beginning again. We had nothing to eat; we had neither door nor windows to our caves. We collected bushes and made a protection of sorts with them, and in that way we were able to use our cave again. The government now organized the people. They got seed-corn for us. Those families with people able to work were given the job of going to fetch the corn. It was a hard spring. But things began to brighten a bit when the maize was harvested that autumn. In 1948, we got 1,200 jin of grain. Then I went back to school, and in the spring of 1949 I joined the League of Youth. In 1949, the harvest was better, and towards the end of 1950 I left school. In our family Father was the only one who worked in the fields, but ever since Hu Tsung-nan's soldiers had flogged him, he had pains in his back and trouble with his legs. He was no longer able to deal with our land alone, so I gave up school in order to help the family.

I was young then and had not worked properly before and did not know so very much. In 1951, we joined Li Hai-kuei's Labour Group for Mutual Help. We managed better there. I had the job of keeping the work daybook and entering the work points. That was because I had some schooling. But the cultivation of the land was still done on an individual basis. The yield per mu had not increased, nor had the number of cattle. In December 1952 I joined the party. During the winter of 1953-4 we discussed the situation. You see, Li Yiu-hua had organized his farmers' co-operative then, and ganbus from the party apparatus and the state administration in our hsien had come out to study what had been done and draw conclusions. Li Yiu-hua's Agricultural Co-operative now had seven oxen and a few donkeys, and their harvests had been better than ours. Their yield per mu was greater, too. The party then told us that we ought to organize ourselves, so we studied the agricultural co-operative. We members of the labour group for mutual help saw with our own eyes that the agricultural co-operative was superior. After that winter's discussions, we applied to join the agricultural co-operative in the spring of 1954.

I myself realized that Liu Ling Agricultural Co-operative was only a semi-socialistic structure, and that it was necessary to reform it and make it socialistic, a higher agricultural co-operative. This was no problem where I was concerned, but Father was reluctant to start with. This was because he did not want to give up his land. In Liu Ling Agricultural Co-operative he still got a dividend on the land he had; while in the higher agricultural co-operative the land was to become collective property and he would be paid according to the socialistic principle 'To each according to his work'. Father was afraid that we would lose by this. He said that in the agricultural co-operative we got twenty jin of corn per mu of valley land and seven to eight jin of corn per mu of hill land, and he didn't want to lose this.

I now explained the whole thing to Father, as his son and as a communist. I pointed out that we had never been able to manure our hill fields. Our own manure was only enough for the valley land. This meant that we were not exploiting our land rationally or effectively. In the collective, on the other hand, we could work effectively. This meant that all the land had to be cultivated in the way that provided the greatest yield. We would be paid for our work and we would earn many work points, since there were now two of us in the family working. Since I was his son, he listened to me, though he had refused to listen to the others, and after I had had two or three talks with him, he agreed to join.

Our ox was old and not worth much. Together, our animals were valued at thirty yuan. We invested this in the East Shines Red Higher Agricultural Co-operative. It was paid back in five years.

I had only been to school for a few years. In the country, most people cannot read or write. Now I read at night and in the wintertime. I wanted to learn things. To understand what life was like. I was a communist and I was dying to convince people like Tung Yang-chen, who was reluctant in the beginning. In 1956, when the East Shines Red Higher Agricultural Co-operative was formed, I was appointed deputy chairman. That was my first public job. Before that, I had been responsible for propaganda work in our hsiang; that is, the administrative unit there was at that time and which corresponds roughly to our people's commune. After the people's commune was set up, I became deputy chairman of Liu Ling Labour Brigade. That's the same thing.

In the East Shines Red Higher Agricultural Co-operative I was from the start responsible for cultural questions, education and health. This work was later taken over by Jen Yü-chen from Hutoma and I became responsible for the agricultural work. This did not involve any change in organization; it was just a question of persons. I had studied the technique of farming and was transferred to that work, because it was thought to suit me better. Besides that, I work in the labour group for vegetable cultivation.

In the winter, the labour groups put forward their production plans for the coming year. I go through these and collate them into a general plan, which is then discussed by the labour brigade's management committee. I am responsible for the agricultural work. This means that I make regular inspections to see that the work progresses in accordance with our plans. If any problems arise, I have to tackle them. This work, of course, is carried out in the closest collaboration with the responsible persons in the labour groups.

I have, of course, tried to educate myself further. In 1952, I took a course that used a quick method of learning to write the new characters. In that way, I improved my ability to write. Later, I attended evening classes. Besides, I sat up at night and studied on my own. In the League of Youth, between 1949 and 1952, I studied the league's basic course, theory of agriculture and the party's general plan for the socialistic reform of China's agriculture, and read about our bright future under socialism. When I joined the party, I studied the party's programme, the rights and duties of party members, the party's policy, and writings by Chairman Mao. Besides this, I read various things on my own: the history of the party and the selected writings of Chairman Mao.

After that I began on literature. I read novels and collections of short stories. Not so much classic literature. I have read only three of the Chinese classics: *The Eastern Expedition, The Western Expedition* and *The March North*. All three are about war under the Tang dynasty. The modern Chinese authors I like best are Feng Te-yin, Liu Ching and Tu Peng-cheng. Lately, I have been reading Tu Peng-cheng's *Defend Yenan!* This is about how northern Shensi fought Hu Tsung-nan. Then I have read *The Song of Youth* by Yang Mo. This is about the student movement many years ago. It has been made into a film, too. I thought the film was quite good but that the book was much better. No, I have never read any foreign authors. I read in my spare time, and I read when I am resting and I read at nights. I do not need to sleep as much as other people. I like reading and I want to know what things were like in the old days, and I want to learn the technique of writing. When I read, I am always thinking of how what I am reading is constructed, and how one could have expressed it better.

Actually, I am trying to learn to write. I have been thinking of becoming a writer ever since 1954. First, I sent in various things to the local newspapers here in Yenan. Then, after 1958, I began wondering how one could ever describe all that had been happening. I know, of course, that such a lot has happened in the country in the last few years.

But it is very difficult to describe it. I would like to write about how I have experienced it. After all, I am a farmer's son and a farmer myself. I have also published some short stories. Three altogether. They were included in *The Yen River Magazine*. This is a literary periodical printed in Sian. It is published by the Sian branch of the Writers' Association.

I had my first short story published in January 1959. It was called 'We long for our beloved'. It is about how people here in the district have a bumper harvest and how they go into the fields and think about Chairman Mao. That was my first short story. It was a bit fumbly. Then, in 1960, I had my next short story published. It was called 'Visiting Aunt'. I tried to show by describing a visit to an aunt how life had become better and better. How this woman who had been oppressed in the old society had now become a merit worker in a people's commune.

In the summer of 1961 I had my third short story published: 'Two Men Called Hsiu.' In this I tried to describe how the new man who is now beginning to take shape in the countryside loves our collective property. I began by describing two men, who were both called Hsiu. In their brigade there were two oxen which were ill. The oxen were thin and not fit to work. People were talking about them and saying that they ought to be sold for butchering. But these two Hsiu men had a sentiment for collective property, and proposed keeping the oxen. They promised at the meeting to look after them and make them well. Then I go on to relate how they looked after the oxen, and how they thought up every possible way of curing them and so on. And in the end both oxen get well and strong again and are able to work in the fields. The story ends with all the members of the labour brigade honouring the two old men called Hsiu by making them merit workers.

I have not written anything this year. This year I have mostly gone about thinking. I have been thinking of a story, but it won't come right. I haven't been able to get started on it. Perhaps it's not a good idea.

Most people in the village back me up, but they often make fun of me and call me 'the little author'. But they like the idea of me writing. It's as though they liked my writing about them and people's being able to read it. Before I send anything in, I read it out to my close friends. I want to hear their opinion of what I have written. But I don't read out my things publicly, so to speak. One can't call a meeting just so that the deputy chairman of the labour brigade can read out a short story.

What I have written are only just exercises. They aren't master-pieces. But I wanted to see how what one writes looks in print. I am trying to learn the technique of writing. Those in the village who can read have read my short stories. They haven't said much about them. When I have asked them, they have said: 'They are all right as they are.'

The authors in Sian have helped me. They have elected me to the Sian branch of the Authors' Society. They have sent me different study material. I haven't written much. Actually, I am ashamed to be sitting here talking about it. But I have wanted to write for a long time. In April 1960, I also attended a course in Sian itself. It was a study course for amateur writers. We were all workers or farmers. First, we read theory. Then we swotted Chairman Mao's speech about art and literature that he made in Yenan in 1942. Then various well-known authors came and told us about their technique and the methods used in literary work. Then we analysed various short stories. We chose the best stories written by those taking part in the course. None of mine was chosen. We then talked about these stories and tried to arrive at what was good in them and what was bad. At the end of the course, I thought that I knew a bit more about literary theory; I think, too, that it has helped me to describe characteristic people. Since then, I have written very little.

Actually, I would like to write a big novel. It would be like no novel I have ever read. A novel about what actually has happened to us here. I mean a novel about my own life. So far, I have just been practising using words, trying to get a story to hang together and tell something. I have a plan that I have been working on for a long time. I would like to describe everything that has happened here. That would make a long, long novel, a broad description of this region, its people and their destinies. Not an 'I' novel. Not that I am against 'I' novels, but because I am far too young and would like to describe much more than what I myself have been able to witness. To go a long way back in time. The whole revolution, everything that has happened in the country. A big novel.

I don't know when I first thought of it. I think probably I have always been thinking of it in one way or another. But, consciously, I have been thinking about it ever since I met Han Chi-hsiang. He is a blind story-teller and singer. I saw him in Yenan and listened to him. He is engaged on a description of his own life, and I thought that if a

179

blind man can write a novel about his own life, I ought to be able to write one too, having a good pair of eyes. I had read things by him already in 1956, but it wasn't till 1958 that I was able to meet him. He made a profound impression on me. He told me that he was now writing a fat book about his own life. I thought then that perhaps . . . I have met him several times since. He has been out here in Liu Ling telling stories for us.

Chou Chia-fu lives in Yenan, too. He writes about the Red Guard. But he has not made anything like the same impression on me that Han Chi-hsiang did. This is the first time I have spoken about my novel to anyone. Of course, these are things that you can talk about with your friends, and things that you daren't discuss with anyone else but yourself. But now I have said it. Some day I am going to write my big novel. I think about it all the time; and I am usually thinking it over while I am working.

But I have talked about my short stories with Lo Han-hong. I usually start by having a talk with Lo Han-hong about what I am thinking of writing. I talk to him about it, because he is very fond of literature, he reads a lot and himself writes for the newspapers and such. He writes articles mostly and other things. He isn't working on any book, as far as I know.

There is a library here in Liu Ling Labour Brigade. But there isn't much fiction in it. I usually go in to Yenan every now and again and go to the bookshop and buy books. And then we borrow from each other. There are four or five of us in the labour brigade here who read books. Many read the newspapers, but there are only a few who love reading books.

People in the village here laugh at me a lot, as I have told you. But not so much because I write. They like my writing about the village and the country, and they read what I have written. They laugh at me because I sit up at night instead of sleeping. They say that I write in my sleep. You see, everyone else in the village here goes to bed early and falls asleep at once.

I like the cinema and opera. When I was small, I preferred the opera. The music and the costumes and all that interested me. But now that I'm older, I prefer films. I have occupied myself and experimented with play writing a bit. Han-hong and I wrote a play together, or rather a collection of small sketches that were performed by amateurs at the spring festival. It was about what had happened in the brigade. That was a sort of exercise, too. But people liked it. A real opera is something quite different.

My wife cannot read, so she isn't against my writing. But she does not help me either. She does not say anything about it. I never read her what I have written. She has never heard anything that I have written. I only read it for those who can understand what I mean and who can criticize it. She has three children to see to, and if I were to start reading to her, the children would come and disturb us. My parents have no objections to my writing either. But when I sit up late at night, my mother says: 'You'll make yourself tired. It's bad for you to be awake at night. You have to get up early.' But when they heard that my things had been printed and when they saw them in print and could hold them in their hands, she stopped saying anything. Now she is just proud that I, who am only a farmer's son, have had something printed in a real periodical.

I had, of course, begun writing for the local press up here. I didn't, then, even know that there was a magazine called *The Yen River Magazine*. Then a man called Ho Hung-chi came up to Yenan from Sian. He heard about me from the editorial offices in Yenan and came out here to meet me. I told him about my plans. Not about them all, of course, but I told him a lot. Then I showed him what I had written and he criticized it for me. He helped me to work over what I had written. I did not need to change much. Just polish the language and correct mistakes. He also changed the plot in my first short story, the one where they get a bumper harvest and go about yearning for Chairman Mao. After those corrections, he took the manuscript to Yenan and there it was printed. That's how I made my début.

I have also tried writing poetry, but that hasn't been very successful.

At present, I am thinking out my big novel. But I'm not intending to tell anyone about that or discuss it with anyone. Not until it's quite ready.

People say of Tsao Chen-kuei: He is a fortunate person. He thinks clearly and is quick-witted. He is very knowledgeable. Although he is still so young, he is very respected. He is a great enthusiast. People in the village don't say much about what he has written. 'He has been to Liu Ling Basic School for only a couple of years, and yet he publishes things in a proper magazine.' He writes a lot of articles. People are proud that the village possesses its own author. His mother especially is proud of him and says: 'Even though he was just a short time at school, he is learned and has studied. He sits up every night reading. He sits up at night even during harvest and it never makes any difference to his work.' People call out: 'There goes Chen-kuei, our little author.' When Tsao Chen-kuei hears that, he doesn't say anything, but he blushes.

He is an open person, good, and has an even temper. He has a good wife, who has a placid temperament. She is rather silent and a bit uncommunicative, but he talks enough for two. Theirs is a happy marriage. Their children are well brought up and well looked after. His mother loves her grandchildren, sits with them on her lap all day long. The whole family is happy.

It is characteristic of Tsao Chen-kuei that people's moods always change when he comes. Everyone becomes glad and laughs. He is never hard or violent. But even though he's so open, he is a very cautious man. 'You may think him vague and easy-going, but that is just appearance; actually he is very particular and very methodical.'

Lo Han-hong, the book-keeper, aged 28

FATHER'S name is Lo Wen-ming and he comes from Hengshan. I myself was born up there. Things were difficult for us and Father came here to Yenan district when I was five years old. A year later Father came up to us and took my mother, myself and my little sister back with him. I remember almost nothing of that. Father rented land here in Wangchiakou from a landlord called Tsao. This was already a Red area, but it was during the unity period, so Father had to be a tenant. Three or four years after we moved down here, however, the land was divided up, and we were given a small hill for our own. Then there were seven or eight years before Hu Tsung-nan came. During those years Father worked a lot and harvested a lot of corn, 6,000 to 7,000 jin a year. We built three caves, had lots of space and a lot of food and lots of clothes. Life was good. I was thirteen when Hu Tsung-nan came, in 1947. We had an ox then, a donkey and twenty mu of land. We had both valley land and hill land. The K.M.T. destroyed everything and the troops ate our ox. All the animals in the area vanished.

When Hu Tsung-nan came, Father went to the guerrillas. We went into the hills. But at harvest-time 1947 Father came back from the guerrillas and we went down to the village. We could maintain contact with the guerrillas from the village. We had nothing to eat, because the enemy had discovered the place where we had hidden our corn. We had nowhere to live. Most people in the village worked for the guerrillas. The people now hated Hu Tsung-nan. One day some other children and I were out playing. There were eight of us. We were discovered by K.M.T. soldiers and started to run when they shouted to us to halt. They chased us. Then all the soldiers began shooting. Then other K.M.T. soldiers on the hill fired. They were trying to capture us. But they shot at each other instead and killed one of their own men. We children thought that funny. We escaped, but that same night the K.M.T. soldiers came to the village and plundered it. Later that night, some of the older youths went into the hills to join the guerrillas.

Hu Tsung-nan opened a school in Liu Ling and tried to compel us to go to it. But that didn't do him any good, because his troops had plundered so much. There were seven or eight children in our class. Our teacher was called Lei. We didn't try to learn, we just behaved badly, because we knew that the teachers were from Hu Tsung-nan. There were also secret agents going round in ordinary farmers' clothes. But they weren't so dangerous, because in their heart of hearts they were really on the side of the guerrillas. The teachers in the school, however, were real agents. They made propaganda for the K.M.T. They said: 'The K.M.T. is for the people.' But we had seen quite a lot and, being quite big, we said: 'If the K.M.T. is for the people and the K.M.T. is so good, why did they steal our ox?' After that we were beaten. The teachers drank themselves intoxicated in the evenings. We children discussed the different armies: the Red Army and Hu Tsung-nan's army. The teachers heard us and hit us with their steel rulers. The next day I played truant, because I was tired of the school; so then they came and fetched me. But I just sat there pretending to be studying. I wasn't doing anything. Things at school got so bad, and the teachers were so hated by all the children and parents, that the villagers got in contact with the guerrillas and told them that something had to be done. One night the guerrillas came. We had told the K.M.T. agents in the village to go to bed and sleep heavily that night. All the teachers were taken prisoner except Lei, who managed to escape and got away to Seven-mile Village. That night was the end of the village school.

More and more were working for us and, now, the enemy became frightened and fled to the town and no longer dared work out in the countryside. The K.M.T. was short of goods now and their food was bad, and when they came out to the villages to steal food, they were attacked by the guerrillas and things went badly for the K.M.T. in their fights, we were told. In the spring of 1948 the K.M.T. withdrew from northern Shensi.

Then we began building up our home again. The three caves we had built had fallen in and we built new ones. In the autumn of 1948 I began school in Liu Ling. At that time it comprised only the first few classes. It was a lower basic school then. I began in the higher basic school in Yenan in 1953. I went there for eighteen months. In March 1954 my mother died. After that Father wanted me to stop school and come back. I didn't want to stop school at all; I wanted to go on studying. But Father insisted. The family needed me, and I had no choice. I had to go back home to the village at the end of the spring term of 1954. Father was afraid that, if I was able to go on studying, I would start working outside the family. I was the only son, and Father wanted to keep me there in the family. I was very sorry, but I thought of my sister and my father and went back to Wangchiakou village.

The farmers' co-operative had also written to me that they needed someone who could keep books. There were thirty-seven households and not a single person in them who could write. Father had been keeping the books, but he had only been to school for two winters as a child and he was the only one in the village who could read a little. Father found it difficult and the collective was not satisfied. I came back in the month of July 1954, and then our labour group for mutual help was turned into a farmers' co-operative. I was elected book-keeper at the first meeting in which I took part. I was given a big red paper flower as a welcoming present. Although I had been studying for a number of years now, I did not know anything about book-keeping. The party school sent out notices to the villages that it was starting a course for book-keeping and the farmers' co-operative sent me to it. I attended that course from August to December 1954. After that course I did know something about book-keeping and had learned to count with an abacus.

Life was so different in the village. At school, everything had been done at a fixed time and had followed the timetable laid down. Now, in the village, where I was supposed to enter people's work points, it was made difficult, because none of the members of the farmers' co-operative keep any proper hours. I could not get any order in their work and nobody bothered about what I said, because I was so young. I was so agitated I used to weep at nights. I could not get all the house-holds to come every day. When we were to have a settling, there would suddenly be no one there. I thought that life in a farmers' co-operative was intolerable compared with life as a student. I wanted to go back to school.

Then Feng Chang-yeh had a talk with me. He was very serious and upright and talked logically with me. He said: 'You must under-stand that things are like that in the country. That's obvious. We have all farmed on our own and are accustomed to being our own masters and we can't yet be as disciplined as workers or people studying. You have a big future ahead of you if you stay here in the country. We need young people who are gifted and knowledgeable here. We need intel-lectuals of our own kind. Gradually you will learn to work with the villagers, and they will end by keeping to hours and realize that order is necessary. The villagers here rely on you. They have elected you. They have big ideas for your future, and they have great hopes of you. You must remember that they have paid for your studies and that they used their own money to send you to a book-keeping course.' I was very moved when he said that. I remembered how kind everybody had been to me, and I thought how there were thirty-seven households there and no one in them who could read or write properly, and no one able to keep books. So then I decided not to go back to school, but to stay in my village and work.

In the spring of 1955, several of my schoolmates returned. There was Liang Hsing-chen, Li Kwei-ling, Liu Fu-min and Chang Kwei-lin. I was glad to meet them again. We decided to organize a study group, in which we would first make sure of what we had learned in school and then study further on our own. Feng Chang-yeh agreed to this, and we began to study. First, we revised our school lessons, then we collected money enough to subscribe to two newspapers. We read the news-papers out loud to the other members of the farmers' co-operative, and in the evenings we studied and had discussions.

After some time other young people came and asked if they might

1. *The old doctor, Kao Chia-jen, in front of his clinic*

2. *Ma Hai-hsiu, farmer*

3. ABOVE LEFT *Kao Pin-ying, the one who was strung up*

4. ABOVE RIGHT *Li Hung-fu, battalion commander of the people's militia*

5. BELOW LEFT *Tu Fang-lan: "Don't hang us, Father!"*

6. BELOW RIGHT *The Old Secretary, Li Yiu-hua*

7. **ABOVE LEFT** *Feng Chang-yeh, leader of the Liu Ling Labour Brigade*

8. **ABOVE RIGHT** *Li Hsiu-tang*

9. **BELOW LEFT** *Han Ying-lin, the headmaster*

10. **BELOW RIGHT** *Chang Shi-ming*

11. ABOVE *Li Ying-teh, farmer, and the Old Secretary*

12. BELOW LEFT *The cave-builder, Mau Ke-yeh*

13. BELOW RIGHT *The little Liu boy in Tu Fang-lan's house*

14. *Autumn labour: harrowing*

15. *A plough*

16. *A street in the principal village of Liu Ling*

17. *The Chungdreichu ravine*

18. *The melon fields near the temple*

19. *"The Little Author" bringing in his vegetable crop*

20. *A view of the village*

21. *Women working at the manure-heaps*

22. *Latrines*

23. *The author interviewing Tsao Chen-kuei,*
"The Little Author," through an interpreter

24. *The Old Secretary in his cave with one of his grandchildren.*
Behind them are vessels for storing preserved vegetables

25. *The Old Secretary's two daughters-in-law, She Shiu-ying
(the mark on her forehead is from a cupping-glass used in
treatment for headache) and Chang Yü-ying*

26. *Li She-ping and Li Ngai-ping eating noodles during a celebration*

27. *Rock caves. From left to right: the library, the meeting-hall (where interviews took place), the granary, the Old Secretary's house (where the author and his wife lived). The field in the foreground is planted with melons*

28. BELOW LEFT *The stove in Shi Yü-chieh's kitchen*

29. BELOW RIGHT *The kitchen in Shi Yü-chieh's cave. Note the table and chair. This is the only family to have such an arrangement for mealtimes. It is not a typical peasant situation*

30. *First-year pupils at recreation. The school's cook is on the left*

31. *A classroom*   32. *The school*

33. *The school's recreation area. Vegetables for winter are being dried on the platform in the foreground*

34. *A mill near Naopachan*

35. *The mill alongside the temple*

36. *Li Hai-yuan, the one who left the co-operative, at the mill*

join our study group. We told them that we had been hoping from the beginning that our group would grow. Feng Chang-yeh encouraged us to start a reading class. 'Now you should become a teacher,' he said. We used various methods to make more people able to read. We wrote the characters for the different agricultural tools on the tools themselves, so that people would see the character as they used the tool. We had eighteen young pupils. Later, they asked to be allowed to study in books. We could not find any suitable reader for them, so we wrote a book which gave 500 characters specially suited to Wangchiakou village. We had help from various people in the village, who told us what they would think interesting to read. Later our reader was used also in Liu Ling. We, who were teachers, wrote out six copies of it each. There were twenty pages in each copy and this gave us an opportunity to practise our skill in calligraphy.

That year everyone was very enthusiastic. Even the older people wanted to join us. Tung Shen-ming, who was fifty-two and the shepherd, came to us and said: 'Will you also take an old man as a pupil?' We did and he learned to read. In 1956 we had read through this reader and by then all nineteen were able to read. Even the old man. They knew 500 characters; they could write their names, they could read the co-operative's books and no one could any longer diddle them over work points or cheat them over money.

Tung Shen-ming said: 'Before, I was always being diddled. Once, when I went to the market in Yenan to sell corn, I was to have had 2·50 Y for three jin of corn, for that was the market price then; I sold my twelve jin, but got only 2 Y; the buyer reckoned it all out in front of me, but I could neither read nor write and just knew that I was being cheated, but could not prove it. That's what always happened to us farmers in those days. The townspeople cheated us and we couldn't read. I always thought it was my parents' fault for not sending me to school for a winter. But now I can read and no one can cheat me any more.'

That year we formed an amateur group. We sang songs, we wrote short sketches, we made up our own songs, we read newspapers aloud. The members of the co-operative wanted to hear what was in the newspapers. Especially they wanted to hear what was written about farming. They listened to all the farming articles. They were interested in that, and afterwards they discussed the articles.

Then I wrote a small play that I called 'Old Kou joins the farmers' co-operative'. We put this on, and it was a success. Then, one day, I discovered that the young people used to have fights with millet out at the threshing floor. They threw the millet at each other. So, I wrote a little piece I called 'A ridiculous young man took fresh golden rice to fight with. That is good food and it is a silly thing to do.' I posted this up on the wall-newspaper, and people read it and, after my criticizing them, the young people mended their ways.

In 1956 we reformed ourselves into the East Shines Red Higher Agricultural Co-operative. These three groups, the self-study group, the amateur group and the reading group, put a lot of propaganda work into this. I myself kept on being elected book-keeper for Wangchiakou Labour Group, as we were now called. I saw that production was developed at the same pace as that of the bigger collectives. Wangchiakou Agricultural Co-operative had borrowed money and was in debt to the state when we joined the improved farmers' co-operative. But the East Shines Red Higher Agricultural Co-operative paid this loan off in 1957.

In July 1957, I was sent to the School for Agricultural Ganbus in Yenan. We were to learn new methods of farming, and in December I came back. I was very enthusiastic then. I had learned a lot about varieties, fruit growing, manuring, how to fight insect pests, economic sizes of fields, new crops to sow, organization of farmwork, new implements, new types of plough and much more. Besides, I had been able to study politics.

In January 1958, with the support of the Old Secretary, Li Yiu-hua, I formed an experimental group. The young people in this group did not have to do other work. We were given a field in which we could experiment. I was leader of the group, and we experimented with different kinds of seed. We arrived at three good varieties of millet, two of maize and three of wheat. In the autumn of 1958, I had taught them all that I had learned, and the other young people went back to their labour groups. The Old Secretary, Li Yiu-hua, said that we had done a good job and that we in our turn should learn from the old experienced farmers. He said to me: 'They have eaten more salt than you have eaten corn.' At that time, too, there was a party slogan: 'Combine knowledge with experience.'

When Liu Ling People's Commune was set up, I first worked in the loan department of the people's commune. I worked there for two months, and then the book-keeper of Liu Ling Labour Brigade died.

He was old. Then I was chosen book-keeper for Liu Ling Labour Brigade, and I have been re-elected every year since. That was in 1959.

I had joined the League of Youth in 1952, when I was going to school. In 1956 I was elected secretary of the East Shines Red Higher Agricultural Co-operative's branch of the League of Youth. I have been re-elected to this post every year since. In 1960, I was elected deputy secretary of the committee of the Liu Ling People's Commune's branch of the League of Youth. The League of Youth has twenty-four members in the labour brigade. In the two labour groups with which you are concerned, the league has ten members. The main task of China's Communist League of Youth is to act as auxiliaries for the party. We are to help production under the party's guidance. We have one or two branch meetings a month. The groups meet once a week. They discuss their studies, and they discuss production work. Before the meetings, reports are submitted about what has been done during the week. In the League of Youth we study four subjects: (1) The league's programme. This is explained and we have a thorough discussion of each point. (2) Day-to-day politics. We read the newspaper. We discuss the important articles carefully. (3) The works of Chairman Mao. We concentrate on the following works: (a) On practice; (b) On contradiction; (c) Reforming our studies; (d) Presenting a farmers' co-operative. (4) The history of China's Communist Party.

Besides that we read literary works. We read stories about merit workers and the heroes of the revolution. Our study circle meets once a week. We study one thing at a time, and we study it very thoroughly. Just now we are studying a little brochure produced locally up here in northern Shensi: 'How to be a good young communist.' It is a collection of articles. We have been studying this since the winter and we shall continue doing so throughout the year. It will take at least fifty-two meetings. I am not a party member.

People live better than they used to, and they are beginning to have new needs. This began immediately after the East Shines Red Higher Agricultural Co-operative was formed, by people starting to whitewash the caves and get decorations for them. What's happening now is that people are providing themselves with means of transport. Almost every household has already got itself a two-wheeled cart on rubber wheels. These can either be pulled by hand or harnessed to a bicycle. Some have also begun getting bicycles. There are more and more bicycles all the time. And those who have carts and bicycles are now wanting to have radios and alarm clocks. There is no limit to their needs. The better life is, the greater become one's requirements.

The new agricultural implements make farmwork easier. We are hoping for tractors. If you come back in ten years' time, we shall be working all the land down here in the valley by tractor. The same thing will happen with manuring. At the moment, we have carts for manure and that itself is a step forward. That is to say, we have carts for the manure we fetch from the town and the manure we use on the fields down in the valley. The rest still has to be carried. But in ten years' time we shall have manure trucks. In as little as five years we anticipate that our fruit trees will be showing a real profit and bearing plenty of fruit. We are going to electrify more. When we have more power, we shall be able to water our fields more as they should be watered. We are going to drive our mill-stones with electricity instead of by hand or donkey. Life will be much better then. We reckoned that for New Year 1962 one in every three or four households had slaughtered a pig. But for New Year 1963 we reckon that every family in Liu Ling Labour Brigade will be slaughtering a pig. Now every family, or nearly every family, has a goat. Besides them, the number of collective goats is growing the whole time. Things are progressing.

Members are accounted fully able-bodied between the ages of sixteen and fifty. After fifty, members are put along with the sickly and most of the women in the reserve force. Social grants are made by the labour groups first submitting to the brigade committee a list of those in need of social care and of the extent of their need. The brigade committee discusses this and the matter is then referred back to the labour group. If the production plan is exceeded, that is to say, if a certain labour group produces more than anticipated in the plan, the surplus is not divided among all the members of the labour brigade. Once the labour brigade committee has deducted one per cent of the surplus for distribution to merit workers, the whole surplus is divided among the actual members of the labour group in question. The labour brigade does not make any contribution to the people's commune. All that we hand over is the corn tax to the state. This amounts to about ten jin per mu. As corn tax, the state will accept any form of grain, and beans also count as grain. We send roughly twenty-five per cent wheat and seventy-five per cent millet. Oil-yielding plants are counted separately. Last year we planted 130 mu of jute and sold 550 jin of jute-seed. We paid no tax on that. There is also a bit of tax on goats. Last year we had 537 goats and paid 322·20 Y in cattle tax. That means that we pay 0·60 Y in tax on each goat. There is no tax on private goats, private pigs, draught animals and fruit trees, etc. In 1960 the tax was reduced, as the harvest had been so bad. We paid less than ten jin per mu then.

The main aim of our budget is that not more than thirty-five per cent of the total revenue should go to accumulation, welfare funds, taxation, production costs, etc. In reality these items do not amount to more than thirty per cent of our budget. The rest is distributed among the members in accordance with the socialist principle, 'To each according to his work'.

Since the East Shines Red Higher Agricultural Co-operative was formed, we have saved and invested more than 130,000 Y. We have used this to buy donkeys and cattle and goats and instruments, to build caves and to install electric light and to buy an electric water pump for the vegetable group. In the budget we are just working out now for 1963, we shall perhaps increase somewhat the percentage of grain delivered to the state and reduce that of investment, that is to say, purchases. Other items will not be changed and these changes in percentages will presumably be very small. We reckon on a grain harvest of about 320,000 jin and a cash income of about 40,000 Y.

When we sell our corn, we take the actual grain to the grain office of the people's commune. There, a receipt is made out in triplicate. One copy goes to the bank, one copy is retained in the grain office, and the labour brigade has the third copy. Then, when we need money, we go to the bank.

When we got electricity here, we installed an electric pump. The Old Secretary, Li Yiu-hua, came back from a conference he had been attending. He had seen there that other labour brigades had electric water pumps and electric mills. That had made a profound impression on him. When we got back, he said: 'We could have an electric water pump down by the vegetable fields.' At the meeting of the representatives on 29 and 30 August 1961 we discussed this idea. We had calculated that the method we were then using to draw water, by donkey, was costing us 240 Y a year for the donkey power and the person in charge of the donkey, and that the actual drawing cost 200 days' work a year. That meant that the total cost of watering was considerably more than 400 Y a year. We had also talked with people from the electricity works in Yenan and they had told us: 'If you buy an electric pump, this will involve a big outlay the first year, because the motor is expensive, but after that it will pay you.'

We calculated what it would cost to use an electric pump. Purchase price and running costs. We discovered that we should get our money back after little more than a year. If we added to this the fact that we should also have an extra donkey and man to use in the fields, we arrived at the result that it would really involve a gain of almost 400 Y the very first year. Everyone in the brigade committee had been agreed that this was the best and cheapest solution.

The representatives went into the matter very thoroughly. Two of them were strongly against the idea. There were Liu Tsung-hai and Li Wong-shen, both from the village of Wangchiakou. They said: 'Who knows if this electricity really works. It sounds all right, but what happens if we're cut off? If it shouldn't work after we've spent so much money on it, we'll burn up with mortification.' Wangchiakou hasn't electricity. There are plans to electrify the village in 1965. This has been discussed with people from the electricity works. They have approved the electrification plan. When these two from Wangchiakou had spoken like that against the idea, many others, who before had thought a pump a good idea, also began to hesitate. The representatives were on the point of voting that it shouldn't be bought; but then Fu Hai-tsao said: 'I have visited another labour brigade. There they had big vegetable plots and everything was done with electricity. It really is both cheap and efficient.' Then Li Yiu-hua told what he had seen and the discussion continued. In the end, the opponents of the electric pump said: 'If it is true that it functions, that's all right. We only want to be quite sure before we decide. But if you say that it really is so that it is more efficient and cheaper and sure, we are only pleased. In that case we'll vote for it.' After that everyone was agreed, and the proposal was accepted and all the representatives were happy. At the end of the meeting we all forgathered and ate wheat noodles. They bring luck and it was propitious to eat them after making that decision. The noodles were paid for by the welfare fund. This decision that we should eat at the welfare fund's expense was taken last thing at the representatives' meeting.

We have a big library in the brigade here. I have been elected the person responsible for the library, and we now have 2,468 volumes; of these 824 are agricultural textbooks, 681 political literature, 418 belles-lettres and 545 scientific literature. The library was started in 1956. There were a lot of people in the reading class and they thought that there ought to be books in the East Shines Red Higher Agricultural Co-operative. I put the suggestion forward at a committee meeting and was told: 'If people want to read books, we suppose we can vote money for that.' Then I and Tsao Chen-kuei and Kao Liu-chiang from Wangchiakou were given the job of buying books. We went round the villages asking what people wanted, and then one day we went in to Yenan to the bookshop and bought more than 400 books of different kinds. Later that autumn we made another trip to Yenan and bought another 200 books. That was one of the nicest things I have ever had to do. In 1960, we did not buy any books ourselves, but we managed to get an allocation of 400 volumes from the cultural department of Yenan hsien. In 1961, the brigade committee voted twenty yuan to buy brochures containing Chairman Mao's articles. That same year we also got the party school in Yenan to give us 600 volumes. Yenan Intermediate School also gave us books. In 1962 we have not had any money for books voted. We have just got the committee to agree to have the newspapers in the reading-room here.

The reading-room is open two evenings a week during the dead season, and one evening a week during the busy season. I have a book in which people have to register when they borrow a book. They can have one book a week, then they have to re-register. Up to the first of September this year, I have registered 300 borrowers. But that doesn't tell you anything about how many books have been borrowed, because among the borrowers you will find the book members of the labour groups. Each labour group has chosen a book member. In Liu Ling Village Labour Group it is the book-keeper, Chang Chung-liang, and in the labour group for vegetable cultivation, the book-keeper, Li Hai-fa. It does not need to be the book-keeper, but it is easy that way. These book members are chosen by the members at the meeting of the labour groups. They are responsible and usually fetch thirty or forty books a time.

There are several of us young people in the labour brigade who read a lot. We read till late in the evening. At the moment I am reading a Soviet book. It is called *Youth* and is written by a Soviet author with a difficult name. He's called Aleksander Boytchenko (Kiev 1955, Peking 1958).

Actually, I like Chinese books better. Reading foreign authors is difficult, because the characters in their books have such long and complicated names which are difficult to remember, so that it is easy to muddle them up. This book is good. The heroes are very well described and they are all so courageous. They want to defend their country and are prepared to sacrifice their own lives for it. Reading such a book helps me to raise my ideals. This book makes me realize that we in China are poor and backward, but if we work hard we can change our lives as in this book. At the beginning, with the October Revolution, the Soviet people had great difficulties. They had economic difficulties and many other difficulties. But they contended with all these difficulties, and now they have everything and live in affluence. If we work hard, we shall be yet able to have it as good ourselves.

But mostly I read Chinese books. Not just because of the names, but also because the language in Chinese books is so much more comprehensible and alive. Translations always seem so dead in their language, and a translated book is often just the skeleton of a book. I am sure this is not because the foreign authors are like that, but is due to the translation. It is as though our translators only managed to get across the mere idea of the book. The book itself isn't there. I don't know; I don't know foreign languages and don't understand this business of translating. It takes me a month to read a book like this. I have only time to read in the evenings, before I go to sleep.

I try to write little things too. Short reportage and that sort of thing. I write about what has happened in the valley here. I am correspondent for the newspaper in Yenan. I describe what is happening in our sector of the agricultural production front. I know so few characters that it is difficult for me to write. I can now manage 2,000 characters. That is enough for me to be able to write something. I am trying to increase the number of characters I know. I hope soon to know 3,000, and I try to write as much as possible. You see, I didn't go right through the basic school, but even so I read books and newspapers. I write myself, too, but I still come across far too many characters I don't know in the newspapers and books.

I want to work well and be one of the builders of my country. I hope to be able sometime to write something literary, but I don't know if I shall succeed in that field. I want to be a good farmer. If I could write, I would describe the farmer's life. This is an important subject. To be able to describe it, one must oneself both be a good farmer and also have inherited the experience and knowledge that the old people have. I still have a lot to learn from my father.

People say of Lo Han-hong: He is gifted. He is actually very gifted. He has only been a few years in school, but he does his job as book-keeper well. He writes a lot of reports for the newspapers; he often contributes to *The Yenan Daily* and he sometimes even writes in *Shensi's Daily*. He describes what goes on in Wangchiakou Village Labour Group. He has just written a long article about how Wangchiakou Village Labour Group, despite having poorer land and a smaller labour force than Liu Ling Labour Group, has achieved much better results, thanks to better organization and better labour discipline. You could call him Wangchiakou's author. And actually he knows more than 2,000 characters. He is just being modest. He knows quite a lot more. But perhaps he means that he can write 2,000 characters nicely and without thinking about them. He can certainly read twice as many.

He is very fond of reading novels. He is both reader and writer. He is engaged to Li Chin-wa, who is Li Hsiu-tang's daughter. She left the basic school last year. People say that, in Lo Han-hong's opinion, Li Hsiu-tang has not had any bad influence on his daughter. Of course, Li Hsiu-tang was never a landlord himself, he says. They fell in love last year. But he is secretary of the League of Youth and one does not pass comments on him. People are pleased with his work.

Tables

Liu Ling Labour Brigade

Liu Ling Village Labour Group
The Labour Group for Vegetable Cultivation
Wangchiakou Village Labour Group
Hutoma Village Labour Group
Erchuankou Village Labour Group

122 households
2,368 mu of cultivated land (of which 630 mu is valley land)
72 head of cattle, including oxen
40 donkeys
7 horses
4 mules
630 goats
183 pigs, privately owned
640 head of poultry, privately owned

Management Committee

Feng Chang-yeh	Chairman.
Tsao Chen-kuei	Deputy chairman, chiefly responsible for agricultural work.
Lo Han-hong	Book-keeper, youth work.
(Wang Kwang-yung	Treasurer, not a member of the committee.)
Li Yiu-hua	Secretary of Liu Ling Party Association, China's Communist Party, attends meetings *ex officio*.
Ching Chung-ying	Responsible for production.
Fu Hai-tsao	Responsible for production.
Wong Hsin-ying	Responsible for production.
Liu Tsung-hai	Responsible for production.
Liu Ching-tsei	Forestry, cattle.
Li Hung-fu	General security, armed forces.
Jen Yü-chen	Culture, health, communications.
Li Kuei-ying	Women's affairs.

Representatives of Liu Ling Labour Brigade to Liu Ling People's Commune

Li Yiu-hua
Li Kuei-ying
Feng Chang-yeh
Chao Shen-chen

Representatives to Liu Ling Labour Brigade

Ching Chung-ying
She Shiu-ying
Li Hai-fa
Chang Chung-liang
Li Yiu-hua
Tung Yang-chen
Tsao Chen-kuei
Chang Chen-pong
Liu Ching-tsei
Mu Ju-tsai
Wang Hsiu-ying
Kiang Chuen-liang
Liu Ching-hai
Wang Ting-ching
Liang Hsiu-chen
Wang Hung-yün
Chao Shen-chen

Ma Juei-ching
Fu Hai-tsao
Li Hung-fu
Li Hai-ching
Li Hai-kuei
Tsao Chen-hua
Chang Chen-an
Jen Yü-chen
Lo Han-hong
Kao Hsiu-chen
Yang Shu-chih
Chao Chang-ching
Chang Yao-lung
Feng Chang-yeh
Fung Chin-fu
Kiang Hao-wu
Liu Ho-chang

Social grants from the state assistance fund made in 1961 via the management committee of Liu Ling Labour Brigade

Name	Y	Reason
Shi Yü-chieh	26	No fully able-bodied member
Chen Chung-yuan	22	One able-bodied and five in family
Tung Yang-chen	25	Son of a martyr
Li Hai-kuei	34	Father had died
Hseh Shen-kuei	38	One able-bodied and seven in family

Grain production (including bean crops) 1961

Planned production of grain for year 1961	269,985 jin
Actual production	326,784 jin
Planned production exceeded by	56,799 jin

Distribution of 1961 grain harvest

State grain tax	23,680 jin
Sold to state	22,060 jin
Seed	15,980 jin
Fodder	32,700 jin
Social care grant	16,300 jin
Distributed among members of the brigade in accordance with work points	159,265 jin

Distribution of excess grain

Rewards to 20 merit workers	568 jin
To those labour groups which exceeded the plan, for distribution among members according to their work points	56,232 jin

Budget, 1961

Income	Y
Agricultural produce, grain, tobacco, melons, etc.	45,588
Forestry, fruit-growing	1,200
Cattle, slaughtered or sold	8,450
Joinery, repairs, transport work	10,528
Sale of vegetables	14,998
Work performed for other brigades	7,249
Sundries	2,383
	Total 90,396

Expenditure   Y
Production costs: seed, fodder, manure, insecticide, repairs, etc.   13,400
Investments: purchase of oxen, larger repairs   5,360
Welfare fund, social assistance, grant to day nursery and col-
lective dining-hall, rewards for merit workers, etc.   1,675
Administrative costs, purchase of paper, account books,
table for book-keeper, etc.   670
Taxation:
    (a) Grain tax   1,998·13
    (b) Tax on goats   322·20
    (c) Registration fees for bicycles, and horse-drawn vehicles   24·67
Distributed among members of labour brigade   66,946·00
                                                                      ─────────
                                                        Total 90,396·00

Assets at 1 Jan. 1961
  Stores in hand   8,447·90
  Cash   5,126·50
                                                                      ─────────
                                                        Total 13,574·40

Debts at 1 Jan. 1961
  Bank loan   4,000·00

Assets at 1 Jan. 1962
  Stores in hand   17,170·68
  Cash   6,265·32
                                                                      ─────────
                                                        Total 23,436·00
Debts at 1 Jan. 1962
  Bank Loan   4,000·00

Plant, machinery, implements, pump, etc., are not included among the 'assets', nor are any animals. Because of the system used for distribution, neither the real cost of social care nor that of administration can be ascertained from the budget. As each day's work (10 work points) in 1961 corresponded to 2·10 Y and at the same time 144 days' work were credited to members of the brigade injured at work, the true expenditure on social care was 1,977·40 Y.

Four persons are credited annually with 84 days' work each for their work in administering the brigade. These are the chairman, the deputy chairman, the book-keeper and the party secretary. This amounts to 336 days' work. In addition, the brigade has credited those attending various conferences and meetings with a total of 212 days' work. This makes altogether 648 days' work, equivalent to 1,360·80 Y. This makes the total cost of administration 2,030·80 Y.

In addition, there are the days' work the labour groups credit their book-keepers and treasurers. The cost of this amounts to roughly 63 Y per labour group per year.

Five members of the labour brigade work on service duties for the whole brigade. They are paid direct by the labour brigade and do not come under the labour groups. These are two joiners, one repairer, one herdsman and one driver. Each of these receives 280 days' work annually for his work. This amounts to a cost to the brigade of the equivalent of 1,400 days' work, i.e. 2,940 Y.

Budget for 1962

Income	Y
Agricultural production	46,000
Forestry	1,500
Cattle	8,200
Incidentals	14,000
Sale of vegetables	15,000
Work done for other brigades	2,040
Sundries	6,102
Total	92,842

Expenditure	
Production costs	14,400
Purchases	5,460
Welfare fund	2,385
Administration	680
Taxation	1,500
Distributed among members	68,417
Total	92,842

Part VI
Women

Chia Ying-lan, the one who was sold, aged 53

I AM from Hengshan hsien. Li Hai-yuan's wife, Chia Fu-lan, is my sister. Ours was a poor family, and when I was sixteen I was married off to a pedlar and tinker, who took me with him to Hopeh. He began smoking opium and stopped working his land and so he lost it. He began going round the villages mending cooking vessels. He was often away for long times at a stretch.

I looked after our house in Wuan hsien. I don't know what he paid for his opium, but I got less and less from him and in the end I was getting nothing at all. As I did not want myself and our daughter to starve to death, I took a place with a farmer called Sung. He was a medium-sized farmer with his own land. I worked there for four months. I had no pay, but food for myself and my daughter.

When I was twenty-two I was sold. [Weeps.] He came one day and fetched me and my daughter and took us to a slave dealer called Yang. [Weeps.] My husband sold us so as to get money for opium. I never saw him after that. Some years ago I was told that he was dead. When I had been two days with Yang, the slave dealer, he sold me. He sold me and my daughter for 220 silver dollars to a farmer called He Nung-kung.

I was very unhappy. Mr He was an old man. He was twenty-three years older than I was. We did not love each other. But he was kind. I wasn't ill-treated there, neither by him nor by his family. Actually, he was a nice old man. [Weeps.] He had his own household and did not live with his family. I bore him a son, so everyone was kind to me.

Then he fell ill and died. I was thirty-five then. I had a daughter and a son. One child by either marriage. [Weeps.] He Nung-kung died on 29 April according to the moon calendar. That was during the war. It was 1944. [Weeps.] In January the following year, I gave birth to a daughter. She died when she was seven. [Weeps.] I was pregnant when Mr He died, so they had not been able to marry me off again immediately.

I was, of course, a widow and a burden on the village. The landlord wanted to marry me off. My husband's relatives, that is Mr He's relatives, wanted to marry me off, too, in order to get the house and my children. There was a man in the village who was willing to buy me. I don't know how they arranged it, and I don't know who he was. But I didn't want to any longer. I just wanted to be with my children. [Weeps.] In order to get out of this new marriage, I lied and said that I was already forty-one. Then he thought that I would not be fertile any more and wouldn't have me. That was what I had reckoned on. After that I was left in peace.

Some years after that, we were liberated, and the new government protected us widows and the fatherless. In 1958 I began longing for my sister. She, of course, was still living up here in northern Shensi, and my son and I travelled up to visit her. Then she said that we might as well stay here. That's why we are living here now.

My son is working and life is good. But I want him to marry. I have lived in bitterness all my life [weeps] and now I want him to marry so that I may see a grandson before I die.

All in all, the new society is a good one. But my life has been so bitter. I was sold for opium [weeps] and I have never even told my son all this. [Weeps.]

People say of Chia Ying-lan: She has had a hard life. But she can be happy in having a son. If she did not have him, she would be quite alone. She can read and she has taught her son to read. Her son, He Huang-ho, is strong and healthy and works well.

Chia Ying-lan gets very upset because her son hasn't married. He is twenty-five already and he's still without a wife. But in this village there are only one or two girls who are eighteen or nineteen and free. Most of the girls are far too young. It's going to be difficult for him to find a bride. Their neighbours have tried to get someone for him, but they have not been able to find anyone who will have him. He is strong and fit and a good worker, and there's really nothing wrong with him, but the girls won't have him. Probably this is because he speaks Hopeh dialect and has Hopeh ways. People say: 'It's an ugly language he speaks. The intonation is repulsive and one can't understand what he says. People speak so uglily in Hopeh.'

In all probability he will remain unmarried and that worries Chia Ying-lan greatly, because then the family will die out.

Tu Fang-lan, 'Don't hang us, Father!', aged 56

I GREW up in Hengshan hsien. There were six of us children, three sons and three daughters. Mother is still alive. She is seventy-two. Father was drowned. I send Mother money. In 1961 I gave her twenty yuan. All six children send her the same amount and this means that she has proper pocket money. She lives alone up in Hengshan, but her daughters-in-law go and cook for her. She still hears well and still makes quilted jackets for the family.

But life was hard when we were children. [Weeps.] Father was so hopeless. He gambled and drank. We children had to go out and gather edible plants and roots. When I was digging them up, people asked me: 'Has your father been losing again?' It was some game with dice he always played. I don't know it. I would never touch it.

When he lost, he came home and beat Mother. He was angry then and we were all afraid. We children tried to hide. Once he said: 'I'm utterly useless. I can't support them.' Then he took a rope and was going to hang me. Then we all cried out: 'Don't hang us, Father! We can work and help to support the family.' He drank a lot and when he came home he was dangerous. But if he had drunk too much, he just fell over and was so ridiculous that everyone laughed at him. When he became older, even his grandchildren laughed at him.

But sometimes it was better. Father was a good worker. He could work very hard. He was nice then, and then he did support the family and all was well. But then he would meet some friends and they would take him with them and it was as if he couldn't say no, but went with them and drank and gambled and lost and came home and was furious and beat us and didn't work any more. We girls were more afraid of him than our brothers were, but they feared him too.

When I was very young, my feet were bound. Later my mother said: 'This girl has big ugly feet even though we bound her young.' It hurt a lot having your feet bound. It was like someone pinching very hard all the time. But one had to walk on one's feet. I am old now, but I'm still strong; I have good eyes and I no longer feel anything in my feet, even though they were so tightly bound that they are small, like this.

Mother took a long strip of cloth and bound my feet as tight as she could. It was always Mother who did this. Big feet must be soft and lovely to walk on. But you get accustomed to small feet too. When I became older and heard that girls could have big feet, I thought that it must be lovely for them. My youngest sister, who is forty now, has big feet and short hair. When she was small, this business of big feet had been accepted. I remember my mother saying: 'It is good not to have to bind her feet. This sister has been lucky.' She is much younger than I and therefore she has had a better life.

When I was sixteen, I was married off to an even poorer family. It was Mother decided that. I had to marry the person Mother decided on. Father had no say in the matter. He just said: 'Get her married!' I now moved into a different family. Life now became more bitter. [Weeps.] We had to live on potatoes and melons and my stomach was upset. It was bitter being a daughter-in-law. To begin with I used to cry at every meal. I had to sample every suffering. Gradually, however, my parents-in-law became nice to me. But if we had food, my father-in-law and mother-in-law had to eat first, and I had to eat last of all.

Now we were day labourers for a landlord, and some years we were given to eat what the animals had. We even had grass to eat. I was with child eight times in that marriage. Four died. The first three were boys. They survived. The fourth and fifth were boys too. They fell ill when they were four and died. My husband wept and grieved a lot after the fifth child's death. He burst into tears each time it was mentioned. But then I gave birth to a sixth child and that too was a boy and that made him happy. The sixth child survived. The seventh and eighth were miscarriages. The two miscarriages perhaps were daughters. I had wanted to have at least one daughter. But after those miscarriages there were no more.

A daughter is much closer to her mother than a daughter-in-law. But I never had a daughter. Now it is too late.

My parents-in-law died in 1929. Later, we went to Paoan to take service with a landlord. But my husband died five days after we got there. Our eldest son was then thirteen and our second eight. We had of course nowhere to go, so we stayed there in Paoan, and the two elder boys began working as herdsmen in order to help support the family. I worked in the fields, and life was very hard for us. The rich had all the food they wanted. They ate their fill of wheat. But we had nothing. We were poor. I went hungry to such an extent that my hair fell out in great tufts if I pulled at it. That time in Paoan was the worst I experienced. I made shoes for the boys and had to do this at night by the light of the fire in the hearth. It was bitter then. [Weeps.] If second brother had not helped me with a little rice, we would have starved to death.

Then, in 1939, we came here to Yenan. There were communists here and the boys began working as herdsmen. For that they were given corn. There was land here too. I worked harvesting jute-seed and pressing oil. We lived in the town of Yenan then. When the town was bombed, we hid, but I was wounded in the arm by a piece of flying steel. I still have a scar. Then, during the war, the boys all married, one after the other. They joined the guerrillas, but came back alive.

When Hu Tsang-nan came, he stole our pig and four hens. We had moved out to Thirty-mile Village then, and there we had twenty mu of land. They ate up our little ox and all our corn and destroyed everything we had, and because of that, my grandson, who was three years old, died.

I moved to Liu Ling in 1955. I began making shoes for people. In 1961, I married Ching Chung-wan. You see, my relations in Yulin wanted me to go back up there, but I liked the maize here in Liu Ling; here the millet is good too and so are the potatoes. The labour brigade did not want me to work in the fields, but I told them that I had always worked and intended to go on working till I died. 'Everything that a young girl can do, I can do. And I'll do it better,' I said to them. They had to give in, and in the end they even gave me a diploma as a merit worker.

People say of Tu Fang-lan: She has had a hard life. She was badly treated by her mother-in-law and she weeps a lot. She comes from a poor family. Up in Hengshan hsien she did not eat all that well. Her mother-in-law ate millet and she had to make do with grass. She was not entitled to eat with her parents-in-law, of course; she was just the daughter-in-law. She became ill up there; the bad food gave her stomach disease, and her stomach is still delicate. She has a lot of pain, especially in the winter, and the women in Liu Ling are sorry for her. But sometimes she gets a bit muddle-headed and all at once she will start talking nonsense, and if you ask her about a thing, she will answer about something quite different.

She works well. She does more work than the young women. That comes out when the income from the harvest is distributed. If the young women get nine yuan, she will get twelve yuan. She was obliged to marry Ching Chung-wan. It's the custom for people to marry. Women marry, even if they are over forty. They can even be fifty when they marry. After all, a woman can't live alone. If a middle-aged woman wants to marry, people will have no objection. Tu Fang-lan was known to be wanting to marry. She wanted to get hold of a man. She needed a man.

She married Ching Chung-wan. He is eight years younger than she is. He is the younger brother of Ching Chung-ying, leader of the labour group for vegetable cultivation. As I said, people remarry a lot here in Liu Ling. As soon as the husband or wife has died, the survivor tries to remarry. 'People should not live alone, and if a woman can remarry, she should do so. Who is going to carry water for her otherwise?'

But the Ching family has a great sorrow. It is on the point of dying out. There is no young generation in the Ching family. Ching Chung-ying married a woman who already had children. He himself had no children. So he expected his younger brother Ching Chung-wan to have children. They particularly expected a son who could continue the family. But Ching Chung-wan had no children by his first marriage, and when his wife died he was so old that no young woman would have him. The young women all refused to marry him and, in the end, he had to marry Tu Fang-lan.

But that marriage hasn't been a happy one. He's thinking all the time that he is childless, and that he is going to die without an heir. Tu Fang-lan, of course, is already too old to have children. Their mutual relations therefore are not good. He couldn't find anyone else, of course, but had to make do with her. He had lived alone for many years without being able to get hold of a woman, so in the end he married Tu Fang-lan, because he had to have a woman. After all, someone had

to cook for him. Now he nags at her and says: 'I want to have a son.'
But she just replies: 'I can't help you there. I am too old. You should
have married a younger woman. But the younger women wouldn't
have you, would they?' He ought not to nag at her, because he knew
this before they married. And it isn't her fault either that she is too old.
She has had sons too. He isn't a particularly good worker. He is a
mediocre fellow. But she works well, and she's to be pitied.

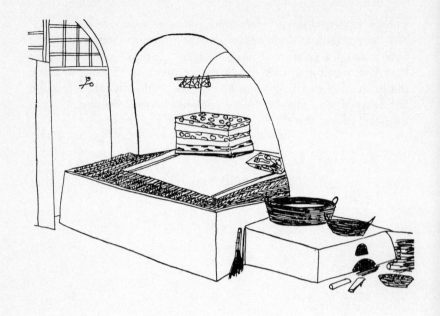

Ma Hung-tsai's wife, aged 25

My husband's father is Ma Hai-hsiu. My husband's mother is dead. She was Tuan Fu-yin's younger sister. Li Hung-fu is my husband's eldest stepbrother. They had the same mother. My own mother lives in Koumen Village twenty li from here. I moved here when we married. I have two children, a boy of seven and a girl, who is three. My husband's grandmother, old Mrs Tuan, looks after the children while I am out working. Today, I have my monthly trouble and am not feeling too well, so I am at home today.

My husband goes out to the fields at daybreak. When he has gone, I make breakfast for myself and the children and for him. A special food carrier from his group fetches him breakfast. He is ploughing today. There is a lot to do now, but in the winter he usually stays at home till he has had breakfast, about seven o'clock.

I myself usually go out to work at about seven or eight o'clock. I get home to the cave about twelve and make dinner. My husband rests while I am preparing the food, then we eat and he has a little sleep. Sometimes he helps me. He looks after the children then. We do help each other at times. We are a young couple, of course. At two in the afternoon, we go out to work again, and we usually get home about eight in the evening. Then we have supper and go to bed.

I feed the pig, the hens and the goats before I go to work in the morning. I also see to the animals in the evenings. That's my responsibility. Sometimes my husband helps me clean up, sometimes I do it by myself. The men have four free days a month; women have six free days. We can take our free days when we need them.

Our family has a private plot of $1\frac{1}{2}$ mu. We grow maize, potatoes and beans there. My husband does most of the work there on his free days, but I help him. Every year we discuss what we are going to grow there. In the older families, it is the husband alone who decides, but my husband and I discuss everything together, because we are a young couple. Sometimes he gives in and sometimes I give in. We have just re-whitewashed our cave. We do that ourselves. I want it to look neat and tidy here. We are going to slaughter the pig for the New Year.

Li Shang-wa, the young girl, aged 16

MY mother died long ago. My father, Li Yü-hsin, is Li Yü-teh's older brother. I left school this spring.

Actually, I would have liked to go on studying, but as my mother is dead I had to start working in the household instead. We have a pig and two goats; I look after those. But we have no hens or chickens. I like cooking and I look after my small brothers and sisters. Although, really, I would have liked to go to Yenan Middle School. But then someone has to take care of the family, too. Just now I'm laying down turnips and lotus for the winter.

I haven't joined the League of Youth, and I'm too old for the pioneers now that I've left school. I like singing and usually sing to myself all the songs that my teacher, Kou, taught me. I go into Yenan to shop and to go to the cinema once a week. I like adventure films best and war films and films about heroes. I like reading and I read different children's books. Both where films and books are concerned, I prefer those books and films that improve my morale and enhance my quality.

I don't like opera. I don't understand about the operas. Everything in operas is all so peculiar. I like the song-and-dance shows. I often go to the school in order to be able to sing with my schoolmates.

I am proud of being able to work on the land. Agriculture is the foundation of society. No society could exist without agriculture. Or course, I would be happy with whatever work the party gave me to do. We who are young now have a bright future ahead of us. I hope to be able to make my contribution on the agricultural front and be a good 'swallow', as the teachers in school taught me. I'm not contemplating marriage. I shall marry late. I'm altogether too young to be able to think of love. I'm running the house for my father. Later, I am going to work on the land.

People say of Li Shang-wa: She is a sweet, nice girl. She is pleasant-looking and efficient. She and Li Hsiu-tang's daughter, Li Ai-liang, were the only ones from Liu Ling to finish school this spring. They had roughly the same marks. Li Ai-liang's were very slightly better. Li Shang-wa would have liked to go on to Yenan Middle School and she is the type for it; but her father did not want her to. It was Li Hsiu-tang's daughter who went on to do higher studies. People say that the party and the brigade committee talked with Li Yü-hsin to try to get him to let his daughter continue her studies, but when he wouldn't she had to stay at home. Li Yü-hsin thinks it's good to have her at home to run the house.

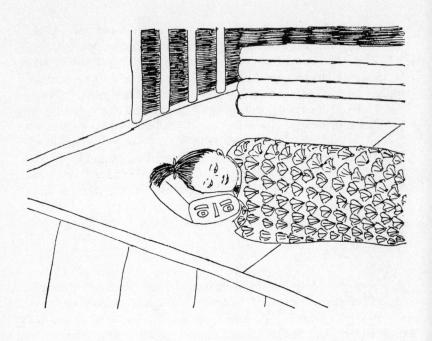

Li Kuei-ying, woman pioneer, aged 32

I HAVEN'T much to tell. I haven't many experiences. I was born into a farming family. I grew up in the country and have never been anything but just a country woman.

We moved to Yenan in 1950. I don't remember anything of our life in Hengshan. But my father, Li Yiu-hua, and my mother say that they worked for a landowner, and that, though they worked hard, they did not have enough to eat. There were six of us in the family when we moved: Father, Mother and four children. Father carried two worn quilts and a felt rug on his back. I walked and walked, and I was so tired that I cried. When we reached Yenan, we still had to work for a landowner. Father worked for Li Hsiu-tang's family. Then he broke new ground for himself up on the slopes. Mother looked after our pig, and I plucked grass.

I don't remember exactly what year that was, but we children worked too. We worked in Father's labour group. He had organized one. When Hu Tsung-nan was coming with his troops, Uncle took us children with him to Ansai. That was a week before the enemy occupied Liu Ling. Father and Mother went somewhere else. In Ansai, we lived with another of Mother's brothers. It was a small village of four or five households. When the K.M.T. troops finally came there, all the villagers were afraid. They hid all the young girls and women. They were put into abandoned caves and the entrances blocked up with bushes and branches. In that way they tried to protect them from the soldiers.

Now all we children were living in Ansai and we ate lots. The soldiers plundered Uncle, too, and he had difficulties. When the guerrillas came that way, he got out some corn and gave it to them; but when Hu Tsung-nan's troops came he didn't give them anything, but hid everything from them.

One day, when the troops came to the village, my little brother and I were ill. We had high temperatures with bleeding at the nose and mouth and diarrhoea. Uncle's only child was ill too. One of Uncle's female relations was staying with us in the cave to look after us and Uncle. The woman's husband was a stretcher-bearer for the guerrillas. She was living with Uncle, as she had been left alone in the village. Now she was to look after us children. That is why she was not hidden when the soldiers came. They stood outside the cave and told us to come out. We replied: 'All those who are well are away, it is only we ill ones left.' Then they asked what illness we had. 'It's catching.' At that they took two paces back. Then they said: 'Those who are not ill must come out, otherwise we shall shoot.' After that Uncle and the woman stepped outside. They did not bother with Uncle, but they took the woman away with them. Two hours later she came back. Her face was quite grey then, and she was quite silent. She just sat and sat and never said a word. That night her husband came. They sat side by side for a while, then they stood up and walked out, in the middle of the night. No one has heard of them since. No one knows where they went. They just walked out into the dark.

In July, we children went back to Liu Ling. Uncle had no more corn to give us and our parents had already returned. Father had moved across to this side of the village. The whole village was in great disorder. Many families had disappeared and their caves were abandoned.

Everything had been smashed, cooking stoves, windows, everything had been destroyed. Everyone was depressed and unhappy. We had breakfast, but no dinner. The corn had been growing in the fields, but the troops had cut the maize before it had had time to ripen and used it as fodder for their horses. Sometimes they had set fire to it. At night, the fields would burn. In the end people became quite indifferent. It was as if nothing mattered any longer. No one went out to the fields any more. Not even to the fields high up on the hillside. Nobody worked. People just lay on their backs and slept. It was as if people no longer wanted to live.

In the autumn, there was almost no harvest to get in. We had no hope for the future. That winter Mother and I did washing for the troops. In that way we survived. Father had no work and it was difficult for him. That was the first time in his life he hadn't worked, and he was so upset. He wasn't accustomed to not working.

In March or April 1948, Hu Tsung-nan withdrew. We then had no grain at all. Father went to Lochuan to fetch seed-corn. My two younger brothers were working in the fields although they were very young. Father went back to Lochuan to fetch more corn. This he sold. He carried the sacks on a carrying-pole. He kept on doing this right till the maize could be harvested. Then he stopped carrying grain from Lochuan. The harvest that year was not too bad. I don't remember exactly when it was, but I think it was the year after that that Father organized a labour group for mutual help. In this the families worked for each other and helped each other. Our family was very poor, and I used to go up on to the hill and pluck grass for our pig. I was also supposed to look after the goats and the group's cattle.

In 1951, we were told that the party school in Yenan was having a training course for female ganbus. It was said that as half the population consisted of women, trained women were needed as well. Our labour group for mutual help was now to be turned into a farmer's co-operative. It was Father who forced that through. It was the first of its kind and it was an experiment. The labour group for mutual help told the party school about me, and I was accepted and sent off to attend the course and study for six months. Ever since I had been small, 1 had dreamed of being able to learn to read and write. I had dreamed daydreams of becoming a student. Yet when they talked with me and told me that I had got permission to go to the party school, I became worried. Because what could a farm girl learn at school? I was worried about the housework too: the spring sowing was about to start and there was so much that ought to be seen to at home.

When I got to the school, I met a lot of women and men there. After a couple of weeks, I had got accustomed to being in school. The main object was for us to learn to read and write. To begin with, it was rather difficult for me to live a collective life, but afterwards it went quite all right. I decided to learn all that I could. Now that I had managed to get to a school I was not going to lose a minute. I thought of how things were in the new society and how they had been under Hu Tsung-nan's occupation and I promised myself that, when I was finished with the school, I would organize all the women in the village for this new life, and I read seriously.

At the school, I got up as early as in the village. First, we had a lesson of forty minutes, when our homework was corrected. Then, after a short break, we had another lesson, which was either arithmetic or Chinese. At eight o'clock we had breakfast. We usually got steam bread and vegetables. Then we had three lessons of arithmetic and Chinese. We had fifteen minutes' interval between each lesson. Then we had a rest period of one and a half hours. After that a further three lessons of arithmetic and Chinese. Then we had dinner. We used to get steamed millet and vegetables. Once a week we had a meat dish. This, of course, was better food than we were accustomed to at home, but we needed it, because we were working hard and had to learn everything at once. After dinner, we had ninety minutes' prep. After that we did different kinds of personal activities. We did not have any political studies. This was a course at which we were to learn to read. In the evenings we used to sing and discuss things. We learned lots of songs and talked a lot about our home villages and all the things that could be done. We all knew that we must learn to read as soon as possible. Six of us women shared a room. I still see a lot of two of them; they live near by; but I have lost touch with the others. We were free on Sundays. I used to go home to the village then and help in the fields. I was needed there too.

That time at the party school was the decisive time of my life. It was then I realized what I must do with my life. I came back to Liu Ling in July 1951. I could then read and write, and I took part in the autumn harvest and, in the winter, I began organizing the women to study. When I got back, the women said: 'We didn't think grown-ups could learn to read and write, but you have.' Because of that, the younger women now wanted to learn to read too, and I told them all how good it was to be able to read and write; that she who could read could see; and she who couldn't was blind.

That winter I taught ten women to read and write a hundred characters each. That isn't enough to be able to read a newspaper or such, but it is enough to be able to write simple accounts and receipts and to keep notes. They have gone on with it since, but it has been difficult for them. They can't read much more now after ten years, though I have been working with them the whole time.

I continued studying on my own. I got hold of old books of legends which I read. I swotted up more characters; I read newspapers and began reading simple new stories. In 1952, I married. That was in August and I was very happy. It was a marriage of free will. We had met at the party school and fallen in love with each other. He was attending a different course. When I told Mother that I was in love and wanted to get married, she said nothing at all, but Father said: 'If it's so that you really want to, then I don't intend to oppose it.'

There were three labour groups in the farmers' co-operative in 1953. Two of men and one of women. I was chosen leader of the women's group. At the meeting, the women said: 'She is young and hard-working and she can read.' So I thought that, if they had such faith in me, I must show that I was worthy of their opinion of me. That I must work much harder than before. I wanted to get the women as a group moving. I wanted to get them to break away from the past. I was thinking of the time when Hu Tsung-nan had occupied the area. There was a cavalry regiment quartered here in Liu Ling then. Its duties were to track down and capture deserters. They shot the deserters in our potato plot. Every day I used to stand by my cooking stove in the cave and see them shoot deserters down there. I thought then that that must never be allowed to happen again. That we women must all get together to see that it never happened again.

That winter I opened a winter school. We had lessons in the school and in the homes of Shi Yü-chieh and Li Hai-kuei, who had large caves. We helped the women to make shoes and clothes and to improve their agricultural tools. We gave them lessons in feeding poultry and in spinning. We had discussions after the lessons. We tried to get the women to tell us themselves what things had been like before, and how it was now, and how it ought to be in the future. For example, they said: 'My feet were bound so that I could not walk. In the old society, a woman was not supposed to go beyond the threshold of her home for the first three years of her marriage. We weren't allowed to eat on the kang, but had to sit on a stool when we ate, and if my parents had decided to marry me off with a cur, then I had to be content with a cur. But now you are allowed to see your husband before you marry, and you can refuse to marry him if you don't like the look of him. The old society was bad and the new is good.' We discussed whether women are men's equals or not, and most said: 'Within the family, man and woman are equal. We help the men when they work in the fields and they should help us in the house.' But many of the older women said: 'Women are born to attend to the household. A woman cannot work in the fields. That can't be helped. It is just that men and women are born different. A person is born either a man or a woman. To work in the fields or in the house.' We had long discussions. The young ones were all on the side of equality and freedom. It had now become quite usual with our generation for husband and wife to discuss the family's problems and decide about them together. Women now no longer work just in the house; they also work in the fields and earn their own money. But the men of the older generation still say: 'What does a woman know? Women know nothing! What's a woman worth? Women are worth nothing!' In such families the men decide everything and their wives say: 'We are just women. We are not allowed to say anything.'

The first time we women took part as a group in an open discussion was at the meeting about whether or not we should turn Liu Ling Farmers' Co-operative into the East Shines Red Higher Agricultural Co-operative. Officially, we had the same political and economic rights as the men. We were citizens too, so She Shiu-ying and Li Yang-ching asked to speak and stood up in the middle of the meeting and said: 'The old women still say that they don't understand things and are just women, and that it is the men's business to decide and that the women should do as the men decide. But we say that we do understand. We are women and we know what this discussion is about. Everything has to progress. We must increase production. It isn't fair to pay a dividend on land. That can mean that a person who works a lot can be paid less than one who works less well. That is not right. We must increase our investment instead, so that we can all increase production and be better off by doing more work. Therefore we must join forces and do away with land interest. That is progress and we stand for that.'

Li Ying-teh, who is an old man and Li Hsin-chen's father, then said: 'We should not listen to women when it is a question of serious business. They understand nothing. After all, they are only women and ought not to disturb our discussions. We do not need to concern ourselves with what they have said.' But my brother, Li Hai-tsai, replied to this: 'Why shouldn't we listen to the women? Every other Chinese is a woman. There is a lot of sense in what they've just said about investment and production and land interest and joint effort. I am entirely with them.'

We won. Gradually the others were voted down and persuaded and got to agree. I was elected a member of the committee of the East Shines Red Higher Agricultural Co-operative. Besides this, I had three children. We wanted to have three children, so I had a boy in 1953, a boy in 1957 and a girl in 1958.

I joined the party in 1955. There were women party members in the other villages. We often had meetings with them. Then Yang Fu-lien said: 'Why don't you join the party? The party needs women ganbus.' But I didn't want to join. I said: 'I can work just as well for the people without being in the party.' 'No,' Yang Fu-lien said, 'you can't. You will do better work if you are in the party.' I thought a lot about what she said. Then I went home to my parents and borrowed Father's copy of the party programme and read it through. I realized then that I would be able to work better and train myself better if I joined the party. So I sent in an application. Yang Fu-lien and Li Hai-kuei recommended me. This was in the middle of the discussion about the change to a higher agricultural co-operative. My husband had been a party member since 1948 and he had tried to talk me over several times, but I had not listened to him. It carried more weight when other comrades, who didn't belong to the family, talked to me about it.

After joining the party, I studied the party programme, the series of articles called 'How does a party member serve the people?' Comrade Liu Shao-chi's 'How to become a good communist', our party's history and different articles on topical questions. We studied together in the party association and after the studies held discussions. Besides this, we studied on our own. After this, I thought that everything had become more clear and easier to understand. I have become more assured in my work. After studying those questions, I could understand the whole implication of them. If I make mistakes, the others come and tell me and help me to put things right.

In 1958, we formed Liu Ling People's Commune. It was even bigger than the higher agricultural co-operative. It took in the whole of our hsiang. We had only a short discussion before we agreed to it. Most people were convinced from the start, but some, like Kao Kuei-fang, said: 'Why cause all this trouble? Why go on altering everything all the time? It's going well as it is. I think it's a mistake just altering and altering.' But Wang Yü-lan replied: 'What Kao Kuei-fang says is not correct. She is forgetting that production must go on increasing if we are to be better off. The people's commune will provide better possibilities for accumulation. We will be able to carry out more new building works that require capital, and we can have better-arranged social care. We must keep our objective in view the whole time. If we are on our way to Yenan, we can't stop in Seven-mile Village and settle there.' The discussion was very short. The introduction of the people's commune did not involve any great changes in our work. It was mostly that it made it possible for us to do without a number of salaried officials, who had previously been in the hsiang administration and who were no longer needed once we were doing the administration ourselves. Besides that, it gave us the ability to carry out works requiring capital, and we set up a proper system for exchanging labour between the brigades. We had heard it said that in different parts of the country they had food and other things free, but that did not sound right to us. At all events, it wouldn't suit us in northern Shensi. We decided not even to discuss the idea. It was never put on the agenda for any of our meetings.

We carried out great irrigation works in the winter of 1958–9. We built terraced fields and were able to do so because we had arranged for exchange of labour between brigades in the people's commune. There was a bad drought in 1959. We had to fight a hard battle with nature. But the 1959 harvest was not bad at all and that strengthened the members in their belief that the people's commune was the right form. We would not have got through that drought without a people's commune.

In the winter of 1959–60 we had a discussion about our work among the women. I sent a proposal in to the committee of the party association for setting up a special women's committee for our work among the women. I told them that, in my opinion, so far I had been the only one working on the women, and that we could not let so important a matter be dealt with like that. It mustn't be left to a few comrades to do the work more or less on their own. The party itself must be responsible, both politically and organizationally. We discussed the matter thoroughly, and in the end my proposal got a majority of votes and went through. The party association decided to set up a labour group for work with women. Ma Ping and I were elected Liu Ling's representatives in the group. This group now has regular meetings. It has representatives from the various villages, and we now plan our work among the women properly.

I was head of the women's organization in Liu Ling from 1955 to 1961. It wasn't a real organization. It automatically comprised all the women in the village. It was one way of activating the women in social work and getting them to develop and accept responsibility and get up at the different meetings and give their opinion. We abolished it in 1961, because it was no longer needed. We had quite enough women then who realized that women can be in the ordinary organizations and speak at their meetings. Instead, we formed a women's work group. I was chosen leader of this. We work directly in production.

But the party group for women's work still functions. It has five different tasks: (1) To organize women to take an active part in production; (2) To spread literacy among women and get them to study and take an interest in social questions; (3) To help them do their domestic work effectively and economically, to help them when any economic problem arises in their family; (4) To teach them personal and public hygiene; (5) To give help and advice over marriage or other personal problems of wedded life.

I have already told you about our work in teaching and production. Otherwise, there are no great problems. One gets those mostly with the older people. That goes for marriage: some of the older people do not believe in marriage of free will. 'How can a girl run off with the first chap she sees?' the older women ask. We have to talk to them and make propaganda for the new marriage. We have to remind them of how they felt when they were young and how they were made to suffer under the old system of marriage. It isn't so often it ever comes to a real conflict, but we did have a case in 1960.

That was when Tuan Fu-yin's eighteen-year-old daughter, Tuan Ai-chen, fell in love with a boy from Seven-mile Village. But her parents refused to let her marry. They said that the boy was poor and that they wanted to marry her to somebody better off. One evening Tuan Ai-chen came to me and wept and complained. I went with her to her cave and talked with her parents. I said to them: 'You have no right to prevent your daughter from marrying, you know that, don't you? Purchase marriage is not allowed in the new society. It is a crime to sell your daughter these days. Before, you could sell your daughter like a cow, but you can't do that any longer.' I told them about the things that used to happen in the old days, about girls drowning themselves in wells, of girls hanging themselves and that sort of thing, about all the unhappiness purchase marriage caused. At first, Tuan Fu-yin tried to stand up to me. He said: 'I had to pay dearly for my wife. Now I have been giving this girl food and clothes, I have brought her up and she just goes off. It isn't right. I just lose and lose all the time. I must get back something of all the money I have laid out on her. If she can't fall in love with a man who can pay back what she's cost, then it isn't right for her to marry.'

I talked a long time with them that evening, and in the end I said: 'You don't live badly in the new society. If you ever have difficulties, your daughter and son-in-law will help you. They are not rich, but they won't refuse to help you.' Then they replied: 'We must think about it.' The next time I went there, only the girl's mother was at home. She had thought about it and she now told me her own story. I hadn't known it, otherwise I would have made use of it on the first occasion. She said: 'I was sold to Tuan Fu-yin when I was a little girl. I was sold in the same way you sell a goat. But my parents got a lot for me. Tuan's father had to take out a loan. That made them nasty to me. I was forced to work hard so as to make the loan worth while. They were all nagging at me. I can remember how much I used to cry. Now that I think of that, I don't want my daughter to marry someone she can't like.' Then she wept. Tuan Fu-yin didn't say anything more. But such cases are rare. It is the only one I remember. Tuan Fu-yin's own sons had been allowed to marry in the new way, of course, because that meant that he did not need to pay anything for his daughters-in-law.

Another thing we have to deal with now and again is that the old women find it difficult to understand that nowadays women laugh and joke with men. They scold their daughters and daughters-in-law and granddaughters for not observing decent behaviour. When that happens, we have to speak with the old women about the equality of the sexes. We tell them that, now, a woman is the equal of a man in the family and in society. She does not just look after the home, she also works in the fields. She has to vote and she can be elected. It is obvious that she also talks with men and jokes with them as comrades. We remind the old people about their own bitter youth and keep telling them that as women now are equal, they also have the right to chat and joke. The old people say that they agree we are right. But in their heart of hearts they always feel uneasy and uncertain when they see girls joking with men. But we are patient with the old people. They can't help their attitude. Perhaps not all old women are like that, but most, I'm sure, think it indecent and immoral and shocking that young people talk with each other. The young people, of course, are all agreed. None of the young people think like the old ones on this question. So it will solve itself in time.

We have continued our work with hygiene and public health all the time, especially since 1958, when we formed the people's commune. The public health work was better organized after that. We go to see the women who are pregnant and talk with them about what to do in their pregnancy. We instruct them in the new delivery art and tell them how to look after their infants. Before, a woman had to be sitting straight up and down on her kang three days after having her baby. And you can understand how that must have felt. Now we say to them: 'That is all just stupidity and superstition. Lie down with the child beside you and rest. You're not to sit up at all.' We tell the women to let themselves be examined regularly and follow the doctor's advice. We instruct them in birth control and contraceptive methods. The women follow our advice because they have found that with the old methods many children died, but with our new scientific methods both mother and child survive.

Birth control is primarily a matter of propaganda. Firstly, many say: 'We want to have more children'; secondly, after all birth control is voluntary. We have discussed which contraceptives are best. Personally I find the condom to be the most reliable. They are rather inexpensive too: Thirty-three pieces for one yuan. But there are other methods, too, and certain of the families don't use any contraceptives at all but only simple techniques. A lot of women still believe that they can't become with child as long as they are suckling. And each time, they are as surprised as ever, when they find they are pregnant again. But we are working to enlighten them.

In certain families with lots of children, the women would like birth control, but their husbands won't. In those families the husbands say: 'There's not going to be any family planning here!' Then we women go to them and try to talk sense into them. We say: 'Look how many children you have. Your wife looks after the household and sees to all the children and she makes shoes and clothes for both you and the children, but you don't think of all she has to do or of her health, but just make her with child again and again. Wait now for three or four years. Then you can have more if you want.' Usually, they will eventually say: 'If it isn't going to go on all one's life, then all right. But if she's going to go on with birth control for ever, then I'm not having any.' In those cases, all goes well and usually they do not decide to have any more afterwards. But in other cases, the husband just says: 'No.' Then we women speak to him about it every day, till he agrees to birth control. No husband has yet managed to stand out for any length of time, when we are talking to him. Actually, of course, they know that we are right. They know, of course, that they are responsible. It's only their pride that stands in the way, and we have to tell them that such pride is false and not at all right. But there are, too, families, where both husband and wife are agreed that they want to have children all the time. We can't do anything there. The whole thing's voluntary. The chief thing is to have a healthy family, and that the mother feels all right.

Since 1958, we have also established a children's day nursery and a collective dining-hall. These are used in the busiest of the harvest season, when it is important that as many as possible work, and so the women have to be relieved of their domestic work for a time. It's the same at the ploughing. Li Hai-ching is in charge of the collective dining-hall, and Wang Yü-lan of the children's day nursery. They were elected by the representatives of the labour brigade. Those are positions of trust. During harvest and ploughing, the women who are pregnant and the old ones with small, crippled feet do the work in the day nursery and the collective dining-hall. All the others are out in the fields. It works very well. In that way the women earn money. They like that. Neither the day nursery, nor the collective dining-hall is free. But the labour brigade contributes a certain share of the cost. This, too, was discussed and decided at a meeting of the representatives. Every child that spends a month in the day nursery entails a cost of thirty work points, that is to say three days' work. Of this the child's family pays fifteen work points and the labour brigade fifteen. The collective dining-hall serves three meals a day. For these, those who eat there pay seven or eight work points a month and the labour brigade pays three.

That's how we women work in Liu Ling Labour Brigade. We are making progress all the time. Every year the labour brigade chooses a few merit workers. They are given various prizes as a token of appreciation. I have had a pair of socks, a fountain-pen, a hoe, some notebooks and some diplomas. In 1960, the women elected me their delegate to a conference of merit workers that was being held down in Sian. They did that because I had taught them to read and write. I was very touched by it. I could not help thinking how they were commending me, though really I had not done all that I ought to have done. I determined to work even better, seeing that the women believed in me. I want to solve all our women's problems here. You see, not all women by any means are aware that they are their husband's equals. Some still look up to their husbands as in the old days, before women became free. They suffer because of that, and that they must be freed from it.

People say of Li Kuei-ying: She is always clear and sensible. She speaks in a low voice, but she always knows what she wants, and when she says a thing, then it is so. She does not like loose talk and she is not much of a one for laughing or joking. One has no need to be shy with her. One can talk with her about everything and she understands everything. She likes children and children like her, but they have respect for her too. If children are making a noise and fighting and she comes along, they will stop fighting at once. She is like her father, she is unselfish and hard-working and straight and helpful and serious. But she does not condemn and, whatever one discusses with her, she will help over it. She is the sort of person you can discuss your gravest problems with. She helps the women to earn money. If anyone in a family is ill, she organizes the neighbours to help. She is liked and no woman has ever said anything nasty about her. Even the old women respect her. Besides this, she is a good housewife and a good cook.

She studied for six months at the party school, and her husband is a ganbu. All the women admire her, because she has always decided exactly when she is to have children or not have children. Chi Mei-ying said: 'I am not like Li Kuei-ying. We too, tried, to be clever and plan, but it went wrong and so I had my last child. Not everyone can be as decided as Li Kuei-ying.'

Li Yang-ching, housewife, aged 29

I AM married to Liu Chen-yung. Li Hsiu-tang is my uncle, he is my father's younger cousin. Li Yü-teh is my half-brother. We have different mothers. My mother is dead, my father is dead, my mother-in-law is dead, my father-in-law is dead. I look after the house and work in the fields when I have time. We have three children. My sister-in-law, old Mrs Li, looks after them when I am working. My oldest daughter is ten and goes to school.

I work in the fields, when it is possible for me to do so. I have to look after the cave, too, of course. My year is roughly like this, going by the moon calendar. I don't know the sun calendar.

January, February. I make clothes and shoes for the family.

March, April. I work in the fields, turning the earth in places they can't get at to plough with the oxen, and preparing the manure for spreading.

May, June. I weed the fields, beans, wheat, millet, potatoes.

July, August. We weed a second time, then we begin cutting the wheat.

September, October. We take up the potatoes, harvest the beans and jute, and plough the fields for wheat, manure them and sow the wheat. We have brought the harvest down from the fields up on the hillside to the threshing floor and we thresh it. Towards the end of October, the threshing will be almost finished.

November, December. There is less to do in the fields, and we women do not need to go out and work on the land. The men gather firewood and are busy with the manure. Then the year begins again.

We women who are working in the fields leave home around half past seven in the morning. We come home about twelve to prepare food for the family. Then we sleep for an hour. At about three o'clock, we go out again and get back home at seven or eight o'clock in the evening. My husband and I get up at the same time in the morning. That's before five o'clock. Then he goes to work at five, has breakfast out in the fields later; I get breakfast ready, clear away and do the cave, dress the children, feed the pig and see to the hen and her six chicks. After that, it is time for me to go to work. In the midday break, when I come home, I cook a meal, and, when I come home in the evening, the first thing is to feed the family; then I feed the pig, the hen and her six chicks, then I see to the children and when they're asleep, I do my sewing and make clothes and attend to such things, until about ten o'clock, when I am tired and fall asleep.

In the busiest time in the summer, when the days are longer, we get up before four and my husband goes to work at four. We then work on until it is so dark that we can't see to do any more. We have dinner in the middle of the day, but then we have it at the collective dining-hall so as not to lose time. But at such times I don't sit up at night making clothes. It isn't so hard; people have always done it.

In the dead season, we stay in bed a bit longer. We don't get up then till six o'clock, with the dawn. Then I make breakfast and my husband has it with us. After that I see to the animals and perhaps go down to the big donkey-driven collective mill to mill flour. That takes half a day and I do it now and then during the winter. Then I make quilted coats for the family, sew shoes and that sort of thing. At midday, my husband comes home and we eat. In the winter he does not need a midday rest after dinner. He has slept longer in the morning and it is cool outside. In the afternoons he works outdoors and I sit at home making shoes and clothes. He comes home at dusk and if there isn't anything special on, we go to bed immediately after supper.

He has one rest day a week. Being a woman, I have a little more. In the summer, we use these to work in our private plot. We grow maize and millet and 'sticky millet' of two kinds. We have both our own private plot of good land down in the village and the new land we cleared for ourselves last year. You are allowed to clear as much as you like up on the hill; it's just a question of what you can manage. Last year our private crops brought us in about 800 jin of grain. In the winter, he uses his rest day to cut wood or do other of the heavier household jobs.

We don't often go into Yenan. Once a month roughly, and then to shop and see the opera. I don't go regularly, but if a good, famous opera company comes, I'll go in more often, otherwise not so often.

We never go together. I go in the daytime and he in the evenings. That's because of the children. When one's working and has children, one can never go out together in the evenings. I like the Shansi opera best. Sometimes films come to the village. Then I see them. We have a film show every month or six weeks. But I don't like films all that much. Opera is much better. When we have a film show, it is in the collective dining-hall.

I go more often to Seven-mile Village. I go there every fortnight to buy salt and soya and that sort of thing. Every fortnight we in the family use roughly:

Salt (we salt down a lot)	2·5 jin
Soya	1·0 jin
Vinegar	1·0 jin
Cooking oil	1·0 jin
Biscuits	1·0 jin
Sugar	2·0 liang

That's the food we buy. The biscuits and sweet cakes are for the children. The whole thing usually costs about four or five yuan.

We women usually sit together by day, so that we can chat. That makes the work go easier. Sometimes there are two or three of us, sometimes five or six. The more we are, the more fun it is. In summer we haven't time to see each other, but in the winter our work is of such a kind that we can sit together. We who meet to chat and sew are all of the same age. We haven't much to chatter about with the older women.

You can also divide the year by the festivals. I'm still speaking of the moon year. We haven't anything to do with the sun year. We butcher our pig and goats for the New Year festival. Then we make millet cakes and 'Chinese bean pudding'. We eat dumplings filled with pork and lots of other things. Then we go visiting, and our neighbours come to see us, and, on New Year's Day, everyone eats until you can't squeeze another bit of food down. We drink home-made wine and spirits from the shop. We paste paper cut-outs on the paper windows of the cave. My sister does that. She is clever at that sort of thing. We fix up verses beside the door, but I can't read those, because I can't read.

Then comes the mid-spring festival. We go to our ancestors' graves then to make offerings. We take food and wine with us and offer a little at the graves, pouring out a little wine in front of them. I and my husband and the children all go together. Everyone in the whole village goes to their ancestors' graves on that day. No, there isn't anyone who neglects to do so. In the old days, people used to make pilgrimage to the pagoda in Yenan. Now they have a fair there, instead. There are plays and performances, story-tellers and lots of other things. The whole family goes for the fun of it. It doesn't cost much if you are careful; but if you don't look out, you can run through all your money.

Our next festival is on 5 May. I don't properly know why it is celebrated. Some old custom, I expect. The only thing we do then is to eat triangular cakes of 'sticky millet', filled with dates.

On 6 June summer has come, and we have a summer festival and eat cold buckwheat pudding; 15 July is the 'harvest's birthday' and we celebrate it by eating better food than usual and as much as we can; 15 August is the full moon and then we eat moon cakes with sweetmeats inside. On 9 September the buckwheat has just ripened and we celebrate that by making buckwheat noodles. They bring you good luck. On 1 October the millet has just been harvested and we have a millet festival with cakes of steamed 'sticky millet'.* Then we have a festival in November, when we eat golden millet bread and the second kind of 'sticky millet'. On 18 December we eat gruel made of 'sticky millet'.

On these feast days the men go to work as usual and the women stay at home in the caves to prepare the food. Otherwise, we eat the same things the whole year round. Millet is our main food; we cook it in various ways. Mostly, though, we eat it as porridge. We have meat at the New Year. We have a proper meat meal then; afterwards we salt down the rest of the pig and use a bit for each of the festivals when one eats meat. Sometimes, if we have guests, we will buy meat in the market and make something. This year we must have had meat three or four times in addition to the festivals. Vegetables we have according to the season. We don't grow tobacco. My husband does not smoke.

In October, I put down cabbage. This lasts then through the winter until into March, when fresh vegetables start. I boil up the water, put

* Not China's national day, 1 October, but the first day of the tenth month of the lunar calendar. According to the lunar calendar the year consists of 354 or 355 days divided into twelve months. To make the lunar year agree with nature's year, an intercalary month of 29 days is added every so often. Such years then have 383 or 384 days in them. Now, the Gregorian calendar is used in China.

the cabbage in, take it out again quickly and put it in cold water. Then I put it in a big earthenware jar in layers with lots of salt. One layer cabbage, one layer salt. Then I press it all together with a big, well-cleaned stone. This same month, too, I lay down turnips and radishes. I cut them into narrow strips and layer them with salt in a stoneware jar and press with a stone.

In the spring I dry vegetables. I cut mustard-root into pieces, steam it and then let it dry in the sun; the beans dry on their own, and maize and potatoes can be stored in a potato pit.

In December, I begin making my red wine. I leave some 'sticky millet' to soak overnight; then I pour off the water, grind the millet and steam it. It is then like thick gruel. Then I mix in some yeast and pour the mixture into a jar. I put the jar on the warm kang. It has to stand there fermenting for four or five days, then the wine will be ready. When you want to drink it, you take some of the gruel from the jar, mix it well with water, then sieve it so that the liquid is almost clear. Then you boil it up, and it is drunk hot. I give the mush to the pig. It loves it.

If this wine is made the right way, it will be sweet and weak. If you let it stand fermenting for a long time, it becomes sour and strong. I prefer sweet wine, but there are people who want it strong, so they leave the jar a long time on the kang, because the longer it stands, the stronger the wine will be. I only make this in wintertime, because in the summer it isn't so easy to ferment it. Besides that, we buy spirits in the shop. We usually buy two bottles every New Year. My husband isn't very fond of drinking, and I myself think spirits altogether too strong. After all, it's sixty per cent. This year I am putting by six jin of millet to make wine with.

This week, my husband hasn't had a free day. He took two free days the week before last. He has thus worked all week without one. Yes, our food is pretty monotonous. There's not much variety. Our menu this week has been:

*Monday, 20 August 1962**

Breakfast. Millet porridge and maize bread and a vegetable dish of tomatoes, beans and potatoes, chopped up and fried in oil. We have fried chili with this and all our meals. The children don't like this, so we fry it separately and each mixes it in with the food as he likes along with vinegar. We don't drink water or tea with our food, but have

* Author's dating according to the solar calendar.

234

broth instead at every meal. At breakfast this consists of watered gruel.

Dinner. Steamed 'golden rice', that is millet, the same vegetables as in the morning and a broth of vegetable water.

Supper. Millet porridge.

Tuesday, 21 August 1962

Breakfast. Millet porridge with pumpkin. That makes a thick sweet gruel. Potato chips fried in oil.

Dinner. Noodles made of bean flour and wheat meal, fifty/fifty; tomatoes, beans and potatoes, chopped and fried in oil. With noodles we always have a strong sauce made of chives, strong pepper and salt. First, the chives are ground, then salted and peppered.

Supper. Millet porridge.

Wednesday, 22 August 1962

Breakfast. As Tuesday.

Dinner. Steamed 'golden rice' of millet, fried beans.

Supper. Millet porridge.

Thursday, 23 August 1962

Breakfast. Millet porridge, turnips, maize bread and fried vegetables.

Dinner. Thick maize porridge made with potatoes and fresh cabbage.

Supper. Millet porridge.

On this day we also ate a watermelon and three jin of small yellow melons.

Friday, 24 August 1962

Breakfast. As Thursday's.

Dinner. Wheat noodles with strong sauce and a vegetable dish of tomatoes and cabbage.

Supper. Millet porridge with maize cobs and steamed pumpkin. We have started to harvest our maize and so are eating a lot of maize cobs.

Saturday, 25 August 1962

Breakfast. As Tuesday's.

Dinner. Steamed cakes of finely chopped potato kneaded with wheat flour. With this we had fresh green beans, onion and garlic. We have onion and garlic with all meals, but that's obvious at this time of the year. It goes without saying.

Supper. Millet porridge. Maize cobs. Steamed pumpkin.

Sunday, 26 August 1962

Breakfast. Millet porridge and maize bread.

Dinner. Steamed wheaten bread with a vegetable dish of beans and tomatoes.

Supper. Millet porridge. Maize cobs. Steamed pumpkin.

We always cook our vegetables the same way: they are chopped finely and then cooked briefly in vegetable oil. Just now I am busy making ketchup, because there are plenty of tomatoes. I put the tomatoes in boiling water for a short time, take them out, peel them, take out the seeds and such, and then the tomato mush is boiled for a long time with salt and black pepper. We use this sauce for noodles.

I usually reckon on a good five jin of grain a day for the family. That does us. We are two adults and three children after all.

For the New Year I make salt patties of 'sticky millet'. I leave the 'sticky millet' soaking overnight, pound and steam it. Then I make a filling of potato and salt or grated carrots and salt; this filling is given a quick fry, stirring strongly. I roll out the dough and make it into patties with the salty mass as filling. Then I fry the patties in oil. If you want to make sweet patties, you do just the same, but fill them with pumpkin and sugar or beans and sugar. This filling is fried just the same as the salt filling, and the patties are made in the same way. Children like them. If you want to make 'sticky millet' cakes, the recipe is basically the same, but you don't use any filling and the dough is fried in oil as square cakes. They can be eaten with sugar or with gruel or how you like.

Bean curd is made for the New Year. I take some black beans and let them stand in water overnight. Then I peel them and grind them. I put the pulp in a piece of cloth and squeeze out the water. Then I boil them up in a pot, then I put in a little soda, which makes it like jelly. Then I put in a cloth again and press it till it becomes quite hard. Then I cut it into bits and fry or boil them and serve.

We got electric light in 1961. In the winter it costs us roughly 1·80 Y a month. In July we paid about 0·80 Y. Last month it had gone up to 1·47 Y. We haven't a dog or a cat, because our cave is new and there are no rats or mice here.

I make all the family's clothes. That is a lot of work, because the children are growing and wear things so. I either make a new, or re-make, a quilted coat, an unquilted coat, a pair of quilted trousers and a pair of unquilted trousers for everyone in the family each year. Last winter I bought twenty chi of cotton material; we had quite a lot left over from the year before; and I also bought five jin of cotton wadding. I mixed the new wadding with the old, which I had first cleaned, washed and carded. When I unpick an old garment, I use the old material as lining or for the children's clothes. But I wash it well first. No, I don't use a sewing-machine. There is only one person in the village who has a sewing-machine. That is Yang Fu-lien, who lives in Shiaoyuanchihou on the other side of the valley. That's a good way from Naopanshan, here. I make a whole new quilted coat for each member of the family every other year. In between, I unpick, wash and mend the old one.

I also make all the family's shoes. I make two pairs per person. Ten pairs each winter. The children have wadded shoes, but we grown-ups are hardened. No, I'm not cold in winter. The cave is warm. Each pair takes almost ten days to make. The winter's long and I work at the shoes whenever I get a free moment. First, I collect all the old worn-out cloth that can't even be used as lining any more. I wash it carefully, then I paste the pieces together, on top of each other, between layers of new cloth. When this has dried, I cut it out into soles. I make thicker soles for my husband and thinner soles for the children. Then I sew them with jute thread. That is the most laborious. You have to stitch very close and pull hard. The wear of the shoes depends in the first place on how the soles are sewn together. It is the jute you wear, not the cloth. I make the paste myself; I take roughly equal quantities of wheat and bean flour, mix it with water and boil it. I also make the jute thread myself. I cut the jute, remove the leaves, etc., then I put it in the stream. I dam this up with stones, so that the jute is quite covered with water. I put stones on the bundles of jute to keep them in place, and there they have to stay for a week, rotting. After that, I take the jute out, peel it and there the fibres are. I wind these into thread by rolling them on my thigh.

My husband knits. In this district, it is the husband's job to knit. He does this in the winter, when he's resting. Last winter, he knitted four pairs of stockings. One pair for himself and one for each of the children. I don't need any. I'm indoors most of the time, you see.

Yes, I'm from Liu Ling here. I learned how to run a cave from my mother and sister-in-law. I helped my sister-in-law when I was young and unmarried. I never went to school and I was never a pioneer. Instead, when I got a bit older, I looked after the family's children.

I was married when I was eighteen. I was betrothed when I was thirteen. My husband was then fourteen. It was our parents who decided it, but we were shown to each other and accepted it. I have never thought of anyone else. When we married, my parents-in-law were still alive and we lived with them. Life was much harder for me then, and I had much harder work than when I was a girl.

Talking of marriage and that, has anyone told you that Li Chin-wa, who is Li Hsiu-tang's daughter, has become engaged to the brigade book-keeper, Lo Han-hong, who is secretary of the League of Youth?

Well, life became more difficult for me when the children started coming. It isn't easy being a woman. My husband brings up four buckets of water a day from the well. I myself go down to the river to wash clothes once or twice a week. We often go down, a lot of us together. We do that when we have our day off. Or we do it during the midday rest, when our husbands are asleep. When we have our rest out in the field, we take out clothes to make or shoes to sew. The men either sleep then or walk about collecting fuel.

Women work much more than men. We have two jobs: we work both in the fields and in our caves. I know my husband helps me, we're a young family, of course, but he isn't as particular about housework as a woman is. Life is a lot of hard work. I don't take part in any kind of women's activities, political or otherwise. I just meet a few friends and chat with them.

I would, of course, like all my children to be able to study. I hope that they will work properly at school, so that they can be of some use here in the world and do something for people. The party and the school will have to decide what they are good for. But I am proud of my daughter. She is clever at school and helps me at home with the housework. She works hard. I hope that we shall be able to work and be healthy, so that we can live better and that our children will grow up into good people.

People say of Li Yang-ching: She loves a chat and jokes a lot. She is a gentle, well-brought-up woman and talks lovely Chinese with elegant phrases. She talks all the time when she's working in the fields, chattering and laughing. She talks a lot about the men in the village. She is very orderly and knowledgeable, though there isn't anyone of the older generation in her home. Everything in her cave is well looked after, and her children are well brought up and she works hard. She does more than other women. Most other women stop working in the fields when they have their first child, and don't find the day long enough even to look after the children; but she does work in the fields and sees to her home and the children, and has time to chat with her friends and run her home properly.

Her husband, Liu Chen-yung, is good. Most men here, or at least half of them, anyway, go straight to the kang and lie down and sleep when they get home from work; but he helps her and does things in the home. He is calm, quiet and doesn't speak much. They never quarrel; everyone considers them a happy family. He was anxious during her last pregnancy, in case she wasn't going to give birth to a son. She had had two girls before, you see. But she just told him not to worry, because she had decided to have a son. Then, when she did give birth to a son, all the women in the village were talking about her and envying her for being able to decide about such things herself. But, of course, she had been just as anxious in case it should be another girl.

Li Yang-ching is economical and thrifty. In 1961, they made a new cave, and the same year she went in to Yenan and bought a bicycle for her husband in the shop. She bought it with money she had earned herself. Liu Chen-yung is proud of his wife. She put a hundred days' work into that bicycle. He says: 'We haven't inherited what we have. We have worked for it.' They have also bought a two-wheeled cart with rubber wheels. That's a happy family.

Part VII
The People's Militia

The People's Militia

EVERY person *with civic rights*, only excepting invalids or the disabled, is a member of the people's militia: men between the ages of 16 and 45, women between 16 and 35. The people's militia is, however, a voluntary organization. It is at one and the same time a mass organization, with leaders elected at meetings of its members, and the ultimate backing of the power of the state: the people under arms acting as the organized violence in the defence of democracy and socialism.

There are three people in Liu Ling who do not belong to the people's militia: Tsao Chen-yung, because of an injured leg; Ai Ke-kao because of bad eyesight; and Li Hsiu-tang because he has been deprived of his civic rights. He is not regarded as a citizen.

Between the ages of 16 and 25 the members of the militia are in the armed militia, the crack unit of the people's militia. After that age, members are in the ordinary militia.

The duties of the people's militia are to ensure public safety; to see that order is maintained and that laws and regulations are complied with, to prevent and combat crime and track down any criminals there may be; to provide local defence in the event of war and, in the event of occupation, to act as guerrilla forces and local support forces.

Elected to the staff of Liu Ling Battalion

Battalion commander	Li Hung-fu
Political commissar	Li Hai-kuei
In charge of women	Li Kuei-ying
Battalion scribe	Lo Han-hong
Squadron leader★	Li Hai-ching
Group commander for the armed unit	Ma Hung-tsai
Group commander of the ordinary militia	Tung Yang-chen

★ The squadron leaders for the other villages are not given.   J.M.

Li Hung-fu, battalion commander, aged 33

I HAVE worked on the land as long as I can remember. I cannot remember any time in my life when I wasn't doing that. I began when I was so small that I no longer remember anything of that time. I was never able to go to school. We were poor and rented eighteen mu of land from Li Hsiu-tang's family. We had to pay more than fifteen jin of corn per mu in rental. Later, when the K.M.T. fled and the Eighth Route Army came, the land was divided up and we got thirty mu of good land in the valley, as well as 100 mu of poor, dry land up on the hillside. After that, life was better. Having land and not needing to pay rent to anyone, there was enough for us to eat. We got ourselves an ox and a donkey. We weren't so well off for clothes, of course; ours were poor, but we could eat our fill.

After that Hu Tsung-nan came. We fled into the hills. We took the donkey with us, loading our baggage on it. It starved to death, because there was no fodder up there. We made our way to the village of Kelaikou, some fifty li from here. I had joined the Young Pioneers when I was twelve, and I entered the Self-defence Corps when I became sixteen. We were to help the guerrillas. We were to get them information about the enemy; we were to examine strangers and question them, find out which were enemies. Of course we knew all the people in the villages round about, but we had to check up on any strangers who came to the village. This was still my job when we moved to Kelaikou.

Hu Tsung-nan also organized something he called a 'Self-defence Corps'. Their agents came to the village. We captured two, tied them up with rope and sent them to the guerrillas higher up in the hills. I don't know what happened to them. We didn't ask. We had other things to think about.

One day I was keeping watch in the village, when one of Hu

Tsung-nan's soldiers came, quite on his own. I called the others and we hid, so that he could not see us. We let him come right into the village. He went into a cave. We caught him there, as in a trap. He had a grey uniform. Hu Tsung-nan's soldiers had both grey and yellow uniforms. People said that they had got the yellow ones from the U.S.A., but I don't know. It was in May this happened. When the man saw us, he dropped the corn he had managed to grab. He made an attempt to escape. One of the chaps caught hold of him and we two others had a rope ready and we wound him up in that, so that he could not move. Then we sent him up to the guerrillas. He looked very anxious when we carted him off. When he got to the guerrillas, he said to them: 'Don't kill me. I'm just a farm boy too. I don't like being a soldier at all. I was forced into the army.' The guerrillas replied: 'We shan't kill you. We communists don't kill our prisoners. We are going to convert you.' So then they gave him instruction and after that he was let go, so that he could go back to his own village, where he was to tell people what the Eighth Route Army was and what our aims were and how we treated prisoners.

Then we went back to Liu Ling. That was under the occupation. When we got back, we saw that Hu Tsung-nan had destroyed everything. We had had both a house and a cave. But the troops had torn down the house, they had used the window-wall of the cave for firewood, and they had smashed all our cooking-pots and jars and things. They had used a lot of force to smash our things. That's what they were like. They had eaten our ox and found and stolen our corn. We borrowed a cave from Chang Chen-pong. He lives in Seven-mile Village now. That year we were only able to till three or four mu.

By the spring of 1948, our corn was all at an end. After that we ate elm leaves and chaff. People were very hungry. When the Eighth Route Army came back, they gave people loans. I borrowed twenty dollars. Then I carted supplies for the Self-defence Corps for a time. After that we began tilling the land again.

I was living then with my stepfather, Ma Hai-hsiu. He joined the labour exchange group. This was later turned into the labour group for mutual help. There was no great discussion about it. My ox was a miserable one, and I found it difficult to manage. The labour group for mutual help was useful for us. I had been leader of the labour exchange group, but Ma Juei-ching became leader of the labour group for mutual help.

After that we discussed the idea of an agricultural co-operative. We said: 'Let us plough up the marches. They are just in the way.' Besides that, it had always been difficult to decide whose turn it was to have his fields ploughed or harvested, when we had the labour group for mutual help. That was a long discussion. On the first day twelve families applied to join the agricultural co-operative. I was one of them. On the second day, five more families applied. Li Hai-yuan, who had been one of the founders of the agricultural co-operative, then resigned from it, saying that he wanted to farm on his own again. But things did not go as well with him as he had thought they would. They went as we had told him they would; and in the end he had to apply to join again.

I now married and moved from Stepfather's, setting up my own household. That was in 1952. A lot of people were joining the League of Youth then. I saw that and wondered about it. I realized that I could serve the cause of the people better if I was organized. It was Jen Teh-wan's son, Jen Huai-wan, who recommended me for the League of Youth. But the person who really made me decide was Li Hai-chun, who is now in charge of the loan department of the people's commune. He was the sort of person I wanted to be. Everything he said and did was honest, moderate and restrained. He was always correct, always helping the people in the village, without favouring anyone. He was always calm and collected and always able to say the right thing to relieve a situation. I understood that this was because he was organized. Therefore, I considered that I ought to join an organization too. Being a member of an organization meant that you were trained and educated by the organization and your comrades. My first teacher, though, had been my stepfather, Ma Hai-hsiu. When I was a child, he had often talked to me about the fight for the people's cause, and how one must be honest and impartial and always serve the cause of the people. He was a communist, and he often talked to me about the future and the time when the people would be victorious in all countries. What he said and what he did had always been the same thing. He helped me a lot, and he brought me up to be a conscious being.

I was now working as group leader in Liu Ling Agricultural Co-operative and in the League of Youth. I joined the party in 1955. Then came the discussions about the higher agricultural co-operative. During these, Li Chung-ying said that he would not join. He had enough land to manage on his own, he said. He would hire a farmhand. Well, there were no farmhands to be had any more. We all told him that, in the new society, all that with farmhands and day labourers was over. He had to sweat in his fields by himself. And while he was sweating by himself and not getting much of a harvest, we were working together in the agricultural co-operative and singing as we worked. So, in the end, he applied to rejoin.

The three people who from the start were the most enthusiastic advocates of the higher agricultural co-operative were the Old Secretary, Li Yiu-hua, my stepfather, Ma Hai-hsiu, and Mau Ke-yeh.

In 1957, I became leader of the labour group. The following year, we formed Liu Ling People's Commune. That was better than the East Shines Red Higher Agricultural Co-operative. It was stronger and had a more comprehensive economy; it enabled us to terrace and that sort of thing. We had begun with big water-regulation works already in the spring of 1958, before the people's commune. We built a dam at Yuanchihkou. We began building it immediately after the spring sowing, and we finished some time in October or November. We borrowed people from the other brigades in the people's commune, because the people's commune was set up while we were in the middle of working on it. We ran the building work in the same way before and after the formation of the people's commune. We borrowed labour from other places and kept count of their days' work. That is to say, we paid them back either in days' work or in money. When we began, it was an exchange of work between higher agricultural co-operatives and, when we ended, between labour brigades. The people's commune did not really involve any change there.

Since that, we have done certain terracing jobs in Liu Ling Labour Brigade. We have done them within the frame of the people's commune, in the same way as we worked in 1958, and afterwards we helped other labour brigades with their terracing work. Since 1959, we have mostly been occupied keeping the big dam in good order. It keeps filling up with mud the whole time, of course. Besides that, we have made smaller irrigation dams and terrace fields. We did not begin any new project in the winter of 1961–2. And it will be the same in the coming winter. We shall be content to keep what we've already built in good repair. After harvest in 1959 we made some iron. But I hadn't anything to do with that. I stick to agricultural work. Feng Chang-yeh was the one responsible for that job.

With the years, life has got better. We are making progress all the

time. In the old days, for example, we had few possessions. Now we have thermoses, galoshes, blankets, hand-carts with rubber wheels, bicycles. There's no comparison between what it was like before and what it is like now. We had been hoping for a long time to be able to buy a bicycle. We had planned to buy one. Eventually, in 1959, we had got enough together to buy one. We use it for transporting things, for bringing things home when we have been in the town shopping, and I usually take it to ride over to my relations in other villages. Sometimes I take my wife and children with me. I give them a lift then. It's a quick way of getting there. Women walk so slowly. I also take the bicycle when I am going into the town to go to the opera or the cinema. I like the opera and cinema; but on the other hand I am not particularly amused by the song-and-dance troupes. It's mostly operas that are already classics that I like. Of the films I remember, I can mention 'The Monkey King Conquers the White Bone Spirit Three Times', that is a filmed opera, and 'Hwa Mountain is Conquered'. I like films. My ten-year-old son can't get on with opera, but he likes films, he wants to see films like 'A Warrior of Steel'. He wants adventure and excitement and war and that sort of thing.

I am in charge of the people's militia within Liu Ling Labour Brigade. I have been a member of the militia for twenty years, ever since I was twelve years old. I was chosen battalion commander three years ago, since when I have been re-elected each year. The battalion includes the whole of Liu Ling Labour Brigade. It has 180 members who are capable of carrying arms. Here, in the village of Liu Ling—Liu Ling Village Labour Group and the Labour Group for Vegetable Cultivation—we have roughly eighty members. Small labour groups organize themselves as militia groups, and the larger labour groups as militia squadrons. The whole people's commune comprises a regiment. Up to battalion commander, we are elected by direct vote at general meetings. Beyond that, this would be too long-winded, so we battalion commanders elect the regimental commander and so on. I myself was never a squadron commander.

We are responsible for public order and security, and if there is war and the enemy dares to come here, we form guerrilla forces. There is no actual police as such. We provide our own police service. We have no badges of rank, by the way; we don't call ourselves lieutenants or colonels or suchlike. We are just elected leaders.

There are, of course, wholetime employees in the hsien administration who are concerned with police work. We can call on these if we need help. In the towns, too, there are traffic police and that sort of thing. But, in the country, we see to all that ourselves. We don't get any pay for it; nor are we credited with any days' work for taking part in manœuvres and that sort of thing, nor do we commanders get any sort of remuneration. The regimental commander in charge of the whole of the armed forces of Liu Ling People's Commune is at the same time one of the ten wholetime administrative ganbus employed in our people's commune. The people's commune, of course, constitutes a regiment, and this regiment is commanded by a regimental staff, which meets every three months. As battalion commander, I am a member of the regimental staff.

In this way we are, on the one hand, a mass organization with meetings and elections, and, on the other hand, a military organization which is responsible for security and which has military duties in time of war. For that reason, our order system is of a military kind. The commanders are elected at general meetings of the members, but their orders have to be obeyed while on duty. Our firearms are stored centrally by the hsien administration. The people's militia is an organization of the whole people. If the people have the political and economic power, it must also have the real power. In this way, we can be sure of not losing the democracy we fought to get.

But, of course, not everybody is in it. There are always some who are ill or lame or blind and thus unable to bear arms. Also, our counter-revolutionaries are not in it. We really don't want to give them weapons. It was difficult enough once to take their weapons from them. Nor can they be in it, because their civic rights have been taken from them by decision of the court. If they had reformed and if they really had been re-educated, they would get their civic rights back and thereby be able to be taken into the people's militia as members. But Li Hsiu-tang's children are in the people's militia. They are very efficient. They do a lot in the people's militia. They belong to the new age.

We have a ceremony at the annual meeting, when we take the new members in, those who have turned seventeen and can apply for admission. At the same time, we say thank you to those who have to leave the militia because of age.

In wintertime we hold manœuvres lasting one or two weeks. We chose the time so as not to interfere with production. We practise shooting then and have a programme of gymnastics and sports. We who have been elected commanders have more lectures than the ordinary members, but our training is the same. During training, people from outside come to help us. Also, we choose the best of us to lead the manœuvres. We get trainers and lecturers from the people's commune and the hsien administration. But we have never had an officer or trainer from the Chinese People's Liberation Army.

We have various courses and lectures and discussions among ourselves. We hold the larger meetings in the collective dining-hall, smaller gatherings are held in this cave, and the talks we have in the fields during the rests. Besides, we usually go into the town on 1 May and 1 October and listen to what is said at the big meetings, at which leading comrades speak. We also have a lot of material sent to us. We read this aloud to the members and then discuss it. We do this mostly out in the fields during rests. We usually hold all these meetings and lectures at some time that cannot be used in production. So it is mostly in the winter evenings. We study three subjects in the people's militia: military science, politics and agricultural theory.

In the old days, there was a lot of stealing and many unpleasant things happened. I remember that, when I was a child, we had our donkey stolen once. But since the Eighth Route Army came and our lives changed, things have been better. In the last ten years nothing has happened. Of course, our task is first and foremost to prevent crime and see that nothing disturbs peace and order. We are not a police organization that busies itself tracking people down; we are the might of the people itself which comprises the whole people and therefore prevents crime.

But we have had one case of theft which we discovered. That was in April 1960. There had been opera in the town and we were patrolling the highway in the evening. Then a man came along pulling a hand-cart. He was from a village farther on. We wondered why he was pulling a hand-cart in the middle of the night, and we asked him that. He could not give us a clear explanation and behaved so strangely that it looked as though he had a bad conscience. So we took him and the hand-cart to the office of Liu Ling's People's Commune in Seven-mile Village. It later transpired that he had been to the opera and, when he had left the town and was on his way back to his own village, he had seen the hand-cart standing outside a house and had just taken it with him. And the family from whom the hand-cart had been stolen got it back before they even discovered that they had been robbed. That's the only case there's been. Because, if the people itself is responsible for order, crimes are prevented before they are committed. In this village, there hasn't been anything at all. Nothing that I know of, at least.

In 1959, I was chosen, as a merit worker, to attend a conference of merit workers in our hsien. On 28 December 1961 I had a diploma conferred on me by Liu Ling People's Commune for 'Good work in production and good work in the people's militia'. That was given me in part for my agricultural work, and in part because there had been no accidents nor any crimes committed within the area for which I am responsible. In June this year I was given yet another diploma. The text was the same, but this time the citation was for 'Services in organizing the people's militia for agricultural work; meritorious leadership in agricultural work; exemplary style of working, hard work and simple way of life; good security work, no accidents, no crimes'.

My wife does not do any political work. She has never been elected to any post; she isn't a member of either the League of Youth or of the party. I have, of course, talked politics with her on occasion, but that hasn't been often. I myself was never able to go to school as a child. Since then, I have been working on other matters and have not been able to spare much time for learning to read and write. But I have attended various reading courses in my spare time in the winter, and I now know roughly a hundred characters.

But that also means that I do not know enough characters to be able to read a newspaper. But I can keep notes of a kind.

People say of Li Hung-fu: He is good-looking. He is an ordinary person. He is taciturn and never speaks unnecessarily. He is quite respected, but the women do not like joking with him. He does not understand joking, and laughing and that sort of thing. 'Though he doesn't like chatting and never jokes, and though he can go days at a stretch without opening his mouth or saying a word to anyone, there's a lot in his head.' He is a good organizer. He understands how to get people to work. He himself spares no effort and is always an example in any situation calling for energy and endurance. His manner of living is that which the party recommends: hard work and a simple way of life.

He has married again. His new wife is very young. She is not the least interested in politics. She talks a lot, sings and laughs and jokes, and they are utterly different. He often asks her to be quiet. She wants to sing, but he prefers to have quiet. She is an easy, pleasant person. Life is a game to her. She does not bother much about looking after the children; they have to manage on their own; and the house just has to get along too. But she is very young. She was scarcely eighteen when they married after his first wife's death. But she treats her stepson very well. She is just as fond of him as if he was her own. 'She is lazy and sings and laughs all day long, but she is nice to her stepson.' Her stepson is also very fond of her. Most children are.

The women say: 'Li Hung-fu is a stylish chap, but she is just a child. If she had married some young fellow, who was as fond as she of talking and laughing, they would have starved to death. It was lucky for her she married Li Hung-fu, who is always calm and sure and never fusses her, but just does his bit and gets on with his work.'

Part VIII
Liu Ling Labour Brigade's Supervisory Committee

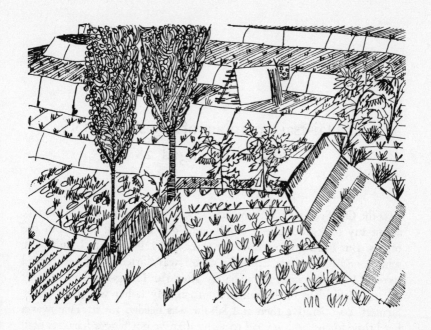

Members of the Supervisory Committee:

Mau Ke-yeh, Chairman	Labour Group for Vegetable Cultivation
Li Kwang-yung	Wangchiakou Village Labour Group
Han Fu-chieh	Hutoma Village Labour Group
Li Hai-tsai	Liu Ling Village Labour Group
Chiang Hao-wu	Erchuankou Village Labour Group

Li Hai-tsai, member of the supervisory
committee, aged 28

I AM the Old Secretary, Li Yiu-hua's second son, so I do not need to talk
about my background and childhood. You know all that from the
others. But I did go to school for three years. It was Liu Ling's basic
school, and I was there from the time I was thirteen till I had turned
sixteen. I began school immediately after Hu Tsung-nan had to buzz
off, and I finished in the winter of 1950. My father was head of the
farmers' co-operative then and labour was needed for it. That was a
hard time for us, and we had to show that we got bigger harvests than
either those farming on their own or the other labour groups for mutual
help. And this in spite of our land not being so good. One of Father's
difficulties was that there was no one in his farmers' co-operative able to
read or write. There was no one who could even keep a work daybook.

Father told me then that I ought to come home. He asked me if I
would not leave school and start work in the farmers' co-operative
instead. It was a hard choice for me. I loved school and had hoped to
be able to go on studying, but I thought that farmwork was glorious
too. Besides, I saw how hard Father had to toil and what difficulties he
was up against, so I told him that I would leave school and start working on the land instead. I have been working as a farmer ever since.

I have not joined any organization of any kind. I have been
wondering for a long time about joining the party, and now, at last, I
have sent in my application. The party is in the course of considering it
just now. They are testing me to see if I am worthy. I have never been a
member of the League of Youth. I am too old to join now, and when I
was young I was too immature. When I matured, I found I was too old.
When I was young, I was not very politically minded: I liked singing
and acting and playing. I thought the League of Youth dull and boring;

I just wanted to laugh and sing in those days. I used to sing every morning on my way out to the fields. That irritated some people. Of course, there's no harm in singing, but somehow I and the League of Youth just did not fit in.

I arranged my own marriage. I am of the first generation of the new society, and nobody else arranged my marriage for me. You attend to that sort of thing yourself these days. I was on a visit to another village, had gone to see a relative we had there. And there I saw a girl. I liked her. After that I used to go often to visit that relative. And mostly I saw the girl. Then we got engaged. Her parents agreed to it without much opposition. Mine were just happy. That was 1956. She was nineteen and I was twenty-two then.

I was working on the land the whole time. From 1950 to 1958 I kept the work daybook and calculated people's days' work. After that, I was just an ordinary worker until December last year. We were due to have the annual meeting. At this we were to elect a new member for the supervisory committee, to replace Fu Hai-tsao. People said: 'You are just and you are known not to be easy-going or the sort of person to look through your fingers at other people's mistakes. So, at the annual meeting of the representatives we are going to elect you to the supervisory committee.' Fu Hai-tsao's place was to fall vacant because he was going to be elected deputy labour leader of the labour group for vegetable cultivation, and, besides, he had been proposed for election to the management of the labour brigade. So I was asked: 'Will you stand?' I said: 'I'll stand. But only if I really am going to be elected, and if the voting is unanimous. I don't want to have any discussion about it. Either people have confidence in me or they don't have confidence in me. If they have, then I shall be happy to have their trust and shall do my best to be of service.' Well, the meeting was held and I was elected, unanimously.

The supervisory committee has a whole lot of duties. Its members, of course, are unpaid. And we are not allowed to be on any other committee or board. We have to supervise how the ganbus work, see that they are doing their bit and organizing the work in the right way. We have to supervise the implementation of production plans. We have to keep an eye out for extravagance or irresponsibility. We have to supervise the book-keeping. Apart from the different quick checks we make, we have to do an annual audit of the books and the stores and everything. We meet once a month for ordinary meetings, but we can be

259

called for an extra meeting whenever necessary. We have the right to call anyone we wish before us at these meetings. But, of course, no one can invite himself. No one can come and sit down with us and try to influence us.

We have full powers from the representatives and it is to them we are responsible. We are not to have respect for persons, nor be bound by ties of friendship in our work. No one can deny us the right to go through his books and investigate how he is doing his job. That is to say, we do not investigate private persons nor people's private lives; that is no concern of ours. We just investigate the various people who have been elected to positions of trust and how they are discharging their duties, dealing with the money and common property in their charge and so on.

We make our most important reports at the annual meeting. What happens is this: there is the annual meeting of the representatives. First, the chairman of the committee of the labour brigade makes his report. Next, the labour brigade's book-keeper makes his. After that, the chairman of the supervisory committee makes his report. He reports on what the supervisory committee has done during the year, and also on the results of the annual audit of the labour brigade's books, funds and stores. Only then does the general discussion begin. After that, the report is accepted, unless there is any reason to find fault with it, and after that there is the voting for the posts for the coming year.

But, of course, we submit reports at every meeting of the representatives during the year: what the position is and what action we have taken. We are duty-bound to report everything directly to the representatives. But the annual meeting is the most important. I can give you some examples of what we do:

A complaint against Tung Yang-chen, deputy labour leader of Liu Ling Village Labour Group, was made to us at our meeting on 15 August this year. It was made by the older farmers, and they wanted us to check his work. This was because, when they were ploughing for wheat, he had simplified the work and adopted a subjective attitude. He was a newly elected labour leader and did not have a great deal of experience. The old farmers had said: 'Remove all the weeds from the headlands.' But Tung Yang-chen had refused to listen to them and had said: 'We are short of labour. We are not going to waste time on the headlands. Just get on with the ploughing.' He decided simply to let the headlands go. All the others were against him, but he would not listen. He just gave the order.

The old farmers were thoroughly upset by this. They came to us and demanded that we take the matter up. The chairman of the supervisory committee, Mau Ke-yeh, was given the job of discussing the matter with the old experienced farmers. They all said: 'It is best to weed the headlands straight away, so that next year's harvest isn't a bad one.' Then we discussed the matter; and then we sent for Tung Yang-chen and had a serious talk with him. In the end, he admitted his mistake; the older and more experienced farmers were right, you see, and his conduct had not been what a labour leader's should have been: he had disregarded their advice and instead tried to give them orders. The headlands were then weeded. That is one sort of problem that we have to deal with.

Another kind of problem with which we have to deal is the book-keeping problem. In July, the book-keeper of Liu Ling Village Labour Group, Chang Chung-liang, came to me one night. Chang Chung-liang's cave is just next to Wang Kwang-yung's office. He is the treasurer of the labour brigade. Once a month he and the brigade book-keeper, Lo Han-hong, go through their books. The two books have to agree. But on this night, when Lo Han-hong and Wang Kwang-yung were sitting checking their books, Chang Chung-liang heard them say that there was a discrepancy of a hundred yuan or so. He came to me as soon as he heard that, since I am Liu Ling Labour Brigade's representative on the supervisory committee. Chang Chung-liang then left and went home to bed. I went to the chairman of the supervisory committee, Mau Ke-yeh, and we had a brief discussion about what ought to be done, and, as I had been to school and also had done a bit of book-keeping at the beginning of the 'fifties, we decided that I should go through the books.

So then we both went down to Wang Kwang-yung's cave and confiscated both his and Lo Han-hong's books, and made a quick check. They were taken by surprise. I worked all night going through the books and checking each item. In the end, by which time it was already noon the following day, I had found the error. One of the members, He Huang-ho, had handed in a certain cash sum to the treasurer, and the book-keeper had entered this in his books. But the treasurer, Wang Kwang-yung, had forgotten to enter the amount in his book. It was a sum of 100 Y. But when we went through the cash—

we had naturally confiscated that along with the books—we found the hundred yuan there. The cash in hand agreed with the book-keeper's books; but the treasurer's own books did not agree with his cash in hand. There was thus no question of misappropriation, but there was gross negligence. The treasurer, Wang Kwang-yung, was subjected to sharp criticism. We pointed out to him that this was irresponsibility. This he admitted. He promised for the future to endeavour to be more accurate.

We then reported to Chang Chung-liang what had been done and what the discrepancy had amounted to. It is our duty to do this. We have to report at once to whoever has informed us of any irregularity or proposed a check. This is very important. If the supervisory committee was not obliged to do this, it could happen that a soft member of the committee failed to act on an unpleasant report, out of friendship. As it is, we have to show that we really do do our jobs, otherwise the informant is entitled to demand our removal at the next meeting of the representatives. If we neglect our duties in any way—though I have never heard of anyone doing so really—the representatives can dismiss us, even in the middle of the year. Thus we reported the result to Chang Chung-liang, and he was satisfied. We did not summon any extra meeting of the supervisory committee, however. We did not think that was necessary, since there was an ordinary meeting due in two days' time. Later, the whole matter was put before a meeting of the representatives.

We have not had any more serious case. We have never discovered any embezzlement or that sort of thing. But we are constantly on the watch. It is a big responsibility to have to look after the people's money. That is why we check all books and stores very carefully. We go through every item. We do this as thoroughly as we can.

Every member of the supervisory committee has the right to make an on-the-spot investigation, if he suddenly comes across anything that seems not right. But he must get into touch with the chairman of the supervisory committee immediately afterwards and confer with him. There are five of us in the supervisory committee. Four members and a chairman. I am, naturally, proud of the fact that people have trust in me. Because it is a great proof of trust to be elected member of the supervisory committee. No one may be on the supervisory committee if he has relatives or friends in charge of funds. However honest he is, one can never know if he won't one day temper justice with mercy. He might, perhaps, shut his eyes to mistakes. But a member of the supervisory committee must never shut his eyes to any mistake, whoever has made it. Our chairman, Mau Ke-yeh, is an old and experienced party member, who has been in many positions of trust, and who knows a lot about organizations and economic associations. You ought to have someone like that as chairman of a supervisory committee. Someone one can rely on absolutely, and whom one knows not to have any personal ambition in his work, but who can stick to a fixed line of principle the whole time.

People say of Li Hai-tsai: He is never tired. He works hard and he talks the whole time. But his isn't exactly a mild or gentle nature. He often gets angry, and it does not take much to make him fly off the handle. His wife is just the same, and they have fearful quarrels. They can be heard all over the village. But no one interferes in their squabbles, because after a bit they will be laughing together again. They just like slanging-matches and say what they think, straight out.

He is incredibly frank. He will say anything to anyone. He is no respecter of persons. He has never seemed to be afraid of anything, but says exactly what he thinks. That is why we chose him for the supervisory committee: he is both honest and frank. And his temperament is such that no one could influence him and get him to do anything dishonourable.

But he jokes with his wife even when they are out among other people, and that is a bit peculiar. He does not care what people think, but will say to her: 'I'm not handsome, but that doesn't matter, you being as ugly as you are.' Then they both laugh. One doesn't say that sort of thing. Nor does one talk about one's own looks or joke about someone else's appearance. But Li Hai-tsai does. He'll joke with anyone, and never bothers what people think. But he is gay and friendly, too, and he isn't nasty or resentful. It's just that he's so incredibly outspoken.

Part IX
The Counter-Revolutionary

Li Hsiu-tang, aged 38

I AM of a landowning family. My father died when I was a child, and I do not remember so very much of my early childhood. But it was happy. We lived well, even after Father died. We had good food and life was pleasant. We ate pork every day, we had chicken and eggs and wheat noodles and stuffed wheaten bread. I practically never tasted millet as a child. That is grown a lot round here, but we didn't eat it. It was only the ordinary people who ate millet; we ate rice and wheat. We had a big house in Old Yenan. It does not exist any longer. The whole of the old town was wiped out during a bomb raid in the war. But I remember our house very well. There was a big hall in it, and it had lots of rooms. Our family consisted of over forty people. Father had four brothers, but I was his only son. Mother, though, was just a concubine. There were many relations and they were all nice to me. I remember Li Han-hua as one of my older uncles. I met him when I was ten. He was my bride's brother. Mine was a happy childhood.

When my father died, the inheritance was divided into five shares. The eldest of the cousins, Li Niu, became the head of the family, and he got the land. Another cousin took over the shops; he was responsible for the finances. A third cousin had all the cash. My mother and my elder sister and I got the property in the town. That brought in a lot in rentals. The youngest cousin got the animals, the oxen, sheep and goats. After that, we each moved into a house of our own. That was easily arranged, because we owned a lot of property, and we only had to give notice to a few tenants and move in.

Li Niu, who had got the land, moved to Liu Ling. I did not know much about what was going on out there. We didn't hear anything about Liu Ling. That was partly because I was so young, and partly because the land was in Li Niu's share. On the other hand, I knew a lot about our house property. Mother used to discuss the management of it with me. Though I did know that, later on, Li Niu's land was divided up. He was living then in the cave where Tung Yang-chen lives now. The cave was taken from him when everything was divided up, and given to Tung Yang-chen, because of what had happened to his father. At that time there were only seven or eight households in the village, and they were all able to have good land. We also had a plot. Later, Li Niu moved to another cave and, when he did, I took his over. But that comes later.

I went to Kao Hsiao's school in Yenan. It was a good school and I liked being there. We studied Chinese language and literature, mathematics and history and Sun Yat-sen's principles. Nothing serious happened in my life until the Red Guard entered the town. Mother had never spoken to me about the Red Guard. I knew, of course, that other people did not dare leave the town and were short of food, but my mother was a widow and had only been my father's concubine, so she always went outside the town to buy things and used to come back with lots of food. I know that there were people in Yenan who were starving and in difficulties during the blockade, but I myself noticed nothing. Our table was the same as ever. We had lots of courses.

Then the Red Army came. They summoned a mass meeting. It was to be held at the East Gate. There was a rumour that the communists were going to cut people's throats, and we wondered. I went to the meeting with my school class, because the schools had all been ordered to attend. The meeting was held in the middle of the day and was well attended. Everyone wondered what the communists would have to say. Three people made speeches. Liu Chih-tan was one of them, I remember. I had heard his name. He said: 'Be calm, don't worry, carry on with your ordinary work. There is no reason to run away.'

Mother had been worried before this and wondered if we should try to get away, but after this she decided to stay. Many of our tenants were tradesmen from Shansi. One of them, who was head of the town's chamber of commerce, came to see Mother. He said: 'There's no reason to be afraid. The Red Guard has spoken with me and promised to protect trade and safeguard the interests of the tradesmen. They asked me whose house I lived in, and I told them: '"A poor widow's house", so there's no cause for anxiety.' Then women ganbus from the Red Guard came and talked with us.

School was closed for ten days. Then it opened again. Now certain teachers had been replaced. We had the same timetable as before, but there was more talk of Sun Yat-sen's three principles and the teachers told us that we must fight against Japan. Till then, nobody had spoken to us about Japan. Then I joined the Young Pioneers. The main thing was that one helped the teachers see that everyone studied properly. Besides that, we sang songs. Then the school was incorporated in the Normal School and I left. I did not see the fun of going to school and, anyway, I was Mother's only son. She was afraid that I would abandon the family if I went on studying. I was to learn to be a tradesman instead.

I now began working in a shop. I had no difficulty in getting work, because most of our tenants were tradesmen and, in many cases, we owned half their shops. I began by keeping the yards clean and sweeping out the floor of the shop, but then gradually I was also allowed to serve in the shop. I liked that better than going to school. I had always dreamed of becoming a merchant. I still went to the Pioneer meetings once a week. There, we discussed abolishing gambling games and that sort of thing. We still lived as well as we had before. Actually, the arrival of the Red Army did not cause any change in our lives. We still ate pork and chicken and eggs. I did not need to eat millet. I liked my work and had great hopes for the future.

Then came the bombing. Most of our houses were demolished. The others were damaged and had to be pulled down. The whole town was destroyed. The bombing was a hard blow for us. Mother wept, because we had lost all we possessed. My mother's uncle came to help us. We moved to Liu Ling. There we had a mill and the land that we had got ourselves allotted, and we were hiring day labourers to look after it. We now had twenty mu of valley land and thirty mu of hill land. We did not work on the land ourselves. The day labourers did that. We were exploiters, as it's called.

We got on well with the people in Liu Ling right from the beginning. When we moved out there, everyone was kind to Mother. She was a woman and a concubine, and she had always been courteous and friendly to the people there when Father was alive. But when our second cousin wanted to come out there, too, people said no. So he never came to Liu Ling. But life had become worse than before. We no longer had any income from our houses, of course. All that we had to live on was the land, the mill and a little trading. We ate better than our neighbours, to be sure, that was obvious, but life wasn't what it had been.

I had married before we moved out from Yenan. That was in 1938. It had been arranged by my parents before I was born. After that we were four in the family: Mother, Mother's uncle, I and my wife. I now began working as a street trader. There was a big co-operative here down by the road, and I used to go there in the morning and sit down by the roadside with my wares. I sold cigarettes and melon seeds and walnuts and groundnuts and that sort of thing, and when the villagers from roundabout came to the co-operative to buy or sell, they stopped and talked with me and bought something. It was something of an event for them to go to the big shop, so it all fitted in well that I should be there and could sell them a few delicacies.

Mother's uncle was in charge of the land and the mill. The day labourers came from Yulin. We made quite a lot from the mill. Between twenty-eight and thirty jin of grain yielded roughly twenty-two jin of wheaten flour; for milling we charged two jin of flour and all the bran. My income from peddling was not large. It perhaps bought my food. I came and went as I liked; I was my own master, and I did not need to over-exert myself. I liked trading, I liked chatting with people and doing what I wished. That's the life that has always suited me best. I have always wanted to be a tradesman. And we lived much better then than we do now. Much better. We felt better and ate better.

Mother kept saying: 'If it hadn't been for the Japanese, we would still have been there in the town. We would have had our houses and not needed to live like this. But their bombs destroyed it all.' Then we heard that the Japanese had been beaten, but that there was a new war between the communists and the K.M.T. government. Now the situation hardened, and I gave up my street trading and ran the mill instead. I often used to think of what might happen. Actually, I wanted to live a more comfortable life. I had been accustomed to that since childhood. Though life was not as good as before, it was still better than most people's. The mill milled 300 jin a day. That brought in a good lot. There was a lot of talk about the war between the communists and the K.M.T., and I wondered what was going to happen. To be on the safe side, I joined the militia. You see, I had always been a Young Pioneer. Mother used to say: 'If we hadn't had the misfortune to live in Yenan, but had been in the K.M.T. area, what happy lives we should have led.' All the elder members of the family said that, and I thought the same.

Then we heard that the Eighth Route Army was to retreat and that General Hu Tsung-nan's troops were coming. A mass meeting was held in Yenan before it was evacuated. At this they quoted Chairman Mao, who was supposed to have said: 'Hold Yenan, lose Yenan. Surrender Yenan, keep Yenan.' But that just bewildered me and didn't know what to think. I was so worried. One did not know what was going to come of it all, and it was important to steer the right course. It's always like that in war. You can never be sure. We were anxious, and Mother kept saying: 'If only we had been in K.M.T. territory all the time. Now nobody knows what can happen.' Then Yenan was evacuated, and I saw the Eighth Route Army withdraw. After that, General Hu Tsung-nan's troops arrived, and I had never seen so many soldiers before. They had modern weapons and guns and everything, and I thought: 'Well, at all events the communists have had it.'

I remember the day the K.M.T. troops marched in. Our mill was on the other side of the river. We had tried to protect that. People had been told to evacuate their possessions and bury their grain. This had been done rather tardily. It was only in the last few days that people made any attempt to hide their grain. Now, I and Tuan Fu-yin and some others had taken ourselves up on to Naopanshan, just here beside us. We had several bottles of spirits with us and sat up there on the hillside, drinking and talking. Then we saw the troops arrive. It was ten o'clock. It was just as people were due to go out with the goats. General Hu Tsung-nan made his troops march on Yenan in two detachments. One came from Kanchuan and the other from Ichuan. This was the one from Ichuan arriving. As we sat there talking, one of us suddenly said: 'Now they're coming!' We stood up and watched them. The troops came marching along. First came the cavalry on big horses. Then the infantry. There were soldiers everywhere; they were spread over the whole landscape; they occupied all the eminences along the road, there seemed no end to the soldiers. Uniforms and weapons everywhere and the cavalry riding along on big fine horses. We stood there watching them, Tuan Fu-yin and a person from the co-operative shop, he has gone back to Shansi now, and another from Michi, he has gone back there too, a man called Yen Chu-tsai who is in Shansi now, and another called Yen something, and myself. Then we saw the police troops coming towards the village. Then Tuan Fu-yin called: 'Quick! Quick! Let us boil up water and bid these troops welcome. Let us not wait until it's too late.'

I thought: 'These K.M.T. troops are not going to do anything to me. But if I don't go down and meet them now, something might happen to my property.' Then we finished off the last of the spirits and ran down to the village to welcome the troops.

There we were taken prisoner. They told us to fetch water for them, and then we had to guide them the safest way into the town. We did this. Three days later the others were released and ordered to get back to their home villages as quickly as they could. But I was kept. They interrogated me. They did not trust me. You see, I did not dress as a farmer in those days. I wore European clothes and cut my hair the European way. I had trousers and a jacket with three pockets and wore a hat on my head. The officer took hold of me and said: 'Are you from the Eighth?' 'No, I am not,' I replied. He looked at me and said: 'You are not dressed like the farmers.' 'But I'm still not from the Eighth Army,' I said. He did not believe me, but said: 'You're an inveterate communist and now you're going to tell us about the communists' illegal organization and where the Eighth Army is and what plans the guerrillas have.' But I couldn't tell them anything, because I didn't know anything. 'I don't know any military secrets. After all, I'm just a mill-owner.' But the K.M.T. did not believe me, but took me to a cell. They locked me in. The prison was in the garrison. A judge called Kao interrogated me. Then they tortured me. They sat me on a chair and tied my knees down and stretched out my feet and put bricks under them. More and more bricks. But whatever they tried, I could not tell them anything, because I didn't know anything. Then they let me alone.

We prisoners were now divided into different groups. They called us prisoners-of-war. Each group was attached to a unit. One of the K.M.T.'s difficulties was that they had taken Yenan without getting any prisoners, and that there hadn't been a fight. The Eighth Route Army and the communists had evacuated in time and avoided fighting. But the K.M.T., you see, had to be able to show that it had won a victory. The officers needed prisoners to show off with. They were given prize money for every prisoner. They now brought visitors in to see us and said: 'These are our prisoners. They are from the Eighth Route Army.'

Then, we were to have more important visitors. We were given old worn uniforms. Foreign journalists were coming. I was to tell them that I was from the Eighth Route Army and belonged to the 358th Detachment. Several delegations of journalists came to look at us. Some of these foreigners had yellow hair and long noses. Others looked more normal. Some wore big boots with spurs, others tall boots with laces. Some of them had K.M.T. caps and others sheepskin caps. They spoke to us, and a K.M.T. officer stood in front of us and translated their questions, and we answered as we had been told to answer. Then they photographed us, and some had cameras like yours and others had film cameras. Then they took group pictures of us.

Then, in June, more peculiar things happened. We were ordered out to dig false graves up on the hillsides. I had to dig them up on Lokoushan beyond the vegetable plots. There were no corpses in the graves, but we were to say that this was where this or that communist officer was buried. People then came to see them and inspected the graves and interviewed us as witnesses. We told them how the communist officers had died and that we were local farmers. After that the

273

K.M.T. officers were given tens of dollars for each of the graves. But later that same month my period of being a prisoner ended.

Two officials came to Yenan. They were both from the town here. One, who was called Yuan, had served in Yenan earlier, and the other, Chu, was also from the district. Both used to come to my family's house. When they saw me, they said: 'But why in the world are you in prison?' I told them the truth, that I was suspected of being a communist, and that I had been tortured and had not been believed when I said that I was a mill-owner and a landowner's son. Then they saw to it that I was released at once.

I was now made a batman in the garrison headquarters. My officer was called Wong. He was from the General Staff and was responsible for prisoners-of-war. I had to tidy up and serve at meals and all that sort of thing. I worked for him like this for a month and he got to know me. Then all the so-called prisoners-of-war were to be transported down to Sian. Hundreds of people were to be sent off. Then Hsia, the General Staff officer responsible for army intelligence, sent for me and said: 'We need twelve men to work in the radio communications department and run the intelligence service in Yenan.' It was to be a secret organization, and therefore was to be called the 'north-western News Bureau'. My officer Wong selected the men. Most were from Yenan. I was made leader of the group. I don't know how it happened that they chose me. It must have been pure chance. I hadn't done anything.

We were not paid. We were just given our food. One day a month, we put on uniform; that was the day the pay was supposed to be paid. But after that they took our uniforms away again, and the officers held on to our money. That was customary in the K.M.T. army. It was a common trick. There were always more men on the roll than there were in reality, and in that way the officers were able to get more money.

Our group was stationed behind the buildings that now house the offices of Yenan hsien. In the mornings we had to start up the motor that supplied the garrison with electricity, and then we were supposed to go out into the town and listen to what people were saying. We always wore civilian clothes. What the two officers, Wong and Hsia, wanted to hear about most was what people were saying about the Eighth Route Army and the guerrillas. We had strict orders not to say anything about our working for the intelligence service. But people knew it, of course, and it wasn't much we heard. We didn't get any money, because the officers took our pay, so we couldn't go in anywhere and eat and drink and listen to what people were saying, but had to walk about in the streets and try to listen. I heard that my mother had said that she was anxious about me and my work. I wasn't earning anything for the family, of course, and it wasn't work that had any advantages. My deputy and I had each been given a pistol with ten cartridges, but I was careful not to carry mine on me. I locked it up and never touched it and never fired a single shot, because there was no knowing what might not happen in the future.

We had orders not to go more than ten li from our garrison. Out there were the guerrillas, and they might capture us. I had been given the pistol to use against the guerrillas, but I preferred to keep it hidden and try to avoid getting in contact with the guerrillas. I was the one who gave the others in the group their orders, but I made them report direct to Hsia. I never interrogated any prisoners. We did duty in the radio communications section at night, between ten in the evening and four in the morning. During the first month, all went well and we liked our work, but then people became more and more reluctant to have anything to do with us and that made us feel uncomfortable.

At first, no one dared make a fuss, but then our wives and mothers came and cursed us for not earning anything, and those working in the group began to be discontented. People in the group began saying that they were working for the K.M.T. intelligence service, yet their families still had to starve. Besides, it did not look as if the communists were as thoroughly beaten as we had thought.

Then the garrison headquarters was to be moved and the Seventeenth Division transferred to Yenan. At first, the garrison wanted to take us with them, but we did not want to go on with this work and I went to see our official, Chu. The other official I knew, Yuan, had already left Yenan. I spoke frankly to Chu and told him the whole thing, and as he had known my father and wanted to do me a good turn, he said: 'You can go off if you like.' So then we handed in our pistols and cartridges, and, in September, I went home to Mother.

The family was then living in Seven-mile Village. They had moved there from Liu Ling. When Mother saw me, she said: 'I am afraid.' I was at home only one night. Mother had a talk with me. She had not been expecting me home so soon. She was worried that I had brought no money home. She did not like me working for the K.M.T. 'Don't get yourself mixed up with that sort of thing,' she told me. 'Take up trading instead.' I said: 'One has to say yes when those who hold the power ask one. If you want to get away from here, we must find a way.' You see, at the beginning we had thought that the K.M.T. would win for good, but now, that August and September, we all understood that the K.M.T. would soon have to get out again. The guerrillas were active all the time, and the K.M.T. troops and K.M.T. officers themselves no longer even believed that they had won. We talked a lot that night about what we were to do. Now everything had become rather dangerous for me. The guerrillas might come at any moment and capture me, and on the other hand the K.M.T. might decide to fetch me back for its intelligence service again, so we decided that I should go to Lochuan that very night.

I had a lot of friends in Lochuan. There, I borrowed 400 silver dollars from a friend and bought cloth in Fuping. It was good homespun, and there was, of course, a shortage of goods up in Yenan. A month later, I was back in Seven-mile Village with my cloth. There, in October, I opened a shop. But I did not dare serve in it myself, because I might either be taken by the guerrillas or by the K.M.T., and I would have fared just as badly with either. So I was very cautious and went into partnership with a man called Pai Hsin-hwa. He was to serve in the shop, while I would be out in the countryside buying up more cloth. He is a book-keeper in Yenan now. For myself, I tried to make myself as unobtrusive as possible.

One evening, when I was at the opera in Yenan, I heard rumblings in the street outside. When the opera was over and I went out, I saw that General Hu Tsung-nan's troops were in the act of leaving. They were fleeing. They were so scared, they were quite ridiculous, yet there wasn't a single guerrilla soldier anywhere near, nor yet one man from the Eighth Route Army. They did not arrive until the following afternoon.

As I was going home that evening, I thought: 'Now I really have made a mess of things. The K.M.T. appeared to be so strong when it came, and now its troops are running away like dogs with their tails between their legs. This is going to be serious for me.' But we never thought of leaving Liu Ling and escaping along with the K.M.T. You see, we could not have taken our possessions with us. Our land must lie where it lay. If we lost that, we should have become beggars, and what future could we have looked forward to then? But I was afraid of the Eighth Route Army.

Yet when it came, nothing happened. The people in Liu Ling and Seven-mile Village were reasonably all right to us. I began driving a horse and cart, being carrier and transporter. I had gone into partnership over this and I was always on the road. We wound up the shop gradually and closed it in November 1946. We had also closed the mill. I drove my horse and cart for two years; then little by little I began tilling the land again, and rejoined the people's militia and began exchanging work with other people. Life was better than under the occupation, but far from as good as it had been before General Hu Tsung-nan's time. Then it happened.

It was the fifteenth or sixteenth of February 1950 or 1951, I don't remember exactly. I was working in the fields, when two men came. One was the district chief and the other, Liu Pao-ying, the battalion commander of the Self-defence Corps. They came up to me and said: 'Hsiu-tang, have you had dinner?' I replied that I hadn't. 'Then go and have it,' they said. I invited them to come home and eat with me, but they just said: 'We have eaten.' As I set off for home, they said: 'Eat quickly, because we want a word with you.'

I went home to eat. I realized that something was going to happen, but I didn't know exactly what. I had been anxious immediately after the Eighth Route Army had come back, but then, as time passed, I had begun to think that the authorities were letting bygones be bygones. I supposed that they were now going to have a talk with me. I had not much appetite and had soon finished. They were waiting for me when I came out. They showed me a paper and said: 'Now you are under arrest.' And I would never have believed that they would arrest me straight off like that.

Then I was taken to the Office of Public Security. There was I locked up for the night, and the next day I was taken to the court in Yenan. When I was brought before the court, they said to me: 'Li Hsiu-tang, do you know that there is a big campaign now to suppress counter-revolutionaries?' 'No, I didn't know that,' I replied. 'I haven't heard anything about that.' Then they told me about the big campaign and told me to tell the truth about what I had been guilty of doing. They said: 'The party and the state are lenient and forbearing and prepared to let bygones be bygones and carry on, if you are frank and honest and confess everything. But if you conceal the truth and try to get out of it, it won't be so nice for you. You should not be afraid of confessing. Your mistake in life has already been made and cannot be

277

unmade. But what was done was done several years ago, and if you tell us, you have many years in front of you. You are still young, and your future lies in your own hands. But if you keep anything back, you will be suppressed. Now you are to go to your cell and think this over.'

I was prepared to confess everything straight away, but they wanted me to go back to my cell and have time to think. The next time I was brought before the court, I made a complete confession. I had nothing to hide, because I had not interrogated prisoners and I hadn't shot anyone or even carried my pistol, but kept it locked up. But they had a fair amount of evidence from other quarters too, and the third time I was taken before the court it was to be sentenced. There were only a few in the court that day. There was just the judge, his assistant, a guard and me. I was condemned to three years. Then I was taken back to my cell.

It was hard, of course, to be condemned to three years, but I was also relieved, because, though before I had thought that the authorities had forgotten me, while in the cell I had remembered that counter-revolutionaries usually had a pretty bad time of it. They told me that, if I worked and behaved well, I would return to society and be accepted back into it and the past would be forgotten for ever. I said that I accepted everything.

After that, I was twenty days in the cell. This was the time which I had to appeal in. I told them that I had no desire to appeal and didn't want to go before any higher court, but just to start serving my three years straight away. But they said that whether I wanted to appeal or not, I still had to stay in the cell and wait till the period for appealing was over; because such was the law.

When the twenty days were up, I was transferred to a reformatory farm called Hunsze, which was near Thirty-mile Village. We worked there to be reformed. We were given food, clothes, hand towels, soap, shoes and stockings, but no money. The food wasn't so bad: we had maize bread, millet, sometimes rice and even meat now and again. Once a week we had steamed wheaten bread. We were considered mild cases. That was a reform farm for little counter-revolutionaries. Our families often came to see us.

We had an eight-hour working-day, and the work was the same kind of thing as at home in the village. There were no guards, but sometimes prisoners who did not belong to our farm came to work with us in the fields, and they had armed guards with them. They were more serious cases. They were people who had been responsible for executions and that sort of thing. We had nothing to do with them and made no contact with them. I don't know exactly where their camp was, but it must have been somewhere in the neighbourhood. It was certainly a much stricter place, with locked cells and armed guards.

We had no guards, and we slept in ordinary rooms. There were two of us to a room, and the rooms were never locked. If we wanted them locked, we had to provide our own locks. We could ask for leave to go home and see our families. Every time I drove the horse and cart into Yenan to fetch things or deliver our products, I used to stay the night with the family. At this juncture, my cousin Li Niu died, and the family moved into his cave in Liu Ling.

I do not know the details of the administration of that reform farm. I never became anything more than a labourer in the fields at that farm; but there were thirty of us small counter-revolutionaries and one director. All the organization's work was done by the prisoners: the cooking, the selling, everything. There were no guards and, as far as I know, the director had no firearms.

We had a meeting and entertainment every Monday and Tuesday afternoon. We played cards and sang, and we had discussions. We were told that we were now having to be useful and repay society for all the harm we had done. We had to study the party's policies. Those who could not read or write had to learn to do so, and we others read the newspapers.

During the three years that I was there, there was only one case of a person running away, and he came back of his own accord after a time. He had found it difficult to manage. He hadn't, of course, been able to live in his own village, but had had to stay in hiding. Then he realized that he would be taken sooner or later, and that that would make it more difficult for him to be freed later. When he came back of his own accord, we held a meeting. We prisoners had a long talk with the authorities and we passed a resolution that, since he had himself thought better of it and come back of his own accord, he ought not to have his sentence increased, but that it should be enough to say that he had been guilty of a foolish action. The authorities agreed with us, and his sentence was not increased. Then, gradually, some of the prisoners were freed. One after the other they served their sentences. One or two preferred to stay on the farm, and so they were made fully paid farmhands. They had no families to go to and they did not think things would be so easy for them in their home villages any longer, so they preferred to stay among friends on the farm. There were, perhaps, some who had other ideas too. I don't know. People are so different, aren't they? But there weren't many. Most of us wanted to get back home as quickly as possible.

I think it was in December 1954 that I was released. I was glad when I was told that I could leave the reform farm. I hadn't kept a proper account of the months, which were very monotonous, and I was surprised when they told me that I had done my time. They said: 'You have done your time now. You can leave us. The authorities in your home village will look after you and see that you get a proper start.' People were nice to me when I got back to Liu Ling. Nobody mentioned my term of imprisonment or anything about it. They all pretended it had never been. For one year I farmed on my own. My mother's uncle, who had been looking after our land while I was away, moved back to his own home; Mother was happy, and I thought it was very pleasant to have got away from the reform school. Then I joined the East Shines Red Improved Farmers' Co-operative.

What happened to the others in my group, I do not know. Some were punished and others were so insignificant that they were just given a warning. There was no one else from Liu Ling in the group, and I haven't tried to get in touch with any of them since. Life is different now. There is a lot of work; there are many mouths to feed and not much manpower in the family. But we manage.

People say of Li Hsiu-tang : His is the only cave with flowers to grace it. The whole family is well looked after and well fed. He always has a big store of food. His children are the healthiest in the village. They are always the best dressed, the best washed and the best behaved. No one mentions his past any more. He never speaks of it himself. The younger people scarcely even know that he was ever an active counter-revolutionary. He and his wife have not yet been granted civic rights. They have never shown the least interest in regaining them.

He does not work hard and shows no signs of being reformed. His way of thinking hasn't altered. But he never says anything against socialism. He prefers to say nothing about public matters. He prefers easy work. If he is given a choice, he will always find an easy job that gives him a good return in the form of work points. He is clever at that.

But when he likes, he can really get down to it, though mostly he can't be bothered. 'Once a landlord, always a landlord.'

His manner is gentle and friendly and he gets on well with everyone, yet at the same time he does not worry about having friends. He is shrewd and cautious and is good with mechanical things. He likes doing repairs to bicycles and motors. As he avoids all really heavy work, he spends most of his time driving the shit-carts from the town. That lets him go about Yenan a bit, too.

The family is badly off for manpower, but his wife is very clever. She is one of the best housewives in the village. Her children are always the best looked after, her cave is the cleanest. But she has a very sharp tongue. He would never have been able to manage without her. Otherwise, he would perhaps have become like Tuan Fu-yin. People never mention her family, and the young ones don't even know that Li Han-hua was her brother. They have two children in Yenan Middle School. There are only four children from Liu Ling in the school altogether. One of their daughters has just become engaged to the secretary of the League of Youth, the Labour Brigade's book-keeper, Lo Han-hong. One laughs at this; but one does not comment.

Part X
Old Doctor Kao

Kao Chia-jen, aged 72

I was born under the Ching dynasty, in the seventeenth year of the government named Kuang Hsu, 'Brilliant Course'. I come from this valley here. Father was a farmer. He rented his land. When I was a child, the old people in Yenan used to tell about the Moslem rising in which many people lost their lives. The armies had marched through the land, plundering and pillaging. There was a big battle at Thirty-mile Village, where the Moslems fought the troops of the Ching dynasty. One general was killed and many fell. A little stone plaque has been set up on an eminence there.

The family wanted me to start school. Father sent me to the school in Yenan. At that time, there was still the old system of state examinations. The family, I suppose, would have liked me to become a hsiu tsai, but I was not so ambitious; Father also thought that the main thing was for me to learn to read and write. In those days there were very few of the ordinary people who could read and write. There were eleven of us poor children in the school. It was not too easy for us. And even if I had taken my examination, there were several more exams to be passed before you could hope to be a government official. And it wasn't so easy to become one, even if you had passed the necessary exams. You had to have influence and pay bribes as well.

At school I studied the four classics. Later, the whole of this system of examinations was abolished. My family was also too poor to keep me at school any longer; so, when I was fourteen, I left the school, after having studied for four years. I was not sorry to have to leave school; quite the reverse. The masters were old and they required you to know the texts by heart. If you faltered, you had to hold out your hands and the master hit you.

I now began working on the land. First, I was herd-boy in Louping village, fifty li from here. I worked for some rich people, and they gave

me food and I must have got a sort of wage too. When I was nineteen,
I got myself sheep and goats of my own, and two years after that we
heard that there was a revolution. I ran off to the hills. Then we were
told that now we were called the Republic of China, and that the Ching
dynasty was at an end. That was all. We were old country people, and
we seldom went into the town and never talked about such things as the

emperor or government. Nobody would have dared do that. And we never saw them either. The officials in the nearest yamen watched over us, and they were the same after the revolution as before it.

Ordinary people did not like going to see the officials. That was a thing one did only if compelled. If one met them, one had to kneel before them. It was exactly the same after the revolution. I could not see that there was any difference at all.

But at that time we did, at all events, hear it said that there were foreigners in China. I had known, of course, that there were barbarians beyond China, but now I heard about foreign countries and that there were foreigners in China. But we did not bother ourselves about that. We were farmers and it was not our business to worry about that. We lived in our village and everything else was very remote. When I was living in Louping, three or five years could pass between my visits to Yenan.

Then my father died, and I began farming. I rented twenty to thirty mu. This was freshly cultivated land quite close to the village. I rented it from a small landowner called Mr Pei. We called him Old Third Pei, because he was the third of three brothers Pei. He had only just become a landowner. After the Moslem revolt, there was a lot of abandoned land, and if you paid the authorities a small sum you were entitled to take possession of this land and keep it as long as you paid your taxes every year. Well, for that reason, the rental of this land I had from him was low too. I had to pay only fifteen jin for three mu. The rent was paid only once a year. Those were good years. The rent was low and the harvests good. It was then I began studying medicine.

When I was twenty-three or twenty-four, I had gone to the doctor with a stomach complaint. He treated me for two years, and I began to get interested in medicine. He was one of my neighbours. He was called Chang, and his father and all his ancestors before him had been doctors. But his own sons could neither read nor write; they were not interested in the art of healing and preferred working on the land. Chang had some mu of land and was both a doctor and a farmer. That was usual. When Dr Chang saw that I was interested, he said: 'You have talent. You could become a doctor.'

Chang had many old medical books. He lent them to me. 'Read them properly,' he said. 'Then I will help you to learn to be a doctor.' We were neighbours and he took no payment for this. But every year I used to send him a present of a little corn. After all he was my teacher and like a second father to me. He was over sixty then and used to explain the books to me. 'It's important to learn all this properly,' he said, 'because, when you become a doctor, you must be able to help people.'

To begin with, I was just his pupil and watched while he treated his patients. He explained to me what he was doing and let me feel the pulse and understand about it. Then, gradually, I was allowed to treat the less serious cases myself, under his supervision. When he considered me fully trained, he said: 'I am old now and cannot go on being a doctor any longer. You are to have my books and take over the work.' He then gave me his books. They were old books that had been handed down from father to son for many generations. Immediately after that, he died. Chang was both my teacher and my friend.

In this way, I worked as a farmer, studied medicine and practised as a doctor in Louping Village right up to 1923. By then life had begun to get more and more unsafe, and there were many bandits up in the hills. I no longer dared live on in Louping and, Chang being dead, there was no longer anything to keep me there, so I moved back to Yenan. I had my practice there and, at the same time, I rented land in Seven-mile Village. I rented it from a man called Hu. I rented twenty mu and was to hand over twenty per cent of the harvest to him. Now, I was worse off than before. Times were worse and taxation heavy.

I had a sign outside my house in Yenan saying that I was a doctor. In the beginning, I did not get many patients, one or two, perhaps three a day. I examined them and wrote out prescriptions for them, and they took the prescriptions to the chemist. Patients usually paid 200 cash for a consultation: 4,000 cash went to a silver dollar, so for a consultation fee I could buy roughly three jin of rice or two jin of wheat. Sometimes they paid for the next consultation, sometimes they didn't pay. I lived mainly by farming.

In 1928, we had a lot of refugees from the famine areas. They came from Hengshan and Yulin. The first time I was told about the communists was in 1933. I was told how awful they were and how they murdered and plundered. Then, eventually, the Red Army did come, but it was certainly not as bad as people had said.

The Red Army took Yenan, but that changed nothing for me. The years passed exactly as before. I still had to pay Hu the same as before for the land I rented from him. This stayed at twenty per cent of the crop from 1922, when I moved to Yenan, right till Hu Tsung-nan's troops came, in 1947. The only thing that happened during those years was that I began gradually to get more patients. I was older then and more experienced and better known. Besides that, the Japanese had bombed Yenan, so I had moved from the town and settled in Seven-mile Village. Otherwise, I could call that quarter of a century in Yenan uneventful.

In 1947, Hu Tsung-nan's troops came. I fled up into the hills and lived far away in a remote hill village. I stayed there hidden throughout the occupation. I came back when Hu Tsung-nan's troops had fled. By then I had lost everything: my books, my corn, even the doors of my dwelling. I was very sad and felt that I hated the K.M.T., because they had stolen or destroyed all my books. I had loved those books so much. I have bought new medical books since then, but they are not like my old books. Hu Tsung-nan ruined everything for me. As everything had been destroyed, I could not bring myself to take up farming again. I could no longer face starting all over again. Anyway, I was already an old man. So, in April 1948, I set out as itinerant doctor. I went from village to village in the neighbourhood, curing people. They knew me, of course.

My son and my daughter-in-law worked in the fields. I sent them a little corn now and again. I liked going round the villages. One met so many people. The other doctors had suggested my doing this. In this way we shared the burden of work. Later, when I was getting altogether too old and it had become more and more difficult to walk the roads, I was sent back to Seven-mile Village. I was told to take charge of the chemist's, but I did not like that. I found it difficult too; because there were a lot of Western medicaments in it and I did not know anything about Western medicine. I had never studied it.

Then, one day, the Old Secretary, Li Yiu-hua, had a talk with me. We had known each other for many years. We were, of course, neighbours. 'Why don't you come to our brigade?' he said. 'You will then be near Seven-mile Village, and we would be glad to have a doctor of our own, whom we know and who knows us.' I, of course, knew all the people in Liu Ling. I had treated almost all of them. In 1960, I moved to the village here. My family stayed on in Seven-mile Village. I now get thirty-eight yuan a month. I have my own little plot and grow maize and beans. I am content with that. I am having a peaceful life in my old age. I have money, I have food and clothes; people are friendly. I usually have eight or ten patients a day. These last few days, it has been more, because the weather has been changeable.

I gather herbs, and I buy herbs. I take roughly one yuan from each patient. The brigade has given me an assistant who sees to the book-keeping and finance and all that. This is Li Kuei-lien, the Old Secretary's daughter. I think this is a good way of spending one's old age. I don't know how the whole thing works out financially; I don't deal with that. But we are not altogether part of the labour brigade. We constitute an independent unit that pays for itself. Part comes from the brigade's welfare fund, and the brigade provides us with dwelling and that sort of thing.

I have spent all my life in this hsien. I have only once been outside it, and that was at the age of sixty-five, when I went to Sian. One of my patients was working there and had fallen ill and, having no confidence in any other doctor, he had sent for me. I took the bus down to Sian. He paid for the journey. Then I treated him and, when he was well again, I came home. Many things have happened during my lifetime. The thing which grieves me most is that my old medical books were destroyed by Hu Tsung-nan. Because books are like old friends: one knows them and one likes to associate with them. I have never bothered about reading other books, novels and that sort of thing. But now I am happy: all is peaceful and I have a grandson who is growing up healthy and strong.

People say of Kao Chia-jen: He is good for children's complaints and women's ailments. He is known for that. Therefore, we were all glad when he agreed to come and live in Liu Ling. Chiao Kuei-lan used to have bad pains in her womb every day, but now that she has had Dr Kao's help, she is much better; the pains have gone. Tung Kuei-ying, her mother-in-law, had a constant cough. Some people said that it was her lungs were finished; others said that it was tuberculosis. She went to many doctors, but never became any better. When Dr Kao moved to Liu Ling, she went to see him. He examined her and said: 'This is weakness of old age and inflammation of the bronchii.' In wintertime she had trouble with asthma and could scarcely breathe; but now that Dr Kao is treating her, she is much better. She scarcely coughs at all and she has been better and better every year. Chen Chung-yuan's youngest son, who is four, had continual diarrhoea and became very thin and weak. His mother took him to Dr Kao and he has been healthier since. His stomach is still not quite in order, but he is almost well now and Dr Kao says that in a year's time he will be quite all right.

Part XI
The School

Han Ying-lin, headmaster, aged 28

I AM the head of Liu Ling Basic School. I was born in 1934 in Lochuan. My mother is dead and my father is a farmer. He can neither read nor write. I went to school in Lochuan. By the time I was ten, I had been through the first section of the basic school, and I then went to Lochuan Normal School. In 1949, I joined the League of Youth. In 1953, I joined the party. That same year I began as a teacher. In 1958, I began as assistant to the head in Yenan Middle School. In 1960, I studied at Yenan University. In 1961, I was appointed headmaster of Liu Ling Basic School.

I was fourteen when Hu Tsung-nan's troops withdrew from the area. All my conscious life has been spent in the new society. I am a rural intellectual of the new type.

The school has ten teachers, one of whom is an assistant teacher

293

who works in the whole of our district, helping school-teachers with their own education. Most of the teachers are new. Our experience is short. The most experienced of us has ten years' service. Three of the teachers are women. We all belong to the trade union. The school is, of course, mixed; 109 of our pupils are boys and 68 girls. We have six classes. The first four classes constitute the lower basic school and the two highest the higher basic school. The school was started in 1940 with 24 pupils. It closed down during the occupation, but reopened in 1949 with 8 pupils. The higher basic school was opened in 1956. Our pupils come from this and surrounding labour brigades, and also from Seven-mile Village.

Our school fulfils the task the party has given us. Teaching has to serve the policy of the proletariat, and teaching has to be combined with productive work. We are to inculcate the fundamentals of knowledge and basic techniques. The pupils study, but after lessons they have to contribute, as well as they can, in productive work in the school's vegetable garden. They have to know the honour of working, so that they don't look down on work. There are many good little workers among our pupils. I myself can remember that in my schooldays the pupils never cleaned out the latrines. If we met a farmworker carrying a couple of buckets of human excrement, we felt unclean and hid. But now, in our school, the pupils have such a feeling for the honour of work that they will crawl down into the latrines with enthusiasm and bring up the shit. This teaches them cleanliness and respect for work.

At the parents' meetings, people often say that, before, their children had not helped in the house, but that now they sweep the yard, carry the rubbish away and collect grass for the pig. But it is not just a question of production. It is also a matter of proletarian policy. Of knowing how. The teachers are young and enthusiastic and they work hard and prepare their lessons well. Before, the teachers never bothered about anything. Now they all study so much that I have to go round at night and myself see that they put their lights out and go to sleep.

The pupils have two kinds of preparatory work: that which they do in school during private study hours, and proper homework. We have rather a problem with this latter. It is often difficult for the pupils to study undisturbed at home in their caves. We have discussed this with the parents at the parents' meetings. The teachers are, besides, in touch with parents over various questions. If any problems arise with pupils, if their work is not satisfactory, or if there are difficulties at home, we discuss this at the parents' meetings and in the school management. Teachers will also go to a home and have a talk with a pupil's parents. They discuss how the pupil concerned is studying, how he lives, how he works at home. They assess his good and his bad sides. We try to foster his good side and correct his bad side. It may also happen that parents do not consider that their children should go to school. Perhaps the family is badly off for labour and want to have the child at home in order to put it to work. We then have a talk with the parents about the necessity for education. We try to get them to understand this and to agree. We had one of these problems some time ago. Tuan Fu-yin, whose son, Tuan Shao-tang, is one of the best pupils in the school, forbade him to go to school. This was during the spring term 1962. Tuan Fu-yin wanted to have his son at home, so that he could work and earn money. It took three visits before we could get this father to agree to his son's staying on at school.

All forms of physical punishment are forbidden. For a teacher to raise his hand against a pupil is a crime, no matter what the circumstances under which it is done. We discuss problems with the pupils, we discuss them with the parents. In extreme cases we can expel a pupil. But that is only on paper. We have never had to expel anyone. We have never come up against a case as grave as that. We also have different kinds of activities outside school hours. We organize the children's play, because children ought to learn as they play. Then we have the work in the vegetable garden I mentioned.

The methods we use are different from those of the old days. We have no learning off by heart. We try to stimulate the pupils' own interest in what is being studied. They must want to learn the thing. School education must be such that they of their own accord long to go to school and love their studies and understand why education is necessary. The new school must be attractive. Especially now, when education is still not compulsory, and it will certainly be some time before that can be introduced.

Before, school used to train bookworms who had no understanding of real life. One of my classmates had a father who was a farmer, too. When this father came to visit his son at his school in Lochuan, the boy used to run away and hide, because he was ashamed before the others of having a father who worked with his hands. Now, pupils are brought up to do work with their own hands and to love their parents and have respect for all who are elderly. Children no longer learn mere theory, but practice as well. In mathematics, for example, we teach them to work with an abacus. One of our pupils from Seven-mile Village is already doing all the family's book-keeping.

Because we explain to the children that the purpose of their studying is to make them fit to build up their country, our pupils now work with great enthusiasm. That was not the case in the old days. Then, one just learned things by heart. In general, the children do obey us. Their grades are not particularly good, but they themselves are good. We attach great weight to their moral education. We hold up various models and heroes as moral examples for them. We tell them what they should do, and what they should not do. We make it clear to them where the line runs between right and wrong. If something seems not clear or doubtful to them, we announce a class discussion, and, when this has been held, the teacher draws the conclusions from it for them, emphasizing right and wrong.

We instruct the children in hygiene and cleanliness. They do not know much about this when they first come to school. This is, of course, a backward, dirty part of the country. People here do not have good habits in hygiene. After our training, the children become better. We help their families to change their habits. We teach the children gradually to persuade their parents to change their habits, where hygiene is concerned. We certainly do not encourage them to argue stubbornly with their parents. On the contrary, we attach great importance to their respecting their elders. Our task is to collaborate with their parents. School and home must stand united. Our aim is to turn the children into healthy bearers of culture, willing to work with others and loving their socialist country.

We do not want any smooth, slippery personalities. But it is very necessary that they should have the feeling of being ready to work and be collective-minded. Children ought to be group-conscious. We teach the children to help each other. Not to compete with each other, but to help each other. Take, for example, the river-crossing down here. After rain it is not easy, and so the older children have to help the younger, and the boys the girls. The older ones carry the young ones across. We also train them to be honest. If they find anything on the road, they are to bring it to school. We have had two examples this month of our pupils' moral growth:

After the rain we had a few days ago, two boys in the older classes noticed an old woman with crippled feet standing down by the river.

The river was up, and she could not get across. The boys at once picked her up and carried her across and saw her home to Ten-mile Village. Later, that old woman came to me and said: 'The school does not just foster good pupils, but also respectful, good social beings.'

One boy found a pocketbook with a lot of money in it on the road. He brought it to me without opening it. Later, the owner thanked us.

Those who go through our school become good people. Some go on to higher studies, like Li Hsiu-tang's daughter, Li Ali-liang, who left us this spring and is now in Yenan Middle School. Others are doing their bit on the production front, like Lo Han-hong and others. We have former pupils who have become merit workers, and others in high administrative and other posts. But none of these has been from the village of Liu Ling. They came from other villages. Our pupils are hard-working and show great interest in their studies. In the spring term of 1962, there were fourteen pupils who had the highest grade in all subjects. But none of them was from Liu Ling.

Our timetable follows that generally laid down for schools. In the lower basic school the lessons are of forty minutes and the breaks of fifteen. The school day begins at 08.00 and goes on till 12.00. Afternoon work starts at 14.00 and goes on till 17.00 Between 08.00 and 08.20 and between 14.00 and 14.25 the classes join up for reading aloud without a teacher. This is to allow those who have a long way to come to get here. They are allowed to arrive later.

First Class

Mathematics, 6 periods a week:
    addition, subtraction and multiplication up to 100.
Chinese language, 14 periods a week, of which 3 are calligraphy:
    no fixed number of characters.
Drawing, 2 periods a week:
    the teacher presents a simple model which has to be copied. The principles of drawing.
Gymnastics and sport, 2 periods a week:
    games and exercises for small children (running, etc.).
Music, 2 periods a week:
    Various choral songs.
Private study, 16 periods a week:
    Going through preparatory work under supervision of a teacher.
Homework is reckoned to take one hour a day.

No garden work.
No form of handicraft.

Second Class
Mathematics, 6 periods a week:
> multiplication and division with 2-figure numbers. Addition and
> subtraction of larger numbers.

Chinese language, 14 periods a week, of which 3 are calligraphy:
> studying characters. No definite number.

Drawing, 2 periods a week:
> copying.

Music, 2 periods a week:
> choral singing.

Gymnastics and sport, 2 periods a week:
> games and exercises suitable for children.

Private study, 16 periods a week.
Homework is reckoned to take one hour a day.
No garden work.
No form of handicraft.

Third Class
Mathematics, 6 periods a week:
> multiplication and division of big numbers.
> Telling the time and the clock.
> Solving practical problems.

Chinese language, 14 periods a week, of which 2 are periods of calligraphy and 2 periods of composition:
> writing simpler essays. Describing a picture.
> 'My Family'. 'What does my mother do?'

Drawing, 1 period a week:
> copying.

Music, 2 periods a week:
> choral singing. Those who are musical now start singing solo.

Gymnastics and sport, 2 periods a week:
> exercises and games. Simple sport. Football, running.

Private study, 17 periods a week:
> pupils should now be keeping a diary.

Homework is reckoned to take one hour a day.
No form of handicraft; but the pupils are now allowed to weed in the
vegetable plot, sweep the floors and sweep the yard, if they wish.

Fourth Class

Mathematics, 5 periods a week:
> calculation of time. Calculation of area.
> Conversion from Chinese measure to metric scale. Practical use of the four rules of arithmetic.

Use of abacus, 2 periods a week:
> addition, subtraction, multiplication, division and decimal calculation on the abacus.

Chinese language, 14 periods a week, of which 2 are of calligraphy and 2 of composition:
> understand all composite characters in the textbook. Simple descriptive compositions: 'What we did at the New Year'. Be able to read simple newspapers specially written for children.

Drawing, 1 period a week:
> copying, somewhat more difficult objects than before, but still just the principles of drawing. Still just black and white.

Gymnastics and sport, 2 periods a week:
> exercises and games. Simple sport.

Private study, 17 periods a week. A weekly diary is kept.

Homework is now reckoned to take one and a half hours a day.

Garden work, 80 minutes a week:
> voluntary, but organized.

No form of handicraft.

Fifth and sixth classes comprise the higher basic school.
Periods are 45 minutes and breaks 10 minutes.

Fifth Class

Mathematics, 6 periods a week:
> practical tasks. Use of abacus included, but not an independent subject. Calculation of cubic content.

Chinese language, 12 periods a week, of which 1 period for calligraphy and 2 periods for composition:
> compositions are no longer just descriptive, but should be in the form of essays. Pupils should understand all terms in the text read and be able to give an independent summary of a newspaper text that has been read out.

Nature study, 1 period a week:
> the air, soil, simple mechanical principles.

Geography, 1 period a week:
China's geography, China's provinces, China's climate.
Agriculture, 2 hours a week:
climate, fertilizers, cattle, poultry, grain.
Only theory.
Drawing, 1 period a week:
start water-colours. First colour work.
First creative sketches. Theory.
Music, 1 period a week:
choral singing. Simple theory.
Gymnastics and sport, 2 periods a week:
ball games. Athletics.
Private study, 15 hours a week.
Garden work, 80 minutes a week after school hours:
looking after the school garden.
Handicraft, in spare time after school, no fixed period:
making stones for grinding colour for Indian ink. Simple wood-work.
Homework reckoned to take one and a half hours.

Sixth Class
Mathematics, 6 periods a week:
decimal system, fractions, statistical tables, book-keeping. Use of abacus included.
Chinese language, 12 periods a week, of which 1 for calligraphy and 2 for composition:
describe a person, a landscape. Acquire a fine style and a correct way of writing. Read aloud with the correct Peking pronunciation.
Nature study, 1 period a week:
the air, soil, simple mechanical principles.
History, 2 periods a week:
only Chinese history. From Peking man to the Big Leap Forward.
Agricultural theory, 1 period a week:
climate, fertilizers, cattle, poultry, grain.
Only theory.
Drawing, 1 period a week:
more complicated sketches.
Gymnastics and sport, 2 periods a week:
ball games. Athletics.

Music, 1 period a week:
    songs. Simple theory.
Care of garden, after school hours, 80 minutes a week. Handicraft, in
    free time after school hours, no fixed period:
    clay work, making colour-grinding stones for Indian ink. Simple
    woodwork.
Homework reckoned to take one and a half hours a day.

That is our timetable. Teachers stay with their classes from the
first to the sixth class. The school year begins on 1 August and ends on
20 June. The school works six days a week. Together, the year's holidays
amount to seventy-five days. The time of the winter holiday depends
on the weather. There are eight individual holidays: two at the
National Day in October, one on 1 May, one at the New Year, one on
International Children's Day and three at the spring festival, if this does
not coincide with the winter holiday.

The teachers are quite free during the holidays. They can go home
if they wish, they can go away somewhere, they can do further study
or anything else they like.

If a pupil fails in two basic subjects, like mathematics and Chinese
language, he cannot move up to the next class. If a pupil fails in one
basic subject, he has to be re-examined before the autumn term and can
move up if he passes. If a pupil fails in three other subjects, he cannot
move up. If he fails in two other subjects, he can move up. Last year,
we had seven who had not moved up. A pupil who has failed to move
up twice and then again gets such grades that he cannot be moved up
has to leave the school. Pupils can be absent owing to sickness or with
the special permission of the head.

The numbers in our classes are high, of course. Last year the
numbers in the different classes were:

First Class	42	Fourth Class	24
Second Class	31	Fifth Class	37
Third Class	28	Sixth Class	21

Certain children transfer to other schools or leave school altogether.
There are also children of school age who do not attend school. We
speak with their parents and often succeed in persuading them to send
their children to school. Though not always. Sometimes the children
themselves don't want to go to school. They manage to get their
grandmother to feel sorry for them, and some parents are unable to

stand up to their elders. Then, of course, there are also parents who want to exploit their children's labour.

We did, however, succeed in getting Hu Yen-ching back to school. Last year, when she was eight, she ran away and refused to live with her parents. She went to her grandmother, Ching Chung-ying's wife. Granny thought the poor child was made to work far too hard at school, and she even accused the teachers of having a grudge against her. She loved her granddaughter and let her stay with her. But now we have managed to persuade Hu Yen-ching to go back to her parents and to come to school again.

We have no real difficulties over discipline. The only difficulty is that certain children are late for school. Of course, we have this period both in the morning and afternoon with reading aloud to give them time to get to school, and we try to get the children to help each other keep to the hours. But some of the children have a long way to come, and it is difficult for them to keep to the hours. The farthest any of our children has to come is eight li. Seven of the children have so far to come that they do not go home for the midday rest. They bring food with them, and the cook heats it up in the staff kitchen, then they have their rest in the school. We have one room for the boys to sleep in and another for the girls.

Another difficulty is that certain children find it difficult to sit still and be quiet. Thus, in the first class there is not much discipline. There everything's more of a game. The children must think all the time that school is fun. Then gradually, as they become older, they see the necessity of work discipline, and then we require more of them.

There is a certain amount of fighting and quarrelling. We try to quell this and sort it all out with discussion and persuasion. As I've said, no teacher must ever try to settle anything by striking a child. We have to check disorder by other means. And it always succeeds. Before, in the old days, schoolmasters used to beat their pupils, but then the children had no real respect for their teachers. They were just afraid of them. That was why the teachers found it difficult to keep order. Now teachers and pupils love one another, and all goes well.

We take certain fees from the parents. There is an instruction fee of 1 Y per pupil per term. Then there are certain school costs which the pupils have to pay themselves: gymnastic apparatus, water for the children's tea and heating during the winter. The gymnastic costs are 0·50 Y per pupil per term; the boiled drinking water costs 1·50 Y per

302

pupil per term; the cost of fuel for the winter works out at 1·50 Y per pupil for each autumn term. Parents also pay the cost of school material. In the first class this amounts to 0·30–0·40 Y per term for each pupil, and in the higher classes it rises to 0·50–0·70 Y.

The teachers' salaries are paid by the hsien authorities. This school in Liu Ling is, of course, wholly state-supported. With us the highest salary is 49·50 Y a month and the lowest 35 Y. Salaries are calculated according to education and length of service. On questions of salary, the teachers make suggestions, and the amount is fixed by the hsien authorities. Free dwelling quarters and a cook paid by the state are supplied in addition to the salary. We receive full pay during the school holidays. We are not expected to take other work. Teaching is an exacting task, and for a teacher to be able to give of his best, it is preferred that he both rest and continue his own studies. Then there is the staff garden. This is not the same as the school garden. We look after the staff garden ourselves. In it we grow vegetables and corn and keep chickens and pigs. This does not mean that we are anything like self-supporting as far as food is concerned. We eat communally, and we usually reckon on having to contribute five yuan a head each month to the catering fund for outside purchases.

Teachers are duty-bound to spend nine hours a week on private study over and above their teaching duties. The teachers' timetable is three hours for teaching subjects, four hours for pedagogy, and two hours for private study. Lu Huan-ping is in charge of this instruction and supervises it.

The school's budget is quite simple. In the spring term 1962 it was as follows, apart from wages to staff, headmaster, teachers and cook:

Income	Y
From Education Office in Yenan hsien	1,375·33
Fees from pupils	177·00
Total	1,552·33

Expenditure	
Installation of electric light	1,100·00
Two-wheeled hand-cart with rubber tyres	125·60
Indian ink, paper, chalk, sickles, mattocks	236·24
Total	1,461·84
Balance at the end of spring term, transferred to following year	90·49

Expenditure on gymnastic apparatus, water and heating have its own budget, since it is paid direct by the pupils:

Income, Spring Term 1962   **Y**

Gymnastics fees	88·50
Water fees	305·50
Fuel fee (not applicable in spring term)	
Fuel in hand, carried over from autumn 1961	69·72

Total 463·72

Expenditure, Spring Term 1962

Gymnastic apparatus	84·96
Boiled water	216·28
Fuel in hand consumed	69·72

370·96

Balance at end of spring term, carried over to next school year   92·76

The staff garden comprises four mu. There we grow food for our own account. Any surplus we sell. In 1961, my share of the year's crops sold amounted to twenty yuan.

The children's garden, the school garden proper, in 1961 produced goods to a total value of 740 Y. Of this we sold produce to the value of 147·19 Y in the market and bought prizes for the pupils.

Each pupil got some sort of prize. Its size depended on his or her grading. These prizes consisted of such things as pens, books, notebooks and similar things. When we had put aside what was needed to increase the following year's production, we were left with produce to a value of roughly 300 Y. This the pupils ate.

The school garden, you see, is not run for income, but to teach the pupils to love agricultural work. That, too, is why we do not distribute the produce in accordance with the amount of work put into it by the pupils. We sell or exchange part of the produce in order to buy food-stuffs, and with these the school cook makes one or two 'feasts' every year. All the pupils come to these feasts, even those who have not done any garden work. We do this to induce a right attitude to work. It is part of the pupils' moral upbringing to grow their own food and eat it, sharing it and their labour with others.

The school is run by a headmaster's council. This consists of five people: the headmaster, convener and representative of the party; Li Juei-chen, deputy head; Chang Chang-li, in charge of administration; Chang Chung-fang, representative of the staff; and Lu Huan-ping. This headmaster's council is there to discuss the school's educational work and its internal administrative problems. Questions raised at the headmaster's council are taken up at the staff meeting, attended by every member of the staff in the school: the head, the nine teachers and the cook. There, they are discussed, decisions are reached and recommendations may be sent to the education office in Yenan hsien.

Another group which is of great significance is the school council. I am the chairman of this. On it are representatives from all the labour brigades from which we have pupils. The school council studies relations between the labour brigades and the council, between the pupils' homes and the school; it investigates any problems that may arise. Last year there was, for example, electrification: that was a question that had to be solved in collaboration with the labour brigades. The school council can, on the one hand, only recommend measures to the education office in Yenan hsien; but, on the other hand, it has the power of decision in certain questions, namely those concerning co-operation with the different labour brigades.

There is yet another school group, the parents' representation. In each village, the parents of our pupils choose one to represent them. There are seven of these representatives, and they come under the headmaster's council. I am their chairman by virtue of being head. Their duties are undefined; but one can say that the school council concerns itself with the practical problems, whereas the parents' representatives deal with the more personal problems. One can discuss the children's work with them and any faults there may be in the liaison between school and home. The parents' representatives have only advisory powers.

If, for example, you could imagine one of the children behaving so badly that it really became necessary to consider expulsion—but I must once again emphasize that this has never happened here—the matter would be discussed first at a meeting of the parents' representatives. If no solution of the problem was found, then the headmaster's council would have to discuss it and finally propose expulsion. After the school council had discussed this decision, it would have to be referred to the education office in Yenan hsien and approved by it before it could be put into effect.

All the teachers are members of the trade union. The trade union's duty is to help the teachers in their studies and to see to their social welfare. One per cent of the teacher's salary goes to the trade union's funds. The union receives an equal amount from its central office, and this is used to ensure the teachers' material welfare, to buy study material for them and for other similar purposes. I am the head of the trade union here in Liu Ling Basic School.

It is essential for the school to have good contacts with the people in the village. The pupils are expected to help teach at the reading classes in the winter; that is, of course, only the older pupils in the highest classes. The school has its own library, but here, too, we have established close co-operation with Liu Ling's Labour Brigade. We have over 300 volumes, and we have borrowed a further 300 from the labour brigade's library. These are mainly works of fiction suitable for children and pure children's books. The older children borrow them. In addition, each class has a class library. That of the sixth class comprises almost forty volumes.

The children elect a leader for each class. The leader's job is to help the teacher maintain order; and he also has to help organize the pupils when on excursions and that sort of thing. He also presides over the committee of three that the pupils of each class elect to manage the various jobs the class does jointly. The committee of three consists of the class leader, a study leader and one who is responsible for practical matters, such as keeping the classroom clean, work in the garden, etc.

Kou Chao-lan, schoolmistress, aged 25

I STARTED school when I was ten. Having gone through Yenan Middle School, I passed the entrance exam for Sian Normal School, and there I studied at the faculty of history for one year. After that I had to ask for sick leave. After I had been away from my studies for a year, I was still too ill to be able to resume them. Later, when I became fit for work again, I was partly too tired and too much of an invalid, and partly had fallen so far behind my classmates in Sian Normal School, that I decided not to continue with higher studies, but to start work instead.

I had dreamed of becoming a schoolmistress ever since I was in the first few classes of the middle school. So I was sent as schoolmistress to Liu Ling and began work here on 1 October 1961. I began by teaching mathematics and history in the sixth class and Chinese language in the second class, and I also taught all classes music and singing.

I am fond of my work, but I am inexperienced. The children are lively and I have always loved children, but when I came here, I did not know much about pedagogy and, naturally, I made a number of mistakes. I was too hasty-tempered and too easily became irritated with the children. The other teachers helped me. There are special ways of dealing with difficult children. You have to go about it in the right way. Now things are better. I am fond of children and I am fond of my work, and that is a prerequisite for being a pedagogue.

As we teachers go with the children from class to class, we get to know them. After six years of working together teacher and pupil know each other very well. I remember that from my own schooldays. This makes the school-teacher a better educator.

You see, we do not just help the children during lessons, but afterwards, too. We sit with the children during the private-study periods and help any who have problems. That is why we are there during these periods. I was put in charge of the second class when I came. The children there are about eight or nine. They are fond of playing and find it difficult to maintain order and to sit still. To a large extent, this is due to the fact that they have had no prior training. What upbringing they have had at home does not amount to much.

My children have now reached the third class. If I look at those who come from Liu Ling, they are all different.

Tuan Shao-tang, Tuan Fu-yin's son, is very gifted. He studies hard and his homework is always thoroughly done. He is good at mathematics and Chinese language. He is fond of singing and dancing and is one of the best in his class. But he is also a fidget and a chatterbox; he can never sit still and is never quiet. He always starts playing with something under the desk. He gets many admonitions and bad marks. Of course, he is the youngest son in his family and very spoiled by his mother. I have gone to his home to talk about this with Tuan Fu-yin, but he is seldom at home and does not bother much about what I say, either.

Li Shung-chen is Li Yu-hsin's youngest son. His mother is dead. He is quite gifted and high-spirited. He sings and dances with enthusiasm and loves to take part in physical work, if we allow him. He likes organizing the children in this and is responsible in his class for practical matters. But he is also inattentive and lacks interest in book learning. He is not persevering, and he is careless. The reason why his grades are so bad is that his mother is dead and his father works in the fields, so that it is only his older sister, Li Shang-wa, who looks after him, and he has to help with a lot of work in the home.

Tsao Shan-nü, daughter of Fu Hai-tsao, is not very gifted, but she is industrious and painstaking. She lives near the school and sometimes comes here in the evenings to sit in the school and read. Her results are average. Her family has given her a better upbringing at home than is usual. Her mother is strict and sees that she studies properly. Her mother is high-spirited, and the family background is better than with the two previous ones.

Liu Lan-shuan is Liu Chen-yung's daughter. She studies hard, but is rather dull-witted. Her way of studying is not a good one. She won't study alone; she likes collective studies best. She is always wanting the teachers to gather everyone together and have singing and dancing. Her mother is strict and the girl is almost too docile.

Tung Er-wa is Tung Yang-chen's daughter. She is very hard-working. If she isn't told not to, she will come back to the school every evening. She says that she likes being here so much. She is a little slow in grasping things, but she is fearfully particular about hygiene and cleanliness. She loves school and is always bringing different things from home to give to the school. In a country school like this there is always so much that is needed.

Li Yu-shen is Li Hai-kuei's son. He is one who has failed to move up, and I don't know him so well. Everything goes so desperately slowly with him. But this year he really is trying to work. But even though he makes great efforts to read, he finds it difficult to understand. He is older than the others in the class and likes to try and be their leader.

I am fond of my children, and, when I consider them, it seems to me they have a bright future ahead of them. Some will study and follow that path; others will leave school to work in agriculture or some other field of activity. They are going to make good builders of their country; they are calm and steady. I have a very strong sense of this. I often wonder what this one or that will make of life. One does, when one is a teacher. But it's still too early to say anything.

They don't even know themselves yet. They are so young. If they have seen a film about the Chinese People's Liberation Army, they all want to be soldiers; and, if they have seen a film about tractor drivers, they all want to be tractor drivers. Some time ago, I gave them a composition to write: 'What are you going to be when you grow

309

up?' Some said they were going to join the Chinese People's Liberation Army. A couple wanted to be airmen, in order, as they said, to 'defend China's wide frontiers'. One girl wanted to be a schoolmistress. 'There have to be some who educate those who later are going to build up communism in China,' she said. Several wanted to be tractor drivers. Many of these were girls: 'We must harvest more grain, and one does that with machines.' A couple just said that they wanted to become merit workers in agriculture. One wanted to be a navvy.

We tell the children that, now, women can have any post in society, so it's natural that some girls also want to be soldiers or air-women. All their ideals are the same, both the girls' and the boys'. They read things in the newspapers and see things at the cinema, and then talk among themselves about what they want to be. But, in general, you can say that the girls in my class are more obedient and quieter and work harder than the boys. But there are more boys who are gifted.

Of course, at this age, all children are still very naïve and touching. When the 26th World Table Tennis Championship was held in Peking, most of the pupils told me in confidence that they thought they would be world champions at table tennis when they grew up.

Chi Chung-chou, in charge of the Young Pioneers, aged 24

I AM from the country too. My parents and my ancestors were all farmers. I was eleven when I began school in Lichiachi Basic School, thirty li from here. By the time I was seventeen, I had left the basic school and begun in Yenan Middle School. After three years there I took my exam and was sent here to Liu Ling as schoolmaster in 1961.

I had decided to become a schoolmaster when I was still only in the first class of the basic school. We had a very good master there, an old man called Ma Sze-chao. When I was a child, I thought that he knew everything and could answer everything. He had educated so many children, who had then grown up and yet still respected him. It was glorious to be a teacher. Wherever you went, you would meet your pupils. That's what I thought when I was a child. Later, in middle school, I still wanted to be a schoolmaster. I thought that was a profession that would suit me. The teachers in the middle school agreed with me. My parents had no special views about this, and my father just said: 'I suppose you must do as you like.'

When I came here, I was put in charge of the fifth class. That's the sixth class this year. I now teach Chinese language in the sixth class, nature study in the fifth class and drawing in the fourth, fifth and sixth classes. Before Kou Chao-lan came here, I also had music and singing in the fifth and sixth classes. Besides that, I am responsible for the school work with the Young Pioneers.

Of the school's 177 pupils, 103 are members of the Young Pioneers. Most of the seventy-four who are not members are too young to join. The age for being a Young Pioneer is from nine to sixteen. But there are also cases like Li Shung-chen. He dreams of being a Pioneer, but he hasn't been allowed to join. He is far too undisciplined, and he does not

311

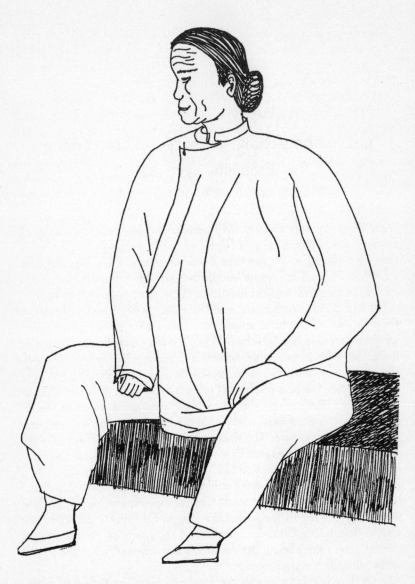

work at his studies. So he has not been accepted as a member. It's not his dull-wittedness that is the obstacle—he can't help that—but the fact that he neglects his work. Li Shuei-ming is definitely subnormal where ability is concerned, but nevertheless he is a pioneer. Li Shung-chen longs so much to join, but now we have had a serious talk with him and told him that, if he is good, he may join. He has promised to improve. Now he is trying to do his best. At least, he is doing so for the time being; one will have to see how long it lasts.

I have two pupils from Liu Ling in my class, the sixth class:

Tsao Ming-wa, Fu Hai-tsao's son, who is continuing the name of his father's stepfather, Tsao Shen-yung. He is fifteen and very fond of books. He reads everything he can lay hands on. He is very quick at grasping things and is serious about his work. He does his homework most excellently. But he is pig-headed and stubborn, and also hasty-tempered and impetuous. He has to be coaxed along. If one wants to get him to do anything, one has to be very careful to speak to him about it in the right way. We praise him for his good work, but criticize him for his behaviour in other respects. He ought to go on to Yenan Middle School. He is not the dreamy type. He reads a lot, but I don't think he has any special daydreams. He writes a composition once a week, and these show that he has read a lot outside the school curriculum, but he cannot express himself on paper all that well. He himself wants to study. He wants to become an engineer. He draws well; he has a dashing way of drawing with wide sweeps.

Tsao Shi-lien is Tsao Chen-kuei's sister. She is older than Tsao Ming-wa. She is seventeen and very sensitive. She is honest and sturdy, and she makes great efforts to study well. Her family background is not bad, but she is a little slow and dull-witted. She has difficulty in understanding. She struggles hugely to overcome her difficulties. She does work hard. Her homework is well done. If she makes the least mistake in writing, she prefers to start again from the beginning. No one had asked her to do that. She does it on her own. But she makes a lot of mistakes and has to work hard, and it all takes her such a long time. She is always particular about being clean and neat. When she draws, she is very accurate and carefully draws in every little detail. She cannot draw a flower without drawing both pistil and stamen. She has just entered puberty. In general, pupils manage to get through basic school before that happens. She wants to be a tractor driver.

Most of the pupils in my class will go on to the middle school. They say: 'Our studies are of value to the party and country, too.' But they will joyfully take up agricultural work, even so, if necessary. Most of their career dreams are connected with agriculture. They want to be tractor drivers, book-keepers, merit workers in agriculture and so on. Those who think they will be able to study further want to be engineers.

We have certain difficulties in our work. The greatest is that we teachers are so young and inexperienced. For that reason our results are not so satisfactory. You can see for yourself what grades the children have. That is our fault. Another difficulty is that, when they come to school, the children have had no previous training. Farmers don't really bring their children up at all. They simply do not have time to attend to their children. So, when the children do go to the school, they are quite undisciplined. They are also quite unaccustomed to keeping fixed hours. At home, you see, they have been allowed to come and go as they like.

Hygiene and cleanliness is another difficulty. Before they come to school, some of the children are used to drinking unboiled water. If they become thirsty and are by the river, they just bend down and drink. We make them boil their water. We tell them about bacteria and disease: 'Bacteria are tiny animals that make you ill. They are so small that they cannot be seen by the eye.' We teach them to clean vegetables before they eat them, to wash their hands and their faces, and to cut their nails. We show them various posters and pictures and try to inculcate good habits of hygiene. In the lower classes, we usually go round and inspect the children to see that they are clean and newly washed. In the upper classes this is not necessary. There the class is itself responsible for the pupils' cleanliness.

But country children are robust. They are seldom ill. If any child is away ill for any length of time, we go to its home and work with it in the cave. They don't like being at home. 'It's deadly boring not going to school.'

In the two highest classes, the children often ask for permission to help the family. But they are not usually granted it. We talk with them and query whether it really is absolutely necessary. We suggest that they help their fathers on Sundays, instead.

People say of Chi Chung-chou: He is a good teacher. The older ones say that he loves children and understands them. His colleagues say that he works very well. He has already had three distinctions for good work as a schoolmaster. He is a merit worker. The children are said to set store by him.

314

Tables

The Staff of Liu Ling Basic School
I Educated in a higher training institution
II Educated in a normal school, medium level
III Educated in a normal school, basic level
P Party member
U Member of League of Youth

	Name	Sex	Age	Years' service	Wage	Remarks
I	Han Ying-ling	M	28	10	49·50 Y	Headmaster P
II	Chi Chung-chou	M	24	2	43·00	In charge of Pioneers P
II	Li Juei-chen	M	21	3	43·00	Deputy head
I	Wu You-yün	F	25	2	47·00	P
I	Kou Chao-lan	F	25	1½	35·00	U
III	Chang Chang-li	M	21	3	37·00	Administration U

	Name	Sex	Age	Years' service	Wage	Remarks
III	Ho Kai-chuan	M	19	1	35·00 Y	U
III	Chang Chung-fang	F	24	6	43·00	Staff repre- sentative
III	Ho Hsiu-chen	F	25	7	35·00	Freshly ap- pointed, 1962

Assistant employed to help the teachers in their further education, paid by Liu Ling School:

	Name	Sex	Age	Years' service	Wage	Remarks
II	Lu Huan-ping	M	23	4	47·00	U

There is also a cook who is paid 43 Y a month

Pupils from Liu Ling Village in Liu Ling Basic School, autumn term 1962, and their grading, spring term 1962.
Grading is from 1–5. 1 and 2 do not pass.

Beginners from Liu Ling village in first class of Liu Ling Basic School, autumn term 1962:

Name	Sex	Age
Li Ai-ping	M	8
Liu Yuan	M	8
Li Ai-shen	M	9
Jen Chiu-yen	F	8
Li Shi-ming	M	7

Pupils from Liu Ling Village who left Liu Ling Basic School in the calendar year 1962:

Name	Sex	Age	Reason for leaving
Li Shuei-ming	M	12	Under-developed. Unable to follow
Li Shang-wa	F	16	Left to run the home
Li Ai-liang	F	17	Transferred to Yenan Middle School

Pupils from Liu Ling Village in Yenan Middle School, autumn term 1962:

Name	Sex	Age
Li Chi-shen	M	17
Yen An	M	17
Li Ta-min	M	15
Li Ai-liang	F	17

Class	Name	Sex	Age	Chinese Language	Mathematics	Counting on the Abacus	Natural Science	Geography	Agricultural Theory	Drawing	Gymnastics	Music	Member of the Young Pioneers
6	Tsao Ming-wa	M	15	4	5	5	4	4	3	4	3	5	Yes
6	Tsao Shi-lien	F	17	3	2	3	4	4	3	3	3	5	Yes
5	Chang Niu-ming	M	14	2	4	4				4	4	4	Yes
5	Li Shuan-tsai	M	12	2	3	2				3	5	5	Yes
4	Chen Nü	F	11	5	5					4	5	5	Yes
4	Li Shung	F	12	3	3					4	4	4	Yes
3	Liu Lan-shuan	F	10	4	3					4	3	4	No
3	Tsao Shan-nü	F	9	3	4					3	4	4	Yes
3	Tuan Shao-tang	M	11	5	5					5	4	5	Yes
3	Li Shung-chen	M	11	2	3					5	3	4	No
3	Tung Er-wa	F	10	3	3					3	4	5	Yes
3	Li Yun-shen	M	12	2	2					3	3	3	Yes
2	Mau Ying-shin	M	8	2	3					2	3	4	No
2	Chang Shun	M	9	2	2					4	4	4	No
2	Hu Yen-ching	F	9	3	3					3	3	4	No

Part XII
Lao Dung

'By the intellectuals observing the four "with's":
Live with the masses
Eat with the masses
Work with the masses
Discuss problems with the masses,
they will transform themselves until they have acquired
the working people's attitude to life.'

Ching Chi and lao dung: how physical work taught her the proletarian attitude to life, aged 29

In 1953 I joined the League of Youth, and, in 1956, I became a member of China's Communist Party. My work is that of secretary in Intourist in Sian. I earn seventy-four yuan a month, am married and have two sons, one of eight and one of five. I did thirteen months' lao dung, from the spring of 1959 to the spring of 1960, that is voluntary physical work. I did this in Liu Ling.

I come from a milieu that is not proletarian. We have always been well off. My father is a doctor, and when I was small he was in charge of a clinic in Szechwan. My mother went to college. My father was a Christian. He despised traditional medicine, which he called quackery. What he thinks about it now, I don't know. I expect he was reformed after the liberation, along with the rest. At the moment he is in Moscow studying neuro-surgery. I don't know whether or not he is still a Christian. I was sent to a school run by Canadian nuns. They taught me to play the piano. We used to sing psalms.

Life was never difficult for us, nor were we ever short of food. My father loved cleanliness above all else. I was forbidden to go out to the kitchen; if I did so despite this, then I was beaten. He would give me ten strokes. This was because in Szechwan food is cooked over wood fires, and I could have made myself grimy. I looked down on our servants. They were dirty. I grew up thus and became lazy. I could not use a broom or even wash myself. Those were not things that I needed to do. After 1949, I became a bit better, perhaps. At school I was on my own and had to wash and dress myself; but my sentiments were far from being those of the workers. I knew nothing of the seriousness of life either. I did not know where the food that was set on my table came from. Nor did I bother about it. After the liberation, I learned a lot about how the proletariat felt, it is true, but actually I myself looked down on the poor, because they were uneducated and uncouth and filthy.

I know that I was always saying: 'The farmers are good. The working class and the poor farmers are the leading classes. All honour to work. All honour to the workers. Physical labour is the highest.' I often said that at meetings, but I didn't mean anything by it. I really thought the working class and the poor farmers an uneducated, dirty lot, and even though I did in a way believe what I said—in that I believed in the liberation of the Chinese people—I was only paying lip-service by saying that. I considered it to be our, the intellectuals', job to be the leaders. Which we have always been. I had no contact with working people. As far as I was concerned, this business of class and class struggle was something quite abstract. Those were just words.

But after the liberation, I did at least start washing myself. Before, I had had a servant to do that for me. In 1953, when I was twenty, I got married. But I did no housework, and I did not run the house. My mother-in-law did that. When I had my first baby, I just lay in bed. I did not bother about doing anything. My mother-in-law saw to everything and looked after the baby for me.

In 1958, the party exhorted all young ganbus to do their share of physical labouring and go out among the people. We decided that all the ganbus in our organization must go and spend a year in the country.

I was a town girl and had never lived in the country, nor even been in a village, and I volunteered in 1958. But I wasn't accepted that year. It was not till 1959 that I was selected to go on one year's lao dung, voluntary physical work. I was in the third group to be sent out from our office. As it is, half of our ganbus have done their lao dung. At the moment the fifth group is out doing it. Each group consists of eight to ten people and is away one year. Our office comprises the following organizations: Intourist, Sian Hotel, Sian Representative of the Protocol Department of the Foreign Ministry, and the local Sian section of the Chinese People's Society for Cultural Relations with Foreign Countries.

There were nine of us in the group I was in.

We were to be re-educated and given a proletarian attitude to life. We were to fortify our physique and help the people's commune, to which we were sent, in its work. We were five women and four men. I had discussed all this with my husband. Of course, it was a pity being unable to be together for a year; but we had discussed it all thoroughly and come to the conclusion that one year was not of such great significance in a whole life. It was important to do one's share of physical work and also necessary for me, if I was to be a true revolutionary woman. My mother-in-law promised to look after the baby, which she loves dearly, and my husband said he would write to me often. In general, he is inclined to be lazy, but where I am concerned he has always been most punctilious. We love each other. People say of us Chinese girls that we are cold, just because we don't go about kissing and holding hands in the street and that sort of thing, but that isn't true.

We are like blast-furnaces: we may be cold outside, but we are red-hot inside. So we decided that a year was not such a long time, and that it was important for me to counteract my laziness and become a better person. My husband works at the university. He teaches Russian. He was going to use this year for further study.

So we took the train to Tungchwan, where we changed to the bus. We were very excited to see where we were being stationed. All that we knew was that we were going to the Yenan district. We reached Yenan on 28 February 1959. It was cold and snowing, and we were frozen. We were quartered in the hotel, where many groups from Sian, which were also going out to do lao dung, were staying. We stayed at the hotel for a few days, while the hsien authorities discussed where we were to be sent. Finally, my group was attached to Liu Ling People's Commune. The commune decided that we should join Liu

Ling Labour Brigade, so all nine of us drove out to Liu Ling. That was on 2 March 1959. It was a warm afternoon, and the Old Secretary, Li Yiu-hua, was sitting outside the cave here, smoking. He gazed at us for a while, then he said: 'I know that most of you have never done any real work before in your lives. We will try to help you. You won't have to do too much to begin with. I shall try to find simple jobs for you at first, so that you can accustom yourselves to working with your hands. The best thing, perhaps, will be for you to start by trundling up dry dung and helping to carry soil. After that, we shall see.' Two in our group had done physical work before, but the other seven of us had never done a thing. The first fortnight was difficult for all of us. We ached all over and fell asleep the moment we lay down. But at least nobody laughed at us. Then, little by little, things began to go better. But even the two who said they had done physical work before were as tired as the rest of us, although we were only doing the lightest jobs, the sort of things that otherwise were only given to the old men, and to the women whose feet had been bound, to do.

We had two caves, one for women, one for men. The women's cave was the one Tsao Chen-yung lives in now. We had a man who cooked for us. He cooked for his family at the same time. We were still paid by our office and got the same salary as we had had in Sian. Twice a week I got a letter from my husband. We helped build the collective dining-hall behind here, which they were going to use at harvest-time. Sometimes we would show a film there in the evening.

In July, I was chosen to lead the women's group. We held the meeting on the open space in front of the cave here. We held meetings once a month to discuss our work and plan the next month's work. The brigade leader had had a talk with me, at which he said: 'The women's group needs your help. There are now three work leaders among the women here and not one of them can either read or write. Your job is not only to lead the work, but also to teach the other leaders to read and write. You'll have six months in which to do it.' I said to him: 'If it really is so that the women are relying on me and have chosen me themselves, of course I shall do my best.' At the meeting, I was elected. I was very happy that the women believed in me. That was my first position of trust. At first, I was a bit scared by the job, because, after all, I was a town girl, so how could I take charge of things in the country? Everything there was so different. But after a month I had become one of the group. Actually, I am from Hopeh, though I was born and grew up in Szechwan. I had lived for more than ten years in Chengtu. Well, when I left Liu Ling, at least one of the women labour leaders was able to read and write sufficiently well to be able to keep a work daybook and calculate the day's work. Before, they had had to go to the book-keeper every day and ask him to make the entries. That had been a lot of trouble both for him and for them.

Well, after that I worked all the time. I ploughed and I weeded. I dug and I sowed. I had to learn everything. Every Monday and Tuesday evening, I went to the three leaders of the women's group and taught them reading and writing. Otherwise, when off duty, I went round visiting the families. I was supposed to be on the look-out for difficulties, such as a child ill or anything else. Where there were any, I would help the women in the cave or try to find some other woman in the vicinity who could come and help her. But it was out in the fields that I talked most with the women. We have occasional rests, and then the women sit and chat.

At the same time, I worked at my own ideological re-education. I had, you see, to transform myself from a bourgeoise to a human being. This was done partly by physical work and partly by reading. I read a book called *Steel Yourself in the Fight with a Hundred Thousand Difficulties*. I read Liu Shao-chi's *How to Become a Good Communist*. I read a variety of articles. We had a leader of our group. He had been chosen even before we left Sian. At first, we all found it very difficult. Even the two who came of farming stock found everything primitive and difficult, but in our second month we had grown accustomed to the work and had adjusted ourselves. We tried to spend as much time as possible with the people of Liu Ling. We were not going to huddle together or make a sort of urban clique. We were to learn from the people and become one with them.

We paid nine yuan a month for our food. We ate a lot because, of course, we were now doing physical labour. Before we went out to the fields in the morning, we helped the families where the husband was working in the town or elsewhere. The women in such families had a hard time of it. We fetched water from the well for them, and we also swept up outside their caves. We helped the women wash the clothes and make quilted winter coats. We also tried to help the women to learn a few characters. What we did was to draw a picture of something, a pig for example, and write the character for pig beside it. We gave ten such pictures to every woman who was interested, and they put them up on the walls of their caves, so that they should have them in front of their eyes all day long. After a week, they were supposed to exchange pictures with each other. The schoolchildren also helped in this voluntary study. But it did not work as well as we had hoped. There are very few women in the village of Liu Ling who can read or write. It is much more difficult to learn to write our characters than you imagine. It is especially difficult for adults. But it is also true that they are much more beautiful than letters.

After the winter harvest was in, that was December 1959, there was less work in the fields. That is the time of year when life in the country quietens down and people occupy themselves with minor jobs. We then embarked on serious criticism and self-criticism. For two months we kept at this and held discussions about it. We went through each one's faults and judged whether they had corrected them and how. We probed into ourselves and examined each other and tried to get to the bottom of all our personal problems and each of our incorrect attitudes to life and work. Sometimes, these meetings lasted half a day, and we went on day after day. Altogether we had seventy or more meetings. This meant that each of us in the group was analysed and corrected for anything up to fifty hours. These meetings were attended by the different ganbus in the village. Li Yiu-hua spoke at them, and so did the different leaders of the brigades and the labour groups and the party organizations. Even the villagers got up one after the other and told us what they thought about us and our work.

This was very important. You know that most of us come from non-proletarian milieux, in which we never come in for harsh, caustic criticism. In the old days, one never told people the truth to their faces. In my home we had always to be polite. It was not fitting to criticize another person. It was only servants one could tell off properly. But these farmers spoke frankly to us. Of course, we were doing lao dung in order to be transformed. Often enough this criticism hurt, but it helped. The village women considered that one of the girls in the group was arrogant; but they talked her out of it. You know, the old person has to go, so that the new can emerge and take her place. I was told I had said that I would teach the leaders of the women's group to write and read, but when it came to it, I had only been able to teach one of them to read.

All that winter we went through our work and our behaviour in this way. Afterwards, there was not much left that we had not analysed and criticized. When you go on as long as that, you have no possibility of hiding behind fine phrases. Then, after thirteen months of lao dung, the time came for us to go home. I felt torn in two. On the one hand, I was longing dreadfully for my husband, but on the other hand I felt fearfully unhappy at having to leave Liu Ling. I had grown to the place and become part of it.

I shall never forget the morning we left. People had come down to the flat here to say goodbye. The women and I were in tears. They begged us to stay. Then they gave us eggs and pumpkin seeds, which are lovely. I wept very much. You see, I had been working with the women's group and now I was having to leave them. I knew all the women and had associated with them all the time and knew them better than I had ever known anybody in my life before. I had never been so close to people before. In my home, one did not behave like that. Then the car moved off and we drove away from Liu Ling.

I believe I learned a lot during those thirteen months. I became a different person. I had acquired a fundamentally proletarian attitude to life. For example, before, in the summer, if I thought it too hot, I used to hope it would rain, without stopping to think whether the rain would be good for the harvest or not. I can never do that again. Now, I automatically think first how the weather will affect the harvest. That year also gave me self-confidence. I learned to rely on myself and on my own capabilities. I am young and actually rather strong, and always have been; yet, before, I could scarcely even wash myself. When first we were told that we were to break new ground up on the hillside, I stood down there in the valley and looked up and almost burst into tears, because it all seemed so impossible. It was so high up and far away and the ground so hard. But there was nothing else to do but to climb up and start work. There was no way of my getting out of it. It was so hard, and it looked so hopeless. But then I noticed that we were making progress, and that I could work. And in the end I realized that nothing was impossible, and that it had only been my bourgeois up-bringing that had prevented me from relying on myself. The work went ahead quicker than the Old Secretary, Li Yiu-hua, had expected.

Yes, that year gave me the working people's attitude to existence. I became a completely different person. I had learned to work, and, when I returned home to my husband, he too thought I had changed. Since leaving Liu Ling, I have written to them all the time and heard from them too, and I am so happy to have been able to come here with you.

I have longed for this the whole time. I have put my name down as a volunteer for another year's physical work, but they haven't given me much hope. First, I must do my work in Sian and make use of all the education I have had. And I cannot expect to be sent out for a second year's lao dung until all the others who have not yet been have done their year. Then it is possible that I may. But I'm told that society has invested a lot of money in my education, and that I must exploit it.

People say of Ching Chi: She is healthy and strong and gay. She loves eating and chattering, and she can get through a lot of work. She loves to talk and laugh and is always helpful. At first, when she came here in 1959, she was like most town girls, but after only a few months she had become a thoroughly ordinary person. She is like one of the village's own daughters. She has no town airs left, and she does not behave in the least as if she were an intellectual. She likes best to sit with the women eating and talking about having babies and men and that sort of thing, like all the rest. But she is a sensible girl, too, and knows what she wants.

Part XIII

The Party

The Communist Party of China

Has twenty-three members in Liu Ling Labour Brigade.

Li Yiu-hua is secretary of the party association in Liu Ling Labour Brigade.

Li Hsin-min is party secretary for Liu Ling People's Commune.

Thirteen members of the party live in the village of Liu Ling:

Li Hai-kuei, leader of Liu Ling Village Labour Group's party group, member of the committee of Liu Ling Labour Brigade's party association

Li Kuei-ying, leader of the women's group. Member of the committee of Liu Ling Labour Brigade's party association

Li Hai-ching

Tsao Chen-kuei

Mau Ke-yeh, member of the committee of Liu Ling Labour Brigade's party association

Li Hung-fu

Fu Hai-tsao, president of the party group of the labour group for vegetable cultivation

Ma Chen-hai

Liu Ching-tsei

Liu Chen-yung

Ma Hai-hsiu

Li Yiu-hua, secretary of the party association of Liu Ling Labour Brigade

Yang Fu-lien

China's Communist League of Youth

Has twenty-four members in Liu Ling Labour Brigade.

Lo Han-hong is secretary of the League of Youth in Liu Ling Labour Brigade

Nine members of the League live in the village of Liu Ling:

Tsao Chen-hua

Tsao Chen-yung

Chiao Kuei-lan

Chi Mei-ying

Wang Fung-li, member of the youth association of the Liu Ling Labour Brigade

Ma Hung-tsai

Ma Tsuei-chang

Ma Ping

She Shiu-ying, member of the committee of the youth association of the Liu Ling Labour Brigade

One member of the League of Youth has moved from Liu Ling to Seven-mile Village:

Li Kuei-lien in charge of the women's group.

Li Yiu-hua, the Old Secretary, aged 57

IT is possible that I may be mistaken in my dates occasionally. You see, I cannot read; farmers of my generation cannot read or write. Not that my sons have been properly to school, but they have learned to read and write. So have their wives. This was the cause of considerable difficulty for us when we formed our first labour group for mutual help and the early farmers' co-operatives. None of the farmers could read or write, and therefore nobody could keep books or a work daybook, and often the children had to keep our books for us. In the old days, it often happened that there was not anyone able to read for several villages around, and so, if one received a letter, one went from village to village searching for someone to read it for one. But even though I cannot read properly and cannot always remember calendar dates accurately, there is nothing wrong with my memory, and I remember all that has happened to me in life.

I, too, am from the north. From Hengshan hsien. There were eleven of us children, eight brothers and three sisters. We were half-brothers and half-sisters, because we had different mothers. I was the eldest child of Father's second wife. I had a younger brother and a younger sister. Father was a tenant farmer. He used to say: 'Your great-grandfather lost our land.' My great-grandfather had owned a lot of land in Yangchiakoushan, but he was a bad farmer and also a lazy man; then he gambled all our land away on some gambling game, so Grandfather had to move to the village of Yuehyoushan, where he became a tenant of the local landowner, Yang Shen-you. I can remember Yang Shen-you; he was very old. Father died when I was eight, and then my eldest brother, Li Fong-hua, Li Hai-ching's father, became head of the family. But he didn't do well. He took to gambling and lost a lot, and several of the brothers had to go out as day labourers.

Then my eldest brother took the family and moved to the village of Hsiaotuwa, where he rented land from a man called Tung Shen-chi. We rented roughly twenty mu, for which we paid about 2,000 jin of corn a year in rental. Besides this, there were various taxes: I cannot now remember them all in detail, but we paid tax every month, and, once the rent and the taxes had been paid, there wasn't much left, and in springtime we went hungry. It was especially bad when my eldest brother had been out and gambled the family's money away. Gambling was a real curse up here in the old days. We were a big family of twenty. But my eldest brother managed things badly and, when I was thirteen, I had to go out as a day labourer. When I was sixteen, Mother died. Life became more and more difficult. The six older brothers were now married; the two younger ones bachelors. Now, we divided up the family possessions, and, since I had neither wife nor child, all I got was myself. The others had more mouths to feed and they shared what there was.

What happened was that every year we had run out of corn and had had to borrow from the landlord, paying the loan back after harvest. The interest varied a bit from year to year, depending on what sort of harvest it had been. The lowest interest was when we borrowed 300 jin and repaid 390, the highest when we borrowed 300 and paid back 450. The worse things were for us and the worse the crop, the higher interest we had to pay. In that way, the landlord always gained, whether the harvest was good or the crop failed. He always won. When we had paid the rental, our debt and the interest on it and the taxes, there was not a great deal left. We had to borrow money for clothes and tools. In the beginning, the interest on money was around three per cent a month, but then it rose to five per cent a month and finally it was up at ten per cent a month. We could not always pay it, and our debts grew with interest being charged on the interest. When we divided up the family possessions, we had a debt of 400 silver dollars and assets of 6,000 jin of grain, plus various small possessions. Being unmarried, I was excluded from the distribution, so that my older, married brothers each took a share both of the debt and of the grain. I, of course, got no grain, but on the other hand I was free of debt. My younger sister was already married then. I was sixteen and able to look after myself, so I went to Yaping, a village thirty li away.

There I took a place as farmhand with a landowner called Chang Ming-liang. I intended to work hard, save money and so gradually get enough to enable me to marry and found a family. We of northern

Shensi have always worked hard. We have a saying that in northern Shensi one lives on a pig's fodder and works like a horse. In the old days, under the old society, there was a small group that lived in luxury, but not even they had brocades or silks or that sort of thing. The rest of us had to live on bran and chaff and wild herbs for six months of the year. Now, life is better, but it is still hard and far from what we want it to be. But work we have always done. And it has been an honourable thing to work, too. A person known to be able to work hard has always been held in honour. When people from lower Shensi come to us here on lao dung, for example, we notice that. Even if they were farmers down there, they don't understand what we mean by work up here in northern Shensi. They just cannot work as we do.

Well, I began as farmhand with Chang Ming-liang. I had said to him: 'I intend to work hard, but I shan't take any wages until I marry. I want twenty silver dollars a year plus food and lodging.' He agreed to that. I worked in that way for four years, and as I did so much, we had no quarrels. When I was twenty, I became engaged. I was on my own, of course, and so I arranged my own marriage. I married when I was twenty-one. I then had eighty silver dollars lying with Chang Ming-liang, but I needed a hundred dollars to marry; so I borrowed twenty dollars from him. He did not charge me interest. 'As you didn't take interest from me for the money you did not draw, I shan't charge you interest on the loan,' he said. I went on working as his hand till 1934. There were now two of us and I took my wages in both cash and corn. My employer took a couple of silver dollars a year to pay off my debt. I was known as a good worker and a couple of other landowners came to me and offered me a higher wage to go to them. When my employer heard this, he was afraid to lose me and increased my wage. In the end, I was foreman and got thirty silver dollars a year. You see, it was the same in the old society too; a person who worked properly was respected, even if he was just a farmhand or a day labourer.

But a lot had happened in those years, too. It had been a hard time: 1928–9 was a period of famine. The 1928 harvest was bad and, in the spring of 1929, the slave dealers began coming to the villages of northern Shensi. They were out to buy children, and many were sold then. Children from northern Shensi were usually sold to Shansi and Hopeh. The boys went to childless families which wanted their name to continue, and the girls were sold as brides or to the towns. When girls were sold, the slave dealers just took them away, and we did not know

335

what happened after that. Most were never heard from again. There was just silence. There are several here in Liu Ling who have experienced that. Two of Ching Chung-ying's younger brothers were sold to Shansi, and Chia Ying-lan was himself sold to Hopeh, and it was not till after the liberation that he got in touch with his sister and turned up again. Later that spring, people were dying of starvation.

The landowners were inhuman and cruel. They themselves had grain enough. They had big stores of grain. But they did not let those who had no land to pledge have any. They demanded security for a loan. They did not worry about people's distress. I worked hard, and we two managed all right. But then there were just the two of us. Yet, if Chang Ming-liang had sold his corn at normal prices, no one in our village would have starved to death. He had a big enough store. We thought he had, even then, during the famine, and later, in 1935, when we expropriated him during the revolution and examined his stores, we found a big hoard of grain dating back to before 1929. But he was a landowner.

The first time we heard any mention of the revolution was in 1929–30. People said then that the landowners' property was all going to be shared out, and that the poor farmers would have the power; but at first we just thought it a joke. At that time, we had not even heard of Sun Yat-sen and the K.M.T. That came later. And then people were also talking about someone called Chu Mao. He was supposed to be a general away down in the south. We thought then that it was just one person.

Later, there was a lot of talk that the students in the cities were demonstrating and saying that the land ought to be divided up equally, and that the students would serve the people. We thought that sounded fine. But it sounded mostly to be just a lovely dream. We thought it would be pretty difficult to put into practice. I don't remember now who it was told me about this. It was mostly just general talk. What the students were saying in the cities made a great impression on us, as did the fact that there was a revolution in the country, led by General Chu Mao among others, and that the revolution was dividing up the land and giving it to the poor, and that all people were equal. All that made a great impression. It was about 1930 that people in the villages were talking of this. It was not till many years later that I realized that General Chu Mao was really General Chu Teh and Chairman Mao Tse-tung, and that they were the leaders of the communists.

In 1934, I went back to Yuehyoushan and worked there for our old landlord's son, Yang Kung-shan. The thing was that I had worked for Chang Ming-liang for a long time and in the end had become fed up with him and no longer liked him, so that when young Yang came and asked me to come back and told me how well off I should be, I thought that I might as well go back to Yuehyoushan. I took out half my wages in cash and half in grain. My brothers had moved away to different villages. Our life was the same as ever, poor people remained poor people. A quilted coat had to last you ten years. You washed it every year and patched it, till it was nothing but patches. One day, when I was sitting having supper, Yang Shen-hsi came to me. He was the old land-lord, Yang Shen-you's brother. He had just come from the town. He said to me: 'My friend, there's a lot of talk now of revolution and that you are going to divide up the landowners' land. So you wait, and before long you'll be sharing out our land and our goats.' Then he laughed, because he thought it a great joke. But I thought: 'But this is quite possible. And it would be a good thing, if it did come.'

After that, people began talking about the Red Army. I was working from sunrise to sunset and did not have much time for talking, but I listened to what people said about the Red Army. It was led by Liu Chih-tan. He divided the possessions of the rich among the poor. The landowners were no longer joking about this. Instead, they began coming to us and saying: 'The communists are only wanting to take your wives and share them with each other. Because the communists share everything. They also share their wives with each other.' We wondered how much of this was true.

In March 1935, the first propagandists from the Red Army began to arrive. But they did not come to our village, because that was where the landowner himself lived. They kept to the other villages. That summer, in June and July 1935, the landowner began to feel afraid. He dug caves into the hillside and hid his possessions away and kept a watch at night. People said that he was afraid, but he said that it was because there were so many bandits about those days. Then everyone said: 'He's afraid of the Red Army.' Now, all the surrounding villages were doing what the Red Army said. The landowner, Yang Kung-shan, himself went to the Red Army and said: 'I believe in the revolution. I want to follow the Red Army.'

But he only just said that. Actually he hated the Red Army and was afraid and wanted to run away. To me he said: 'It's a pity the Red Army is so persecuted. I shall help them.'

But nobody bothered about him, and then the propaganda started among us, his dependants. He was quite hemmed in and had to pretend to be Red. He began saying that all people were brothers. There were only seven families in our little village, besides the proprietor and his family, and we all worked for Yang Kung-shan. Now, when the propaganda became stronger, we farmhands stopped working for the landowner and revolted.

Then he tried to run away. He wanted to get to Yulin, 240 li away, or to Hengshan, 120 li away. He had managed to remove a good deal of his possessions to the town earlier on, and he now came to me and said: 'Come along with me. As long as I have corn for myself and my family, you and your family will have enough to eat.' But I thought: 'Why should I go along with you any longer?' At that time, I had three children, and I did not want to go with him. Then he said: 'As you will. Stay here then. My corn is stored. You will be responsible for it. See that my cave is kept in repair and that it doesn't collapse.' 'Yes,' I replied. Then he left.

He set out that evening and hoped to reach Hengshan before it grew light. Most of the households in our village went with him. They were related to him and did not dare do otherwise. They thought he was more powerful than the Red Army. My family and I were the only ones to stay behind in the village. When the villagers in the other villages round about heard that he had fled, they took up the chase; but they did not succeed in catching up with him. Just as they had sighted him, he reached a K.M.T. post forty li away, and after that, they could not catch him, but had to turn back. They came back then to our village, and at dawn began dividing up his corn. They were all his tenants. Now, too, the landless farmhands and day labourers from the surrounding villages came and joined the revolution. We shared the land and the grain. I got 300 jin of corn, and I thought: 'Corn I can eat and then no one can take it from me. But what about the land?' There was no detachment of the Red Army in the neighbourhood when we made our revolution. There were only Red Guards with spears from the neighbouring villages.

We now had to register for land. Each got as much land as he could till. The rest was set aside to be cultivated by the Red Army. That was our form of grain tax during the revolution. It was organized by the president of the people's militia in our district. He was called Shang Wen-zu. I don't know what happened to him afterwards. He stayed on in his village after the power of the people was broken, and I have not heard anything of him since.

Now a lot of propagandists and ganbus were coming to the village, sent by our government. They used to spend the night in my cave. One day, a ganbu called Chang came. He was the battalion leader of the Red Guard, and he had a talk with me and said: 'The revolution is for the poor. In our revolution, the poor must themselves take power. You shall be responsible for setting up the Red Guard here.' I had seen this Chang before. He was from a village a bit farther on. We trusted each other, because we came from the same district and we were all poor. One of the things that made our revolution possible was that we always talked to the poorest. Another thing that had a lot of significance was that we heard of the revolution from members of our own family. We had most trust in the family, and when the family started saying that the revolution was necessary, this was better propaganda than anyone coming from outside to talk to us. An uncle can say things that an outsider cannot say.

I now had thirty mu of land. It was the first time I had had my own land, and it was good land. I had chosen it myself. My wife said nothing. That was still in the old society, in which women did not talk about such things. Now that I was in charge of the Red Guard in our village, I took part in the distribution of land in other villages. When we went to those villages, we first got in contact with any we had known for a long time and had a serious talk with them. I took part in the distribution of land in Yaping. I was a platoon commander, and we of the Red Guard came to Yaping armed with spears. We had arranged this with the leader in Yaping. We had walked all night and got there in the morning. We came from a number of villages, as we always did. Hundreds and hundreds of poor farmers and tenants and day labourers and farmhands, all with spears, came from all the villages of the neighbourhood. By the morning, we had all arrived and then we accomplished the revolution.

Three hundred men were assembled in the village of Yaping. The propagandists went up to the landlord, Chang Ming-liang, and talked sense to him. He saw that all resistance was hopeless and he acquiesced in his land being divided up without more ado. He himself shared out his grain and his land and his tools, and then became just one of the ordinary village farmers. He talked with me as with an old acquaintance, but he did not let on that he was against the distribution of land. He behaved well. Later, he fell ill and died, but his son continued to cultivate his land and he never mentioned the dividing up of it, but was an ordinary villager. Most of the landowners were sensible. They accepted the inevitable. Some fled. Yang Kung-shan, who had fled to Hengshan, later went on farther to Yulin, when we were approaching Hengshan. Then, when the counter-revolutionaries defeated us, he returned; but that is another story.

After that, we kept this whole area as a liberated area for two years. If the counter-revolutionaries had not attacked, all the farmers would gradually have got land and oxen, and corn enough to eat their fill every day of the year. During these two years we carried our revolution through at the same time as we were growing grain. Half the time we spent out and about fighting in the revolution, and the other half of the time we were at home cultivating our fields. In those days we had enough corn.

In every village there was a leader of the Red Guard and a president of the Poor Farmers' Union. He was responsible for the grain and for Red Army men being quartered, if any came to the village. The grain we expropriated was shared out among the farmers, except for a small part which was kept for the Red Army. The president of the Poor Farmers' Union was responsible for the grain store. We elected him at a meeting, and this was our first bit of independent administration. Life became easier for us. We had no rents to pay, no taxes, no interest, all we had to do was to work and eat. At that time we paid no grain tax on our production. There were so few Red Army men, and only a couple of ganbus running the entire administration. We had a small plot that we cultivated for the Red Army. The farmers paid nothing whatsoever. The only impost we had, apart from cultivating the plot, was that every woman had to make one or two pairs of shoes a year for the Red Army.

We held lots of meetings. Everything had to be decided in open assembly. Small things as well as big. As soon as a matter cropped up, we arranged for a meeting. Then, the Red Guard in the village had its own meetings, and there were youth meetings and women's meetings. And the communists used to meet at night in some old temple or other, because no one had time by day. At first, things went rather slowly at our meetings. Nobody dared say what he really thought. Naturally, it

341

was difficult at first, for we were only farmers and had never held meetings before or voted or held discussions or made decisions.

We did not hear much about what was being done in the cities, but there was a lot of talk about which areas had now been liberated in northern Shensi and what Liu Chih-tan and Hsien Tse-chiang had said. We also heard about other liberated areas and about Mao.

We used to talk about how big and powerful our Red Army in northern Shensi was. You see, in 1935 and 1936, no one ever thought of the K.M.T., and it never occurred to us that the landlords would come back, or that the counter-revolution would be victorious and defeat us. When Liu Chih-tan and Hsien Tse-chiang led the Red Army against Hengshan, I was there making a delivery of grain. We were besieging Hengshan then, and it was the first time I had seen an army of that size. They had weapons and uniforms. We had come with the grain carts and, when we had delivered the grain to the army, we stayed on for the rest of the day and ate in the mess. As we sat there eating, Liu Chih-tan came in. He walked right past me, but he did not speak to me. He had great responsibilities then, as commander of the Red Army. But I had at least seen him.

Our government was in Anting—the town is now called Tsechiang —and all the villagers were talking of how our army exercised there and how strong it was. We held a lot of political mass meetings at that time. We had meetings about the Soviet Union, and at these, ganbus came and told us that we had learned from its experience how to make a revolution. The Soviet Government had also begun with only a few rifles. We had meetings at which we talked of how all humanity was to be freed of all oppression and all misfortune and need, and how all peoples were to become brothers and live as equals all over the world. We had meetings about imperialism and what the imperialists had done in China. There were different sorts of meetings, and we talked about the three mountains that weighed on the people of China. These three mountains were bureaucratic capitalism, the feudal landowners and the foreign imperialists. We had all to help and topple them over.

We often held our meetings on the tops of hills, and then we had flags with us and posted Red Guardsmen with spears round about as guards. And we had red streamers fixed to the spears. At the start of the meeting we sang. We sang lots of songs and both men and women sang. We all sang together. There were great differences between our life then and what it had been before. The greatest difference was that all landlords, despots and bureaucrats had disappeared and the land been divided up, and that the farmers were free. We never saw a single tax collector those years. Before, the dogs used to come every month, and, even if one paid the tax, they would say: 'But I have walked such a long way, I must have some journey money for myself too.' If one had no money to pay the tax with, they hit one with chains. But in those years the dogs never came near us.

The women too were liberated. The three mountains may have weighed heavily on the people of China, but they had weighed most heavily on the women. A woman's sufferings were unspeakable. When she was fourteen or fifteen she was married off to someone twenty years her senior. Many girls committed suicide then. Their feet were bound. No one would marry a 'big foot'. None dared cut her hair. They all wore theirs in a bun on the nape of their necks, as my wife still does today. When a young girl's feet were bound, the bindings were pulled so tight that she could not walk. It hurt so much that she could not stand. But she was forced to get up and walk; she was hit with a broom till she did so. And this was not done because people were evil. They only wanted what was best for the girl. Nobody wanted to hit their child, but if her feet weren't bound, she would have such an unhappy life that one was compelled to be hard for her own sake. At first, after having their feet bound, girls just stumbled about.

Now, after our revolution, all the women's feet were to be freed. We removed the bindings from the feet of all little girls. Many women took part in our discussions and meetings. Women were elected to different committees and different posts in the villages. The women also formed their own propaganda groups. Then we sang about women's emancipation. I can still remember many of the songs of those days about women's rights. We made propaganda for the equality of women and free choice in marriage. There were lots of divorces in those days, for most people's marriages had been arranged for them and they did not care for each other. We held meetings about love then. Most did not go back to their former marriage partners, but looked for new ones with whom they would be happier. The class enemy then slandered us and flung mud at us, saying that we had no morals. But we wanted everyone to be free and equal, and the new marriages were both happier and more enduring than the old. The upper classes still tell lies about us.

But this new equality certainly was a problem. Li Hai-fu's first

343

wife left him in 1935. She went off with a troupe of women propagandists. She was going to make propaganda for the revolution. Her father-in-law was still very feudal in his attitude. He said: 'Do you want to run away? Then I'll break your leg so that you won't be able even to limp along.' Then I told him: 'If you break her leg, you will regret it. How could you even think of such a thing?' 'She wants to run away from us,' he said. 'She isn't running away,' I said. 'She's transferring to different work.' He had to give in. The power of the people would not let him break her leg and she went with her propaganda troupe. She did a good job for the revolution. Later, when the K.M.T. came, she was taken prisoner and badly tortured. We succeeded in freeing her in the end, but she died soon afterwards. Her son is grown-up now.

In July 1935, I joined the party. It was very simple. The party was holding a meeting in the old temple above the village. There were four people there. Two party members came and fetched me and took me to the meeting. There we discussed revolutionary work, after which they said to me: 'Are you prepared to become a member of the Communist Party of China?' 'Yes, I am,' I said. That was how I became a party member.

Right up to the end of May 1937, when the enemy attacked us from Hengshan, we had no idea that they were going to launch an attack. The enemy's troops reached our village in September. They rounded up us farmers and made us build fortifications in the hills. There had been many fights in the years before this, but in the great attack of 1937 the Red Guard could not do much against the enemy's troops. We had knives and spears and muzzle-loaders, but they came with machine-guns and cannon and modern weapons. There were many enemy troops. They were advancing the whole time. They advanced ten li, then they compelled the villagers to build them a fort, and, when it was finished, they advanced another ten li. Our guerrillas were retreating the whole time. We never saw the Red Army. When we farmers saw the enemy's troops coming, we said: 'We are helpless. There's nothing we can do.' We could not even defend ourselves when the enemy rounded us up to build forts for them. While we were working on the forts, we kept asking each other: 'When will our government come back? When will our Red Army come? If only we could hear from them, and if only we knew where they are now, so we could work for them.' But however much we asked, nobody knew where our government had gone or where the Red Army was, and we never heard from the party and just wondered. We could not do anything. We were conscript labourers and were beaten by the K.M.T. soldiers while we were building fortifications for them, and the poor people suffered.

Now, too, the owner of the land, Yang Kung-shan, returned. The year before, 1936, when we still were in power, he had led an enemy force to the village of Shiwan, forty li away, and there had stolen goats and corn and plundered us, but on that occasion we had been able to drive him off. The enemy was always bloodthirsty. In November 1935, the enemy had gone to Yushomou, where my sixth brother, Li Shu-hua, Li Hai-chun's father, was president of the Poor Farmers' Union. They cut off my brother's head and those of eleven other poor farmers that same night. When enemy troops re-entered the village in 1937, they cut off the heads of five farmers and one ganbu from the district administration who was in charge of youth matters. I knew them all, because we were neighbours. But of us brothers, it was only the sixth who had his head cut off. The landowners wanted their revenge. They had good relations with the K.M.T. and dragged the farmers before their courts and said: 'This peasant has done this and this.' At first, that was quite enough. But afterwards the K.M.T. came to see that it would be dangerous to cut off too many people's heads.

So, when Yang Kung-shan came back and took me prisoner and hauled me before the K.M.T. court in Shiwan in 1937, he said: 'He has eaten up my corn and divided up my possessions.' Then I replied: 'I was not the only one to make revolution. We all did so and it was your own fault. You weren't worth anything better.' Yang Kung-shan wanted them to cut my head off, but they didn't. They just beat me till I lost consciousness and then poured water over me to bring me round and then beat me again. They kept on with that for a bit. The enemy had a special committee called 'Committee for Quelling the Revolution', and after being thus tortured, I was brought before their committee. There they interrogated me to find out if I was a communist. Then they tortured me again. I never told them anything, and they got nothing out of me, and in the end they put me in prison and left me there. Then friends in Shiwan stood guarantee for me and so got me out of prison. I had been tortured so much that I was unable to walk, and they had to hire a donkey to transport me home. There I lay on my kang for three months unable to get up.

345

But Yang Kung-shan did not like my being released. He would have liked to have me condemned to death and my head cut off. Not only because he disliked me, but because he would then have been able to sell my widow and my children and in that way get his money back. He never forgave me for having helped to divide up his property. I had scarcely got on my feet again before he had me in prison a second time. Then people in the villages round about said that they had all helped to make the revolution, and not just me, and that it was unfair to treat me in that way. If Yang Kung-shan wanted his money back, he could demand rental for those years from me in the ordinary way, but he could not just have them cut my head off and take my family as pledge. The K.M.T. authorities had now become more circumspect. They wanted the district to be calm and quiet, so the officers just said to me: 'It doesn't matter now you being in the Red Army. Just confess and get it off your chest. We only want to help you become a better person.' But I didn't confess anything and people stood guarantee for me and I wasn't even tortured, but released again. Yang Kung-shan could not endure that and, having twice failed to get my head chopped off, he now drove me out of the village and refused to let me live there any longer.

So I moved to the village of Yuanmukou, which was fifteen li farther on. My employer's name was Ma Tse-yuan. He owned his land. He had been in Shiwan when I was in prison there the first time. I worked for him as a farmhand for two years, 1938 and 1939. All cash I earned I had to pay to Yang Kung-shan; the children were growing up and there were many mouths to feed.

I used to wonder where the Red Army had gone. Some said that it had taken itself down to Yenan, others did not know. We tried to get in contact with the party, but could not do so. Now and again a few of us used to meet in secret, but we had no regular activities and we did not dare meet too often, because we were all poor and all members of the party and all suspected of being so. There were very few members left. Only a few in every other, or every third or so, village.

It was difficult to get into contact with Yenan. Our village, of course, lay inside K.M.T. territory. But some of my family had moved down there long before, before our revolution began in northern Shensi. You see, in those days one was moving the whole time hunting for land and better conditions; and in the old Yenanfu, all ten hsiens were short of people, and so people were always moving. The old people said that famine and wars and revolts under the Ching dynasty had de-populated the area. In October 1939, I went down to Yenan to see if there was work for a farmhand there. My sister, Li Fong-lan, who is Tung Yang-chen's grandmother, was living in Liu Ling, and she said: 'We need someone to work for us.' Then I went back to our village and stayed there for the winter. When we had eaten up our corn, we all went to Liu Ling.

That first year, I worked for Tung Yang-chen's family. I was the only worker there. I got one jin for every ten I harvested for them. In 1940, the harvest was good and we had lots of food. Tung's family had good land down in the valley and they harvested 300 jin per mu. They had a good ox too. But then Tung Yang-chen's mother married and so brought a pair of hands into the family again, so I began working for Li Hsiu-tang's family. I worked there for a year. When I began work-ing for him, I had to borrow 300 jin. I repaid 600 jin. I worked in his fields with his ox, and we divided the harvest fifty-fifty.

I'd known Li Hsiu-tang since he was very young. I know him in-side out. His father owned half the valley and many shops and houses in the town here. Li Han-hua, who was Li Hsiu-tang's brother-in-law, owned the west half of the valley and the Date Garden, where the Cen-tral Committee had its headquarters. You could almost say that Li Hsiu-tang's brother-in-law has been Mao Tse-tung's host. But he was a very reluctant host. Li Han-hua was a very dangerous man. He was rich and powerful, and he commanded the armed combat forces of the landowners. He had many people's blood on his conscience. Yenan's third big man owned even more. He was the richest of the three. But Li Hsiu-tang's father was one of the three big men of the old Yenanfu. Now, we are trying to bring his children up to be good citizens. They are so young that they have no experience of what used to be.

The Red Army was down here in Yenan, of course. It was called the Eighth Route Army. Here, too, there was the Communist Party and its central committee and the government of the Shensi-Kansu-Ningsia Frontier Region. In 1942, the Central Committee proposed a big production campaign, and then I organized and led a labour exchange group. This consisted mostly of my relatives. Those who had come down here earlier had been given good land in the distribution, and they did not want to join in any sort of co-operative cultivation. But we, who had come here later, had to be content with the hill land

and that called for co-operation. So I went up to Hengshan and fetched more of my relatives and started a labour exchange group. It was the first permanent labour exchange group in the Shensi-Kansu-Ningsia Frontier Region. It had no special name. It consisted of eight families: I, the organizer and leader; Li Hai-fu; Li Hai-kuei; Li Hai-chun, who works now in the people's commune; Li Hai-chen, who also works in the people's commune now, and three families from Hengshan who fled from Hu Tsung-nan back to Hengshan and are still there. We worked one day for one family, the next day for another family, and so on. We broke new ground and cleared fields, and we worked well together. All the fields you see up there on the hillside on the other side of the valley are ones we cleared. We did it all by hand: we had no oxen, just mattocks.

The other farmers in the valley had good land and they did not co-operate. That came much later. But we co-operated. We had to co-operate, if we were to get on. We had discussed it thoroughly in our group. 'Our land is poor,' we said. 'We have no level ground, we have no oxen, but we can work.' At the end of the year we had a lot of corn, and it had all been harvested on the fields we had cleared. As, after this harvest, we all had enough to eat, we bought pigs. Two families clubbed together to buy the beasts, and that winter the group owned six. So we worked on till the winter of 1946-7. By then, every household in the group had animals and a store of corn. I had three beasts and a donkey. I thought the whole time that organization meant strength. The more people, the greater the labour force. In some few short years we had all achieved prosperity through hard work and co-operation. The others down in the valley said: 'They work very hard and they get incomes out of it. They are doing well.'

When I went down to Yenan, our party group had lost contact with the party, as I said. At first, I did not get into touch with the party in Yenan either. I never thought there was anyone to contact. I had no connexions there, you see. Things were different here in Yenan than they had been with us. The Central Committee was here, though, and the government and everything, and one could not just go up and talk with them. But when I was working for Li Hsiu-tang, I was responsible for public safety in the village. Then I organized the labour exchange group. After that, the party got in touch with me and asked me if I would be willing to start working for the revolution. We had many talks, and, in 1945, I joined the party again.

When I was in Hengshan, even in the latter part of my time there, it was very little we knew about the outside world. For example, we had not heard of the war with Japan, even in 1939. I never heard of it till I came down to Yenan.

A lot has happened in Liu Ling in these years. When I came here, there were only a few households and a few caves in the hillside. Then the co-operative built its centre down by the well, and had its big shop on the other side of the river. That was the Southern District's Sellers' and Consumers' Co-operative. All the farmers had shares in it. The co-operative developed very quickly. In 1942, it built a number of proper houses and big sheds. Its employees lived here in long rows. Chiang Kai-shek was trying to blockade the frontier region, so Mao said: 'We must create plenty with our own hands.' By 1943 the co-operative had 800 transport mules. The communist party was poor in those days and had no motor-cars. The mules fetched salt from Ting-pian. Most of the villagers were members of the co-operative, and we elected representatives. Each member had one vote irrespective of the size of his share. Little by little the people had to learn to be masters of the country. It was not easy to begin with. The co-operative was a school in which we learned how to run a business with elected delegates and how to run the country with popularly elected power.

We had our difficulties too. In 1942, the river flooded. The old people said that it was the worst flood in living memory. The co-operative shop was under water and even some of the ganbus lost all hope, but Liu Chien-chang, president of the whole of the Southern District's Sellers' and Consumers' Co-operative, said: 'A single-storey house can be flooded; so we shall have to build two-storey houses.' And we did. We also built an assembly hall and many other buildings. So, gradually, things went better and better for the co-operative. The transport of goods and salt gave it a big income. The dividend on the shares rose to five times the shares' value. Some people—those who were hard up—took out their money, but most people left their money in the co-operative. Five shops were opened and we built workshops, where we produced wine and oil and Chinese bean pudding. We were beginning to put Li Hsiu-tang's mill out of business, by starting a lot of other small co-operative mills, which were driven by donkey power and which charged the farmer less than Li Hsiu-tang did.

But exploitation still existed in those days. There were many who lived wholly or partly on other people's labour. But we controlled this exploitation and kept an eye on it. Those who had been given land, when it was parcelled up, had got very good land. They had valley land and too much of it for a family to be able to cultivate alone. So they had begun hiring hands and day labourers during the busy season. In this way, some farmers, who before had been poor, now became exploiters; or, rather, they were beginning almost to be exploiters. This was the way things went, for example, with Tung Yang-chen and Ma Hai-hsiu. Their family's labour force was too small and so they employed others. In this way, class differentiation was starting again after our land reform. If this had gone on, there would have been new landlords and new big farmers in the valley here. I thought a lot about this at the time. We were up on the hill there breaking new ground. I felt that it was essential to get co-operative farming, if we were not to get a new rich class.

At that time, then, we had our relics from the old days, people like Li Hsiu-tang, who still lived on part of his land and lived on income that he didn't work for. But after our land reform, we had three different tendencies of development among the ordinary farmers: *nouveaux riches* farming on their own, people who had been given good valley land and were beginning to employ day labourers and farmhands and thus starting to live in part on other people's labour; the sellers' and consumers' co-operative, and the labour exchange group working up on the hill land. Li Hsiu-tang and similar relics still fulfilled a certain function.

The winter of 1946–7 was marked by preparations for war. Evacuation was planned and the authorities made propaganda to encourage the farmers to evacuate the valley. All corn was to be buried and all tools hidden. 'The enemy is going to attack and will occupy this area, that much is certain,' we were told. As early as October 1946, ganbus began coming to us telling us that the enemy was going to attack. Then more and more was said about Hu Tsung-nan's coming attack. The ganbus told us to hide our corn, so that we should have it once the enemy had withdrawn, and to prevent it from benefiting them. But I thought: 'Surely Yenan is the headquarters of the Central Committee? How can it be abandoned? And how could the Central Committee ever come back here after having fled?'

In January 1947, a representative of the government came to the village to try to get us really to hide everything. A great deal of propaganda was now being made. The ganbus told us that Mao had said that the enemy was going to capture Yenan, and not just the town but the whole of the surrounding countryside as well. In fact, the whole frontier region would fall to the enemy. Mao was also supposed to have said that if we wanted to lose Yenan, we should defend it. Mao had also said that Hu Tsung-nan would be in Yenan seven or eight months, or a year at the most. I thought that the propagandists must have heard wrong. It couldn't be true. The Central Committee and Chairman Mao had been in Yenan for many years. Why, then, was the Central Committee going to run away from the enemy?

The farmers were not good about hiding their corn. What was hidden was only hidden because a government representative stood over them to see it done. In February, the propagandists were saying: 'Don't be afraid. You will manage under the enemy. Just don't have a change of heart.' Then they went away and our troops marched off northwards. I had sent my children to Ansai, and there was only my wife and I left. Certain families, which came from Michi and Heng-shan, went back to their home country, including three of the families in our labour exchange group. But as we had no land up there, we stayed where we were. The Southern District's Sellers' and Consumers' Co-operative had 800 mules. These were loaded up and driven to Wayapo. After that, the farmers began digging pits to hide their grain in and, by the time the enemy marched in, we had gone up into the hills.

We were living in a little village. When the enemy came, it was with thousands and thousands of men. They marched in and swept the valleys and the branch valleys and the hills clean. There was a couple of households here who thought that the communists had been defeated for good and all, and they hurried to offer the K.M.T. troops boiling water, and to show them the way into Yenan town. They were so impressed by the K.M.T.'s good weapons that they went over to them entirely. Li Hsiu-tang and Tuan Fu-yin did that. After our victory, we re-educated them and they are now treated kindly.

The K.M.T. began making its old propaganda, saying that the communists were evil and that the K.M.T. wanted to save us farmers from their clutches. But nobody believed them. 'We are the troops of the Central Government,' they said. 'We have crushed the communist bandits, and now we are going to see that you live well.' But at the same time as they said this, they were plundering the farmers. Where their troops had been, you would not hear a hen cackle, nor find a pig left. They even dragged the shoes off people's feet. They plundered Li Hsiu-tang's and Tuan Fu-yin's caves just as thoroughly as all the others. It made no difference to the soldiers whether they had gone over to the K.M.T. or not.

We were profoundly depressed when we saw the K.M.T. troops. They were so heavily armed, and they had weapons we had never even seen before. Our soldiers in the Eighth Route Army had nothing similar. I stayed up in the hills for a fortnight, but the enemy was roaming about up there too and, when those who had gone back to Liu Ling came up and told us that it would be all right to go back, we did so. When we got back, we heard that not a single shot had been fired in the valley. Our men had retreated without a fight. But lots of graves were being dug on the hills, and they were being made out to be those of Eighth Route Army men. This was because the K.M.T. needed a victory.

Many of these graves were dug, especially on Lokoushan. We did not properly understand the enemy's purpose in digging them. After the liberation, when we ploughed up the ground there, we examined all the graves before ploughing them, but did not find a body in any of them. They were just bluff.

When I returned to Liu Ling, half the village had been destroyed. The enemy had plundered it most thoroughly. Yet, at the same time, the K.M.T. tried to organize the people into groups and sections. They chose various people and gave them various posts, but those they chose had all had something to do with the K.M.T. before. In Liu Ling, the K.M.T. appointed Tuan Fu-yin its group leader. They appointed a section leader in Seven-mile Village. This was Tuan Shi-tsai. He had been a pedlar. He worked as informer for the K.M.T. He, of course, was from the district and he went round pointing out communists and communist sympathizers to the K.M.T.'s secret police. He was arrested after the liberation, and we re-educated him through work. He got three or four years. He returned to Seven-mile Village in 1954 or so.

Most of the young people of the village were out with the guerrillas. No one from this village fell in the fighting. The guerrillas fought when they were able to defeat the enemy, but otherwise they kept clear and hid from the enemy. Hu Tsung-nan held this area occupied for thirteen months. In March 1948 he had to withdraw. Everything had been destroyed by then. The co-operative had had eighty buildings in its premises in the village, and they had all been pulled down and destroyed. They had stood where the school is now. We had no corn to eat and no seed to sow. When the enemy had been driven out, we had to begin at the beginning all over again. Despite the destruction, however, we were glad to be rid of the K.M.T. The authorities now organized farmers to carry seed-corn from Lochuan, where there were stores of grain. I acted as porter then. We each carried seventy to eighty jin in two sacks on a arrying-pole. It took us roughly a week to walk to Lochuan, get the corn and walk back. Your back ached, life was bitter and I wanted to cry, because everything was so smashed and ruined; but at least the enemy had been sent headlong. We had to work hard to get going again.

All labour was mobilized and organized at the time. Certain of us had the job of fetching corn from Lochuan, others stayed at home in the village. We had almost no animals. The young men had to draw the plough and the women ploughed. Now Li Hsiu-tang emerged once more. He is very sly. He applied for membership of the militia again, just as if nothing had happened; but we would not have him. His hopes were vain. We gave him an official refusal.

Mao got to Peking in 1949. He never returned to Yenan and still has not been here again. But, in 1949, the whole country was in the process of being liberated. He then sent us in the old liberated areas telegrams, exhorting us to organize our work and heal the wounds of war. We were to increase production. Then we began to recall that Mao had been right in saying that the enemy would hold Yenan occupied for about a year, and so we felt that we could rely on the Central Committee and Mao. In Liu Ling, we called a meeting to discuss Mao's telegram and to organize ourselves for production.

That year we set up four labour groups for mutual help, which included every household in the village of Liu Ling. They built on the experience we had gained with ours, before the occupation. I was in charge of the first labour group for mutual help, which had the same members as before the occupation, with the exception of the three families which had moved back to Hengshan and now did not wish to return. Also Li Hai-yuan joined it. We took the land we wanted upon the hills on the other side of the valley. I had chosen this area right from the beginning, because there is good water there and it is easy to get fuel up on the hills, nor was the soil so bad either. We had five beasts.

The second labour group for mutual help was led by Ma Juei-ching. The third was led by Jen Huai-wan, Jen Teh-wan's son, who is now party secretary at the pottery in Yenan. Fu Hai-tsao was in charge of the fourth labour group for mutual help.

But there were certain difficulties in running this kind of co-operative work. When there were eight households working jointly in a labour group for mutual help, it meant that one of the households had its land sowed roughly eight days earlier than the last household's. That involved a financial gain for the one and a financial loss for the other. This led to a lot of discussion. We had lively discussions of the whole question in our group and finally we said: 'Let us try cultivating it all together and then just sharing the produce.' That was in November 1949, after the harvest. But we had no knowledge of how a co-operative farm should be run. We did not even know that we were a co-operative farm. We did not know how we were going to calculate a day's work or how each person's work was to be assessed. But we were not all agreed. Li Hai-fu and Li Hai-kuei refused. They took out their two beasts and went and joined Fu Hai-tsao's labour group for mutual help. That left only four families of us, and we had three beasts.

But I still thought that we ought to try. To start with, we did not have work units, but each of us had a certain labour value. We did not assess the actual work, but the worker in person, acting on the assumption that each of us would always do his best. We were all good workers. We had difficulty over the book-keeping. We were all uneducated and had no one who could keep accurate notes.

Li Hai-chun and Li Hai-chen were the ones who had to do our book-keeping. They had the head for that sort of thing, and both have since transferred to administrative work. It was I who led the discussions in November 1949, and I was able to force the change through, partly because I was leader of the labour group and partly because the members were all my relations and, I being one of the older generation in the family, they had respect for me. I told you before that the ties of family have been of great significance in our revolution. It wasn't so strange that Li Hai-fu and Li Hai-kuei did not want to be in on this. They lived on this side of the valley and they had beasts. We, on the other hand, had nothing but hillside fields on the other side of the valley and so had to join forces. Of those who remained and built up the first farmers' co-operative, Li Hai-chen and I were the better off. I had an ox and Li Hai-chen had two beasts. The other households had nothing but their hands. They owned nothing. But Li Hai-chen and I had been to many meetings and taken part in lots of things, and we were more aware and decided to help the other two families. The Party was interested too. The Party secretary for Yenan hsien came out in person to listen to our discussion. But at that time he only listened. He didn't say anything.

There was no great enthusiasm for our work that first year. The 1950 harvest was good, it is true, but our method did not work. We had decided that every worker had a certain value. A good worker had ten points, a not-so-good worker, like my young son who was not then yet fully grown, was given five points. At the end of the year, when we shared out according to this system, the shares were not related to the work actually done. We did not yet know how to keep books with actual work reckoned in days' work.

We had a very serious discussion after the harvest in 1950. The income per household was big, it is true, but when we examined the distribution of income more closely, we found that there still was exploitation in our co-operative. The oxen were exploiting the people. Each ox brought its owner 900 jin of corn a year, but its feed came from the co-operative.

Even so, despite the fact that our system was a bit lame, people thought that the co-operative was a good idea. That autumn, we acquired two new members. Li Hai-fu came back to us after a year in Fu Hai-tsao's labour group for mutual help, and he brought his ox. Then a family, Ma Chan-wan, came from Hengshan. They moved back to Hengshan some years later. So now we were six families and four oxen. We decided then to value the oxen. We valued the three at 200 Y, that was roughly 3,000 jin of corn. This was to be paid to the owners over five years. Li Hai-fu's ox was valued in the same way. The other families were not so well situated, so the payment period was made longer. We had no dividend on land in our co-operative, because all the land was newly cleared, and we were clearing more the whole time collectively.

In November 1951, I was chosen to attend a conference for merit workers in agriculture being held in Sian. I was to report on our work. The provincial Party authorities heard me before the meeting and decided that what we had actually made was a co-operative farm. We were the only one in Shensi at the time. They also said that we must have a name and gave us mine, calling us Li Yiu-hua's Farmers' Co-operative. I was not quite sure that that was the right thing to call it:

the name might not go down in Liu Ling, but I gave the conference a report on how to organize a labour group for mutual help and how to found a farmers' co-operative. I was given a diploma for good work on the agricultural front and a money prize of sixteen yuan, and, in addition, I was chosen to attend a conference for merit workers for the whole North-western District. There, too, I reported and there too I was given a diploma and a money prize of 200 Y. It was unusual to get such big money prizes. With the 216 Y I bought two oxen, so that now we had enough draught animals. We also bought a donkey.

Now we went over to a better system of book-keeping and, instead of putting a value on the individual, we valued each job and reckoned incomes in days' work performed per year. We were now well off for labour and also for animals. We had six oxen and a donkey. But the land was poor. Down there in the valley were the labour groups for mutual help and, if we were to beat their production, we had to work harder and organize our work better than they.

In April 1952, we were able to borrow forty goats from the hsien authorities. We were to look after them, and half of the kids were to belong to the state and half to us. We also bought another donkey. Our production now increased considerably. The three labour groups for mutual help had not been able to increase the numbers of their stock, nor had they increased their production of grain, so that we did better than they, despite their having the good land. In October 1952 a calf was born increasing our stock to 7 beasts, 2 donkeys and 120 goats, 40 of which belonged to the state.

At the same time, Ma Juei-ching's labour group decided to form its own co-operative. They had good land and thought that what we had done they could do too, and even better, and with less work because of their good land. Then the Party committee of Yenan hsien intervened. It organized a little propaganda troupe to help us and this stayed in Liu Ling for twenty days, and we had great discussions about forming a proper big agricultural co-operative. Ma Juei-ching said: 'We are not going to join Li Yiu-hua's co-operative farm. We can organize one of our own. We have better land.' That was because our fields lay rather far off, well up on the hillside. The other two labour groups were still keeping out of it. Ma Juei-ching's labour group was the only one that had already decided to form a co-operative farm.

With the help of the Party group, we now reported to the others

356

the lessons we had learned and emphasized that it was a question of organization. Better organization gave a greater return. Ma Juei-ching agreed with this, but he refused to join our co-operative. I had always thought it bad policy to give our co-operative farm my name, and now this was proving of considerable significance emotionally. This was exactly what I had feared when I had first discussed it all with the provincial committee in Sian. There was also another matter: who should be elected in future to the various posts in the farmers' co-operative. I now had a frank talk with the responsible comrades from Yenan hsien's Party committee and said: 'If you want us to incorporate the other labour groups into our farmers' co-operative, then we must first change its name from Li Yiu-hua's Co-operative Farm to Liu Ling Co-operative Farm. In addition, there must be guarantees that all posts will be occupied by actual members properly elected. We must introduce real democratic principles into the farmers' co-operative.' The ganbus from Yenan hsien accepted this. When this had been done, many households joined our co-operative.

But Li Hai-yuan said: 'If they come in, I go out. If they come, I'd prefer to be on my own. And I'll never come back. Never.' Then he left us. To get the others in, we also had to put through certain other organizational and financial changes. The organization of the Party association was strengthened. We elected a proper management committee for Liu Ling Co-operative Farm. As the new members had good land and were worried in case they lost it, we had to switch over to paying dividends on land. The previous owners were to be paid ten jin of grain per mu of valley land and three to four jin of grain per mu of hillside land. This was to be done annually. Donkeys were also to remain private property. The new members were to keep their donkeys as private possessions. This was, in a way, a retrograde step, but it was necessary in order to expand the co-operative and include more members. If the collective had need of the donkeys, it was to pay the owners so much a day.

As both Ma Juei-ching and Jen Huai-wan, who were both leaders of a labour group for mutual help, had gone in with us, Li Yü-teh became leader of one labour group for mutual help, and Fu Hai-tsao remained leader of the other. These two groups which had not joined the farmers' co-operative together comprised less than twenty households. We now had two-thirds of the valley land, and sixteen households were members. Ma Chan-wan was homesick for Hengshan and left us. When we got home, he led a movement to organize a farmers' co-operative in his own village there. We bought a horse and a cart, and all went well for us. In November 1954, we again began considering taking in more members. This time we had no need of outside help. It was all voluntary, and we made our own propaganda. In January 1955, people began applying for membership. Then all the households joined Liu Ling Farmers' Co-operative. There was one exception, Li Hai-yuan, who said that he did not want anything to do with us. He was now farming on his own and intended to go on doing so. He was pig-headed.

Our success in 1954 had been so great that it did not need much propaganda to convince people of the advantages of the farmers' co-operative. They could see them themselves. There were now thirty-two households in the co-operative. We had divided ourselves into two labour groups. Li Hai-kuei was leader of the one, and Li Hung-fu deputy leader. Ma Juei-ching was labour leader of the other, and Fu Hai-tsao deputy labour leader.

In October–November 1955, we turned the whole thing into a higher agricultural co-operative, forming the East Shines Red Higher Agricultural Co-operative. This included Liu Ling Co-operative Farm, Wangchiakou Co-operative Farm, Hutoma Labour Group for Mutual Help, and Erchuankou Labour Group for Mutual Help, as well as those who had still been farming on their own. Now, at last, Li Hai-yuan joined again. He was the last in the entire district to go in for collective farming. We now comprised a total of 104 households.

We now also carried out great changes. All cattle and other animals were owned collectively. We arranged this in the same way as we did when we first pooled our animals. That is to say, we valued them and the owners were paid over five years. In addition, we abolished dividends on land. It was to be actual work that brought in the income. But we also, for the first time, brought it in that families which had no member able to work should receive help from the co-operative. This was something quite new. We had never had any definite rules and regulations as such, and we did not draw up any now. That wasn't usual out in the country. After all, we were just ignorant farmers; we had no education, and it was simpler for us just to decide how we were going to have things. We only made the decisions that we thought right. So we did not write down any rules and regulations.

I became party secretary of the East Shines Red Higher Agricultural Co-operative. It is, of course, through the Party that everything is discussed, and it is the Party which draws up the aims of future development.

It was in August 1958 that we began preparing the formation of a people's commune. This was discussed at various levels. We had the decision of the Central Committee to go by, of course. The people's commune was set up on the basis of the Great Leap and the need to increase capital investment. Before the people's commune was set up, we had begun building a dam that was to serve three different improved agricultural co-operatives. But it had been difficult getting them to collaborate. The people's commune made it possible to systematize joint effort. We needed a larger unit in order to be able to carry out the big works required.

We had always had a hsien administration before, one with many employees. In the people's commune we fused our economic organization with the state power. This entailed a big saving, and made it possible for us to get rid of several ganbus from each area and gave us greater possibilities for collaboration and rational working without unnecessary loss of time. In our people's commune we have constantly stuck to the socialist principle 'To each according to his work', and we have never departed from it. In addition, we introduced certain social benefits and also a certain amount of social welfare. The people's commune also acquired a repair workshop of its own, which is now beginning to grow into almost a little factory.

Personally, I consider that the advantages of the people's commune are that it makes it possible to make better use of labour power during the dead season. At those times, the brigades can exchange days' work and carry out big undertakings. There is unified management. There were several other brigades that helped us carry out our terracing work. Though latterly we have not done so much in that direction.

We grow a lot of millet up here. Half a jin of millet will satisfy a man, but after a jin of wheat he will still be hungry. Our revolution was victorious on millet and rifles. China's farmers have liberated themselves by revolutionary struggle and fighting for their emancipation. I have always hoped that all the farmers of the world should be freed and achieve socialism. We Chinese farmers started from a bad initial position: we were oppressed and poor, and our oppression was great. In your countries, the farmers are in a much better position. After

359

all, you are living under capitalism. But we lived under feudalism. I have often thought about this. Our fight was such a difficult one. We had no weapons. But the bureaucrats and the landowners and the warlords had armies and weapons. It was very difficult for us.

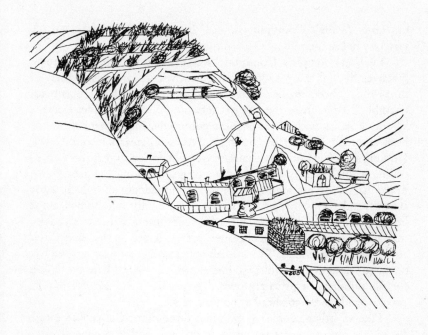

Liu Hsin-min, young ganbu, aged 32

I was born in Twenty-mile Village. Apart from the time of Hu Tsung-nan's occupation, I have lived in the new society for as long as I can remember. My father was made chairman of Liu Ling hsiang in 1939, under the Shensi–Kansu–Ningsia Frontier Region. I began school in 1943. After Hu Tsung-nan's withdrawal, my father remained chairman of Liu Ling hsiang for one year, then he transferred to the bank. I stopped school that same year. I never joined the Young Pioneers. Nor was I ever in the League of Youth. I did farmwork till I joined the revolution in October of 1952, when I became chairman of Liu Ling hsiang and thus a ganbu. In June 1957, I joined China's Communist Party. That was the first organization I had been in. When Liu Ling People's Commune was set up in 1958, all paid posts in the hsiang administration were done away with, and I then became president of

Liu Ling People's Commune instead. In April 1961 I became party secretary in Liu Ling People's Commune.

Liu Ling People's Commune was formed in September 1958, when eight higher agricultural co-operatives, comprising a total of thirty-nine labour groups, sent their representatives to a constituent assembly. After that, the higher agricultural co-operatives became labour brigades within the people's commune. Since then, there has been a certain amount of administrative re-organization and, today, Liu Ling People's Commune consists of eighteen labour brigades, comprising a total of fifty-seven labour groups. Liu Ling People's Commune has 1,401 households with 5,039 individuals, of which 2,461 are men and 2,578 women. Of these, 1,938 are fully able-bodied, 1,194 being men and 744 women. The people's commune comprises 360,000 mu, and of this 30,027 are cultivated; 2,124 mu are on the valley floor and 27,903 hillside land. The animals collectively owned comprise 933 oxen, 403 donkeys, 20 mules, 30 horses and 816 goats. I have no figures for the numbers of privately owned goats, but there are 850 pigs in private hands and 6,564 head of poultry privately owned.

Like all other people's communes throughout China, Liu Ling's People's Commune was set up in accordance with the general party line and with the advice of the Central Committee and Chairman Mao.

The people's commune is based on the triumph of collectivization. At the beginning of 1943, Chairman Mao exhorted the people to organize exchange labour groups. These were then formed in our area on both a bilateral, as well as a multilateral, basis. In 1950, the party and Chairman Mao exhorted the people to organize, to help each other and to co-operate. Then, we here formed 45 labour groups for mutual help comprising 431 households, amounting to 46.5 per cent of the total number of households. Then, in the spring of 1950, the first farmers' co-operative was formed. It was run by Li Yiu-hua and comprised four households, which had pooled their land and animals. In its first year, it had a record harvest, cropping an average of 131.2 jin per hillside mu. That was 53.6 per cent more than what the labour groups for mutual help were getting. People now saw the advantages of collectivization and actively asked to join the farmers' co-operative. After that, farmers' co-operatives were set up one after the other, in a string.

In 1953, the party made four resolutions on the organization of agricultural co-operatives. This was a demand from the broad mass of the farmers. That year, 632 households were organized, comprising 65·2 per cent of the total number of households. Of these, 295, that is to say, 46·7 per cent of the organized households, joined the seven farmers' co-operatives that were set up then.

In 1955, Chairman Mao wrote his report on co-operation in agriculture, and, therefore, the winter of 1955–6 saw a flood of collectivization. Labour groups for mutual help were transformed into farmers' co-operatives, and farmers' co-operatives into higher agricultural co-operatives. After these changes, we had, in 1956, eight higher agricultural co-operatives with a total of 958 households. That is to say: 96·3 per cent of all the households in Liu Ling hsiang were organized in higher agricultural co-operatives. That year, the average production of the higher agricultural co-operatives was 107·8 jin per mu more than the return per mu of the farmers' co-operatives in 1954, and 27·4 per cent more than what the labour groups for mutual help had obtained in 1951.

Then came the year 1958. That was the year of the Great Leap and it was then that the broad masses of the farmers saw the necessity of co-operation in order to master the forces of nature, expand production and raise the standard of living. So, on the basis of the higher agricultural co-operatives, collaboration between agricultural co-operatives was organized. They required unified management, and their big investments of capital also called for a unified plan. Work was exchanged between agricultural co-operatives on a basis of equal value and mutual advantage. Then, that summer, the Central Committee passed its resolution to set up people's communes in the countryside. This met with warm support from the farmers, and so, in September, we set up up Liu Ling People's Commune on the foundation of the improved agricultural co-operatives. During the four years that have passed since then, we have done much to perfect our people's commune.

We have striven to overcome nature's catastrophes and achieve record crops. We have had great results in our efforts to expand the collective economy, and we have carried out comprehensive water-regulation works. The people's commune is now an entrepreneur, carries out afforestation and herds cattle.

In 1959, it had 18,015 mu under corn, and the average crop per mu was 146 jin: the total harvest was 2,630,248 jin, 35 per cent more than in 1957.

In 1960, it had 19,832 mu under corn. Owing to a severe drought, the average crop was 123 jin and the total harvested 2,439,336 jin.

In 1961, the area under corn amounted to 29,183 mu and the average yield was 147·5 jin per mu, the total harvested being 4,304,483 jin.

The 1962 plan is for an average yield of 150 jin per mu. I have no figures concerning the number of mu put down to corn and have no knowledge either of the size of the total crop. I seem to remember that we were going to increase production somewhat. There must be a plan, but I do not have it.

As production rises, the members' incomes go up.

Income per head in 1959 was 80·20 Y in cash and 642 jin of grain; figures for 1960 were 84·72 Y and 519 jin, and for 1961 92·00 Y and 720 jin. I have no comparable figures for 1958, nor for the time before the formation of the people's commune.

We have also carried out big water-regulating works. At the end of 1957, we had only 30 mu of irrigated land. Since then we have built 5 dams, 3 canals and 400 mu of terraced fields, and in 1962 the total irrigated land amounted to 8,320 mu. We have been continuing with this work all the time. I do not have the figures for how much has been done each year.

Since the formation of the people's commune, we have had workshops run by the commune, and this has solved the farmers' repair problems. We repair carts and tools and semi-mechanized implements. This workshop was started in 1959, when the blacksmiths came to us with their tools. We then borrowed 5,000 Y from the bank. This was repaid in 1961. We are expanding now and planning to be able to produce motors, turbines, etc. In general, our products are sold within the people's commune, but outsiders can, of course, buy if they wish. But we are far too short of agricultural implements to sell any of these, so that if others than members of the people's commune make use of our workshop, it is for repair work; 85 per cent of the workshop's income goes on wages and materials, and 15 per cent to the people's commune. The monies invested in the workshop came from the commune. The labour brigades have different workshops of their own.

By 1962, we had nine basic schools in the area of the commune. Four of these are state schools, and five are run by the labour brigades jointly with the hsien authorities. The labour brigades in these cases pay for them out of their welfare funds. Proportions in the different schools vary. In 1957, we had 375 pupils, and this year we have 592. Now, in 1962, fifty-eight per cent of those over school age, but still under forty, can read at least 1,000 characters. They can thus read *The Yenan Daily* and make notes. I do not know how many were able to read in 1957.

In 1957 we had a small clinic here, but now the people's commune has a hospital, a clinic and five health centres. Eighteen of the labour brigades are on the telephone network. These costs have been paid by the labour brigades themselves. They have paid all the cost of the wire and posts and that sort of thing in their area. I believe the people's commune did make a certain contribution, but I don't know what, and I do not have any figures available. Sixty-three households in Liu Ling Village and Seven-mile Village have got electricity. This has been paid for by the labour brigade.

Here, in Liu Ling, we have always had private plots of land. This helps the collective economy and the country's supplies. We have never made any departure from this policy and have never made any changes.

We have carried out a lot of ideological work to strengthen the farmers' proletarian class-consciousness and their socialistic sense of collective thrift. Since the formation of the people's commune, we have made great progress under the party's leadership and with the 'three flags'—the party's general line, the Great Leap and the people's communes—before us. But we have no experience of how to run and administer a people's commune. Agriculture is still backward. We have no machinery and the yield per mu is low. Because of various natural disasters, our agricultural production has not been steady from year to year, but we believe that, with the guidance of the party and Chairman Mao, this backwardness will disappear and grain production will be stabilized. We are not content with our progress, but want to achieve more.

Our preliminary calculation is that, after a further three five-year plans, we shall have achieved a stabilized yield of 180 jin of grain per mu. Our income then will be twice what it was in 1961. That is to say that we are reckoning on a *per capita* income of 180 Y cash and 920 jin of grain in fifteen years' time. The area used for industrial purposes is to be increased from 423 mu this year to 1,321 mu. The afforested area is to be doubled to become 8,000 mu. We are to get up to a collective stock of animals corresponding to two oxen and seven goats per household and a privately owned stock of two pigs and two hens or ducks per head.

We are convinced that, led by the Central Committee of the party and Chairman Mao and with the 'three flags' before us, we shall by the work of our own hands, with industry, thrift, hard work and a simple way of life, be able to achieve this.

The turn of the year 1958-9 saw us busy making iron by the age-old methods. We used our own ore and, for four months, from October 1958 to January 1959, we had 67 men employed on this. We expended a total of 8,040 days' work at 1·10 Y, so the wage costs amounted to 8,844 Y. We used 150 tons of twenty per cent iron ore, which we quarried ourselves. We bought in 78·6 tons of coke at a price of 25 Y a ton. We spent 340 Y on special bricks and 498 Y on tools, and a further 143 Y went on various administrative costs. The total expenditure on iron production was 11,790 Y.

We produced a total of 39·3 tons of iron. The cost per ton amounted to 300 Y. At the time, we could buy iron in the shop for 289·40 Y a ton. This meant that we were producing our iron at a cost 10·60 Y above the shop price; or, in other words, that every ton of iron we produced involved us in a loss of almost ten days' work. We decided, therefore, to stop the experiment. At the same time, it must be said that our people learned the technique, which has a certain value, and also that at the turn of the year 1958-9, which was during the Great Leap, it was difficult to buy iron. At the meeting at which we discussed the question after this first experiment, the main argument was that we were then able to buy iron once more and thus were able to use our labour in agriculture, where we could make better use of it.

The people's commune receives no administrative fees from the labour brigades. Its administration is paid for by the state. We, of course, fulfil the functions of the state. Every year we send in a budget to the hsien authorities for our administrative costs. Our finances are supervised by the supervisory committee of Liu Ling People's Commune and that of Yenan hsien. In addition, auditors may be sent by the province or the central government without prior notice, and if leading comrades from the provincial capital or from Peking come, they too can have a look at our accounts.

The following expenditure is covered by the states' administrative grant: (a) wages of the ganbus of the people's commune. There are ten of us and our cook. The highest wage is 62 Y a month and the lowest 37·50 Y a month. We are not entitled to our own plot of ground. If we do voluntary manual work, we are not paid for it. The introduction of the people's commune meant a saving to the state. Prior to that, there had been fifteen ganbus in the hsiang administration. This meant a reduction in the amount spent on wages of more than thirty per cent. The five who had to leave went to other areas; (b) postage, telegrams and similar administrative expenditure; (c) various journey allowances, mostly for the Liu Ling People's Commune's representatives and the party conference of Liu Ling People's Commune. Those attending these get an allowance of 0·30 Y a day. This is paid out of the state grant to the administration.

In 1961, we received 8,154 Y from Yenan hsien. We spent 7,875 Y and transferred 279 Y to the 1962 budget. For 1962 we have had 8,925 Y from Yenan hsien.

In addition to this budget, we send Yenan hsien bills for day allowances paid to delegates from our commune attending meetings in the commune called by state authorities. These receive 0·20 Y a day from us. For meetings called by the Yenan hsien authorities within Yenan hsien, but outside Liu Ling People's Commune, delegates receive 0·30 Y a day direct from Yenan hsien.

The income of the people's commune comes from the workshop it runs, Liu Ling People's Commune's Agricultural Implement Factory. This factory's costs amount to 85 per cent of its income. The remaining 15 per cent is taken by the commune. In 1961, the 15 per cent amounted to 5,600 Y. Of this, 5,000 Y was re-invested in the factory. The commune bought a truck for the factory. For 1962 we reckon to receive 6,000 Y and re-invest 4,200 Y in the factory. We have already had 2,000 Y. The surplus goes to the investment fund. This is looked after by the finance and credit department, and the representatives of the people's commune decide on the use to which such means shall be put. It can be used to buy tractors, trucks, cattle, film projectors, etc. At the moment, the fund has about 15,000 Y.

On the recommendation of the management of the commune, short-term, interest-free loans can be made from this fund to a labour brigade, labour group or factory. But this applies only to short-term loans. For proper loans, they have to go to the State Bank. For these, a recommendation from the commune's management is also needed.

In a way, the factory can be said to be a labour brigade. But it does not have the same authority to control its economy as the labour brigades have. The workers in the factory can elect their own book-keeper and their president of the factory management committee and also their representative on the people's commune, but they cannot decide about the factory's finances and economy. That is a matter for the commune's management. On the other hand, the factory pays no taxes.

In 1961, the grain tax paid by Liu Ling People's Commune amounted to 135,250 jin. That is an average of 4·6 jin per mu. This tax was fixed after the land was divided up. It is based on a certain percentage of the 1948 harvest. It has been calculated for each individual field. There is no tax for the first three years after ground is first cultivated. In our commune, we have not changed the grain tax since the commune was formed. That is to say that it is based on the ground that was under cultivation in 1955. This is an incentive to increased production. In this way, the proportion of the total production going in tax is decreasing the whole time. This does not mean that the grain tax has been exactly the same all the years that the people's commune has been in existence. It has fluctuated a few hundred jin, because we have exchanged certain fields with neighbouring communes in order to obtain a more uniform area and to straighten out our boundaries.

We also pay a tax on stock, that is on sheep and goats. This amounts to two per cent of the animals' value. We usually take the declared value of a sheep at eight yuan and that of a goat at six yuan. There are, in addition, certain registration fees for horse-drawn vehicles, ox-carts and bicycles. These could be called a road tax. The people's commune hands all this over without deduction direct to the authorities concerned in Yenan hsien. Before the people's commune was set up, the tax from the improved agricultural co-operatives was paid to the hsiang administration and this handed the money on without deduction to the administration of the hsien.

The credit department acts as a farmers' exchequer. The members of the labour groups elect representatives, and these, in turn, elect a management committee. The chairman of this committee is at the same time responsible for the commune's credit department. At the same time a supervisory committee of its own is elected for the credit department. Li Yiu-hua is chairman of this committee. In addition the State Bank and the management of the people's commune inspect the credit department. This deals with savings and loans. On 8 September 1962, the last day for which we have a report, the savings of the labour groups in the credit department amounted to 10,358 Y, and the private savings accounts totalled 19,485 Y. The total of loans was some few thousands of yuan. Assets are lodged with the State Bank in the credit department's account there. I don't know what interest the bank pays. Nor do I know what interest the labour groups receive. I don't know what interest private savers receive. During 1961 and the first eight months of 1962, the following loans have been made to individuals in Liu Ling:

5 May 1961. Chen Chung-yuan for purchase of sucking pigs, 15 Y. Interest 0·6 per cent a month. This was repaid on 7 September 1961 with 15·37 Y.

20 March 1962. Li Hai-yuan for purchase of sucking pigs, 50 Y. Interest 0·6 per cent per month. This was repaid on 22 August 1961 with 51·53 Y.

Individual loans are not granted for expenditure on consumer goods, but for various forms of investment. We do not encourage extravagance. But if anyone should want a loan to provide a worthy funeral, that would be considered in order. Normally, this does not happen, for it is the custom for neighbours and relatives to contribute. But there have been cases in the commune.

The party committee of Liu Ling People's Commune consists of eleven members, one of whom is a woman, and five ganbus employed full time. There are 196 party members in Liu Ling People's Commune, of whom seventeen are women, and there are four who are still only candidates for membership.

The management committee of Liu Ling People's Commune consists of seventeen persons. Six of these are ganbus. There are ten ganbus in the whole of Liu Ling People's Commune, that is, persons wholly employed in the revolution. I am on both Liu Ling People's Commune Management Committee and Liu Ling People's Commune's Party Committee. That is why we have five ganbus in the party committee and six ganbus in the management committee, but only ten ganbus in the whole commune. The management committee of the commune corresponds to the old hsiang administration. We have all its state duties, plus the additional duty of being in charge of production. Our duties are thus:

To manage the economy. In actual fact, this means that we do the work of planning. We draw up a plan for production in accordance with the objectives set us by the state and the proposals received direct from the labour groups. We also run the factory and manage its economy. We do this absolutely. We have to decide absolutely about its investments and production.

To inspect that the work being done in the territory of the commune is performed in the correct way.

To ensure the supply of agricultural implements, insecticides, artificial fertilizers and good seed. From January 1961 to September 1962 we supplied the labour groups with 5,527 agricultural tools, 5,162 jin of artificial manure and 1,987 jin of insecticide.

To popularize new agricultural methods and to spread agricultural knowledge.

To run social life; to see to matters of public health; to protect public order and local security; to mediate in disputes between members of the commune, and where possible, get them amicably settled.

We are thus a comprehensive economic organ of state management at local level.

At the organizational level of the people's commune there are two supervisory committees, that of the party organization, consisting of seven members, who have the task of watching over the finances of the party organizations and their work, as well as the work and party behaviour of the members of the party; and Liu Ling's supervisory committee, which has nine members and which has to supervise the finances and work of all organs of the commune from commune level down to labour group level. In addition, they are to watch that no one's rights are infringed and that the liberties and rights of citizens are protected. It has thus four specific duties:

(1) To supervise the carrying-out of the party line and of the resolutions of the representatives of the commune.

(2) To see that there is no breach of the country's laws and/or of the liberties and rights of citizens.

(3) To watch that revenue and expenditure are justified and that they are correctly entered in the books, and that there is no breach of financial regulations.

(4) To watch that there is no waste of public means, and that no sabotage of economic policy or destruction of public property takes place.

Every private member of Liu Ling People's Commune has the right to lay complaints before the supervisory committee, and it is incumbent upon the latter to investigate every such complaint. The committee has the right to examine all books, to attend all meetings and to question any person elected to a position of trust. Its members, however, are not allowed to be on other committees or themselves have any function in the management of the commune or of any of its organs. Nor has the supervisory committee any authority to investigate or interfere in the private life of individual members. The members of the supervisory committee are elected by the representatives of Liu Ling People's Commune at its annual meeting and the committee reports to it then.

Similarly, a mediation committee of nine members is elected. Its duty is to mediate in any dispute between citizens. The most usual is for them to have to mediate between husband and wife. Before the courts can consider an application for divorce, the mediation committee must have tried to mediate between the two partners and to get them to continue their life together on a new and firmer basis. The mediation committee also has to mediate between neighbours. But it has no right of decision and cannot impose any punishment or fine. It can merely advise and try to get the parties to agree. It has no right to prevent anyone from going further, to the court, and suing his or her partner; the committee can merely dissuade.

The Committee of the League of Youth in Liu Ling People's Commune consists of thirteen members. The league has 198 members in nineteen groups. Its tasks are: (1) to train the young people ideologically; (2) to encourage and organize the young people to fulfil the production plan; (3) to direct study activities; (4) to develop the League of Youth, both organizationally and ideologically; and (5) to run the Young Pioneers.

The women's committee of Liu Ling People's Committee consists of nine members. It has to organize the women in production, help the women to study the techniques of farming, help them run their homes, contribute to their ideological and political development. This women's committee does not represent any special women's organization, but has to work among all the women in the commune.

As part of the health work, 1,300 people have twice been vaccinated against smallpox and had injections against typhus. These diseases have now been eradicated. We had 5,300 consultations in 1961. The most common ailments have been influenza, stomach trouble and pneumonia. In 1957, seventy-five children were born, while five children under the age of one and twenty between the ages of one and six died. In 1961, 250 babies were born and seven children under one year of age and twenty-three between the ages of one and six died.

The people's militia has three duties:

(1) To take part in production and protect its fruits.

(2) To guard the public safety and be on the watch for thieves, robbers and secret agents.

(3) To be ready to join up with the Chinese People's Liberation Army and support the front in the event of attack from abroad and, in the event of occupation, continue the fight as armed guerrillas till the enemy has been destroyed.

In principle, all men between sixteen and forty-five and all women between sixteen and thirty-five should belong. Membership is voluntary. Exceptions are those whose health is bad or who have been landowners or counter-revolutionaries.

In 1960, 100 hours were spent in training to shoot. 111 persons took part and their results were: excellent 67, good 35, and pass 9.

In 1961, 100 hours were spent in shooting-training and thirty people took part. We see that this training does not take place during working hours or at times which could be used for productive work. It is not often that the people's militia is called upon to act. We have had extremely few cases. But in June this year a criminal escaped from Matunchun. They rang us up and we mobilized the people's militia. Fifteen men captured the runaway down in the valley at Shiaoyuan-chikyou. We then sent him under guard to the Office of Public Safety in Yenan. We also captured a thief from one of our own labour brigades in 1961. This was Chiang Tsung-chen from Beikou Labour Brigade, who had stolen a two-wheeled cart and was captured by the people's militia in Liu Ling. He was taken to the office of the people's commune, and there we had a serious talk with him. He was severely criticized and also criticized himself. After that he signed an undertaking that he would never do such a thing again and was then allowed to go home. We never let such matters go up to Yenan. We can deal with them ourselves. On the whole, we have never had any crime here and the only person we have ever sent up to Yenan after the campaign against counter-revolutionaries many years ago was that runaway. Whatever happens is just minor stuff. Last year, the militia caught a man cutting firewood in the plantations. He was taken to the commune's office; we criticized him and he was allowed to go home after signing a paper in which he promised not to do this again. We read it out to him, and he put his fingerprint on it.

We elect one of our ganbus to be responsible for the commune's department of public safety and the armed forces. But this is not the same person elected to be regimental commander of the people's militia. The person we have elected to command the regiment is the chairman of the management committee of the people's commune.

In 1961, we received from the social welfare fund of Yenan hsien 710 Y for distribution in social welfare grants within the commune. This year we have already paid out 480 Y; but this will go up a bit in the winter. Last year, there were thirty-seven households comprising 141 persons who received social grants from this fund. This year money has been given to thirty households comprising 136 persons. Three households in the commune receive regular monthly allowances. They get twenty-nine yuan a month. These allowances are outside the scope of this fund. In addition, five households comprising fifteen persons have been credited with a total of 640 days' work as assistance.

Larger undertakings, such as water-regulation works, etc., have to be carried out by several labour brigades collaborating. The work is then managed by a work committee which has its office at the site. The chairman of this committee is always the chairman of the management committee of the commune, while the deputy chairman, who is the one who must always be present at the site, as well as the different labour leaders, are chosen by the labour brigades. Before work begins, the size of each participating brigade's share in the result in the work is fixed. That is, how much of the advantage from the work is for their benefit. In 1958, three labour brigades, Liu Ling Labour Brigade, Kaupo Labour Brigade and Chungchuan Labour Brigade, jointly built the Kaochinko dam. Liu Ling invested 1,900 days' work; Kaupo 1,100; and Chungchuan 890.

As Liu Ling Labour Brigade benefited most by the dam, it transpired at the settling up that Liu Ling Labour Brigade owed the other two labour brigades a total of 494 days' work: 394 to Kaupo Labour Brigade and 100 to Chungchuan Labour Brigade. Liu Ling Labour Brigade repaid this by helping in terracing the fields of the other two labour brigades.

In the winter of 1959–60, Liu Ling Labour Brigade carried out a very big water-regulation project. This cost a total of 14,772 days' work, of which Liu Ling Labour Brigade itself contributed only 4,172. Liu Ling Brigade first repaid a total of 1,568 days' work to the other two brigades which had collaborated, Chungchuan Labour Brigade and the Sun Rises Labour Brigade. They got roughly 800 days' work each.

After that, however, it became difficult to repay in days' work, and, after lengthy meetings and much discussion, we agreed that Liu Ling Labour Brigade could pay in cash. Negotiations took a long time. In the end the parties agreed that payment should be at 0·80 Y per day's work performed. That was roughly 0·30 Y below the current valuation of a day's work. It was a matter of a total of 8,532 days' work. Since then, no labour exchange project of this magnitude has been carried out between brigades.

Where free food is concerned, we felt that the system would not suit us, for several reasons. This is a poor and hilly part of the country; nobody would want free food; it would have meant altogether too much trouble arranging dining-halls and seeing that everybody got food. Therefore, it was never discussed. Neither we nor the farmers thought it at all a good idea.

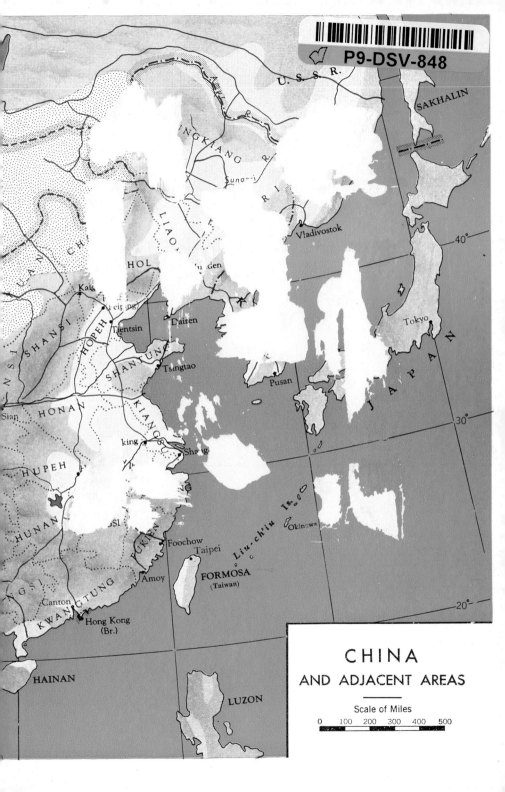

CHINA
AND ADJACENT AREAS

Scale of Miles

0   100   200   300   400   500

The Communist Conquest of China

A HISTORY OF THE CIVIL WAR

1945–1949

The Communist Conquest
of China

A HISTORY OF THE CIVIL WAR
1945-1949

BY

Lionel Max Chassin

Translated from the French by
Timothy Osato *and* Louis Gelas

HARVARD UNIVERSITY PRESS
Cambridge, Massachusetts
1965

End-paper map by A. H. Robinson from
The United States and China by John K. Fairbank
Harvard University Press, 1948
Other maps by T. Osato and L. Gelas

Library of Congress Catalog Card Number 65–22043

Printed in the United States of America

TRANSLATORS' NOTE AND INTRODUCTION

THIS work, which originally appeared under the title *La Conquête de la Chine par Mao Tse-tung*, was first published in France in 1952. Much has been done, both before and since that time, in the study of Chinese communism; but to our knowledge there is little available, in English, to meet the need for a concise history of the climactic phase of the long Civil War through which communism came to sovereign power in China. This work, in our view, helps to meet this need. If it seems at times to stress military factors, there is some justification for this emphasis in the fact that, for China, communism did indeed, as Mao Tse-tung prescribed, come from "the barrel of a gun."

General Chassin, whose poor health precludes the possibility of a preface to this belated English translation of his work, possesses unusual qualifications for the task he completed more than a decade ago. The author, now a retired General of the French Air Force, did most of the research for this book while he was serving, from 1946 to 1949, as Vice Chief of Staff for National Defense. This position gave him ready access to the most authoritative French sources of information on developments in China, notably the reports of the Deuxième Bureau. From this fact alone, the author's account and interpretation of the Communist conquest of China should prove to be of some interest to American readers.

The absence of a bibliography, and of notes regarding the French sources of this work, is best explained by General Chassin in a statement[1] written expressly for this American edition of his work:

Although I never personally served in China during the Civil War of 1945–1949, I was, from 1946 to 1949, Vice Chief of the General Staff for National Defense, and as a member of the highest military body in France and an adviser to the Premier on defense matters, I had access to all National Defense documents. My book, *The Conquest of China by Mao Tse-tung*, is based on the intelligence reports, messages, and telegrams sent by the mission of the French Second Bureau (Intelligence), from China, to the General Staff for National Defense.

These documents, which were extremely copious, were supplemented by personal letters and interviews with officers who had served in the Far East and whom I interrogated, when they passed through Paris, in order to gain a more vivid appreciation of the kind of war that was being waged in China. I might add that when I took command of French Air Forces in the Far East in 1951, I encountered in Tonkin and Cochin China several officers who had served in China during the Civil War, and to whom I showed my work. My thanks go, above all, to Captain Léouzon, who had retained a certain number of papers he had brought back from Chungking, and who was kind enough to review my work in its entirety.

Such are the original sources of my book. Naturally, I also made use of all the (relevant) literature that had been published as of that time, while striving to avoid those sources which might have been tainted by the erroneous political opinions of their authors. Was this not, unfortunately, the case with a large number of works written by Anglo-Saxon authors?

[1] Bien que je n'aie jamais servi personnellement en Chine pendant la guerre civile de 1945 à 1949, j'ai été de 1946 à 1949 Sous-chef d'Etat-Major de la Défense Nationale et en tant que membre de la plus haute organisation militaire en France et conseiller du Premier Ministre en matière de défense,

If some of the author's political judgments seem somewhat contentious to American specialists in Chinese communism, these authorities at least have fair warning!

As to the other sources of this work—notably the State Department's White Paper on China and the words of Mao Tse-tung—the translators have attempted to locate and quote their most authoritative English-language versions, and to identify these in notes for which we, rather than the author, bear the responsibility. We have also sought to clarify, in other translators' notes, matters which may have appeared more self-explanatory to the author than they might to the nonspecialized reader.

A few words must be said regarding the transliteration problems posed in a work of this kind. As the author himself observes, "it is extremely difficult to transcribe Chinese characters into a European language," and "French interpretations of Chinese names are often fanciful indeed." We have

---

j'avais accès à tous les documents de la Défense Nationale. Mon livre: "La Conquête de la Chine par Mao Tse-tung" est basé sur les rapports d' "intelligence," les messages et les télégrammes expédiés de Chine par la mission française du Deuxième Bureau à l'Etat-Major de la Défense Nationale.

L'ensemble de ces papiers, extrêmement copieux, a été complété par des lettres personnelles et des interviews d'officiers servant en Extrême-Orient que j'interrogeais lors de leur passage à Paris — ceci pour me faire une idée plus vivante de la sorte de guerre qui se livrait là-bas. J'ajoute que lorsque j'ai pris en 1951 le Commandement des Forces Aériennes Françaises en Extrême-Orient, j'ai retrouvé au Tonkin et en Cochinchine plusieurs officiers qui avaient servi en Chine durant la guerre civile et auxquels j'ai montré mon travail. Mes remerciements vont surtout au Capitaine Léouzon, qui avait gardé par devers lui un certain nombre de papiers qu'il avait ramené de Chungking, et qui a bien voulu relire entièrement mon travail.

Telles sont les sources originales de mon livre. Naturellement, je me suis servi de toute la littérature qui avait été publiée à cette époque, en tâchant d'éviter des sources que risquaient d'entacher d'erreur les opinions politiques de leurs auteurs. C'était malheureusement le cas pour un grand nombre d'ouvrages anglo-saxons?

L. M. Chassin
General, French Air Force (Retired)
Paris, 22 June 1964

attempted to follow the Wade-Giles system of transliteration in the rendering of Chinese personal names, and that of the Chinese Postal Guide, as exemplified by such sources as *The (London) Times Atlas of the World* and the National Geographic Society's *Index to Map of China* (1945), for the rendering of place names. In a few cases, such as that of "Mukden" (rather than "Shenyang") or "Port Arthur" (rather than "Lushun"), we have departed from this rule in what we regard as the interests of the general reader.

For the sake of simplicity, consistency, and current usage, we have used the name "Peking" rather than "Peiping" throughout this translation, despite the substantial political and historical objections which may, in full justice, be raised against this practice. No disrespect toward the Republic of China, or for knowledgeable purists, is intended.

In translating General Chassin's book, we have chosen to attempt fidelity to the author's meaning and, on occasion, we may have taken questionable liberties with a literal interpretation of his words. We can only submit that the special kind of war described in this history may well be heavy with meaning, not only for the past and present, but for the future.

T.O.
L.G.

Contents

ix

CONTENTS

MAPS

In 1949 there occurred, in full view of our somewhat unperceiving eyes, an event of extraordinary importance: China, a country of almost five hundred million people, and of immense agricultural and mineral resources, passed from the camp of the "Western" powers to that of the U.S.S.R. With this event came a shift, singularly beneficial to the Soviet camp, in the global balance of power. What is strange about this catastrophe is that, as late as 1945, it seemed to be completely unforeseeable. Yet, in only four years' time, the almost unknown leader of a weak and poorly armed political minority vanquished, without benefit of outside aid, one of the world's "Big Five," a champion who for eight long years had led China's resistance against the powerful Empire of the Rising Sun.

The great majority of Europeans still fail to comprehend the incalculable but patently profound consequences of this event. What is more, its genesis—the Civil War of 1945–1949—remains largely unknown to them. To study this fateful conflict in all its fullness, it is appropriate to resort to the historical method, and to consider first of all, if only briefly, the setting of the Civil War, both in time and place.

L. M. C.

Introduction

CHAPTER I ✧

China: A Brief Description

B EFORE undertaking a history of the Communist conquest of China, a few words must be devoted to a description of the ancient arena in which it unfolded, this land of the vanished "Celestial Empire," the "Middle Kingdom" of past millenia.

By virtue of its vast area and population, China is a veritable continent. Its officially claimed area of more than four million square miles equals that of all Europe, and its 483,000,000 people[1] embody one fifth of the total population of the globe. From the fact that one of every five persons on earth is Chinese, one may realize the considerable importance this country can have for the future of the human race.

In geographical terms China extends from the eighteenth to the fifty-fourth parallel North, or from the latitude of Labrador to that of Mexico.[2] In longitude it stretches from 74° E to 135° E—the meridians of Afghanistan and Vladivostok, or Bombay and Kyoto. Since 1949 the country has been divided into six Great Administrative Areas:[3]

(1) *North China,* incorporating five provinces: Hopeh, Shansi, Chahar, Suiyuan, and Pingyuan, a newly created

[1] Population in 1952, according to the Chinese daily *Chieh Fang Jih Pao* (*Liberation*) of Shanghai.

[2] Or, if one prefers, from the mouth of the Elbe to that of the Senegal.

[3] The Communist regime has made several changes in these since 1952. *Tr.*

province of the People's Government carved from the counties of South Hopeh, West Shantung, and North Honan;

(2) *Northeast China,* or Manchuria, divided into six provinces:[4] Liaotung, Liaosi, Kirin, Heilungkiang, Sungkiang, and Jehol;

(3) *East China,* with six provinces: Shantung, Kiangsu, Anhwei, Chekiang Fukien, and, theoretically, Taiwan;

(4) *South-Central China,* with six provinces: Honan, Hupeh, Kiangsi, Kwangtung, and Kwangsi;

(5) *Northwest China,* with five provinces: Shensi, Kansu, Ningsia, Sinkiang, and Tsinghai; and lastly,

(6) *Southwest China,* with four provinces: Szechwan, Sikang, Kweichow, and Yunnan, plus the "autonomous" region of Tibet.

Exclusive of the near-barren borderlands—Tibet, Turkestan, and Mongolia—and of Manchuria, a vast and densely populated sunken plain stretched out between two north-south mountain ranges, China Proper, or the China of the eighteen provinces, is divided into two distinct zones which differ greatly in relief, climate, vegetation, and even in people: North China and South China, which are separated by the wide barrier of the Chin Ling mountains, eight thousand feet high.

In the western part of North China stand the old and coal-rich plateaus of Kansu and Shansi; to the east lie the great alluvial plains of the Hwang Ho, and the mountainous peninsula of Shantung. The climate is harsh, with freezing winters, burning summers, and rain that comes only with the summer monsoon. North China is the land of loess, that famous, fertile "yellow earth," four feet to six hundred feet deep, in which the peasants burrow their cave-like homes. It is also the basin of the Hwang Ho, the Yellow River of terrible floods, which

[4] In place of nine provinces in 1945.

has changed its 2,700-mile course five times in recorded history, and flows within dikes some twenty feet above the plain, past the distant and fearful towns and villages.

Unlike North China, South China is essentially mountainous in topography; its climate, vegetation, and agriculture are of the tropical type; and its great river, the Yangtze, in contrast to its scourge-like northern brother, is a source of life and a central artery of the surrounding region. The "Long River" begins its 3,400-mile course high in the mountains of Tibet, over fifteen thousand feet above sea level. At first it tumbles tumultuously to the south, through the deep gorges of the Szechwanese Alps; then it turns to the north and, reaching the plain, forms a series of basins as richly fertile as they are heavily populated. The first of these, the Red Basin of Szechwan, with its cities of Chengtu and Chungking, is completely surrounded by mountains, and reserves for itself its riches of rice, tobacco, cereals, vegetables, and important mineral resources. Here the population reaches a density of 474 inhabitants per square mile. After traversing the remaining mountainous regions in a series of rapids as redoubtable as they are picturesque, the Yangtze, which at Ichang is now no more than three hundred feet above sea level, slowly flows eleven hundred miles across fertile, prosperous, and well-populated plains, and empties into the sea near Shanghai in a marshy delta where the population reaches densities of up to 3,100 people per square mile. Apart from the valleys of the Yangtze and the Si, and the mountainous region to the east of Kweichow, South China is a scenic land of hills no higher than 2,700 feet, where the rains are regular and plentiful, and the vegetation is very beautiful. The rugged, indented coast shelters numerous ports and harbors, from Shanghai southward through Ningpo, Foochow, and Amoy to Canton and Hong Kong. Off the coast of Fukien lies the fertile and thickly populated island of Formosa, highly developed by the Japanese; in stark contrast is the still savage island of Hainan, which drops away, like a tear, from the coast of Kwangtung.

China's economy is fundamentally agricultural, with rice as the basic crop. For centuries it has been the land of tea and silk; and it is gradually becoming a land of cotton and soybeans as well. From the industrial viewpoint its resources, still unexploited, are immense: coal reserves estimated at 240 billion tons in Shansi, Shensi, and in Manchuria; oil in Sinkiang; iron ore in Manchuria; tin, copper, lead, zinc, manganese, mercury, antimony, bauxite, and very large deposits of tungsten —all these assure an astonishing future, once the country is industrialized and the necessary communications system is constructed. We now know, from the example of Russia, that it takes only a score of years, and a will of iron, to transform an agricultural country into a great industrial power; and China will be aided in this task by the nature of a people who are intelligent, adroit, patient, and hard-working, and whose talents for commerce are superior to those of any other race.

In this history of the Communist conquest of China—an upheaval of as yet little-appreciated importance to the whole world—is reflected a profound change in China itself. Here can be seen a transformation in philosophy and in way of life, through which "classical" China, frozen in scornful and sterile immobilism, gradually rouses itself to become a great power. And this new power will henceforth permit an eager China to take a leading role not only in Asia, but in the entire world.

ORTHOGRAPHY AND NAMES

It is extremely difficult to transcribe Chinese characters into a European language. Since French interpretations of Chinese names are often highly fanciful, the English orthography officially adopted by the Chinese Postal Guide, and used by the Chinese for their Romanized maps, has been followed in the rendering of place names in this work.

As regards the meanings of place names, it is useful to know a few general terms concerning:

(1) Direction: North, *Peh;* South, *Nan;* East, *Tung;* West, *Si;*

(2) Relief: mountain, *Shan;* range, *Ling;* pass, *Shen;* sea, *Hai;* lake, *Hu;* river, *Kiang* or *Ho;* stream, *Chwan;* mouth, *Kow;*

(3) Colors: black, *Hei;* white, *Pai;* red, *Hung;* yellow, *Hwang;*

(4) Numbers: one, *E;* two, *Erh;* three, *San;* four, *Sze;* five, *Wu;*

(5) Positions: high, *Shang;* low, *Hsia;* center, *Chung;*

(6) Finally, administrative subdivisions: prefecture, *Fu;* sub-prefecture, *Chow;* county, *Hsien.* Knowing these, one can comprehend the meaning of the names of the principal Chinese provinces, rivers, or towns. For example, Hopeh means "north of the river"; Shantung means "east of the mountains," and Shansi, "west of the mountains"; Honan means "south of the river," and so on.

As for other proper names, it is well to know that for thousands of years there have been only one hundred family names in China, all of them monosyllabic, such as Chiang, Li, Wang, Sun, Chang, Mao, Lo, Hu. These theoretically represent the hundred legendary families that originally peopled China; until the Revolution of 1911, it was unlawful to assume any other family name. Two persons bearing the same family name were likewise forbidden to marry each other. Given names, in China, come after the family name, and usually consist of two characters with a meaning intended to be descriptive of the particular individual: "Kai-shek," for ex-

7

ample, means "hard rock," or "firm as a rock." Other given names have such meanings as "little dog," "red flower," "little cucumber," "tall building," "precious stone." Christian names also are found among certain families: Eugene Chen, for example. In the past the Chinese would change their given names several times during their lives, childhood names being succeeded by marriage names, graduation names, and so on. The result was enormous confusion in proper identification. The People's Republic has henceforth forbidden these changes in given names.

CHAPTER II

The First Stage: 1911-1945

FOLLOWING the Revolution of 1911, the proclamation of a republic by Sun Yat-sen, Yüan Shih-k'ai's attempt to found a new dynasty and Chang Hsün's attempt to restore the old one, China fell into an era of feudalism. During this period numerous war lords—*tüchuns* such as Chang Tso-lin in Manchuria, Yen Hsi-shan in Shansi, the "Christian General" Feng Yü-hsiang in Peking—succeeded in carving out virtually independent principalities for themselves. Meanwhile Sun Yat-sen and his party, the Kuomintang,[1] had withdrawn to Canton and knotted close ties of friendship with Soviet Russia. In 1923, Lenin had sent Joffe, one of the negotiators of the Brest-Litovsk treaty, to Canton; behind him had come Borodin, to act as a political mentor to the Kuomintang. For his part, Dr. Sun had sent to Moscow an important military mission, the head of which was a young general with the greatest of destinies: Chiang Kai-shek.

Born on 31 October 1887 at Fenghwa, in the province of Chekiang, Chiang Kai-shek was one of the five children of a merchant of modest means. Having lost his father at a very early age, he was brought up, in austere circumstances and Buddhist discipline, by his mother. In 1906 he stood at

[1] Hereafter abbreviated, on occasion, as KMT. *Tr.*

the top of the first class to enter the new Imperial Military Academy at Paoting, and was later sent to Japan to complete his military studies. While in Japan he served three years with a Japanese artillery unit, the 13th or "Takada" Regiment. Returning to Shanghai in 1911, he left the army, joined the Kuomintang, became one of the leading disciples of Sun Yat-sen, and acquired—by means which appear to have been very dubious—a considerable fortune. After an unhappy first marriage which ended in divorce, he resumed his military career in 1923, at the time of his departure for Moscow. He came back in the following year, bringing with him, under the pseudonym of "Galen," the famous Bolshevik general, Vassily Blücher. Together with this Russian colleague, Chiang organized the army of the Kuomintang. In 1926, a year after the death of Sun Yat-sen, Chiang was named Generalissimo,[2] and shortly thereafter commenced, in pursuit of national unification, a victorious campaign against the armies of the *tüchuns*. In 1927 he seized Nanking, and followed this conquest by marrying Soong Mei-ling. With this marriage, Chiang was not only led to become a Protestant by his bride; he also became the brother-in-law of Sun Yat-sen's widow, and of T. V. Soong and H. H. Kung, the famous Chinese financiers.

Suddenly there was a reversal in Chiang's relations with the Reds: now feeling himself to be strong enough to do without them, he abruptly broke off the Communist connection. By his order the Communists were excluded from all the higher posts in the Kuomintang. Borodin and Blücher fled back to Moscow; in all the cities where the Communists had begun to form autonomous groups, they were disarmed. Hesitating to unleash civil war, Ch'en Tu-hsiu, at this time the head of

---

[2] A purely unofficial title, probably reflecting Chiang's designation as "Commander in Chief of the Revolutionary Armies" in 1926, shortly before the Northern Expedition. As hereafter used, "Generalissimo" invariably refers to Chiang Kai-shek. *Tr.*

the Chinese Communist Party,[3] submitted. He was replaced by such extremists as Li Li-san, who declared China to be in a state of "permanent revolution" and tried, without success, to foment mass uprisings in the large cities. At Canton the Red revolt of December 1927 was drowned in a bath of blood.

Meanwhile, as Chiang moved north and made himself the master of Peking,[4] a certain number of Communist leaders who had escaped the repression resorted to guerrilla warfare in the mountainous regions, where regular troops could be easily resisted. This was the case with two leaders who were to become famous—Chu Teh and Mao Tse-tung.

General Chu Teh, whose name means "Red Virtue," was born in 1886 at Ilung, in Szechwan province. His family were landlords, and quite well off. A graduate of the Yunnan Military Academy, where he studied under European instructors, Chu distinguished himself as a battalion commander in 1912; as early as 1916 he was promoted to brigadier general, then made Chief of Public Security of Kunming, and then Commissioner of Finance for Yunnan. He was now immensely wealthy; he possessed nine concubines and a sumptuous palace, in which he devoted himself to opium smoking and a life of debauchery. Suddenly, in 1922, he became a convert to Communism. Abandoning all his riches, he took the "cold-turkey" cure for his opium habit by signing on as a sailor with an English river boat on the Shanghai-Hankow run. He soon made contact with the Kuomintang revolutionaries, who looked upon him with suspicion. In 1923 he went to Germany and then to Paris, where he founded some Chinese Communist cells; then he went to Moscow, where he studied Marxist doctrine. Returning to China, he became one of the

---

[3] Hereafter abbreviated, on occasion, as CCP. *Tr.*
[4] It was at this time, the spring of 1928, that the Nationalists renamed the city Peiping, or "Northern Peace." *Tr.*

Kuomintang's most highly regarded military leaders. But in 1927, when Chiang Kai-shek declared war against the Communists, Chu Teh refused to fight the Reds, and left Nanchang to join the rebels. With a band made up of workers, peasants, deserters, and students, he started in to wage guerrilla warfare in the Hunan-Kiangsi-Kwangtung border area.

In 1928 Chu Teh joined forces with Mao Tse-tung. Mao, a cultivated and ironical young man, a country schoolteacher turned politician, had at first centered his political activity at Changsha; then he too had been forced to seek refuge in the mountains which border Kiangsi. The two leaders set up their command post in the Chingkanshan mountains, where they created a small Communist state, Mao occupying himself with the political direction of the movement while Chu Teh became commander in chief of the army. By 1933 they had succeeded in forming four army corps, and had amassed some fifty thousand rifles and several hundred machine guns. For his part, Chiang Kai-shek had called upon a German military mission to fashion his army along modern European lines. Successively, Colonel Bauer, then Colonel Kriebel, General Wetzell, General von Seekt—the former Chief of Staff of the Reichswehr—and finally, General von Falkenhausen, formed and trained Chiang's cadres until Hitler, under the pressure of Japanese protests, recalled Falkenhausen.

In September 1933 Chiang launched a great "extermination campaign" against Mao and Chu. Despite Chiang's commitment of hundreds of thousands of trained troops, supported by artillery, tanks, and aircraft, the Nationalists were held at bay for more than two years; then, finally, the Communists were forced to abandon Kiangsi and set out upon their "long march." Taking everything with them—women, children, and baggage—the Communists marched more than six thousand miles, through Kwangtung, through Kwangsi, through Yunnan and Szechwan, fighting all the way, until finally, in October 1935, they reached the dusty plains of North Shensi. Here they established a "Soviet base," with Yenan as its capital. Of the 300,000 people who had left Kiangsi, no more than forty thousand reached Shensi.

Chiang tried to oust these remnants from their ultimate haven, because he understood very well the danger of leaving his adversaries free to establish direct links with Mongolia and the U.S.S.R. But in December 1935, during a trip to the Northwest which took him to Sian, he fell into the hands of Chang Tso-lin's son, the "Young Marshal" Chang Hsüeh-liang, who had decided to revolt against the Generalissimo. What really lay at the bottom of this incident has remained a mystery, because at the end of eight days of talk Chiang was released by his mortal enemies—and at the instigation, according to reliable evidence, of Mao Tse-tung himself! The precise conditions of this extraordinary liberation are unknown. It should be recalled, however, that the Chinese do not think like Europeans: during the campaigns of 1945, for example, they never failed, despite the formal orders of their American instructors, to leave a way of "honorable retreat" open to encircled Japanese troops. It has been said that the Chinese Communists, obedient to Moscow's directives in this matter, were satisfied with extracting Chiang's promise to adopt a clearly anti-Japanese policy and join with them in a struggle for the liberation of China.

It is certain that Chiang at that time considered his fight against communism to be more important than a struggle against the Japanese invader. Profoundly imbued as he was with the old principles of Chinese civilization, and with those of the Christian faith as well, Chiang's war upon the movement led by Mao and Chu Teh had been a virtual war of religion. But after the Sian "incident," Chiang, who did not abandon his desire to crush his Communist adversaries, nevertheless gave first priority to the struggle against the invader.

As early as 1931 the Japanese had commenced to carry out their plan for continental conquest. During the night of 18–19 September, following the Mukden incident (in which a Japanese officer, Captain Nakamura, who had conducted a "military reconnaissance" while in mufti, was arrested and executed by the Chinese), they had invaded Manchuria. Shortly thereafter, in February 1932, they had organized their conquest as a satellite state called "Manchukuo." In the spring of 1933 Japan seized Jehol, and the Tangku Truce gave her control of Liaoning, Kirin, and Heilungkiang, which were incorporated into Manchukuo. Moreover, the terms of this truce also compelled the Chinese to withdraw their troops from the entire region between the Great Wall and the outskirts of Peking. In 1935 Japan obtained Chinese demilitarization of eastern Hopeh and all of Chahar, Shansi, Shantung, and Suiyuan; an "autonomous regime" was sponsored by the Japanese in Chahar and Hopeh. Not feeling strong enough to resist, Chiang Kai-shek submitted to all these encroachments, despite the violent protests of enlightened opinion in China.

But to the aggressors themselves, their success seemed insufficient. On the night of 7 July 1937, an incident[5] took place at the Marco Polo Bridge, on the outskirts of Peking, which gave them the occasion to present new demands. This time Chiang Kai-shek refused to submit. And so began a war which was to last eight years and end in Japan's defeat.

In a Kuomintang-Kungch'antang[6] agreement signed on 22 September 1937, the warring brothers united in a common front against Japan.. The Nationalists officially recognized the

[5] Following the disappearance, during maneuvers, of a Japanese soldier, Chinese authorities refused to permit Japanese officers to make a search inside the town of Wanping.

[6] "Kungch'antang" is Chinese for "Communist Party." *Tr.*

"Shensi-Kansu-Ningsia Border Region." Chu Teh's Eighth Route Army, three divisions strong, was also recognized by the Nationalists and theoretically integrated into the 18th Group Army under Marshal Yen Hsi-shan, the "model governor" of Shansi. A representative from Red Army headquarters at Yenan took a seat in Chiang Kai-shek's Military Council[7] and, beginning in the summer of 1938, Communists also sat in the "People's Political Council." As early as 1937 a second Communist field army, the New Fourth Army, was formed, with the Kuomintang's assent, to operate to the north of the Yangtze.

The war against Japan gave the Communists the opportunity to expand their influence throughout all of Northeast China. As the government's troops retreated, Communist guerrillas would infiltrate behind the lines of the advancing Japanese, organize resistance, and take over the administration of these "liberated" areas. Chiang Kai-shek soon perceived that he had put too powerful a weapon into the hands of his enemies. He thus began a close blockade of the Communist zone in Shensi and Kansu, which he ringed with a fortified line of more than ten thousand blockhouses and pillboxes manned by several hundred thousand troops. By such means the area of the Red "Border Region" was reduced to about ninety thousand square miles.

But all this effort was in vain: little by little, and despite the presence of the Japanese, the Communists came to dominate all of Northeast China. What is more, Mao Tse-tung, profiting from circumstances, broke his promises and slipped his New Fourth Army to the south of the Yangtze. Now for Chiang to permit a Communist intrusion into South China

---

[7] Chou En-lai represented the Yenan regime in the Political Department of the National Military Council, of which Chiang was the chairman, from 1937 until his walkout from that body in 1940. Tr.

was absolutely out of the question. On 18 January 1941 he ordered the arrest of the offending Red commander, General Yeh T'ing, and announced the dissolution of the New Fourth Army—a dissolution which, unlike the arrest, was never brought about. In the face of invasion, civil war broke out anew. As for the Japanese, they were always careful to refrain from a westward attack across the Yellow River against Yenan —a possibility which, in their view, would only play Chiang's game against the Reds.

To the Chinese people, deeply anti-Japanese as they were, Chiang's policies at this time were no more comprehensible than they were to the West. Mao Tse-tung became increasingly popular in Central China. Here, his disciples, following the classic Communist tactics of the "first phase," brought with them no doctrines of total collectivization, but an "agrarian democracy" in which the peasant owned his land and collective efforts were limited to such major tasks as the harvest.

Mao Tse-tung's principles were set forth in a book, *On the New Democracy*, for which he had asked, as an obedient Stalinist, the imprimatur of Moscow, and which he aimed at Western opinion in particular. In this work he declared that China was not yet ripe for socialism, but only for a "democratic revolution." He observed that such a revolution had been brought about in Europe by the bourgeoisie, for ends which were strictly capitalistic. But because of China's backwardness, and because of her Communist Party, it would be possible to avoid classical capitalism and create a "new capitalism" which would function in the interests of all the people. For the same reasons, Chinese democracy would be of neither the bourgeois nor the Russian type, but a "new democracy" characterized by the coalition of all revolutionary classes:

peasants, workers, the petty bourgeoisie, and even those capitalists who showed themselves to be antifeudal and patriotic.

Faithful to these theories, the Communists contented themselves with only one third of the key political posts in the zones under their own occupation, leaving the other two thirds to non-Communists. They plied the people with skillful and appropriate propaganda, cleverly blending free theatrical shows with the presentations of itinerant political agitators. They assigned control teams to take over immediately in the administration of newly occupied areas, and these Red officials were more honest than their Kuomintang predecessors. They carried on an energetic resistance against the Japanese, and their troops were under iron discipline. Incredibly, they even succeeded in restoring respectability to the soldier's calling, so strongly discredited in the eyes of the populace. In so highly civilized a country as China, soldiers were looked upon as a plague, or as obnoxious parasites at best. In the words of an old proverb:

> Hao tieh pu ta ting
> Hao jen pu tang ping

or:

> "Good iron is not used to make a nail,
> Nor a good man to make a soldier."

Meanwhile the war had spread throughout the entire world, and after December 1941 China no longer stood alone. But General Joe Stilwell, America's top military man in China, rapidly came to a realization of the unbelievable situation that prevailed there: the best Nationalist troops, with the most modern matériel, were occupied in mounting guard on Yenan, while the Japanese gradually overran the whole country. To him, this state of affairs appeared inadmissible. But the Generalissimo met Stilwell's objections with strategic conceptions of astounding remoteness:

> For me the big problem is not Japan, but the unification of my country. I am sure that you Americans are going to beat the Japanese some day, with or without the help of the troops I am holding back for use against the Communists in the Northwest. On the other hand, if I let Mao Tse-tung push his propaganda across all of Free China, we run the risk—and so do you Americans —of winning for nothing. I say this because behind Mao there is the religion of Communism—and in consequence, Russia.[8]

At that time, this plain language could come only as a mystery to the Americans; and it was American refusal to recognize reality that was to lead to Stilwell's departure in 1944. However, his replacement, General Wedemeyer, did succeed in persuading Chiang to shift some of the troops from his *cordon sanitaire* against the Reds to Kwangsi, in order to meet the Japanese attack on Kweiyang.

At the beginning of 1944 President Roosevelt had sent Vice President Henry Wallace to China "to see what could be done to increase the Chinese war effort against Japan." Wallace concluded that a solution would have to be based upon achievement of a real agreement between the Communists and the Nationalists. Following this advice, the President in September 1944 dispatched to Chungking his personal friend, General Patrick Hurley, to act as mediator between the two adversaries. Shortly after his arrival, Hurley also replaced Clarence Gauss as American Ambassador to China.

Hurley, like Roosevelt, was a devoted champion of democracy. At the time of his arrival in China, he believed that it would be possible to form a coalition government and bestow

---

[8] The source of this account is a highly placed Nationalist general officer whose identity the author cannot disclose. *Tr.*

upon the Communist Party a legal basis for its existence. In November 1944 he personally drew up the draft of a five-point agreement, to which he obtained the signature of Mao Tse-tung. He flattered himself that he would get Chiang Kai-shek to sign it, too; but he was quickly disabused of this notion by the snail-like pace of Chinese-style negotiations, and by counterproposals, lies, and broken promises. Moreover, he soon came to share the ideas of Chiang Kai-shek, who convinced him of the noxious and intrinsic peril that the Chinese Communist Party posed for the future of Western civilization and the interests of American democracy. Hurley also discovered that many American diplomats, amazed by the efficiency of the Communists and their ability to gain popular support, were secretly favorable to Yenan. This is what brought him to resign, on 26 November 1945, and to quit China with such a slamming of doors behind him.

Be that as it may, by the time of the Japanese surrender the Communists had gained control of a territory of almost 400,000 square miles, inhabited by one hundred million people, and divided into sixteen "semi-independent" anti-Japanese base areas. Their regular armies had grown to a strength of 900,000 men, and their people's militia now numbered about two million men. The Communists hoped to retain a certain amount of autonomy within newly liberated China, keeping their dominant position in some of the provinces, leaving the others to the Nationalists, and relying upon peaceful propaganda as the means to attain their final goal.

For their part, the Nationalists were set in their determination to wipe out the *imperium in imperio* Mao had established in the heart of China, a task in which they could profit from the modern matériel and military training they had acquired during the war against Japan. Before undertaking this operation, Chiang Kai-shek made sure of Moscow's neutrality. On

14 August 1945 he concluded an accord with the U.S.S.R. in which he agreed to recognition of the independence of Outer Mongolia, to the establishment of a joint Sino-Russian base at Port Arthur and of a free port at Dairen, and to a thirty-year concession for joint exploitation of the Manchurian railroads. In return the Soviet Union promised to give its support to the Nationalist government, to refrain from intervention in China's internal affairs, and to respect Chinese sovereignty in Manchuria. Having thus secured the rear, Chiang now prepared for war.

✧ PART ONE ✧

1945
THE ADVERSARIES
MOVE INTO POSITION

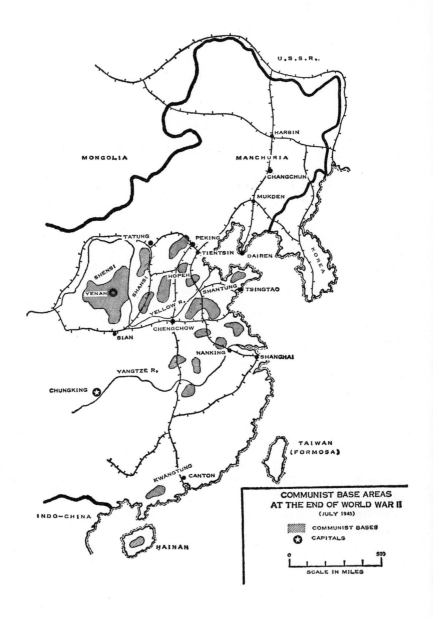

U.S.S.R.

HARBIN

MONGOLIA

MANCHURIA

CHANGCHUN

MUKDEN

TATUNG

PEKING

TIENTSIN

DAIREN

KOREA

SHENSI

SHANSI

HOPEH

YENAN

SHANTUNG

TSINGTAO

YELLOW R.

CHENGCHOW

SIAN

NANKING

SHANGHAI

YANGTZE R.

CHUNGKING

TAIWAN
(FORMOSA)

KWANGTUNG

CANTON

INDO-CHINA

HAINAN

COMMUNIST BASE AREAS
AT THE END OF WORLD WAR II
(JULY 1945)

▨ COMMUNIST BASES
✪ CAPITALS

0   500

SCALE IN MILES

CHAPTER III

The Two Camps on the Eve of Civil War

LIKE all modern wars the Chinese Civil War was, within China's means, a total war, in which the military factor was only one of several determinants. To draw a true picture of the opposing forces it is therefore necessary to analyze not only the military factor, but political, social, and economic factors as well.

THE POLITICAL SITUATION: THE NATIONALISTS

With the surrender of Japan, China realized all her national aspirations in the field of foreign relations. The unequal treaties had been abolished; except for Hong Kong, all foreign concessions—those thorns embedded in China's living flesh —had been returned to her. Foreigners no longer enjoyed the right of extraterritoriality, which had so greatly humiliated Chinese self-respect. China was about to recover her lost lands: Formosa, occupied and exploited by Japan since 1895, and Manchuria, the richest region in the Far East. Her international position had never been so favorable: China had become one of the Big Four, before even France gained admittance to this holy of holies; and she held a position of authority in the United Nations, especially in the Security Council. With the obliteration of Japan, China had become the great Asian nation of the world, her prestige enhanced by her long resistance against the common foe. Japan having been crushed, China had no more enemies. She had the support, both moral and material, of the United States. With Great Britain, there were no problems other than Hong Kong, and each side strove to avoid aggravation of this issue. Chinese troops occupied Indo-China north of the sixteenth parallel, and the inevitable incidents with the French were settled without any serious repercussions. Only the Soviet Union could have constituted a threat to China. But in August of 1945 the U.S.S.R. had signed in Moscow a treaty by which it pledged itself to respect the territorial integrity of China, to recognize the Nationalists as the only legitimate government of China, and to withhold its support from the Chinese Communists. In return the U.S.S.R. had obtained the right to establish a naval base at Port Arthur, joint administration with the Chinese of the port of Dairen, and certain advantages in Manchuria. In signing this accord China's hand had, of course, been somewhat forced by the United States, at a time when the Americans believed in the advantages of a Russian intervention in the war against Japan. But if Russia were to respect the terms of the treaty, the few concessions agreed to by China would be amply compensated. Deservedly or not, the credit to be gained from all these achievements accrued, within China as well as abroad, to the Nationalist government and to its leader, Generalissimo Chiang Kai-shek, who had been variously depicted by wartime Allied propaganda as a sort of Chinese Napoleon or Cincinnatus.

Unfortunately, the internal situation of the country was far less favorable than its world position. China's push toward progress, started in 1930, had been halted by the war against Japan; even worse, China seemed incapable of resuming its forward movement. She had known no peace for thirty years, and now she was exhausted. She needed tranquility in order to rebuild; but civil war was at the door. She needed far-reaching reforms; but the Kuomintang, in former times her engine of progress, showed itself to be almost completely worn out.

In his political testament Sun Yat-sen had entrusted the tutelage of China to the Kuomintang, until the day when the political maturity of the country would permit the functioning of democratic institutions. This day had seemed in sight, and then came Japanese aggression to delay the transition to democracy. After the first access of popular enthusiasm died down, and as soon as the failings of the Kuomintang were revealed by the tests of war, numerous critics arose to contest the validity of the Kuomintang's tutelage and its capacity to exercise sole leadership of the embattled nation. Lacking an organized liberal party,[1] these critics were isolated and powerless; since they lent some weight to the Communist viewpoint, they were also ruthlessly suppressed within the Kuomintang itself. Although it had been organized along the same lines as the Russian Communist Party, the Kuomintang had lost the monolithic aspect of its model; it had a right wing, a center, and a left wing—or, rather, a certain number of cliques which more or less represented these tendencies. To the right there was the CC clique, so named because of its leaders, the brothers Ch'en Li-fu and Ch'en Kuo-fu, conservatives for whom the salvation of China lay in a return to the sound traditions and paternalistic philosophy of Confucius. In the center, the clique of the generals, named after the Chinese

---

[1] The Democratic League, which attempted to create an opposition party, was dissolved as pro-Communist in 1948, without ever exerting any real influence.

St. Cyr,[2] Whampoa, constituted a sort of Mafia, grouping certain graduates of this institution who had few political views other than loyalty to Chiang Kai-shek. There was also the clique of "the two Kwangs," so called for the southern provinces of Kwangtung and Kwangsi, led by the ex-war lords Li Tsung-jen and Pai Ch'ung-hsi. To the left was the "Political Science Group" of bankers, administrators, and technicians, who, liberal by education, favored a transfer of power from the hands of the military to their own. Lastly, certain other groups, of varying importance and distinctness of definition, oscillated opportunistically from one side to the other. All these cliques were jealous of one another and undermined each other, overtly as well as covertly. The Kuomintang was not, however, the only influential political element on the Nationalist side. Traces of pure feudalism had not completely disappeared with the unification of China in 1927. Several war lords retained an attitude of independence toward the central government, and ruled as virtually absolute sovereigns of their own domains. Such were Yen Hsi-shan, the famous marshal of the "model province" of Shansi; the Moslem generals of the Northwest, Ma Pu-fang in Tsinghai and Ma Hung-k'uei in Ningsia; Teng Hsi-hou in Szechwan, and so on. There was also "The Family," the Soongs: T. V. Soong; his brother-in-law, H. H. Kung; and the three Soong sisters. Ch'ing-ling, Sun Yat-sen's widow, had withdrawn into self-imposed isolation since 1927, deeming that her brother-in-law Chiang had betrayed the revolutionary ideal of her husband, and devoted herself to charity. But all the rest of the family constituted a new sort of ruling dynasty, thanks to its supporters and to its fabulous wealth; and when public opinion forced T. V. Soong's withdrawal, it was Kung who would take his place, and vice versa. What cement held all these clans and cliques

2 The French equivalent of West Point. *Tr.*

together? For one thing, their common enemy—communism; for another, Chiang Kai-shek.

The Generalissimo had aged since 1927, and the exercise of power had hardened him. He had always had an almost inhumanly iron will, which held him to his course when everyone else yielded to contrary evidence and to the crushing onslaught of events; he had a limitless self-confidence, warranted by his rapid ascent to power and the perpetual approbation of his entourage; he had a blind, pure faith in the sacred character of his mission. His sly peasant cunning lacked, however, any breadth of view, and he had the shortcoming of all dictators: nepotism, and a weakness for the comrades of his early days. With these qualities and these faults, his moral authority today remains unchallenged in Nationalist China; everyone knows that when he dies the Nationalist camp will immediately fall into chaos. He is irreplaceable, though his power is far from absolute. Given the structure of his government, Chiang could enjoy neither the advantages of a democratic regime nor those of a dictatorship. He kept on top of the system by playing one group off against the other, and wasted all his energy in that sterile game, accomplishing nothing positive except in the international field, where his crafty Chinese mentality worked wonders.[3]

From top to bottom of the administrative hierarchy, the picture was the same, but complicated by local problems.

[3] On this point, the evidence of General Stilwell, taken from his book *The Stilwell Papers* (New York: William Sloane Associates, Copyright, 1948, by Winifred A. Stilwell), pp. 315–316, is of interest:

I never heard Chiang K'ai-shek say a single thing that indicated gratitude to the President or to our country for the help we were extending to him. Invariably, when anything was promised, he would want more. Invariably, he would complain about the small amount of material that was being furnished. He would make comparisons between the huge amounts of Lend-Lease supplies going to Great Britain and Russia with the meager trickle going to China. He would complain that the Chinese had been

And a fact of primary importance must be noted: in the countryside, authority and wealth were merged in the local cell of the Kuomintang, which alone held power.

The great question at the end of 1945 was that of political reform. Everyone knew its urgency, but the Kuomintang was scarcely inclined to undertake reform. The Sino-Japanese War had furnished justification for the continued tutelage of China by the Kuomintang; now, with the war's end, the Communist danger became the excuse to strengthen the party's control. In fact, what the Kuomintang feared most, and rightly so, was the verdict of a genuine popular consultation. The party was worn out; it had renewed neither its men nor its ideas. Corruption and nepotism ruled shamelessly—corruption as the almost necessary result of inflation and the ridiculously low salaries of officials; nepotism as the legacy of ancient traditions which had survived the upheavals of revolution. Hon-

---

fighting for six or seven years and yet we gave them practically nothing. It would of course have been undiplomatic to go into the nature of the military effort Chiang K'ai-shek had made since 1938. It was practically zero.

Whether or not he was grateful was a small matter. The regrettable part of it was that there was no quid pro quo. We did what we could, furnished what was available, without being allowed to first ask what he would do, etc. The result was that we were continuously on the defensive and he could obstruct and delay any of our plans without being penalized.

[I have] faith in Chinese soldiers and Chinese people: fundamentally great, democratic, misgoverned. No bars of caste or religion. . . . Honest, frugal, industrious, cheerful, independent, tolerant, friendly, courteous.

I judge Kuomintang and Kungchantang [Communist party] by what I saw:

[KMT] Corruption, neglect, chaos, economy, taxes, words and deeds. Hoarding, black market, trading with enemy.

Communist program . . . reduce taxes, rents, interest. Raise production, and standard of living. Participate in government. Practice what they preach.

Obviously, General Stilwell saw only the early stages of communism in China.

est people were powerless. The government had so often denounced these evils, and so often promised to eradicate them, with so few results, that it seemed all hope was lost.

THE COMMUNISTS

In contrast to the Nationalists, the war against Japan yielded no diplomatic advantages to the Yenan government, which came out of the war as it had gone in—an armed political party. No government recognized it. In 1945, thanks to Ambassador Hurley's insistence, the Communists were granted representation in the Chinese delegation to the San Francisco Conference of the United Nations, but not, obviously, representation as a sovereign state. In this regard, it is curious to note that the CCP never sought formal recognition of its rights until its final victory, perhaps because such a move would have alienated the sympathies of the Chinese people, reluctant as they were to admit the *de facto* existence of two sovereign Chinese governments. The Chinese Communists shared the ideology of the U.S.S.R.; but this tie did not prevent the Russians from abandoning their Chinese comrades to their difficult fate in 1927, or from reserving their material aid for the Nationalists only in 1938, or from signing an agreement with the Nationalists in 1945. Strangely, this attitude failed to shake the Marxist faith of the Chinese Communist Party which, without rancor, continued in its adherence to the Stalinist line.

Although the CCP was more united than the KMT, certain cliques were nonetheless discernible in 1945, at a time when a Communist victory was still far from certain.

The first of these was made up of the sincere partisans of Mao Tse-tung: Liu Shao-ch'i, his old comrade from Hunan, who had the title of Minister of Organization, and his deputy, Jen Pi-shih, the Vice Minister; Lu Ting-i, the Minister of Propaganda; Li Fu-ch'un, Minister of Finance; and lastly, among the members of the Central Committee, T'an Cheng, Ch'en Yün, Kao Kang, Wu Yü-chang, Hsieh Chüeh-tsai, and Tung Pi-wu. Among the military chiefs this group numbered P'eng Te-huai, deputy commander of the Red armies; Hsiao K'e; T'eng Tai-yüan; Ch'en Keng; and Lin Tsu-han, who held the important post of Chairman of the Shensi-Kansu-Ningsia Border Region Government.

Opposing this clique was a group of Communists who in 1945 still set themselves against Mao Tse-tung. Their leader was Li Li-san, the former leader of the CCP who, ousted by Mao and his supporters, had returned from a subsequent sojourn in Moscow with all the prestige of one who had resided within those sacred precincts. Around him were grouped Ch'en Shao-yü, Chang Wen-t'ien and, above all, the two great military leaders: Lin Piao, "The Invincible," commander of the Army of Manchuria; and Ch'en I, commander of the New Fourth Army, which held the provinces of Shantung and Kiangsu.

Between these two groups stood the "Opportunists," who waited to see how things would turn out and who gathered around K'ang Sheng, a crafty and brutal ex-pupil of Moscow's OGPU who as chief of Social Affairs controlled the secret police; Chou En-lai, the diplomatist of the party; and Yeh Chien-ying. General Chu Teh, the chief of the Red Army, and Liu Po-ch'eng, the "One-Eyed General" commanding the Army of the Central Plains, maintained a strict neutrality. In general, the "Hunan Clique" controlled the party, while the "Szechwan Clique" controlled the army.

These internal disputes were of little importance, however, and the government of the Red zone clearly profited from the advantages of dictatorship. The CCP enforced its authority without having to take into consideration either cliques or an opposition. Yet it always attached great importance to public opinion, and did not hesitate to make timely concessions. Even though the Communist government was no more the product of popular elections than was that of the Nationalists, it succeeded in avoiding the stigma of dictatorship. At village and district levels the Communists set up administrations which were, to a certain extent, democratic. In the local soviets the CCP made sure that the proportion of Communist members was no more than one third, the other two thirds being reserved for the regularly elected representatives of the people. In these assemblies criticism was not only permitted but encouraged. The Communists therefore represented progress to the majority of peasants, who had hitherto known only oppression or, at best, governmental neglect, and who did not dream of questioning the abstract and long-range implications of communism. On the other hand, those who opposed communism on principle, and those who deviated from the party line, were denied any means of spreading their views. The party "forgave" errors made in good faith; to correct and prevent such errors, it had established "political study centers" which all party members, whatever their positions in the hierarchy, were compelled to attend. For those who did not submit to persuasion, there were "rectification camps." Moreover, the traditional character of the Chinese, inclined as he is to accept circumstances over which he has no control, made him a docile instrument. In the Red zone, opposition was a negligible, if not nonexistent factor.

The party alone had a decisive voice in the highest circles of power. At the summit, Mao Tse-tung showed himself, more and more, to be a statesman of the first order. When the Marxist jargon is cleared away, his speeches reveal a wide breadth of view and a profound realism; his words seem to translate themselves into concrete acts; and Mao has the gift of sound judgment of men and situations. He is far more than the poet so often depicted in France. It should be noted that Mao, though he has carefully read all the Marxist, Leninist, and Stalinist literature, is nonetheless a self-made man; and, also, that he is the only party leader never to have traveled outside China.[4]

Around Mao Tse-tung were Chu Teh, Chou En-lai, and Lo Fu, his close associates. Beneath them, the structure of the CCP, organized along classical Communist lines, remained changeless: between the central committee and the village soviet was the usual chain of command, with its responsible officials, its political commissars, and its unceasing mutual surveillance. There is no need to expand upon the discipline of this party. Decisions made at the top of the hierarchy were implemented right through to the bottom, and the political commissars corrected, sooner or later, whatever mistakes were made. The tremendous superiority of the CCP, it must be emphasized, lay in the absence of corruption among the officials placed over the people at this time. On this point, the testimony of all witnesses is unanimous. Party discipline suppressed with impartiality the personal intrigues which otherwise would certainly have manifested themselves on the battlefield. In brief, facing a worn-out party rotted by corruption and intrigue, there was a young party, ardent, disciplined, full of faith—and clever enough to conceal the long-range goal toward which, with carefully graduated steps, they led the Chinese people.

---

[4] As the author later points out in Chapter XVIII, Mao did travel to Moscow in December 1949, to conclude the Sino-Soviet treaty of 1950. *Tr.*

Broadly speaking, the history of China can be summarized as follows: the reigning dynasty becomes rotten with corruption; the people revolt; a successful chieftain seats himself upon the throne and founds his own dynasty. The first sovereigns of this new dynasty rule the country well; but their successors become progressively weaker, and the cycle begins all over again. The most astonishing feature of this history is that, despite the often violent convulsions characterizing the transition from one cycle to another, the social structure of China remains untouched. It is as if this structure had found, after centuries, its most satisfactory form and its final equilibrium. Now, unlike its predecessors, the upheaval of the twentieth century entailed a profound transformation of the social order in China. Three new factors appeared in the nineteenth century: the end of China's isolation; the growth of its population; and the industrialization of the Western world. In the face of such an assault, the millenial traditions which had for so long maintained the framework of Chinese society were suddenly swept away.

It should not be forgotten that the Revolution of 1911 was, above all, a nationalistic uprising against the Manchus. Its objective, the unification of China, was achieved by the Koumintang in 1927, if one excepts the Communist rebellion. But though the Kuomintang had made real progress in the political field during the decade that preceded the Sino-Japanese War, little if anything had been accomplished in the field of social reform. Superficially, Chinese society in 1945 did not differ essentially from the appearance it had presented for the past twenty centuries. To realize this, one had only to take a short walk in the streets of any Nationalist-held town, where daily life appeared to go on at its traditionally slow pace.

Yet, beneath the surface, there seethed the dangerous phenomenon of a profound social unrest. To this unrest contributed not only the three new factors brought into play by the nineteenth century, but the unprecedented fact that, unlike all previous dynastic changes, the upheaval of 1911 had failed to produce the traditional improvement in public administration.

Eighty per cent of China's population were peasants, of whom only twenty per cent were landowners. Landless peasants hired themselves out as agricultural laborers, or rented small plots of land at exorbitant rates. Because landowners also represented the local political authority, it was easy for them to escape taxes, compulsory labor duties, and military conscription, the burdens of which thus fell even more heavily upon the peasantry. When it came time for the peasant to sell his crop, prices invariably fell. Because of the poor transportation network there was no nation-wide market in China, which might have played a regulatory role, and there were incredible fluctuations in farm prices from one week to another and between one district and another. Hunan province could die of starvation while Szechwan wallowed in a superabundant crop. As a consequence, the market was at the mercy of wealthy manipulators. When the peasant wanted to buy seed, prices suddenly went up; the peasants were thus permanently in debt, with no possibility of recovery. This in turn bred banditry, still a seasonal occupation in certain parts of China. Before the opening of China to foreign commerce, the peasant could work as an artisan during the off-season, earning enough to make ends meet; but with the influx of cheap manufactured goods from abroad, this source of income rapidly disappeared. In short, it was the peasantry, more than any other class of Chinese society, who always paid the costs of war and of the chronic disorder of the country.

34

The great majority of the Chinese population being peasants, and the economy of China predominantly agrarian as it was, the pattern of land tenure urgently required a radical reform. It is true that the Kuomintang had enacted a law limiting land rents to reasonable levels, but since the party contained precisely those elements with the greatest interest in maintaining the status quo of a country whose 450 million inhabitants led the harshest of struggles for existence, it is easy to understand why this law was never enforced.

The Chinese proletariat did not yet constitute an important part of the population. Concentrated in a few industrial centers, such as Canton, Shanghai, Tientsin, and Hankow, it was easy to keep under surveillance and was always under a tight rein. Its misery was no less acute than that of the peasants. The worker, buffeted by inflation and foreign competition, was also ruthlessly exploited, despite the Nationalist social legislation which—like agrarian reform—remained always a dead letter. Sporadic riots and looting of rice shops reflected the unrest of the workers. The only measure taken to remedy this situation was to pay a portion of wages in kind, a measure extended also to the swollen ranks of the bureaucracy, inevitable victims of inflation.

Students, traditionally involved in the political life of the country, vested with the privilege of voicing their sometimes abusive opinions, in consequence made up a social category that was particularly feared by the government. Most of them being poor, the Spartan existence of the students was subsidized by the government, and they enjoyed exemption from conscription. Despite these relative advantages, their sympathies did not lie with the Nationalist government; their juvenile intolerance, inflamed by reading and propaganda, made them bitterly resent the immutability of a social order in which they had no real place. Yet technicians were numerous in China and, had they been properly utilized, their numbers would have sufficed to bring progress to the country. Unfortunately, the student without personal connections was in most cases without chance of a suitable job. As examples, there was the case of a statistician who, after eight years' study in France, could find no employment upon his return to China except as a grade school teacher; and the Belgian-trained chemical engineer who could find in Chungking no other way to make a living than to concoct artificial *apéritifs*.

In stark contrast to all this misery, often made even more tragic by famine, flood, and war, a small minority of the regime's new rich happily accommodated themselves to the situation, becoming major stockholders in American firms, and selling, on the black market, U. S. goods and drugs sent to China under Lend-Lease.

In the social field, the Kuomintang must be given credit for advances in public education. A similar effort was made to improve sanitary conditions, which had remained the same since the days of Confucius. This effort achieved only a partial success. Although large epidemics were held in check, infant mortality remained as high as ever, and notions of personal hygiene had reached only a small minority of the bourgeoisie. Opium, the scourge of China and a major target of the Communists, was effectively controlled by the Nationalists, but it should be noted that tobacco had everywhere replaced opium, with Mao Tse-tung himself chain-smoking some sixty cigarettes per day.

To conclude this brief sketch, the fact must be emphasized that Chinese society, unlike that of the Hindus, has never known a hereditary caste system. With luck, a coolie could become a mandarin. This is a very important fact, for the existence of a caste system has always been a considerable obstacle to profound social change.

THE SOCIAL SITUATION: THE COMMUNISTS

The great fault of Chiang Kai-shek, then, was his failure in the field of social reform; and it was precisely here that the Communist Party put its emphasis, focusing its principal effort upon the number-one social problem, agrarian reform. To solve this problem, the party pushed programs for the redistribution of land, improvement of productivity, elimination of corruption, and equitable distribution of the tax burden.

When the local soviets were first established by the Communists, the landowner was expropriated, even massacred, and his lands redistributed; but soon, as the result of Mao's influence, expropriations were halted in order to retain control of rents. In 1946 the Communists revived their program of land redistribution, but this time there was no liquidation of landowners, who were permitted to retain the maximum legal holding, fixed at about 1.5 acres per person, with local variations according to the quality of the land and the density of the population. The distribution of plots was determined by the local soviets. With 1.5 acres per person there would no longer be "feasts for the few and famine for all the rest." Since about three quarters of an acre is estimated to be the area needed in China to feed one person, one wonders about the long-range effects of this radical reform upon the birth rate in a country already overpopulated, and the effects upon agriculture, where the modern trend has been toward the large holdings which alone permit the efficiency of mechanization.

Be this as it may, the Communist program apparently gained the approval of the majority of the peasantry. Moreover, the Communists implemented this program in appropriately gradual steps. In areas long dominated by the Communists, where land redistribution had already been accomplished, they sought to improve redistribution and increase crop yields. In areas occupied during the war, they concentrated on land redistribution alone. In areas only recently conquered, they limited their reforms to reduction of rents and taxes. A good example of the flexibility of Communist policy in this field occurred in the spring of 1948 when, the majority of the population of Honan province proving to be opposed to land redistribution, the Communists deemed it necessary to delay this move "until the time when political education would permit the application of this reform."

The improvement of productivity offered a practically untouched field to the reformer. Since time immemorial the Chinese peasant has cultivated his land according to precepts adhered to by reason of their very antiquity.[5] In China such modern techniques as seed selection were completely unknown, and entire regions were permitted to lie fallow because no one had even heard of such a thing as dry farming. It was in just such a region that the Communists established themselves in 1935. Popularizing the new methods worked out by their experimental farms, the Communists obtained results that not only permitted them to survive the Nationalist blockade, but provided a surplus which could be traded, in the black markets of the Nationalist zone, for the manufactured products that they lacked.

Since there were no major industries located in the Communist zone, there were very few industrial workers, and Communist social reforms involving labor remained perforce only promises as of 1945. The Communists had, however, developed small industries and artisanry; and their concern for the worker's lot was tempered by their realization of the need to produce enough to make themselves independent of imported

---

[5] The peasant is sometimes right. Take, for example, the case of the missionary in Chahar who, in attempting to demonstrate the merits of deep plowing to peasants who seemed content with merely scratching the land, lost all his topsoil to the spring winds blowing in from Mongolia.

manufactured goods. For this reason the CCP kept a close watch on the maintenance of satisfactory labor-management relations.

In the field of education the success of the Kuomintang was limited by lack of schools. Many children went without schooling, and nothing had been done for adult illiterates. The Communists attempted to fill this void by a method as simple as it was effective. In each village, in each military unit, in each party group, those who knew one thousand characters of the Chinese language were to teach them to those who knew only five hundred. These, in their turn, became the instructors of the illiterate. Hygiene was popularized in the same way: instructors trained in higher schools of the party trained other instructors, who in turn fanned out to teach at lower echelons.

In summary, the Communist Party in social matters had succeeded in persuading the people that their methods brought undeniable progress. It understood very well indeed that without popular support it would be impossible to carry on the military struggle against the Kuomintang.

THE ECONOMIC SITUATION: THE NATIONALISTS

Contrary to appearances, the economic situation of China at the end of World War II offered good reason to hope for a rapid recovery. Its compartmentalized agrarian economy had not suffered, except in the areas directly exposed to the combat operations of 1943–1944. Its industrial production, except for textiles and mining, had increased under Japanese exploitation. The rail system, and inland and coastal navigation, had suffered some damage, but not to any grave extent. The important problem was thus not so much reconstruction as revival of the flow of exchange and distribution.

Inflation was the second major problem. Deprived of its principal sources of revenue by the Japanese occupation, the Nationalist government had been forced to resort to the printing press in order to finance its war effort. The American loan of $500 million in 1943 had failed to check the fall of the Chinese currency; from one American dollar for two Chinese dollars (*fapi*) in 1937, the rate of exchange had reached 1,200 *fapis* per dollar by 1945.

With victory in World War II, the Nationalist government now had the means to solve both of these problems. It was in the process of recovering practically all the resources it had possessed before the war. Particularly important was the fact that, controlling as it did all the ports except Dairen and Chefoo, it could count on the customs duties which, for all the various Chinese governments of the previous three decades, had constituted the greatest and most stable source of income. Moreover, among its assets was a credit of 900 million U. S. dollars, the largest amount ever possessed by any Chinese government. It also had $800 million worth of Chinese holdings abroad. The reoccupation of Manchuria, highly developed by Japan, would give the Nationalists an industry four times greater than that of China Proper, and agricultural surpluses as well. To be sure, these expectations were soon to be nullified by the looting of Russian troops, who sent all the industrial machinery home to Russia, and permitted the local population to pillage all the rest. Nevertheless, Formosa, developed by fifty years of Japanese occupation, brought a prosperous industry (cement, aluminum, lumber, oil) and surplus food production (sugar, canned goods, and so on). The government also inherited the Japanese holdings in China which, whether directly exploited or transferred to private enterprise, assured important new sources of income. Also, it could count on Japanese reparations, to which China could lay legitimate claim for a substantial amount, and on aid from UNRRA, which was eventually to reach a total of $660 million. Finally, it was almost certain of obtaining American financial and material assistance, in the form either of loans or of surpluses sold to China at one tenth their real value.

Military expenditures constituted the immediate cause of inflation: eighty per cent of the budget was devoted, with little accountability, to the maintenance of an army as burdensome as it was inefficient. If the defeat of Japan brought urgent new tasks for the military, it also furnished an excellent opportunity to reform the army and to limit, without risk, military spending. In any case, even if this reform were not undertaken, the government's new resources should have assured so favorable a margin of income that it could easily have been able to balance its budget. That it was unsuccessful in this endeavor is clear evidence of the corruption and wastefulness of the Nationalist regime, even when the Communists' attempts to destroy the government's material advantages are taken into account.

The Nationalist economy was certainly very vulnerable. The reoccupation of southern China, a food-deficient area, and the reoccupation of large cities such as Shanghai, Tientsin, Peking, Tsingtao, and Mukden, imposed enormous supply burdens upon the government. Thus, the solution of the problem depended upon the agricultural production of the countryside and the smooth functioning of the transportation system.

THE ECONOMIC SITUATION: THE COMMUNISTS

The Communists enjoyed none of the advantages mentioned above. Their share of UNRRA aid, which in theory was to be distributed *pro rata* to the population without regard to political affiliations, never reached ten per cent of the total. They received no financial aid whatsoever from the U.S.S.R. and, lacking seaports, they were completely cut off from foreign trade. Their economy thus remained primarily agrarian. This posed a serious disadvantage in that the Reds, who held no major industrial centers and had no foreign trade except for the uncontrollable traffic which later developed between northern Manchuria and Siberia, depended on the output of their artisans and trade with the Nationalist zone for the minimum of manufactured goods necessary to them. Fortunately for them, their needs were limited, and they had developed small industries as much as possible. Also, it was easy to carry on trade with the Nationalist zone, since the Nationalist government needed the agricultural production of the Red zone to feed its food-deficient regions and its great commercial centers. This trade was strictly controlled by the CCP, which saw to it that demand in the Communist zone did not get out of hand and that imported products were distributed through cooperatives kept under their close surveillance. This system conferred an enormous advantage upon the Communists. The Communist-held regions, thanks to their uniformly primitive state of economic development, were interchangeable. Thus, the Communists could sacrifice a region without decisive loss; their economy was effectively protected against military setbacks.

The inflation of Nationalist currency had, of course, repercussions in the Communist zone, but the Communists were cushioned against its effects by the economic compartmentalization of their zone, in which each region had its own bank of issue, as well as by the effectiveness of their ever-present controls. There was practically no black market and, like it or not, neither producers nor retailers could possibly evade the price ceilings fixed by the party.

The administration, and above all the Red Army, which required continuous expansion, necessarily absorbed a major portion of the Communists' revenues. As the party did not want to lose the good will of the population, it was reluctant to raise taxes. Thus, except for inflation, the only solution was to make the administration and the army not only productive, but self-supporting. This was the solution adopted, and the efforts undertaken as early as 1934–1935 succeeded in bringing partial relief to the Communist budget. Each official, with Mao Tse-tung himself in the lead, was required to work his small plot;[6] each army unit, when not engaged in combat, tilled the land assigned to it, or lent a hand to the peasants. School children also were brought into this program. The organization of the Communist armed forces, with a nucleus of regular troops supplemented by local units of militia mobilized for particular operations, permitted the release of large numbers of troops at sowing and harvest time.

THE MILITARY SITUATION: THE NATIONALIST CAMP

Without any doubt, the best appraisal that can be found of the quality of the Chinese Nationalist Army in 1944 comes from General Stilwell:

In 1944, on paper, the Chinese Army consisted of 324 divisions, 60-odd brigades and 89 so-called guerrilla units of about 2,000 men each. This looks formidable on paper, till you go into it closely. Then you find:

1. That the average strength per division instead of 10,000 is not more than 5,000.
2. That the troops are unpaid, unfed, shot with sickness and malnutrition.
3. That equipment is old, inadequate, and unserviceable.

[6] Mao, of course, grew tobacco; Chu Teh grew lettuce.

43

4. That training is nonexistent.

5. That the officers are jobholders.

6. That there is no artillery, transport, medical service, etc., etc.

7. That conscription is so-and-so.

8. That business is the principal occupation. How else live?

How would you start to make such an army effective?[7]

At the end of 1945, a serious effort had nonetheless been made. The strength of the army was raised to about 2,500,000 regulars, formed into 278 brigades which were reorganized beginning early in 1946.[8] The elite of this army consisted of thirty-nine divisions which had been trained and equipped by the Americans; although some of these had not yet received all of their equipment at the time of Japan's surrender, the Americans left enough matériel in China to fully equip these divisions. Among these thirty-nine divisions, those of

[7] *The Stilwell Papers*, pp. 316–317. *Tr.*

[8] During this period of reorganization—as well as before and after it—the terms "brigade" and "division" appear to have been loosely synonymous, since both referred to a formation of about 10,000 men supported by one battalion of organic light artillery (usually 75 mm. pack howitzers). When the infantry firepower of a brigade attained the planned levels prescribed by U.S. military advisors—or when an "army" was reorganized and trimmed down to such a level—the term "division" would be applied to a force of this strength and firepower. In general, a Chinese Nationalist infantry division of the Civil War period had about two thirds the personnel strength, and less than one third the artillery, of a World War II-type U.S. infantry division. A Chinese Nationalist "army," with three divisions, was therefore the rough equivalent of a small U.S. corps in strength, and of a U.S. division in artillery firepower. A Nationalist "group army," consisting of a variable number of armies, had the approximate strength of a large U. S. corps or, in the case of a large group army, of a U.S. field army. For more detailed discussions of Nationalist organization and reorganization, see Charles F. Romanus and Riley Sutherland, *United States Army in World War II, China-Burma-India Theater, Time Runs Out in CBI* (Washington, D.C.: Office of the Chief of Military History, Department of the Army, 1959), pp. 232–233, 382; see also the Chinese Ministry of Information, *The China Handbook, 1937–1945* (New York: The Macmillan Company, 1947), p. 286, and The China Handbook Editorial Board, *The China Handbook, 1950* (New York: The Rockport Press, Inc., 1950), pp. 187–188. *Tr.*

the New First and New Sixth armies[9] had fought with distinction in Burma; and "Youth Divisions," originally made up of student volunteers, could also be counted among the army's elite units.

But the bulk of the Nationalist Army had not been affected by the work of reorganization undertaken by the Americans during the war. It was made up of units of mediocre quality, which were deeply rooted in obsolete military traditions; the worst were the troops of Wang Ching-wei's puppet government, who were taken into the Nationalist Army after the defeat of Japan. To these units, directly subordinate to Nationalist command, could be added local troops in the pay of the war lords, as well as a large but indeterminable number of miscellaneous militiamen (1,500,000, at least). All of these units, with the exception of one armored and several cavalry brigades, were infantry brigades. Each brigade consisted, at least theoretically, of three infantry regiments and one or two battalions of artillery. Their light weapons were in general abundant, though sometimes mixed in origin; a third were of American make, a third were of Japanese origin, and the rest came from Chinese and various other sources. The state of discipline was extremely uneven, being very poor in most of the armies, and barely acceptable in the armies of the central government. Although the quality of junior commanders was generally satisfactory, command at the higher levels was deplorable. Good Nationalist generals, such as Fu Tso-yi, Pai Ch'ung-hsi, and Chiu Ching-chuan, were very few. Finally, the technical services were practically nonexistent. Generals never gave due consideration to the importance of regular re-

---

[9] The designation, "new" army, referred to Chinese forces (the "X-Force") originally organized and trained in India by General Joseph Stilwell, who led them in the invasion of Burma in 1944. See F. F. Liu, *A Military History of Modern China, 1924–1949* (Princeton University Press, 1956), p. 215. *Tr.*

supply of weapons, rations, or ammunition. The medical service was wholly inadequate. The soldiers—ill-fed, ill-paid, short of ammunition—thought mostly about looting. Although those Nationalist field armies that had been trained by the Americans were of comparatively good quality, thanks to the relative regularity of their supply and pay, most of the Nationalist forces bore a far greater resemblance to the Chinese hordes of the past than to modern armies.

Consequently, morale was low. Undernourished conscripts, forcibly drafted by the uncontrolled authority of village bosses, arrived in training camps, often completely exhausted, only to find a more deplorable and harsher life. Yet, when well trained, well fed and well led, the Chinese peasant, extremely enduring and patient, intelligent, and not without courage, can become an excellent soldier—provided he has faith in a cause. The Communists undertook to prove this point; but Nationalist officers never proved themselves to be capable of infusing their men with faith in the cause for which they fought. These officers, themselves extremely poor because of miserable pay, afflicted by a fearful feeling of inferiority toward their adversaries, often indulged in corruption and ended, finally, in treason.

The Navy

The Nationalist Navy, though relatively small, enjoyed total superiority over the Communists, who had no naval forces at all. It consisted of a small core of warships, the largest of which was the ex-British cruiser *Aurora*, rechristened *Chung-king*, and a large number of gunboats. To these there were soon added 131 landing craft (LCT, LSM, LCI, LST, and so forth) turned over to China by the United States shortly after V-J Day. Also, the Americans rapidly established a naval training center at Tsingtao, where a total of three hundred officers and ten thousand enlisted men of the Nationalist Navy were trained in modern methods.

The major missions the Nationalist Navy should have accomplished were interdiction of arms-smuggling by junks on the big rivers (especially the Yangtze), and attack of enemy forces moving close to the coasts (for example, along the Liaoning corridor). The Chinese Navy was incapable of accomplishing either of these tasks. Its morale was low and its officers, among whom corruption was rife, often found it more profitable to protect smuggling than to stop it.

The Air Force

It was in 1929, at the time the Central Military Academy was founded at Nanking, that the Chinese bethought themselves of the need for an air force. Two years later, in 1931, a Central Aviation School was established at Hangchow, near Shanghai, under the auspices of a private American mission supported by T. V. Soong. While this school vegetated for lack of means, all the war lords decided to create their own private air forces. Thus, in Yunnan and Szechwan, in Kwangtung, Kwangsi, and Manchuria, a hodgepodge of aviation units appeared, each with assorted types of aircraft lacking in spare parts as well as in standardization. Actually, there was no Chinese Air Force. Fortunately, toward the end of 1936 a retired American colonel, Claire Chennault, was able to hire out to China some Northrop, Douglas, and Martin aircraft, and about one hundred trained American pilots, who fought heroically at the outbreak of the war against Japan. The Russians also contributed to the struggle by sending a mission with some IL–15 and IL–16 fighters. In 1938 even an international squadron was organized in China.

During the war (November 1943) the "Flying Tigers" became an official Sino-American force, designated the "Chinese-

American Composite Wing" and equipped with P-40 fighters, B-25 light bombers, and C-47 transports.

This force achieved some remarkable successes, shooting down six hundred Japanese fighters and sinking seven thousand boats along the coasts. Little by little the Chinese Air Force became independent, thanks to pilots and mechanics trained in the United States, and to the eight schools[10] set up in China. Organized with five fighter groups (one with P-40's and four with P-51's), two medium bombardment groups (B-25), one heavy bombardment group (B-24), one reconnaissance squadron (P-38), and two transport groups (C-47), this air force had a grand total of 500 aircraft—including 200 fighters, 60 medium bombers, 30 heavy bombers, 15 reconnaissance and 120 transport planes. At war's end the supply of spare parts for these aircraft, left in place by the departing Fourteenth U.S. Air Force, was theoretically sufficient. But soon the Nationalists' lack of organization, of skill, and of honesty diminished the number of operationally ready aircraft on line, despite the efforts of the Air Advisory Division of the Joint U.S. Military Advisory Group. The same was true of the infrastructure—airfields and radio installations—which, left in place by the Americans, would have been more than adequate had they been properly maintained. The Nationalist Air Force should have played a considerable role in the civil war against the Communists. But its poor organization, its poor doctrine, its poor leadership, the dissimilar training and poor morale of its key personnel, made its services far fewer than those which could normally have been expected of such a force. It was only in transport operations that it gained some

[10] These schools were the following: General Staff School at Nanking; Air Academy at Hangchow; Logistics School at Nanking; Meteorology School at Shanghai; a school for mechanics and radiomen at Chengtu; Antiaircraft Defense School at Peking; Medical Service School at Hankow; and a recruit training center at Chungking.

measure of success by supplying encircled garrisons until the arrival of relieving forces.

THE COMMUNIST ARMIES

On paper the regular Communist forces appeared to be very much inferior to the Nationalist armies. To be sure, they had grown very rapidly, increasing from 10,000 men in 1928 to 300,000 in 1945; but only half of these men had firearms, and the weapons of those who had them were of largely obsolete and widely assorted varieties.

These forces were at first organized in regiments of one thousand men; but eventually the "column," with an average strength of ten thousand men, became the standard tactical organization. The column comprised two light divisions, each division consisting of three or four regiments of fifteen hundred men each. Equipment was obtained, very soon after V-J Day, by the disarming of Japanese units in Manchuria as well as in China; but it was American matériel, captured from the Nationalists, which was to provide the great bulk of Communist equipment. As for Russian matériel, it was almost never seen in the hands of Chinese Communists. They went into the Civil War with fewer than six hundred pieces of artillery, and with no tanks at all. Ammunition was procured from the primitive arsenals which the Communists were to perfect gradually during the war, or captured from the enemy, or purchased from smugglers. The real strength of the Communist armies was to be found not in material factors, but in their morale, their discipline, and their leadership. Thanks to their program of daily "indoctrination," the Communists succeeded in infusing their troops with a faith which was to sustain unhesitating willingness to fight to the death for the triumph of their cause. They were thus to succeed in making the Chinese soldier an upright and disciplined fighting man, who was to obtain the help and friendship of the people because, for the first time in centuries, he would pay for what he took and would never pillage the peasantry.

Communist officers, trained at the Yenan military academy in an atmosphere of austerity and enthusiasm, were to enjoy the advantage of being led by intelligent and audacious chiefs whose aggressive spirit was to provide a striking contrast to the conservatism and defensive spirit of Chiang Kai-shek's commanders.

Finally, the Red Army was to find, in the joint leadership of Chu Teh and Mao Tse-tung, a high command of extraordinary quality.

As early as 1936, Mao, in his book *The Strategy of Revolutionary War in China*[11] had prescribed with remarkable clarity the strategy and tactics the Red Army was to employ until the time of its success in attaining equality of force with the enemy:

A vast semi-colonial country that is unevenly developed politically and economically and that has gone through a great revolution; a powerful enemy; a weak and small Red Army; and the agrarian revolution—these are the four principal characteristics of China's revolutionary war. They determine the guiding line for China's revolutionary war and its strategic and tactical principles. The first and fourth characteristics determine the possibility of the Chinese Red Army growing and defeating its enemy. The second and third characteristics determine the impossibility of the Chinese Red Army growing speedily or defeating its enemy quickly, or in other words, they determine the protracted nature of the war and, if things go wrong, the possibility of the war ending in failure.

These are the two aspects of China's revolutionary war. They exist simultaneously, that is, there are favorable as well as difficult

[11] Usually known in this country by the title *Strategic Problems of China's Revolutionary War. Tr.*

conditions. This is the fundamental law of China's revolutionary war, from which many other laws are derived. The history of ten years of our war has proved the validity of this law. He who has eyes but does not see these laws of a fundamental nature cannot direct China's revolutionary war, cannot lead the Red Army to win victories.

It is quite clear that, in order to determine correctly our strategic direction, it is necessary to solve correctly all problems of principle, as for instance: *against* adventurism during offensive operations, *against* conservatism while on the defensive, and *against* flight-ism when shifting our forces; *against* guerrilla-ism in the Red Army, yet *for* its guerrilla character; *against* protracted campaigns and a strategy of quick decision, and *for* a strategy of protracted war and campaigns of quick decision; *against* fixed operational fronts and positional warfare, and *for* fluid operational fronts and mobile warfare; *against* the mere routing of the enemy, and *for* a war of annihilation; *against* the principle of striking with both fists, and *for* the principle of striking with one fist; *against* a large rear area and *for* a small rear area; *against* absolute centralized command and *for* a relatively centralized command; *against* the purely military viewpoint and the idea of roving insurgents, but *for* the view that the Red Army is a propagandist and organizer of the Chinese revolution; *against* banditry and *for* strict political discipline; *against* warlordism and *for* a democratic way of life within limits and authoritative military discipline; *against* an incorrect sectarian cadres policy and *for* a correct cadres policy; *against* isolationism and *for* the winning over of all possible allies; and finally, *against* keeping the Red Army at its old stage and *for* striving to bring it to a new stage.[12]

Such a doctrine, perfectly executed due to unity of command and complete agreement among all the army leaders, was to prove itself extremely effective. Yet the final victory to which it led was far from easy to foresee.

[12] The English translation is from *Mao Tse-tung: Selected Works*, vol. I: *1926–1936* (New York: International Publishers, 1954), pp. 197–198. Quoted by permission of International Publishers. *Tr.*

In addition to its regular units, the Red Army was composed of two other kinds of forces. The *ming ping*, or militia, were charged with local defense and support of the regular forces. Formed mainly from peasant volunteers, they were poorly armed but capable of reinforcing the regulars when needed. These men made their own primitive weapons— medieval scythes and bills, hand grenades stuffed with nails, wooden cannon firing stones or shrapnel balls, old muskets dating back to the T'ai-p'ing Rebellion. At the end of 1945 these militiamen numbered about 700,000. Lastly, the Red forces included innumerable guerrilla groups, based in the mountainous wilds of Shantung and South China, on Hainan, in Kwangtung, Kwangsi, even in Fukien. These groups attacked local Nationalist forces, cut communications, and devoted themselves to intensive propaganda work. Chiang Kai-shek, who concentrated all his efforts upon the regular Communist forces in the north, neglected them. But when the over-all balance of opposing forces started to change, these guerrillas were to play a considerable role.

In brief, when the Civil War broke out all foreign observers predicted a quick victory for a Chiang Kai-shek, who, haloed by the nimbus of triumph over Japan, was assured of American aid as well as the neutrality of the U.S.S.R. But the factor of morale was to show itself, once again, to be decisive in war. It is not enough to have soldiers and weapons: soldiers must have the will to use their weapons, or nothing can be done. Behind matériel, there is always man. In our own times, as in the days of Marshal de Saxe, "It is deep in the human heart that one must seek the secret of victories."

CHAPTER IV ❖

From Japan's Surrender
to the
Arrival of General Marshall

A̲ᴛ the time of Japan's surrender the situation, so far as geography was concerned, favored the Communists. Red guerrillas held almost all of North China, and had reached as far south as the Yangtze. On 4 September Yenan announced: "We hold the entire region stretching from Kalgan to the mouth of the Yangtze, and from Shansi to the China Sea, except for the largest cities and some fortified points along the railroads." In September Weihaiwei and almost all of Shantung, as well as more than half of Hopeh and all of Kiangsu north of the Yangtze, fell into the hands of the Reds. Aided by the cells they had established in all the large cities, there is no doubt that the Communists could have occupied Shanghai and Wuhan, had they not feared diplomatic complications.[1] In any case, they were well poised to seize political power in North and Central China, to occupy the historic cities of Peking and Tientsin, and to be the first to enter Manchuria.

[1] They nevertheless occupied Wuhu, a large rice port on the Yangtze.

A good strategy for Chiang, whose prestige was now at its zenith, would have been to consolidate his position south of the Yangtze and then move forward cautiously, at the same time trying to regain the confidence of the peasants by implementing a program of agrarian reform. For the Generalissimo, however, any loss of face was unthinkable. Thus the mastery of North China had at all costs to be his, and the Nationalists had to be the first into Manchuria. In view of the vast distances which separated these territories from the Nationalist bases in South China, Szechwan and Yunnan, such an operation could not but be extremely difficult. But Chiang Kai-shek counted on American support, which he was indeed to obtain.

For the Communists, abandoned by Russia as they were, the problem was to take as many territorial bargaining counters as possible, in order to negotiate for a coalition government which would permit them to persist in their propaganda.

The Russians, little desirous of diplomatic complications with the United States, adhered fairly strictly to the "Big Four" agreements, and did not help the Chinese Reds significantly in their rush to occupy Manchuria. As for the Americans—misled as they were by Hurley, by the charm of Mme. Chiang, and by the craftiness of Chinese diplomats in Washington—they committed themselves completely to the military and economic support of the Nationalist government.

In China, two acts were to be played simultaneously: the negotiations at Chungking and, throughout the entire country, the race to occupy strategic points.

At Chungking the two sides reached agreement, in principle, on many points, but remained opposed on the two main questions: the army, and control of the regions liberated by the Reds. With regard to the composition of a new national army, the Reds laid claim to a proportional strength of forty-eight divisions, while the Nationalists, projecting a peacetime total strength of no more than one hundred divisions, would grant the Reds only twenty. As for the second question, the Chungking government wanted to name all the governors of provinces and the mayors of large cities, while the Reds wanted to retain their own men at the head of the regions they had occupied.

On 11 October the government published the record of its conversations with the Communists. This text reflected the same difficulties. The Communists had agreed to withdraw their troops from Kwangtung, Chekiang, southern Kiangsu, southern and central Anhwei, Hunan, Hupeh, and southern Honan, and to a gradual concentration of these forces to the north of the Lunghai railroad[2] and in northern Anhwei and Kiangsu. After prolonged discussion, they had indicated that they would be satisfied with the governorships of Shenkanning,[3] Jehol, Chahar, Hopeh, and Shantung; the vice-governorships of Shansi and Suiyuan; and the installation of Communist deputy mayors in Peking, Tientsin, and Tsingtao. Finally, they had asked for authorization to accept the surrender of Japanese troops. On these major points, agreement could not be reached. Mao Tse-tung, who had come to Chungking for the negotiations, went back to Yenan, and the Civil War was on.

As the fighting began, the Nationalist government received the support of the Japanese, and of puppet troops, who attacked the Communists in Central China. On 21 October, Mao, a better strategist than Chiang Kai-shek, announced that he was evacuating his forces from regions south of the Yangtze; in North China, he concentrated his forces and destroyed all

[2] This line, which runs from Tunghai westward through Suchow, Kaifeng, and Loyang to Sian, was to play a highly important role in military operations of the Civil War.

[3] The Communist Border Region, incorporating parts of Shensi, Kansu, and Ningsia. Its principal town was Yenan, Mao's capital.

the railroads in order to slow down the movements of the Nationalists.

Influenced by Ambassador Hurley, the government on 10 November presented new proposals to Mao. Regarding the political problem, it proposed that the Political Consultative Conference, the supreme legislative organ, be composed of eight Nationalists, seven Communists, thirteen members from other parties, and nine non-party members. In the military sphere, the Communists were to cease the cutting of communications and remain where they were until the government decided upon new zones to be assigned each division. The Communists refused to accept these proposals; on 25 November Chou En-lai, in his turn, left Chungking.

In the face of this complete failure, General Hurley resigned, vehemently accusing the professional diplomats, especially George Atcheson and John Service, of undermining his policies and playing the game of the Communists. The fact was that they had simply shown more discernment and foresight than Hurley had. So too had General Wedemeyer, who had written, on 20 November:

I have recommended to the Generalissimo that he should concentrate his efforts upon establishing control in north China and upon the prompt execution of political and official reforms designed to remove the practice of corruption by officials and to eliminate prohibitive taxes.[4]

He further stated:

The Generalissimo will be able to stabilize the situation in south China provided he accepts the assistance of foreign administrators and technicians and engages in political, economic and social reforms through honest, competent civilian officials.[5]

[4] U.S. Department of State, *United States Relations with China, with Special Reference to the Period 1944–1949* (U.S. Government Printing Office, 1949), p. 131. *Tr.*
[5] *Ibid. Tr.*

On the other hand, Wedemeyer did not believe that it would be possible to stabilize the situation in North China unless there was an agreement with the Communists; as for a Nationalist occupation of Manchuria, it was impossible without an agreement between Chiang, the Chinese Communists, and the U.S.S.R.[6]

But Chiang did not care to follow this wise advice, and persisted in sending his best armies into Manchuria—a strategic trap from which they were never to escape.

THE MILITARY OPERATIONS

As soon as the Japanese government announced its intention to accept a cease-fire, the Communists, on order of Chu Teh, took the offensive in all of Northeast China.

On 19 August Chiang Kai-shek, whose troops were very poorly positioned for occupation of the large cities in the north, ordered the Reds to stay put. Yenan refused to obey: "We consider," wired the members of the CCP, "that you have sent us an erroneous order: this error is very serious. We are thus obliged to inform you that we refuse to carry out this order." Chiang Kai-shek then turned to the Americans for help. By his General Order No. 1, General MacArthur directed Japanese troops to surrender only to Nationalist forces and, pending the arrival of the latter, to "maintain order" in the areas they occupied. As American planes prepared to transport Nationalist armies to the north, clashes broke out between the Japanese and the Reds, and between the Communists and the Nationalists as well. The Japanese, who in a moment of post-defeat depression had evacuated Kalgan on 20 August, now pulled themselves together and prevented the Reds from laying hold of Peking, Tientsin, and Shanghai.

[6] See *ibid*, p. 132, for this portion of Wedemeyer's report of 20 November 1945. *Tr.*

57

As rapidly as possible, the Nationalists sent their troops into the large cities. On 25 August the New Sixth Army, of Burma fame, entered Nanking. On 10 September the Ninety-fourth Army moved into Shanghai. A few days later the Third Army occupied Hankow. As early as 9 September, General Li established a forward echelon of Chiang Kai-shek's headquarters at Peking. On the 16th, Yenan voiced bitter complaints about attacks on its Eighth Route Army in Shantung and Shansi, where the Reds had been forced to abandon Chaocheng and Wencheng. On the 17th, the first Nationalist units entered Peking.

Meanwhile, General Wedemeyer had moved to Shanghai, whence he declared that his government would assist China "in evacuating Japanese occupation troops," whose number amounted to some two million men. Also, on 20 September Chiang requested the United States to land American troops at Shanghai, Nanking, Peking, and Tientsin, "to aid the Chinese in disarming the Japanese." The next day, ships of the British Navy and the U.S. Fifth Fleet entered the great harbor of Shanghai. The American action induced the angry Communists to withdraw their troops, little by little, from Central and North China. They hoped for better breaks from the Russians, who now occupied all of Manchuria, and they did, in fact, succeed in infiltrating the countryside and in disarming numerous groups of Japanese.

Because it throws light upon the Chinese mentality, it is interesting to note that the two sides now adopted strategic plans which were curiously reminiscent of maneuverings in the bygone days of the ancient Chou and T'ang dynasties. In China, from earliest times, kingdoms based in Shensi always attempted to apply what the classics call the "horizontal plan": the conquest of a strip of land which, following the course of the Yellow River, would extend eastward from Shensi to the sea. The states of the south, on the other hand, always sought

58

to apply the "vertical plan," which called for the formation of a north-south bulwark capable of confining their enemies to the west. "A study of the map of North China," says C. P. Fitzgerald,

will show that these rival plans embody abiding strategic verities conditioned by unchanging geographical facts, which will remain true in all ages. Similar plans were framed in the civil wars of 1923–30, and during every contest between the western hill provinces and the great eastern plain, the "horizontal" and "vertical" plans of the ancient Chou strategists reappear in all essentials unchanged.[7]

It was American aid to the Nationalists which alone prevented Mao from accomplishing the horizontal plan. On 30 September the U.S. 1st Marine Division landed at Tientsin; on 1 October the Marines were at Tangku; on 7 October they received, in the name of Chiang Kai-shek, the surrender of eighteen thousand Japanese troops. In a parallel move, Russian naval forces under Rear Admiral Tichanovitch landed at Port Arthur on 2 October. Chinese Red forces, armed mostly with weapons captured from the Japanese and their Chinese collaborators, were moving into Manchuria by way of Jehol; the Manchurian soviets, which had been founded in 1935 and had gone underground during the Japanese occupation, were being resurrected. On 7 October Admiral Daniel Barbey's Seventh U.S. Amphibious Force entered the harbor at Chefoo, but then withdrew in order to avoid incidents with the Reds, who controlled the city. On 9 October, two thousand American Marines arrived at Peking. The next day they occupied Tsingtao, where they established an important base. A total of 53,000 U.S. Marines took over from the Japanese in the historic key cities, to the accompaniment of mounting Com-

[7] C. P. Fitzgerald, *Son of Heaven: A Biography of Li Shih-min, Founder of the T'ang Dynasty* (Cambridge University Press, 1933), p. 51.

munist anger and incidents which flared up, almost everywhere, between their forces and the Americans.

The Americans were now too deeply involved to be completely neutral. On the contrary, General Stratemeyer, complying with Chiang Kai-shek's desire to move forces into North China as rapidly as possible, put the U.S. Tenth Air Force at his disposal. Under General Hegenberger, 235 Dakotas[8] airlifted three Chinese armies, totaling 110,000 men, from the south to the north in record time. The Ninety-fourth Army was transported from Liuchow to Shanghai, and thence to Peking, where it arrived on 26 October; the Ninety-second Army was lifted from Hankow to Peking on the 28th; lastly, the Third Army was moved from Chihkiang to Nanking. These were elite troops, equipped and trained by the Americans.

The northward movement of the Nationalists continually produced local clashes with the Communists and, as the situation became more and more confused, each side accused the other of provoking civil war. Yenan's communiqués accused the central government's troops of attacking—sometimes with Japanese assistance—and occupying Communist-liberated areas in various regions of China from Canton to the Inner Mongolian province of Suiyuan. For his part, General Fu Tso-yi, Governor of Suiyuan and commander of the 12th War Zone, on 26 October accused the Communists of attacking the government troops in his province with forces amounting to some 100,000 men. In rebuttal, a Communist communiqué claimed that the government troops had attacked Red forces as they were withdrawing from Chekiang toward the north, and that a Communist brigade had suffered severe losses in a sixteen-hour battle near Hangchow. General Ho Ying-ch'in[9] had

[8] C–47 (or DC–3) aircraft. *Tr.*
[9] At this time General Ho was Chief of the Supreme Staff of the Nationalist armed forces. *Tr.*

already stated that the Chinese Communists wanted to obstruct the movement of Nationalist troops from Chungking to Peking and Tientsin, where they were to receive the surrender of the Japanese. Battles were being waged along the Peking-Hankow railroad; localities in Hunan were under attack by the Communists, who controlled two thirds of Shantung; on 28 October new outbreaks of fighting were reported in Shansi, whose governor accused Communist forces, coming from Hopeh, Honan, and Shantung, of cutting his communications.

At the end of October the general situation was as follows: in Central China, Nationalist troops were swamping the retreating Reds, who destroyed the railroads and implanted stay-behind guerrilla cadres as they withdrew. The Nationalists occupied almost all the large cities, and were attempting to assure their control of the major lines of communication. But the big question remained that of Manchuria, for the invasion of which Chiang had concentrated in the Peking area the Third, Eighty-fourth, and Thirty-second armies. Indeed, as the Nationalist information minister once remarked to Chiang: "Without Manchuria, China is like Italy; with Manchuria, it is like India."

By virtue of its geographic position, its resources, its communications, and its ease of exploitation, Manchuria is destined to become one of the key regions of the world, like Pennsylvania, the Donets Basin, or the Ruhr. With an area of over 500,000 square miles—as large as France, Germany, and the British Isles combined—Manchuria is an immense sunken plain lying between two mountain chains: the Great and Little Khingans in the west, and the crystalline chain of the Korean and Chang Pai ranges in the east. Its exceptional importance is due, above all, to its mineral resources. It has enormous reserves of coal, estimated at ten billion tons, echeloned between Mukden, Kirin, Ningan, and the lower Sungari.

61

The best known of the Manchurian mines are those at Fushun, about twenty-five miles east of Mukden, which is the largest open-pit mine in the world, with reserves estimated at four billion tons; and those at Taluyentai, about twenty-eight miles south of Mukden. Before the war the annual production of coal exceeded ten million tons; under the Japanese, Manchurian coal production reached thirty million tons per year, as much as the output of all the rest of China.

Coal alone would be insufficient, but Manchuria also possesses the second element necessary to the build-up of a powerful heavy industry: iron. Although yielding only ores of low grade, the mines of Liaoning (at Anshan, Kungchuling, and Penki), and those of the Suanlung district in Chahar, have produced up to three million tons of cast-iron. Moreover, the Japanese discovered large beds of excellent ore at Tungpientao, in the valley of the Yalu in Korea, where they promptly built numerous blast furnaces and thermal electric power plants under the direction of a very powerful trust, the Manchuria Heavy Industry Company. In addition to iron and coal, Manchuria also possesses hydroelectric power (as witnessed by the dams on the Yalu and the Sungari), gold, copper, silver, lead, magnesium, and large saline deposits.

In fifty years its population had by 1945 risen from twenty to forty million inhabitants; factories of all kinds had been built; lastly, by 1939 its communications net had reached a total of over six thousand miles of railroads, eighteen thousand miles of roads, and 2,900 miles of airways.

For these reasons Chiang Kai-shek considered the conquest of Manchuria to be absolutely necessary. Despite the difficulty of achieving such a conquest, one can understand why he undertook the campaign which was to lead to his defeat.

The agreements signed on 14 August between the Chinese

Nationalists and the Russians[10] called for the evacuation of Manchuria by Soviet troops to begin on 15 November, a provision which presupposed the arrival of Nationalist troops to relieve the Russians. But the Communist Eighth Route Army, by active resistance as well as destruction of railroads, effectively barred the movement of Chiang's armies into Manchuria by land. Some other way had to be found to prevent Manchuria from falling prey to the Communists; and it was the U.S. Navy that offered the solution to the Generalissimo's problem. Under the command of Vice Admiral Barbey, the transports of Admiral Kinkaid's Seventh Fleet embarked two Chinese armies at ports in southern China and set forth for Manchuria. The most suitable ports of debarkation were Dairen and Port Arthur, from which the railroads would have afforded the Nationalist divisions rapid access to the heart of Manchuria. But the Russian authorities, taking cover in the clause of the Sino-Soviet agreement of 14 August which limited the use of the ports to Russian or Chinese ships, refused entry to the American transports.

There remained the small fishing ports, such as Antung, Yingkow, and Hulutao. But here a new difficulty arose: the Russians had evacuated these ports several days in advance of the planned date, and had been replaced by Chinese Communist forces that were firmly determined to prevent any Nationalist landings. Admiral Barbey, refusing to run the risk of becoming directly involved in the struggle between the Nationalists and the Communists, ordered his ships to withdraw. Finally, on 1 November, troops were disembarked at

[10] The Sino-Soviet Treaty was signed in Moscow by T. V. Soong. In return for the Chinese concessions regarding Port Arthur, Dairen, and the Manchurian railroads, the Russians agreed to evacuate Manchuria and turn the region over to Nationalist forces. Also, Chiang Kai-shek's regime was the only Chinese government recognized by Moscow.

Chinwangtao, which the Japanese had retaken from the Chinese Communists and turned over, in October, to the U.S. Navy. This port was located on the Tientsin-Shanhaikwan railroad, which was being guarded by American Marines as well as Nationalist troops. The Communists accused the U.S. Navy of another landing of Nationalist troops at Shanhaikwan, a port near the eastern end of the Great Wall. In this embarrassing situation, Admiral Barbey on 4 November conferred with the Nationalists and the Russian authorities regarding the possibility of his access to Yingkow, where—as at Chinwangtao—the Chinese Communists held the hinterland. On 8 November the Communist newspaper *New China Daily* declared that General Chu Teh, commander of the Communist 18th Group Army, had written to General Wedemeyer in protest against the following facts: (1) American forces had seized Communist office facilities at Tientsin, and disarmed and interrogated the office personnel; (2) American planes had strafed Communist-held Antze, in Hopeh; (3) American planes had dropped propaganda leaflets calling for Communist withdrawal from Kuan, in Hopeh.

These complaints led General Wedemeyer, on 8 November, to define the American position. He declared that for the protection of American lives he was determined to keep lines of communication open in North China with all the means at his disposal. At the same time, he specified that the American forces had no other mission than that of assisting the central government in its task of reoccupying strategic positions formerly held by the Japanese, and of disarming Japanese troops. Mr. James Byrnes[11] supported Wedemeyer by emphasizing the fact that the surrender of two million Japanese soldiers had not yet been effected. General Wedemeyer

[11] The Secretary of State at this time. *Tr.*

further specified that American forces would, in any case, stay completely out of China's civil conflict and that, beginning on 15 November, the 53,000 American Marines would evacuate North China. Despite these assurances, the Communists on 10 November appealed to President Truman and the American people to bring Wedemeyer's intervention to an end, while the *New China Daily* voiced further complaints against the alleged use of American aircraft to provide daily resupply for Nationalist troops engaged against the Communists.

As for the Russians, they carefully kept out of the conflict. On 10 November Marshal Malinovsky informed General Tu Yü-ming that the Soviet evacuation of Manchuria would be effected in three phases: (1) evacuation of areas to the south of Mukden in the period from 2 to 10 December; (2) evacuation of areas to the south of Harbin by 25 November; (3) evacuation of the remainder of Manchuria prior to 2 December. However, the Soviet command informed Chinese authorities that it would be unable to guarantee the security of Nationalist troops disembarking at Hulutao, in the Gulf of Liaotung, or near Antung, in the Gulf of Korea, due to the weakness of the small Russian detachments in these sectors. Following this phased withdrawal of Soviet troops, Chinese Nationalist forces would be free to land anywhere in Manchuria.

After all these difficulties the Nationalist forces found themselves compelled to enter Manchuria along the axis of the Tientsin-Mukden railroad which, skirting the coast beneath the steep cliffs of the Liaoning corridor, was easy to block. On 4 November some Yunnanese troops were redeployed from Indo-China and the Canton region and landed at Yingkow, which was evacuated by the Russians on the eighth; but they ran up against Communist blocking positions along the Liao River and made no progress. Along the main axis of the Nationalists' advance, fighting raged for two weeks around Shanhaikwan; on 16 November the Nationalists, who had attacked in force with tanks on the 10th, broke through the Communist defenses and resumed their slow northward advance along the railroad. Hulutao was taken on 24 November, but by now Chiang Kai-shek was beginning to realize that the occupation of Manchuria was going to be a long and arduous undertaking.

Chiang now feared that if the Russians evacuated Manchuria according to the planned schedule of withdrawal, the Chinese Communist forces that had penetrated the region by way of Chahar would have time to consolidate their hold before the arrival of his own troops—unless these were to be transported, once again, by air. Thus, he initiated negotiations with the Soviets, asking them to postpone their evacuation until the Nationalists could make good their occupation of the large cities; to permit his forces to use the airfields at Changchun, Mukden, Harbin, and Tsitsihar; and, finally, to prevent the penetration of armed Chinese Reds into the zone occupied by the Soviet Army. The Russians consented to a delay in their evacuation, a concession which permitted them to carry away with them, as prizes of war, all the heavy machinery, machine tools, railroad ties, and even office furniture —as well as 700,000 Japanese prisoners from the Kwantung Army. On the other hand, it appears that they scrupulously kept their promises, and that they refrained from any systematic aid to the lodgment of Lin Piao's Red forces in Manchuria. But the Red Chinese, proceeding as they did in the days of Japanese domination, contented themselves with infiltrating the countryside and bypassing the Russian-held population centers.

Lin Piao's forces, which had come from Yenan and the Communist base in northern Shansi, now controlled all of Chahar and rural Manchuria. As of November 1945 their strength, according to a statement by General P'eng Te-huai, was about 300,000 men, 100,000 being regulars of the Eighth Route Army or the New Fourth Army, supplemented by Manchurian volunteers and soldiers from the Tung Pei Army of Chang Hsüeh-liang, whose brother was proclaimed governor of Liaoning. These forces, gathered under the name of the "Democratic Army of the Northeast," had taken Chengteh, encircled Tatung, and occupied a large part of Jehol. Applying their methods of instituting "agrarian democracy" and popular representation, the Communists solidly established themselves in the northern and western parts of Manchuria, disarmed small groups of Japanese troops and their collaborators, and awaited only the departure of the Russians before jumping off against the cities.

Yet Chiang Kai-shek continued to rush his troops to the north: before the end of November, three Nationalist armies had been successively concentrated in the area north of Peking. On 22 November some of these forces stormed the pass at Nankow and chased the Communists out of Jehol. By the beginning of December the Nationalist advance guard was at Tahushan, about sixty miles southwest of Mukden. On 12 December the Soviets confirmed their intention to permit Nationalist entry into Manchuria by air, land, and sea; on the 13th, some air-transported Nationalist troops were landed at Mukden, which the Russians had not yet evacuated.

Two days later President Truman made an official statement on American policy in China in which he announced that, having accepted the resignation of General Hurley, he had decided to send General George Marshall, the illustrious soldier who had led the American armies to victory in World

War II, to the Far East, as an arbiter charged with the mission of making peace between the Nationalists and Communists in China.

On 23 December, the date of Marshall's arrival in China, the strategic situation was as follows: the Nationalists had regained almost complete control of the large cities to the south of the Lunghai railroad, except for a small area in Kiangsi. In North China they held Peking, Tientsin, the Mukden railroad, Taiyuan, Tatung, and the western part of the Pingsui railroad (Peking to Paotow). But they had failed to clear, in their entirety, the vital Peking-Hankow and Tientsin-Shanghai railroads, a failure which seriously handicapped the logistical support of the crack armies that the Nationalists had hurled into Manchuria. For their part, the Communists, still based primarily in the Shenkanning Border Region, remained powerful in Shansi, Hopeh, Jehol, and in Chahar, where they held Kalgan. They were strong in the western parts of Manchuria, and retained isolated but important nuclei of power in Kiangsu, Honan, and the near vicinity of Hankow.

American aid to Nationalist China continued, and the plan to equip thirty-nine divisions and eight and one-third air groups was still in effect. Without any doubt, it was the American navy and air force that enabled Chiang Kai-shek to gain the considerable Nationalist successes which marked the end of 1945. From this fact resulted the mounting exasperation of the Communists, and a clearly discernible change in the tone of their pronouncements regarding the United States. General Marshall was to find himself confronted by an insoluble problem. Rapidly realizing this, and yet faithfully striving for a solution, he was destined to end his mission in discouraged departure.

PART TWO

1946

THE MARSHALL MISSION, ITS
FAILURE, AND THE PERIOD OF
NATIONALIST SUCCESSES

CHAPTER V ✧

The Marshall Mission

Hurley's failure and Marshall's arrival in Chungking forced the Kuomintang—at least theoretically—into the path of reform. Chiang Kai-shek knew that he would not be able to dupe the former American Chief of Staff as he had the ex-cowboy;[1] so he decided to play the "good democrat" in order to retain American aid and convince the new envoy of his good faith.

Thus, as early as 31 December 1945, the government announced that the Political Consultative Conference, agreed upon in principle by the Kuomintang and Yenan in October 1945, would convene on 10 January 1946. At the same time the government suggested the formation of a "Committee of Three," composed of a representative from each of the two sides with General Marshall as chairman and arbiter. Yenan accepted and designated Chou En-lai; Chungking named General Chang Chun as its representative. The committee went into action immediately, and held its first meeting on 7 January 1946. Right at the outset, General Marshall voiced his view that, given the international agreements which had been signed by the United States and the U.S.S.R., the Nationalist

[1] Before he became one of the most powerful members of the Republican party, Patrick Hurley had been a cowboy, a miner, and a lawyer.

government ought to be able to reoccupy Manchuria without any interference from the Communists. In an extraordinary development, Chou En-lai agreed. Thus, on 10 January 1946, Marshall could report to Truman that a truce had been concluded on the following bases:

All units, regular, militia, irregular and guerrilla, of the National Armies of the Republic of China and of Communist-led troops of the Republic of China are ordered to carry out the following directive:

a. All hostilities will cease immediately.

b. Except in certain specific cases, all movements of forces in China will cease. There also may be the movements necessary for demobilization, redisposition, supply, administration and local security.

c. Destruction of and interference with all lines of communications will cease, and . . . obstructions placed against or interfering with such lines of communications (will be cleared at once).

d. An Executive Headquarters will be established immediately in Peking for the purpose of carrying out the agreements for cessation of hostilities. This Headquarters will consist of three Commissioners; one representing the Chinese National Government, one representing the Chinese Communist Party, and one to represent the United States of America.[2] The necessary instructions and orders unanimously agreed upon by the three Commissioners will be issued in the name of the President of the Republic of China, through the Executive Headquarters.[3]

This declaration then went on to specify that the order did not apply to the military movements south of the Yangtze provided for in the government's plan for military reorganization, nor to movements of Nationalist forces into (or within) Manchuria for the purpose of restoring Chinese sov-

[2] Mr. Walter S. Robertson, American Chargé d'Affaires in China, became the U.S. representative. Tr.

[3] U.S. Department of State, United States Relations with China, with Special Reference to the Period 1944–1949 (U.S. Government Printing Office, 1949), p. 609. Tr.

ereignty. This "Cessation of Hostilities Order" was made effective as of midnight, 13 January, and the Executive Headquarters at Peking began to function as early as the 14th.

In a parallel move, the Political Consultative Conference opened its session by hearing a declaration from Chiang Kai-shek which promised the people democratic rights and freedoms and the end of the period of tutelage provided for by Sun Yat-sen. It was all there: freedom of thought, of speech, of assembly, of association; equality of rights for all; liberation of political prisoners. This magnificent program was approved by all the parties—the Communists, the Democratic League, the Young China Party—but it aroused severe criticism within the reactionary faction of the Kuomintang. Meanwhile, the Conference agreed upon numerous projects: reorganization of the government, reconstruction, revision of the draft Constitution of 1936; it set 5 May 1946 as the date for convocation of a National Constituent Assembly, to consist of 2,050 members; finally, it passed an important resolution on military problems. This resolution started off with a statement of fundamental principles: the Army belongs to the State; the soldier's duty is to protect the nation and love the people, and so on; the armed forces must be separated from the parties; they must keep out of politics; they must be under civilian control. The resolution then tackled the problem of a progressive reduction in army strength by calling for an initial cut to ninety divisions, and then reduction to a final strength of sixty divisions.

But the most difficult question was the division of troop strength between the Nationalists and the Communists. On 25 February 1946 the committee composed of Chang Chih-chung, Chou En-lai, and General Marshall[4] announced that

---

[4] This was the Military Sub-Committee, of which Marshall was the adviser, which held its first meeting on 14 February 1946. Tr.

agreement had been reached on this question, based upon the following points:

At the conclusion of 12 months the armies shall consist of 108 divisions of not to exceed 14,000 men each.[5] Of these, 18 shall be formed from Communist Forces.

The deployment of the armies at the end of the first 12 months shall be as follows:

NORTHEAST CHINA—5 armies, each consisting of 3 National divisions, each army with a National commander; and 1 army consisting of 3 Communist divisions with a Communist commander —total 6 armies.

NORTHWEST CHINA—5 armies each consisting of 3 National divisions each with a National commander—total 5 armies.

NORTH CHINA—3 armies each consisting of 3 National divisions, each with a National commander; and 4 army groups, each consisting of 1 National and 1 Communist army of 3 divisions. 2 army group commanders shall be National officers and 2 army group commanders shall be Communist officers—total 11 armies.

CENTRAL CHINA—9 armies, each consisting of 3 National divisions, each with a National commander; and 1 army consisting of 3 Communist divisions, with a Communist commander—total 10 armies.

SOUTH CHINA (including Formosa)—4 armies, each consisting of 3 National divisions, each with a National commander—total 4 armies.[6]

Following this initial reorganization, a second partial demobilization was to take place over a period of six months so that, within a total of eighteen months' time, the strength and deployment of the armed forces would be as follows:

NORTHEAST CHINA—1 army consisting of 2 National and 1 Communist Divisions with a National commander and 4 armies each consisting of 3 National divisions, each with a National commander—total 5 armies.

[5] The type-army was to consist of three divisions of not more than fourteen thousand men each, plus about 6,300 service troops, for a total of about 48,300 men (the rough equivalent of a U.S. corps. Tr.).

[6] U.S. Relations with China, pp. 623–624. Tr.

NORTHWEST CHINA—3 armies, each consisting of 3 National Divisions each with a National commander—total 3 armies.

NORTH CHINA—3 armies, each consisting of 1 National and 2 Communist divisions, each with a Communist commander; 1 army consisting of 2 National and 1 Communist divisions with a National commander; and 2 armies each consisting of 3 National divisions, each with a National commander—total 6 armies.

CENTRAL CHINA—1 army consisting of 1 National and 2 Communist divisions with a Communist commander and 3 armies each consisting of 3 National divisions, each with a National commander—total 4 armies.

SOUTH CHINA (including Formosa)—2 armies each consisting of 3 National divisions, each with a National commander—total 2 armies.[7]

Finally, by July 1947 the Chinese Army was to be reduced to sixty divisions, of which fifty were to be Nationalist and ten Communist. The maintenance of a "Peace Preservation Corps," in a strength not to exceed fifteen thousand men per province, was permitted, and its armament restricted to pistols, rifles, and automatic rifles. Pro-Japanese puppet troops, as well as irregulars, were to be disbanded as soon as possible.

This politico-military agreement was applauded throughout the entire country, which hoped that it would prove to be the means by which civil war could be avoided. The agreement clearly recognized the preponderant position of the Nationalists; but the Communists intended to profit from its recognition of their party by pursuing their propaganda efforts and winning the people over to their ideas. This frightened the right wing of the Kuomintang, and there were malcontents in Yenan, too; but, such as it was, the agreement was a victory for General Marshall, who sincerely believed that he had found the solution to an insoluble problem. In reality, each side remained fully determined to fight through to the complete destruction of its adversary.

[7] *Ibid.*, p. 625. Tr.

The agreement had hardly been signed when disorders broke out in Manchuria, where Nationalist troops, as agreed, were preparing to move in on the heels of a Russian withdrawal. At this time the Nationalists had only a few administrative delegates in Manchuria, charged with re-establishing the authority of the Nationalist government under the aegis of the Russian garrisons, plus some token forces in the cities. Outside the population centers, out in the countryside, the Red forces of Lin Piao were in control, and were infiltrating into all of northern and central Manchuria. Chiang Kai-shek and the Russians were playing a double game. On the one hand, Chinese public opinion clamored for the departure of the Russians, and students demonstrated in Chungking on 21 February; yet Chiang had asked the Russians to prolong their occupation until his own forces could replace them. For their part, the Soviets were quite content to prolong their sojourn in Manchuria, in such a manner as to dismantle and carry off to Siberia all the industrial machinery installed by the Japanese; yet, wishing to let the Chinese Communists take over Manchuria, they did not want to wait too long for the arrival of the Nationalists. By the end of February, Nationalist troops had occupied virtually all of the Liao Ho valley to the south of Mukden. As for the theoretically neutral Americans, they continued their aid to Chiang Kai-shek. On 10 March they transferred 271 small naval auxiliary craft to the Nationalists; they also formed at Nanking, on the same date, a "consultative commission,"[8] headed by Major General Robert B. McClure, for the purpose of reorganizing the Chinese Army along modern lines.

[8] The American designation for this body was Nanking Headquarters Command, which included the advisory groups for the three services and a Joint Advisory Staff to coordinate dealings with the Chinese government in general and the Ministry of Defense and Supreme Staff in particular. In September 1948 the designation was changed to Joint U.S. Military Advisory Group—China, or JUSMAG. See *U.S. Relations with China*, pp. 339–340. Tr.

On 23 March Chiang Kai-shek, pressed by public opinion, formally requested the Russians to evacuate Manchuria. Thanks to the American ships which had transported seven of his armies to the ports of the Gulf of Liaotung, he now felt strong enough for Manchuria. Marshal Malinovsky replied that he expected to complete his withdrawal by the end of April and, in any event, "before the Americans leave Chinese territory." The Russians did, in fact, evacuate Mukden on 12 March. Lin Piao's Communist forces immediately moved in, but were driven out on 13 March by the Nationalist Twenty-fifth Army, which was soon joined by the Fifty-second Army. Chiang Kai-shek's son, Chiang Ching-kuo, was made Governor of the Northeast Provinces. But, at the same time, the Communists were proclaiming people's governments in the provinces of Kirin and Heilungkiang.

The two sides now commenced to accuse each other of violating the truce. On 13 March, Ch'en Chi-ch'eng, the Nationalist commander in North China, claimed that the Reds had launched 220 attacks against the Nationalists, occupied 1,330 railroad stations, and invested twenty-six localities. Lu Chung-lin, the government's official representative in North China, declared that the Reds had practically isolated Peking, Tientsin, and Tsinan. For their part, the Communists charged that the Nationalists had attacked their troops in southern Manchuria and refused to send in a mixed pacification commission, or "field team,"[9] that they had encircled sixty thousand of their troops in the region of northern Hupeh and southern Honan, and, finally, that they had attempted to massacre Red forces in the Canton area. Officially,

[9] On 24 January 1946 General Marshall had proposed that a field team be sent out from Executive Headquarters in Manchuria to stop the fighting at Yingkow, and that similar action be taken in the event of further outbreaks of fighting between the Nationalists and the Communists. The Communists approved this proposal, but the National Government did not give its limited assent until 27 March 1946. See *U.S. Relations with China*, pp. 145–146. Tr.

Chiang Kai-shek abided by the rules of the game. On 15 March he freed General Yeh T'ing, former commander of the New Fourth Army, whom he had held prisoner since 1941; and he continued to proclaim his willingness to resolve the Manchurian problem by political means. Nevertheless, he refused to permit the entry of field teams into Manchuria, and deferred *sine die* the opening of the National Assembly. The question of Manchuria was becoming paramount, a growing seed of discord whose only fruit would be a renewed outbreak of civil war.

General Marshall, who had already begun to grasp this situation, left for Washington on 11 March to make his report to President Truman, leaving Lieutenant General Alvin C. Gillem, Jr., to represent him in the Committee of Three. Marshall had realized that American aid to the Nationalists was scarcely compatible with the position of a neutral arbiter, but he still hesitated to impose an embargo on the continuing flow of arms to Chiang Kai-shek. He also thought it necessary to withdraw American forces from China as soon as possible, and was determined to hasten their departure. But when he returned from Washington on 18 April the irreparable had occurred; open civil war had broken out on 15 April, just as the Russians were evacuating Changchun, the capital of Manchuria.

As early as the 8th, Communist forces, forewarned of the imminent departure of the Russians, moved on Changchun from the north and east. By the 9th they were in the outskirts of the capital. On 14 April at 1020 hours, the last Russian left Changchun. By the next morning the Reds had seized the airfield and infiltrated into the city, which was defended by only four thousand men of the Peace Preservation Corps, against whom the Reds had concentrated 35,000 men. After severe street fighting on the 16th and 17th, Ch'en

Chi-ch'eng's forces capitulated to the Communists on 18 April, with relieving Nationalist armies still no nearer than some 130 miles to the south of the Manchurian capital. Indeed, as late as the 15th, the New First Army had come only as far as Szepingkai, an important rail center.

Meanwhile, Nationalist forces had methodically fanned out from Mukden. The New Sixth Army and the Seventy-first and Ninety-fourth armies cleared the Mukden-Yingkow railroad by way of Liaoyang, while the Fifty-second Army advanced along the Mukden-Kirin railroad to Fushun, which it held against the attacks of five Communist divisions on 7 and 8 April. The Nationalists succeeded in running a train from Mukden to Peking on 18 April, but the line remained exposed to Red attacks in the vicinity of Shanhaikwan. While the Nationalists were trying to disengage Mukden and resume their advance upon Changchun, Lin Piao, without firing a shot, occupied all the rest of the country. Hard on the heels of the withdrawing Russians, his forces entered Kirin on 22 April, Harbin on the 25th, and Tsitsihar on the 28th. Everywhere, the representatives of Chiang Kai-shek's government were forced to flee; they sought safety with the withdrawing Russians, who later returned them, via Vladivostok and the sea, to China.

Little by little, the Nationalist armies pushed northward along the Changchun railroad. They were well equipped with heavy weapons, even with tanks, and the Communists could not stand up to them in open battle. Thus, when the New First and Fifth armies attacked on 21 April, the Communists were forced to fall back and, after a bitter, month-long resistance, to yield Szepingkai to the Nationalists on 19 May. On the 21st the government troops seized the pass at Kungchuling, about thirty-five miles south of Changchun. Finally, on 23 May, Nationalist armored units entered the Manchurian capi-

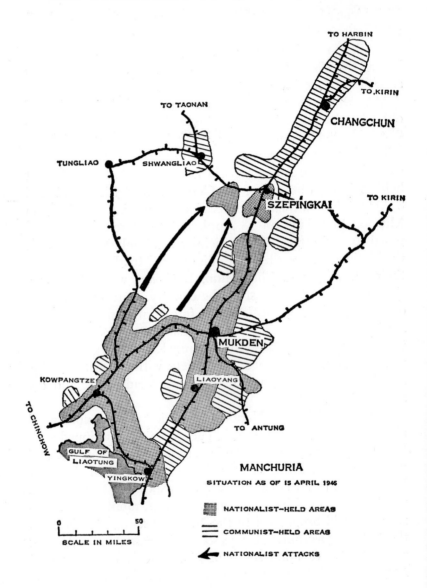

TO HARBIN

TO KIRIN

CHANGCHUN

TO TAONAN

TUNGLIAO SHWANGLIAO

SZEPINGKAI

TO KIRIN

KOWPANGTZE

MUKDEN

LIAOYANG

TO ANTUNG

TO CHINCHOW

GULF OF LIAOTUNG

YINGKOW

MANCHURIA

SITUATION AS OF 15 APRIL 1946

NATIONALIST-HELD AREAS

COMMUNIST-HELD AREAS

NATIONALIST ATTACKS

0 50

SCALE IN MILES

tal. Exploiting this success, they occupied Kirin on the 29th, crossed the Sungari river, and on 5 June took Schwangcheng, about thirty miles to the south of Harbin.

At this time Chiang Kai-shek was at Mukden, where he had arrived in General Marshall's personal plane for a tour of inspection. The capture of Changchun increased Chiang's confidence and his certainty of victory through force. For their part, the Communists, enraged by the fact that Chiang had flown to Manchuria in Marshall's own airplane, found it increasingly difficult to credit the impartiality of the American mediator.

While the fighting had been going on in Manchuria, two major developments had unfolded elsewhere.

In the first place, the Communists had been very active in Shantung and Kiangsu. In Shantung P'eng Te-huai's forces had come down from their mountains and, advancing along the Tientsin-Pukow railroad, had encircled Tsinan and threatened Peking. The effect of these significant successes was to force Chiang to divert forces from the Manchurian theater. In Kiangsu the Communist New Fourth Army, while retaining its hold on the coastal area between the mouth of the Yangtze and the former mouth of the Hwang Ho, took the offensive and threatened Nantung.

Secondly, the negotiations which continued throughout these operations were becoming more and more difficult for General Marshall. After proving a Communist violation of the armistice in the Red occupation of Changchun, he was obliged to recognize that the Nationalists, too, had committed numerous transgressions: encirclement, to the north of Hankow, of parts of the Communist New Fourth Army; troop movements in prohibited areas, such as Jehol; refusal of the government to report its troop movements south of the Yangtze; arrest of Communists and closing of Communist newspapers in Peking; bombing of the airfield at Yenan;[10] arrest of the Communist members of the field team at Mukden. For their part, the Communists, after their victory at Changchun, requested modification of the force ratio initially prescribed for the Northeast. General Marshall refused, pointing out that Chiang Kai-shek, in asking only for the evacuation of Changchun and not, as the initial agreements entitled him to, of all of Manchuria, was showing great good will. Moreover, fully realizing that his mediation was becoming more and more difficult, and that the field teams were never obeyed, Marshall declared his desire to withdraw from mediation.

With the Nationalist recapture of Changchun, however, Chiang became more amenable. On 24 May he proposed a truce, even though he continued his offensive against Kirin and Harbin. Returning to his restored capital at Nanking on 3 June, he approved on 5 June a cease-fire which, with Communist consent, was established for a fifteen-day period commencing 7 June 1946. Chiang declared that this truce would "give the Communist Party an opportunity to demonstrate in good faith their intention to carry out the agreements they had previously signed."[11] Invoking the Sino-Soviet treaty, he pressed his claim to Nationalist sovereignty in Manchuria. In response, Chou En-lai self-righteously recalled that the Chinese Communist Party had never ceased its efforts to bring an end to civil war.

Taking up the agreement of 25 February 1946 regarding the demobilization, reorganization, and integration of the armed forces, the two sides fruitlessly negotiated throughout the fifteen-day truce. On 22 June the truce was extended by eight days, with no results. On 30 June the Civil War, which

10 The White Paper uses the term "buzzing," rather than "bombing," to describe this action of Nationalist planes over the airfield at Yenan. See *U.S. Relations with China*, p. 151. Tr.

11 *Ibid.*, p. 641. Tr.

had never really ceased, was officially resumed—to the accompaniment of telegraphed orders from Chiang and Mao, each of whom directed his troops not to attack, but to fire only when fired upon.

Each side threw upon the other the responsibility for the failure of the negotiations. In fact, the fundamental question remained that of the areas occupied by the Red Army. The Nationalists demanded Communist evacuation of Jehol and Chahar; of the Manchurian cities of Harbin, Antung, Tunghwa, Mutankiang, and Paicheng; of the greater part of Shantung, and all of Kiangsu.[12] "This would be," declared Chou En-lai, "a return to the system of military districts, or outright annexation. It would not be a democratic measure. The demands of the government are thus unacceptable."

Regarding the reallocation of armed forces in Manchuria requested by the Communists, Chiang accepted a strength of three Red divisions in place of the one division initially prescribed, but refused the figure of five proposed by Chou En-lai. There were long discussions about the concentration zones to be left to the Communists, and about the cities the Reds were to evacuate. Chiang Kai-shek showed himself to be as intractable as his adversary. He seemed, at this time, to be absolutely sure of victory through force. As for the Communists, they were beginning to realize that, apart from his "American" divisions, Chiang's armies were really quite weak. Considering the strategic situation to be more favorable to themselves, so long as they held Shansi and Shantung, they prepared their troops, and the weapons they had taken from the Japanese in Manchuria, for the continuation of the Civil War. They, too, could see only victory as the outcome.

[12] The importance Chiang attached to these demands is reflected in the fact that he was to persist in his attacks until most of these objectives, announced on 17 June, were attained in November.

In July fighting resumed in earnest—despite the restraining orders which had been issued by both sides—and raged with particular severity in Shantung and Kiangsu. In Shantung the Nationalists, who had concentrated some twenty divisions in the province, succeeded in recapturing control of the Kiaochow-Tsinan railroad and regaining freedom of movement around Tsingtao and Tsinan. It proved impossible for them, however, to drive the Communists from the mountainous region of the province.

At this time (10 July) the Nationalists also launched a great offensive in Kiangsu. This operation was part of an overall, coordinated plan which aimed at the successive reduction of the Communist zones in Central China by concentration of overwhelming force upon each in turn, in such manner as to facilitate a final thrust into North China and Manchuria. This offensive, directed by General T'ang En-po, Deputy Commander in Chief of the Chinese Army, and General Li Mo-an, Commander of the First Pacification Zone, was supervised by Pai Ch'ung-hsi, the Minister of National Defense, and by General Ch'en Ch'eng, the Chief of Staff of the Chinese Army. The result of this multiplicity of chiefs was orders, counterorders, and disorder. Eight Nationalist armies (the Fifth, Seventh, Twenty-first, Twenty-fifth, Forty-ninth, Seventy-fourth, Ninety-ninth, and 100th) supported by one hundred aircraft (the Fifth Group) were launched against the 130,000 men of General Ch'en I,[13] the Red commander coordinating operations in Kiangsu and Shantung. Clearly, the

---

[13] Not to be confused with the notorious General Ch'en I who was relieved as Nationalist governor of Taiwan in 1949, and executed by the Nationalists in 1950 for his plot to kidnap Chiang Kai-shek and defect to the Communists. All subsequent references to Ch'en I in this work are to the Communist general of that name. One of the Communists' most brilliant commanders in the Civil War, this is the Ch'en I who is currently (1965) Foreign Minister of the People's Republic of China. *Tr.*

Nationalist forces possessed numerical and material superiority. But their morale was low; once again, one was to witness inexplicable surrenders. For example, the 19th Brigade of the 89th Infantry Division (100th Army), and part of the Forty-ninth Army as well, laid down their arms without having fired a shot—a capitulation which permitted the elusive Communists, who were employing guerrilla tactics *con brio*, to conduct a successful defense along the Tientsin-Shanghai railroad between Suhsien and Nantung. The capture of Jukao by the Nationalists failed to bring any decisive results.

Meanwhile, the Communists had vented vehement protests against American policy in China, and Chiang's untimely departure for Kuling[14] on 14 July led to a slowdown in negotiations. The adversaries again accused each other of violating the truce, but now a stiffer attitude was apparent on both sides. On the Kuomintang side the reactionary faction was becoming, like the Communists, anti-American, and they now viewed American mediation as positively injurious to the Nationalist cause. At Kunming the secret police assassinated two professors who belonged to the Democratic League, and terrorized the liberal leaders. For their part, the Communists provoked serious incidents with the U.S. Marines and on 29 July ambushed an American convoy at Anping, near Peking. The convoy, consisting of members of an Executive Headquarters field team, some UNRRA supplies, and a Marine escort detachment, lost three killed, twelve wounded, and one jeep. The Communists alleged that the Americans had been fighting side by side with Nationalists. The commander of the Seventh U.S. Fleet, Admiral Charles M. Cooke, formally denied these accusations and warned that henceforth the Marines would fire when fired upon.

[14] Chiang's summer residence in Kiangsi, where he would take an occasional vacation.

Meanwhile, General Patrick Hurley had yet to be replaced as American Ambassador to China. General Marshall felt a need to be backed up by a man of integrity who was an expert on China, and who would be capable of replacing him when he departed—a departure he was beginning very strongly to desire. He asked Truman to name Dr. Leighton Stuart, President of the American Yenching University at Peking, to the vacant post. Stuart arrived in Nanking on 26 July, and promptly began his efforts at mediation. Paving the new ambassador's way, Marshall warned Chiang Kai-shek against his self-delusions of rapid victory through force, pointing out to Chiang the diminution of his prestige, the deterioration of China's economic and financial situation, and the misinformation the Generalissimo was receiving from his entourage. On 1 August Dr. Stuart proposed to Chiang the creation of a Five-Man Committee, to consist of two Communists and two Nationalists, with the ambassador himself as chairman.[15]

Once again Chiang imposed preliminary conditions: withdrawal of Red forces in Kiangsu to the north of the Lunghai railroad; withdrawal from the zone of the Tsinan-Tsingtao railroad; withdrawal from all of Jehol south of Chengteh; withdrawal of all Red forces in Manchuria into the Manchurian provinces of Hsingan, Heilungkiang, and Nunkiang; finally, Communist withdrawal from all places in Shansi and Shantung occupied after 7 June. In reply, the Communists declared that they would not withdraw so long as the question of administration of their occupied territories was not resolved in a satisfactory manner. Actually, Chiang regarded the "truce" as favorable to himself, even if its terms were not respected, and he pressed on with military operations, especially in Hopeh and Jehol. The Communists having encircled Tatung at the

15 The Nationalists were represented by two generals, Wang Ta-ch'en and Chang Li-sheng, and the Communists by Chou En-lai and Tung Pi-wu.

end of July, the government announced a Nationalist offensive against Kalgan, the only large city in the hands of the Reds. Mao Tse-tung's reply was to order, on 19 August, general mobilization in all territories under Communist control.

On 20 August the Thirteenth and Fifty-third armies advanced on Chengteh, the capital of Jehol, which they took on the 28th; the Communists, following their custom, fell back and avoided pitched battle in open country. In contrast, General Ho Lung's sixty thousand Reds tightened their grip around Tatung, despite the dispatch of a Nationalist relief column from Peking by General Fu Tso-yi. As for the stalled negotiations, nothing could break the deadlock: a message from President Truman, the explanations and supplications of Stuart and Marshall—all were to no avail. Truly, as pointed out in the American White Paper, "General Marshall was being placed in the untenable position of mediating on the one hand between the two Chinese groups while on the other the United States Government was continuing to supply arms and ammunition to one of the two groups, namely, the National Government."[16]

The American military aid program, which called for the equipping of thirty-nine Nationalist divisions and eight and one-third aviation groups, was still in effect. Thus, in order to convince the Communists of his good faith, Marshall in August imposed an embargo on American arms shipments to the Nationalists.[17] But Chiang had ample reserves of war matériel at this time, and he continued his military operations without abatement as the fruitless negotiations dragged on. On 28 August the Generalissimo proposed Red participation in a coalition government. In reply Yenan prescribed, as

[16] U.S. Relations with China, p. 181. Tr.

[17] The embargo, in the form of a ban on the issuance of export licenses for shipment of arms and ammunition, was lifted by the Secretary of State on 26 May 1947. See U.S. Relations with China, pp. 355–356. Tr.

the first condition of its acceptance, a general cease-fire; without this, the Communists feared that they would be forced by the Kuomintang, which would have a majority in the State Council,[18] to submit to conditions imposed by the Nationalists. As for Marshall, he had long since realized that there were no peaceful ways out of the Chinese impasse. He continued, however, to struggle courageously, but without hope. Session after session, the futile palaver continued, with each side always finding good reasons to reject the other's proposals.

Chou En-lai's departure from Nanking for Shanghai, on 16 September 1946, showed very clearly that the Chinese Communists regarded an agreement with the Nationalists as increasingly improbable. The Red leader released to the press a vehement protest against the aid provided the Kuomintang by the Americans, who had expended at least $600 million for the support of Nationalist China since V-J Day, and who had continued since then to supply Chiang with arms and ammunition. Nevertheless, the negotiations continued, while Nationalist attacks sought by force to obtain what the government had asked for in its June proposals. But with each defeat, the Communists only became more unyielding in negotiation. Gradually, they came to realize that they were losing far fewer men than the Nationalists, whose morale was not always proving to be of the best. And they were beginning to gather the fruits of their guerrilla campaign, which not only served to keep their regular military forces intact, but, by

---

[18] In January 1946 the Political Consultative Conference had passed a resolution to make an enlarged State Council, with appointed representatives of the KMT "as well as non-members of the Kuomintang," the "supreme organ of the Government" pending the convocation of the National Assembly. A major (and unfulfilled) purpose of Ambassador Stuart's August proposal for a Five-Man Committee was to reach an agreement on the organization of the State Council, which it was hoped would "give a form of genuine legislative action for control or guidance of the Government." See *U.S. Relations with China*, pp. 610, 174–175. *Tr.*

severing communications, was separating the cities from the countryside and slowly driving the government into an economic crisis.

Meanwhile, the Nationalist attack on Kalgan, the second capital of the Reds, gave Chou En-lai the opportunity to demonstrate the bad faith of Chiang Kai-shek and lodge vigorous protests with General Marshall. Marshall then asked Chiang to stop the attack and make new proposals. The Generalissimo's minimal concessions were rejected by Yenan. Clearly Chiang wanted to exploit his military superiority and resolve the issue by force. At this point Marshall threatened to withdraw from mediation and go home, thus wringing from Chiang his agreement to a truce and a halt to his advance on Kalgan. But now it was the Communists who managed to find reasons for rejecting the truce, thus leaving Marshall high and dry. In Manchuria and in all regions under Communist control, mass demonstrations against the Americans proliferated; even though the U.S. Marines had evacuated Tientsin and Chinwangtao as early as September, their continued presence at Tsingtao sufficed as fuel for these protests. On 11 October the Generalissimo, whose troops had now taken Kalgan and Chengteh, announced that the National Assembly would meet at Nanking on 12 November, whether or not the Communist Party saw fit to participate.

For the moment all was calm in Manchuria, where the Nationalists had attained almost all of their June objectives. But the Communists were preparing for open war, and they recalled the missions of negotiation they had until then maintained at Nanking, Shanghai, and Chungking, their personnel being repatriated, by courtesy of American aircraft, to Yenan. There was a last ray of hope when the "Third Party Group"[19] succeeded in persuading Chou En-lai to return to

[19] Leaders of minority parties other than the CCP. *Tr.*

Nanking and begin a last round of talks. But the Communists continued to lay down as their preliminary conditions the withdrawal of government troops to the lines of 13 January in China, and of 7 June in Manchuria. The Reds also asked for a total of fourteen seats on the State Council for the CCP and the Democratic League, thus giving them a check upon majority decisions. Chiang Kai-shek refused and presented counterproposals of his own. The situation grew worse and worse. On 24 October the Nationalists occupied the last important stations of the Kiaochow-Tsinan railroad, moved forward in southern Hopeh, and in Manchuria launched an attack on Antung. The Communists withdrew their personnel from the field teams and from the Executive Headquarters at Peking, whose activity had long been negligible at best. On 26 October Chou En-lai declared that continuation of the government attacks would mean the end of negotiations.

Announcement of the fall of Antung on 27 October filled Chiang's entourage with joy, and General Marshall felt himself bound, the very next morning, to give the Generalissimo his frank personal estimate of the general situation. In this interview with Chiang, Marshall drew his hearer's attention to the illusions nourished by his advisers. In Marshall's own view, the Nationalists had succeeded in occupying cities, but they had failed to take any weapons or prisoners from the Red forces, which remained intact. He added that even the fall of Harbin itself would solve nothing, and that the Generalissimo could not resolve the issues by force. On 8 November, Nationalist troops having occupied Tunghwa in Manchuria, Chiang declared that the time had come for a general cease-fire.

CHAPTER VI

The Military Situation at the End of October and Operations During the Last Months of 1946

A study of the zones occupied by the Communists as of the end of October 1946 shows that the situation of the Reds remained very strong in North China, owing not only to the territory they held, but to the threat they posed, from Kiangsu to Manchuria, to all the Nationalist lines of communication. They continued to implement their "horizontal plan," and to prevent the rail movement of Nationalist troops to the Northeast. Chiang Kai-shek's only important success had been the almost complete clearing of Hupeh, southern Honan, and South China; the Communists had even been compelled to evacuate their forces from Kwangtung by sea to Shantung. Those who remained, and particularly those on Hainan, had been rebaptized as "bandits" by the Nationalists, who continued to wipe out or at least neutralize the Red remnants in these areas.

The events which befell Communist forces in what had been the central zone of operations, Hupeh and Honan, can be summarized as follows: pressed by a food shortage and resupply difficulties, Li Hsien-nien, whose forces had been a source of serious trouble for the Nationalists in the Hupeh-Honan border region during the winter of 1945–1946, in April requested a truce that would permit the free passage of his troops into Kiangsu. The Nationalists refused, fearing that Li would profit from the proposed lull by moving his forces into Shantung and thence to Manchuria, where the situation was critical. Nonetheless, the Generalissimo's headquarters at Wuhan granted the hungry Reds a loan of 400 million *fapis*[1] for purposes of resupply. Early in May, General Byroade, Chou En-lai, and Hsu Yung-ch'ang arrived to investigate the situation of these troops, and signed an agreement which delimited, as a fixed zone for Li Hsien-nien's troops, an area to the east of the Pinghan[2] with Loshan as its center. But at the end of the month, Li, on the pretext that the Nationalists were attempting to encircle his forces, crossed the line of the Pinghan and marched westward, gathering up on his way other Communist elements that had survived the earlier Nationalist push and were in the process of recuperation, as well as the advance guards he had sent forward to clear the way. In one month, Li, hard-pressed as he was by the Nationalists, still managed to take a dozen towns, including Suihsien, Tsao-yang, Sinyeh, and Sichwan, and then moved northward up the valley of the Tan. In order to ease the supply problem the Reds quickly divided their forces following the fall of Suih-sien, and General Wang Chen, commanding the southern column, crossed the Han and took Icheng, Nanchang, Pao-

[1] At this time the *fapi*, the Chinese nonconvertible legal-tender note, had an official exchange rate of about $2,000 Chinese to $1 U.S., and was rapidly depreciating in value. See the China Handbook Editorial Board, *China Handbook, 1950* (New York: Rockport Press, Inc., 1950), pp. 470–471, and U.S. Department of State, *United Relations with China, with Special Reference to the Period 1944–1949* (U.S. Government Printing Office, 1949), p. 221. Tr.

[2] The Peking-Hankow railroad.

kang, and Chusan. By the end of July the two Red columns had established themselves in two well-protected valleys, that of the Nan, near the Honan-Shansi-Hupeh border, and the valley of the Chu, near the Shensi-Szechwan-Hupeh border. The Communists had suffered severe losses during this march and they needed a respite in which to regroup. A new armistice of three weeks' duration, effective at midnight of 6 August and covering a zone which included Hupeh, Shensi, and Honan, gave them the needed break. Once regrouped, the Reds crossed the armistice line of the Wei River near Sian, and on 30 August entered the Shensi-Kansu-Ningsia Border Region, the official seat of Chinese communism.

Thus, at the cost of abandoning South and Central China, the Communists had succeeded in effecting a strategic concentration of their forces—a concentration which stood in marked contrast to the dispersed deployment of their adversaries.

On 15 November the National Assembly met at Nanking without the participation of the Communists or of the Democratic League, whose combined quota of seats, according to the proposals of the Political Consultative Conference, should have amounted to 610 of the total of 2,050. The Kuomintang and its affiliates should therefore have elected only 1,440 members; but the National Assembly had 1,580 of them, which gave Chou En-lai a new opportunity to protest, this time against the illegal seating of 140 representatives of the KMT.

On 19 November Chou left for Yenan. General Marshall, too, was packing his bags, for he fully realized not only that his mission had failed, but that Chiang Kai-shek, whose situation appeared to be so favorable, was actually headed for an impasse from which he had little chance of emerging. Seventy per cent of the government's budget went to the financing of the war; only twenty-five per cent of this budget was met by taxes, with another ten per cent covered by gold reserves and various fiscal devices. The missing sixty-five per cent explains an inflation that was becoming catastrophic: during 1946 prices rose by 700 per cent, while gold reserves dwindled by fifty per cent. Pleading its poverty, the government incessantly clamored for American aid, while corruption reigned unchecked at all levels of the poorly paid public service. As for the troops, they were underfed, poorly led, and without morale.

In Marshall's view the Chinese Communist Party had been sincerely desirous, in the spring of 1946, of reaching an understanding with the Nationalists; it was the Kuomintang government that had wrecked the negotiations by its incessant violations of the truce and continuation of its military action up to October, thus undermining his peace proposals even as they were being advanced. Marshall again demonstrated to Chiang that Nationalist forces were incapable, since the departure of the American Marines, of keeping open the vitally important Tientsin-Chinwangtao railroad, or of clearing the Communists from Hopeh. The Generalissimo's reply was that, in his opinion, the Chinese Communist Party had never been sincerely willing to cooperate, and that its real goal was to drive, with the help of the U.S.S.R., the Nationalists from power in China. In his view the sole solution was war, and he expected to finish off the Reds in less than a year. As for the economic situation, it did not appear so catastrophic to him, since China's compartmentalized agrarian economy made the provinces almost autarkic and only the large cities would have to be provided for.

On 4 December the Communists again demanded the dissolution of the National Assembly and withdrawal of Nationalist troops to the cease-fire line of 13 January. Stiffening more and more against the United States, they also rejected any mediation by the Americans. For the second time, Marshall, prior to his departure, personally intervened and tried to show Chiang the sensible solution. Marshall insisted upon the primordial necessity of popular support for the Kuomintang, and the consequent requirements for agrarian reform and a democratic constitution. He begged the Generalissimo to rid himself of the reactionary clique of the brothers Ch'en, and of the secret police, and to rally the liberals to his side. Quite understandably, he refused to remain in China as Chiang's adviser. With this, Chiang made what seems to have been a real effort to escape the reactionary influence of the CC clique.[3] His pro-democratic pronouncements to the National Assembly regained much of his prestige, and his efforts resulted in the adoption of a new and liberal constitution. But the Ch'en brothers continued to be active within the inner circles of the party, and maintained their hold upon the cadres of the Kuomintang.

On 6 January President Truman recalled General Marshall, who left China on the 8th. The American attempt at mediation had ended in complete failure. On the one hand, the Communists, who had long been somewhat sympathetic in their attitude toward the United States, and especially toward Marshall, had now become resolutely anti-American. On the other hand, the United States, which had proved incapable of formulating a sound China policy, now found itself more and more involved in support of the Kuomintang, when it should have been clear that its ward's chances of winning were becoming fewer and fewer. With Marshall's departure all official American organizations also left China, except for the "naval training group" at Tsingtao.

[3] The name of this clique was derived from that of the brothers Ch'en Li-fu and Ch'en Kuo-fu, Chiang Kai-shek's adopted nephews and the leaders of the KMT's extreme right.

Marshall left the Nationalists in a catastrophic position. The Communists, seeking to hasten economic collapse, were systematically destroying communications and isolating the cities from the countryside. The American dollar, worth 2,020 Chinese dollars as of 1 January 1946, had reached an exchange rate of 6,500 Chinese dollars by December of that year. Kuomintang finances were completely adrift, with no control over expenditures and each level of command indulging in embezzlement, the "squeeze," and outright theft. The enormous army—poorly employed, pent up in useless garrisons, always on the defensive—was a crushing financial burden, as was the resupply of Manchuria.

Yet, beginning as early as V-J Day, the Chinese government had received considerable foreign aid. During 1945, UNRRA had sent 300,000 tons of food, clothing, and other supplies. From 1945 to 1947, UNRRA had also contributed $685 million in financial aid, $475 million of it from the United States. Through the Export-Import Bank $82 million had been advanced to the Nationalist government, and a credit offering of $500 million had been made, for purposes of reconstruction, to Chinese companies.[4] In June 1946, Canada lent $60 million, and the United States $51,700,000, for purposes of reconstruction. Surplus military matériel of American forces in the Pacific (vehicles, spare parts, engines, electrical and medical equipment, tools, chemical products, aviation spare parts, and construction materials), worth $900 million, was turned over to the Nationalists for $175 million, payable on easy terms. Unfortunately, this enormous effort was in vain. Civil war, corruption, and incompetence prevented the Chinese government from maintaining a healthy economy and a truly strong army.

4 The outbreak of civil war led the bank to withdraw this offer.

MILITARY OPERATIONS FROM OCTOBER
TO DECEMBER OF 1946

Military operations during the period of October-December 1946 may be described as follows: in Kiangsu, the Nationalists failed in their attempts to clean out the Communist enclave. After some success, their offensive failed when General Ho P'eng-chu, who held the eastern part of the Lunghai railroad between the Grand Canal and the sea, went over to the Communists. Although the Nationalists took Lienshui and Fowning in December, Red guerrillas reappeared behind them in the Nantung and Jukao areas. In Shantung the Communists remained invulnerable in the mountainous part of the province, while in the south they repelled a Nationalist offensive along the Taierhchwang-Yihsien front. Meanwhile, in order to separate Red forces in Shantung from those in Hopeh, the government had undertaken an enormous engineering effort. In repairing the embankments of the Yellow River which had given way, in 1938, between Kaifeng and Chengchow, they now sought to divert the river eastward into its old course. This would flood Anhwei and Kiangsu, dry the former river bed into a mud flat at best, isolate Hopeh from Shantung, and make the movement of Red troops exceedingly difficult.[5] This posed a serious threat to the Communists, for their "horizontal plan" required the maintenance of contact between the Kiangsu-Shantung region and that of Hopeh-Shansi-Shensi. In December General Liu Po-ch'eng moved to oppose the Nationalist troops of General Ku Chu-t'ung who, despite several successes which included the seizure of Taming, failed to clear the Reds from the Peking-Hankow railroad. In Hopeh the Reds continued to be extremely active, and Na-

[5] Work on this project was halted in 1947, and the river resumed its course to the Gulf of Chihli.

97

tionalist communications between Peking and Paoting, and between Paoting and Shihkiachwang as well, remained severed. By the end of December, only fifty-three of Hopeh's 133 *hsien*, or districts, were held by the Nationalists, while the Communists held forty and the other forty remained in contention. In Shansi, where the Reds were trying to lay their hands on the Luliang Shan range (the mountain chain which separates the Fen Ho from the Yellow River), the situation remained in doubt. In the Mongolian provinces, the Nationalists expanded their zone of influence to Chahar, achieving the conquest of Jehol despite the severe cold which made operations difficult and very hard on the men. In the Yenan region, General Ma Hung-ku'ei, the Nationalist governor of Ningsia, attacked the Yenchih salt-works, but was pushed all the way back to his starting point. Lastly, in Manchuria the Nationalists established lines of defense around Changchun and around their bridgehead on the Sungari, while clearing the country to the south. They were particularly successful in Liaoning, where, after encircling the Red zone around Antung, they seized practically all of the peninsula. Red guerrillas still survived in this zone, however, as well as in the Szepingkai area, where trains were continually machine-gunned by the Communists.

Toward the end of the year the Reds reorganized the five Manchurian provinces over which they held complete control: Sungkiang (with its capital at Harbin); Hokiang (Kiamusze); Heilungkiang (Lungchen); Nunkiang (Tsitsihar); and Hsingan (Hailar). This Communist zone had about twenty million inhabitants, half the total population of Manchuria, and an area of over 300,000 square miles. It was governed by a People's Council composed of twenty-seven members and directed by Lin Feng and Chang Hsüeh-szu, brother of Chang Hsüeh-liang, the young war lord who had kidnapped Chiang

Kai-shek at Sian in 1936. Theoretically, these men were not Communists, and the government was "democratic." But the presence of Lin Piao's army, 300,000 strong, gave the Reds a far from negligible instrument for the kind of pressure other Communists brought to bear in Hungary and the Balkans.

The disposition of Nationalist forces in Manchuria was now as follows: the commander in chief (General Tu Yü-ming) had established his headquarters in Changchun, and had divided his forces into two major groups. The northern group consisted of seven divisions organized in three armies. It covered the Changchun-Kirin zone, and held the Nationalist bridgehead on the Sungari. The stronger southern group, consisting of twelve divisions, was centered around Mukden and faced toward the Korean frontier; farther west, Nationalist units facing toward Jehol covered Mukden against possible attack from Inner Mongolia. Lastly, the Sixty-third Army was in process of disembarkment at Chinwangtao.

All these divisions were equipped with American weapons and vehicles; they were well supplied with ammunition; and they enjoyed considerable superiority in numbers. The Nationalist Air Force, though weak, held a self-evident mastery of the skies, since the Communists had no aircraft at all. The Nationalists could thus readily spot enemy concentrations, and rapidly airlift reinforcements or supplies to threatened points. Theoretically, then, the general situation was in their favor, so far as the pitched battles of positional warfare were concerned. But the Red armies of Lin Piao, composed of equal numbers of Manchurians and northern Chinese and supported by numerous Mongol cavalrymen, had succeeded in seizing many Japanese arms depots, particularly at Mukden, Tsitsihar, and Harbin, immediately after the Russian withdrawal. Moreover, they were in a strategically favorable position, which they improved by employing aggressive guerrilla warfare and sever-

99

ing the Nationalists' umbilical cord of rail communications, despite the presence of "peace preservation corps" and "pacification columns."

Finally, it must be recognized that man for man, Mao's troops were clearly superior to Chiang's. The Nationalist armies, except for those composed of the veterans of the Burma campaign, were fully representative of the classical tradition in Chinese armies: in other words, they were undisciplined, poorly trained, completely lacking in morale, and ready, from corporal on up to general, to change sides whenever circumstances beckoned. With the Communists, things were far different. Once again, the historical lesson of the wars of religion was to be repeated: the more fanatical side is always more daring, more enterprising; the majority, trusting in its superior strength, lacks nerve, and invariably garners only defeats.

Superficially, the military situation at the end of 1946 seemed very favorable to Chiang Kai-shek, and the Nationalist press services circulated a constant stream of victory bulletins. In reality, however, the Communists were as strong as ever, and the Kuomintang was digging its own grave.

CHAPTER VII

The Last Attempts at Reconciliation

THE day after General Marshall's departure from China, the State Department published a personal statement in which this great and good man analyzed, with his customary frankness and clarity, the situation in China.

In the first place, the greatest obstacle to peace has been the complete, almost overwhelming suspicion with which the Chinese Communist Party and the Kuomintang regard each other.

On the one hand, the leaders of the Government are strongly opposed to a communistic form of government. On the other, the Communists frankly state that they are Marxists and intend to work toward establishing a communistic form of government in China, though first advancing through the medium of a democratic form of government of the American or British type.

The leaders of the Government are convinced in their minds that the Communist-expressed desire to participate in a government of the type endorsed by the Political Consultative Conference last January had for its purpose only a destructive intention. The Communists felt, I believe, that the government was insincere in its apparent acceptance of the PCC resolutions for the formation of the new government and intended by coercion of military force and the action of secret police to obliterate the

Communist Party. Combined with this mutual deep distrust was the conspicuous error by both parties of ignoring the effect of the fears and suspicions of the other party in estimating the reason for proposals or opposition regarding the settlement of various matters under negotiation. They each sought only to take counsel of their own fears. They both, therefore, to that extent took a rather lopsided view of each situation and were susceptible to every evil suggestion or possibility. This complication was exaggerated to an explosive degree by the confused reports of fighting on the distant and tremendous fronts of hostile military contact. Patrol clashes were deliberately magnified into large offensive actions. The distortion of the facts was utilized by both sides to heap condemnation on the other. It was only through the reports of American officers in the field teams from Executive Headquarters that I could get even a partial idea of what was actually happening and the incidents were too numerous and the distances too great for the American personnel to cover all of the ground. . .

I think the most important factors involved in the recent breakdown of negotiations are these: On the side of the National Government, which is in effect the Kuomintang, there is a dominant group of reactionaries who have been opposed, in my opinion, to almost every effort I have made to influence the formation of a genuine coalition government. . . They were quite frank in publicly stating their belief that cooperation by the Chinese Communist Party in the government was inconceivable and that only a policy of force could definitely settle the issue. This group includes military as well as political leaders.

On the side of the Chinese Communist Party there are, I believe, liberals as well as radicals, though this view is vigorously opposed by many who believe that the Chinese Communist Party discipline is too rigidly enforced to admit of such differences of viewpoint. Nevertheless, it has appeared to me that there is a definite liberal group among the Communists, especially of young men who have turned to the Communists in disgust at the corruption evident in the local governments—men who would put the interest of the Chinese people above ruthless measures to establish a Communist ideology in the immediate future.

The dyed-in-the-wool Communists do not hesitate at the most drastic measures to gain their end as, for instance, the destruction of communications in order to wreck the economy of China and produce a situation that would facilitate the overthrow or collapse of the Government, without any regard to the immediate suffering of the people involved. They completely distrust the leaders of the Kuomintang and appear convinced that every Government proposal is designed to crush the Chinese Communist Party. I must say that the quite evidently inspired mob actions of last February and March, some within a few blocks of where I was then engaged in completing negotiations, gave the Communists good excuse for such suspicions.

However, a very harmful and immensely provocative phase of the Chinese Communist Party procedure has been in the character of its propaganda. I wish to state to the American people that in the deliberate misrepresentation and abuse of the action, policies and purposes of our Government this propaganda has been without regard for the truth, without any regard whatsoever for the facts, and has given plain evidence of a determined purpose to mislead the Chinese people and the world and to arouse a bitter hatred of Americans.

It has been difficult to remain silent in the midst of such public abuse and wholesale disregard of facts, but a denial would merely lead to the necessity of daily denials; an intolerable course of action for an American official. In the interest of fairness, I must state that the Nationalist Government publicity agency has made numerous misrepresentations, though not of the vicious nature of the Communist propaganda. Incidentally, the Communist statements regarding the Anping incident . . . were almost pure fabrication, deliberately representing a carefully arranged ambuscade of a Marine convoy with supplies for the maintenance of Executive Headquarters and some UNRRA supplies, as a defense against a Marine assault. The investigation of this incident was a tortuous procedure of delays and maneuvers to disguise the true and privately admitted facts of the case.

Sincere efforts to achieve settlement have been frustrated time and again by extremist elements of both sides. The agreements reached by the Political Consultative Conference a year ago were a liberal and forward-looking charter which then offered China a basis for peace and reconstruction. However, irreconcilable groups within the Kuomintang, interested in the preservation of their own feudal control of China, evidently had no real intention of implementing them. . .

I have never been in a position to be certain of the development of attitudes in the innermost Chinese Communist circles. Most certainly, the course which the Chinese Communist Party has pursued in recent months indicated an unwillingness to make a fair compromise. It has been impossible even to get them to sit down at a conference table with Government representatives to discuss given issues. Now the Communists have broken off negotiations by their last offer which demanded the dissolution of the National Assembly and a return to the military positions of January 13th which the Government could not be expected to accept.

Between this dominant reactionary group in the Government and the irreconcilable Communists who, I must state, did not so appear last February, lies the problem of how peace and well-being are to be brought to the long-suffering and presently inarticulate mass of the people of China. The reactionaries in the Government have evidently counted on substantial American support regardless of their actions. The Communists by their unwillingness to compromise in the national interest are evidently counting on an economic collapse to bring about the fall of the Government, accelerated by extensive guerrilla action against the long lines of rail communications—regardless of the cost in suffering to the Chinese people.

The salvation of the situation, as I see it, would be the assumption of leadership by the liberals in the Government and in the minority parties, a splendid group of men, but who as yet lack the political power to exercise a controlling influence. Successful action on their part under the leadership of Generalissimo Chiang Kai-shek would, I believe, lead to unity through good government.[1]

It is quite clear that this last sentence was no more than the expression of a pious hope, and that Marshall had fully grasped the true nature of the situation.

---

[1] U.S. Department of State, *United States Relations with China, with Special Reference to the Period 1944–1949* (U.S. Government Printing Office, 1949), pp. 686–688. *Tr.*

Nevertheless, the Nationalist government at the beginning of 1947 proposed an unconditional cease-fire; but the Red response was to demand, as preliminary conditions, the abolition of the constitution and the withdrawal of Nationalist forces to the line of 13 January 1946.

On 10 January, in a speech broadcast by the Yenan radio, Chou En-lai clearly indicated a reversal of Communist policy. Taking clever advantage of Marshall's criticisms of the Kuomintang, he said:

General Marshall admitted that there is a reactionary group in the Kuomintang which constitutes a dominant one in the Kuomintang government, and which includes military and political leaders. They oppose a coalition government, have no confidence in internal cooperation, but believe in the settlement of problems by armed force. They have no sincerity in carrying out the PCC resolutions. All these remarks are true. But what is to be regretted is that he did not point out that Chiang Kai-shek is the highest leader of this reactionary group. . . He continues to act against the PCC agreements in massing 280 brigades (formerly divisions), 90 percent of his total military strength, to attack the communist-held liberated areas. Up to the end of last year, his armies invaded 174,000 square kilometers and took 165 cities in the liberated areas. . . When it was advantageous for Chiang to launch an attack, he would not hesitate to attack. But when he was defeated and required time to regroup his troops, for instance (he was in such a pass last January and February), he would favor the halting of the war and conducted the so-called peace talks. . .

The Chinese Communists have unremittingly exposed and lodged protests against American aid to Chiang Kai-shek's government troops in the form of transportation, lend-lease materials, surplus property, warships and airplanes, military advisors and technical training, and the colonial policy of the American imperialists. . .[2]

At the same time, the Communist information chief, Lu Ting-i, published a memorandum entitled "Explanation of

[2] *Ibid.*, pp. 707–709. Tr.

Several Basic Questions Concerning the Post-War International Situation,"[3] in which the pro-Russian and anti-American attitude of the Chinese Communists was clearly spelled out. He commenced by citing Mao Tse-tung: "There is now a strong U.S.S.R. in the world, and peoples who are organized and awakened. The victory over the Fascists (Germans and Japanese) has opened the road to victory for the people's struggle in the post-war period." As a result of this post-war situation "the anti-democratic forces will be compelled to attack and the democratic forces will, inevitably, be victorious." As for the United States, "American imperialists have taken the place of German, Italian, and Japanese fascists in the world, aided by reactionaries in some countries: Churchill in England, de Gaulle in France, Chiang in China, and by Fascist remnants in others: Franco in Spain, Yoshida in Japan, Schacht and von Papen in Germany." After a violent attack against a United States which was accused of arming to the teeth, establishing its bases everywhere, and searching for ways to unleash war against the U.S.S.R., Lu asserted that "the Soviet Union is the defender of world peace" while "the real policy of the United States is to oppress the American people and the peoples of all the capitalist, colonial, and semi-colonial countries." It was the approach of an American "economic crisis" which forced the imperialists to increase the violence of their attacks, and Lu did not hesitate to declare that "the American economic crisis will come this year (1947) or the next." At this point, what were the relative strengths of the two sides in this world struggle? The people's democracies, and the Communist parties in France, in England, in the colonial and semicolonial countries, were all making progress. Strikes were spreading everywhere. "The international position of the most progressive nation in the world, the U.S.S.R.,

[3] For the full text, see *ibid.*, pp. 710–719. *Tr.*

has greatly improved." The reactionaries were still strong, but they were isolated and their strength was diminishing. "In summary, world-wide progressivism, the successes of the U.S.S.R., and the American crisis are three factors of decisive significance in the history of the future development of mankind. Let us march then," Lu concluded, "down the road to victory. The struggle will be a hard one, but we will win. We need only look at our adversaries' lack of confidence, their fear of the U.S.S.R., their abhorrence of the truth, to know that we shall prevail. It can be categorically predicted that, within three to five years at the most, the face of China and of the world will be completely changed."

Despite this public position, which should have shattered the last illusions of those who had maintained that the Chinese Communist Party was in no way an orthodox Communist party, Dr. Stuart forwarded to Yenan new truce proposals from the Nationalist government. His effort was in vain. On 1 February 1947 the Central Committee of the CCP denounced all agreements which had been signed after 10 January 1946. On 5 March the Nationalist government "invited" the last Communist representatives remaining in Nanking, Chungking, and Shanghai to leave its territory. The Communist newspaper in Chungking was shut down. Despite a last maneuver by Molotov in the Council of Foreign Ministers at Moscow on 10 March, the break was complete. Now the guns would speak: *Ultima ratio regum.*

PART THREE

1947
THE COMMUNISTS RESTORE
THE SITUATION AND
TAKE THE OFFENSIVE

CHAPTER VIII

1947: The First Six Months

MILITARY operations in China during the first half of 1947 can be characterized as follows: strategically, the Nationalists sought to split the Communist zones in North China by gaining firm control of the main lines of communication—first of the Peking-Hankow railroad, in order to cut off Communist bases in the Shantung-Kiangsu region from the Red stronghold of Shensi-Shansi; and then of the Tsinan-Pukow and Kiaochow-Tsinan railroads, in order to slice up the Shantung zone itself. Concurrently, in Manchuria they strengthened their positions along the Sungari river and prepared an offensive against Harbin, while attempting to consolidate their rear areas in Liaoning and Jehol. Lastly, in order to obtain a spectacular success and enhance their prestige, they launched an attack against the Red capital at Yenan. This attack, mounted by the best troops the Nationalists had, was to succeed in taking the city; but it was to have no influence upon the course of operations other than to permit the Reds to perform a very pretty maneuver which put the attacking Nationalists, stranded in the wastes of Shensi, in an extremely tenuous position.

For their part the Communists, who sought to implement a strategy which would maintain at all costs the "horizontal" link between Yenan and Shantung, conducted a fiercely determined defense in North China. In Manchuria, which was to become Chiang's "strategic trap," the Reds launched diversionary offensives designed to draw and fix as many enemy divisions—which would be difficult for the Nationalists to resupply and reinforce[1]—as possible. Tactically, the Nationalists' superiority in numbers and armament[2] was to force the Reds to continue the practice of their cherished methods of guerrilla warfare: the refusal of battle in open country, the fast-moving raids on garrisons and isolated units, the rapid retreat and "disappearance" when the Nationalists concentrated in strength. For the Red leaders, the paramount point was to inflict more losses upon the enemy than they themselves suffered and, above all, to seize the maximum amount of modern arms. Remarkably well led and well trained, Communist units were to succeed brilliantly in the accomplishment of these ends. With their rapidity of movement, their discipline, their morale, their offensive spirit, the Red troops were gradually to overcome their disadvantages in matériel; by June of 1947 they would begin to abandon their guerrilla tactics, and to undertake the large-scale operations which were soon to prove decisive.

In April 1947 a French observer, commenting on Communist operations in southern Shansi, wrote:

The Communist plan clearly shows not only the sound logic of its conception, but a perfect unity of views in the Communist high command, since it calls for close coordination between the

[1] As of March 1947, 227 of Chiang Kai-shek's total of 248 regular brigades were committed either at the front or as garrisons in active theaters of operation. This left him a reserve of only twenty-one brigades.

[2] At the end of 1946 the government had 2,600,000 men under arms, against a Communist strength of 1,100,000. With regard to rifles, the Nationalists—despite the capture of large stocks of Japanese weapons by the Reds in Manchuria—still had a three- or four-to-one superiority.

theaters of operation commanded by General Ho Lung and by General Liu Po-ch'eng. This is in marked contrast to the Nationalists, who have always found it extremely difficult to get their generals to work together, and even more so to get them to do it on their own initiative.

As regards tactical operations, this observer gave the following examples:

The capture of Houma cost the Reds two hundred killed and wounded, but brought them eighteen hundred prisoners, including a brigadier general. The capture of the town of Sinkiang cost them four wounded, and they took six hundred prisoners from the seven hundred militia who tried to defend the place. The capture of Kuwo, defended by two Nationalist regiments and attacked by three Red regiments, yielded the Communists two thousand prisoners—the entire garrison. Taking into account the fact that the Nationalists do not bother to destroy their weapons before they surrender, these operations were the kind of "paying propositions" General Chu Teh likes to talk about. The lack of fighting spirit shown by the common soldier demonstrates the degree to which the Nationalist army has disintegrated. The easy successes of the Communists can be explained only by their superior morale. After Communist indoctrination and political instruction, the ex-Nationalist soldier, typically passive and disheartened until then, becomes an enthusiastic and aggressive fighting man.

And this perspicacious observer concluded:

When they are not positively hostile, the people show no sympathy at all for the Nationalists. Nationalist generals pay no attention to one another. Their troops do not want to fight. They have no effective weapon against a resolute and elusive enemy. The American aid they get ends up in the hands of the Communists, often right after the first fight. If military factors alone were involved, there would be no doubt at all about the outcome of this war.

OPERATIONS IN MANCHURIA

After the operations of late 1946, the front in northern Manchuria stabilized along the arc of the Sungari River. But within the triangle Taolaichao-Changchun-Kirin, during the first half of 1947, the Reds were to launch, one after the other, five offensives. Originally diversionary in nature, these offensives were at first designed to diminish Nationalist pressure in Shantung; but they were to end in a major Communist victory. General Lin Piao, who had only about 300,000 men for this vast Manchurian front—a relatively small force, despite the almost total support of the population—launched his first attack, with sixty thousand men, on 6 January 1947. Three groups crossed the frozen Sungari and headed for Changchun and Kirin. Advancing southward down the Harbin-Changchun railroad from Wukoshu, the northern group isolated Nationalist garrisons, cut communications, and by 13 January reached Chengtzekai, about fifty miles north of Changchun. The second group, which moved out to the west from Paikitun, located on the Sungari to the south of the Willow Wall, seized the power station at Kiutai on the 15th, thus depriving the Manchurian capital of light and water. Finally, the third group, which departed from Wulakai, advanced southward to the immediate vicinity of Kirin.

The success of the Reds was short-lived. As early as 15 January the Nationalists, having concentrated their forces at Kirin, unleashed a counteroffensive which, moving northward along both banks of the Sungari, threatened to trap the advancing Red forces. Retiring in haste but leaving few prisoners to the Nationalists, the Communists were forced to recross the Sungari, pursued by forces from Changchun. On the twenty-fifth Wukoshu was retaken by the Nationalists. Lin

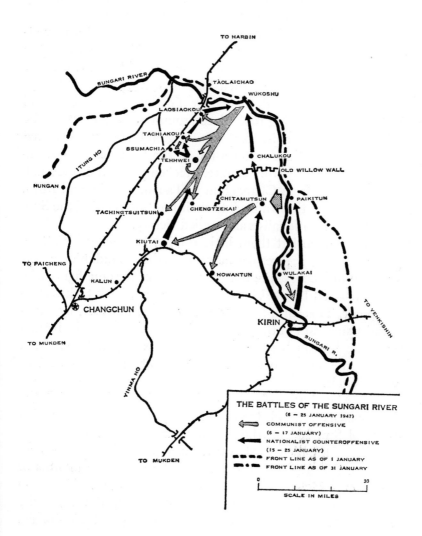

THE BATTLES OF THE SUNGARI RIVER
(6 — 25 JANUARY 1947)

COMMUNIST OFFENSIVE
(6 — 17 JANUARY)
NATIONALIST COUNTEROFFENSIVE
(15 — 25 JANUARY)
FRONT LINE AS OF 1 JANUARY
FRONT LINE AS OF 31 JANUARY

0   30
SCALE IN MILES

Piao had been completely defeated. The Nationalists, noisily optimistic, announced a forthcoming attack on Harbin.

Nevertheless, on 16 February the Reds launched a new attack to the northwest of Changchun, and then crossed the Sungari on the 23rd at the same places as in January. Moving as rapidly as they had in their first offensive, the Reds by the 24th again threatened to deprive Changchun of light and water. Severe fighting took place around Kirin and along the Kirin-Changchun railroad. But once again Red strength proved to be insufficient and, after a lull in the fighting, the government's New First Army counterattacked along the three railroads running from Changchun to Taoan, Harbin, and Kirin. The Reds were thrown back to their positions behind the Sungari, and the Nationalists again cried victory.

But Lin Piao left them little respite. Renewing his attack on 10 March, a three-day advance again found him a few miles from Changchun; but once again, as in some figure of a well-rehearsed ballet, Lin was forced to fall back to his starting point. This third failure was balanced, however, by Communist successes in the area to the east of Kirin and Mukden near the Korean border, where the Reds invested Tunghwa, and in the Tungliao valley, about seventy-five miles west of Changchun.

The Manchurian front remained quiet in April, and the Nationalists were able to effect a change of command in which General Sun Li-jen,[3] the defender of Changchun and commander of the New First Army, was replaced by General P'an Yü-kun. The Red offensives during the first three months of the year had worn out the Nationalist troops. Dissension among their commanders, poor leadership, the insecurity which prevailed outside the cities, had sapped their morale.

[3] A V.M.I. graduate and veteran of the Burma campaign, Sun was regarded by Stilwell as the ablest of the Nationalist field commanders. *Tr.*

Thus the Red offensive in May, perfectly prepared and executed, was to be an overwhelming success.

For this offensive, Lin Piao divided his forces into four groups. The first, in the north, commanded by Lu Cheng-ts'ao, was composed of two columns which were concentrated to the west of the Sungari between Talai and Fuyu, along the Changchun-Taoan railroad. The second group was north of the Sungari in the Yushu area. The third group was concentrated in the Hweinan area to the east of the Mukden-Kirin railroad, about fifty miles to the east of Szepingkai. Finally, a fourth and weaker group, consisting of Mongolian cavalry, was concentrated to the west of Mukden. To these regular forces were added the Red guerrillas, who were already in action along the railroads. On the Nationalist side, part of the forces were concentrated as garrisons for Changchun, Kirin, and Mukden, but a large number were scattered along the railroads to defend the stations and bridges.

The Red offensive, their fifth, was launched on 10 May 1947. The northern column marched south, isolated Nungan, and threatened Changchun by seizing, as early as the 18th, the city's airfield. Continuing its advance, it took Kungchuling on the evening of the 19th, but the Seventy-first Army retook the city on the 23rd. Szepingkai was encircled by the Reds on the 25th. Simultaneously, the southwest group, in a move designed to prevent the Mukden garrison (New Sixth Army) from coming to the aid of Changchun, attacked and took Faku and Kangping on the 24th. A state of siege was proclaimed at Mukden. The eastern group reduced the Nationalist bridgehead on the Sungari, to the east of Kirin, crossed the river, and on 17 May encircled Kirin, whose garrison shut themselves up in the city and proclaimed martial law. Lastly, the Communist group in the southeast cut the Mukden-Kirin railroad at Tsingyuan on 15 May and took Tunghwa on the

25th. Confronted by this catastrophic situation, the Nationalists made a grave decision: they abandoned the Liaotung Peninsula and concentrated their forces around Mukden. Thanks to a massive effort by their attack aircraft and their unhindered use of air transport, the Nationalists succeeded in the resupply and reinforcement of their encircled garrisons, and finally managed to re-establish a precarious link between Mukden, Changchun, and Kirin.

The Communists used the early days of June to exploit their successes. By 10 June, only Szepingkai still held out in the area between Mukden and Changchun. In the southeastern sector the Fourteenth and Fifty-second armies, which had held Liaotung for the Nationalists, succeeded in making their way north and concentrating anew at Mukden; but this success, requiring as it did the abandonment of Antung, led to the fall of that city, and of considerable matériel, to the Reds on 10 June. On the 20th Liaoyang, in its turn, succumbed to the Reds. By 16 June the Communist tide was at its height. Kirin and Changchun had been isolated. The Reds had entered Szepingkai. Mukden was now threatened from the north, the east, and the south. Finally, all of Liaotung was now in Communist hands.

Nevertheless, the arrival of the Fifty-second and Fourteenth armies at Mukden now permitted the Nationalist high command to retake the offensive. These two armies attacked along the railroads leading out of Mukden, while the New First Army and the Eighth Army (formerly a puppet army of the Japanese) launched similar attacks from Changchun and Kirin. Jumping off simultaneously from Mukden and Changchun, the attacking Nationalist forces succeeded in linking up on 2 July, after retaking Szepingkai. On 9 July the Nationalists announced the "liberation" of the Mukden-Changchun railroad. Contact between Changchun and Kirin had been restored on 29 June; but the greater part of the Kirin-Mukden railroad remained in the hands of the Reds, who also retained their hold on the line from Yingkow to Tashihkiao.

As of 10 July, when torrential rains brought operations to a halt, the balance sheet of battle reveals the disaster that had befallen Chiang Kai-shek: loss of half the Nationalist-occupied territory in Manchuria; abandonment of two thirds of the railroads; enormous losses of matériel, weapons, and supplies of all sorts. The low morale of the government's troops had caused a great number of desertions which, when added to combat losses, had reduced the strength of all Nationalist units by an average of over fifty per cent. Some units had been particularly hard hit: after the battles at Hwaite and Kung-chuling, the 88th Infantry Division of the Seventy-first Army, for example, had been reduced to the strength of a battalion. All the fleeing garrisons had abandoned considerable amounts of matériel, leaving entire depots and supply trains to the Reds, and many organic vehicles and weapons as well. Along the railroads, bridges had been destroyed, the ties torn up and burnt, the rails thrown into the fires and twisted into uselessness.

Although the Reds were not yet capable of standing up against continuous and massive attacks employing modern matériel and air power, they showed a degree of mobility and flexibility which enabled them to evade most of the blows leveled against them. Their discipline and morale were incomparably better than the Nationalists'. This is proved by the ratio between the weapons lost by the Communists and the number of Red prisoners and dead: one rifle, five prisoners, fifty dead.[4] If after two months of uninterrupted operations they stood in need of a certain amount of regrouping and re-

[4] It is interesting to note that figures from Nationalist sources, though undoubtedly exaggerated in absolute terms, reflect the same ratio.

equipping, they had lost little of their combat effectiveness. This fact is even more remarkable when it is realized that in Manchuria the great majority of Communist troops, cadre as well as fillers, were local recruits whose training, in theory at any rate, could not be compared with that of Chiang's "Burma veterans" or the Japanese-trained puppet troops of what had formerly been Manchukuo.

The American Consul General at Mukden reported the real situation at the end of May 1947:

In past two months [the] morale [of] Nationalist forces has deteriorated at rapidly accelerating pace. Present serious state of their demoralization has been confirmed to us by many sources ... and has become matter of wide public knowledge and talk. It is reflected in jumpy nerves of military garrison, efforts to evade conscription, and reliable information from all sectors of Nationalist territory (including points distant from current fighting) indicating that Nationalists in a panicky state are feverishly building trench systems everywhere with only "Maginot" defense strategy in mind. There is good evidence that apathy, resentment, and defeatism are spreading fast in Nationalist ranks causing surrenders and desertions. Main factors contributing to this are Communists' ever-mounting numerical superiority (resulting from greater use [of] native recruits, aid from underground and Korean units), National soldiers' discouragement over prospects [of] getting reinforcements, better solidarity and fighting spirit of Communists, losses and exhaustion of Nationalists, their growing indignation over disparity between officers' enrichment and soldiers' low pay, life, and their lack of interest in fighting far from home among "alien" unfriendly populace (whereas Communists being largely natives are in position of fighting for native soil).[5]

Confronted by such a situation, it would appear that Chiang Kai-shek should have written off Manchuria com-

[5] U.S. Department of State, *United States Relations with China, with Special Reference to the Period 1944–1949* (U.S. Government Printing Office, 1949), pp. 315–316. Tr.

pletely, in order to concentrate all his forces in North China while he still had a certain superiority in numbers and armament. But the Generalissimo did not want to "lose face." He satisfied himself with firing a scapegoat, General Tu Yü-ming. Persisting in his attempt to hold on in Manchuria, an increasingly difficult operation, he was to bury his best troops in this "far-off land." As the American White Paper so rightly concludes, the Communist victories must be attributed primarily to the "military ineptness of the Government,"[6] reflected by this overextension in Manchuria; and it was in Manchuria that the Kuomintang cause was lost.

THE BATTLE OF SHANTUNG

While these disasters were befalling the Nationalists in Manchuria, a bitter struggle was raging in Shantung, a major Communist stronghold which the Nationalists wanted to seize before moving on into Hopeh, Shansi, and the Red "Border Region" of Shenkanning. Once again the struggle centered around the control of the railroads. Shantung is crossed from north to south by the Tsinpu railroad (Tsinan-Pukow), and from east to west by the Kiaotsi (Kiaochow-Tsinan) and the eastern part of the Lunghai (Sian-Kaifeng-Suchow-Tunghai). The Nationalists had controlled almost all of the last two lines since late 1946; they now sought to open a way to the north, so as to link the Tsinan-Tsingtao corridor to the rest of the territories under their control.

But Chiang, always seeking particularly prestigious successes, decided to commence his campaign with the capture of Lini, an important commercial center, the capital of the Communist zone in Shantung, and the headquarters of General Ch'en I. The battle, which pitted eight Nationalist divisions

[6] *Ibid.*, p. 314. Tr.

—half of them mechanized and American-equipped—with air support, against no more than six Red divisions, opened in December with a Nationalist advance which carried as far as Tsangshan. But on 1 January the Reds counterattacked with their customary dash, hitting the Nationalist flanks with night and dawn attacks boldly executed after rapid marches and carefully coordinated with guerrilla harassment of the Nationalist rear. By 23 January the Reds were threatening Taierhchwang and the Grand Canal; they had also made prisoners of several Nationalist generals, cut the Lunghai railroad, and seized the mining center of Tsangshan. The situation of the Nationalists had clearly become critical when a new defection of General Ho P'eng-chu, who suddenly changed sides and went back to Chiang Kai-shek on 23 January, forced the Communists to break off their attack toward Suchow. During the war against the Japanese, Ho P'eng-chu had commanded the Nanking puppet government's forces in the Shantung region; he had rallied to Chiang in 1945 and then, on 9 January 1946, had gone over to the Reds with his four divisions, totaling forty thousand men, who held the coast of Shantung between Liangcheng and the mouth of the Shu. Although Ch'en I had never really trusted Ho's "New United Army of Central China" and was quickly able to react to its loss, the new threat to his capital from the east forced him to abandon his offensive.

The defection of Ho P'eng-chu brought with it an inordinate increase in the confidence of the Nationalists, who now wanted to do three things all at once: capture Lini; clear the Tsinpu railroad to the north; and trap Ch'en I's troops between the Kiaotsi rail line and the Nationalist troops advancing from the east and south. Despite a vigorous Communist counterattack in the first days of February, Ch'en I was forced to evacuate his headquarters, and the victorious Nationalists entered Lini on 15 February. As usual, they found their prize to be completely devoid of Red troops, all of whom had vanished. Once again the Nationalists were faced with the same dilemma: they had either to mass their forces, in order to push the Reds back and seize the cities—a ponderous solution incapable of bringing the elusive enemy to decisive battle; or they could scatter out to clear the countryside—a hazardous solution which ran the risk of exposing thinly deployed forces to defeat in detail. In view of General Ch'en I's exceptional talents, this last possibility became a strong probability.

In 1947 Ch'en I was forty-eight years old, a short, stubby man, quick-moving and quick-talking. He always wore a beret, pulled down almost to his ears; beneath a scraggly moustache a cigarette perpetually protruded from his mouth, one side of which continually drooped in a sardonic sort of half-smile. At first sight he gave, with his rough manner, an impression of coarseness; but this impression would soon yield to an awareness of the lively intelligence reflected in his eyes. And this man, a master of disconcerting irony, was also a poet and an ardent lover of art and the theater. He had studied in France, where he won his degree in electrical engineering. His inquiring mind had led him to take a job as a common workman in the Michelin plant at Clermont-Ferrand, where he worked for some time, and in the Creusot works as well: it also led him into a new belief in Communist doctrine. Upon his return to China he immediately joined the Red troops in the Kiangsi-Fukien region,[7] where he commanded a band of guerrillas. When the Chinese Red Army started off on its "Long March," Ch'en was left behind with General Yeh T'ing, and took command of one of the divisions in Yeh's newly organ-

---

[7] According to several other authorities, Ch'en returned to China in 1921, and did not join the Red Army until 1927, at the time of the Nanchang Uprising. *Tr.*

ized Fourth Army. He also became Yeh's second-in-command, and took over the New Fourth Army as its acting commander when Yeh was arrested by the Nationalists in 1941. Upon Yeh's death in a plane crash in 1946, after his release from Nationalist captivity, Ch'en was officially confirmed as commander of the Communist New Fourth Army. He also confirmed his reputation as a master in the art of prompt retreats and unexpected reappearances, becoming so famous for this in Shantung that the peasants would say, of each Red victory: "Ch'en I is back at the front."

Meanwhile, following their capture of Lini, the Nationalists undertook to move back up the Tsinpu railroad, and entered Yihsien on 17 February, Tenghsien on the twenty-fourth, and Tsowhsien on the 25th. They found nothing before them but a void, the Reds having suddenly withdrawn to the east. On the 28th, Kufow, the home of Confucius, fell into their hands. To the Nationalists, everything now seemed to be going their way. In a move designed to trap Ch'en I's elusive forces, the government's Twelfth and Seventy-third armies, under General Wang Yao-wu, now pushed southward from Poshan, near the Kiaotsi rail line, toward a link-up at Lini with the Nationalist forces in the south.

The Red reaction was truly remarkable. While Ch'en I's troops hit hard at the flanks of the Nationalist armies moving southward and also harassed the Kiaotsi railroad in their rear, the Red forces of General Liu Po-ch'eng, coming all the way from Hopeh, crossed the Lunghai railroad and threatened Suchow from the southwest in a move calculated to compel the Nationalists to withdraw from northern Shantung.

In the face of the concurrent Communist threats to Tsinan and Suchow, the Nationalists were forced to abandon their southward march on Lini and pull back for the defense of the Kiaotsi railroad. They tried in vain to trap the forces of Liu Po-ch'eng, which had ventured far from their base in Hopeh;

but Liu, after having saved Ch'en I from a serious threat of encirclement, at the end of February withdrew to the north of the Lunghai rail line. Better yet for the Reds, they had succeeded in cutting the Kiaotsi railroad between Weihsien and Yehsien, thus restoring a direct link between their zones in Hopeh and northern Shantung.

In March, however, a mighty effort by the Nationalists brought their southern forces, which took Tawenkow on 27 March and arrived at Taian on 1 April, to a successful link-up with the forces of General Wang Yao-wu, who pushed southward from Tsinan to meet them at Taian on 2 April. A precarious connection was thus established between Tsinan and Suchow, but the rail line continued to be subjected to the unceasing attacks of Communist guerrillas. In April the Nationalists attempted a link-up at Mengyin, moving Ou Ch'en's forces eastward from the Tsinpu railroad and T'ang En-po's troops northward from Lini; the attempt failed under the counterattacks of ten Communist columns, numbering about ten thousand men each. Ch'en I's skillful maneuvering had denied the Nationalists any decisive results.

Resuming their efforts on 1 May, Ou Ch'en and T'ang En-po finally succeeded, at the price of considerable losses, in effecting their junction in the Mengyin area. In the erroneous belief that they had destroyed the enemy, they made the dangerous mistake of dividing their forces and venturing forth in divergent directions. Ou Ch'en moved northward toward Poshan, while T'ang En-po charged off to the east against Ishui, which he attacked in conjunction with other Nationalist forces moving northward from Lini. On 16 May, the left flank of the forces which were moving on Ishui from Mengyin was hit by a Communist counterattack that threw the troops of T'ang En-po into a complete rout. The Nationalists were forced, at least temporarily, to give up their attempts to cut off the Shantung peninsula from the rest of China. Moreover, the following months saw them become bogged down in a series of difficult mountain operations which cost them enormous losses in men and matériel and brought them nothing in the way of really positive results. As of 1 July the Communists still retained their hold upon the peninsular portion of Shantung, more than half of the central plain, and the Weihsien-Yehsien isthmus.

But also by 1 July the Nationalists, for their part, had succeeded in completely clearing the Tsinpu railroad between Tsinan and Suchow and carving out a large corner of southern Shantung. This dearly bought success led Mao and Chu Teh to decide upon a major redisposition of Red forces. In Shantung, Red guerrillas, militiamen, and newly formed regular columns were left with the task of spreading confusion throughout the enemy's rear areas and harassing the Kiaotsi and Tsinpu railroads. From Hopeh, Liu Po-ch'eng attacked southward along a broad front. Since this attack denuded southern Hopeh of Red troops, Ch'en I's regulars were moved out of Shantung to replace Liu Po-ch'eng's forces in southern Hopeh. The Nationalists were unable to prevent this major shift of Communist forces. Although Ch'en I's departure permitted them to reach the Gulf of Laichow and thus, in theory, to accomplish their mission, they never really conquered peninsular Shantung. This hard campaign, which cost the Nationalists considerable losses, did little to diminish the Communists' powers of resistance.

OPERATIONS IN HOPEH AND SHANSI, AND THE ATTACK ON YENAN

During the first half of 1947 the struggle in Hopeh and Shansi was characterized by the inability of the Nationalists to exert effective control in the territories which, theoretically, were under their authority, and by the ease with which Communist guerrillas severed communications and gradually became a threat even to the large cities. In Hopeh, a key position which permitted the Reds to implement their "horizontal plan" and maintain contact between the Shenkanning Border Region and Shantung, General Liu Po-ch'eng had no difficulty in repelling the attacks of Hu Tsung-nan, whose twelve divisions were little more than equal in strength to Liu's. As for General Fu Tso-yi, who held Peking for the Nationalists, he kept open the Peking-Paoting-Chengting portion of the Pinghan railroad; but he never succeeded in clearing even a short stretch of the Tsinpu line.

In Shansi, General Hu's government troops received no support at all from the forces of Yen Hsi-shan, who was satisfied merely to protect the Chengtai railroad (Chengting-Taiyuan). This inaction delivered almost all of the province into the hands of the Reds, who also seized the arsenal at Chaoyi on 21 January 1947. When they perceived that the Nationalists, inspired only by the desire to obtain a prestigious success, had made the strategic error of committing considerable force to the sterile conquest of Yenan, the Reds gradually built Shansi into their principal base of maneuver. Repeated Red attacks hemmed Nationalist forces in Shansi into a few cities, whose garrisons were resupplied only by air. The Communists also harassed Yen Hsi-shan's troops along the Chengtai railroad and launched violent attacks against Shihkiachwang, near Chengting.

The Nationalist attack on Yenan was long in the making. For several months there was indecisive fighting around the fringes of the Shenkanning Border Region, particularly in the southern salient of the area. On 20 January the Nationalists seized the town of Malanchen, in the center of the salient, declaring that this operation was purely defensive in nature. In reality, major troop concentrations were effected there by the Nationalists, who then launched simultaneous attacks from four directions. In the north, the 22nd Infantry Division, operating under the orders of General Fu Tso-yi, pushed southward from Yulin. In the west, General Ma Hung-ku'ei's troops advanced eastward from Ningsia. From the southwest two cavalry divisions, based at Kingchwan, pushed to the north along the valley of the Tung. And from the south, General Hu Tsung-nan, with five well-trained and Russian-equipped divisions, on 15 March attacked in force northward between the Lo Ho and the Yellow River.

Facing these forces the Communists had barely half-a-dozen poorly equipped brigades, two of which were training units; they also had some militiamen, armed only with pikes, or rifles of venerable vintage. The Communists had long since anticipated the attack and were well prepared to evacuate the miserable "Border Region" and set themselves up in Shansi, where they now decided to establish the new seat of their government. Ho Lung's defending Red troops were therefore quite content to fight only delaying actions.

The Nationalists' main effort attacked in two columns, the right wing moving up the Yellow River and the left advancing directly upon Yenan from Lochwan. The left wing took Fuhsien on 15 March and Kanchuan on the 16th, and on the 18th was stopped at the Tahsiaolao pass by the last fortified position in front of Yenan. The right wing took Linchenchen on 15 March, veered to the left to seize Chengchiakou on the 17th, infiltrated the Yen Shui hills on the 18th, and arrived, during the night of 18–19 March, on the heights which dominate Yenan from the southeast. At 0800 hours on 19 March the 1st Division (of the left wing) led the Nationalist entry into Yenan, which was found to be completely empty. By this time the party's Central Committee was at Wayaopu, about

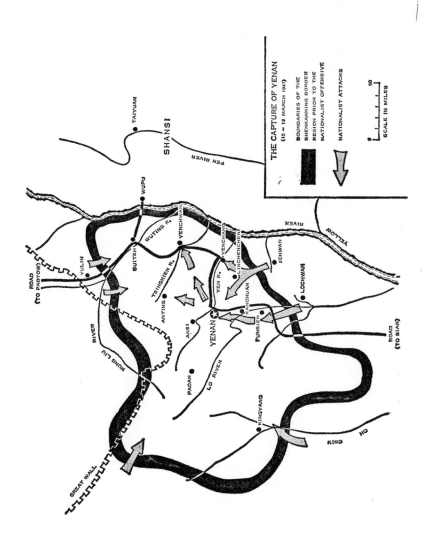

THE CAPTURE OF YENAN
(15 — 19 MARCH 1947)

BOUNDARIES OF THE
SHENKANNING BORDER
REGION PRIOR TO THE
NATIONALIST OFFENSIVE

NATIONALIST ATTACKS

SCALE IN MILES

fifteen miles north of their "capital," heading for a leisurely withdrawal down the Suiteh-Wupu road toward Shansi; the families were already at Suiteh, the radio transmitter at Wayaopu, and the administrative services at Anting.

The capture of Yenan, the capital of Chinese communism, was proclaimed to the world as a great triumph for Chiang Kai-shek. In reality it was only another false victory. The Nationalist armies had cast and drawn their net around a void. Henceforth, as they ventured forth into northern Shansi, they were to find themselves in a strategic situation which would lead only to their defeat.

CHAPTER IX

1947: The Last Six Months

Two Communist campaigns constituted the major developments of the last half of 1947. On the one hand, there were Lin Piao's sixth and seventh offensives in Manchuria which, without being decisive, achieved appreciable results and drained the Nationalists of their last reserves; on the other, southward envelopments by the armies of Ch'en Keng, Liu Po-ch'eng, and Ch'en I succeeded, to everyone's amazement, in establishing new Communist bases in Central China, near the north bank of the Yangtze itself. By the end of 1947 the Communists were to have almost made up their previous inferiority in numbers and armament, and were ready to undertake massive offensive operations.

THE NORTHEASTERN THEATER OF OPERATIONS

Following their defeat in the summer of 1947, the Nationalists had reorganized their high command in the Northeast, and the dualism that had existed between the Peace Preservation command (General Tu Yü-ming) and the Generalissimo's headquarters in this region (General Hsiung Shih-hui) had been suppressed through dissolution of the former. Both generals had been relieved of their commands and replaced by Chiang's Chief of the Supreme Staff, General Ch'en Ch'eng. The new commander had twenty-five divisions, divided into four groups; some of these troops were cooped up in the cities—Changchun, Kirin, Szepingkai, Mukden, and Fushun—which were the Nationalists' centers of resistance, and the rest were scattered among the isolated strong points along the railroads. No reserves were available, but Chiang had promised to send ten to twenty divisions as reinforcements.

On the Communist side, Lin Piao had somewhere between 250,000 and 300,000 men, twenty-five divisions, twenty of which were concentrated to the east of the Mukden-Changchun line around Meihokow, plus five "independent divisions." Supplementing these purely Chinese forces were some Koreans (who arrived, in fully trained and organized units, direct from North Korea), some Mongols, and some Japanese. The Communists were armed with Japanese matériel, taken from the Kwantung Army with Russian permission, and with weapons captured from the Nationalists. The Reds were well trained, fairly well supplied in ammunition by their arsenals, and well led. Their artillery consisted of horse-drawn 75 mm., 105 mm., and 155 mm. pieces, which they employed, following Russian practice, in massive concentrations. Gradually, they increased recruitment and training of Manchurian peasants to the point where they were to have no difficulty in replacing their losses.

During the breathing spell that remained to them, the Nationalists made feverish efforts to re-establish rail communications between Peking and Mukden, which were absolutely necessary to them if they were to receive reinforcements and resupply. Unfortunately, it is much easier to sabotage a railroad than it is to repair it or, what is even more difficult, to protect it. Despite the construction of thousands of pill boxes, and the parceling-out of tens of thousands of troops to man them, the Communists practically always succeeded in their sabotage, either by raids against small stations and bridges, or by mine-laying, rail removal, and razing of telephone poles. According to a Nationalist officer, there were, in September 1947, no more than one hundred Communists engaged in sabotage against the Peking-Paoting, Peking-Tientsin-Shanhaikwan, and Peking-Kupehkow railroads. Yet, during this single month, sixty-two successful sabotage operations, which destroyed 201 rails and 876 ties, were carried out by the Reds against these three lines.[1] Despite these difficulties, Nationalist railroadmen, with astonishing patience and great ingenuity, persisted in repair work which permitted the passage of several trains. But the necessary materials became increasingly scarce, and eventually the Nationalists were to find it impossible to assure the proper functioning of their transport services.

The sixth Communist offensive in Manchuria began on 15 September 1947. Carried out by troops of the Hopeh-Jehol-Liaoning military zone, it was directed at the Peking-Mukden railroad, between Chinchow and Shanhaikwan, with the isolation of Manchuria from North China as its strategic objective. Despite the reinforcement of the defending Nationalists the offensive was a complete success for the Communists, who cut the railroad about ninety-five miles south of Mukden and seized the molybdenum mines at Chinsi as well.

The second phase of the offensive opened on 1 October. Its objectives were to isolate the cities of Changchun, Kirin, and Szepingkai from Mukden, and to cut Mukden itself off from the ports at Hulutao and Yingkow. At the same time, the Communists organized foraging sweeps to seize the harvest in the areas controlled by their adversaries. In accordance

[1] Earlier, in July, comparable figures were: twenty-nine sabotage operations, fifty-five rails, and 534 ties.

133

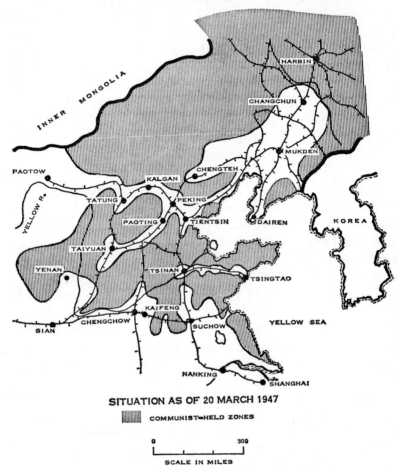

SITUATION AS OF 20 MARCH 1947

COMMUNIST—HELD ZONES

0   300

SCALE IN MILES

with their plans for a hedgehog defense, the Nationalists, as expected by the Reds, withdrew into the cities, which were rapidly surrounded by the Reds. Kungchuling, a town halfway between Szepingkai and Changchun, fell to the Communists on 4 October. South of Szepingkai, the Reds took Changtu and Kaiyuan on the 5th, but were stopped at Tiehling by fierce resistance from the forces of General Liao Yao-hsiang.[2] Between Mukden and the sea the Nationalists lost Tashihkiao and Haicheng, but continued to resist at Yingkow. In the face of arriving Nationalist reinforcements (one division came from Jehol and two divisions from North China were disembarked at Hulutao) the Communists—who had not yet committed the bulk of their forces, which remained to the east of the Mukden-Changchun line—broke off their attacks and momentarily withdrew. But the Reds maintained their grip upon the large cities they had previously surrounded; and it was only by the most painful effort that the Nationalists, during the two-month lull (15 October–15 December) that followed the sixth Red offensive, succeeded in establishing a precarious link between Szepingkai and Mukden by retaking Kungchuling on 1 November. The same kind of effort was required for the relief of Kirin, which was accomplished on 13 November.

The Reds launched their seventh offensive on 15 December. It soon became evident that, once again, Lin Piao's goal was the isolation of Mukden from the rest of Manchuria. In order to strengthen the defense of the city, General Ch'en Ch'eng was forced to shift there from Changchun two good divisions of the New First Army (the 30th and the 38th), which were replaced by two divisions airlifted from Fukien. This shift prevented the Communists from taking Mukden, but it permitted them to concentrate the bulk of their forces—eight columns of regulars, reinforced by independent units—well to the south of Changchun, in an area northwest of Mukden and between the main north-south railroad and the border of Jehol.

[2] General Liao Yao-hsiang, born in 1906, was a product of French training, including the Military Academy at St. Cyr (1931–1933), the Cavalry School at Saumur, and service with a French cavalry regiment at Strasbourg. During World War II, he commanded the New Sixth Army in Burma. He took command of the 4th Group Army at Mukden shortly before the Communists launched their sixth offensive in Manchuria.

Adhering to the strategic precepts of their great leader, Mao Tse-tung, the Communists did not yet attempt to reduce the large cities, such as Changchun and Mukden; but one could sense that an all-out Communist offensive would not be long in coming.

On 1 January 1948 Chiang Kai-shek reassuringly declared that "the threat of Mukden's encirclement" had "disappeared." On the same day, General Chang Chun[3] proclaimed that the critical period in the Northeast had passed and that "Nationalist troops were ready to launch their winter offensive." He added that the Reds had made a great mistake in overextending their lines of communication, and in ignoring the rigors of winter; as for the Nationalists, concentrated at several well-defended points, they could "contemplate the future with serenity." Nothing could have been further from the truth. The Communists, who lived off the land and obtained their arms and ammunition from the enemy, did not even have, properly speaking, lines of communication, which were so important to the Nationalists. And far from being spent, the Communist columns ceaselessly grew in strength. Very soon, on 5 January 1948, the Nationalists—who had hoped for a respite of two months—were to undergo an eighth Communist offensive in Manchuria.

OPERATIONS IN NORTH CHINA

Manchuria, where the Nationalists continued to pour in their best troops and use up what remained of their transport aircraft in extremely costly operations, was not the only scene of Nationalist reverses during the last half of 1947. The period also witnessed the Communists' consolidation of their great

---

[3] At this time Chang Chun was President of the Executive Yüan, or premier, of the National Government. *Tr.*

base in Shansi; the Nationalists' loss of Hopeh, and their failure to clear Shantung; the breakout of Communist forces to the south of the Lunghai railroad; and, finally, the establishment of a Red base in Honan, high in the Tapieh mountains to the northeast of Hankow.

Operations in Shansi and Shensi

Following their loss of Yenan to the forces of General Hu Tsung-nan, the Communists maneuvered very skillfully in Shansi. While Ho Lung's forces in the northeast of the province conducted delaying actions in their slow withdrawal to the north, General Ch'en Keng, in the south, launched an attack westward toward the Yellow River which threatened to take Hu Tsung-nan's forces in the rear. The Nationalist commander in Shansi was still, as always, the old war lord Yen Hsi-shan, whose sole thought was to hold on to Taiyuan, his capital, with his own private army; he cooperated little, if at all, with Hu Tsung-nan, or with Fu Tso-yi, who commanded in Chahar as well as in Suiyuan and Hopeh. Having isolated Taiyuan, Ch'en Keng's Red forces took Yicheng on 5 April and crossed the Fen river, after defeating the Nationalist reinforcements sent out from Shensi by Hu Tsung-nan.

The Red forces in northern Shansi, aided by forces from Inner Mongolia and Suiyuan, pushed northward and threatened Tatung with encirclement. In the eastern part of Shansi, the Reds further protected their grip on the province by mounting a bold attack against the Chengtai railroad, an attack coordinated with a threat to Shihkiachwang by their forces in Hopeh. By May, practically all of Shansi was in Communist hands, except for a strip along the Peking-Suiyuan railroad in the north, a few Nationalist strong points undergoing gradual reduction, and the beleaguered capital at Taiyuan.

137

In the neighboring province of Shensi the Nationalists, after their capture of Yenan, had been stopped by the threat of a westward movement against their rear by Ch'en Keng's forces in southern Shansi. A link-up between the forces of Fu Tso-yi and those of Hu Tsung-nan, along the line Yulin-Yenan, was now the goal of the Nationalists. This goal seemed to be in sight in July, after the capture of Suiteh and Micheh, but the Nationalists' successes had overextended their highly vulnerable lines of communication, and they failed to reach it. Moreover, Red forces moved up the Yenan-Yulin road from Yuhopao in March 1947 and attacked Yulin, reaching its outskirts on the 27th. This town, which Fu Tso-yi's forces seemed incapable of defending, was saved by a relief column of thirty thousand men dispatched by the governor of Ningsia (General Ma Hung-ku'ei), who until then had refused to commit his troops outside his own province. The Red forces pulled back to the western border region of Shensi, south of the Great Wall.

Operations in Hopeh

In Hopeh the Nationalists were exposed to unceasing guerrilla warfare within the triangle Peking-Tientsin-Paoting and, as early as 9 April 1947, to the attacks of Liu Po-ch'eng's regulars in the Shihkiachwang area. As of September the Nationalists still had a firm grip on the Peking-Suiyuan railroad, the Peking-Tientsin-Mukden line, and the Pinghan (Peking-Hankow railroad) as far as Paoting. But Paoting itself was almost completely encircled by the Reds, who also took Chengting, in the vicinity of Shihkiachwang.

In the last months of the year the situation took a sudden turn for the worse, changing the forced optimism of Nationalist officers into the darkest pessimism. The principal causes of this abrupt change were the fall of Shihkiachwang and

Yuanshih to the Communists, and the reinforcement of General Nieh Jung-chen's forces by two Communist columns which had hitherto been part of Li Yung-chang's command in eastern Hopeh and southeastern Jehol. The fall of Shihkiach-wang, taken by the Communists after the crushing defeat of General Lu Li-fung's forces in a pitched battle fought in open country, was a heavy loss for the Nationalists. It not only freed large numbers of Red regulars for further operations; the loss of this important town also meant the loss of much railroad matériel to the Communists. And Mao Tse-tung, moving in behind his conquering troops, soon established his new capital at Shihkiachwang.

Thus, as of 1 January 1948, except for the Tientsin-Peking-Kalgan-Tatung corridor, still firmly held by Fu Tso-yi, and the encircled cities of Taiyuan, Paoting, and Anyang, the Reds were in possession of all of Shansi and Hopeh. For the Nationalists this was a major defeat.

Liu Po-ch'eng's Offensive in Central China

During the night of 11–12 August 1947 the Red columns of General Liu Po-ch'eng, about fifty thousand strong, crossed the Lunghai railroad to the east of Kaifeng and, meeting with no resistance, flooded southward toward Honan. Advancing at the rate of thirty miles per day, they reached the mountainous Tapieh Shan region where, in conformity with classic Communist doctrine, they established a new base. Swerving then to the east, their advance guards reached the heights overlooking the Anking-Hofei highway on 11 September. While passing through Liuan,[4] Liu's columns cleaned out the Nationalist arsenal there, carrying off some 150,000 rifles. Almost simultaneously, on 22 August, the twenty thousand troops of General Ch'en Keng, one of Liu Po-ch'eng's prin-

[4] A town in Anhwei, about 130 miles west of Nanking.

cipal subordinates, crossed the Yellow River in the vicinity of Yuanku, cut the Lunghai railroad between Loyang and Shanhsien, and marched east to join up with Liu. To counter this perilous threat, the Nationalists reinforced the Hankow region with units from Chungking and Canton. But the ceaseless growth of Communist strength, fed by numerous volunteers, soon made it apparent to the Nationalists that a major operation would be required if they were to succeed in wiping out the new Communist base. Thus, the center of gravity of the fighting had suddenly moved south, almost to the Yangtze. For Chiang Kai-shek, who managed to keep up a show of optimism, this was a very severe blow.

Meanwhile, Liu Po-ch'eng's movement to the Tapieh mountains had left a gap in southern Hopeh. The forces of General Ch'en I, based in Shantung and threatened by a Nationalist offensive against Chefoo, received Chu Teh's order to fill this gap. Crossing the Lunghai rail line on 27 September with five columns, Ch'en I bypassed Suchow and on 8 October cut the Tsinpu railroad on either side of Suhsien, as well as the Pinghan line in the vicinity of Hsuchang.

During December the struggle raged in the region between the Yellow River and the Yangtze, where three Communist armies were now in action. Ch'en I's force of seven columns was operating on both sides of the Lunghai line, to the east and south of Kaifeng. Liu Po-ch'eng's six columns were in the Tapieh mountains and adjacent areas to the south and west. Ch'en Keng, with two columns and the Thirty-eighth Army, was fighting in the area west of the Pinghan line up to the Honan-Shansi border.

The activity of these three groups was both intense and important. They severed Nationalist lines of communication, interdicted river traffic on the Yangtze, and destroyed protective outposts along the Lunghai and Pinghan rail lines, all in order to isolate the cities and aggravate the supply problems of the Nationalists. In December Liu Po-ch'eng further widened the action by thrusting two columns, against stiff Nationalist opposition, to the west of the Pinghan railroad near Liulin. And everywhere the presence of these Red forces gave rise to numerous guerrilla bands which threatened the large population centers and spread anarchy and desolation throughout the region.

The End of the Shantung Campaign

Having failed in their attempt to conquer Shantung by land, the Nationalists organized an amphibious operation. On 27 August a landing took place at Shihkiuso, about sixty miles southwest of Tsingtao, followed by another at Chefoo. A third landing, at Weihaiwei on 30 September, was repulsed by the Reds.[5] The capture of Chefoo was hailed as a great victory by the Nationalist press; but it brought no decisive results and, in spite of Ch'en I's departure for the Kaifeng area, the remaining Red columns in Shantung escaped the Nationalist pincers. Moreover, the forces of General Su Yü, who had replaced Ch'en I as Red commander in Shantung, succeeded in maintaining control of the peninsula, Weihaiwei included, and of their important bases in the Chucheng area. In November the Reds retook Laiyang, Chiaohsien, and Kaomi and then, pushing southward, reoccupied all the ground they had lost as far as the borders of Anhwei and Kiangsu. The Shantung campaign, into which the Nationalists had poured up to half-a-million men, ended in bitter defeat. And they were never to regain the initiative.

[5] The Nationalists took only Linkung, the island off the port of Weihaiwei.

CHAPTER X ✧

Political Developments in 1947

ON 2 March 1947 T. V. Soong resigned his post as premier,[1] very probably because he felt that China's financial situation was incapable of sustaining Chiang Kai-shek's program for all-out war, which in Chiang's view would be "all over in three months."[2] Increasingly influenced by the reactionaries of the CC clique, Chiang refused to give credence to the demoralization of his troops; in his view, the reason for their defeats was always treason. His response, in the face of student demonstrations against the Civil War, was to intensify the repressive action of the secret police.

To Chiang the capture of Yenan came as a ray of hope; but for the liberals in the Kuomintang, Nationalist defeats in Manchuria soon led to a realization that the situation was continuing to worsen. The government's only real solution was to take the road of radical reform. The Americans did all they could to bring this about. But such reforms as the reorganization of the Council of State, the naming of Dr. Sun Fo as Vice President and of General Chang Chun as premier,

[1] Soong's official title was President of the Executive Yüan. *Tr.*
[2] It should also be noted that the Constitution of 1947, under which the President of the Executive Yüan is appointed by the President of the Republic with the consent of the Legislative Yüan, was promulgated before Soong's resignation, on 1 January 1947. *Tr.*

effected in April 1947, were to mean little in actual practice. The CC clique continued to dominate the party, and the corruption and inefficiency of the Nationalist officials, who were miserably paid, led to a total lack of popular confidence in the party and in the Generalissimo himself. In an attempt to galvanize the troops the Standing Committee of the party's Central Executive Committee on 30 June decided to integrate the *San Min Chu I* Youth Corps into the Kuomintang, and to intensify punitive action against the Communists. At the same time an anti-Kuomintang plot was uncovered at Peking, and numerous arrests were made; the Democratic League, the left wing of which was indeed communistic, was compromised by the plot and subsequently outlawed. On 4 July the Communists were proclaimed to be "in open rebellion," and a general mobilization of all Nationalist resources was ordered.

Yet, while the Americans could see no other solution than far-reaching internal reforms, the Nationalists saw American aid as their sole source of salvation. This is why General Wedemeyer's arrival in China was greeted with satisfaction by the Nationalists. Charged by President Truman with a fact-finding mission covering the entire situation—political, economic, psychological, and military—Wedemeyer arrived at Nanking on 16 July and remained in China until 24 August. Upon his departure he summed up his findings in a public statement that came as a severe blow to Chiang Kai-shek. In it Wedemeyer criticized "the abject defeatism of many Chinese, who are normally competent and patriotic, and who instead should be full of hope and determination."[3] He declared that "the existing Central government can win and retain the undivided, enthusiastic support of the bulk of the

[3] U.S. Department of State, *United States Relations with China, with Special Reference to the Period 1944–1949* (U.S. Government Printing Office, 1949), p. 763. Tr.

Chinese people by removing incompetent and/or corrupt people who now occupy many positions of responsibility in the government, not only national but more so in provincial and municipal structures."[4] He insisted upon the urgent necessity of radical reforms in the army (equalization of the burden of conscription, increase in pay), and in the administration as well (pay increases for officials, lowering of taxes, and so on).

In the lengthy report presented to President Truman by Wedemeyer on 19 September, the general examined the problem in all its aspects. From a purely military point of view, he found the situation to be extremely serious:

Total Nationalist forces of about a million and a half combat troops plus another million service troops are opposing less than a million Communist combat troops and militia supported by an unknown number of service troops . . .

The underlying military reason for Communist success is that they retain the initiative, striking at places of their own selection with local superiority of forces and with a mission of *destruction* [author's italics]. Nationalist forces, on the other hand, with a mission of *protection* [author's italics], are forced to what amounts to a perimeter defense of scattered areas and of long connecting lines of communication. Such widespread defense offers little chance of lateral coordination and mutual support, thus immobilizing forces that would otherwise be available for offensive action. Communist drives appear to meet with little substantial resistance, while Nationalist withdrawals are generally premature and the words "strategic retreat" have lost all significance . . .

All in all, the military situation in China appears to be governed predominantly by Communists enjoying substantial military successes in Manchuria, in Shantung and in Hopeh. These successes can be attributed mainly to the lightness and efficacy of their hit-and-run guerrilla type forces, to their mission of destruction as opposed to the Nationalist mission of protection, to the ineptitude and incompetence of Nationalist high command, to the shrinkage of Nationalist communications, to the general depreciation and

4 *Ibid.*, p. 764. Tr.

depletion of Nationalist equipment and supplies, both ground and air, to increased friction between military forces from the south and civil administration in the areas under attack, and to the stigma attached to troops which so often live off the local civil population.[5]

After describing the situation, Wedemeyer came to the important matter of recommendations. He recommended:

That the United States provide as early as practicable moral, advisory and material support to China in order to prevent Manchuria from becoming a Soviet satellite, to bolster opposition to Communist expansion and to contribute to the gradual development of stability in China.

That China be advised to request the United Nations to take immediate steps to bring about a cessation of hostilities in Manchuria and request that Manchuria be placed under a Five-Power Guardianship (the U.S.S.R., the U.S.A., Great Britain, China and France) . . .

That China be advised to take steps to reduce its military expenditures in the national budget and at the same time increase the effectiveness and efficiency of the military establishment.

That China give continuing evidence that urgently required military reforms are being implemented.

That China, with the advice and support of the United States, develop and implement a sound program of equipment and improved logistical support.

That arrangements be made whereby China can purchase military equipment and supplies (particularly motor maintenance parts), from the United States.

That China be assisted in her efforts to obtain ammunition immediately.[6]

That the 8⅓ Air Group Program be completed promptly and that consideration be given to expansion of its air transport (two groups of C–47 aircraft).

[5] Ibid., pp. 808–809. Tr.
[6] The embargo on arms shipments imposed by Marshall in August 1946 had been lifted in May 1947.

That the China Mapping Program be extended in scope where practicable.

That the program for transfer of ships to China be completed as rapidly as China is able to utilize them effectively . . .

[That] military advice and supervision be extended in scope to include field forces, training centers and particularly logistical agencies[7] . . .

Thus Wedemeyer, recognizing that the National Government was "incapable of supporting an army of the size it now has in the field,"[8] was led to propose to Truman intensification of American aid to Chiang Kai-shek. In view of the Generalissimo's increasingly slim chances of victory, this proposed action risked troublesome consequences for the future course of Sino-American relations. As Brigadier Field, the British military attaché at Nanking, remarked at this time: "I would be most embarrassed if my government, finding itself in the situation of the United States, were to ask me to propose a solution to the problem."

American hopes for a sound and reasonable response from Chiang Kai-shek were soon dashed. The fourth session of the KMT's Central Executive Committee, which opened at Nanking on 9 September 1947, was to see the triumph of the reactionary clique and the consolidation of its hold upon the Youth Corps. The appointment of T. V. Soong as governor of Kwangtung was without doubt the result of a deal with the brothers Ch'en, who wanted to get Chiang Kai-shek's brother-in-law out of the way. It is true that Chiang tried to combat corruption, to put real power into the hands of the Control Yüan, and to re-establish, by augmenting the authority of the local police at the expense of the secret police, a certain degree of individual freedom. These fragmentary measures proved to

[7] *U.S. Relations with China*, p. 814. Tr.
[8] *Ibid*. Tr.

be insufficient. In October 1947 the military situation became increasingly bad; turning in anguish to the United States, Chiang met a deaf ear from the Americans, who held fixedly to their own plan. On 28 October, the Democratic League was outlawed. Carson Chang's Democratic Socialist Party rapidly crumbled. The political situation degenerated into anarchy. Eroded by factional intrigue, the political power of Chiang Kai-shek was steadily diminishing.

In contrast, Mao Tse-tung's power over the Communist movement became ever greater. In November 1947 he had established his capital at Shihkiachwang, reorganized his services, and placed political commissars at the side of the generals who were in command of armies. In the Central Committee, where he continued to lean upon the faithful shoulders of Liu Shao-ch'i, Jen Pi-shih, Lu Ting-i, and K'ang Sheng, his authority was never questioned; events had always borne him out, and his methods were showing themselves to be victorious. Following the successes of the last half of 1947, Mao on 25 December gave a speech to the Central Committee of the CCP that was a veritable victory chant. He proclaimed his conviction that the Communists now possessed all that was needed for the final victory he foresaw in 1949. Magisterially, he prescribed the strategy and tactics of the Red Army, and the necessity of agrarian reform. Finally, he violently attacked the United States, declaring that "reactionary American imperialism was the great enemy of humanity and the agent responsible for the continuation of the Chinese civil war." From a military viewpoint the principal passages of Mao's speech are well worth quoting at length.[9]

[9] The quoted passages are from the English translation of Mao's speech of 25 December 1947, "The Present Situation and Our Tasks," in *Mao Tse-tung: Selected Works*, vol. V: *1945–1949* (New York: International Publishers, 1956), pp. 157–163. Quoted by permission of International Publishers. *Tr.*

I. A *Turning Point in History*

The Chinese people's revolutionary war has now reached a turning point. That is, the Chinese People's Liberation Army has beaten back the offensive of several million reactionary troops of Chiang Kai-shek, the running dog of the United States of America, and gone over to the offensive. Already in the first year of the present war, from July 1946 to June 1947, the People's Liberation Army beat back Chiang Kai-shek's offensive on several fronts and forced him onto the defensive. And beginning with the first quarter of the second year of the war, July-September 1947, the People's Liberation Army went over to the offensive on a national scale and wrecked Chiang Kai-shek's counter-revolutionary plan of continuing to carry the war into the Liberated Areas in order to destroy them completely.

Now the war is no longer being fought chiefly in the Liberated Areas but in the Kuomintang areas; the main forces of the People's Liberation Army have carried the fight into the Kuomintang areas. In this land of China, the People's Liberation Army has turned back the wheel of counter-revolution—of U.S. imperialism and its lackey, the Chiang Kai-shek bandit gang—and sent it down the road to destruction and has pushed the wheel of revolution forward along the road to victory.

This is a turning point in history. It is the turning point from growth to extinction for Chiang Kai-shek's twenty-year counter-revolutionary rule. It is the turning point from growth to extinction for imperialist rule in China, now over a hundred years old.

This is a momentous event. It is momentous because it is occurring in a country with a population of 475 million and, having occurred, it will certainly culminate in victory throughout the country. Furthermore, it is momentous because it is occurring in the East, where over 1,000 million people—half of mankind—suffer under imperialist oppression. The turn of the Chinese People's War of Liberation from the defensive to the offensive cannot but gladden and inspire these oppressed nations. It is also of assistance to the oppressed people now struggling in many countries in Europe and the Americas.

II. Chiang Kai-shek's Counter-Revolutionary War and Its Direction by American Imperialism

From the day Chiang Kai-shek started his counter-revolutionary war we said that we not only must defeat him but can defeat him. We must defeat him because the war he started is a counter-revolutionary war directed by U.S. imperialism against the independence of the Chinese nation and the liberation of the Chinese people. After the conclusion of World War II and the overthrow of Japanese imperialism, the task of the Chinese people was to complete the new-democratic transformation politically, economically and culturally, to achieve national unification and independence and to change China from an agricultural into an industrial country. But at that time, after the victorious conclusion of the anti-fascist Second World War, U.S. imperialism and its lackeys in various countries stepped into the shoes of German and Japanese imperialism and their lackeys and formed a reactionary camp against the Soviet Union, against the People's Democracies in Europe, against the workers' movements in the capitalist countries, against the national movements in the colonies and semi-colonies and against the liberation of the Chinese people. At such a time the Chinese reactionaries headed by Chiang Kai-shek acted as the running dog for U.S. imperialism, just as Wang Ching-wei had done for Japanese imperialism, sold out China to the United States and unleashed a war against the Chinese people to check the advance of their liberation. At such a time, if we had shown weakness or given ground and had not dared to rise resolutely to oppose counter-revolutionary war with revolutionary war, China would have become a world of darkness and the future of our nation would have been forfeited. The Communist Party of China has led the Chinese People's Liberation Army in firmly waging a patriotic, just and revolutionary war against Chiang Kai-shek's offensive.

The Communist Party of China, having made a clear-headed appraisal of the international and domestic situation on the basis of the science of Marxism-Leninism, recognized that all attacks by the reactionaries at home and abroad not only had to be defeated but could be defeated. When dark clouds appeared in the sky, we pointed out that this was only temporary, that the darkness would soon pass and the sun break through. When the Chiang Kai-shek bandit gang launched the country-wide counter-revolutionary war in July 1946, they thought it would take them only three to six months to defeat the People's Liberation Army. They reckoned that they had a regular army of two million, more than a million irregulars and another million or more men in the military establishments and armed units in the rear, making a total military strength of more than four million; that they had taken time to complete their preparation for the offensive; that they had regained control of the big cities; that they had a population of more than 300 million; that they had taken over all the equipment of a million Japanese invading troops; and that they had received huge military and financial aid from the U.S. government. They also reckoned that the People's Liberation Army was tired after fighting for eight years in the War of Resistance Against Japan and was far inferior to the Kuomintang army in numbers and equipment; that the population of the Liberated Areas was only a little more than 100 million; and that in most of these areas the reactionary feudal forces had not yet been cleaned up and the land reform had not yet been universally and thoroughly carried out, namely, that the rear area of the People's Liberation Army had not yet been consolidated.

Proceeding from this appraisal, the Chiang Kai-shek bandit gang ignored the Chinese people's desire for peace, finally tore up the truce agreement signed by the Kuomintang and the Communist Party in January 1946, as well as the resolutions adopted by the Political Consultative Conference of all parties and launched an adventurist war. We said then that Chiang Kai-shek's superiority in military forces was only transient, a factor which could play only a temporary role, that U.S. imperialist aid was likewise a factor which could play only a temporary role, while the anti-popular character of Chiang Kai-shek's war and the feelings of the people were factors that would play a constant role, and that in this respect the People's Liberation Army was in a superior position. Patriotic, just and revolutionary in character, the war waged by the People's Liberation Army was bound to win the support of the people of the whole country. That was the political foundation for victory over Chiang Kai-shek. The experience of eighteen months of war has fully confirmed our judgment.

III. The Military Principles of the People's Liberation Army

In seventeen months of fighting (from July 1946 to November 1947; December figures are not yet available), we killed, wounded and captured 1,690,000 of Chiang Kai-shek's regular and irregular troops—640,000 killed and wounded and 1,050,000 captured. Thus we were able to beat back Chiang Kai-shek's offensive, preserve the main territories of the Liberated Areas and go over to the offensive. Speaking from the military aspect, we were able to do this because we employed the correct strategy.

Our principles of operation are:

1. Attack dispersed, isolated enemy forces first; attack concentrated, strong enemy forces later.

2. Take small and medium cities and extensive rural areas first; take big cities later.

3. Make wiping out the enemy's effective strength our main objective; do not make holding or seizing a city or place our main objective. Holding or seizing a city or place is the outcome of wiping out the enemy's effective strength, and often a city or place can be held or seized for good only after it has changed hands a number of times.

4. In every battle, concentrate an absolutely superior force (two, three, four and sometimes even five or six times the enemy's strength), encircle the enemy forces completely, strive to wipe them out thoroughly and do not let any escape from the net. In special circumstances, use the method of dealing crushing blows to the enemy, that is, concentrate all our strength to make a frontal attack and also to attack one or both of his flanks, with the aim of wiping out one part and routing another so that our army can swiftly move its troops to smash other enemy forces. Strive to avoid battles of attrition in which we lose more than we gain or only break even. In this way, although we are inferior as a whole (in terms of numbers), we are absolutely superior in every part and every specific campaign, and this ensures victory in the campaign. As time goes on, we shall become superior as a whole and eventually wipe out all the enemy.

5. Fight no battle unprepared, fight no battle you are not sure of winning; make every effort to be well prepared for each battle, make every effort to ensure victory in the given set of conditions as between the enemy and ourselves.

6. Give full play to our style of fighting—courage in battle, no fear of sacrifice, no fear of fatigue, and continuous fighting (that is, fighting successive battles in a short time without rest).

7. Strive to wipe out the enemy through mobile warfare. At the same time, pay attention to the tactics of positional attack and capture enemy fortified points and cities.

8. With regard to attacking cities, resolutely seize all enemy fortified points and cities which are weakly defended. Seize at opportune moments all enemy fortified points and cities defended with moderate strength, provided circumstances permit. As for strongly defended enemy fortified points and cities, wait till conditions are ripe and then take them.

9. Replenish our strength with all the arms and most of the personnel captured from the enemy. Our army's main sources of manpower and matériel are at the front.

10. Make good use of the intervals between campaigns to rest, train and consolidate our troops. Periods of rest, training and consolidation should in general not be very long, and the enemy should so far as possible be permitted no breathing space.

These are the main methods the People's Liberation Army has employed in defeating Chiang Kai-shek. They are the result of the tempering of the People's Liberation Army in long years of fighting against domestic and foreign enemies and are completely suited to our present situation.

The Chiang Kai-shek bandit gang and the U.S. imperialist military personnel in China are very well acquainted with these military methods of ours. Seeking ways to counter them, Chiang Kai-shek has often assembled his generals and field officers for training and distributed for their study our military literature and the documents captured in our war. The U.S. military personnel have recommended to Chiang Kai-shek one kind of strategy and tactics after another for destroying the People's Liberation Army; they have trained Chiang Kai-shek's troops and supplied them with military equipment. But none of these efforts can save the Chiang Kai-shek bandit gang from defeat. The reason is that our strategy and tactics are based on a people's war; no army opposed to the people can use our strategy and tactics.

On the basis of a people's war and of the principles of unity between army and people, of unity between commanders and fighters and of disintegrating the enemy troops, the People's Liberation Army has developed its vigorous revolutionary political work, which is an important factor in winning victory over the enemy. When we abandoned many cities on our own initiative in order to evade fatal blows from superior enemy forces and shift our forces to destroy the enemy in mobile warfare, our enemies were jubilant. They took this to be their victory and our defeat. They became dizzy with this momentary "victory." On the afternoon of the day he seized Changchiakou (Kalgan), Chiang Kai-shek ordered the convening of his reactionary National Assembly, as though his reactionary regime had from that moment become as stable as Mount Taishan.[10] The U.S. imperialists, too, danced with joy, as though their wild scheme for converting China into a U.S. colony could now be realized without obstruction.

But with the lapse of time, Chiang Kai-shek and his U.S. masters began to change their tune. Now all our enemies, domestic and foreign, are gripped by pessimism. They heave great sighs, wail about a crisis and no longer show any sign of joy. In the past eighteen months, most of Chiang Kai-shek's high-ranking field commanders have been replaced for losing battles . . . Ch'en Ch'eng, too, was relieved of his post as Chiang Kai-shek's chief of staff in over-all command of operations and demoted to command a single front in the Northeast. However, it was in the very period when Chiang Kai-shek himself assumed over-all command in Ch'en Ch'eng's place that the situation changed and that his armies shifted from the offensive to the defensive, while the People's Liberation Army went over from the defensive to the offensive. By now the reactionary Chiang Kai-shek clique and its U.S. masters should have realized their mistake. They had regarded as signs of cowardice and weakness all the efforts for peace and against civil war which the Communist Party of China, representing the wishes of the Chinese people, had made over a long period after the surrender of Japan. They had overestimated their own

[10] One of the five legendary mountains of ancient China.

strength, underestimated the strength of the revolution and rashly unleashed the war and so were caught in their own trap. Our enemy's strategic calculations failed completely.

These remarkably sound principles were very skillfully applied by Red armies that were manifestly well trained, well led, and possessed of an iron-like morale. And their victories were made all the easier by the fact that they were opposed by Kuomintang armies whose disintegration was becoming increasingly widespread.

✧ PART FOUR ✧

1948
THE DECISIVE YEAR

CHAPTER XI

The Situation at the Beginning of 1948

THE decisive year of the Civil War was 1948. On the one hand, Chiang Kai-shek's last attempts to renovate the economy failed, and President Truman refused to renew an American effort foredoomed to failure by the deepening disintegration of the Nationalist regime and its increasing unpopularity. On the other hand, the wear and tear on Nationalist forces was such that the Communists, having attained numercial parity, were now able to launch truly coordinated offensives, to attack large cities, and to fight and win pitched battles in open country; lastly, by securing all of Manchuria, the Reds were able to redeploy the additional forces that were to assure their final victory. There being no need for the Communists to guard conquered areas with regular troops, they could free such troops for further operations elsewhere; but Nationalist-conquered areas, because of guerrilla activity and the hostility of the populace, required enormous garrisons.

It is difficult to study simultaneously operations that were as entangled and confusing as those of the year 1947, which saw the Reds reach the Yangtze, continued fighting in Manchuria, Communist guerrilla activity in Kwangtung, and the

GENERAL DISPOSITION AND STRENGTH OF NATIONALIST AND COMMUNIST FORCES AS OF 1 JANUARY 1948[a]

Theater of operations	Nationalists	Communists	Nationalist margin of superiority
Manchuria	TOTAL: 400,000 men Nine armies under General Ch'en Ch'eng	TOTAL: 320,000 men General Lin Piao	80,000 men (25%)
Yellow River Valley	TOTAL: 280,000 men (28 divisions) 1. *Forces of Ku Chu-t'ung:* a) 75,000 men (8 infantry divisions), in the Suchow area. b) 75,000 men (8 infantry divisions), in the Kaifeng area. c) 70,000 men (7 infantry divisions), in Shantung. 2. *Forces of Hu Tsung-nan:* 60,000 men (5 infantry divisions). *Note:* all of these were reorganized divisions	TOTAL: 180,000 men 1. 60,000 men under Ch'en I in Shantung, western Honan, northern Anhwei. 2. 40,000 men under Ch'en Keng in western Honan. 3. 40,000 men under Ho Lung in southern Shansi. 4. 40,000 men under Su Yü in Shantung.	100,000 men (55.6%)

North China	TOTAL: 430,000 men 1. 230,000 men under Fu Tso-yi (20 to 25 divisions, not reorganized) in Hopeh, Chahar, Jehol, Suiyuan, northern Shansi. 2. Fu Tso-yi's "personal" troops amounted to 100,000 men. 3. 200,000 men under Yen Hsi-shan in central Shansi (inactive troops).	TOTAL: 120,000 men 1. 60,000 to 80,000 men under Nieh Jung-chen in Hopeh and Chahar. 2. 40,000 men under P'eng Te-huai in northwestern Shansi.	310,000 men (258%) Exclusive of Yen Hsi-shan's troops, the difference is 110,000 men (92%)
Yangtze Valley	TOTAL: 140,000 men Twelve divisions under Pai Ch'ung-hsi, whose command extended to the valley of the Hwai.	TOTAL: 80,000 men 1. 40,000 men under Liu Po-ch'eng in the Tapieh Shan. 2. 20,000 men under Li Hsien-nien in the valley of the Han. 3. 20,000 men under Wang Hung-kun in the area northwest of Hankow.	60,000 men (75%)

RECAPITULATION: Communists: 700,000 men   Nationalists: 1,250,000 men

[a] Nationalist strength figures are exclusive of troops located to the south of the Yangtze and in Szechwan. The Communist strength figures are for regulars only, and do not include guerrillas or militia.

faithful adherence of the northwestern provinces (Ningsia and Kansu) to the Nationalist cause. It is clear, however, that numerical parity between the two armies had not yet been arrived at as of 1 January 1948. The table on pages 158–159 gives the strength and general disposition of the opposing forces at this time. It shows that the Nationalists still had a two-to-one superiority. Nevertheless, they had suffered enormous losses. Even though Mao Tse-tung's claims of 640,000 killed or wounded and 1,050,000 prisoners for the period July 1946–November 1947 were doubtlessly exaggerated, the government itself admitted Nationalist losses of 400,000 killed, wounded, and missing during 1947. As for the Nationalist claims of 638,000 Communist dead and 127,000 prisoners, it is certain that they were far more exaggerated than those of the Communists. In any event, the really important factors were the cohesion of Communist troops, their discipline, and their tremendous moral superiority over their adversaries.

Mr. M. Keon,[1] a reliable non-Communist newspaperman from Australia who spent several months of 1947 with the Reds in Shantung, has provided extremely interesting information on this subject. As soon after each engagement as the situation permitted, a small unit would assemble to listen to its leader's explanation of the operational results obtained, his criticisms, and his answers to the questions all were free to ask. Mr. Keon once witnessed the return of a small detachment from the front with half its strength wounded; one of the casualties had lost an arm and was still in tourniquet, and another had a bad stomach wound; the customary critique

---

[1] Michael Keon, in 1947 a correspondent for the Melbourne newspaper *The Age*, later served as Press Attaché of the Australian Embassy in China. He also covered the guerrilla war in Malaya. He is the author of two novels dealing with Communist guerrilla warfare, *The Tiger in Summer* (1953), and *The Durian Tree* (1960), and is currently news editor of the *Rome Daily American*. Tr.

took place anyway, and the wounded asked questions like everyone else. In another case, a telephone line was being strung over a fast-flowing river by a fifteen-man detail; when three of the men fell and drowned, they were rapidly replaced, without the others ever faltering in their task. Numerous other incidents testifying to the energy and courage of Communist troops appear to have deeply impressed Mr. Keon, especially after what he had seen on the Nationalist side.

The behavior of the Red Army toward the population was always scrupulously correct, and its soldiers everywhere received a joyful welcome. Red troops were forbidden to interfere in village politics, and they actively aided the peasants whenever help was needed. Products of the same political education, soldier and peasant thought alike, and the Red Army was truly one with the *lao pai hsing*.[2]

Although there was conscription, the great majority of Communist soldiers were volunteers. Of peasant origin, the volunteer valiantly defended the lands newly acquired by his own kind, and fought with an enthusiasm heightened by awareness of the honor now accorded the role of soldier. He could also derive some degree of material or educational advantage from service with the Red Army. He was generally well armed with either Japanese or captured American weapons, and large stocks of Japanese small-arms and artillery ammunition came from Manchuria, by junk, for distribution to all units. Locally manufactured hand grenades were favorite weapons, but there was also great stress on bayonet training. Radio and telephone communications, benefiting from Japanese and American equipment, were excellent, with some telephone lines extending over hundreds of miles. Motor vehicles were quite plentiful, and fuel was supplied as needed by whole convoys of wheelbarrows (Mr. Keon saw convoys

[2] The "hundred thousand," or common people.

of up to three thousand wheelbarrows, each with a two-man team). The Communists continued to free their prisoners en masse, even the officers, usually after a period of political indoctrination; by this means, they riddled the Nationalist zone with spies and agitators.

There is no doubt that the Nationalist Air Force hampered the movement of Communist troops, which almost always took place under the cover of darkness. Bombing of villages by B-25's was seldom effective, especially since the bombings always occurred at regular, set times; strafing attacks, usually by P-51's, were feared far more by the Communists. The Reds had no active antiaircraft defenses, but an excellent warning system existed in all the villages.

At this time (late 1947), Mr. Keon estimated that at least sixty per cent of the peasants were pro-Communist, most of the others being neutral and a few discreetly hostile. Essentially, the Communists' success with the peasantry was due to their program of land redistribution and to the relief they promptly provided whenever scarcity threatened; it was also the result of a state of mind which Communist propagandists so well knew how to create. For the first time in Chinese history, the peasantry had become the object of attention and intensive education. Mr. Keon has described a typical village of the time: schoolchildren, like ambulant apostles, would teach the elders, read the wall newspapers to them, help with the household chores and sometimes in the fields, and set up mutual aid and cooperative organizations. The Communists found their most ardent adherents among young children and adolescents, upon whom they bent their greatest efforts. The younger generation was especially useful in keeping tabs on public opinion, and frequently practiced a familial sort of espionage. There was also a great change among women, most of whom came to be strong supporters of the Communist Party.

Although there was an active political life in the villages, complete with elections, town meetings, and leaders who very often were non-Communists, the all-powerful political commissar was always there to rectify errors and maintain adherence to the party line. This kind of politico-administrative organization of the village tended to supplant the traditional family organization; thus the village, where every measure was discussed and decided upon in common, was replacing the family as the basic unit of Chinese society. At higher levels of government, such as the provincial, there was a large proportion of non-Communist administrators; former officials of the Kuomintang's central or provincial regimes, they were kept on by the Communists because of their technical skills. They were what the Russians call "specialists." Staying on because of sentimental regional attachments, job interest, or a taste for responsibility, most of them were remarkable individuals who indirectly did much to help a movement whose own administrative personnel were still lacking in experience.

Both in theory and in apparent practice there was a complete separation between administration and politics. There were, however, numerous propagandists, ninety per cent of whom were students, both male and female. These young people, nourished on Marxist literature and fluent in classical Communist phraseology, were the "pure ones," the "believers," always ready to sacrifice themselves, as well as others, to the continued functioning of a machine they themselves had helped to set in motion. Their energy and devotion to the people were limitless. Together with the army's political commissars, they constituted the vital force of the Chinese Communist Party. But, deeply influenced as they were by the Soviet Union, they were already *more Marxist than Chinese*. Hatred of Americans and admiration for the U.S.S.R. constituted the core of their opinions on foreign affairs. Apart from anti-American slogans and the arguments employed by party leaders, the attacks by Nationalist aircraft—the American origins of which were known to all—resulted in resentments which considerably facilitated the agitators' task. The name of General Marshall was rendered particularly infamous: he was denounced as a double-crosser who had deliberately disguised the machinations of the American "imperialists." It is likely, however, that the real target of this agitation against Marshall was the head of the State Department, responsible as he was for American foreign policy.

In brief, according to Mr. Keon, communism had brought to China a mystique, a faith, which had enraptured Chinese youth and infused them with an extraordinary dynamism classically based upon two slogans: for internal use, "Land Reform"; for external use, "Liberation of the Fatherland from the Imperialists." The success of this propaganda was astounding. And to oppose it there was no real counter-mystique; there was only a decadent and fossilized political party.

By the end of 1947 the Kuomintang was finished, and far beyond redemption by any amount of aid from abroad.

CHAPTER XII ✧

1948: The First Six Months

OPERATIONS IN MANCHURIA

On 5 January 1948 General Lin Piao launched his eighth offensive, with seven columns, to isolate Mukden from China Proper and the rest of Manchuria as well.

In order to isolate Mukden from China, Lin had to do three things: maintain, and if possible enlarge, the incision his forces had made in the Peking-Mukden railroad; cut the Mukden-Dairen railroad; and close off the port of Yingkow. At the first news of Lin's entirely unexpected attack, Chiang Kai-shek hastened to Mukden on 10 January. Here he replaced General Ch'en Ch'eng by General Wei Li-huang, and decided to reinforce the new commander with two divisions transported by sea from Shantung to Hulutao and Chinwangtao; the "Liaoning corridor" had to be held at all costs. Despite these enemy reinforcements, Lin Piao succeeded in taking Kowpangtze on the Peking-Mukden line, and cutting, with the fall of Liaoyang on 4 February, the Mukden-Dairen railroad. The port of Yingkow, which came under heavy attack at the end of January, fell to the Reds on 27 February. Mukden, however, was staunchly defended by its Nationalist garrison, which received strong reinforcement by air.[1] Early in March, Lin Piao shifted the bulk of his attacking forces to the north and displaced his headquarters from Liaochung, about thirty-five miles southwest of Mukden, to Faku, some fifty miles to the north of the city. Although the Red offensive against Mukden had not been decisive, it had forced General Wei to weaken his garrisons at Kirin, Szepingkai, and Changchun in order to strengthen Mukden; and the Nationalists had failed in their attempts to maintain a link between Mukden and North China.

Breaking out anew in the north, the Communist offensive took Kirin—abandoned by the Sixty-ninth Army for Changchun[2]—on 9 March, and Szepingkai on the 13th. Changchun, some 120 miles to the north of Mukden, was now completely isolated; and Mukden itself was now the center of a circular Nationalist-held area no more than sixty miles in diameter.

The situation in Manchuria was desperate. Unwilling, at any price, to lose face, the Generalissimo had refused to evacuate his troops while there was still time, as he had been advised to do by General Barr, the director of JUSMAG.[3] The garrisons of Mukden and Changchun were now being resupplied only by air (seven to ten aircraft per day), and it was clear that such airheads could not be held indefinitely. Consequently, a Nationalist offensive to reopen the Liaoning corridor, at all costs, was clearly necessary. But to the Nationalists, frozen as they were in a defensive mentality, no attack was conceivable without a numerical superiority of at least three to one. None of General Barr's suggestions was accepted.

[1] Following the fall of Liaoyang, General Wei had assigned forty C–47 "Dakotas" to the transport of troops from northern Manchuria to Mukden.
[2] This shift came about at the insistence of Chiang's American advisers, who felt that all of Manchuria should have been evacuated at this time. Chiang, however, consented only to the evacuation of Kirin.
[3] The Joint U.S. Military Advisory Group to China.

To his increasingly strong and even angry representations, the sole response was new requests for more weapons and matériel. Yet the Mukden garrison, consisting of the Fifty-second Army, the Thirteenth Army, and the New Sixth Army— 200,000 men, well trained, well armed, supported by ample artillery and even tanks—could easily have broken out to link up with relieving forces from Chinchow. But General Wei Li-huang could think only of static defense.

Thus, for two months all was quiet on the Manchurian front. Only the Nationalist Air Force was active, bombing— to no great effect—Tsitsihar, Meihowkow, Hailung, Tunghwa, and Yingkow, and attacking trains on the Harbin-Kirin, Kirin-Tunghwa, and Tashihkiao-Yingkow lines, which had been restored to operation by the Reds. Profiting from the inaction of his adversaries, Lin Piao sent part of his forces to the aid of his comrade Li Yung-chang in Jehol, and devoted his time to training his troops and organizing new columns. As the summer went by there were only small skirmishes, with the Nationalists attempting a sortie to the south in May and the Reds continuing their close investment of Changchun, where famine gradually set in. Yet one could sense that the last round in Manchuria was drawing near.

OPERATIONS IN NORTH CHINA

In North China, at the beginning of 1948, General Fu Tso-yi, with his headquarters at Peking, kept a firm hold upon the Tientsin-Peking-Kalgan-Tatung-Paotow line with 230,000 troops of his own private army. His forces thus were able to maintain contact with the troops of Ma Hung-ku'ei, the governor of Ningsia, who had won the battle of Yulin. In contrast, the situation in Shansi was much less favorable to the Nationalists: Marshal Yen Hsi-shan, with 200,000 men, was practically encircled at Taiyuan, and Nationalist forces in the south of the province now held no more than the town of Linfen and a small bridgehead across the Yellow River. In Shensi, General Hu Tsung-nan[4] still held Yenan, but was experiencing difficulties accentuated by Communist guerrilla attacks which gradually wore down his forces. Finally, three fourths of Jehol and Chahar was in the hands of the Communists. Here the Reds had reinforced Nieh Jung-chen, who had eighty thousand regulars, while in Shansi and northern Shensi, Ho Lung and P'eng Te-huai together had only fifty thousand men.

THE BATTLE OF ICHWAN AND THE RED DEFEAT AT PAOKI

The first important operation was the battle of Ichwan, in Shensi, which ended in the recapture of Yenan by the Reds. The offensive was launched on 29 February 1948 by General P'eng Te-huai, who had spent most of January and February in reorganizing his twelve columns along the regulation lines prescribed for Communist columns. Debouching from the Anyi area and attacking toward the northwest, P'eng's forces encircled and annihilated four brigades of the Twenty-ninth Army; the army commander, General Liu Kan, who had taken Yenan the year before, was killed on the battlefield, and numerous other generals were killed or captured. Ichwan fell on 3 March, its capture by the Communists accompanied by their destruction of a new brigade of the 76th Infantry Division. Kanchuan fell to them on the 5th and Fuhsien the next day. By 10 March the Reds had arrived in front of Loch-

---

[4] It is interesting to note that this Nationalist commander's troops were equipped with *Russian* matériel, given to Chiang Kai-shek by the U.S.S.R. at the beginning of the war against Japan.

wan where the Nationalists, pulling themselves together, managed to put up a staunch resistance. In the belief that he had sufficiently weakened the enemy, P'eng Te-huai left the siege of Lochwan to part of his forces and, concentrating four of his columns and two cavalry divisions about sixty miles north of Sian, on 17 April launched an audacious raid toward Szechwan, with only his 3rd Column as rear guard.

The Nationalists then decided to evacuate Yenan and abandon the city to the Reds. At the price of this hard blow to their prestige, they were to gain a real success. After leaving Yenan and relieving and gathering up the defenders of Lochwan, the 27th and 17th infantry divisions set off in pursuit of P'eng Te-huai. It was high time: the Communists had by now crossed the King river at Pinhsien and cut the Lanchow-Sian road between Changwu and Kienhsien; by 27 April, they had taken Paoki, on the Wei river at the western extremity of the Lunghai railroad, a town in which the Reds found much valuable booty. P'eng now posed a direct threat from the north to the province of Szechwan, the Nationalists' holy of holies, and they bore in on him from all sides. A division coming from the east retook Paoki on 28 April. A Moslem cavalry division from General Ma Pu-fang's command rushed down the Lanchow-Sian road from Tsinghai. Finally, the divisions moving down from Yenan cut off P'eng Te-huai's retreat. A decisive battle then ensued within the triangle Linyu-Fengsiang-Kienyang; the Reds lost half their strength, and were forced to pull back into northern Shensi. Despite this defeat, the Communists managed to keep their hold on almost all of Shensi, and their base in Shansi remained sheltered from Nationalist attacks. And even P'eng's defeat itself had served to demonstrate that, henceforth, Szechwan was vulnerable to Communist attack.

THE BATTLE OF LOYANG

The second major operation was the battle of Loyang, a strategically important city on the Lunghai railroad taken by Ch'en Keng's army in a northward attack from Honan. Loyang fell to the Reds on 12 March, only to be retaken by the Nationalists on 18 March; it changed hands for the last time when the Reds, in their turn, retook the city on 7 April 1948. Thus, the Communist base in Shansi was now and henceforth linked to Liu Po-ch'eng's newly organized Red base in Central China. The Reds rounded out their victory at Loyang by taking Linfen, the last island of government resistance in southern Shansi; the city and its 25,000-man garrison fell to the Communists on 17 May. The Red troops freed by its fall immediately moved north to join in the siege of Taiyuan.

OPERATIONS IN SHANTUNG AND KIANGSU

Despite the departure of Ch'en I's forces from Shantung, the Communists, during the first half of 1948, continued to gnaw away at Nationalist strength in the province. This strength was further reduced by the need for Nationalist reinforcements in Manchuria, and for the formation of a reserve against the threat of Liu Po-ch'eng's columns along the Yangtze. Slowly, the Red guerrillas regained the upper hand. They reduced, one by one, the Nationalist strong points along the Kiaotsi railroad. On 27 April they seized Weihsien and entered Weihaiwei, which had been "voluntarily" abandoned by the Nationalists; they now could block off Tsinan, defended by 100,000 men, and Tsingtao, still occupied by American forces (a naval task force, three thousand Marines, and fifty combat aircraft).

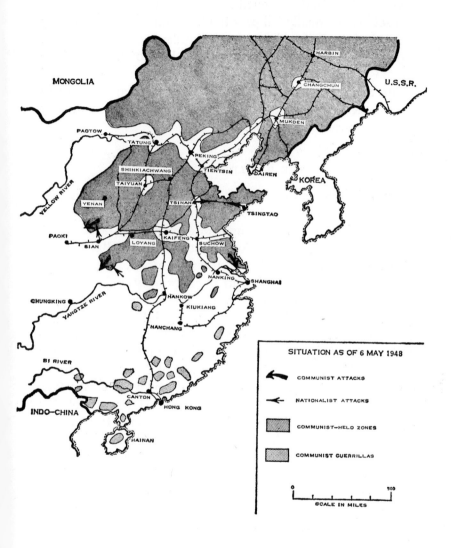

SITUATION AS OF 6 MAY 1948

COMMUNIST ATTACKS

NATIONALIST ATTACKS

COMMUNIST—HELD ZONES

COMMUNIST GUERRILLAS

0   500
SCALE IN MILES

While their leaders argued among themselves, the Nationalist soldiers gradually fell prey to Communist propaganda. By the end of April the Shantung peninsula, except for Chefoo, had been completely mopped up by the Communists. The last of Ch'en I's columns were now free to move westward and isolate Suchow, as Su Yü's forces made their appearance in southern Kiangsu with the capture of Honancheng, about sixty miles to the east of Nanking.

THE BATTLE OF KAIFENG

Following the fall of Loyang the Communist objectives in Central China became Chengchow and, above all, the city of Kaifeng. The battle of Kaifeng is of capital importance in the history of the Civil War. For the first time, the Reds, abandoning guerrilla tactics for positional warfare, were to join battle with the Nationalists in open country and maneuver large masses of infantry, artillery, and even some tanks.

Preceding this major milestone, some interesting politico-military developments took place within the Nationalist camp during May 1948. After the re-election of Chiang Kai-shek as President by the National Assembly at Nanking in April, the Vice Presidency became the object of a bitter struggle. The election of General Li Tsung-jen, who was not the Generalissimo's candidate for this post, appeared to be a sure index of Chiang's waning influence. The political crisis which followed this election was ended, on 24 May, only by the naming of Dr. Wong Wen-hao as premier,[5] with General Ho Ying-ch'in as Minister of National Defense and Dr. Wang Shih-chieh as Minister of Foreign Affairs. Simultaneously, General Ku Chu-t'ung became Chief of the Supreme Staff, and was replaced as Commander in Chief of the Army by General

[5] Or President of the Executive Yüan. Tr.

Yü Han-mou. These two generals were known for two principal characteristics: their professional mediocrity, and their fierce loyalty to Chiang Kai-sek. Their incompetence was promptly proved by the battle of Kaifeng.

Kaifeng, the capital of Honan province, is a city of about 300,000 inhabitants, surrounded by ramparts and served by two airfields. Its military significance lies in its covering location to the east of Chengchow, the strategically important junction of the Lunghai and Pinghan railroads. In May 1948 the Nationalists had twenty-five brigades in the Chengchow-Kaifeng area, about 250,000 men; added to these regular troops were about fifty thousand men of the Peace Preservation Corps, railroad guards, and various auxiliary units. These forces were divided into three group armies, commanded by generals Chiu Ching-chuan, Huang Po-tao, and Ou Shou-nien. Against these considerable numbers the Reds threw eighteen columns, about 200,000 regulars, supported by guerrillas, and organized into five groups assigned to the armies of Ch'en I, Ch'en Keng, and Liu Po-ch'eng. General Ch'en I had over-all command of the entire operation.

The Red attack started at the end of May. One group moved down from Shantung, took Taian on 30 May, and advanced southward along the Tsinpu railroad, while another group, coming from Shansi, crossed the Yellow River at Puhsien and advanced as far as the area around Kinsiang and Chengwu. The latter group was then blocked by the Nationalist Fifth Army, which sought to prevent the junction of the two Communist groups. The Fifth Army being thus engaged, Ch'en I moved from the center of Honan toward Chengwu with a third Red group, his initial idea being to hit the Fifth Army from the rear. In pursuit of this plan he crossed the Lunghai railroad, reaching the Lanfeng-Kaocheng area on 15 June. Then, receiving intelligence on the weakness of the

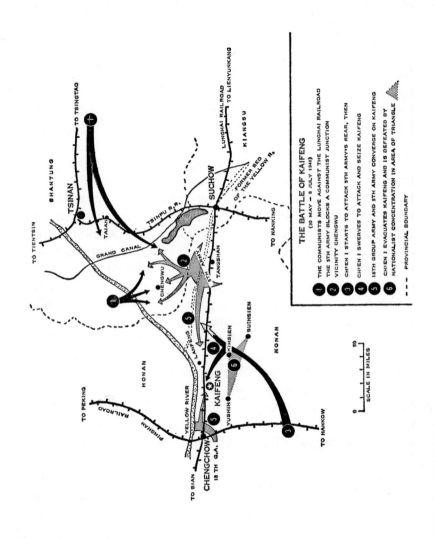

garrison at Kaifeng, Ch'en abandoned his initial scheme of maneuver and improvised a swift descent upon the capital of Honan, with the aim of looting its large depots and gaining a success of enormous psychological value. He thus launched his three columns against Kaifeng and, after a brief struggle against weak resistance, took the airfields on 17 June and the city itself on the 19th.

The capture of Kaifeng did indeed produce a considerable effect: since the fall of Kalgan, it was the first provincial capital to be taken by the Reds. The Generalissimo himself hastened by air to Chengchow, where he took over personal direction of operations. At his orders Kaifeng was bombed by the Nationalist Air Force which, flying much too high, obtained no militarily significant results and contented itself with killing civilians. Meanwhile, the Nationalists hurried their troops to the scene of Ch'en's audacious victory. The Fifth Army and part of the 16th Group Army closed in on Kaifeng from the east and west. In the face of this threat, Ch'en I slipped smoothly out of the city on 25 June and, well covered by the columns of Ch'en Keng and Liu Po-ch'eng, withdrew his forces eastward to the south of the Lunghai railroad. Within a triangular area bounded by Suihsien-Kihsien-Yushih there now took place a great battle. It lasted until 8 July and ended in a partial defeat for the Communists who, seeing clearly that they could not win, rapidly dispersed to the north, south, and southeast, leaving a void before the victors. But the Reds had inflicted ninety thousand casualties upon their foes; and the Nationalists, despite their final success, had shown in this battle a marked tactical inferiority to an adversary who had continually kept the initiative and dominated the situation.

Moreover, the behavior of Communist troops at Kaifeng had greatly impressed the populace: perfect discipline, no pillage, no arbitrary arrests, the helpfulness constantly shown by the Red soldiers to the sorely tried inhabitants of the city —all this added to the prestige of the Communists. And the Reds now had well-organized fifth columns in all the cities. As soon as they arrived in Kaifeng, for example, they readily found the local personnel needed for the establishment of a provisional administration; the Nationalists discovered, to their angry consternation, that even the head of the Kuomintang's propaganda office in Kaifeng was a Communist agent!

With respect to the Nationalist high command, the record of an interview with one of the Nationalist field army commanders[6] after the Kaifeng offensive is of interest:

In March 1948, Ch'en I moved north of the Yellow River to regroup. Three months later we were warned that he was preparing an offensive. At this time we were south of the Yellow River, facing the 1st, 4th, 6th, and 11th columns, plus the Two Kwangs Column and the Rapid Column. Then two of Ch'en I's columns south of the Lunghai railroad, the 3rd and the 8th, started moving west toward Shangkiu. Those *fumbling bunglers* in the National Defense Ministry ordered me to displace to the south to intercept these two columns. I wired back that if I were to do so, the Communists would move the main body of their forces south of the Yellow River. They replied that if the Reds were to do this, I would still be able to get back in time to stop them. So I obeyed the order and moved south. We marched over thirty miles a day, getting only two hours' sleep out of the twenty-four, but before we could catch up with the 3rd and 8th columns, Ch'en I slipped across the Yellow River with his main body. The Defense Ministry then ordered me back to my former positions. My soldiers were furious, but we turned around and went back. . .

On 26 June, I was all set to move into Kaifeng. The Generalissimo wired me from Sian: "Enter Kaifeng." But the Ministry of Defense panicked: before I ever got the Generalissimo's message about Kaifeng, the Ministry ordered me to move south imme-

---

[6] The energetic General Chiu Ching-chuan (who was later killed in the fighting around Suchow in January 1949. Tr.)

diately to Kihsien, and ordered Ou Shou-nien to displace from Shangshui to Suihsien. . .

On 30 June the Ministry ordered me to go to the rescue of General Shen.[7] I started moving out toward the east on 1 July, with my 83rd Infantry Division taking heavy losses. On 2 July a plane dropped a message to me from the Ministry: five new Communist columns, under Liu Po-ch'eng, were about to hit me from the rear. I turned around, but there was nothing there. This false report must have been put out by the Communists . . . and the Ministry, as usual, fell for it.

THE RELATIVE SITUATION OF EACH SIDE AS OF 1 JULY 1948

In a secret session of the Legislative Yüan on 24 June 1948, generals Ho Ying-ch'in and Hsiao Yi-shu, the Minister and Deputy Minister of Defense respectively, revealed some very interesting information regarding long-term changes in the strength of the two sides. At the time of Japan's surrender, the government had had 3,700,000 men, of whom 1,620,000 were armed, and six thousand artillery pieces.[8] Against these, the Communists had had 320,000 regulars, of whom 166,000 were armed, and six hundred artillery pieces. By late June 1948 the situation had changed drastically. While the strength of regular troops in the Nationalist Army had been reduced by about one third, the number of Red regulars had quintupled, and the Communists had attained parity with their adversary in combat matériel. The Nationalists now had no more than 2,180,000 men, 980,000 of them armed, and 21,000 artillery pieces. Opposing them now were 1,560,000 Red regulars and 700,000 guerrillas, with a total of 970,000 rifles and 22,800 artillery pieces. And it is easy to guess where the

[7] Commander of the Nationalist 75th Infantry Division, then engaged at Suihsien.

[8] Including 37mm. guns and mortars.

greater part of all this Red matériel came from: it had been captured from the Nationalists.

For their part, the legislators sharply criticized the poor organization of the high command, the unfair rewards and punishments, the favoritism and empire-building of influential generals. They broke out in particularly harsh denunciation of the officers who set themselves up in business with military funds, and used army trucks for the transport of their "merchandise."

In reply, General Ho Ying-ch'in declared that he was sending inspectors to all troop units in an effort to restore proper discipline; he had prohibited the trafficking denounced by the legislators; he was struggling against the practice of officers to pad payrolls and pocket the pay of nonexistent enlisted men; he was seeking to raise the pay of officers and men alike, which by now had dwindled to one fourth and one fifth, respectively, of prewar levels.

This memorable session clearly revealed the deep malaise and discouragement which prevailed among the Nationalists, at a time when their adversaries were gaining one success after another—as shown by the appearance of Communist guerrillas in every province of Nationalist China, and especially in Kwangsi, in Kwangtung, and even in Szechwan.

It was in North China that the situation of the Nationalists, thanks to the quality of Fu Tso-yi's troops and his good administration, remained the most stable. But the government's need to withdraw troops from Chahar and Jehol, in order to reinforce Manchuria, had permitted the Reds to intensify increasingly numerous attacks against the Tatung-Kalgan-Peking-Tientsin railroad and the Tientsin-Shanhaikwan and Peking-Kupehkow lines, which were repeatedly cut, and to keep the entire region south of Peking in a permanent state of confusion. At the end of the first half of 1948 the government still held its essential bastions in North China (the quadrilateral Peking-Tientsin-Mukden-Chengteh) and in Central China (Suchow, Chengchow, Sian), in this manner covering the valley of the Yangtze. Nonetheless, the situation south of the Great Wall was back where it had been in January of 1946. Indeed, the Communists had made appreciable gains since that time:

(a) Occupation of all of Shantung except Tsinan, the Lini salient near the Kiangsu border, and the two hemmed-in ports at Chefoo and Tsingtao; the Nationalists, moreover, had suffered enormous losses in the battles of Weihsien (45th Infantry Division) and Kiaohsien (32nd Infantry Division);

(b) Occupation of all of Shansi, except for the besieged capital at Taiyuan; the capture of Linfen, where the Nationalists' 30th Infantry Division was completely destroyed; the capture in June 1948 of all the towns in the central plain, and the destruction of two thirds of Yen Hsi-shan's forces;

(c) Reoccupation of Yenan and occupation of western Honan, including Loyang.

To offset these Red victories the Nationalists could claim only meager successes: incomplete reduction of Liu Po-ch'eng's bastion in the Tapieh Shan; P'eng Te-huai's check at Paoki; and the reoccupation of Kaifeng.

In the first half of 1948 the directives of Mao Tse-tung and Chu Teh brought about a complete change in the nature of Communist operations. During the first year of war (generally speaking, the period from July 1946 to July 1947), the course of operations had followed an almost immutable pattern. The Nationalists would concentrate their forces in a zone of particular interest, and launch a powerful and sometimes rapid push along the axis of a major road or railroad. Normally, they would reach their objective against little or no resistance. Communist units would then stage only brief and limited attacks against such vulnerable targets as isolated strong points, displacing units, or lines of communication. In nature if not in degree, their actions differed very little from those of guerrillas who attempt to make an occupied region untenable for the enemy. Except for the first battle of Szepingkai, this early period saw the careful avoidance by the Communists of any prolonged, positional battle, and very few sieges on their part. Only in regions of reputedly impregnable terrain did the Reds ever seek to make a serious stand.

September and October of 1947 marked the beginning of a profound change in this pattern, not only in Manchuria but in China Proper as well. Without renouncing its traditional hit-and-run tactics, the Red Army now showed that it no longer feared to undertake sieges: Weihsien, Linfen, Tzeyang, and Loyang were taken; Tatung, Changchun, Chengteh, and Tsinan were attacked; Kaifeng, though subsequently retaken by the Nationalists, had fallen to the Reds. But of far greater significance was the increasing frequency of Communist operations in open country, at first in Manchuria and then in China Proper. And these movements were being made in ever greater strength: P'eng Te-huai attacked between Lanchow and Sian with six columns, and no fewer than sixteen Red columns had been concentrated in the course of the battles at Kaifeng and Kihsien. Communist operations now appeared to be better coordinated, more precise in their goals, more extensive in the choice of their objectives. Although they could not yet be compared to the operations which have unfolded upon the battlefronts of Europe, they at least showed an evolution in Communist strategy and tactics which more and more approached the scale and level sustained by their adversaries in the early months of the war.

A second important development was the southward shift in the war's center of gravity. The main theater of operations in 1946 had been in Manchuria; in 1947, Manchuria and, above all, Shantung, were the great cockpits of conflict. In October 1947 the strength of Red regulars to the south of the Lunghai railroad had totaled no more than eighty thousand men (forty thousand under Ch'en I, twenty thousand under Liu Po-ch'eng, and twenty thousand under Ch'en Keng). Now, in July 1948, official Nationalist estimates put the strength of regular Red troops in Central China at 450,000 or 500,000 men—a five-fold increase in less than one year. Where, in the previous year, Communist units had been chased from both sides of the Lung-hai and Pinghan railroads, it was now they who were doing most of the chasing, and who penned the Nationalists into the few population centers which remained to them. Three or four times in the past the Nationalists had pushed the Communists back into western Honan, and restored the Chengchow-Hankow section of the Pinghan rail line. Now they seemed too tired to do so, or incapable of doing so—even during the Kaifeng crisis, when they were stopped in their northward advance from the Sinyang area. As of 1 July 1948, *fully half the strength of both the Communists and the Nationalists was now in Central China.* This region had become the main theater of operations, without any lessening of previous activity along the northern fronts. And the regular forces of the Reds, as always under the supreme command of Chu Teh,[9] had now been organized into six field armies: the People's Liberation Army of Northwest China, commanded by P'eng Te-huai, with Wang Wei-chou and Chao Shou-shan as his deputies; the People's Liberation Army of North China, com-

[9] Mao Tse-tung remained Chairman of the Revolutionary Military Council. Yeh Chien-ying was Chief of Staff of the Red Army (by late 1947 known by its present name of "People's Liberation Army." *Tr.*)

manded by Nieh Jung-chen (deputy commander, Hsü Hsiang-ch'ien); the United Democratic Army of the Northeast, commanded by Lin Piao (with Lü Cheng-ts'ao and Hsiao Ching-kuang as deputies); the Shansi-Suiyuan-Shenkanning Field Army, commanded by Ho Lung (with Chang Tsung-hsun as deputy); the Liberation Army of the Central Plains, under Liu Po-ch'eng; and the People's Liberation Army of East China, commanded by Ch'en I, with Su Yü as deputy commander and Chen Shih-chu as Chief of Staff.

CHAPTER XIII

1948: The Last Six Months

THE second half of 1948 was to see the collapse of the Nationalists in Manchuria, the loss of their last stronghold in Shantung, and the fall of Kaifeng, Chengchow, Paoting, and Taiyuan to the Communists. The loss of these cities was in turn to bring about the total isolation of Fu Tso-yi's forces in the Peking-Tientsin-Kalgan area. And this area, in turn, was thenceforth cut off from Central China and the two provinces of the West, Ningsia and Tsinghai, which still remained faithful to the Nationalists.

THE BATTLE OF TSINAN

Tsinan, the capital of Shantung, is a city of about 700,000 inhabitants. The old walled city is adjoined, to the west, by a modern industrial section with many textile factories. On the north, the city is bordered by the lower course of the Yangtze. It is on the Tsinpu and Kiaotsi railroads, and until April 1948 the trains were still running between Tsinan and Suchow. There were two airfields, one to the northwest of the city and the other to the south, which were dominated by hills the Nationalists had taken care to enclose within the defensive perimeter they had set up around the city. Held by the Nationalists since the surrender of the Japanese, Tsinan had played an important role in their operations in Shantung. At first it had been a base of departure for Nationalist offensives; but it gradually became a refuge for the badly mauled units from the central part of the province. Since the Communist offensive of April-May 1948 the city had been completely isolated, except by air. Its garrison, about sixty thousand strong, was commanded by General Wang Yao-wu, who was also the governor of Shantung.

At the beginning of September all of Ch'en I's columns that had taken part in the operations in Honan rejoined his forces in Shantung. These were formed into three groups: one group, composed of four columns, acted as a blocking and screening force to the east and south of Tsinan; the second group echeloned its three columns along the Tsinpu railroad between Taian and Tzeyang; the third group, with seven columns, concentrated in the Kinsiang-Chengwu area. Farther south, the Reds posted two columns around the Nationalist stronghold at Lini. And to the west of the Pinghan railroad, midway between Chengcow and Sinyang, the Communists concentrated eight columns, in groups commanded by Liu Po-ch'eng, Ch'en Keng, and Li Hsien-nien.

The Nationalist reaction to this threat has been described by General Barr:

Decision was made by the Generalissimo to defend isolated Tsinan to the last. (Such decisions have been costly to the Nationalists in troops and supplies.) I pointed out again to the Generalissimo and to the Supreme Staff the futility of attempting to hold cities from within restricted perimeters by purely defensive measures against overpowering enemy forces. Tsinan at this time was isolated from Suchow by Communist forces at Yenchow and Taian. Although in considerable strength in this area the main Communist force was still on the Honan plains, southeast of Kaifeng. An opportunity existed to do one of two things. By offensive action north from Suchow and south from Tsinan, the Nationalist forces were capable of destroying the Communists and reopening the corridor between Suchow and Tsinan. The Nationalists were also capable at this time of evacuating Tsinan and withdrawing into Suchow. Having no confidence in the will to fight of the Tsinan garrison after their ineffective attempt to re-capture Weihsien, and having heard reports of the questionable loyalty of some of the senior commanders, I recommended that the city be evacuated, and the troops be withdrawn to Suchow. Again, as in the case of Changchun, I was told that because of political reasons, Tsinan, the capital of Shantung Province, must be defended. . .

At a meeting in the Ministry of National Defense War Room on 14 September 1948, the following observations were made by the Chinese:

The G3[1] stated that although completely surrounded and isolated, food was still coming to Tsinan from the countryside. He believed that an additional division could be air-lifted into Tsinan to assist in the defense. I recommended strongly against this, believing that the city was lost and that it only meant the loss to the Nationalists of an additional division. One had already been air-lifted in from Tsingtao. I recommended that rather than fly in additional troops, the present Tsinan garrison be air-lifted to Suchow.[2]

Unfortunately, this wise counsel was not followed. In the face of the Nationalists' inertia, Ch'en I—who had nothing to fear from the north, was well covered to the south, and pro-tected, by the latent threat of Liu Po-ch'eng's forces, against any Nationalist counterattack from Kaifeng—launched his eight columns against Tsinan at midnight, 14–15 September. The attacking Reds rapidly seized the airfield to the north-west of the city, interdicted the southern airfield with their

[1] On the Nationalists' Supreme Staff, the G3 was the general staff officer for war plans.

[2] U.S. Department of State, *United States Relations with China, with Special Reference to the Period 1944–1949* (U.S. Government Printing Office, 1949), pp. 330–331. *Tr.*

fire, and hustled the defenders back from the perimeter into the city itself. General Wu Hua-wen, commander of the Nationalist 84th Division and—either through conviction or corruption—a hitherto secret Communist, tried to bring his entire division into the enemy camp. Although his plan was partially foiled by the fidelity of the 155th Brigade's commander, the Communists promptly profited from the confusion produced among the defenders by Wu's treason, and penetrated into the new part of the city. Successively the Two Kwangs Column, the Rapid Column, the 7th Column, launched their assaults; on 24 September, they stormed the north gate of the old city, and Tsinan was engulfed by Red troops who rapidly mopped up the last resistance. On 25 September the Nationalist high command admitted, in veiled terms, the loss of the city, estimating that it had cost the Communists fifty thousand casualties against a Nationalist loss of twenty thousand. But the fact was that the Reds took fifty thousand rifles at Tsinan, and large stocks of ammunition.

In a message to his superiors, the American Consul General at Tsingtao described the causes of the Nationalists' defeat:

Prime cause for swift loss of city is *psychological* [author's italics] rather than material or military. Nationalist garrison had been isolated for two months with no possibility ground support. Previous Nationalist defeats in which Nationalist troops *failed to fight* [author's italics] known to Tsinan garrison and people. Communist victory at Tsinan felt inevitable in view record of failure of Nationalists and consistent victories of Communists who at Tsinan used many of best troops. Nationalist soldiers and population Shantung in general no longer consider Nationalist Government merits continued support in civil war, loss of lives and economic chaos. These factors expressed themselves in outright defection to Communists, immediate surrenders, and failure to stand and fight. Those soldiers willing to fight were unable to trust other units to support them. No mutuality of feelings between regular forces and local Peace Preservation Corps troops. Nationalist regulars were largely from Central and South China and had little interest in defending strange city and people. Communists undoubtedly had organized support within city. No real attempt made to defend perimeter at distance outside of city wall. Antiquated custom of falling back to city walls was speedily observed by Nationalist defenders. Other military causes were poor intelligence, failure to take initiative against Communists when concentrating for campaign and thus keeping them off balance. Belated inadequate improper air support.

In summary, majority troops at Tsinan did not want to fight while those that did fight found their position made impossible by the disaffected. Defection of Wu Hua-wen was merely the manifestation of a general phenomenon. His treason was not of itself the cause of defeat.

Nationalists at Tsinan had ample ammunition and food and assurance of further supplies in event protracted siege.[3]

Disastrous as it was, the fall of Tsinan was only the harbinger of the catastrophe to come in Manchuria.

THE MANCHURIAN CATASTROPHE

The final Communist offensive in the Northeast was launched on 12 September 1948. For this climactic effort Lin Piao had assembled a total of 600,000 men:[4] 65,000 around

[3] *U.S. Relations with China*, pp. 319–320. Tr.

[4] This figure reflects the fact that the strength of Lin's forces had doubled within one year. This increase, moreover, had been achieved through the formation of new units whose personnel came from Manchuria itself. As for his concept of operations, Lin's major goal was to unhinge the remaining Nationalist communications in southern Manchuria. So long as they held their bridgehead at Chinchow, to the north of the Great Wall, and maintained their garrisons between Chinchow and Mukden, it would always be possible for the Nationalists to restore contact between North China and South Manchuria. But the capture of Chinchow by the Communists would result in the confinement of Nationalist forces to the narrow corridor between the mountains and the sea, and the complete encirclement of Mukden: it would then be all over for the Nationalists in Manchuria.

Changchun, 183,000 around Mukden, 179,000 between Mukden and Chinchow, and 180,000 in reserve. To these 600,000 Reds the Nationalists could now oppose only 300,000 men: 60,000 at Changchun, 200,000 at Mukden, and only 40,000 between Chinchow and Chinsi.

Lin Piao threw thirteen columns of Red regulars into his victorious battle of Chinchow. Covering himself against a possible sortie from Mukden, he first snapped up, in succession, the last Nationalist garrisons between Mukden and Chinchow. He then turned the full weight of his attacking forces upon Chinchow. The attempts of the Nationalist high command to relieve the beleaguered city were all in vain. Leaving too late from Hulutao, elements of the Thirty-first Army, which had come all the way from Formosa, were stopped before they could reach Chinchow. The same thing happened to a relief column sent out from Mukden[5] which, instead of heading straight for Chinchow, divided its forces in divergent attempts to re-establish contact with Changchun, on the one hand, and to retake Yingkow on the other. In the meantime Chinchow, together with General Fan Han-chieh and a garrison of 100,000 men, yielded to the Communists on 17 October 1948. With its fall came the destruction of the entire system of Nationalist communications, and the loss of immense supply stocks to the Reds. On 20 October a last attempt to retake Chinchow was shattered by Lin Piao's powerful forces. And the same day saw the fall of Changchun, the capital of Manchuria: part of its garrison, the Sixtieth Army, refusing to attempt a break-out toward Mukden, had turned upon and disarmed, with Communist cooperation, the New Seventh Army. General Cheng Tung-kuo, the garrison

[5] General Wei Li-huang, commanding at Mukden, received Chiang Kai-shek's order to go to the relief of Chinchow on 25 September. Wei did not move out until 7 October.

commander, was a prisoner; five divisions, with all their equipment, had fallen into the hands of the Reds.

After so disastrous a defeat the Nationalists now had no other alternative than to evacuate from Mukden, if possible, the bulk of their remaining forces. Earlier, on 11 October, the Mukden garrison had succeeded in retaking Yingkow and reopening the Mukden-Anshan-Yingkow rail line. But instead of capitalizing on this by using the last way open to them to evacuate their main body from Mukden, and fastening a firm grip around the port of Yingkow, the Nationalists persisted in their attempts to retake Chinchow. While most of the Mukden garrison moved out down the Mukden-Chinchow rail line toward the rail center at Kowpangtze, the eleven Nationalist divisions at Hulutao, by attempting to move on Chinchow from the south, sought to link up with the forces coming from Mukden and assure their evacuation by way of Hulutao.

On 27 October the bulk of the Mukden garrison, which had been formed into a group army commanded by General Liao Yao-hsiang and made up of the New First, Third, and New Sixth armies, plus the Seventy-first Army and elements of the Forty-ninth Army, reached Tahushan, about halfway to Chinchow. Mukden itself was now held by nothing more than the Fifty-third Army and two brigades of the 207th Youth Infantry Division. The Fifty-second Army was strung out along the Mukden-Yingkow rail line. This inviting strategic situation was immediately exploited by Lin Piao, who now maneuvered in a manner worthy of Napoleon's first Italian campaign, or of the Germans at Tannenberg. Leaving only two columns (the 9th and 11th) to watch the Nationalist forces moving northward from Hulutao, the Red commander slipped his main body of eleven columns, some 200,000 men, to the southeast of Liao's advancing group army, and hit it

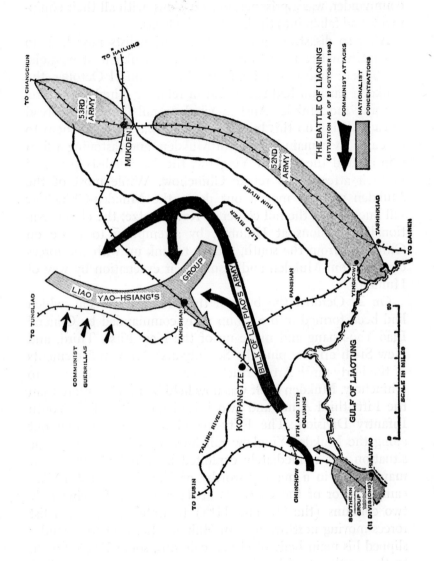

from the flank and rear. As the Nationalist troops in Mukden looked on, the Red columns in seventy-two hours of furious fighting dispersed, destroyed, or captured Liao's entire group army. General Liao, killed in the early hours of the battle, was spared the end of the debacle, which came on 30 October. For the Fifty-third Army, shut up in Mukden, there was now nothing to do but surrender—a fall facilitated by the defection of General Chou Fu-cheng, the garrison commander, to the Reds. As for the Fifty-second Army, it was only the twenty thousand men in the port of Yingkow who were able to escape, by sea, the Red avalanche which flowed over Yingkow itself on 5 November.

This series of disasters had far-reaching effects. The battle in western Liaoning had cost the Nationalists eleven infantry divisions, one Youth Brigade, and three regiments, either captured or destroyed; three generals had been made prisoner, and General Liao Yao-hsiang had been killed. At Mukden, the equivalent of seven divisions had been taken by the Reds. At Chinchow, the Nationalists had lost eight infantry divisions, or 122,000 men—some 88,000 of them, including thirty-six generals and 197 field-grade officers, taken as prisoners. Added to these losses were the division and a half lost at Yingkow and the five divisions lost at Changchun, plus an immense amount of matériel. In total, the loss of Manchuria cost the Nationalists seven armies[6]—some twenty-nine infantry divisions, three Youth Brigades equaling three infantry divisions in strength, two cavalry brigades, four regiments, and numerous nondivisional units—a total of at least 400,000 men. Lost with them were all their weapons, of which about one third were of American make; to these losses were added the

[6] These were the following: New First Army, New Third Army, New Sixth Army, Sixth Army, Forty-ninth Army, Fifty-third Army, and Seventy-first Army.

enormous stocks of military supplies, the entire arsenals—including the one at Mukden, the best-equipped of all—which also became the booty of the Reds. And now the Communists, henceforth relieved of any concern regarding their rear, were free to move Lin Piao's forces to the south of the Great Wall; after losing their last reserves, the Nationalists, driven from Manchuria by Lin Piao's well-trained and combat-tested columns, were again to be confronted by this formidable force of 400,000 crack Red regulars.

Chiang Kai-shek did not, of course, give up. Hastily withdrawing from Hulutao the eleven divisions[7] whose culpable passivity had partially provoked the disaster in Manchuria, he reassigned some of them (General Li Wen's corps) to Fu Tso-yi's command; the remainder, some eighty thousand men of the Fifth, Ninth, and Fifty-fourth armies, went to the Central China command. "The loss of Manchuria," declared Chiang, "is discouraging; but it relieves the government of a formidable burden, so far as military defenses are concerned, and allows it to concentrate its war effort to the south of the Great Wall."

But Lin Piao's forces were already pouring into Hopeh, where they regrouped to form front against the Peking-Tientsin line. Chiang's fate was sealed.

THE BATTLE OF SUCHOW

After the fall of Tsinan, the only important bastions remaining to keep the Red armies from the Yangtze and Nanking were Suchow, the Nationalists' main base in Central China, and Pengpu, a city in Anhwei situated on the Tsinpu

---

[7] These forces did not include the divisions of the Ninety-third Army, which had been annihilated, or of the Sixtieth Army from Yunnan, which had gone over to the Reds.

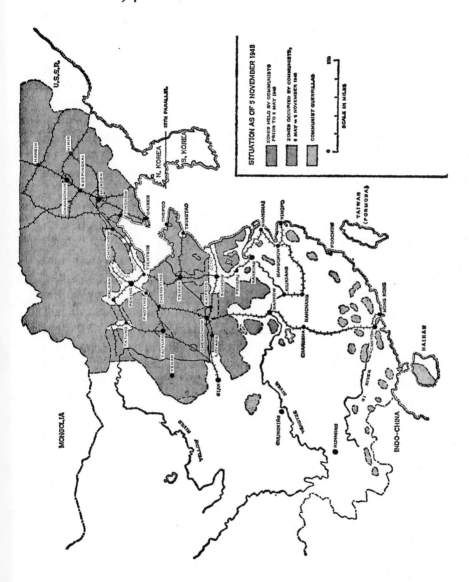

railroad and the river Hwai, at the southern edge of the central plain. Deciding upon a decisive battle and the annihilation of the Nationalist forces in Central China, General Chu Teh concentrated almost 600,000 men—all the columns of Ch'en I, Liu Po-ch'eng, and Ch'en Keng—in the vicinity of Suchow.

To face these Red forces the Generalissimo gave General Pai Ch'ung-hsi[8] fifty-five divisions, organized into ten field armies and four group armies, totaling some 600,000 men. To the west of Suchow was General Chiu Ching-chuan's 2nd Group Army. The 13th Group Army, under General Li Mi, held the city itself. General Huang Po-tao's 7th Group Army was concentrated to the east of Suchow, and General Sun Yuan-ling's 16th Group Army was strung out to the south along the Pengpu-Suchow railroad. All of these forces had ample artillery, both medium and light, as well as tanks and the support of an air force that had absolute mastery of the air. In order to reconstitute a reserve, the Generalissimo had evacuated his troops from Chefoo and Lini, and now held nothing in Shantung except Tsingtao. Possessing as he did a fairly strong and completely unopposed air force, which at will could bomb and strafe the villages and Communist troop concentrations so easily discernible on the open plain, the general situation seemed favorable to Chiang Kai-shek.

But poor morale, inept command, and a fixedly defensive frame of mind were to bring the Nationalists to another terrible disaster. Right at the beginning they adopted a dubious, "mushroom"-type disposition, with part of their forces deployed along the Lunghai railroad, and the rest, like a dangling stem,

[8] According to F. F. Liu, Pai Ch'ung-hsi, "the best of the Nationalist strategists," was not offered this command by Chiang until the "eleventh hour," when he turned it down. It went instead to General Liu Chih, "a man of no particular ability," who had General Tu Yü-ming, "fresh from defeats in Manchuria," as his deputy. See F. F. Liu, A Military History of Modern China (Princeton University Press, 1956), p. 261. Tr.

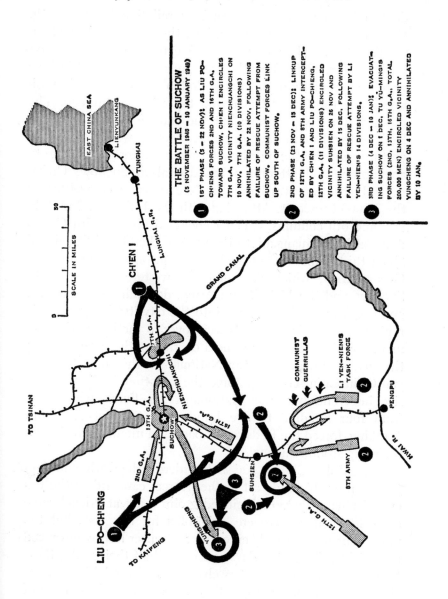

THE BATTLE OF SUCHOW
(5 NOVEMBER 1948 – 10 JANUARY 1949)

1ST PHASE (5 – 22 NOV): AS LIU PO-CH'ENG FORCES 2ND AND 16TH G.A. TOWARD SUCHOW, CH'EN I ENCIRCLES 7TH G.A. VICINITY NIENCHUANGCHI ON 10 NOV, 7TH G.A. (10 DIVISIONS) ANNIHILATED BY 22 NOV, FOLLOWING FAILURE OF RESCUE ATTEMPT FROM SUCHOW. COMMUNIST FORCES LINK UP SOUTH OF SUCHOW.

2ND PHASE (23 NOV – 15 DEC): LINKUP OF 12TH G.A. AND 8TH ARMY INTERCEPT-ED BY CH'EN I AND LIU PO-CH'ENG, 12TH G.A. (11 DIVISIONS) ENCIRCLED VICINITY SUHSIEN ON 26 NOV AND ANNIHILATED BY 15 DEC, FOLLOWING FAILURE OF RESCUE ATTEMPT BY LI YEN-NIEN'S 14 DIVISIONS.

3RD PHASE (4 DEC – 10 JAN): EVACUAT-ING SUCHOW ON 1 DEC, TU YÜ-MING'S FORCES (2ND, 13TH, 16TH G.A., TOTAL 200,000 MEN) ENCIRCLED VICINITY YUNGCHENG ON 4 DEC AND ANNIHILATED BY 10 JAN.

deployed along the Pengpu-Suchow rail line to the south. Frozen in their defensive fixation, they awaited the Communist attacks. The first of these came from the east on 8 November. Defending the eastern approaches to Suchow were the ten divisions of Huang Po-tao's group army, in position along the Grand Canal and the Lunghai railroad. The position was a strong one; but the sudden defection to the Reds of two Kuomintang generals, together with 23,000 men of the army in the northwestern sector, forced Huang to abandon it and attempt a withdrawal to Suchow. Unfortunately, the way was barred by Red columns, as well as by the 23,000 turncoats. Attacking with the 13th, 4th, 2nd, 8th, 9th, and 6th columns, Ch'en I encircled Huang's 7th Group Army at Nienchuangchi, to the west of the Grand Canal and about thirty miles east of Suchow. At the same time, the 2nd Group Army, which defended the western approaches to Suchow, and the 16th Group Army, defending the southern approaches, were forced back into the city itself, where panic rapidly spread. Six regiments went over to the Reds, who momentarily threatened the airfield on the southern outskirts of the city. Fortunately for the Nationalists, the energetic General Chiu Ching-chuan restored the situation, while the massive intervention of the Nationalist Air Force, which flew from four hundred to five hundred sorties per day from Nanking, forced the Reds to fall back and momentarily loosen their grip around Suchow.

Meanwhile, Chiang Kai-shek ordered the 16th and 2nd group armies to send part of their forces eastward to the rescue of Huang Po-tao's encircled group army at Nienchuangchi. Fifteen divisions were assembled for this task, but the movement was so slowly executed that, after having advanced only eight miles in ten days and losing half their tanks, these forces were stopped about twelve miles west of Nienchuangchi. Here they met no more than three thousand survivors of a new Nationalist disaster: Huang's entire 7th Group Army, ninety thousand strong, had been torn to bits; the Reds had captured one thousand artillery pieces; Communist tanks had swept into Nienchuangchi; all the Nationalist generals were prisoners.[9]

On 22 November Ch'en I's victorious forces pressed rapidly southward from Nienchuangchi. Chiang had meanwhile ordered Liu Ju-ming's Eighth Army and Huang Wei's 12th Group Army, located to the south of Suchow, to go to the aid of that city, where there were still twenty-five divisions under Tu Yü-ming.[10] But here again Nationalist execution was pitifully poor. The two forces failed to effect their planned junction at Suhsien, and were soon trapped between Ch'en I's columns, coming from the north, and the forces of Liu Po-ch'-eng, which cut them off from the south. On 26 November it became the turn of General Huang Wei's 12th Group Army, with 125,000 men and many mechanized troops, to be encircled by the Reds at Shwangchiaochi, about fifteen miles southwest of Suhsien.

The Nationalists now made the decision to abandon Suchow and march southward, in order to prevent the annihilation of the 12th Group Army and join up with Liu Ju-ming, who was hastily retiring toward Pengpu. The three group armies at Suchow, with General Tu Yü-ming in over-all command, abandoned the city on 1 December; the Reds entered Suchow the next day. Once again the Nationalists, poorly led and with low morale, let themselves be outmaneuvered by the Reds, who pushed them gradually westward and ended by encircling them in the vicinity of Yungcheng.

As of 6 December the situation was as follows: Tu Yü-ming's twenty-five infantry divisions, some 200,000 men, with

[9] Except for Huang Po-tao himself, who had been killed in action. Tr.
[10] The Generalissimo had put Tu Yü-ming in command of all troops who had taken refuge in Suchow, and of the city's garrison as well.

all their artillery and tanks, were encircled to the west of Su-chow; Huang Wei (whose 110th Division had deserted to the Reds on 30 November) now had eleven infantry divisions, totaling 110,000 men, which were surrounded to the south-west of Suhsien; nine infantry divisions were still at large, and holding the Hwai river along the line Fenyang-Pengpu-Hwai-yuan. The difficulties of the encircled group armies rapidly worsened: the men were eating potatoes stolen from the fields of the peasants, and fought like dogs over the meager rations parachuted to them each day. The morale of the troops sank ever lower and, one after the other, whole divisions went over to the enemy.

Meanwhile Chiang Kai-shek had brought up some troops from the Yangtze region, and had ordered Li Yen-nien's Sixth Army, based at Pengpu, to go to the aid of Huang Wei's en-circled forces with fourteen divisions.[11] In fifteen days Li advanced only seventeen miles against the furious resistance of Red guerrillas and village militiamen, who savagely con-tested every foot of his advance; without reaching Suhsien, Li's forces turned around and retraced their steps. The Reds then launched their final assault against Huang Wei's encir-cled group army. The attack was preceded by an intensive artillery preparation from howitzers, mortars, and mountain guns, which threw the defenses into complete disorder; when the Red assault detachments attacked, the shaken and de-moralized defenders immediately surrendered. By 15 Decem-ber the 12th Group Army had ceased to exist and Huang Wei was a prisoner of the Reds.

The fate of Tu Yü-ming was even more disastrous. His three group armies[12] encircled by the Reds to the northwest

---

[11] This task force included Liu Ju-ming's Eighth Army, as well as Li's Sixth Army. Tr.
[12] The 2nd, 13th, and 16th.

of Yungcheng, he had already lost more than half his forces on 17 December. As demoralization visibly spread, the commanders fell to wrangling among themselves. Earlier, on 6 December, Tu Yü-ming had ordered Sun Yuan-liang, whose forces had already covered the retreat from Suchow, to attempt a sortie; Sun's resentful troops had obeyed only with reluctance, and ended by surrendering to the Reds. Soon all was chaos. Prompted by continual Communist propaganda, desertions multiplied among the now starving defenders. Finally, on 6 January, the Red armies, after twenty days of rest and reorganization, launched their final assault. The encircled Nationalist forces were torn to pieces. In attempting to escape this final debacle, Tu Yü-ming disguised himself as a common soldier and posed as a "prisoner" of his own bodyguards, whom he had disguised as Red soldiers; the subterfuge failed, and he became the real prisoner of real Reds.

By 10 January 1949 the battle of Suchow,[13] which had lasted sixty-five days, was over. The Reds had taken 327,000 prisoners, and Nationalist losses had totaled 600,000 men. The entire region between the Hwai and the Yangtze had been "liberated" by the Reds, and their passage of the historic river barrier was now possible. The Kuomintang had lost its last chance.

THE POLITICAL AND ECONOMIC SITUATION

On 19 August 1948 the Nationalist government, in a desperate effort to check the ruinous inflation, the rise in prices, hoarding, corruption, and famine, decreed a number of stringent measures which, had they been strictly applied and received with confidence by the people, could have succeeded. The first measure taken was to replace the *fapi*, the Nationalist

---

[13] The Reds call this battle, which in the future will be considered one of the decisive battles of history, the Hwai-Hai Campaign.

monetary unit which had sunk to a value of zero, with a new currency backed by gold: the gold *yüan*, which was to represent 0.222 grams of gold, with a conversion rate of four *yüan* to one American dollar. The old currency was to be replaced at an exchange rate of one gold *yüan* for three million *fapis*. This monetary reform was accompanied by other strict measures, such as the freezing of wages, prices, and foreign exchange rates. Severe penalties were prescribed against black marketeers, and General Chiang Ching-kuo, the Generalissimo's son and a forceful personality, was charged with applying the reforms first in Shanghai and then in Nanking and the neighboring provinces.

Despite vigorous action by Chiang Ching-kuo, who conducted a "tiger hunt" against the big black marketeers and speculators of Shanghai, and also succeeded in gaining the support of the workers, the reforms rapidly failed. One reason for this failure was that the younger Chiang was ordered by his father to be "less severe" toward certain tigers, such as David Kung, the president of the Yangtze Development Corporation; but the major reason was that the government, having achieved no increase in revenue or decrease in expenditure, was obliged to print bills which rapidly reduced the value of the gold *yüan*. Prices skyrocketed. On 31 October the ceilings on wages and prices were removed. Resigning in disgust, Chiang Ching-kuo apologized to his fellow citizens in an open letter, characteristically Chinese, to the people of Shanghai:

After the past seventy days of my work, I feel that I have failed to accomplish the duties which I should have accomplished. Not only did I not consummate my plan and mission, but in certain respects I have rather deepened the sufferings of the people which they experienced in the course of the execution of my task ... Today, aside from petitioning the government for punishment so as to clarify my responsibility, I wish to take this opportunity of offering my deepest apology to the citizens of Shanghai. But in so doing . . . I sincerely wish the citizens of Shanghai to use their own strength to prevent unscrupulous merchants, bureaucrats, politicians and racketeers from controlling Shanghai.[14]

China now found itself back in the vicious circle of rising prices and wages. In the provinces everything was disintegrating. Banditry broke out everywhere, and fifty-five million refugees rendered the food problem insoluble. It was only unconditional and permanent aid from the United States which could prevent an immediate collapse. But General Marshall, now the American Secretary of State, in October 1948 redefined American policy toward China: there was to be no more mediation, no more direct intervention in Chiang's favor, but strict application of the China Aid Act of 1948.[15]

Marshall declared:

To achieve the objective of reducing the Chinese Communists to a completely negligible factor in China in the immediate future, it would be necessary for the United States virtually to take over the Chinese Government and administer its economic, military and governmental affairs. . . It would be impossible to estimate the final cost of a course of action of this magnitude. It certainly would be a continuing operation for a long time to come. It would involve the United States Government in a continuing commitment from which it would practically be impossible to withdraw, and it would very probably involve grave consequences to this nation by making of China an arena of international conflict.[16]

This was indeed a grave decision. At the United Nations, Dr. T. F. Tsiang, China's representative on the Security Council, pronounced these prophetic words: "The fate of the entire

---

[14] U.S. Relations with China, p. 880. Tr.

[15] Of the $125 million voted by Congress for special grants to China, the Nationalists used $37,800,000 to buy munitions which were delivered to them in December 1948.

[16] U.S. Relations with China, p. 281. Tr.

Far East is linked to that of China, because the Chinese Communists will help the Communists in Indo-China, in Malaya, in Burma, in India, in all the Far East. Against this tide, you have built in the West a solid dike, in the form of material aid, from Scandinavia to the Persian Gulf. But now this tide will overflow in another direction."[17] But was it possible to do anything useful, considering the actual state of things? General Marshall had no illusions: "The present regime has lost the confidence of the people, reflected in the refusal of soldiers to fight and the refusal of the people to co-operate in economic reforms."[18]

Chiang Kai-shek continued to ignore the advice of General Barr, refusing even to hear it. He wished to direct everything himself, and he was surrounded, as always, by old comrades who were as incompetent as they were corrupt. In the face of a degenerate Kuomintang, the Communists boldly and successfully proceeded to organize the zones under their control. On 1 September 1948 they announced the formation of a People's Government for North China, to include the provinces of Hopeh, Chahar, Shensi, Shansi, and Shantung.[19] Their policy continued to be flexible and adaptable enough to avoid frightening the people, and their establishment of an agrarian democracy which eschewed collectivization and confiscated only the property of landlords, gave satisfaction to the majority. Cer-

[17] For a summary of Tsiang's speech, see *Plenary Meetings of the General Assembly: Official Records of the Fourth Session of the General Assembly, 20 September–10 December 1949* (Lake Success, N.Y.: United Nations, 1949), pp. 15–16. Tr.

[18] *U.S. Relations with China*, p. 282. Tr.

[19] Nine of the twenty-seven members of the government council were Communists. The Chairman of the North China People's Government was Tung Pi-wu, one of the founders of the CCP, a graduate of the Lenin Academy, and a Communist representative at Chungking from 1937 to 1945. The Vice Chairman was General Nieh Jung-chen. The non-Communist members were from the Democratic League, the National Salvation Association, and the Non-Party Democrats.

tain now of victory, Mao Tse-tung toughened even more against the Kuomintang, and published a list of "war criminals" which included all the KMT party chieftains. As his columns prepared for the liquidation of the forces of Fu Tso-yi, Mao's last serious adversary in North China, he tranquilly awaited the peace proposals of his enemies.

In a last effort, Chiang Kai-shek sent his wife to the United States to seek an increase of American aid. Arriving in Washington on 1 December 1948, Mme. Chiang did not get to see Marshall, who was ill, until the 3rd, and was not received by President Truman until the 10th. The visit soon showed itself to be fruitless. Indeed, Mr. Hoffman,[20] who had come to Shanghai on 11 December, went back to Washington on 20 December, and the next day the United States government announced the suspension of its reconstruction aid program for China.

[20] Paul G. Hoffman, head of the Economic Cooperation Administration. *Tr.*

✧ PART FIVE ✧

1949

THE END OF THE CONQUEST

CHAPTER XIV

The Surrender of Fu Tso-yi
and
Chiang Kai-shek's Departure

As the last act opened, it was clear that the Nationalists had no real basis for further hope. On 1 February 1949 the American Department of the Army reported:

The Nationalists entered 1948 with an estimated strength of 2,723,000 troops. Recruitment and replacement of combat losses kept this figure constant through mid-September. By 1 February 1949, however, heavy losses had reduced Nationalist strength to 1,500,000, of which approximately 500,000 are service troops. This represents a reduction of 45 percent of the Nationalist Government's total troop strength, in a 4½-month period.

Communist strength, estimated at 1,150,000 a year ago, has mounted to 1,622,000, virtually all combat effectives. This increase of approximately 40 percent represents the creation of new units, particularly in Manchuria and East Central China. Whereas the Nationalists began 1948 with almost a three-to-one numerical superiority, the Communist forces now outnumber the total Nationalist strength and have achieved better than a one-and-a-half-to-one superiority in combat effectives.[1]

[1] U.S. Department of State, *United States Relations with China, with Special Reference to the Period 1944–1949* (U.S. Government Printing Office, 1949), p. 322. Tr.

The American military attaché at Nanking estimated that, from September 1948 to February 1949, the Reds had captured 400,000 rifles, some 140,000 of which were of American origin; and they had integrated 600,000 ex-Nationalist troops into their own forces, using 400,000 of them as service troops.[2] Moreover, twenty arsenals, including fifteen of major importance, had fallen into Mao's hands.

At about the same time the Communists published their own claims of losses inflicted upon the Nationalists since the beginning of the war. For the period 1 July 1946 to 31 January 1949 these were:

a) *Personnel:* 4,959,000 killed, wounded, or taken prisoner, with the proportion of prisoners seventy-five per cent. Of this total, 2,641,000 casualties had been inflicted upon the Nationalists during the period July 1946 through July 1948, and 2,318,000 in the seven months preceding January 1949. The Nationalists had lost 869 generals; 697 of them had been taken prisoner, sixty-seven killed, and 105 had gone over to the Communists.

b) *Units:* According to the Communists, they had destroyed during this period 380 entire divisions, 615 regiments, and 760 battalions; and the Nationalists had lost the headquarters of two theaters of operations, fifteen group armies, and eighty-six field armies.

c) *Matériel:* The Communists claimed to have captured 1,709,000 rifles, carbines, and pistols; 193,000 automatic weapons; 37,000 mortars and artillery pieces; 250 million rounds of small-arms ammunition; 2,580,000 shells; and 1,900,000 hand grenades. They had taken 513 tanks, and destroyed 140 more. Other booty included 289 armored vehicles; twelve thousand motor vehicles; 857 locomotives; and eighty-six aircraft, more than fifteen of whose pilots had deserted, with their planes, to

[2] *Ibid.,* p. 323. Tr.

the Communists. The capture of this matériel by the Communists—especially the American matériel—for the first time gave Red armies an ample margin of material superiority over the Nationalists, who now retained only naval and air superiority.

THE SURRENDER OF FU TSO-YI

Throughout the fighting in Manchuria and Central China, General Fu Tso-yi, at the head of the Nationalists' best troops, had held firm control of a zone centered around the Tientsin-Suiyuan railroad. This zone included the cities of Peking and Kalgan, through which Fu was able to maintain contact with his province of Suiyuan and with General Ma Hung-k'uei. In the north he held Chengteh, the capital of Jehol, which covered the pass at Kupehkow; to the south, he held Paoting and the port of Tangku. General Fu Tso-yi, whose merit was but little appreciated by Chiang Kai-shek, had long been known as one of the few Kuomintang generals who had the support of the population. Applying Communist methods, he had set his troops to work with the peasants in the fields, and to the repair of the railroads. An excellent strategist, he had succeeded in maintaining effective control over his zone of responsibility, repelling the Red columns of Nieh Jung-chen and Lin Piao.

When Lin Piao attacked in Manchuria, Fu had been compelled to dispatch large forces to Chinchow. The Communists profited from this development by attacking in Jehol, Chahar, and Hopeh. Paoting succumbed to the Reds on 23 October. Immediately after the fall of Yingkow to the Communists on 5 November, Lin Piao and Nieh Jung-chen launched simultaneous attacks against Fu. On 9 November Nieh took Chengteh, the capital of Jehol. On the 18th Lin Piao, in his turn, seized Shanhaikwan; on 2 December, he took Kupehkow, on the Peking-Chengteh railroad. Lin then attacked the defense lines established by the Nationalists to the north of Peking, along the Sino-Manchurian border. Breaking through Fu Tso-yi's front, Lin's forces on 7 December seized Miyun and Hwaiju, about forty miles north of Peking.

Little by little, the front drew ever closer to Tientsin, Peking, and Kalgan; yet Fu Tso-yi, despite his considerable superiority in numbers, fought nothing more than delaying actions. The plain fact was that the Nationalist general had been in secret contact with the Communists since the beginning of December, and was now in the process of negotiating his surrender to the Reds. Following the fall of the coal-mining center at Tangshan on the 13th and of Tungchow on 15 December, Fu permitted Peking to be "encircled" by eight Communist columns and four independent infantry divisions, even though the city was garrisoned by twenty-five Nationalist infantry divisions, of which five belonged to Fu's own personal army.

As for the Communists, their problem was to choose between a conciliatory attitude toward Fu Tso-yi, or the refusal of any concessions. Mao well understood that a bloodless capture of Peking, the ancient capital, plus control of the Tientsin-Suiyuan railroad, were well worth compromise. The necessary assurances were accordingly transmitted to Fu Tso-yi, who continued to withdraw before the outnumbered Red forces. He abandoned Tangku on 19 December, and on the 26th withdrew from Kalgan the garrison of seven infantry divisions supposedly "blockaded" there by Nieh's six columns. Fu, a former governor of Suiyuan, pulled these troops back toward Tsining and Paotow. The westward withdrawal of the Kalgan garrison clearly indicated Fu Tso-yi's intentions: early in January the Nationalist leader officially opened negotiations with Lin Piao, using Chang Tung-sun, a professor at Yenching University and former Secretary-General of the defunct Democratic League, as his intermediary.

Vice President Li Tsung-jen paralleled this move by sending to Peking a former mayor of that city, Ho Ssu-yuan; but anything this envoy might have done was forestalled by his assassination, on 16 January, at the hands of the Ch'en brothers' secret police. Chiang Kai-shek and the Sun Fo cabinet then called a meeting, at Nanking, of the regime's leading generals: Pai Ch'ung-hsi, war lord of Kwangsi and Nationalist commander in Central China; Lu Han, the governor of Yunnan; Yen Hsi-shan, from the beleaguered city of Taiyuan; Hu Tsung-nan, from Sian; Ma Hung-k'uei, from Ningsia; and Chu Shao-liang, from Szechwan. Fu Tso-yi, of course, prudently refrained from attending. During this meeting Chiang decided to entrust each governor with responsibility for the defense of his own province, relying upon the formation of local militia units and appeals to the patriotism of the inhabitants. For all practical purposes this meant the end of coordinated resistance against the Communists.

Nevertheless, Chiang clearly indicated at this meeting his intention to defend the Nanking-Shanghai area to the very end. Throughout Nationalist China this decision was received with dismay by a public opinion which longed only for peaceful compromise. Thus it was that the news of Fu Tso-yi's capitulation at Peking brought forth no great popular indignation. After letting Tientsin go to the Communists on 15 January, Fu had signed a "compromise" with Lin Piao on the 23rd, following a token siege of Peking in which the Communists had done nothing more than sprinkle the city with about 150 seventy-five millimeter shells—most of which failed to explode.

The compromise of 23 January, very moderate in its terms, was to become the "model" for other Nationalist governors. Its thirteen conditions were the following:

1. Hostilities would cease immediately.
2. The two sides would appoint delegates to a joint commission in charge of military and political affairs during the "period of transition."
3. Nationalist troops within Peking would move to the outskirts of the city. Although permitted to retain their original unit designations and insignia, they would be reorganized one month later.
4. For the maintenance of peace and order, some of the Nationalist troops would remain within the city to assist the police and troops already provided for the protection of shops and stores.
5. All government offices, public enterprises, banks, stores, cultural institutions, and schools would retain their current status pending further instructions from the joint commission.
6. The provincial government of Hopeh would retain, at all echelons, its current status, pending further instructions from the joint commission. The personal safety of its officials would be guaranteed.
7. The currency in use, the gold *yüan*, would continue in circulation.
8. All military construction in progress would be suspended.
9. The consular personnel and property of foreign powers in Peking would be protected.
10. Postal and telegraph services would continue without interruption.
11. All newspapers would continue publication, but would be required to renew registration and submit, at a later date, to censorship.
12. Cultural relics, shrines, and historical monuments would be safeguarded, and freedom of worship guaranteed.
13. The normal existence of the population would remain undisturbed.

Promptly, as early as 23 January, a Communist regiment entered Peking and established itself within the city.

The Peking compromise having been arrived at with the assent of Li Tsung-jen and over the opposition of Chiang Kai-shek, the latter now realized that the game was lost; there was nothing left for him to do but retire. This he did on 21 January, relinquishing power to Vice President Li "with the hope," said Chiang, "that the hostilities may be brought to an end and the peoples' sufferings relieved."[3]

[3] *Ibid.*, p. 292. It was at this time that Chiang, although out of office, readied what he regarded as "his" armies, navy, and air force for the retreat to Formosa.

CHAPTER XV

Negotiations and the
Amethyst Incident

From the beginning of February to 20 April 1949, when Communist forces crossed the Yangtze, a scene was enacted similar to that which had unfolded in early 1946. At that time Chiang, possessing the advantage of military superiority, had sought the cover of protracted negotiations while he massed his forces and prepared his attack. He would break off the talks at opportune moments, seize important bargaining counters, and then, in the devious Chinese way so dismaying to General Marshall, reopen negotiations with the Communists. Now it was Mao Tse-tung who had the military might. After the conquest of Manchuria and Peking he needed a few months in which to regroup his forces and prepare his decisive attack across the Yangtze. Consequently, he did not hesitate to undertake negotiations, deliberately foredoomed to failure, in which the concessions of his adversaries were to be met by his ever-increasing demands.

Shortly after the retirement of Chiang Kai-shek—who continued to direct the faithful from the wings—Acting President Li attempted to open negotiations with Mao, who on 14 January had issued his eight conditions for peace. These were:

1. Strict punishment of war criminals.
2. Abolition of the constitution.
3. Abolition of the Kuomintang legal system.
4. Reorganization of Nationalist troops according to democratic principles.
5. Confiscation of "bureaucratic" capital.
6. Reformation of the land system.
7. Abolition of "treasonous treaties."
8. Convocation of a Political Consultative Conference with non-participation of "reactionary elements," establishment of democratic coalition government, taking over all authority of the "Kuomintang reactionary government" and all its strata.[1]

Nationalist compliance with these eight demands would have been tantamount to unconditional surrender. Li rejected them on 31 January, without, however, breaking off the negotiations. He finally obtained the agreement of Yeh Chien-ying, the Chief of Staff of the Red Army and new Mayor of Peking, to the dispatch of an "unofficial" Nationalist mission to the Red capital at Shihkiachwang. This mission, with Shao Li-tzu, Dr. W. W. Yen, and Chang Shih-chao as members, arrived in Peking on 13 February. It was received by three generals, Yeh Chien-ying, Lin Piao, and Nieh Jung-chen, their political commissars Lo Jung-huan and Po I-po watchful at their sides. At Shihkiachwang the mission met with Mao and Chou En-lai. It returned empty-handed to Shanghai on 27 February, Mao having held fast to his eight points.

These negative results caused enormous difficulties for Acting President Li, who had to cope with the opposition of Dr. Sun Fo, as well as that of former members of the Kuomintang who had opposed Chiang Kai-shek. These refugees had now

---

[1] U.S. Department of State, *United States Relations with China, with Special Reference to the Period 1944–1949* (U.S. Government Printing Office, 1949), p. 293. Tr.

ended their long stay in Hong Kong and departed for the "liberated areas," whence on 25 February they addressed their congratulations to an all-conquering Mao. Among them were General Ts'ai T'ing-k'ai, the hero of Shanghai's valiant resistance against the Japanese in 1932; General Li Chi-shen, Chairman of the refugee RCKMT (the Revolutionary Committee of the Kuomintang); Mme. Feng Yü-hsiang, widow of the "Christian General";[2] Mme. Lu Hsün, widow of the "Chinese Gorki"; the writer Mao Tun; and Kuo Mo-jo, the 'poet and archaeologist. The presence of these anti-Kuomintang democrats was to prove useful to Mao Tse-tung, permitting him to create coalition governments which could use well-known personalities who, albeit non-Communists, were completely devoted to the party.

Moreover, in a spirit of broad conciliation, the Communists on 21 February effected an extremely clever reorganization of the Nationalist forces in the Peking area. Although Fu Tso-yi's headquarters was, of course, disbanded, his twenty-five ex-Nationalist divisions were transformed into twenty-five separate divisions within the People's Liberation Army. All officers, regardless of grade, who volunteered to serve in the Red Army were integrated without loss of rank or seniority. Those who preferred to leave the army were given three months' pay and authorized to take with them all their personal belongings; they were even permitted to depart with either one or two orderlies, the number depending upon the officer's rank. All this, of course, was nothing more than a propaganda gesture, aimed at the morale of the beleaguered Nationalist garrisons that still held out in North China.

The month of March brought new convulsions in Nationalist China, where the remnants of the expiring Kuomintang

---

[2] An opponent of Chiang Kai-shek, Feng was for some time a political refugee in the United States. On 4 September 1948 he met a mysterious end aboard the Russian ship *Pobeda*, which burned in the Black Sea while Feng was returning to China from the United States by way of the Soviet Union.

dissipated their dying energies in deplorable internal strife. Dr. Sun Fo, who had taken his Nationalist cabinet and part of the Legislative Yüan with him to Canton, was forced to resign, and was replaced as premier by General Ho Ying-ch'in. More than ever, it was now impossible to know who governed. Generals were practically their own masters in the provinces, and Chiang Kai-shek continued to give orders through the mouths of those who remained faithful to him. Everywhere, weariness and discontent continued to grow. Communist bands increased their strength in Kwangtung, Szechwan, and Yunnan. On 2 March the best warship in the Nationalist Navy, the cruiser *Chungking* (formerly H.M.S. *Aurora*), slipped out of Shanghai and went over to the Reds.[3]

Once again General Ho and Acting President Li sought negotiations with Mao, who was now reorganizing for the final assault and massing his forces along the north bank of the Yangtze. Since Mao wished to avoid the appearance of prolonging the war, the Central Committee of the CCP, meeting in plenary session at Shihkiachwang,[4] on 26 March decided that peace talks would be permitted to open at Peking on 1 April, with Mao's eight points as the basis of discussion. Arriving in Peking on 2 April, the envoys of the Kuomintang found themselves confronted by a stone wall. The Communists were now less willing than ever to make concessions: on the contrary, they set 12 April as the deadline for the acceptance of their conditions and declared that "come peace or come war," the Nanking government would have to accept the passage of Red troops across the Yangtze. The unhappy General Li turned in despair, and in vain, to the United

[3] The ship went to Chefoo, where it was sunk by the Nationalist Air Force on 20 March (according to the Communists, the *Chungking* was bombed and sunk off Hulutao. Tr.).

[4] It was during this session that the Chinese Communists, reversing their previous line, now proclaimed the primacy of the urban proletariat. In Mao's words: "The center of gravity of the Party's work has now shifted from the village to the city."

States; and one of his envoys to Peking, General Chang Chih-chung, who had always been on good terms with Chou En-lai, went over to the Reds!

On 15 April the Communists gave the Nationalist government five days to comply with the terms of their ultimatum. Still struggling feebly against the mortal danger which threatened it, the Nationalist government again appealed to the United States, and sought to bring an end to the divisive wrangling between Li Tsung-jen and Chiang Kai-shek. It was far too late. On 20 April Li rejected the Red ultimatum, but requested an armistice pending resumption of negotiations. The only reply to this request was the crossing of the Yangtze, on orders from Mao and Chu Teh, by the Red armies. On 23 April Li and Ho withdrew to Canton, and Chiang took wing for Formosa. The last act of the tragedy was at hand.

THE *Amethyst* INCIDENT

On 20 April 1949 the 1,480-ton British frigate *Amethyst*, commanded by Lieutenant Commander B. M. Skinner, started up the Yangtze for Nanking. Her mission was to relieve the destroyer *Consort*, bring supplies to the British Embassy, and assure, if need be, the protection of British subjects residing in the Nationalist capital. Upon reaching Chinkiang the frigate suddenly found itself under fire from Communist field batteries positioned along the north bank of the river. She joined battle, but soon, severely damaged, with seventeen dead, twenty wounded, and a mortally wounded captain, she ran aground on Rose Island, about seventy-five miles upstream from Shanghai. Admiral Madden[5] sent the cruiser *London* and the frigate *Black Swan* to her rescue. These ships too

[5] Vice Admiral A. C. G. Madden, second in command of the Far East Station. *Tr.*

were damaged and forced to withdraw, as was the *Consort*, which nonetheless succeeded in making its way downstream from Nanking to Shanghai. It was only with great difficulty that British seaplanes managed to come in alongside the *Amethyst*, which remained, however, in radio contact with Shanghai. For three months the frigate, which had been refloated, remained a prisoner of the Communists, who refused to let the ship weigh anchor so long as her new skipper, Lieutenant Commander J. S. Kerans, would not sign a document admitting British responsibility for the incident and the Communist claim that the ship had "criminally invaded Chinese territorial waters." On 30 July Kerans decided to attempt escape. Weighing anchor under the heavy fire of Communist batteries, and running another gauntlet of fire in passing the Kiangyin forts, the ship finally succeeded in rejoining the British fleet at the mouth of the Yangtze.

Although the frigate's exploit upheld the honor of the British Navy, it is nonetheless true that the *Amethyst* incident, considered in its entire context, constituted a heavy blow to white prestige in the Far East, and gained considerable "face" for the Communists. The Royal Navy enjoyed unequaled respect in China; for more than a century it had been viewed as invincible. In 1860 British ships had silenced the forts of Taku. In 1923 the mere arrival of a British naval squadron off Canton had sufficed to compel the withdrawal of Sun Yat-sen himself. Yet now the Reds had vanquished the invincible. The inhabitants of Shanghai looked on in amazement as the wounded were disembarked from British warships which had been ripped open by Chinese shells. Coming at a time when Chu Teh's armies were closing in on Shanghai, the psychological impact of the *Amethyst* Incident did more for a Communist victory than any strategic maneuver could possibly have done.

CHAPTER XVI

The Communist Offensive
of 20 April

As final battle was joined, Nationalist dispositions, according to American reports, were the following: 350,000 men were in the Nanking-Shanghai area, 175,000 were at Sian, 120,000 in the Northeast, another 120,000 in the Hankow region, and 150,000 were scattered about in isolated garrisons. These figures do not include the 300,000 men of the "armies" that Chiang Kai-shek had already evacuated to Formosa.[1] The situation favored the Reds, all the more since Liu Po-ch'eng, promptly profiting from the conquest of the Peking area, had completely reorganized Communist lines of communication. He had restored to operation the railroads between Peking and Mukden, Kalgan and Shihkiachwang; more importantly, he had established the Peking-Tientsin railroad, with its major spurs of the Tsinpu (Tientsin to Pukow, near Nanking) and the Pinghan (Peking to Hankow), as the arteries of a rear base for logistical support of the Red armies in the field. For the first time in history, Chinese armies could count upon

---

[1] Chiang had also withdrawn "his" navy (some twenty-six gunboats), under Admiral Kuei Yung-ch'ing, and "his" air force, under General Chou Chih-jou, to Formosa

regular resupply of their needs in ammunition and other military stores.

The state of atrophy which prevailed on the Nationalist side stifled the adoption of any effective measures of defense. The admiral charged with responsibility for the defense of the Nanking-Shanghai sector was satisfied with scuttling a preponderance of the junks and sampans of the Yangtze. Nationalist divisions were stretched out over an average front of more than thirty miles. Confronting them, the forces of Ch'en I, which lay along the Yangtze from Nanking to Nantung, infiltrated the south bank of the river at will. Without difficulty or interference from the Nationalists, the armies of Liu Po-ch'eng had regrouped along the northern flank of the Tapieh range. And Lin Piao had been left free to concentrate his armies without opposition from the Nationalists, who once again remained frozen in a sterile and foredoomed defensive posture. The few organized forces remaining to the Nationalists were those of Pai Ch'ung-hsi, whose nine armies were deployed between Kiukiang and Ichang, and the armies on Formosa, which Chiang Kai-shek kept under his exclusive control.

The Communist push was launched on 20 April. On the left, his flank guarded by the sea, Ch'en I crossed the Yangtze without firing a shot, took Nanking on the 23rd, and pressed on toward the bay of Hangchow in a thrust designed to envelop and isolate Shanghai. In the center, Liu Po-ch'eng marched on Fukien, in the direction of Foochow, in order to cut off the retreat of the Nationalist armies. On the right, Lin Piao's Fourth Field Army[2] attacked Pai Ch'ung-hsi's forces

[2] In November 1948 the territorial designations of Chinese Communist armies were dropped, and Red forces were reorganized into four numbered "field armies" plus the North China Army Group, often unofficially called the "Fifth Field Army." It was Lin Piao's Fourth Field Army that was to be the major Chinese force committed in the Korean conflict. *Tr.*

THE FINAL OFFENSIVE
(APRIL — OCTOBER 1949)

●●●● FRONT LINE AS OF 20 APRIL
●●●●●● FRONT LINE AS OF 30 MAY
▬ ▬ ▬ FRONT LINE AS OF 15 JULY
▬ ▪ ▬ FRONT LINE AS OF 8 SEPTEMBER

0   300

SCALE IN MILES

in the Hankow region. The Nationalists put up only a token resistance, even though T'ang En-po and Ch'en Ta-ching, the commanders in Shanghai, loudly proclaimed their resolve to resist to the end and make of the city "a second Stalingrad." Chiang Kai-shek dispatched several armies to reinforce the defenders, and came in person to deliver a speech in which he spoke of "total victory within three years." The defenses of the city were prepared in the typical Nationalist manner, with hordes of coolies set to work upon an all-encompassing ditch and ten-foot palisade of no defensive value whatsoever.[3] Despite their numerical superiority, T'ang En-po's troops remained completely passive within their lines, thereby permitting the Reds to complete their investment of Shanghai without firing a shot.

Hangchow fell to the Communists on 3 May, and on the 7th they took Shaohing, on the road to Ningpo. While Lin Piao's forces in the west took the Wuhan cities, Shanghai by 16 May was completely surrounded. With the first bombardment, the heroic defenders quickly manifested their intention to surrender. The only troops to put up a momentary fight were the reinforcements that had been sent by Chiang Kaishek; aided by air support dispatched from Formosa, they now sought only a safe evacuation from the mainland. On 25 May Ch'en I's troops, in perfect order, entered Shanghai, astounding the inhabitants of the great commercial metropolis with their discipline and decorum. Ch'en I, now mayor of Shanghai, provided for the security and supply of the city, whose fall had yielded the Communists more than 100,000 prisoners and two hundred guns. As for the Nationalists, the government and administration were moved to Canton, where the Ch'en brothers deluded themselves with dreams of a victorious resistance in the heart of the old Kuomintang stronghold. But Kwangtung and Kwangsi were already corroded by communism, and a force of more than sixty thousand Reds controlled a third of Kwangtung province.

At the end of May the Communists' lines of communication were cut by floods which lay waste the lower course of the Yangtze, and the Reds were thus forced to break off their of-

[3] Except to the enterprising officer who profited from the sale of wood for the construction of this medieval barrier.

fensive. They profited from this enforced pause by reorganizing their rear areas and consolidating their control over their new conquests, which in area exceeded that of all France.

Meanwhile, important events had occurred in other sectors since the launching of the Communist offensive on 20 April. On 24 April Taiyuan, the old capital of Shansi, fell after a siege which had lasted since the autumn of 1948. Marshal Yen Hsi-shan, the "model governor" and master of Shansi since as far back as 1911, had made of this province a virtually autonomous and highly prosperous state. More than six hundred miles of good roads had been constructed, as well as two rail lines. One of these, connecting with the Peking-Suiyuan line, ran the length of the province down the valley of the Fen from Tatung to Tungkwan; the other connected Taiyuan with Shihkiachwang, on the main Peking-Hankow line to the east. Yen had reforested the hills of Shansi with firs, and developed agriculture to a level at which the province enjoyed complete self-sufficiency. During the Sino-Japanese conflict, Shansi had almost completely escaped the horrors of war. And to exploit all of these advantages Marshal Yen had established a system of state socialism which, in his view, was far superior to Marxism.

When the Communists moved into Shansi, Yen grudgingly yielded them the field and pulled back into the towns, which fell, one after the other, to the Reds. Taiyuan, however, appeared to be impregnable. Behind its massive ramparts, thirty feet thick, were an excellent garrison and the biggest munitions plant in China, turning out rifles, machine guns, and ammunition. Only by starving it out could the city be taken, and Yen could have stockpiled large supplies of food and ammunition had he only seen fit to do so. Moreover, he had an excellent airfield for resupply by air. Yet he demanded of Chiang Kai-shek five thousand tons of rice per month, an amount sent to him right up to the moment when the Reds seized the airfield. The old marshal then vouchsafed, to an American journalist, that China's salvation would require "two hundred Flying Tigers and 100,000 Japanese mercenaries"; without these, he opined, defeat appeared certain.

Following the failure of a relief column from the south, feebly led by Chang Chih-chung, Yen quickly quitted Taiyuan. Leaving just before the capitulation of his capital to the Communists, he arrived at Canton just in time to succeed Ho Ying-ch'in, on 2 June, as premier of the Nationalist government. Immediately thereafter he went to Formosa to confer with Chiang, with whom he had always maintained good relations. The Nationalists were counting on the prodigious popularity of Yen, a diabetic old despot, to galvanize the last remaining forces of the Kuomintang.

On 20 May, after an offensive led by P'eng Te-huai, the city of Sian, capital of Shensi, surrendered to the Communists. Hu Tsung-nan, an old comrade of Chiang Kai-shek, beat a rapid retreat to the west, calling for help from Ma Pu-fang, the Moslem leader of Kansu who had defeated the Reds at Paoki in 1948. Ma hastened up with his cavalry and delivered a frontal attack upon P'eng's forces about seventy miles from Sian, while a force of 25,000 under his son, Ma Chi-yüan, took the Communists in the flank. P'eng, who had rashly ventured forth upon the "Great Northern Highway" (Sian-Chengtu) in order to invade Szechwan from the north, gave way before this unexpected assault and pulled back toward Sian, pursued by Ma and Hu Tsung-nan. The Nationalists hailed this victory with loud acclaim, and Chiang bestowed upon Ma Pu-fang the title of Commander in Chief in the Northwest, a post which had remained vacant since its treacherous abandonment by Chang Chih-chung. The Generalissimo also promised Ma parachute delivery of the weapons and ammunition so sorely needed by the Moslem leader.

The Nationalist success, however, proved to be short-lived. On Chu Teh's orders Nieh Jung-chen, with two armies, the Sixty-second and the Sixty-third, soon came to the aid of P'eng Te-huai. Moving by rail on the Lunghai line to Sian, Nieh's forces met Ma and his Moslems about thirty-five miles from the Shensi capital and dealt them a decisive defeat, facilitated by the fact that Chiang Kai-shek had failed to fulfill his promises of arms and ammunition. Exploiting their advantage, the Communists pressed on in pursuit of Ma's forces, at first along the sandy roads skirting the river Wei, then through the arid, 8000-foot mountains of Kansu. On 26 August, after a march of nearly three hundred miles, they made their triumphal entry into Lanchow, as Ma Pu-fang, the "Big Horse," sought refuge in Ningsia. The defeat of P'eng Te-huai was avenged; and Red domination of the Northwest, aided by prudent agrarian reforms and a policy of religious toleration toward the Moslems, was firmly established.

Meanwhile, on 2 June 1949 the Nationalists had lost Tsingtao, their last stronghold in Shantung, from which American naval forces had been withdrawn in February. On 20 June the Nationalist government declared a blockade of the entire coast from the mouth of the Liao, in Manchuria, down to that of the Min, at Foochow. The following day a British freighter, the Anchises, was bombed and damaged on the Hwangpu. Despite British protests the Nationalists remained obdurate, and European companies quickly concluded that the risk to their ships was not worth running. Here, at any rate, the Formosa-based air force of the Nationalists obtained undeniable results.

The Nationalists also maintained small garrisons on the islands off the China coast, enabling them to keep in touch with their remaining partisans on the mainland and supply them with arms and money. This insular strategy compelled the Communists to mount numerous landing operations, which went on up to the end of 1950.[4] On 20 August they attacked the Miao islands, in the Po Hai gulf off the north coast of Shantung, a base from which Nationalist ships were blockading Tientsin. As for the Nationalists, on 29 June their air force started a series of bombing raids over Shanghai and Nanking. Fearful of Communist antiaircraft fire, the high-flying planes could only claim a few civilians as victims, and the raids soon showed themselves to be ineffective.

In July of 1949 the first official Soviet military mission arrived in Peking. Headed by Colonel General Andrei Vassilievitch Zhdanov,[5] this mission included an adviser on strategy, Major General Klinmukaiev, and two training missions, one for the army, under Colonel Tikhanov, and the other for the air force, headed by Colonel Voroshilov. There were also a political adviser, N. Pokrishev, who rapidly became a very influential member of the group around Mao Tse-tung; Dr. Tojerkasov, an adviser charged with organizing party propaganda; and two economic advisers. The training mission set up schools for instruction of the Chinese Communists in the use of Soviet equipment. The Reds had made prisoners of more than fourteen hundred Nationalist aviation technicians at Shanghai, and a flying school was established immediately. But primary emphasis was placed upon the training of artillery specialists, in the interests of infantry support: Moscow

---

[4] Despite these operations the Nationalists still hold the islands of Quemoy and Matsu.

[5] Not to be confused with Marshal A. A. Zhdanov.

deemed the training of Chinese pilots to be an excessively protracted and costly process, and a useless task in view of the final victory which was now a certainty.

In truth, the situation of the Nationalists was a desperate one. When the Red offensive resumed, perfectly coordinated by Chu Teh, it was opposed by only a sporadic and uncoordinated resistance, easily broken by the Communists. Despite the levies hastily raised in the south, the Nationalists had only about 1,090,000 men (250,000 in Szechwan, another 250,000 in Kiangsi, 200,000 in Kwangtung, 200,000 in Formosa, and 100,000 troops evacuated from Shanghai). Facing them were 1,500,000 Communist troops, 730,000 of whom were massed in the center, in Hunan and Kiangsi.

In August, Lin Piao attacked Pai Ch'ung-hsi, his main effort thrusting southward along the Canton railway. Pai pulled back to Changsha. Fortunately for him the time-honored bandits of the Tapieh mountains, who made it their business always to oppose the predominant power (they had been Communists in 1930, anti-Japanese nationalists in 1940, and Communists again in 1945), now reverted to militant anticommunism and, posing as they did a formidable guerrilla threat to Lin Piao's rear area, delayed a Communist advance already slowed by floods. The attack on Changsha was marked by the successive treachery first of General Ch'eng Ch'ien, the city's Nationalist garrison commander, and then of his successor, General Ch'en Ming-ch'en, who went over to the Reds with some thirty thousand of his men. For the only faithful Nationalist general, Huang Chieh, there was no other course than to withdraw the remainder of the garrison, and Changsha fell to the Reds on 4 August. Continuing his advance, Lin Piao crossed the Lien river on 12 August and marched on Kwangtung, the cradle of the Kuomintang.

The Nationalists essayed a last and mighty effort. Chiang Kai-shek ordered General Liu An-chi, the Nationalist commander on Hainan, to send north the island's entire garrison of 150,000 men. These, when added to a force of fifty thousand from Formosa and the fifty thousand regulars of Yü Han-mou, the governor of Kwangtung, as well as the troops of Pai Ch'ung-hsi, could together constitute a strong army for the defense of Kwangtung. But once again the personal enmities of Nationalist generals came into play. Pai was a prominent native and former governor of Kwangsi, and Yü Han-mou had no desire to see him move into Kwangtung; he asked Pai to pull back toward the southwest, cover the Kwangsi capital at Kweilin, and keep well away from Canton.

Meanwhile, Liu Po-ch'eng had reached Kanchow, in southern Kiangsi, and Lin Piao had advanced beyond Hengyang, in Hunan, when Pai decided to give defensive battle. He inflicted a serious defeat upon Lin Piao and the thoroughly thrashed Twenty-ninth Red Army was forced to retreat as far north as Changsha. In the meantime, Chiang Kai-shek had laid plans for a clever maneuver designed to prevent Liu Po-ch'eng from rescuing his comrade. From Formosa an army under General Ch'en Ch'eng, Nationalist Commander in Chief in the Southeast, landed at Amoy with Foochow[6] as its objective. General Hu Lien, commanding at Swatow, was to move north and link up with Ch'en Ch'eng. Yü Han-mou, however, ordered Hu Lien to stay put and "cover Canton." Ch'en Ch'eng, who deemed his strength to be insufficient, moved north, was repulsed by Liu Po-ch'eng, and fell back to Amoy for re-embarkment. The Communists then assumed a temporarily defensive posture in the center, where the Hunan "front" stabilized

[6] Foochow had been taken by Liu Po-ch'eng's forces on 17 August.

along the line Taoyuan-Anhwa-Siangtan-Anjen. On their left, the Reds launched a vast envelopment of the Nationalists' right flank. In their rear, Ch'en I readied landing operations against the Chu Shan archipelago, off Ningpo, from which the Nationalist Navy was blockading Shanghai. At the end of August, as in July, floods brought a momentary halt to operations.

CHAPTER XVII ✧

The Last Act

AT the beginning of July, Chiang Kai-shek again took up the conduct of Nationalist affairs. The Central Executive Committee of the Kuomintang was replaced by a Supreme Political Council,[1] with Chiang as its chairman. After once again proclaiming his resolve to fight on to the end, Chiang attempted to create an Asian anti-Communist front. On 10 July he left Formosa for a meeting at Baguio with Mr. Quirino, the President of the Philippines, who declared himself entirely in accord with Chiang on the necessity of facing up to the Red menace. On 7 August Chiang conferred with President Syngman Rhee at Chinhae, in South Korea, where the two men agreed on the idea of a conference of representatives of South Korea, Nationalist China, and the Philippines.

Nor had Mao Tse-tung, on his side, remained inactive. On 15 June 1949 he delivered a speech to the Preparatory Committee of the People's Political Consultative Conference at Peking in which he announced the impending establishment

[1] Also known as the Emergency Council. The Central Executive Committee of the KMT did not go out of existence with the creation of the Supreme, or Emergency, Council on 16 July 1949; but the latter became, "during the period of Communist rebellion," the "highest policy-making organ" of the KMT. See The China Handbook Editorial Board, *The China Handbook, 1950* (New York: Rockport Press, 1950), pp. 134, 239. *Tr.*

of a "democratic coalition government" and hailed the final victory:

The people of the whole country supporting their own People's Liberation Army have won the war. This great People's War of Liberation, begun in July 1946, has now lasted three years. The war was launched by the Kuomintang reactionaries with the help they received from foreign imperialism. In unleashing this civil war against the people the Kuomintang reactionaries perfidiously and unscrupulously tore up the truce agreement and the resolutions of the Political Consultative Conference of January 1946. But in three short years they have been defeated by the heroic People's Liberation Army. Not long ago, after the Kuomintang reactionaries' peace plot was exposed, the People's Liberation Army bravely advanced and crossed the Yangtze River. Nanking, the capital of the Kuomintang reactionaries, is now in our hands. Shanghai, Hangchow, Nanchang, Wuhan and Sian have been liberated. At this very moment, the field armies of the People's Liberation Army are conducting a great march unprecedented in Chinese history into the southern and northwestern provinces. In three years the People's Liberation Army has wiped out a total of 5,590,000 of the reactionary Kuomintang troops. Now the remnants of the Kuomintang forces number only about 1,500,000, including regulars, irregulars and those in the military establishments and academies in the rear. It will still take some time to mop up these enemy remnants, but not long.[2]

Mao proclaimed China's resolve to be free and independent:

China's affairs must be decided and run by the Chinese people themselves, and no further interference, not even the slightest, will be tolerated from any imperialist country...

At the same time, we proclaim to the whole world that what we oppose is exclusively the imperialist system and its plots against the Chinese people. We are willing to discuss with any foreign government the establishment of diplomatic relations on the basis of the principles of equality, mutual benefit and mutual respect for terri-

2 The English translation is from *Mao Tse-tung: Selected Works*, vol. V: *1945–1949* (New York: International Publishers, 1956), p. 406. Quoted by permission of International Publishers. *Tr.*

CHAPTER XVII ✧

The Last Act

A_T the beginning of July, Chiang Kai-shek again took up the conduct of Nationalist affairs. The Central Executive Committee of the Kuomintang was replaced by a Supreme Political Council,[1] with Chiang as its chairman. After once again proclaiming his resolve to fight on to the end, Chiang attempted to create an Asian anti-Communist front. On 10 July he left Formosa for a meeting at Baguio with Mr. Quirino, the President of the Philippines, who declared himself entirely in accord with Chiang on the necessity of facing up to the Red menace. On 7 August Chiang conferred with President Syngman Rhee at Chinhae, in South Korea, where the two men agreed on the idea of a conference of representatives of South Korea, Nationalist China, and the Philippines.

Nor had Mao Tse-tung, on his side, remained inactive. On 15 June 1949 he delivered a speech to the Preparatory Committee of the People's Political Consultative Conference at Peking in which he announced the impending establishment

[1] Also known as the Emergency Council. The Central Executive Committee of the KMT did not go out of existence with the creation of the Supreme, or Emergency, Council on 16 July 1949; but the latter became, "during the period of Communist rebellion," the "highest policy-making organ" of the KMT. See The China Handbook Editorial Board, *The China Handbook, 1950* (New York: Rockport Press, 1950), pp. 134, 239. *Tr.*

of a "democratic coalition government" and hailed the final victory:

The people of the whole country supporting their own People's Liberation Army have won the war. This great People's War of Liberation, begun in July 1946, has now lasted three years. The war was launched by the Kuomintang reactionaries with the help they received from foreign imperialism. In unleashing this civil war against the people the Kuomintang reactionaries perfidiously and unscrupulously tore up the truce agreement and the resolutions of the Political Consultative Conference of January 1946. But in three short years they have been defeated by the heroic People's Liberation Army. Not long ago, after the Kuomintang reactionaries' peace plot was exposed, the People's Liberation Army bravely advanced and crossed the Yangtze River. Nanking, the capital of the Kuomintang reactionaries, is now in our hands. Shanghai, Hangchow, Nanchang, Wuhan and Sian have been liberated. At this very moment, the field armies of the People's Liberation Army are conducting a great march unprecedented in Chinese history into the southern and northwestern provinces. In three years the People's Liberation Army has wiped out a total of 5,590,000 of the reactionary Kuomintang troops. Now the remnants of the Kuomintang forces number only about 1,500,000, including regulars, irregulars and those in the military establishments and academies in the rear. It will still take some time to mop up these enemy remnants, but not long.[2]

Mao proclaimed China's resolve to be free and independent:

China's affairs must be decided and run by the Chinese people themselves, and no further interference, not even the slightest, will be tolerated from any imperialist country. . .

At the same time, we proclaim to the whole world that what we oppose is exclusively the imperialist system and its plots against the Chinese people. We are willing to discuss with any foreign government the establishment of diplomatic relations on the basis of the principles of equality, mutual benefit and mutual respect for terri-

2 The English translation is from *Mao Tse-tung: Selected Works*, vol. V: *1945–1949* (New York: International Publishers, 1956), p. 406. Quoted by permission of International Publishers. *Tr.*

CHAPTER XVII ✧

The Last Act

A̲t̲ the beginning of July, Chiang Kai-shek again took up the conduct of Nationalist affairs. The Central Executive Committee of the Kuomintang was replaced by a Supreme Political Council,[1] with Chiang as its chairman. After once again proclaiming his resolve to fight on to the end, Chiang attempted to create an Asian anti-Communist front. On 10 July he left Formosa for a meeting at Baguio with Mr. Quirino, the President of the Philippines, who declared himself entirely in accord with Chiang on the necessity of facing up to the Red menace. On 7 August Chiang conferred with President Syngman Rhee at Chinhae, in South Korea, where the two men agreed on the idea of a conference of representatives of South Korea, Nationalist China, and the Philippines.

Nor had Mao Tse-tung, on his side, remained inactive. On 15 June 1949 he delivered a speech to the Preparatory Committee of the People's Political Consultative Conference at Peking in which he announced the impending establishment

[1] Also known as the Emergency Council. The Central Executive Committee of the KMT did not go out of existence with the creation of the Supreme, or Emergency, Council on 16 July 1949; but the latter became, "during the period of Communist rebellion," the "highest policy-making organ" of the KMT. See The China Handbook Editorial Board, The China Handbook, 1950 (New York: Rockport Press, 1950), pp. 134, 239. Tr.

of a "democratic coalition government" and hailed the final victory:

The people of the whole country supporting their own People's Liberation Army have won the war. This great People's War of Liberation, begun in July 1946, has now lasted three years. The war was launched by the Kuomintang reactionaries with the help they received from foreign imperialism. In unleashing this civil war against the people the Kuomintang reactionaries perfidiously and unscrupulously tore up the truce agreement and the resolutions of the Political Consultative Conference of January 1946. But in three short years they have been defeated by the heroic People's Liberation Army. Not long ago, after the Kuomintang reactionaries' peace plot was exposed, the People's Liberation Army bravely advanced and crossed the Yangtze River. Nanking, the capital of the Kuomintang reactionaries, is now in our hands. Shanghai, Hangchow, Nanchang, Wuhan and Sian have been liberated. At this very moment, the field armies of the People's Liberation Army are conducting a great march unprecedented in Chinese history into the southern and northwestern provinces. In three years the People's Liberation Army has wiped out a total of 5,590,000 of the reactionary Kuomintang troops. Now the remnants of the Kuomintang forces number only about 1,500,000, including regulars, irregulars and those in the military establishments and academies in the rear. It will still take some time to mop up these enemy remnants, but not long.[2]

Mao proclaimed China's resolve to be free and independent:

China's affairs must be decided and run by the Chinese people themselves, and no further interference, not even the slightest, will be tolerated from any imperialist country. . .

At the same time, we proclaim to the whole world that what we oppose is exclusively the imperialist system and its plots against the Chinese people. We are willing to discuss with any foreign government the establishment of diplomatic relations on the basis of the principles of equality, mutual benefit and mutual respect for terri-

[2] The English translation is from *Mao Tse-tung: Selected Works*, vol. V: *1945-1949* (New York: International Publishers, 1956), p. 406. Quoted by permission of International Publishers. *Tr.*

torial integrity and sovereignty, provided it is willing to sever relations with the Chinese reactionaries, stops conspiring with them or helping them and adopts an attitude of genuine, and not hypocritical, friendship towards People's China. The Chinese people wish to have friendly co-operation with the people of all countries and to resume and expand international trade in order to develop production and promote economic prosperity.[3]

On 1 July 1949, the twenty-eighth anniversary of the CCP, Mao published an article on doctrine which should have swept away all the illusions of those who thought him to be a democratic non-Communist, or merely a future Tito. In this article he clearly proclaimed his Marxist-Leninist faith:

The October Revolution helped the progressive elements of the world and of China to use the world outlook of the proletariat as the instrument for perceiving the destiny of the country, and for reconsidering their own problems. Travel the road of the Russians —this was the conclusion. . .

Under the leadership of the CCP, the Chinese people, after having driven away Japanese imperialism, fought the people's war of liberation for three years and gained a basic victory. Thus the civilization of the Western bourgeoisie, the bourgeois democracy, and the pattern of the bourgeois republic all went bankrupt in the minds of the Chinese people. Bourgeois democracy has given way to the people's democracy under the leadership of the proletariat, and the bourgeois republic has given way to the people's republic. A possibility has thus been created of reaching socialism and Communism through the people's republic, of attaining the elimination of classes and universal fraternity.[4]

In international affairs, Mao emphasized that China

[must] unite in a common struggle with those nations of the world who treat us on the basis of equality and with the people of all countries. This is to ally ourselves with the Soviet Union, to ally our-

---

[3] *Ibid.*, pp. 407–408. Quoted by permission of International Publishers. *Tr.*
[4] Quoted from the English translation of "On the People's Democratic Dictatorship" in Conrad Brandt, Benjamin Schwartz, and John K. Fairbank, *A Documentary History of Chinese Communism* (Cambridge, Mass.: Harvard University Press, 1952), pp. 451–452. *Tr.*

selves with all the New Democratic countries, and to ally ourselves with the proletariat and the broad masses of the people in other countries, to form an international united front. . . Internationally we belong to the anti-imperialist front headed by the U.S.S.R., and we can look for genuine friendly aid only from that front, and not from the imperialist front.[5]

He recognized the necessity of a "people's democratic dictatorship":

The right to vote is given only to the people and not to the reactionaries. These two aspects, namely, democracy among the people and dictatorship over the reactionaries, combine to form the people's democratic dictatorship. . ."Don't you want to eliminate state authority?" Yes, but we do not want it at present, we cannot want it at present. Why? Because imperialism still exists, the domestic reactionaries still exist, and classes in the country still exist. Our present task is to strengthen the apparatus of the people's state, which refers mainly to the people's army, people's police, and people's courts, for the defense of the country, and the protection of the people's interests; and with this as a condition, to enable China to advance steadily, under the leadership of the working class and the CP, from an agricultural to an industrial country, and from a New Democratic to a Socialist and Communist society, to eliminate classes and to realize the state of universal fraternity. The army, police, and courts of the state are instruments by which classes oppress classes. To the hostile classes the state apparatus is the instrument of oppression. It is violent, and not "benevolent."[6]

Finally, after affirming the leading role of the working class and its alliance with the peasantry, he went on to specify the three great lessons derived from the invaluable experience acquired by the CCP over the previous twenty-eight years:

A party with discipline, armed with the theories of Marx, Engels, Lenin, and Stalin, employing the method of self-criticism, and linked up closely with the masses; an army led by such a

[5] *Ibid.*, pp. 453, 456. *Tr.*
[6] *Ibid.*, pp. 456–457. *Tr.*

party; a united front of various revolutionary strata and groups led by such a party; these three are our main (lessons of) experience . . . Our experience may be summarized and boiled down into one single thing, namely, the people's democratic dictatorship based on the alliance of workers and peasants led by the working class [through the CP]. This dictatorship must unite in concert with international revolutionary forces. This is our formula, our main experience, our main programme.[7]

Earlier, on 7 June 1949, the CCP had observed the twelfth anniversary of the outbreak of the Sino-Japanese War by publishing a manifesto which outlined specific party objectives. It called for a peace treaty with a democratized and demilitarized Japan; for the formation of a united Sino-Japanese front against the American occupation of Japan; and for the establishment of a firm Sino-Soviet alliance to shield the Far East against all aggressors. Finally, the CCP called for the ousting of all imperialists from China, appealed to the patriotic elements of the Kuomintang, and reaffirmed the determination of the People's Army to liberate Formosa and bring Chiang Kai-shek back alive.

THE FINAL OPERATIONS

After an intermission of one month, military operations were resumed in October, and the last act was on. Earlier, on 20 September, the Communists had announced the defection of the Nationalist governor of Suiyuan, and on the 25th the end of the struggle in Ningsia, where they had captured six Nationalist armies with all their officers. On the 29th it was Sinkiang's turn to succumb to the Communists. All of Northwest China was in Mao's hands.

Now, with the first days of October, the Fourth Field Army resumed its march on Canton. Chiang Kai-shek had spent all of September trying to stiffen the powers of re-

[7] *Ibid.*, pp. 460–461. Tr.

sistance in the provinces of the southwest. He had ordered
Lu Han, the governor of Yunnan, to dissolve the provincial
legislature, to close the university, to censor the press. All
these efforts were in vain. In Kwangtung the advancing Red
forces encountered, about thirty-five miles north of Canton,
only feeble resistance. On 11 October Li Tsung-jen departed
Canton for Chungking, while Yen Hsi-shan left the threatened city for Formosa. On 14 October the last Nationalist
troops evacuated Canton, after destroying their depots, the
airport, and the three-arched bridge over the River Pearl. On
the 15th the Red forces entered the city and moved up to the
Hong Kong border. Two days later they took Swatow, against
no resistance, as well as Amoy, where the Nationalist rear
guard fought with desperate fury to assure the evacuation of
Chiang Kai-shek's last armies to Formosa. The capture of
Swatow and Amoy gave the Communists complete control of
the Chinese coast, but the Nationalists continued to occupy
many small offshore islands from which, by blocking navigation, landing agents, and sheltering fugitives, they posed a
real threat to the mainland. Thus, the coming months were to
see numerous landing operations, mounted by the Communists in order to rid themselves of this crippling mortgage.

Having liquidated Nationalist resistance in Southeast China,
the Communist armies turned west. Their pursuit of the last
remnants of opposition turned into a veritable military prom-
enade. In early November they overran Kweichow and Szechwan, taking Kweiyang on 13 November and Chungking on the
30th. The few remaining Nationalist "ministers," bolstered
by the arrival of Chiang Kai-shek on the 14th, withdrew by air
to Chengtu, whence they announced that the capital of the
Nationalist government would henceforth be at Taipei, the
capital of Formosa.

With December came the complete collapse of coordinated
resistance against the Communists. On 11 December Lu Han

proclaimed Yunnan's adherence to Peking, a defection imitated by the governor of Sikang on the 15th. The day before, Red forces had reached the frontier of French Indo-China at Mon Cay, sweeping before them some 25,000 Nationalist troops who were disarmed and interned by the French authorities. Finally, Chengtu fell on 27 December, a few hours after the last batch of Nationalist ministers made good their escape to Formosa.

It was all over. For the Nationalists nothing remained on the mainland except guerrilla activity, mostly in Sikang and Yunnan. For Mao Tse-tung there remained the "liberation" of Hainan, Tibet, and Formosa. The first two operations were to be far easier than the last.

The conquest of Hainan was rapidly accomplished. On 17 April 1950 some 110 motorized junks landed the 119th and 120th infantry divisions of Lin Piao's Fourth Field Army to the northwest of Limko, on the north coast of the island, while sixty more junks landed elements of the 121st and 125th infantry divisions to the west of Hoihow. The Nationalist garrison, more than 100,000 men under General Hsueh Yueh (the "Little Tiger"), was simultaneously hit from behind by Communist guerrillas, whose hold on the island's interior had never been loosened. Despite their numerical superiority, Hsueh Yueh's forces, obsessed by the thought of reaching Formosa's safe haven by an evacuation from the southern port of Yulin, were rapidly vanquished by the Reds. In four days the Communists gained complete control of the island, and the Nationalists lost an ideal base for their hypothetical return to the mainland of China.[8]

---

[8] Tibet, too, was later "liberated," without a shot fired, by the armies of Lin Piao, and a treaty signed in 1951 sealed the supremacy of Communist China over the "Roof of the World."

CHAPTER XVIII ✧

Organization of the New Chinese State

From 21 to 28 September 1949 there met at Peking a "Political Consultative Conference of the Chinese People."[1] The 662 members of this body represented not only the CCP, but such other anti-Kuomintang parties as the Democratic League, which sent 142 delegates;[2] regional democratic groups were represented by 102 delegates. There were also representatives of regional governments, of labor and peasant unions, of commerce and industry, of religious and cultural interests, of ethnic minorities, and of the overseas Chinese. All of these conference delegates had been designated by a Preparatory Committee whose own members, though not all Communists, had been picked by the party leaders.

The conference did some important work: election of the members of the central government; adoption of a "Common Programme"; designation of Peking as the official capital of

[1] According to Chinese Communist sources, the session lasted from 21 September to 1 October 1949. *Tr.*

[2] The *China Digest*, VII: 1 (Hong Kong, 5 October 1949), p. 10, lists a total of 142 delegates from fourteen political parties and groups. Of this total, sixteen delegates are listed as representing the CCP, while the Democratic League, also with sixteen delegates, combines with the other twelve non-CCP organizations for a sub-total of 126 delegates. *Tr.*

China;[3] adoption of the Gregorian calendar; adoption of a national anthem ("The March of the Volunteers"); and adoption of a national flag (red, with a five-pointed gold star, surrounded by four smaller stars, in the canton).

The Council of the central government was composed of a Chairman (Mao Tse-tung), and six Vice-Chairmen (three Communists: Chu Teh, Liu Shao-ch'i, Kao Kang, and three non-Communists: Mme. Sun Yat-sen,[4] Chang Lan, and General Li Chi-shen), and fifty-six members. Among the latter were a great number of Red military and political leaders (such as Ch'en I, Ho Lung, Liu Po-ch'eng, Lin Piao, Kuo Mo-jo, P'eng Te-huai, Chou En-lai, Li Li-san, Po I-po, and others), but there were also some turncoat ex-Nationalist generals (such as Fu Tso-yi, Ch'eng Ch'ien, and Chang Chih-chung); a Shanghai industrialist, Ch'en Shu-t'ung; a Chinese millionaire from Singapore, Tan Kah-kee; the widow of Feng Yü-hsiang, the "Christian General"; and minority-group representatives from Sinkiang and Inner Mongolia.

The "Common Programme" was in fact the constitution of the new state.[5] It first of all proclaimed the People's Republic of China to be "a people's democracy under a people's dictatorship, led by the working class and based upon the alliance of workers and peasants, rallying to it all the democratic classes and the nationalities of China." The Republic

---

[3] Chiang Kai-shek, it will be recalled, had renamed the city Peiping, or "Northern Peace," in 1928. The Communists now, on 27 September 1949, changed their new capital's name back to Peking. See *ibid.*, p. 7. *Tr.*

[4] Soong Ch'ing-ling, the sister of Mme. Chiang Kai-shek.

[5] The conference also passed an "Organic Law," which together with the Common Programme was the basic law of Communist China until 1954, when the present constitution was promulgated. For an English translation of these two documents in Chinese Communist sources, see *China Digest*, Supplement to VII: 1 (Hong Kong, 5 October 1949) for the text of the Common Programme, and *ibid.*, VII: 2 (19 October 1949), pp. 7–10, for text of the Organic Law. The excerpts which follow are translated from the French rendering of the author. *Tr.*

was to be "firmly opposed to imperialism, feudalism, and bureaucratic capitalism." It was determined to "abolish the prerogatives of all imperialist nations in China; to confiscate bureaucratic capital; to transform the feudal system into a system of peasant proprietorship; to protect the economic interests and private property of the workers, peasants, and of the small and the national bourgeoisie; and finally, to transform the country from an agricultural into an industrialized nation." All the democratic rights to freedom of thought, speech, the press, assembly, association, correspondence, residence, movement, religion, and so forth, were guaranteed. Women, as well as ethnic minorities, were granted equality of rights. The Republic would of course severely punish all counterrevolutionary activities, all Koumintang war criminals, all reactionary elements, landlords and capitalists. These would be permitted to reform themselves, to become new men; failing such reform, they would be deprived of their political rights. Finally, the People's Republic of China resolutely placed itself on the side of the peace-loving nations, above all the U.S.S.R., to oppose all imperialistic aggression and defend world peace.

After this affirmation of basic principles, the Common Programme went on to delineate the organs of state. At the national level would be an All-China People's Congress, elected by universal suffrage; a Central People's Government Council would govern when the Congress was not in session; there would also be a People's Political Consultative Conference. At the regional level, governments would be elected by universal suffrage, and there would be local People's Political Consultative Conferences.[6]

---

[6] As authorized by resolutions of the National Committee of the People's Political Consultative Conference. *Tr.*

As the constitution itself indicated, this system assured complete centralization of power. For example, Article 15 of the Common Programme specified that the organs of state power, at all levels, were to be established on the basis of the principles of democratic centralism. These fundamental principles prescribed the responsibility and accountability of the Congress to the people, the responsibility of the central government Council to the Congress, and the submisson of Council and Congress alike to the principle of majority rule; but they called also for the submission of lower organs of state power to the decisions made at a higher level, and the submission of all local organs to the central government.

Articles 18 and 19 of the Common Programme can be viewed only as pious declarations of principle. Article 18 asserted that all organs of the state should act in a spirit of simple virtue and dedication to the people: corruption was to be severely suppressed; waste was forbidden; "bureaucratism," and the tendency of officials to isolate themselves from the masses, were to be combated. Article 19 called for the surveillance of governmental activity at all levels by watchdog tribunals, before which any organ or official of state could be haled by any citizen for any violation of law.

In Articles 20 through 25, the Common Programme went on to deal with questions of national defense. It envisaged a navy and an air force, which would join the existing army in subordination to a single unified command. At a "suitable time" conscription was to be introduced.

Questions of political economy were dealt with at length in fourteen articles (26 through 40) of the Common Programme. Here Mao developed his thesis on the necessity of a socialist economy, which in the interests of maintaining production would provisionally permit some forms of private enterprise. Agrarian reform was to be pursued with prudence,

THE COMMUNIST CONQUEST OF CHINA

avoiding excessive "leftism." The position of the middle peasantry, unlike that of the rich peasants, was to be maintained. Reconstruction and economic development were to keep in step with the attainment of budgetary equilibrium and the circulation of a sound currency. As for foreign trade, complete control would be exerted by the state, which would also control currency circulation by means of state banks.

Articles 41 through 49 of the Common Programme proclaimed the need for development of education at all levels. Respect for all nationalities, and representation of minority groups in all organs of the state, were invoked in Articles 50 through 53. The program ended (Articles 54 through 60) by declaring that the foreign policy of the People's Republic of China would be conducted in the interests of national independence and the preservation of peace. Treaties concluded by the Kuomintang regime would be revised: though desiring commercial relations, on a basis of equality, with all countries, the new China would establish diplomatic relations only with those governments which repudiated the Kuomintang regime and adopted a friendly attitude toward the People's Republic.

On 1 October Mao Tse-tung officially promulgated the establishment of the People's Republic of China, and of a State Administration Council of fifteen members, headed by Chou En-lai. Thirty-seven Ministers were named. Chou En-lai combined the posts of Premier and Minister of Foreign Affairs, with Po I-po as Minister of Finance, Hsieh Chüeh-tsai as Minister of the Interior, and Li Li-san as Minister of Labor. Military affairs came under the jurisdiction of a People's Revolutionary Military Council headed by Mao Tse-tung, with Chu Teh remaining as Commander in Chief of the People's Liberation Army. Mme. Shih Liang became Minister of Justice, Mme. Feng Yü-hsiang[7] took over the Ministry of

7 Also known as Li Te-ch'uan. Tr.

Public Health, and Fu Tso-yi, the ex-Nationalist general who had surrendered Peking to the Communists, was named "Minister of Water Conservation." Finally, Shen Chün-ju became Chief Justice of the superior court of justice, or Supreme People's Court.

The new government was promptly recognized on 2 October 1949 by the U.S.S.R., which broke diplomatic relations with the Kuomintang regime. The Russian example was followed on 3 October by Bulgaria and Roumania, on the 4th by Poland, Hungary, and Czechoslovakia, and by Yugoslavia on the 5th. The first non-Communist state to recognize Mao was Burma, on 9 December 1949. India followed suit on 30 December, Pakistan on 4 January 1950, Ceylon, Norway, and Great Britain on the 6th, Denmark and Israel on the 9th, Finland and Afghanistan on the 13th, and finally Sweden, on the 14th. Upon learning that London had recognized the Peking government, Mme. Chiang Kai-shek bitterly reproached a Britain that had "bartered the soul of a nation for a few pieces of silver," and predicted that "one day these pieces of silver will bear interest in British blood, sweat, and tears on the battleground of freedom."[8]

On 16 December 1949 Mao Tse-tung went to Moscow to sign with Stalin a treaty made public on 14 February 1950. This thirty-year treaty of "friendship, alliance, and mutual aid" was directed against the aggression of Japan, or of any other state allied, in any manner, to Japan. The two contracting parties further pledged themselves to press for the prompt conclusion of a peace treaty with Japan; one would never support the adversaries of the other; they would consult together on all important international problems; economic and cultural relations would be developed.

[8] From Mme. Chiang's radio address of 8 January 1950, as quoted in *The New York Times* (9 January 1950), p. 4. *Tr.*

The treaty was supplemented by two agreements. The first of these concerned the railroad running from Changchun to Port Arthur and Dairen. Immediately after the conclusion of a peace treaty with Japan, and in no case later than the end of 1952, Russia was to evacuate Port Arthur and turn the Changchun railroad over to China. In the event of aggression both powers would be entitled to joint use of Port Arthur. The question of Dairen was to be held in abeyance pending conclusion of the Japanese peace treaty, but it was clearly recognized that "administration of Dairen belongs entirely to China." By the second agreement, the U.S.S.R. extended to China a five-year loan, at 1 per cent interest, of an amount equivalent to $300 million. The loan was to help China pay for Soviet material aid in heavy industry, mining, railways, and so forth, and was to be repaid, within ten years, in "raw materials, tea, or American dollars."

These two agreements were followed by three notes exchanged between Vyshinsky and Chou En-lai. The first of these specified Soviet abrogation of the treaty of 14 August 1945 between the U.S.S.R. and the Nationalist government. The second stipulated recognition of the independence of Outer Mongolia by both parties. The third and final note called for the Soviets to turn over to China the Japanese property they had acquired in Manchuria, as well as the buildings of the old Russian military mission in Peking.

This treaty was extremely advantageous to China; it represented one more triumph for Mao Tse-tung, now the all-powerful master of one fifth of the entire population of the globe.

He had won the war; he had now to win the peace, and in this quest lies the key to the future. Foregoing here any prophecy of this future, one may still probe the past, to seek therein the roots of Mao's victory in the Civil War.

CONCLUSION

The Roots of Mao's Victory

IT is always easy to explain events after the fact—even for one who is always wrong in predicting the outcome of events while they are actually occurring. In reading this account one gains the impression that as early as 1946 the defeat of the Nationalists was inevitable. Yet, right up to the end of 1948, the best-informed and most impartial of observers—those who best understood what lay beneath the surface of superficial situation maps—hesitated to predict the complete victory of Mao Tse-tung. To Western observers Mao's solution to the problems of China, with all that it implied for the future of the world, posed the prospect of a disaster which none desired even to think about. They preferred to cling to the most improbable of possibilities. Even after the Communist victory at Suchow and the arrival of the Reds at the Yangtze, many still hoped for a partition of China, as had once occurred in the bygone days of the Sung dynasty.

At the outset, as has been shown, Mao's chances of success were very slim. Clearly outclassed in numbers and matériel, he dominated only a small territory; he had no money, no resources, no allies. Worst of all, the masters of Russian communism had abandoned him; they had recognized Chiang Kai-shek, his mortal enemy, as the leader of China, and yielded

Manchuria to Nationalist sovereignty. Opposing Mao was a man to whom propaganda had given the stature of a giant, a prospective member of President Roosevelt's world-governing Big Four, the master of more than 350 million people, of war-hardened armies, of enormous stocks of modern military matériel, an ally assured of the total support of the great American republic, which in 1945 was the world's most powerful state. Between these two champions, who could have hesitated in his choice?

Four years later Chiang Kai-shek, the Chinese hero, was to find himself a vanquished refugee on the small island of Formosa, while his adversary set himself up in Peking as the master of 480 million human beings. What happened? What were the causes of an event which means so much in the history of humanity?

The profound lesson of the drama that was the Chinese Civil War is this: Even now, in this era of materialism and mechanization, spirit is always predominant, and it is morale that wins battles. Superiority in man power and matériel means little if men make no use of their weapons.

Here, in the Chinese Civil War, the adversaries were of the same race, of the same ancient civilization. How could the same man be a deplorably poor soldier under the Nationalists and then, after a few months of service with the Reds, become a veritable hero? How did hares so suddenly become lions? The answer is that the potential of man is enormous. He is as capable of heroism as of cowardice. But he will not become a hero unless he is inculcated with a faith, a belief, in a doctrine for which he will gladly give his life.

There is no such thing as a degenerate race or generation. The children of today possess the same innate qualities as did those of centuries past. The education of man—or, if one prefers, his "conditioning"—is everything. The cause of Mao's triumph lies in the fact that appealing as he did to ancient and deeply rooted reflexes, he gave a faith, a creed, to the peasants of China. Totalitarian doctrines are always based upon simple slogans, easy to exploit. Hitler chose, as the theme for Germany's external relations, abolition of the Treaty of Versailles; internally, the theme was the struggle against Jews and Communists. Mao had only to follow a beaten track. His external theme was the eternal theme of xenophobic nationalism, of the struggle against foreign imperialists, who themselves but barely emerged from barbarism, had "enslaved" the higher civilization that was China. As for internal themes, he cleverly appealed to the instincts of social justice and proprietorship which are so strong in the human heart. In proclaiming agrarian reform, in despoiling the landlords and lowering taxes, in giving landless farm hands plots to hold as their very own, Mao played the best of cards—to be cynically discarded once victory was won.

But beyond the achievement of these practical goals, it is undeniable that Mao knew how to make of his soldiers dedicated workers for "a powerful China, a respected China, where justice, truth, and peace would reign." He obtained this result by a sustained and patient effort of daily political education. In the everyday routine of the Red soldier, Marxist political indoctrination played a more important role than the manual of arms. Taken in hand by skillful political schoolmasters, the peasant-in-arms rapidly became a fanatic, an apostle of the new religion, ready to sacrifice his life for the better tomorrows. In this lies the essential reason for the victory of Mao Tse-tung. Victory, in a civil war, is almost always won by the side which knows how to gain the support of the people.

In order to win over the Chinese people, this Marxist leader chose the path of prudence. Although he had always been an orthodox Marxist, a believer who would do no rending violence to the classic doctrine, Mao did not hesitate to adopt a course of gradualism, so that the "first steps" would reveal to the peasants only the advantages of the new regime, and none of its fearsome flaws. This gradualistic policy was clearly reflected in the typical sequence of developments which followed upon the entry of the Red Army into a newly taken village. Even in those provinces where there were few landlords and the pattern of land tenure was already one of small holdings—as was often the case in Central China—there were always rich peasants, as well as pro-Japanese collaborators. And, always, there were miserably poor agricultural laborers among the villagers. First the villagers would be deeply impressed by the perfectly correct behavior of the Red troops, who far from giving themselves over to pillage, would ask only to be of help to the peasants. Then the Communist political leader would hold a meeting of all the villagers. He would promptly pillory, to the plaudits of all, the pro-Japanese bourgeois and the exploiting landowner. The lands of the condemned would then be distributed to the landless. The "politruk"[1] would then announce that henceforth the people would be able to elect their own administrators and participate freely in public affairs. Since the officials of the Kuomintang regime were often incompetent and corrupt, the enthusiasm with which the population accepted the new representatives of the People's Republic can be easily imagined.

Moreover, Mao Tse-tung very cleverly resisted "leftism" in matters of agrarian reform, and so was always opposed to the despoliation of the so-called "middle peasants." His reasoning was based on the fact that the Communists had to have the support of the majority of the population; only a minority,

[1] The Russian term for "political leader." Tr.

then, need be despoiled. This was successfully done. Without, of course, renouncing collectivization, the final goal of Marxism-Leninism, it was declared that this ultimate stage of the revolution would not be reached until the distant day of China's industrialization. For the moment the peasants were asked only to give their utmost support to the Red Army, which was liberating them from Kuomintang oppressors who were aided by American imperialists. It is easy to inflame a people against foreigners; in China this task was facilitated by the fact that the Nationalists used American aircraft, and that the bombs which fell on the civilian population were "Made in U.S.A."

The "Red Dragon" thus held important trumps: agrarian reform, xenophobia, the steadiness and discipline of the Red Army, the installation of honest officials, the careful avoidance of premature steps toward statism. But these trumps, without any doubt, would have been insufficient had Chiang Kai-shek been at the head of a strong political organization, and of a state which functioned in a normal manner. But such was not the case. Well before the end of the war against the Japanese, the Kuomintang was already completely rotten.

The drama in the revolution of 1927 was that, unlike all the other revolutions in Chinese history, it failed to conclude with a general clean-up of corrupt officials and local lords. The customary pattern of Chinese revolutions is well known. Thanks to an uprising caused by the incompetence and corruption of a regime which oppresses and starves the people, a new dynasty mounts the throne. The new emperor is a man of strong character, who in the unhesitating implementation of his plans for reform, cashiers corrupt officials and keeps careful watch over public order and the probity of his regime. But then he dies; and his son, already sinking into indolence, replaces him. After a few generations, the new aristocracy falls back into the old Chinese habits, and the tribulations of the people begin again. By nature long-suffering and patient, and brought up to respect their superiors, the people wait, sometimes for centuries, before rising once again. In this traditional cycle each revolution gave the people at least a temporary respite from oppression, if only of a decade or two. But Chiang Kai-shek, when he took power in 1927, was not strong enough to proceed with the necessary clean-up of corruption. On the contrary, Chiang, in order to secure acceptance of his authority, had to bargain with all the great war lords, the *tüchuns* who, like Chang Hsüeh-liang or Yen Hsi-shan, were the veritable proprietors of their provinces. Chinese administration, already corrupt and rotten under the Manchus, remained untouched by the revolution of 1927, and a long-suffering people received no relief.

A second result of Chiang's incomplete victory was that he was never able to put his own ideas into practice, not even in the bosom of his own party. The Kuomintang rapidly fossilized, and soon became a totalitarian instrument for the oppression of the people, rather than a faithful agent of the reforms desired by the dictator. Moreover, the most intelligent doctrinaires of the Kuomintang, the brothers Ch'en Li-fu and Ch'en Kuo-fu, were convinced Confucianists who denied the need for any change in the ancient structure of Chinese civilization. Their opposition to agrarian reform, on grounds of its absolute uselessness, was particularly pronounced. Perhaps they were right, from a philosophical and even economic point of view, China being in general a country of extremely fragmented landholdings. And yet, for all that there was still much that could have been done; at the very least, farm rents and usurious interest on loans could have been diminished. At any rate, by refusing to undertake reforms the Kuomintang deprived itself of a powerful means of influencing the people, who thus were thrown into the camp of the Communist enemy.

Apart from these general reasons, the Chinese Nationalist Party owed its impotence to its immobilism, and to a deplorable conception of the economic and military requisites of the Civil War.

In the first place, despite the enormous sums donated by the Americans, and the wretchedly poor pay of Nationalist soldiers and officials, the Kuomintang was never able to put its financial house in order. Basically, this was because of corruption. Among those around Chiang—himself completely honest—and throughout all echelons of the Kuomintang, everyone stole, everyone made deals. Members of the Soong family prudently invested tens of millions of dollars in America. From cabinet ministers right on down to the local party representatives in the small villages, everyone took such private bites out of public revenue that nothing remained for the coffers of the state. Apart from American subsidies, the sole remedy was the classic recourse to the printing press, a solution which led only to inflation and misery. Under such pressures the people sometimes grumbled; thus the considerable growth of the Kuomintang police. Such growth was initially justified by the struggle against collaborators; but the police rapidly became a powerful instrument of oppression, manipulated solely by the right wing of the party, the CC clique. In these conditions of growing misery, the people, who had manifested great qualities of patriotism and courage during the war against Japan, and had in general joyfully acclaimed the Kuomintang as well as the victory over Japan, became at first apathetic, and then resolutely hostile to the Kuomintang regime. In contrast, they soon favored the Reds, who appeared to the people as liberators: so did the Copts of Egypt, in their day, extend a cordial welcome to the Arabs.

The decline in the morale of the Chinese people, a direct consequence of the maladministration and corruption of the Kuomintang, had a direct impact upon the quality of the Nationalist Army. As pointed out at the beginning of this book, the Nationalist soldier, in the classic tradition of Chinese soldiery, was generally considered to be the scum of humanity. Except in several elite divisions, such a conception could not be changed, and morale remained low despite a multitude of promised reforms. No program of political education was launched, no valid mystique set forth: the soldier of Chiang Kai-shek knew not why he fought. Against the Japanese he could fight for his country and his people; but in this civil war a peasant soldier from Kwangtung had no idea why he should be fighting in Shansi and Manchuria. Poorly fed, poorly paid, poorly clothed, poorly cared for, poorly armed, often short of ammunition—even at decisive moments—unsustained by any faith in a cause, the Nationalist soldier was easy prey for the clever and impassioned propaganda of the Communists.

In turning to military matters of strategy and tactics, one can do no better than quote from the report of General Barr, who as chief of the group of Chiang's American military advisers from 1947 to the end of 1948, observed Nationalist troops and leaders at first hand. Writing early in 1949, General Barr reported as follows:

Many pages could be written covering the reasons for the failure of Nationalist strategy. I believe that the Government committed its first politico-military blunder when it concentrated its efforts after V-J Day on the purely military reoccupation of the former Japanese areas, giving little consideration to long-established regional sentiments or to creation of efficient local administrations which could attract wide popular support in the liberated areas. Moreover, the Nationalist Army was burdened with an unsound strategy which was conceived by a politically influenced and militarily inept high command. Instead of being content with consolidating North China, the Army was given the concurrent mission of seizing control of Manchuria, a task beyond its logistic capabilities. The Government, attempting to do too much with too little, found its armies scattered along thousands of miles of railroads, the possession of which was vital in view of the fact that these armies were supplied from bases in central China. In order to hold the railroads, it was also necessary to hold the large cities through which they passed. As time went on, the troops degenerated from field armies, capable of offensive combat, to garrison and lines of communication troops with an inevitable loss of offensive spirit. Communist military strength, popular support, and tactical skill were seriously underestimated from the start. It became increasingly difficult to maintain effective control over the large sections of predominantly Communist countryside through which the lines of communication passed. Lack of Nationalist forces qualified to take the field against the Communists enabled the latter to become increasingly strong. The Nationalists, with their limited resources, steadily lost ground against an opponent who not only shaped his strategy around available human and material resources, but also capitalized skillfully on the Government's strategic and tactical blunders and economic vulnerability.

Initially, the Communists were content to fight a type of guerrilla warfare, limiting their activities to raids on lines of communication and supply installations. The success of their operations, which were purely offensive, instilled in them the offensive attitude so necessary to success in war. On the other hand, the Nationalist strategy of defense of the areas they held, developed in them the "wall psychology"[2] which has been so disastrous to their armies. As the Communists grew stronger and more confident, they were able, by concentrations of superior strength, to surround, attack, and destroy Nationalist units in the field and Nationalist-held cities. It is typical of the Nationalists, in the defense of an

[2] The "Maginot Line" syndrome.

area or a city, to dig in or retire within the city walls, and there to fight to the end, hoping for relief which never comes because it cannot be spared from elsewhere. The Chinese have resisted advice that, in the defense of an area or a city from attack by modern methods of warfare, it is necessary to take up positions away from the walls where fire and maneuver is possible. Further, they have been unable to be convinced of the necessity for withdrawing from cities and prepared areas when faced with overpowering opposition and certain isolation and defeat, while the opportunity still existed for them to do so. In some cases their reasons for failure to withdraw and save their forces were political, but in most cases they were convinced that by defensive action alone, they could, through attrition if nothing else, defeat the enemy. Because of this mistaken concept and because of their inability to realize that discretion is usually the better part of valor, large numbers of Nationalist troops were lost to the Government.

It must be understood that all through the structure and machinery of the Nationalist Government there are interlocking ties of interest peculiar to the Chinese—family, financial, political. No man, no matter how efficient, can hope for a position of authority on account of being the man best qualified for the job; he simply must have other backing. In too many cases, this backing was the support and loyalty of the Generalissimo for his old army comrades which kept them in positions of high responsibility regardless of their qualifications. A direct result of this practice is the unsound strategy and faulty tactics so obviously displayed in the fight against the Communists.

Cooperation among and coordination of effort between the Armed Forces leaves much to be desired. The Ground Forces, being the old and dominant arm, is the source from which the large majority of top military positions are filled. These officers, mostly old and loyal contemporaries of the Generalissimo, have little or no knowledge of the newer arms: the Air Force and the Navy. The Chinese Air Force, consisting of 8⅓ groups, is far in excess of what a country bereft of gold credits can support. Although it has among its personnel over five thousand United States-trained pilots, it accomplished little, other than air-lifting troops and operating its transports for personal gains. There was an ever-present reluctance to take a chance on losing equipment or personnel, which was clearly reflected in their constant refusal to operate at other than high altitudes. There was an ingrained resentment in the Chinese Air Force against killing Chinese Communists who had no air support. All of these factors are important and unfortunate because the Chinese Air Force, unopposed, could have rendered invaluable support in ground operations had its capabilities been properly employed. From a military viewpoint, the case of the Navy is not so important since its employment, right or wrong, could have had little effect on the final outcome; all operations were land-based. From an economic viewpoint, the Navy could have been of inestimable value in suppressing smugglers in Hong Kong-Canton waters had it been willing to suppress and not participate. It was completely relieved of this mission in March 1948, and reputedly millions of dollars in customs revenue continue to be lost to the Government.

It might be expected that the Communists, being Chinese themselves, would also suffer from these faulty Nationalist traits and characteristics, and to a certain extent they do, but they have wisely subordinated them and made their ideology of Communism almost a fetish. By means of total mobilization in the areas they control, propaganda, and the use of political commissars within their armed forces, they maintain loyalty to the established order. Their leaders are men of proven ability who invariably out-general the Nationalist commanders. The morale and fighting spirit of the troops is very high because they are winning.[3]

There is little to add to this analysis. At most, the additional observation must be made that the lessons of Western-type warfare, when learned by uncritical minds, have sometimes led to disastrous results. For example, even though the Reds had no air force, Nationalist units wasted endless time in confecting artful camouflage and digging innumerable shelters as protection against air attacks which obviously would never come. The emphasis which American instructors placed upon

[3] U.S. Department of State, *United States Relations with China, with Special Reference to the Period 1944–1949* (U.S. Government Printing Office, 1949), pp. 336–338. *Tr.*

the importance of digging-in was further exaggerated by the defense-minded Nationalists, who were convinced that a three-to-one superiority was a minimal prerequisite to engaging the enemy. At each temporary halt, tired men were set to digging trenches. With training such as this, Nationalist troops were incapable of standing up to enemy fire: with the first volley they would hit the dirt and lie there, face down, without reacting. Lastly, the lavish American standards for estimating required expenditures of ammunition induced Nationalist commanders to discover that there was never enough ammunition for attacks.

Confronting the Nationalists was a Red Army with high morale and a remarkable zest for the offense. Frequent bayonet assaults, carefully coordinated with guerrilla activity which sowed a feeling of insecurity in the Nationalist rear, soon vested Red troops with a pervasive aura of invincibility. And by 1949 this army had performed a feat which is unique in the military history of the world: the entire conquest of an enormous country at a rapid pace averaging six miles per day, an advance which swept from the fall of Mukden on 8 November 1948 to the capture of Canton on 15 October 1949. Some of the battles it fought, particularly the battles of Liaoning and Suchow, stand as genuine models of strategy and tactics which merit careful study by the officers of Western countries.

One may well conclude that the Chinese Red Army constitutes a remarkably effective ground combat force. Yet it must be noted that the successes of this army were almost always obtained with ease: never in the Civil War were the Communists confronted by truly resolute, well-armed, and well-led adversaries. In fighting against the Nationalists, the Red Army habitually committed itself only to sure things, to certain victories, in which its own losses would be extremely low. Its strong point was guerrilla tactics, which are excellent in one's own country, but of little use in an alien land. Thus, before the outbreak of the war in Korea, one could rightfully ask how well this army would perform against a Western opponent. The response of the Chinese Red Army in Korea demonstrated that its defensive capabilities are as remarkable as its capabilities for offensive action. When the day arrives that this army is supported by a modern air force, it will prove itself to be a truly formidable foe for even the best of adversaries.

The same may be said for China itself. When this immense agricultural country achieves an industrialization backed by the natural resources of Manchuria and Sinkiang, it will assume a leading role not only in Asia, but in the world. And the average Chinese, who is intelligent, adroit, patient, enduring, and fully capable of manipulating machines, is ruled by a man of eminent qualities who well knows how to exact obedience. It is true that China, for the moment,[4] is confronted by an immense task of reconstruction. But such was the case with Russia in 1918: this precedent proves that only twenty years suffice to industrialize a great agricultural nation—and the pace of history moves ever faster.

We must thus expect to see, a few years from now, the emergence of China as a very great power. For our descendants it will then be interesting to see whether racial instincts are stronger in man than the forces of ideology. In other words, will adherence to the same Communist faith suffice to silence, between a great U.S.S.R. and an enormous China, the antagonisms arising from the color of skin or the shape of eyes? Here is the secret of the future; and there can be no doubt that upon the answer to this question depends, in large measure, the fate of Western civilization and even, perhaps, of the human race.

[4] The author, it will be recalled, was writing in 1952. *Tr.*

Index